CULTURE,
Communication
AND ··········
CHRISTIANITY

CULTURE. Communication AND ·········· CHRISTIANITY

A Selection of Writings by
CHARLES H. KRAFT

William Carey Library
PASADENA, CALIFORNIA

Culture, Communication and Christianity

A Selection of Writings by
CHARLES H. KRAFT

Published By:

William Carey Library
PO Box 40129
Pasadena, CA 91114 USA
(626) 798-0819 • www.wclbooks.com

Library of Congress Cataloging-in-Publication Data

Kraft, Charles H.
    Culture, communication, and Christianity / Charles H. Kraft.
        p. cm.
    Includes bibliographical references.
    ISBN 0-87808-784-2 (alk. paper)
    1. Missions—Theory. 2. Christianity and culture. 3. Intercultural communication—Religious aspects—Christianity. I. Title.

    BV2063 .K7562 2001
    261—dc21

        2001037668

Manuscript Editing & Indexing: Judi Brodeen
Cover Design: Dan Battermann, R&D Design Services

Printed in the United States of America

CULTURE, COMMUNICATION AND CHRISTIANITY
A SELECTION OF WRITINGS BY
CHARLES H. KRAFT

INTRODUCTION

ANTHROPOLOGY

WORLDVIEW

ETHNOLINGUISTICS

COMMUNICATION

THEOLOGY

An Anthropological Approach to Theology

Hermeneutics

CONTEXTUALIZATION

Contextualization of Theology

Examples of Contextualization

INTRODUCTION

It's been thirty-two years now since I joined the faculty of the School of World Mission, Fuller Seminary. At that time I moved careerwise from missionary and African language specialist (1963 to 1973 at Michigan State University and UCLA) to missiologist (1969 to present at Fuller).

Though my whole life has been an interesting and often exciting "ride," these last thirty-two years have been especially fulfilling. I never could have planned things so well. I've gotten to think, theorize, teach, travel, consult, write—and all within the area God originally called me to serve in, missions.

My story is in the first chapter of what follows, so I'll not go further into it here. Following that chapter, then, are 33 articles done mostly during these 32 years, presented here so students and others interested in my thinking can have access to them without having to search for them. All of them, except chapters 3, 7, 31 and 32 have been previously published but often in publications not easily accessible today.

I have arranged the chapters according to topic rather than according to date. The reader must, therefore, be careful to note the date of the writing when comparing what I've said in one place with what I've said in another.

I start the Anthropology section with a 1980 article contrasting worldview assumptions underlying some of the conflict between conservative Christians and anthropologists and suggesting a possible synthesis. One reason I lead with this article is that it outlines what has been a theme of my teaching and ministry. Chapter 3, however, backs up to 1972 to show how I then (and now) attempt to present a perspective that takes seriously both theological and anthropological truths. We then move to my most recent statement (1996) concerning culture from a Christian perspective, a chapter from my textbook *Anthropology for Christian Witness*.

Chapters 5, 6 and 7, then, are applications of this perspective to specific issues. In the 70s there was quite a lot of discussion in missiological circles of what Donald McGavran (the founder of Fuller's School of World Mission) called "the Homogeneous Unit Principle." This occasioned a conference held here discussing the issue. Chapter 5 is my contribution to that conference. Chapter 6 is an attempt to deal with the knotty problem of the ethics of our work in the crosscultural communication of the Gospel. Chapter 7, then, is a revision of a paper done in 1972 for a class I taught for Fuller women entitled *God, Culture and Women*.

With chapter 8 we turn to the subject of Worldview. The broad picture is drawn by another chapter from my 1996 Anthropology text followed by two chapters dealing with worldview in relation to the specific topics of Intercultural Communication (chapter 9) and Bible Translation (chapter 10).

The next section dips back into a specialty of mine that I don't do much with today, ethnolinguistics. Chapter 11 is an application of ethnolinguistics to church planting, published in 1973, my fourth year at Fuller. Chapters 12 and 13, though published in 1975 and 1976, come from my days as an African languages specialist. They are included both to represent that stage of my career and to provide for students of missiology an example of the kind of research that can be done with language material to discover worldview assumptions.

Chapters 14-20 deal with Communication. My aim in these articles is to deal with what we can learn about God's communication and how we can better communicate God's messages. Chapters 14-16 and 19 are four popular articles on the subject, while chapters 17, 18 and 20 are more meaty. Chapter 17 combines two articles presenting the Incarnation as the model we should imitate. This is a theme I have developed more in three of my books. Chapters 18 and 20 elaborate on certain aspects of that theme.

One of my primary concerns over the last 32 years has been to employ the perspectives of anthropology and communication theory in dealing with theology. In Nigeria, I became convinced that theological truths had to be presented in crossculturally appropriate ways rather than in the western philosophical matrix in which we learned them in church and seminary. Chapter 21 is an attempt to present this approach in a theological journal (1985), while chapters 22, 23 and 24 (1977, 1974 and 1978) may be seen as practice presentations of my thoughts in this area as I worked toward the publication of *Christianity in Culture* (1979). Chapter 25, though originally published as chapter 7 of *Christianity in Culture* is notable in that it was chosen by the editor of *The Guide to Contemporary Hermeneutics* (1986) as the only representative from Fuller in that important collection, even though it was not written by one specializing in theological hermeneutics.

The final chapters of this book are devoted to the very important subject of contextualization, an area in which I have been privileged to make what some consider significant contributions. I was invited to write chapter 26 as a part of an issue of *Evangelical Missions Quarterly* (1978) that represented a major step in evangelical acceptance of the term contextualization as a replacement for the term "indigenization" (which, note that we returned to in chapter 34 to satisfy a constituency that helped finance the book in which that chapter originally appeared). Chapters 27 and 28 are, like several earlier chapters, pre-1979 approaches to the topic eventually presented in book form in *Christianity in Culture*.

In chapters 29 through 34, I present several examples of the application of my approach to contextualization. That our attempts at communication need to be contextualized is the subject of chapter 29. This is followed by the earliest of my published writings included in this volume, chapter 30 (1963) on conversion. This article played a part in my being hired at Fuller. Chapter 31, then, though, like chapter 30, written while I was still in graduate school, never was submitted for publication.

Chapters 31 and 32 were written, though never published, to help deal with my anger over the way western missionaries have treated believing polygamists. I wrote them early in my missiological career, when the sting of my own problem with a mission that treated polygamy as an unpardonable sin was very fresh in my mind. I find, however, that there is nothing there that I would retract, even 40 plus years after I challenged my mission on that subject.

The final two chapters of the book deal with contextualization of the church. Chapter 33 (1973) suggests we model churches after highly communicative Bible translations. This is a theme I came back to in *Christianity in Culture* (1979). Chapter 34, then, presents an approach to measuring just how contextually appropriate a church may be.

The volume concludes with an attempt at a complete Bibliography of my professional writings since my first published article in 1961 to the year 2000.

I would like to express my deep gratitude to two people who helped bring this volume into being and one who finished things up. They are David Bjork who, while a student assistant of mine, did almost all of the scanning and original editing of the materials, Anne White who, while working in Fuller's word processing office, did the final editing and shaping of the manuscript into camera-ready form and Judi Brodeen who finished up the details and did the very demanding work of producing an index. Thank you three very much.

South Pasadena, CA
May 2001

CHAPTER 1

MY PILGRIMAGE IN MISSION

Reprinted here with permission from
International Bulletin of Missionary Research 22:162-164 (October 1998)

I was born in 1932 in Waterbury, Connecticut. My family and I attended a rather lifeless Congregational church during my early years. My mother, on the verge of suicide in the mid-1930s, upon rereading a letter from her cousin who served as a missionary in the Sudan and Ethiopia, turned to Christ. With the hope of seeing my brother and me come into the same relationship with Christ, my mother began sending us to various camps during the summers. By 1944 we both made decisions to follow Jesus.

Having come to Christ, I felt that I had to change churches and that I should give my life for the cause represented by the cousin who had led my mother to faith. I joined a small but very mission-minded church and grew rapidly in faith and in knowledge of Scripture. I also spent parts of most summers at a Christian camp where quite a number of the staff, speakers, and musicians recommended Wheaton College, Wheaton, Illinois, as the place to train for missionary service. In addition, I discovered that the missionary cousin (and her husband) who had influenced my mother had gone to Wheaton. When the time came to apply for entrance into college, Wheaton was my only choice. So I headed there in the fall of 1949 with one conscious and two semiconscious motives: to prepare for missionary service in Africa, to find a wife, and to become a good athlete to impress my father.

Path to Mission: Anthropology

Once at Wheaton, I began to ask around to find out what major a prospective missionary ought to declare. Various suggestions emerged, but one made more sense to me than all the others: anthropology. I remember asking an upperclassman who was headed for the Philippines what major I should enroll in. He said, "Anthropology, of course," explaining that this was the only subject in the curriculum that was devoted to dealing with non-Western peoples. Marie Fetzer was our anthropology professor. My enthusiasm was quickly confirmed in her classes, but she left to marry a Bible translator and linguist, William Reyburn, Robert Taylor, who had retired after many years teaching at Kansas State, took over.

As we studied the dynamics of culture, we learned how important it is to respect and love a people for Christ by respecting the only way of life that makes sense to them. We were also put in touch with a movement dedicated to applying anthropological insights to the practice of Christian mission. As a leader of this movement, Taylor in 1953 founded *Practical Anthropology*, a journal that became a very influential vehicle of anthropology and communication theory for missionaries.

As I studied anthropology, played varsity football and baseball, and fell in love with my future wife, Marguerite Gearhart (now professor of intercultural studies at Biola University), I added linguistics to my interests and felt called to become a Bible translator. But with which mission board? I would have joined Wycliffe Bible Translators in a minute if they worked anywhere in Africa. Alas, they didn't at that time, and I felt called to Africa.

So in 1952–53 I did a survey of all the mission boards I could find that worked in Africa, over 100 of them. I asked each what its attitude was toward appointing a person with anthropological training with a calling to do Bible translation. To my dismay, the answers I received were not positive. None of the missions seemed to think of Bible translation as a specialty worth pursuing at that time, except for veteran missionaries, and none was impressed with the value of anthropology.

But my future father-in-law was on the mission board of his denomination, the Brethren Church (Ashland, Ohio). The denomination at that time was working with the Church of the Brethren (Elgin, Ill.) to supply people and funds to open new work in northeastern Nigeria. As we discussed with him this new opportunity, the Lord seemed to be nudging us in that direction. So I wrote to Fuller Seminary, where I had been accepted for the fall of 1953, that I was not coming, and we headed instead to Ashland Seminary. We were accepted as missionary candidates and eventually received ordination from the Brethren Church, with the aim of pioneering in this new Nigerian field.

During the seminary years at Ashland, I took everything I could in Greek and Hebrew in addition to the regular curriculum, preparing for a career as a Bible translator. We also attended the Summer Institute of Linguistics at Norman, Oklahoma, during the summer of 1954. I took the second-year course, my wife the first. Then, after two years and an intensive summer of seminary, we were allowed by our mission board to spend a year (1955–56) studying at the Kennedy School of Missions in Hartford, Connecticut. During that year I was able to continue linguistic study under H. A. Gleason and anthropological study under Paul Leser and also to get into Islamics with Kenneth Cragg. In addition, I was able to build a relationship with Eugene Nida, William Smalley, and William and Marie (Fetzer) Reyburn, both during that year and during summers teaching with them in the Toronto Institute of Linguistics and the Meadville, Pennsylvania, missionary training program. At Meadville we also became acquainted with Ralph and Roberta Winter.

During this time Nida and Smalley, at the American Bible Society, assumed responsibility for Practical Anthropology and made it into a major influence in the lives and ministries of those of us who were open to a culture-affirming approach to Christian mission. I eagerly read and digested the journal as it came out every two months. I also was privileged to be one of a small circle of those who received prepublication papers by Bible Society men and women, sent out as *Translation Department Confidential Papers.* By the completion of the academic year 1955–56, I became a Ph.D. candidate at Hartford and returned to finish the remaining semester's worth of work for my B.D. at Ashland.

The Nigeria Years

In the spring of 1957 we headed for Nigeria. After weathering a six-week trip by sea plus a few weeks within Nigeria to get ourselves, our two-year-old twins, and our baggage to the town of Mubi, we were ready to begin learning the Hausa language. We were under pressure to learn fast, since the mission, eager to test our linguistic ability, had decided that after four months we were to begin teaching the language to four other missionaries. We worked hard at language learning, and by the time the others came, both my wife and I were fluent enough to work out lessons for these others and to bring them to the place where they could work with language helpers on their own.

In December of 1957 we headed for the tribal area to which we were assigned, forty-four miles north of Mubi on the Cameroon border. Bill and Marie Reyburn, who were working several hundred miles to the south of us in Cameroon, came to visit us that Christmas.

Our task was to learn the Kamwe (Higi) language, reduce it to writing, and begin a translation of the Scriptures. I also was in charge of a handful of small churches that had been started without much missionary supervision, largely through the evangelistic activity of two local men: one blind and the other severely impaired by leprosy. As I got into the dual responsibility of learning the language and assisting the church leaders, it fairly soon became apparent that I could not do justice to both. So assuming that I could come back to the linguistic work later, I turned my attention to the churches. I soon found myself in what we learned later to call a people movement. The growth was so rapid that, although converts had to go through a six-month training period before baptism, I was baptizing up to 150 a month!

Though the ground had been prepared and the receptivity was high, my culture-affirming approach probably had a lot to do with not stifling what God had already started. The Nigerian leaders got to do all the preaching, because I refused to, and they did the evangelizing and grassroots teaching. I limited myself to teaching the leaders (in Hausa) and baptizing (required by the mission, since I was the only ordained person working with these churches). The church in our area grew faster than the mission leaders believed a church could grow. This fact, plus a few other things, brought us into conflict with the mission leaders, though we enjoyed the trust and support of most of the Nigerian church leaders. One important issue was the fact that we opposed the mission policy against baptizing believing polygamists. We were in a pioneer area and in a society where in order for a man to be a leader he needed to have more than one wife. So, observing in Scripture that God was patient with this custom, we advocated that we follow God's lead rather than Western sensibilities. The mission leaders, most of whom were not in close enough contact with the people to know what they were thinking, were adamant against our position. In addition, we experimented with Christian dances and other culturally appropriate activities. These too were condemned. So in spite of what looked like success, we were asked not to return after our furlough in 1960. Greatly disappointed that we could not return to Nigeria, we went back to Hartford for me to complete my doctorate.

African Language Specialist

The next three years, 1960–63, were spent at the Kennedy School of Missions completing my doctorate, while Marguerite finished an M.A. I did a dual program, taking comprehensives in both linguistics and anthropology. My dissertation was entitled "A Study of Hausa Syntax." The summer of 1961 saw us returning to the Summer Institute of Linguistics at Norman, Oklahoma, and being accepted as candidates in training with Wycliffe.

The following summer was spent teaching Hausa at Michigan State University. This stint resulted in an invitation to join the MSU faculty as a member of the developing African Studies Center, with Hausa as my specialty. Without being quite sure why, we felt that God wanted us to take the position at MSU rather than going back to Africa (Ghana) with Wycliffe. So we resigned from Wycliffe.

On completion of my degree in June 1963, we headed for East Lansing, Michigan, and stayed five years on that faculty. There we involved ourselves with missionaries studying at MSU and several Peace Corps training programs in addition to my regular professorial responsibilities. In 1966–67 we returned to Nigeria to collect language data on sixty-five unwritten languages (later published in three volumes), with support from a government grant and MSU. During this year we also were able to rebuild our relationship with the mission and to assist them with language instruction and advice on other issues.

Shortly after we returned to Michigan State, an invitation came for me to accept a position in African languages at UCLA. Bill Welmers, who briefly had been my supervisor at Hartford, was now at UCLA and wanted me to join him in that prestigious African studies program. So we checked it out and decided to move there in 1968. UCLA was to be my academic home for the next five years, enabling me to publish several works on Hausa and Chadic languages in addition to teaching.

The Fuller Years

In my very first year at UCLA, we renewed acquaintance with Ralph Winter. This resulted in an invitation to teach in the School of World Mission, Fuller Seminary. After trying unsuccessfully to reduce my UCLA involvement to half-time, I accepted what was essentially a full-time position at Fuller (for half-time pay), starting in the fall of 1969. So, for the next four years I taught classes at each place two days a week, alternating between them for faculty meetings on Fridays! Donald McGavran was our dean, with Alan Tippett the senior anthropologist and Ralph Winter teaching history. I taught introductory anthropology, communication, and courses related to the relationship of Christianity to culture (e.g., conversion in culture, the church in culture). I couldn't have been happier. I had found my niche.

At UCLA, though I continued to do an acceptable job in the classroom, my heart was no longer in linguistic research. So I finished up a couple of books I had been working on and wrapped up my career as an African language specialist there in 1973. Now I could really be full-time at Fuller (and for full-time pay).

I was asked, however, by Clyde Cook, one of our students at the time and then chairman of the Missions Department of Biola College (now University), to help their program by teaching the introductory anthropology course for them. So for the next four years (till 1977) I taught anthropology also at Biola and was instrumental in getting them to hire my wife, at first part-time but then full-time after she earned her first doctorate in 1977.

The opportunity to teach and write in missiology these nearly thirty years has been more than I could ever have hoped for in life. From 1973 to 1979 I was able to work rather intensively on putting together my thoughts concerning the theological implications of the relationships between Christianity and culture. I called my approach cross-cultural theologizing, or "ethnotheology," and suggested that we use the incarnation and informed Bible translation theory as developed largely by Eugene Nida as our models. My call was for churches, theologizing, conversion, and all other aspects of Christianity to be dynamically equivalent within contemporary cultures to the approved models of these things we see in Scripture. This resulted in very fruitful classroom interactions with our experienced student body, the privilege of participating in the landmark Willowbank Consultation, and eventually in the publication of *Christianity in Culture* (1979a), the book many consider to be my magnum opus. It also made me quite controversial in some circles, though very affirmed in others and among our student body and School of Mission colleagues.

Communicating the Gospel God's Way also came out in 1979(b). This was followed in 1983 by *Communication Theory for Christian Witness* (rev. 1991), in which I was able to build from the incarnation a more detailed approach to gospel communication than was possible in *Christianity in Culture.*

In several articles and *Readings in Dynamic Indigeneity* (edited with Tom Wisley), I was able to further develop my approach to contextualization and to point to the importance of seeing indigenizing/contextualizing as a dynamic process, regardless of the name by which we label it. My recent *Anthropology for Christian Witness* (1996) encapsulates nearly fifty years worth of thinking on the relevance of anthropological insight to Christian witness. A forthcoming book on worldview plus a collection of my published and unpublished articles will expand this summary of my thinking.

I see myself in these writings and the teaching that goes along with them as continuing the pioneering efforts of Eugene Nida and his worthy associates of the 1950s and 1960s (Smalley, Reyburn, Loewen), much of the written record of which was published in *Practical Anthropology,* and of Alan Tippett, my esteemed colleague at Fuller for my first eight years.

I have been privileged to have a hand in the development of missionary anthropology, the harnessing of communication theory for Christian mission, and the acceptance and development of contextualization studies by evangelicals.

Christianity with Power

In 1982 a very surprising thing happened to me. Ever since my years in Nigeria, I had been puzzled about the relevance of Jesus' teaching and behavior relating to healing, demons, and other manifestations of spiritual power. The Nigerian church leaders had asked me what they should do about evil spirits, and though I took both their questions and the existence of the demonic seriously, I had no answers for them. In my growing understanding of what is going on in the world in response to gospel witness, I was becoming increasingly aware of the fact that worldwide missionary Christianity was lacking the spiritual power we are promised in the New Testament. Furthermore, I was discovering that many of our missionary and international students were coming from a charismatic background and questioning whether my understandings of the relationships between Christianity and culture took proper cognizance of the presence of spiritual power, whether God's or Satan's.

When we had the opportunity to invite John Wimber to teach us about such things at Fuller Seminary, I was an enthusiastic supporter. His first course, from January to March of 1982, brought about incredible change in my life. For the first time, I was able to see firsthand how the Holy Spirit can work in power for healing, for deliverance from demons, and for any number of other blessings, and all in a matter-of-fact, non-weird way. John became for me and many of the rest of our students and faculty a credible witness to the fact that Christianity is not intended to be powerless.

I remembered a time in Nigeria when the village shaman began to come to church. He soon dropped away, however, probably because there was no power there. And also because most of the Christians came to him rather than going to Jesus or the pastor when they needed spiritual power. I began to see that the biggest problem in worldwide Christianity, the lack of spiritual power, could be solved if we learned what Wimber was teaching—how to work with God to heal, deliver, and bless. And I determined that my students would not go away from my classes as ignorant in this area as I had gone to Nigeria.

So I listened as Wimber taught. I watched as he and others ministered in power. And eventually I began to practice what I saw them doing and then to teach others what God has been teaching me in this area. Missiologically, I am teaching regularly in this area and beginning to write on the contextualization of spiritual power. My *Evangelical Missions Quarterly* article "What Kind of Encounters Do We Need?" (1991) has brought gratifying response, and a forthcoming book on contextualization will develop my thinking in these areas further. At a more popular level, *Christianity with Power* (1989) applies worldview theory to the paradigm shift we evangelicals have to go through to move into this dimension of biblical Christianity. Following this volume, I have published four more semipopular books on inner healing, deliverance, authority, and spiritual warfare.

Moving into the area of spiritual power has made a much more complete missiologist out of me as well as a much more fulfilled servant of Jesus Christ. But, some would say, a strange anthropologist and a strange academic! Such comments, however, prompt me to deny that I am an academic; I simply do academic work to help the cause of Christ. Who I am is a servant of Christ who has learned a few things about how God works in this world. And I am ready not only to talk about those things but also to practice what he gave his life for: to set captives free.

ANTHROPOLOGY

CHAPTER 2

CONSERVATIVE CHRISTIANS AND ANTHROPOLOGISTS: A CLASH OF WORLDVIEWS

Reprinted here with permission from
Journal of the American Scientific Affiliation 32:140–145 (September 1980)

Anthropologists and missionaries as human beings are pervasively conditioned by the values of the cultures of which they are a part. Western anthropologists and western missionaries, as members of the same broad cultural stream, share many of the same values. Similarities in these worldview values, the result of similar cultural conditioning, explains some very basic common concerns and approaches. Among these common concerns is the felt need for both groups to attempt to transcend their own cultural conditioning, at least in cross-cultural contexts. There are, however, differences between the two groups in the ways in which each group attempts to transcend its culture. These differences are seen as differences in basic value orientations, here labeled worldviews. Several aspects of the differing worldviews are dealt with below.

The motivation for this paper stems from the felt need on the part of myself and others who attempt to be both missionaries and anthropologists to explain our understanding of how this is possible both to ourselves and to others. I attempt to do this first by outlining what I observe to be several areas of conflict between the worldviews of the two groups and then by making certain suggestions concerning the possibility for constructing an integrated perspective.

The historical and contemporary intracultural tensions between those who gravitate toward the opposite positions to be described are artifacts of the similarities and differences between the worldviews of the two groups. The influence of the cultural conditioning of the two groups is such, however, that neither is neutral toward the answers that the other group prefers. Historically, for example, western society has moved from a theocentric worldview to an anthropocentric worldview. Given the deeply rooted assumption within the western worldview that any such major change is to be considered progress, it is understandable that those whose worldview is anthropocentric evaluate those whose worldview is theocentric as outdated. Thus, anthropologists tend to see missionaries as behind the times. Missionaries, for their part, tend to see the preferred answers of anthropologists as anti-Christian. The result tends to be a closed-mindedness on the part of each group toward (1) the options chosen by the other group, (2) tolerance of the persons who choose those options, and (3) the possibility of any integration of anthropological and Christian presuppositions into a single worldview.

In addition to the pervasiveness of the distinction between theocenteredness and anthropocenteredness is the fact that missionaries have ordinarily been influenced by the understandings of reality available through the study of the humanities, especially philosophy and history employed for theological purposes. Within these disciplines, especially as they are applied by conservative Christians, the "naive realism" perspective,[1] now being questioned and abandoned by philosophers of science, has continued to be very influential. Anthropologists, however, have been primarily influenced by a disciplinary perspective that is largely in revolt against at least certain of the major emphases of the humanities. In this revolt contemporary anthropologists have largely turned against naive realism.[2] It is understandable that missionaries, and conservative Christians in general, should regard any perspective other than that of naive realism as a grave threat to their core values.

Related to this conflict of worldviews between the older academic disciplines that have influenced the theological perspectives of missionaries and the younger behavioral sciences is the fact that devotees of alternative worldviews often come across to each other as devotees of different religions. The devotion of many anthropologists (and other behavioral scientists) to their man- and science-oriented worldview seems often to be of the same nature as the devotion of missionaries to their theocentric worldview. It is well known in conservative Christian circles that many of the advocates of the behavioral sciences have attempted to promote their cause at the expense of supernaturalistic religion (e.g., Freud, Skinner). Such a fact led William James to contend that the supreme commandment of scientism is, "Thou shalt not be a theist" (James 1904:131). The fact that theological liberals often have virtually abandoned a supernaturalistic perspective in favor of a man-centered concern (often that of sociology) has also tended to turn conservative Christians against the behavioral sciences. Man-centeredness with its concomitant emphasis on cultural, social and psychological relativities has appeared antithetical to a perspective that attempts to focus on God and God-given attributes.

What missionaries, and other conservative Christians, often overlook is the man-madeness and consequent fallibility of every academic discipline, including those on the basis of which Christian theologians have made their interpretations of the Christian Scriptures. Even if, as missionaries contend, the data of the Christian Scriptures are sacred, the perspectives in terms of which they are interpreted are

---

[1] See I. Barbour (1974:34 ft) who describes this perspective as believing that such concepts as scientific theories are "accurate descriptions of 'the world as it is in itself.' Theoretical terms are said to denote real things of the same kind as physical objects in the perceived world." This position thus sees virtually a one-to-one relationship between reality (whether physical or spiritual) and the concept of that reality held by the advocate of this position.

[2] The perspective that Barbour labels "critical realism" is much more in vogue within the behavioral sciences. This perspective, like naive realism, "takes theories to be representations of the world." But, unlike the naive realist, the proponent of critical realism "recognizes the importance of human imagination in the formation of theories ... [He] thus tries to acknowledge both the creativity of man's mind and the existence of patterns in events not created my man's mind. Descriptions of nature are human constructions but nature is such as to bear descriptions in some ways and not in others" (1974:37).

human. A recognition of this fact opens the possibility that even data that are regarded as sacred may fruitfully be analyzed from the perspectives of disciplines other than those traditionally employed.

Are the kinds of polarization discussed below between the concerns of Christian missionaries and those of behavioral scientists a necessary concomitant of the incompatibility of evangelical faith with naturalistic scientism? Or is it simply an artifact of the inability of such competing perspectives to overcome the pressure of western culture to push persons and disciplines to absolutize their specialized insights? One could, for example, infer that in areas of concern to both groups each polarizes in reaction against the other group's position. Anthropologists and other behavioral scientists, of course, do not ordinarily move to their positions in reaction to missionaries—their tendency is not to take missionaries quite that seriously. Their reaction, I believe, has its roots in the overall reaction against the theocentric worldview that our society as a whole has abandoned except within the groups that produce missionaries. Missionaries, however, often react consciously to behavioral science perspectives by moving more firmly into the extreme positions characteristic of their groups.

The Polarization Outlined

Though there is a fair measure of variation within each group, the variations tend to cluster around the pole preferred by the group.

1. The first problem is that of *ultimate authority*. To conservative Protestants (including missionaries), God has been the source of ultimate authority. But, due to the tendency of western culture to absolutize one or the other of two alternatives, conservative theologians have tended to exalt God's authority while demeaning, largely ignoring, or, at best, only vaguely outlining that of human beings. Their treatments in this area often lack balance. Anthropologists, for their part, have been even more guilty of polarization since they have, in reaction, turned completely to human experience as the source of authority. This is, of course, in keeping with the naturalistic humanistic worldview that western science espouses.

2. The second area where these groups differ is in *how to arrive at truth*. Conservative Christians have focused on revelation from God as the source of at least the most important truths, whereas anthropology looks to scientific discovery via empirical research as the source of truth. To conservative Christians (under the influence of their theological tradition) truth tends to be primarily a cognitive, propositional kind of thing, derived from faithful interpretation of the once-for-all revelation given in the Scriptures. For anthropology, on the other hand, the key to finding truth is a never-ending process of sense perception leading to theory building, testing and modification.

3. A third problem of concern to both groups is that of *determinism and free will*. Conservative Christian theorists have seen man as circumscribed by God. And those theologians who have gone to the determinist extreme have seen him as

absolutely determined by God. In reaction against such theological determinism, other Christian theorists have focused on human freedom. Both Christian groups have, however, tended to deal rather imprecisely with the circumscribing, sometimes determining, effects of culture. Anthropology, has, of course, tended to ignore the possibility of divine limitation and focused on the interaction between human beings and culture.

4. A fourth concern pertains to the matter of *what (if anything) is absolute and what is relative.* Conservative Christians consider it essential that their perspectives be firmly based upon and give strong witness to theological absolutes. They seek to discern from the Bible divinely ordained absolute truths that are applicable to all humans at all times. Naturalistic anthropology, in reaction, has made the culturally relative aspects of human existence its primary focus. Anthropologists have been quick to criticize conservative Christians for regarding as absolute certain aspects of western culture. And many Christians have fallen into a kind of "worldview shock" by being forced to admit the validity of at least certain of these contentions.

5. Closely related to the opposing emphases with respect to absolutes and relativities is a polarization over whether to be primarily concerned with *human commonality or with human diversity.* Conservative Christians, interested in discovering the "once for all" verities with respect to God have focused likewise on that which is regarded as the same for all human beings. Differences stemming from culture and/or psychology have often been noted but either minimized or condemned as heretical. Behavioral scientists, while retaining a commitment to basic human commonality, have tended to react against both (1) what they see as a naive overemphasis on the extent of such similarity and (2) the ethnocentric basis on which many of the generalizations concerning similarities are based. Within anthropology, then, there has developed a rather total preoccupation with cultural diversity on the part of many (though not all). At one extreme, many conservative Christians overestimate the number of similarities between "human nature" and basic western values. At the other, many behavioral scientists and many liberal Christians seem to have "sold out" to a relativistic perspective, acting as if nearly everything about peoples of different cultures is totally different. Many conservative Christians have blamed the behavioral sciences for such liberal perspectives as "situation ethics" (see Fletcher 1966). This has further alienated the conservative Christians from the insights of the behavioral sciences.

6. A sixth difference that can be noted relates to what I here call a *preference for "static models" versus a preference for "dynamic models" of reality.* The "once for all" preoccupation of conservative Christians has pushed them toward the adoption of perspectives that have very little room for "give" or growth in them. Behavior is understood as good or bad, black or white. A person is either a Christian or a non-Christian, in or out on the basis of one decision. The dynamic processes tend to be ignored by means of which one becomes a Christian and moves toward maturity or by means of which one changes one's behavior from sub-ideal toward more ideal. The behavioral sciences, though themselves also plagued by static models, have at least lately come to be more concerned with the dynamic processes by means of which changes in human behavior come about.

7. A seventh concern is the problem of *imperfection.* To conservative Christians, the immediate cause of evil is in human nature corrupted by sin. Anthropologists have, however, tended to go to an opposite extreme. They have taken a positive view of human nature. Evil, therefore, has largely been seen as a function of imperfect sociocultural systems rather than of imperfect people.[3]

8. Another area of polarization to be highlighted here involves the *focus on concepts recorded primarily in books versus a focus on people and their behavior.* The academic tradition of which conservative Christian theology is a part conceives of research as book-based and largely centered on thinking behavior. Anthropologists, as a part of the behavioral science reaction against the excessive preoccupation of many with the purely conceptual, have turned to studying the totality of human behavior. The field method called "participant-observation" has been developed by anthropologists in an attempt to serve this aim (see Pelto 1970). Conservative Christianity, minus this ability to study the totality of human behavior in culture, has continued to be concept and book-centered. This concept and book-centeredness has enormously hurt missionaries working in preliterate societies. Their background and training has provided them with no tools by means of which to get inside the hearts and minds of the peoples with whom they work.

9. A ninth area that may be designated is the fact that *both groups are active proselyters.* Conservative Christians, and especially missionaries, are, of course, openly committed to winning people to their point of view. Anthropologists, and other academicians who feel that their discipline has led them into new truth, often appear to be equally "conversionist." I once had to counsel a distraught graduate student who was nearly denied admittance to a doctoral program because, despite otherwise impeccable credentials, his professors questioned his commitment to the discipline.

10. A final point to be considered is the fact that *each group has its own "Golden Rule" that it tends to forget or ignore* when interacting with the other group. For Christians this doctrine is expressed as, "Treat others as you would like them to treat you" (Lk. 6:31). For anthropologists there is the equivalent in the doctrine of cultural relativity (or, better, "cultural validity"). We are to respect and take seriously every other cultural way of life just as we respect and take seriously our own culture.

These are a few of the major issues on which the worldview of conservative Protestantism (from which the majority of the missionaries here in view have come) differs from that of anthropologists. The fact that many of the members of each group spend a considerable amount of energy criticizing the perspective of the other group indicates the extent to which the views are seen to be in competition with each other and mutually exclusive. It is not uncommon, for example, to find critical allusions to missionaries in anthropological publications and to find critical allusions to anthropologists (and other behavioral scientists) in statements made by conservative Christians. Not infrequently those of us who attempt to do anthropology on the basis of a conservative Christian ideology are regarded with suspicion by members of both groups. We question, however, whether the polarization that has

---

[3] Anthropologist Walter Goldschmidt (1966:134–136), however, shows a mediating position.

occurred is necessary. For in so many areas we see the concerns of the two groups to be more complementary than mutually exclusive, once the tendency to polarize completely at one extreme or the other is overcome. In what follows I seek to outline a possible synthesis of the worldviews in the hope that such a model might suggest a fruitful basis for understanding and, for some at least, for building a new worldview.

Toward a Synthesis

Human beings need some sort of worldview allegiance (or faith). Conflict at the worldview level between missionaries and anthropologists is, therefore, a conflict between faiths—not a conflict between faith and non-faith. The fact that one faith has a supernatural object while the other denies the relevance of that object cannot, I believe, mask the fact that even the anti-supernatural position is a faith position.

Crucial to the conservative Christian worldview is an allegiance to a supernatural God. This worldview value would be regarded as non-negotiable in any attempt by Christians to take seriously the anthropologically preferred alternatives to the positions traditionally taken by Christians on the above issues. But, I believe, a conservative (better "evangelical") Christian could modify considerably in the direction of the anthropological position and remain true to the essentials of his faith. In fact, I would maintain (as argued elsewhere) that certain of the anthropological positions allow a Christian to be more true to biblical guidelines than do the traditionally held positions.

I further argue that an anthropological perspective does not require an anti-supernaturalistic worldview assumption, and that, therefore, those committed to supernaturalistic worldview assumptions can do valid anthropology. Indeed, given a commitment to the anthropological doctrine of "participant-observation," an anthropologist who is himself committed to supernaturalistic worldview assumptions is likely to be in a better position to study peoples who have supernaturalistic assumptions than is an anthropologist with a naturalistic worldview. A committed Christian (even a missionary) might, therefore, be able to adopt a validly anthropological perspective—but only if he/she adopts an understanding of Christianity that is not bound to the extreme positions outlined above. For example:

1. I believe it is possible to develop a perspective that denies neither the authority of God nor the authority of human beings—a perspective that holds to the ultimate authority of God, without denying either the importance of the delegation of certain authority to humans or the fact that on occasion God limits himself to that human authority. The Psalmist asked, "What is man?" and concluded that we are "but little less than God" (Ps. 8:4-5). Jesus became human and trusted humans (in spite of many good reasons for mistrust) to carry on his work after him. Perhaps the insights of the Science of Man (anthropology) concerning this marvelous creature that Christians believe was created by God are not incompatible with Christian understandings, as long as human authority is not absolutized. Perhaps, further, anthropological insight can assist conservative Christians to overcome their bondage

to the so-called "Puritan" negativeness toward human beingness—a negativeness that lies behind much of the antagonism that many missionaries exhibit toward other cultures.

2. Informed Christians are forced to recognize that the search for truth is much more than a matter of receiving revelations from God. Even the study of the Bible, considered to be God's revelation, involves interpretation based on human conceptualization and perception. More Christians are coming to believe that such interpretation can be validly done from a variety of points of view—perhaps even from an anthropological perspective. There is, I believe, room within missionary-minded Christianity for an approach that takes seriously both divine revelation and the human discovery processes by means of which that revelation is made vital to Christians and to the life of the world around them. I am, in this regard, experimenting with an approach that postulates the revelational validity of the biblical data and the interpretational validity of a cross-cultural anthropological perspective applied to the understanding and application of the insights available from the biblical data. The results of this approach are in some respects quite different from those of traditional monocultural theological approaches. Many of the missionaries with whom I interact find the new approach much more promising. So do those with whom they work within other cultures.

3. Those with a supernaturalistic faith (and especially Christian missionaries) can no longer ignore the mass of anthropological data concerning the influence of culture on human beings. Though committed to a belief that God is in ultimate control, informed Christians can no longer be content to deal with the relationships between human beings and God with only imprecise, passing reference to culture. For it is evident that even if one believes that it is God who ultimately circumscribes human beings, one must accept and try to understand the fact that culture also circumscribes humanity. Furthermore, conservative Christianity maintains that God interacts with human beings in history (culture). Understanding the nature of that milieu and its relationships both to humans and to God is, therefore, of prime importance to Christians. Anthropology's strength at this point is in an area of one of conservative Christian theology's greatest weaknesses. For anthropology is the discipline that has devoted the most attention to the development of an understanding of culture. Christians can employ anthropological perspectives and methodology just as they have for years employed historical perspectives and methodology without fear of compromising their faith.

4. In the area of absolutes and relativities, we face perhaps the most sensitive issues. Conservative Christians, without the jarring experience of having to really face cross-cultural diversity, have tended to absolutize much more of western culture than even western interpretations of the Bible allow. Missionaries have often been much less ethnocentric. But even those with the most intense exposure to other societies have often been extremely reluctant to accept the validity of the perspectives of those peoples.

This leaves conservative Christians committed to a faith once clothed in the trappings of a Middle Eastern culture but now pressed into Euroamerican cultural forms and taken to the ends of the earth as if inseparable from these forms. Anthropologists and others with a relativistic bias have, I believe, rightly criticized

Christians for regarding as absolute certain aspects of western culture. And many Christians have seen the validity of at least certain of these contentions. Conservative Christians stop short, however, of seeing the essence of Christianity as simply the product of western (or any other) culture and, therefore, devoid of transcultural validity.

A committed Christian with an anthropological perspective seeks to distinguish between the relative cultural forms, in terms of which even transculturally valid Christian meanings must be expressed, and those meanings. He adopts and supports from the Bible (cf. Nida 1954:48–52) a "relative cultural relativism" and adds to the list of cultural universals acceptable to naturalistic anthropologists a category of "spiritual universals" or "universally experienced spiritual felt needs" to which he sees essential Christianity speaking. He attempts to learn from anthropology how to become expert in interpreting and applying his non-western source of revelation (the Bible) without sacrificing his supernaturalistic worldview, in such a way that the interpretations he makes are cross-culturally valid rather than ethnocentric. There is much potential conflict in this area between the practice of most anthropologists and that of most conservative Christians. I believe that this is mostly at the surface level, however. The conflict, while the result of the different faith positions as they are actually held does not indicate the impossibility of working out an informed anthropological approach based on a biblical faith.

5. In the area of whether to focus on human commonality or on human diversity, I believe both groups have begun to show more concern for the focus of the other. Anthropologists seem to speak more today of cultural universals while conservative Christians—especially those, like missionaries, who work cross-culturally—speak more acceptingly of cultural diversity. In my judgment, conservative Christianity still has a ways to go toward overcoming its absolutized ethnocentrism. A cross-cultural perspective learned from anthropology but wedded to a supernaturalistic worldview could provide an approach that is both more satisfying and more in tune with the Christian Scriptures.

6. Conservative Christians can and, I believe, must learn from anthropologists and other behavioral scientists concerning the dynamics of human life. It is often at least as important to understand the cultural processes by means of which people move (or are moved) from one state to another as it is to understand the goals toward which one desires that they move. Such understanding is important to an informed interpretation of the Bible. For the Bible shows God accepting people whose belief is sub-ideal and who have not attained to a particular ideal behavior. He accepts people who are "in process toward," even though not yet having attained God's goals for them. It is the imposition of western cultural models on biblical interpretation that has staticized the conception of what God approves to conform to western "either-or" values. The input of more dynamic anthropological thinking can contribute to freeing essential Christianity from its enslavement to traditional western modes of thought.

7. With respect to the problem of imperfection, biblical Christianity requires a belief that there is something radically wrong with human nature. There is, however, so much to learn from the findings of anthropologists concerning the outworking of evil in sociocultural systems that Christians dare not ignore its insights. For

conservative Christianity needs to deal in an informed way both with the evil in human beings and with its outworking in sociocultural systems.

8. Conservative Christians, especially those who work cross-culturally, can learn from anthropology how to study people and human behavior more effectively and with less dependence on books. This would be of great positive value both to the cause of the missionaries and to the people they seek to reach. It should, furthermore, constitute no threat to the missionaries' worldview.

9. Conflict between proselytizers may never be fully reconcilable. But this situation could, perhaps, be rendered more tolerable if it is recognized that the two faiths are not at the same level and are not, therefore, mutually exclusive. Christian faith is an ultimate sort of commitment to a God who exists outside of the historical and cultural milieu within which human beings operate. Anthropological faith, on the other hand, is faith in a perspective in terms of which to view the historical and cultural milieu. If such faith posits a naturalistic or humanistic object or perspective as its ultimate, it is at that point that it conflicts with Christian faith. If, on the other hand, Christians insist that a particular perspective on history and culture is concomitant with their commitment to God, there may be conflict with anthropology at that point.

I would contend, though, that the ultimate faith in God exercised by Christians is combinable with the anthropological perspective (or perspectives) on history and culture. The perspective(s) on history and culture ordinarily associated with conservative Christianity are, I believe, artifacts of the marriage between Christian faith and the western academic perspective traditionally associated with the humanities (especially certain schools of philosophy and history), rather than essential parts of that faith. Likewise, the close association between the anthropological perspective(s) and naturalistic faith is an artifact of the fact that anthropology has been largely developed by those who espouse such a faith. If this is true, it is at least thinkable that a different non-ultimate perspective (such as that of anthropology) could be employed by those committed to the ultimate perspective of Christian faith. It is also thinkable that those whose present commitment is to an anthropological perspective wedded to an ultimate naturalistic faith could legitimately replace the latter with a Christian ultimate faith without doing injustice to their anthropology.

Whatever proselytizing goes on between these groups should be recognized for what it is and conducted on the proper level. The advocate should understand whether he is seeking to win his hearer(s) to an essential faith or to a new perspective that will, of course, have implications for how one understands his faith but is not mutually exclusive with that faith.

10. With respect to the Golden Rule, perhaps the only thing to say is that one wishes that each group would obey its own version. I have attempted above to provide at least the start toward a rationale that would make toleration and respect between the groups more possible.

Conclusion

I have sought in this paper to make explicit ten areas where anthropologists and conservative (Protestant) Christians share similar concerns but follow different paths in seeking to deal with them. I have suggested that we are dealing here with a matter of similarity and difference between worldview values. The development of differing positions and the concomitant antipathy between the groups is understandable as a normal result of the historical backgrounds of the two groups. Though the focus chosen by each group in each of the ten areas tends to be in opposition to that of the other (in keeping with the differences in their respective worldviews), I maintain that that opposition is not necessary. By recombination (in Barnett's sense—Barnett 1953) of a Christian ultimate faith with a largely anthropological perspective on history and culture one can, I believe, both resolve the majority of the conflicting issues and develop a more satisfying worldview than either alternative has traditionally provided.

CHAPTER 3

GOD, HUMAN BEINGS, CULTURE AND THE CROSS-CULTURAL COMMUNICATION OF THE GOSPEL

Slight revision of an unpublished article written in 1972

Introduction

It is the purpose of this chapter to explore the relationships between God, human beings, and culture with primary attention given to three aspects of these relationships: 1) the development of a general perspective that takes all three seriously, 2) a consideration of how God reveals himself to humans and 3) the implications of all of this for cross-cultural and cross-subcultural communication of the gospel.

Christian theology (as developed within western Christianity) has traditionally focused on God, humans and the interactions between them. Evangelical theology has strongly asserted the transcendence, omnipotence, omniscience, perfection, absoluteness and personality of God while asserting that humans are finite, in rebellion against God, pervasively affected by sin yet unable to find real meaning in life apart from a relationship with God. God, furthermore, seeks to bring humans back into a relationship with himself and for this purpose reveals himself to humans in acts and words, a selection of which, centering around God's interaction with the Hebrew people and his entering the human scene in the person of Jesus Christ, have been recorded in the Bible. Central to both God's revelation of himself to us and his seeking to bring us back to himself are the incarnation, the written Word and (though to some extent less understood by western theology) the continuing work of the Holy Spirit.

This presentation assumes all of this plus the great majority of the concomitants of these basic tenets that go to make up what is know as evangelical theology. It is notable, however, that in all of this focus on God, human beings and their interaction, evangelical theology says very little if anything about culture, the setting in which humans operate and in which all God-human interaction takes place. Theology only deals with God and human beings.

Anthropology, on the other hand, speaks of culture and human participation in it. And it is to anthropology that we must look for the filling in of the information we need to understand the cultural medium of the God-human interaction. Anthropology, however, focused as it is on the human context and operated as it largely is by naturalistically-oriented scholars, says virtually nothing acceptable to evangelical Christians about God. In fact, insofar as anthropology speaks of God at all, it does so only at the perceptual level—as humans within culture perceive God to be. And since anthropologists usually do not hold to the existence of an absolute, transcendent God who exists above and outside of culture, these differing cultural perceptions of God look to anthropologists like just so many culturally-defined gods (which, indeed, they may often be) rather than (as they frequently are) merely differing culturally-defined perceptions of the one true "supracultural" (see below) God.

The perspective we need, then, to adequately deal with God, human beings *and* culture must draw insight from both theology and anthropology while avoiding the extremes that either often goes to in touching upon the other's territory. For theology in its disregard of culture is often found to be absolutizing not only the Christian functions and meanings (see below) that God (we believe) desires to see worked out in the human context but the very *forms* in which these functions are embodied in a particular (usually western) culture. Thus, for example, within western theology it usually goes unquestioned that such things as a western philosophic approach to formulating doctrine, a purely monologic definition of "proclamation," a democratic form of church government, a largely impersonal, money-oriented approach to charity and the like are the God-endorsed ways of doing these things. In ignorance of the fact that the forms in which each of these Christian functions (i.e., theologizing, proclaiming, governing and giving) in embodied are culturally determined (by western culture) not ordained by God, many theologically trained but culturally naive Christians have sought to simply convert persons of other societies to these forms rather than to communicate to them the Christian functions while assisting them to clothe these Christian functions in the forms appropriate to their culture.

But if this extreme is to be avoided, even more must the Christian turn from the extreme to which anthropology goes when dealing with the subject matter of theology. For anthropologists tend to relativize God and deny the existence of absolutes and, indeed, of any reality outside of the cultural context.

What we need, then, is a wedding of the central perspectives of the two sciences into a new approach that might be termed "Christian ethnotheology." This approach (to be employed here) takes God, human beings and culture seriously and seeks to draw insights from both theology and anthropology to deal with such subject-matter as that which this paper treats. It looks to theology for most of its information concerning God and much concerning humanity—particularly with regard to our sinful condition and our ultimate need. It looks to anthropology, however, for understanding of culture in general and of the implications of our immersion in culture for our perception of and interaction with God. The proposed relationship between the sources of the informational content employed to provide the perspective here termed "Christian ethnotheology" may be diagrammed thus:[1]

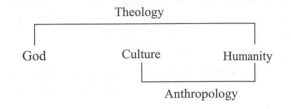

Figure 3.1 Relationship of sources in Christian ethnotheology

Culture and Human Beings

> The culture of any society consists of the sum total of the ideas, conditioned emotional responses, and patterns of habitual behavior which the members of that society have acquired through instruction or imitation and which they share to a greater or less degree (Linton 1936:288).

Every society has its own culture and every person is subject to the culture of the society of which he or she is a part.

Human beings are thoroughly immersed in culture. Each human individual is born into a particular society and immediately begins a lifelong training process (technically known as *enculturation*) by means of which he or she is thoroughly indoctrinated into that society's culture. Much of this training is performed in such a way that the individual is unaware of it. But the training is thorough and all pervasive so that before children are very old they have made the values, attitudes, worldview and the majority of the basic patterns of the society's culture their own. What then seems natural and normal to the rest of the society seems natural and normal to them. What seems unnatural to the rest of the society seems unnatural to them.

If, for example, one's society regards the universe as something one submits to rather than something one conquers or divides time into two categories (e.g., present and a combined past-future) rather than into three (past, present, future), or believes that disease is caused by personal malevolent spirits rather than by impersonal germs, or feels that women are so valuable to society that they must be provided as much security as possible (one of the primary rationales for polygamy) rather than that women are so important as individuals that they must be given as much freedom as possible, etc., the child born into that society will soon come to accept, without argument, that these attitudes are those which are most normal and natural. He or she is probably, in fact, blissfully unaware of the possibility that anyone anywhere could hold to any of the alternative attitudes listed above.

---

[1] See Kraft 1972 for a more detailed discussion of "Christian ethnotheology."

Each child, therefore, is thoroughly conditioned by the adults around her or him to see reality as that society sees it. And, anthropology tells us, the number and variety of such culturally defined perspective on reality is vast. Such perspectives, often referred to as "worldviews," provide the unconsciously-subscribed-to attitudes and value systems by means of which the members of the various societies live. And when such unconsciously subscribed to worldviews meet each other some very interesting misunderstandings are likely to occur—misunderstandings that to the perceptive observer demonstrate just how widely divergent cultures can be.

It may not, for example, even occur to people whose worldview sees the environment as something to which we are expected to unthinkingly submit that they have the right to manipulate land (e.g., by the use of fertilizer) to produce better crops. Nor may they think it legitimate or possible to take certain preventive measures to ward off disease or to develop certain curative techniques to prevent death from disease, lest they be interfering with God or fate. To societies with such a worldview, such matters belong only to God or fate, and humans have no right to assert themselves by attempting to manipulate the factors involved.

Other societies (such as those of European nations), however, take an opposite view of the proper relationship between humans and our environment. These societies, operating from this opposite perspective, encourage their members to exploit natural resources, and to develop both preventive and curative measures with respect to disease. They may even (as Euroamerican societies do) go so far as to give the impression that these areas are of no concern to God if, indeed, there be a God at all.

Both types of society start with the same question: "What is the proper relationship between humans and their environment?" But they come up with radically different answers because each approaches the problem from a different perspective—a perspective determined not by the environment nor by a common humanity (both of which may be very similar for both societies) but by that which we call "culture."

The majority of the problems faced by human beings—such as how to relate to the physical environment, how to relate to the social environment, how to constructively control and channel human drives, how to invest life with meaning, what value to put on any given person, thing or event, and the like—are universal human problems. For, and anthropologists and theologians are in agreement on this point, down deep beneath the culturally-conditioned surface of human societies lies a human common ground—sometimes referred to as a "common humanity"—that is so basic that it has prompted one noted anthropologist to remark that "people are more alike than their cultures." There is, he continues, "a good deal of evidence that, for instance, the average Zuni and average Kwakiutl man behave a good deal more like each other than the normative patterns of the two cultures are alike." He further suggests that this recognition be interpreted not merely as "an expression of the limitations of culture," but as an insight into "the nature of man *to which culture must adapt*" (Goldschmidt 1966:134–135).

And it is on the basis of this common humanity that it is possible to communicate from one cultural "world" to another in spite of the radical differences in perspective, perception of reality and overall worldview that have been observed between cultures. For this common humanity includes (again, according to Goldschmidt who, for an apparently disinterested anthropologist, sounds remarkably like a theologian) both 1) the presence of deep dissatisfaction, selfishness, exploitiveness and conflict in every culture and 2) a longing for escape from all of this into "some kind of symbolic eternity" (1966:136). That is, in theological terms, men of every culture have a basic sin problem and a basic longing for salvation.

Still, since cultural conditioning is so pervasive and results in such radically different conceptions of reality, Nida, in discussing the bases for cross-cultural communication of the gospel, prefers to label these commonalities "points of contact" rather than "common ground." He says

> the valid common starting points ("points of contact" in contrast with "common ground") are the human needs shared by all: mental and physical health, fulfillment of hopes and aspirations, satisfactory training of one's children, security for the future, relief from family tensions, personal conflicts and moral failures, and a faith as to the ultimate meaning of life. In these matters all mankind finds a common starting point, even though the cultural expressions may vary (1954:261–262).

The Relative Equal Validity of Cultures

The presence of basic similarities between peoples does not mean that culture can be ignored. On the contrary, in spite of deep and basic human commonality, the all-pervasiveness of culture is also a fact and must be taken seriously at every point. Furthermore, the study of culture has demonstrated that every culture is extremely complex. Naive approaches to culture have tended to label the cultures of other people as "primitive" or "advanced" according to how closely they approximate one's own culture. It was, in fact, once in vogue to line cultures up in an evolutionary sequence from "most primitive" to "most civilized" (that is, most like our own). The assumption was that "primitive" peoples possessed "primitive" or simple cultures. Further investigation, however, has demonstrated that there is no such thing as a "simple" culture. All cultures are very complex and intricately put together, whether or not they resemble ours.

One thing learned from those early attempts to classify cultures was that when we look at other cultures we tend to evaluate them in terms of that which we in our culture value most highly. That is, our scale of primitivity was set up on the basis of similarity to or dissimilarity from the cultural emphases which we consider to be most important. These emphases tend to be technological, individualistic, and in every other way to approximate the value system that our society has bought into. Thus it was that western culture invariably appeared at the top of the list as the "most civilized" culture while the cultures of nomadic herders—those who from our point of view did not even know enough to settle down in one place—tended to come out near the bottom of the list, with "hunters and gatherers" who don't grow their own food at the very bottom.

This ethnocentric and evolutionary view of culture has, however, been abandoned by the majority of anthropologists—though unfortunately, it is still very much a part of the thinking of many non-anthropologists, including many Christians (who often allow an overestimate of the effect that Christianity has had on western culture to further cloud the issue). In its place has developed a perspective that regards cultures as basically mixed in terms of superiorities and inferiorities. One culture, for example, may manifest superiority to another culture in technology yet the second culture may outshine the first with respect to such things as family solidarity and other aspects of social organization. Cultures are no longer, therefore, regarded by anthropologists as absolutely superior to or inferior to each other but rather, as relatively equal to each other—especially in terms of the adequacy with which each culture handles the felt needs of its participants.

We thus see emerging an attitude toward the cultures of humanity very similar to an informed attitude toward individual persons. Just as it is necessary to evaluate a given person in terms of his or her own particular strengths and weaknesses (rather than in terms of the strengths and weaknesses that someone else may have), so it is appropriate to evaluate different cultures in terms of their own strengths and weaknesses with respect to the adequacy with which they handle the problems of life as they perceive them. Moreover, just as in dealing with individuals it is of utmost importance to take each person seriously (whether or not one agrees with her or his positions), so in an approach to cultures the informed attitude must be that each culture be taken seriously in its own terms.

God and Culture

It is crucial, though, in treating a topic such as this to ascertain just what God's attitude toward culture is. Is God a cultural relativist? Or did he, as some seem to contend, once create a model culture (Hebrew culture)? Or, as many seem to assume, is he in the process of developing a more and more "Christian culture" out of western "civilization"?

In a now classic statement of the relationships that western theologians have seemed to understand between Christ and culture, H. Richard Niebuhr (1951) treats three basic positions: Christ against culture, Christ in culture and Christ above culture. In a similar vein one might designate at least five possible understandings of the relationship between God and culture: God in culture, God against culture, God endorsing a culture, God above and apart from culture, and God above but interacting with humans in terms of culture. Though each of these perspectives captures some truth with regard to God's relationship to culture, it is here maintained that only the last understanding is true both to the Bible (the theological source of our understanding of God and humanity) and the insights of anthropology.

1. Those who see God as contained in culture typically see him merely as the expression of a longing on the part of humans to deify ourselves. "Man creates God in his own image," they say, and then bows down in reality not to someone who really exists but to a concept that we ourselves have created. In support of such a contention its advocates (including perhaps the majority of anthropologists) point to the widely differing culturally-defined perceptions of deity abroad in the world, maintaining that these differing perceptions have each developed wholly or largely as the result of the human quest for suprahuman sanction for the kind of life that a person's society prescribes for him or her.

The Christian must, of course, reject this kind of complete relativization of God. We do, however, need to note how true it is that the members of different societies do perceive deity in quite different ways and that there are major differences between the worldviews (including values, ideals and beliefs) of these societies. When, therefore, one focuses *only* on culture-bound perception it is not impossible to suggest that even Christians to a great extent "create God in their own image." Americans, for example, so focus on the love (as we idealize it) of God that we not only have difficulty interpreting scriptural passages displaying the judgmental side of God but often fail miserably in understanding *that* God could ever condemn. Likewise early Hebrew culture, focused in as it was on the majesty and righteousness of God, while finding it relatively easy to understand his judgments, often failed to understand his love. In such ways, at the perceptual level only, humans "create" God.

2. The second view is of those that maintain that there is an absolute God but regard him as basically antagonistic toward culture. These often point to passages such as 1 John 2:15, 16 and 5:19 where Christians are told not to love "the world," since the world "is in the power of the evil one," as indications that God is dead set against human culture since the latter is wholly under the power of Satan. To those who hold this view the essence of "culture" is the evil that they see around them and the way to holiness is to escape from and condemn "the world."

This group, while rightly understanding that Satan makes use of human culture for his ends makes two very serious errors. First they equate the term "culture" with but one of the New Testament uses of the word *kosmos*,[2] and secondly, they assume that because Satan has power over the limited areas of culture they focus on, that, therefore, all of culture is evil. They, however, continue to live by and endorse the major part of their way of life (their culture) even while condemning and attempting to escape from that which they define as culture. They even do such things as seeking God's guidance in socially-approved (i.e., culturally appropriate) ways when they look to God to lead them through prayerfully considered circumstance rather than, as with the Hebrews via visions and dreams. In this and a multitude of other ways they demonstrate that God as well as Satan is able to employ cultural forms to perform his functions and convey his meanings.

3. The third of these views of God's relationship to culture sees God as either creating, developing or endorsing a given culture or subculture and ordaining that everyone in every place and time be converted thereto if they are to be considered

---

[2] The word, though frequently and prominently employed in this negative sense especially by John, is widely employed with less negative and technical connotations as well. In no case, as far as I can determine, may *kosmos* be interpreted as coextensive with the term culture as used by anthropologists.

Christian. This concept may take the form of an absolutization of some historical culture such as Hebrew, Greco-Roman (often referred to in these contexts as "first century Christian culture," "biblical culture," or "New Testament culture"). Or, more often in the last few centuries, the recommended culture is some form or modification of western "civilization," often referred to as "Christian culture." Quite often the recommended culture is conceived of in terms of a particular denominational or transdenominational (e.g., conservative or evangelical) subculture, at least with regard to its theological, ethical and ceremonial beliefs and practices. And other subcultural variables such as democratic government, capitalistic economics, "middle class values" (including often even such trivia as hair length and clothing styles), and the like may also be specified.

People holding such views, though correctly seeing that there are major cultural differences between Christians and non-Christians, fail to properly distinguish between the fact that Christians can operate the forms of a given culture to serve Christian functions and the labeling of the forms of a culture (or subculture) as "Christian" (whatever this would mean). Even slavery, for example, as counter to Christianity as we feel this cultural form to be, was operable by Christians with a maximum of Christian considerateness and, therefore, employable to Christian ends (functions). Likewise dictatorship, warfare (as in the Old Testament), death (e.g., martyrdom), secularism, etc. (though not, apparently, murder, stealing, covetousness, adultery, etc.). It is the functions and usage, though, not the forms, that may be Christian. Similarly, cultural forms that might be designated as "more Christian" than any of these are continually operated both by non-Christians and (often unconsciously) by Christians to serve functions that are completely counter to Christianity. Even the cultural forms of "Christian" charity, church organization, evangelism, etc., as we know too well, are often operated in very unchristian ways.

The weakness, therefore, of this type of understanding of God's relation to culture is that it interprets Christianness of culture primarily in terms of the forms of culture rather than in terms of the functions to which those forms were put which may or may not be Christian. "Christianness" as a measure of culture, however, is more properly applied to functions than to forms. At one point, though, this perspective has produced a valuable insight—certain cultural forms allow for a greater possibility that they may be employed to serve Christian functions than others. Therefore, when there is opportunity for the Christians within a society to bring about change from less usable cultural forms to more usable forms, such opportunity should be taken. Thus the influence of Christians to abolish slavery, define and set up democratic government, work toward racial equality and the like should be applauded and encouraged but not because there is any hope of ultimately producing a culture which we can label "Christian."

4. The fourth of these views is that of Deism and much popular thinking within western societies and of many African cultures as well. It holds that God is above and outside of culture and no longer really concerned with human affairs. He may be regarded as having programmed the whole thing before he left or as having started something which he is no longer able to control but he is gone and virtually unreachable and it is useless for us to waste time calling to him for he no longer listens or cares.

In animistic societies such as those in Africa, the view is often that there is a "high god" who is good and who, therefore, can be ignored. Between him and humans, however, are a multitude of spirits, many of whom can hurt us. To prevent these spirits from doing their evil, we must offer sacrifices, perform rituals and/or do other prescribed things to appease them and keep them happy. The result is that people's attention is turned from God and focused on the spirits.

Except for the truth of God's transcendence that this position appears to have carried too far, it is difficult to say anything positive about such a perspective. It cannot, of course, be reconciled with the biblical portrayal of a concerned and communicating God and, in fact, appears to have so little to offer by way of insight into the God-culture-humanity relationship (which it denies) that it seems pointless to discuss it further here.

5. The God above-but-through-culture understanding of this relationship, however, appears to put it all together and will be the view assumed through out this chapter. This view sees God as transcendent and absolute, completely beyond and outside of any culture but so concerned with humans and desirous of interacting with us that he chooses the cultural milieu in which we are immersed as the arena of his interaction with us. Thus, when he speaks to Adam or Abraham or Moses or the disciples or us he does so whether directly or indirectly by employing human, not divine language—language that participates in human culture with both its strengths and its weaknesses, its heights and its depths, its glories and its sinfulness, its facilitating of communication and its limiting of it and encompassed by its finiteness, its relativity and its assured misperception of infinity.

Yet when God sought to communicate with Hebrews he did not first demand that they learn a language and culture that allowed them, for example, to better understand his lovingness.[3] He employed Hebrew-linguistic and cultural forms in spite of their inadequacy in this respect, even to the extent of endorsing (for them, though obviously not for everyone at all times) at least major portions of Hebrew culture, even though he knew that their culturally conditioned fear (terror?) of him would constitute a rather serious impediment to his getting across to Hebrews his lovingness. Likewise, though Jesus and his disciples operated in terms of Aramaic culture and language (God showing his willingness to employ that culture for the sake of those immersed in it), when the events of the New Testament were recorded it was for a Greek audience and, therefore, Greek was employed. And this in spite of the well-known difficulties (including both losses and gains in information) inherent in the process of translation. God, however, appears from the biblical record determined to communicate himself to people within their own linguistic and cultural framework. That is, God chooses to work in terms of human language and culture to interact with us. More of the implications of this choice on God's part will be developed below.

---

[3] Which may account for the fact that God chose to work with Jews in terms of a culturally known covenant relationship that may have been the closest they could come to the God-man relationship that the New Testament sees as grounded in love. Jewish culture, at least at the time of the earlier Old Testament writings, may not have been able to comprehend "love as pure expression of psychical reality apart from legality" (Kittel 1951:11) the legality of a covenant.

A Christian Attitude toward Culture

Many Christians, probably because they feel that a relativistic attitude in other areas of life is incompatible with Christianity, shy away from a whole-hearted acceptance of cultural relativity. They have, furthermore, so long regarded western culture as essentially "Christian" that they find it difficult to allow for the possibility that western culture is but one among a number of essentially equally valid approaches to life, rather than *the* most valid approach.

Yet study on the part of a growing number of dedicated Christians of the evidence provided by anthropology has led to the development of a perspective on the cultures of humankind that attempts to integrate the insights of anthropology with those of Christian theology. This perspective, while not going all the way with those anthropologists who hold to a completely relativistic attitude toward cultures, finds both common sense and the Bible on the side of what might be termed a "relative cultural relativism."

Dr. Eugene A. Nida summarizes the biblical position as follows:

> The Bible clearly recognizes that different cultures have different standards and that these differences are recognized by God as having different values. The relativism of the Bible is relative to three principal factors: 1) the endowment and opportunities of people 2) the extent of revelation, and 3) the cultural patterns of the society in question (1954:50).

The Parable of the Talents, the Parable of the Pounds and the clear statement of Luke 12:48, for example, teach that expectation of accomplishment is relative to a person's (or society's) endowment and opportunities. The extent of revelation that a people possesses will, furthermore, figure in the final judgment (see Luke 12:47–48; Rom. 2:14).

But it is the cultural relativity of the Bible that particularly interests us here. And this shows through most clearly in two areas. The first of these is in relation to customs that God allows in the Old Testament (within Hebrew culture) but treats differently within the different cultural milieu of the New Testament. God in his approach to ancient Jewish culture, for example, approves of polygamy (2 Sam. 12:7–8) and the enslavement of Gentiles (Lev. 25:39–46) while providing for relatively easy divorce (Deut. 24:1–4). Within the Jewish culture of the first century in which Jesus operated, however, divorce is proscribed (Matt. 5:31–32) and neither enslavement of Gentiles nor polygamy—which, though still legal, was apparently not a problem in that day—were mentioned (passages such as Matt. 19:4–5 and Mark 10:7–8 seem to assume that monogamy was the accepted norm).

The second indication of biblical endorsement of a relativistic attitude toward culture lies in Paul's statement that he attempted to be "all things to all men" buttressed by several illustrations of his application of this principle. In 1 Corinthians 9:20–21, for example, he indicated his movement back and forth over the cultural barrier separating Jews from Greeks. Furthermore, in spite of his insistence that the adoption of Jewish culture was not necessary to Christianity (see e.g., Gal. 2:11–16), he circumcised Timothy "out of consideration for the Jews" (Acts 16:3 NEB) and underwent the Jewish ritual of purification to demonstrate that he was still "a practicing Jew" (Acts 21:24).

"Biblical relativism" says Nida, "is not a matter of inconsistency, but a recognition of the different cultural factors which influence standards and actions" (1954:52). In fact, he adds in a footnote, "Biblical cultural relativism is an obligatory feature of our incarnational religion, for without it we would either absolutize human institutions or relativize God" (1954:282). Biblical Christianity, unlike for example, Islam, "clearly establishes the principle of *relative relativism*, which permits growth, adaptation, and freedom, under the Lordship of Jesus Christ. The Bible presents realistically the facts of culture and the plan of God . . ." in order that Christians of many cultures may thereby understand that under God they are freed to go beyond mere "static conformance to dead rules" to a culturally appropriate "dynamic obedience to a living God" (1954:52, emphasis mine).

Perhaps, therefore, far from being a threat to an evangelical Christian perspective, the development of an understanding of biblical cultural relativism should be regarded as a part of the leading "into all truth" that is one of the important functions of the Holy Spirit today.

Christians may, therefore, regard the Bible as supporting at least the following contentions concerning culture: 1) culture is all-pervasive, 2) the diversity of worldview and value systems manifested in human cultures is to be taken seriously, 3) whole cultures are more properly regarded as possessing a relatively equal overall validity than as superior or inferior to each other in any absolute sense. This general perspective should not, however, be taken to mean either 1) that individual aspects of a culture cannot be compared with the corresponding aspects of another culture and rated as of greater or lesser efficiency (or validity) than those aspects of that culture or 2) that the "Christianness" of parts of cultures cannot be measured by comparing them to revealed "supracultural" truth (see the next section). On the contrary, such comparisons can and will be made and judgments made as to relative efficiency (e.g., guns are more efficient than bows, airplanes are more efficient than bicycles) and Christianness" (e.g., love is more Christian than hate, patience is more Christian than impatience) of various aspects of culture. The point is simply that since each culture is a "mixed bag" of more efficient and less efficient elements (e.g., the culture that invented airplanes has such an inefficient, antiquated spelling system that untold hours and energy are wasted trying to induce adequate performance and motivation in reading) and of more close and less close approximations to Christian ideals (e.g., western culture, which in the name of Christianity abolished formal slavery, in its commitment to industrialization and capitalism endorses such non-Christian ideals as human depersonalization and exploitation for the sake of financial gain), it is not proper to consider one culture as better or more valid than another *in its totality*. It is rather both more anthropologically accurate and more Christian to regard cultures (as one should regard individuals) as of equal overall validity or value. Such an approach recognizes the fact that each of us without such recognition would tend to weight evaluations of this sort (with regard both to individuals and cultures) in such a way that we place ourselves and our strengths in a favorable light and others (including their strengths) in an unfavorable light.

The Supracultural and the Cultural

If cultures are relative, what then is absolute? Nida says, "The only absolute in Christianity is the triune God. Anything which involves man, who is finite and limited, must of necessity be limited, hence relative" (1954:282). William A. Smalley, longtime editor of the influential Christian journal *Practical Anthropology*, amplifies Nida's statement by developing a concept that he calls "the supercultural" (here termed the "supracultural"), to refer to that which theologians refer to as transcendent with respect to God. This term, says Smalley, refers to

> that which is truly beyond culture— . . . God Himself, His nature, attributes, and character . . . the moral principles which stem from what He is . . . His plan and total will (1955:60).

God's immediate will for specific people and specific events is not supracultural, since that part of God's will is necessarily "relative to the people and the events." This represents rather, the outworking within culture of a part of God's supracultural will as it relates to those particular people and events. Likewise any given church, its organization, worship, etc., is a relative, cultural manifestation of the supracultural church, the "bride of Christ."

In such expositions as the Ten Commandments (especially as Jesus summarizes them in Matt. 22:37–40), the Sermon on the Mount, the listing of the fruits of the Spirit (Gal. 5:22–23) and the many similar statements, the Scriptures come closest to a clear statement of a portion of the supracultural will of God for man's conduct— perhaps as close as possible within the limits of human language and culture. Yet,

> a little reflection will show that even in the Ten Commandments there are touches of cultural . . . the making of "graven images" is relative to the use to which they are to be put . . . the word "Sabbath" is relative, for we observe not Saturday but Sunday. . . . The commandment against killing . . . (is) decidedly relative. God commanded the Israelites to kill in war, and to execute the murderer. The soldier and the executionist were, therefore, not covered by the sixth commandment. Adultery, stealing, "false witness" and covering cannot be considered outside of the cultural setting (Smalley 1955:65).

Throughout the Scriptures we are provided with glimpses of the supracultural, clothed in specific events taking place within specific cultures at specific times. Frequently, as with the Ten Commandments, the Sermon on the Mount and numerous direct statements of God and Christ, we get the impression that we are looking at supracultural truth with a minimum of cultural distortion. More frequently, however, we are exposed to supracultural truth by means of its application in a specific situation and in terms of a specific culture, the account of which is recorded in a specific language and translated for us so that we see such truth as "puzzling reflections in a mirror" (1 Cor. 13:12, Phillips). Among these "reflections" Smalley feels that

> those parts of Scripture which give us evaluations of human motives and emotions, human attitudes and personalities, give us the deepest insight into God's ultimate will, and that to understand the revelation in terms of God's will for our behavior we will have to learn to look behind the cultural facade to see as much as we can of what the Word indicates about those questions. The cultural examples given us are thereby not lost. They provide most valuable examples of the way in which God's will was performed in another cultural setting to help us see how we may perform it in ours (1955:66).

In this way it is possible for Christians to learn something of the supracultural even though this, like all human knowledge, is perceived by us in terms of the cultural grid in which we operate. Yet by searching out the supracultural truths embodied in the cultural forms of Hebrew and Greco-Roman culture and recorded in the Scriptures we are enabled by the indwelling Spirit to learn what he desires to be the cultural outworking of his will in our lives as we live them out in terms of our cultural forms.

God's Revelation within Culture

The fact that humans are totally immersed in culture means, then, that we are utterly dependent upon revelation from the realm of the supracultural for any knowledge that we might gain of the supracultural. We cannot see supracultural truth apart from our culture but only in terms of the perceptual categories of the cultural frame of reference in which we are immersed. God, therefore, in seeking to reveal himself to us does so in terms of human language and culture.

This revelation consists of at least four parts: 1) a natural revelation in nature and basic cultural heritage, 2) a written revelation in the Bible, 3) a personal revelation in Jesus Christ, and 4) a continuing revelation (part or all of which some would term "illumination") through the activity of the Holy Spirit in the lives of individuals and in the life of the church. And each aspect of God's revelation is in cultural terms so that it can be understood by human beings who are immersed in culture.

1. The revelation of the supracultural God in nature and basic cultural heritage—that is, that vouchsafed to man at creation and passed on through natural cultural processes—is that referred to by Paul in Romans 1 and 2 and called by theologians "natural revelation." Acts 14:17 seems to imply that God has never allowed a people to go without some witness to him. It is apparently possible for men to "stifle" this revelation (see Rom. 1:25, etc.), but not possible for them to completely obliterate it (Rom. 2:11–16) and people are to be held accountable for it. It is, according to Paul, possible, by means of this revelation, to see at least God's invisible attributes, that is to say his everlasting power and deity . . . in the things he

has made" (Rom. 1:20 NEB) and, apparently, on this basis to carry out the precepts of the law (Rom. 2:14).[4]

2. The Bible, God's written revelation, likewise, presents supracultural truth in cultural trappings—recording as it does, in casebook fashion, specific events occurring in the lives of specific persons acting out and/or interpreting their interaction with God in accordance with the specific cultures in which they were immersed. The most striking differences, in fact, between the presentation of supracultural truth in the Old Testament and that in the New are more easily explained in terms of cultural differences than in terms of differences in theology between Old and New Testaments. Often, as with a comparison between the experience of covenants in the Old Testament and love between God and humans in the New Testament, the apparent theological difference disappears if one takes cultural factors into account and, in addition, focuses on the function of the item under consideration rather than its form.

3. God's revelation par excellence was, of course, in the person of Jesus Christ—supracultural God himself who became for a time a participant in one human culture. In this way God's ultimate revelation of supracultural truth was presented from within culture, not only in human language but in human life, not only indirectly through the words and deeds of ordinary human beings but (although the records are by witnesses) directly in the life and words of God-man. Because of Jesus, we now know at least a bit (since the Gospel writers were selective in their reporting) about how God would act if he were immersed in culture as we are because he actually became immersed in human culture.

4. There is, furthermore, the continuing activity of the Holy Spirit within and through his people which, at least insofar as it involves new insight into supracultural truth, must be regarded as a part of God's revelation from within culture. Evangelical theologians do not ordinarily contend that the Holy Spirit reveals *completely new* supracultural truth in these days, but to the extent that the discovery of new individual or corporate insight into the Scriptures and God's working among humans (called "illumination" by theologians) may be considered parallel to God's activity within culture in any of the above three ways, to that extent we may consider the work of the Holy Spirit today to be a part of God's revelational activity within culture.

---

[4] I would suggest that it is perhaps even probable that such natural revelation is theoretically sufficient to lead one to salvation (though I would not press the matter since we have very little light to go on). Even if this is possible, however, natural revelation by itself may seldom *actually* be sufficient since, while it may provide enough *information* to bring one to salvation, it is doubtful that it often provides a great enough *stimulus* to get one to act on the information. For I take it to be a universal of human nature that people characteristically know what they should do much more frequently than they actually do it. Hebrews 11:6 may also bear on this matter since it seems to suggest that anyone who believes that there is a God and sets out to find him will find God. If this is true they will only be able to come to God through Christ (whether or not they are aware of the fact that it is through Christ that they are coming) since there is no other way. It may, however, still be possible for people to come *through* Christ but without specific knowledge of him (as Abraham did). In any event, Christians must proclaim the way to God through Christ not because men *cannot* be saved through faith without knowledge of him but because most *will not* without a greater stimulus than that provided by knowledge alone.

In these ways the supracultural, transcendent God has chosen to make himself knowable to culturally immersed human beings without requiring us to move outside of our culture (even if we could). That is, the supracultural God has chosen to reveal himself in terms that are comprehensible to us from within the human cultural context, chosen to commit his revelation of himself and his supracultural message to human life, human language, human culture in order to effectively communicate with human beings.

Thus we read in the Old Testament the record of the supracultural God communicating his revelation to Jewish people in terms of Jewish thought patterns and accepting from them typically Jewish responses to his supracultural message which for their sakes he clothed in Hebrew language and culture. In the Old Testament, therefore, God is perceived primarily in terms of his majesty, power, justice and the like—attributes that are both true characteristics of the supracultural God and expected characteristics of God from a Jewish cultural perspective. God, however, also went beyond Jewish expectations and revealed himself in addition as a God who enters into covenant relationships with humans.[5] Even this (and other) non-expected revelation, though, God communicated by both starting where the Jewish recipients of the revelation were and by revealing new insights in a manner comprehensible to them through the voices and pens of thoroughly Jewish preachers and writers.

In the New Testament likewise we see this method of God's revelation of himself both in terms of first century Palestinian culture (Gospels, Acts, Hebrews, James, Peter) and in terms of Greco-Roman culture (Paul's epistles). In each case we see God starting (though not ending) where people are culturally for the sake of revealing himself to them comprehensibly. And the apparent differences between the loving God of the New Testament and the stern judgmental sacrifice-demanding God of parts of the Old Testament are to be interpreted not as indications that God changes his approach to humans every few thousand years (as some seem to imply) but, rather, that the unchanging supracultural God chooses to reveal himself in such a way that the members of various societies may focus in on those aspects of God's nature and activity most amenable to their cultural expectations as to what God should be like and to respond to him in faith (a supracultural requirement) expressed in ways appropriate to their cultures.

The revelation recorded in the Bible should not, therefore, be looked upon as a linear, evolutionary type of presentation of God and his workings with man, as if it started from a simple concept and proceeded to a more complex concept within a single cultural framework. It should, rather, be seen as a "zoom lens" presentation focusing at different times on quite different cultural understandings (each Spirit-guided) and tending toward a comprehensiveness of presentation concerning God that far exceeds that which could be given in terms of any single culture. Jewish culture, for example, allows for certain insights into the nature of God that Greek culture completely misses. Greek culture, on the other hand, allows for insights that Jewish culture misses. And Euroamerican and Asian and Latin American and

---

[5] Though covenant relationships were already an important part of Jewish culture and in this sense not new, the employment of such a concept with regard to the relationship between humans and God appears to have been very new and in this sense "beyond Jewish expectations."

African cultural insights also have, under the leading of the Holy Spirit, important contributions to make to the comprehesiveness of the truth that God seeks to reveal[6] concerning himself and his interaction with human beings.

Human Perception

As God's message is proclaimed in various societies (either the biblical societies or those in which the Scriptures are translated or Christian preaching performed) it becomes clothed in very distinctive cultural forms—forms which, though very meaningful to one group of people, may be meaningless or convey a completely different meaning to another. Thus, in communicating the supracultural message that Christian women should not risk being identified as prostitutes, it was appropriate for Paul writing to Greeks to speak strongly against haircutting (since haircutting was a characteristic of immoral women).[7] The same proscription of haircutting on the part of American Christian women, however, communicates a very different message—a message that is unlikely to be related to the original message, since the meaning of haircutting in American society is very different from that attributed to it by first century Greco-Romans. Likewise the literal application in American society of Paul's command to "greet one another with a holy kiss" (2 Cor. 13:12, etc.) could be interpreted in a very unholy manner since the meaning of kissing, especially between members of the same sex, is quite different in our society than it was among Greco-Romans.

It is necessary, therefore, for those of us living in societies other than those in which the biblical revelation occurred to interpret the recorded message in its cultural context if we are to understand it aright. If, then, we seek to communicate this message to those within our own society we must reclothe the supracultural message in forms appropriate to our culture. Thus the message concerning the inappropriateness of allowing an easy identification between Christian women and immoral women can be communicated to Americans by talking about styles of clothing rather than of hair. And the meaning of Paul's admonition concerning the "holy kiss" may be gotten across by recommending warm handshakes as J. B. Phillips does in his New Testament translation (see below for further discussion of this type of substitution).

A much greater problem than that of attempting to understand a message presented in one cultural context from the perspective of another culture faced the supracultural God in his desire to communicate supracultural truth within human cultures. How does one communicate infinity to finite human beings? Can God communicate absolute truth in human language and culture in spite of their relativity? Can this greatest of all cultural gaps be bridged?

---

[6] Largely, since the closing of the canon, through leading Christians to new insights into biblical truth, never, though, in contradiction to truth revealed in the Bible.

[7] See commentaries on 1 Corinthians 11:6.

Apparently so. It happens first and least adequately via natural revelation, then more adequately in the lives of countless human beings who either once lived or are now living in contact with God. Some of these stories are recorded in the written Word and in other books and films for the benefit of succeeding generations. But God has revealed himself most adequately of all in the person of Jesus Christ, God incarnate in human life and culture. And this too is recorded in the Book as seen and witnessed to by human beings who knew him in the days of his flesh.

Since infinity cannot be contained by finite language, culture or humanity, however, these glimpses of absolute truth are less than 100 percent with respect either to their comprehensiveness or their absoluteness. Yet we know both from our own experience and from the recorded experiences of countless others that God has succeeded in communicating a message that is entirely *adequate* to his purpose—the salvation and spiritual growth of all who respond positively to his invitation. We see, then, a revelation of absolute truth communicated in culturally understandable terms for the purpose of eliciting from us culturally immersed human beings a faith response to the God who stands outside of any culture but who is willing and anxious to work within any society, in terms of any culture, with those therein immersed who respond to him in faith.

Culture-Bound Humans

We have seen that humans are completely immersed in culture and that this immersion affects us pervasively. We have seen, further, that God reveals himself within culture for the sake of reaching culture-bound human beings and that this revelation (though perceived by us within the human cultural context and though less than 100 percent of all there is to know about God and his workings) is adequate to elicit a saving faith-response on our part.

This initial response, however, and the subsequent "inculturating"[8] of supracultural Christianity into appropriate cultural forms will also be pervasively affected by the fact that the people doing the inculturating are totally immersed in their culture. Thus, a twentieth century American church if it is true to its culture will not look very much like a first century "New Testament church" in, for example, worship, organization, forms of fellowship, language, etc., since the cultural setting is so different.

Nor should it since, as we have seen, it appears to be God's desire to adapt his approach to human cultures in order to be experienced by humans as relevant to the needs of those enmeshed in each particular cultural context. A twentieth century American church should, therefore, differ in most external respects (though not in basic theology or commitment to Christ) from a first century Greco-Roman church to

---

[8] This term signifies the process of introducing supracultural truth into a cultural context and the embodying of that truth in appropriate cultural forms. It parallels on the cultural level the theological term "incarnate." It should not be confused with the standard anthropological term "enculturation" that refers to the process of acquainting a child with his or her culture.

the same extent that our culture differs from theirs. That is, though each church pledges its allegiance to the same Lord and seeks to fulfill his will in the cultural world of which it is a part, functioning as the body of Christ within its own culture, the *forms* in terms of which each church lives out its Christian functions should differ as much from each other as do the cultural settings. To the extent that this is not true, the process of inculturation of supracultural truth within twentieth century American culture has been interfered with—perhaps due to a failure to distinguish the supracultural from the cultural in Scripture.

If, therefore, we find an American church employing Latin (or, even, the Protestant "neo-Latin" of certain Bible translations, liturgies, prayer forms, etc.) or forms of organization, worship, policy, communication, etc. more appropriate either to some culture other than ours or to a previous form of our own culture, we judge this church to have improperly inculturated supracultural truth in the present American scene and should not be surprised if modern Americans write it off as irrelevant. And yet many Christian groups fall into this trap because they fail to understand that God is primarily concerned with similarity of perceived meaning rather than sameness of form in the expressions of Christianity from culture to culture.

This distinction between form and meaning is perhaps most easily illustrated by means of a comparison between a literal Bible translation (e.g., King James Version, American Standard Version, Revised Standard Version) and a more idiomatic or meaning-based translation such as that by J. B. Phillips. A literal translation attempts to stick as closely as possible to the *form* of the original and, in the process, comes up with non-English sounding expressions such as "bowels of mercies" (a word-for-word translation of an idiom meaning *compassion*), "The valley of the shadow of death" (a word-for-word rendering of a Hebrew idiom which simply refers to a valley characterized by fear-inspiring deep darkness) and "through a glass darkly" (indistinctly through a window or in a mirror).

A meaning-based translation, on the other hand, is one that does "not sound like a translation at all" but, rather, like an original work in the receiving language. Such a translation aims at producing "in the hearts and minds of its readers an effect equivalent to that produced by the author upon his original readers" (Phillips 1958:vii). That is, such a translation aims at conveying an *equivalent* meaning in the receiving language rather than merely carrying the *forms* of one language and culture over into the other culture, thereby forcing readers to do a good bit of extra study if they want to derive the intended meaning from a given passage. The intended meaning, in fact, may be very badly distorted by such a literal translation due to the fact that the form employed in the translation may well convey implications that are incompatible with the intention of the original (see the discussion of haircutting and the "holy kiss" above).

The inculturating of supracultural Christianity within a given culture involves, therefore, the attempt to embody the gospel message so completely in forms specifically appropriate to that culture that the people within the society understand it and respond to its meanings as if it were an indigenous rather than a foreign thing. The supracultural message should speak to their felt needs (not those of another people immersed in a different culture) and the forms of, for example, organization, worship, proclamation, witness, expression and outworking of the faith-relationships with God, etc., should be appropriate to their culture if we are to be true to what we understand of God's approach to culture-bound humans.

And this principle applies even though the perception of any given supracultural truth on the part of the members of another society may differ to a lesser or greater degree from our own culture-bound perception of the same truth, just as our perception may differ to some degree (and quite predictably in terms of the differences in culture) from that of the first century Christians.

With regard even to such a clear command as "Don't steal," for example, there may be different culturally conditioned perceptions as to how the command is to be interpreted. Within our society we are taught that we should regard as stealing any appropriation without permission of something belonging to someone else. In discussions with Nigerians, however, I discovered that something taken without permission by a brother would not be considered stolen. I asked one man if he would regard it as stealing if his brother, without permission, simply took his best suit of clothes, kept it, and eventually wore it out. He said he would still not regard it as stealing, "because he is my brother." In that part of Nigeria, property owned by one member of a family is (or at that time, at least, was) considered to belong to every member of the family. So, if the member of the family who bought the suit wasn't wearing it, it was fair game for another member of the family so that his use of it, even without permission, was not considered stealing.

To these Nigerians, reacting in terms of their cultural perspective, the command "Don't steal" was understood virtually the same as I, coming from my cultural background would understand it but with at least this one difference. Thus, their reaction to a similar act on the part of a non-brother turned out to be virtually the same as mine, but we differed, at least in theory, with regard to such action on the part of a brother. Actually, many westerners would make the same exception for a brother, though we can call it stealing. These Nigerians couldn't. Probably, though, the Jews to whom the command was first given understood it more like the Nigerians than like westerners do. This leaves us with the possibility that God is in favor of their interpretation rather than ours! In any event, we see here one supracultural command with two at least partly different cultural perceptions of the meaning of that command. Similar illustrations can be given for each of the other Ten Commandments.

Yet God apparently chooses to accept such culture-bound understandings of himself and his will as the *starting points* (though not the end points) for his interaction with people, for he accepts as equally valid the faith-response of an American directed toward a God whom he perceives of as a kind of Santa Claus and that of a Jew to whom God is more like an oriental king. Furthermore, in order to appeal to the American—who expects to find God via reason and circumstances— God employs such vehicles as reason and circumstances, in spite of the fact that he often approached Jews through dreams—since they, unlike Americans, *expected* God to reveal himself in this way.

Culture and Subculture

God's desire to reach human beings where we are, however, extends even beyond the adaptations required by culture. Ultimately, in fact, God adapts his approach to meet each of us where we are as individuals. But in between the cultural level and the individual level are a variety of levels that may be termed "subcultural."

Just as with language (especially larger ones), people develop different subvarieties of speech that linguists call "dialects" (e.g., the terms "standard American English," "Brooklynese," "a Boston accent," "a Scottish accent" are popular terms meant to designate dialectal differences within English), so people develop subcultural varieties within cultures. Such subcultures may be focused on at various levels. It is possible, for example, to speak of distinctly German, French, British and American cultures, as subcultures within the broad designation "western culture." It is also possible to speak of several fairly well-defined varieties (some of which may be termed "social classes") within any of these cultures. Within American culture, for example, we can identify such varieties as "youth subcultures," "ghetto subcultures," "white-collar subcultures," "rural subcultures" and, within Christianity, each of our denominations.

Some see such divisions within society (especially the denominational divisions within Christianity) as things that "ought not to be." And in a sense, perhaps, they are right. But people don't work by "oughts" and God's approach to people starts where people are, not where they ought to be. God, therefore, also takes subcultures (including denominations) seriously and seeks to approach us in terms of our subcultural as well as our cultural involvement.

One very important positive feature of many denominations, in fact, is precisely the fact that they embody and encourage the kind of understanding of and response to the supracultural God that is appropriate to the particular subculture(s) to which they cater. Thus it may be assumed that just as God is desirous that distinctively American churches be developed for the purpose of inculturating supracultural Christianity within American culture so he favors the development of, for example, distinctively "white-collar" churches to meet the spiritual needs of "white-collar" type people, distinctively youth oriented churches to communicate with the youth subculture, "Baby Boomer" churches for the sake of reaching that subculture, etc. One necessary concomitant of this understanding is that in approaching subcultures in this way we recognize that it is unnecessary to convert from one subculture to another (say from Boomer to Traditional) in order to be "truly Christian." That is, such an approach takes subcultures completely seriously—it is not simply a tactic for gaining entrance into a group for the sake of winning them over to some more "acceptable" way of life.

Communicating the Gospel across Cultures

As we have seen above, it is God's desire to reach people through and in terms of each human culture or subculture. The process by means of which each communication is effected is, however, complex. Quite typically this process involves persons who have come to faith in Christ within their own society crossing cultural boundaries in order to communicate Christ to another people. Not infrequently, however, such cross-cultural communication is attempted on the basis of an inadequate understanding of what is involved.

The assumption is often made, for example, that the superiority of Christianity to the religious beliefs of the people of "culture (or subculture) X" does not need to be demonstrated. Once they are simply presented with the claims of Christ, this type of thinking contends, it will be obvious to them that Christianity is superior since all their religion consists of is "a lot of senseless taboos and meaningless rituals." If, then, they do not convert to Christianity it is "because of their own perversity and desire to remain in their sins." Similar attitudes regard the "heathen" mind as an empty vessel into which Christianity merely has to be poured or his "primitive mentality" is so inferior that this decisions have to be made for him—preferable by representatives or a "superior" "Christian" culture, such as ours.

Each of these attitudes, however, betrays the egocentric, ethnocentric approach to the cultures of man that we have seen to be untrue to the best insights of both anthropology and Christianity. Such views, further, seriously underestimate the pervasiveness of culture and its tenaciousness. People's minds simply are not "empty vessels," nor is the superiority of Christianity that apparent to those whose worldview has been shaped without reference to Christ. The way of Christ has to be *communicated to* the people of culture X, not simply *paraded before* them.

Furthermore, if we are to be true to our calling, it must be *supracultural Christianity*, not simply the religion of western culture (that happens to be called by the same name), that we communicate. It is a good thing for us (judging from the understanding of God's attitude toward culture discussed above) that supracultural Christianity has been inculturated within our culture. But it is a bad thing if we simply assume (as the Judaizers did in Paul's day) that the (cultural) forms in which Christianity has become meaningful to us are the only forms in which Christianity can be meaningful to anyone. It is easy, for example, for us to assume that our moral ideals (though frequently differing from our practice), our kind of marriage (including free choice of partners, monogamy, and a church wedding), democratic church government, tithing of money, monological preaching, the particular ways in which we express justice, mercy, brotherhood, and charity, the prohibition of dancing-type bodily movements in Christian worship, etc., are necessary elements of Christianity in every society, rather than merely parts of a specifically western-cultural outworking of Christianity in ours.

The Judaizers who followed Paul from place to place on his missionary journeys believed that entrance into Christianity on the part of the Gentiles could only be attained through prior or concurrent conversion to Judaism. And this embracing of Judaism implied the adoption of a sizable portion of the Jewish cultural accouterments of Judaism including circumcision, minute attention to the keeping of the law (as defined by Jewish theologians), and the keeping of Jewish food taboos (such as those against the eating of the meat of strangled animals or of blood). Paul and Peter, of course, stood solidly against the necessity for such conversion from one culture to another (see Acts 10 and 15) as a prerequisite to or concomitant of conversion to Christianity. Many present-day missionaries and those who support them, however, have slipped back into the Judaistic mentality by requiring adherence to some modified (frequently regarded as "purified") from of our culture as a concomitant of conversion to Christianity.[9]

As Smalley points out, "missionaries generally approve of and strive for culture change which makes people more like themselves in form (. . . even though they may overlook the meaning of this form)" (1958:54).

Truly Christian conversion, however, results in the inculturation of supracultural Christianity to the extent that the cultural "changes which take place under the guidance of the Holy Spirit meet the needs and fulfill the meanings of *that* society and not of any outside group" (Smalley 1958:54, emphasis mine). And such converts "are not necessarily cleaner than their (non-Christian) neighbors, not necessarily more healthy, not necessarily better educated" (1958:57). It is, in fact, frequently true that when such converts attempt to adopt our customs with regard to cleanliness, health, education and the like, that they (and their church) lose contact with their own society and become themselves the agents of "cultural" (as opposed to truly Christian) conversion.[10]

The aim of effective cross-cultural proclamation of the gospel, is, however, the kind of communication of supracultural Christianity that results in a truly indigenous (contextualized) church:

> a group of believers who live out their life, including their socialised Christian activity, in the patterns of the local society, and for whom any transformation of that society comes out of their felt needs under the guidance of the Holy Spirit and the Scriptures . . . If other patterns are forced upon a church by missionaries, consciously or unconsciously, such a church will not be an indigenous one (Smalley 1958:54).

But at this point cross-cultural communicators face, perhaps their greatest challenge. For they only know supracultural truth as it has come to them in terms of their own culture—truth that has come from outside of culture and has come to us through the intermediacy of the various cultures represented in the Bible. It is this truth, minus the accouterments of the culture in terms of which we have come to know it, that we are called to communicate in meaningful terms to the members of another society. Diagrammatically we may indicate these facts as follows:

---

[9] See Kraft 1963 for a fuller treatment.

[10] The term "cultural conversion" (employed in Kraft 1963) is intended to signify the kind of conversion to another culture as a prerequisite to becoming a Christian that the Judaizers and many mission organizations to this day require.

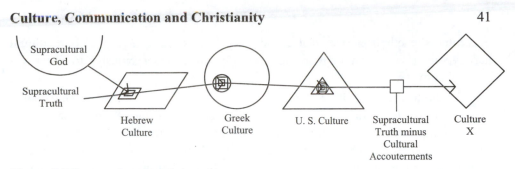

Figure 3.2 Supracultural truth in culture

Yet, as pointed out above, this situation is analogous to that which God faced in seeking to communicate with humans across the supraculture-culture boundary. And his primary method was by means of the incarnation. God became human for several reasons. One of the most important of these, however, was so that he could communicate supracultural truth in terms that would be maximally intelligible to culture-bound humans. To reach humans he became a human—appealing to culture-bound people from *inside* of culture, on the basis of commonly experienced needs and frustrations, ideals and limitations, desires and disappointments. He identified with us in order to communicate with us, turning his back on the prestige and position that was rightly his, seeking to *win* a hearing as a man from within the cultural context rather than to simply *demand* from outside the culture the allegiance due him as God. And in so doing God not only effectively communicated, he also provided the model par excellence of effective cross-cultural communication of the Christian message.

There are, of course, certain features of God's model that are impossible for us to imitate. Chief among these is the impossibility of our being born into the culture within which we seek to communicate (although frequently those whom God calls to work across subcultural boundaries, both within our culture and within other cultures do have this advantage). Nor is it usually possible for us to undergo the long process of training and education that children and youth go through in becoming full participants in their culture. Yet, a large degree of participation in, and identification with the cultural context in which these people live is possible. And to this end we need to bend every effort toward learning all that we possibly can about what it is like to be inside the skin of a member of the culture.

For this purpose the recent large-scale development of the science of anthropology and the application of its insights to the problems of cross-cultural communication of the gospel are very welcome. And the recognition of the need to understand the place of culture both in human life and in the purpose of God, plus the availability of specific training in techniques of cross-cultural communication now make it possible for the average missionary to go a longer way toward an incarnational approach to the cross-cultural communication of the gospel than was formerly possible. Of course, as Nida says, "good missionaries have always been good anthropologists" (1954:xi). That is, there have always been (and always will be) a good number of perceptive persons who, without benefit of formal training in the techniques of cross-cultural communication, naturally operate in terms of such techniques. These are "the naturals." But a primary need for the majority is the kind of training that will enable us to first discover and then as much as possible to overcome the ethnocentrism that causes us to think more highly of our cultural heritage than we ought to think and (usually quite unconsciously) to strive for cultural conversion.

On the basis, then, either of natural perception or of the perception engendered by training (or both) the modern cross-cultural communicator of the gospel can be freed to approach the people of another society incarnationally—as one who first seeks to discover the felt needs of the people to whom she or he goes (the questions *they* are asking about the realities of life, the problems that *they*—not we—recognize to be problems) and then to adapt his or her approach to "scratch them where they itch." In this way it is possible to discover "points of contact"—areas where people are reaching out for something, seeking the answer to some problem, concerning which God speaks.[11]

Often one such area is concern for the fact that God seems so far away. Sitting with a Nigerian chief one day, I chanced to ask him what his people believed about God before the missionaries came. He told us a tribal myth concerning a previous era during which God "and his son" lived on earth with humans. This era ended abruptly, however, when, through the carelessness of a woman God's son became ill and died, whereupon God left in a huff. "God," the chief continued, "hasn't been heard from since." Then, looking squarely at me, the chief asked, "White man, can you tell us where God has gone?" The chief had exposed a felt need and at the same time provided a point of contact between his own culture-bound understanding of reality and the supracultural message that I had come to communicate to him. An incarnational approach would take the chief's story seriously (in spite of certain factual inaccuracies), latch onto the truths of God's distance and our responsibility for having brought about the rift, and respond to the chief's question in terms of what God has done to overcome the rift.

Other areas that provide such points of contact and tend to expose human needs that are even more basic than cultural differences often tend to cluster around the individual's need to satisfy certain fundamental drives such as those for self-assertion, self-protection and self-preservation. But perhaps the most important basic need from the point of view of the Christian witness (though it is by no means divorced from other basic needs) is the craving for some sort of meaning in life that seems to be a common need of all human beings regardless of cultural diversity. An incarnational approach to cross-cultural witness seeks to discover the culture-bound ways in which such needs are expressed and to apply the gospel in culturally relevant ways at those points. For it is with respect to such ultimate problems that the answers advanced by the peoples of the world are least satisfying and the participants in these societies at least theoretically most likely to be open to the possibility of change.

In this way, then, on the basis of an understanding of and participation in the culture or subculture to which God has called him, the effective cross-cultural communicator seeks to apply supracultural truth to the felt needs of culture-bound humans. But he must understand not only the bases and processes of such communication but also the type of response that God desires.

---

[11] See Nida 1960:211–215 for a valuable treatment of this subject.

Many missionaries are willing to approach the people to whom they go incarnationally. And they probably will also be committed to the principle that the proper result of such communication is the development of an "indigenous" (contextualized) church. But, as Smalley points out, one disturbing feature of a truly indigenous church is that missionaries typically do not like it! "Often a truly indigenous church is a source of concern and embarrassment to . . . mission bodies" (1958:55) since, if the church is truly inculturated, it will be rather completely conformed in every outward respect to the cultural patterns of its society though, as we have seen, the motivations will be Christian and, therefore, different from those of the rest of the society. This will mean, then, that it will be characterized by thoroughly indigenous forms of worship, doctrinal formulations (if such are even important to the culture), interpersonal and group communication, fellowship and recreation, etc.

That is, the response of truly indigenous Christians to God will be direct, and their expression of their relationship to God appropriate specifically to their own culture—rather than, as it often the case with churches established by missions, the response to God and expression of Christianity being conformed to a cultural model other than their own (such as the culture of the missionary). Diagrammatically we may represent the ideal cross-cultural communication plus the response engendered as follows:

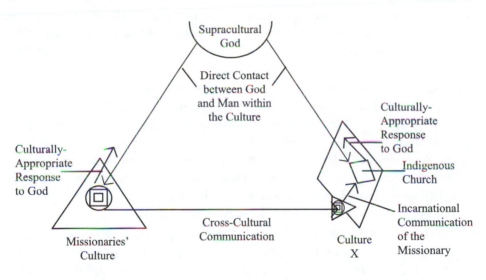

Figure 3.3 Ideal cross-cultural communication plus response

Even though, then, the message comes indirectly to the members of society X via a person from another society and, in so coming is not completely able to shed all of its other-cultural accouterments, nevertheless it is possible in this way to plant truly African churches in Africa, truly Asian churches in Asia, truly Indian churches among Indians, truly Boomer churches among Boomers, etc., and thus to fulfill the will of God vis-à-vis the communication of the supracultural gospel to culture-bound humanity.

CHAPTER 4

A PERSPECTIVE ON CULTURE

Adapted with permission from
Anthropology for Christian Witness, chapter 3 (Orbis 1996)

Introduction

The term *culture* is the label anthropologists give to the complex structuring of customs and the assumptions that underlie them in terms of which people govern their lives. Every society has its own cultural way of life. Apparently, human beings cannot live without such structuring. At least, no group of people has yet been discovered without culture.

A culture may be likened to a river, with a surface level and a deep level. The surface is visible. Most of the river, however, lies beneath the surface and is largely invisible. In a river, what happens on the surface is both a reaction to external phenomena and a manifestation of the deep level characteristics of the river. For example, if something is thrown into a river, there will be a splash as the surface of the water is affected by the external phenomenon. That item, however, will in turn be affected by subsurface phenomena such as the current, the cleanness or dirtiness of the river, the presence of other objects in the river and the like.

So it is with culture. What we see on the surface of a culture is the patterning of human behavior. This patterning or structuring of behavior, though impressive, is the lesser part of the culture. In the depths, then, are the assumptions we call worldview (see chapter 4 of Kraft 1996) in terms of which the surface level behavior is governed. When something affects the surface of a culture it may result in a change at that level. The nature and extent of that change will, however, be influenced by the deep level structuring (worldview) of the culture.

With humans, unlike with rivers, there is a still deeper level. We will call this the level of person. Culture (including worldview) is a matter of structure or patterns. Culture does not *do* anything. Culture is like a road. It provides a surface with boundaries on which people may walk or drive. Or, people may choose to walk or drive off the road. They may creatively forge a new path, develop a new custom that may or may not be followed by others. If that new custom is followed by others, it becomes a part of their culture as well. If not, it remains idiosyncratic and dies with the person who invented it.

Ordinarily people govern themselves by habit. Though people are creative and some very creative in devising new strategies, most of what we do and think is more habitual than creative. And it is our regular habit to follow the cultural guidelines (roads) taught to us as we were growing up. The apparent power of a culture to govern a person's behavior, then, lies in the human propensity to live by habit. Culture has no power in and of itself. The interaction between people and cultural structuring will be explored further below and becomes an important part of the undergirding or our whole treatment.

I am frequently asked, Where did culture come from? And how did there get to be so many of cultures? My assumption is that God both created into humans a culture-creating (and modifying) capacity and gave Adam some kind of culture to start with. Since we know of no language without a culture, the fact that Adam spoke a language would seem to indicate that he also had culture.

As for the vast number of cultures in the world (probably more than the 6,000 languages that have been counted), my theory is that the primary reason for such diversity is *human creativity* (a part of the image of God in humans). In spite of our propensity to behave habitually, humans are just too creative to continue to do things, think things, say things in the same way(s) all the time. So people innovate. And enough innovation and isolation (geographical and/or social) over a long enough period of time results in cultural and linguistic divergence and splitting.

Cultures Are to Be Respected

We cannot live without culture. It is that matrix within which we "live and move and exist" (Acts 17:28), the non-biological, non-environmental part of our lives that we learn from our elders, that we share with our community, and in which we are totally submerged from one end of life to the other.

Cultural structuring is both outside of us and inside of us. We relate to it in many ways as a fish relates to water (though it is more influential in our lives than even water is to fish). But we are usually as unconscious of it as fish must be of the water in which they exist or as we usually are of the air we breathe. Indeed, many of us only notice culture when we go into another cultural territory and observe customs different from our own. And then we often feel sorry for those people and, if we are able, seek ways to rescue them from their customs.

Historically, many have reacted to other people's customs by trying to rescue the people from them. They responded to other people's ways like the monkey in the southeast Asian story of the monkey and the fish. It seems Monkey and Fish got caught in a flood. As the waters rose higher and higher, Monkey found a tree and climbed to safety. As he got above the water level, he looked down and saw his friend Fish still in the water. So, out of concern for his friend, he reached down, rescued Fish, and held him tight to his chest as he climbed higher in the tree.

Human beings, like fish, can live inside a culture but not outside of one. Thus, any person "rescued" from one culture can only survive if he/she is quickly immersed in another. Some from the Two-Thirds World are studying or living in America, because they've been "rescued" from their culture and no longer fit in the society in which they were born. When they're in their home country, they don't any longer feel at home. They have been pulled out of their home culture. The sad thing is that, having been pulled out of one culture, they have usually not been made to feel completely at home in the other. They feel, as one of my Nigerian friends put it, like the bat—they don't get along either with birds or with animals.

The way of Jesus is, however, to honor a people's culture, not to wrest them from it. Just as He entered the cultural life of first century Palestine in order to communicate with them, so we are to enter the cultural matrix of the people we seek to win. If we are to witness effectively to human beings, we have to take account of the culture in which these human beings live. If we fish for fish, we have to know whether the fish are swimming in deep water or shallow water, in water that is running rapidly or is stagnant, in water that is clean or dirty, cold or warm. We have to know these things if we're going to fish for fish. This text is designed to help us learn about the cultural water in which people live and move and have their being and without which we are not human beings.

We who are missionary anthropologists believe that we really can't do what we seek to do very effectively if we live in ignorance of the cultural dimensions of human beings. Much good Christian witness has resulted from the activities of perceptive people who, though working cross-culturally, have dealt with people sympathetically and understandingly in terms of the kinds of principles we are talking about. As Eugene Nida states "Good missionaries have always been good 'anthropologists'" (1954:xi). What he means is that good missionaries didn't need a basic anthropology course to alert them to these things. They did the right things naturally. Unfortunately, too many of us, like those who have sought to rescue people from their cultures, don't do the right things naturally. We need books like this to inform us concerning the relationships between people and their cultures to enable us to be the kind of cross-cultural witnesses we intend to be.

People and Culture

As mentioned above, we need to distinguish carefully between people and the cultural structures in which we operate. It has been too common with both nonspecialists and specialists to confuse the two. For example, it is common to hear statements such as "Their culture *makes* them do such and such," or "A people's culture *presses* them into its mold," or "A people's worldview *determines* their view of reality, enabling them to see certain things clearly but blinding them to other aspects of reality," or "Their culture *doesn't allow* them to . . ." Note that the italicized verbs in these statements convey an assumption of personal initiative and power on the part of culture.

Such statements represent what has been labeled a *superorganic* view of culture or cultural superorganicism. People who subscribe to such a view picture culture as if it were an enormously powerful being that molds and pushes people around, determining or at least strongly influencing their beliefs and behavior, sometimes helpfully, sometimes harmfully. A culture, from this point of view, is a living organism, existing independently of those who practice it, with great power to influence their lives.

Those who hold to a superorganic view of culture are attempting to deal honestly with what is a big problem. The question they seek to answer may be stated as follows: How do we explain the fact that people within any given society behave in incredibly similar ways? All anthropologists have to answer that question. Some choose to see the source of such conformity in culture. Some choose to see it in the people themselves. I choose the latter.

For this reason I attempt to make a clear distinction between culture as structures and patterns and people as the active agents either in maintaining those structures and patterns or in changing them. This position, then, has great theoretical significance both for our approach to anthropology and for our approach to Christian witness.

As I have written elsewhere in a treatment of worldview

Culture is not a person. It does not "do" anything. Only people do things. The fact that people ordinarily do what they do by following the cultural "tracks" laid down for them should not lead us to treat culture itself as something possessing a life of its own. Culture is like the script an actor uses. He follows it most of the time. But occasionally, either because he has forgotten his lines or because he thinks he has a better way of reaching the goal, he departs from the script and does something else.

The "power" that keeps people following the script of their culture is the power of habit, not any power that culture possesses in itself. People ordinarily follow the patterns of their culture, but not always.

Cultural (including worldview) patterns, then, do not force people to follow them. *It is force of habit that keeps us following custom.* But even a habit can be changed with some effort. If the change is considered serious, however, others in the society will exert great pressure on the one who is deviating to get him or her to conform. If the deviation is not considered serious, little or no pressure may be exerted to get the person back in line (1989:56–57).

The distinction we are making is embodied in the contrast between the words *culture* and *society*. Culture refers, as we have pointed out, to the structured customs of a people. Society refers to the people themselves. Note in the final paragraph of the above quote that it is the pressure of people (i.e., social pressure) that is brought to bear to keep people obeying certain customs while the lack of such pressure leaves them free to make changes. There is no power in culture to press for conformity.

The chart below summarizes the distinction I am making between the behavior of persons and the cultural structuring of that behavior. Note that on the left (personal) side of the chart, we describe the activities by using verbs. People behave and assign meaning. On the right (culture) side of the chart, then, we use nouns to indicate the static nature of the patterns people learn by means of which they guide their behavior. Note the distinctions made between habitual and creative behavior and between overt behavior (doing and speaking) and covert behavior (thinking).

I have included the deep structure (worldview) part of the chart to give the whole picture even though we will not deal with the specifics of worldview until the next section.

		PERSONAL BEHAVING	**CULTURAL STRUCTURING**

S U R F A C E		*BEHAVING*
		
		Habitual Behaving
		Overt (Doing, Speaking, Emoting)
		Covert (Thinking, Feeling)
		Creative Behaving
		Overt (Doing, Speaking, Emoting)
		Covert (Thinking, Feeling)
			PATTERNS OF BEHAVIOR
			
			Overt Customs that Pattern Doing,
			   Speaking, Emoting, etc.
			
			Covert Customs that Pattern
			   Thinking, Feeling, etc.

D E E P		*ASSUMING* (Usually Habitual, Often
		   Creative)
		
		PRIMARY LEVEL ASSUMING
		   Willing
		   Emoting
		   Reasoning
		   Assuming Motivations
		   Assuming Predispositions
		
		ASSIGNING MEANING
		   Interpreting
		   Evaluating
		
		RESPONDING TO ASSIGNED
		   MEANINGS
		   Explaining
		   Committing/Pledging Allegiance
		   Relating
		   Adapting
		   Seeking Psychological
		   Reinforcement
		   Striving toward
		   Integration/Consistency
			PATTERNS OF WV
			ASSUMPTIONS
			
			PATTERNS UNDERLYING
			   PRIMARY BEHAVIOR
			   Willing (Choosing)
			   Emoting
			   Reasoning
			   Deciding Motivation
			   Being Predisposed
			
			PATTERNS OF MEANING
			   ASSIGNMENT
			   Ways of Interpreting
			   Ways of Evaluating/Validating
			
			PATTERNS OF RESPONSE TO
			   MEANING
			   Ways of Explaining
			   Ways of Committing/Pledging
			   Allegiance
			   Ways of Relating
			   Ways of Adapting
			   Ways of Getting Psychological
			   Reinforcement Ways of
			   Integrating/Attaining Consistency

Figure 4.1 Surface and deep, personal and cultural

We may liken the interaction between people and their cultures to that between actors and their scripts. In preparation for performing a play, an actor memorizes his script. During the performance, then, he speaks his lines as creatively as possible within the limits set for him by the script and the physical setting on the stage. There are, however, conditions under which the actor will depart from the script. For one, he may forget some lines or make a mistake and have to improvise. For another, one of the other players may miss a cue or do something the first actor hadn't counted on requiring him to improvise. Or, some external circumstance (e.g., a prop misplaced or falling over) might motivate him to say or do something other than what he has memorized. Or, he may simply create something new right on the spot to spice things up.

Though cultural lines are carefully memorized and most of the cultural performance proceeds according to habit, there is also room for creativity. When people follow the patterns, whether by habit (ritual) or by conscious choice, they are, in a sense, "performing their culture." They are following the cues. When, then, they make mistakes or innovate, they are also performing, but in a more creative way. This kind of performance relates to the cultural script but does not follow the guidelines exactly.

In the drama of cultural performance, it sometimes seems good to change the script. This is done by agreement between the parties concerned: director, actors and actresses, stage manager, etc. Cultural patterns (scripts) are both maintained and altered by the people who use them. The performance of people as they use their cultural patterns results in the continuance of most of the patterns, though always with some changes.

Culture Defined

Culture may be defined as the "total life way of a people, the social legacy the individual acquires from his group," a people's "design for living" (Kluckhohn 1949:17). Or, to be more specific, we may see a culture as *a society's complex, integrated coping mechanism, consisting of learned, patterned concepts and behavior, plus their underlying perspectives (worldview) and resulting artifacts (material culture)*. Diagrammatically we may display this definition as follows:

A complex, integrated coping mechanism	Belonging to and operated by a society (social group)	Consisting of: 1. Concepts and behavior that are patterned and learned 2. Underlying perspectives (worldview) 3. Resulting products, both nonmaterial (customs, rituals) and material (artifacts)

Figure 4.2 A definition of culture

Let's now look more closely at our definition.

1. First, culture is seen as *a coping mechanism*. Another term that might be used is *a strategy for survival*. The idea is that culture is the mechanism by means of which every human group and individual copes with human biological makeup and the surrounding geographical and social environment. We experience three basic givens: our person (including biological, mental, psychological and spiritual components), the environment in which we live (including both physical and social components) and the culture in terms of which we relate to the other two. The latter provides us with the plans (strategies) and patterns that we employ in dealing with the givens of our psychobiological makeup and those of our geographical and social environments. We will come to understand more of this coping mechanism as we go along.

2. Secondly, we have labeled a culture as *belonging to and operated by a social group (society)*. A culture is owned by the people who are trained in it and who live according to it. As pointed out above, it is a "social legacy," an inheritance from a people's ancestors. It is very precious to a people and under ideal conditions is operated happily and confidently by those for whom it is the only "life way" or "design for living" that makes sense to them. A people perceives their culture as having been created by concerned and revered forebears to enable them to deal effectively with the concerns of life.

3. Such a cultural system *expresses ideas or concepts*. These ideas are where things start. There is no lever to enable us to move large rocks without an underlying concept, no wheel, no wedding ceremony, no eating custom, no pottery or basketry, no naming or puberty rite. Underlying every custom, every cultural strategy and, probably, historically prior to each is one or more concepts in the head of the originator and of each one who practices the custom or employs the strategy.

4. The thing that these concepts underlie, then, is *cultural behavior*. Behavior is simply what we do with body or mind, alone or in groups. It is the most visible type of cultural activity. Some examples are listed in the above paragraph.

5. The concepts and behavior of a culture are *patterned*. In the past certain westerners (often missionaries or travelers) went to other parts of the world, observed the behavior of the people there, and made statements such as, "These people don't have any organization to their life. They just do what they feel like, without rhyme or reason to their customs."

As anthropologists and others began to really study other people's cultures, however, they discovered that that is not an accurate point of view. Every group of people has rules and regulations according to which they live. There is always structuring, always regularity, always system, and a very high degree of predictability since most cultural behavior (thinking as well as doing) is quite habitual. People act habitually and unconsciously according to the patterns they have been taught.

Due to these patterned regularities and the habitual behavior that stems from them, cultural behavior is interpretable by insiders—the other members of the cultural group. If cultural behavior were random, there would be no way for other members of a society to understand what that behavior means. Suppose, for example, a given person greeted others sometimes by waving, sometimes by punching them in the nose, and sometimes by disrobing in front of them. Unless everyone in the society agreed that each of these methods was appropriate greeting behavior, this person would be greatly misunderstood. For *understanding requires agreement. And agreement requires predictability, which, in turn, requires patterning.* So cultural behavior is (and must be) patterned.

6. Culture is, furthermore, *learned*. We get it from our parents and others from whom we learn. It is not transmitted biologically. Nor does it come from the environment. It is a human thing, passed from generation to generation very effectively via familiar processes of imitation and teaching. Most of these processes, however, take place quite unconsciously, leading us often to underestimate the difficulty of culture learning and the complexity of what we have learned.

Sometimes I'm asked, "How come you westerners with all your education and intelligence can shoot rockets to the moon, but you can't even learn our culture and language, the simplest in the world?" I tell them we had the wrong mothers! If we had their mothers, we would have learned their culture and language. But we didn't. Our mothers didn't know their culture and language and so didn't teach it to us. But there's a fair chance that these people won't understand what I'm saying unless they try to learn another culture and language themselves.

7. Culture also consists of the *underlying perspectives (worldview)* on the basis of which the cultural concepts and behavior we have been discussing are generated. As pointed out already, this constitutes the very important deep structure of culture.

8. Lastly, we point to the *products* produced by people as they follow cultural rules and patterns. These products may be non-material or material. The majority of the products are non-material. These include the concepts and behavior patterns practiced by a people. All the customs and rituals practiced by a people are non-material cultural products. So are the ideas that underlie the material artifacts produced by a people. Those artifacts are the material cultural products of a people. These include the tools, containers, utensils, houses, vehicles, clothing, etc. that people use in their cultural behavior. Some anthropologists (e.g., Spradley and McCurdy 1975) would exclude material products from a definition of culture, contending that culture is totally a matter of knowledge and ideas. It has, however, been traditional to include them, and I here follow that tradition.

Levels and Types of Culture and Society

The terms culture and society can be used at several levels. Though, as mentioned above, these two terms are often carelessly used interchangeably, we need to be careful to use *culture* when referring to the structuring of life and *society* when referring to the people who live by that structuring.

Since each person is immersed in a culture, it is possible to speak of the most specific level of cultural structuring as a *personal culture*. At the other end of the spectrum, then, we may lump together large groupings of cultures that manifest similar characteristics. Such terms as *western culture(s)*, *African culture(s)*, *Latin American culture(s)* are used to label such groupings. Equally appropriate as designations of the peoples who live by these cultures would be *western society(ies)*, *African society(ies)*, *Latin American society(ies)*.

A sequence of terms to designate cultural structuring may be charted as follows:

```
            Personal Culture
         Family Culture (or Subculture)
       Community Culture (or Subculture)
        Regional Culture (or Subculture)
      National Culture (e.g., American Culture)
     Multinational Culture (e.g., Western Culture)
```

Figure 4.3 Different levels and types of cultural structuring

Another way of grouping cultures and societies is on the basis of one or more shared characteristics. Such labels as *traditional cultures/societies*, *peasant cultures/societies*, and *industrial cultures/societies* are often employed to distinguish cultural structures and peoples on the basis one set of economic features. Another set of economic features is in focus when anthropologists designate a people as participating in an *agricultural* or *settled farming culture* or a *herding* or *cattle herding culture*. The people, then, may be called an *agricultural society* or a *herding society*. Sometimes social characteristics are used as the basis for grouping as when reference is made to *polygamous* or *monogamous cultures/societies* or when peoples are grouped according to family characteristics such as *extended family cultures/societies* or *nuclear family cultures/societies*. Religious designations are frequently used to lump cultures and peoples, e.g., *Muslim cultures/societies*, *Buddhist cultures/societies*, *Roman Catholic cultures/societies*, *Hindu cultures/societies*.

The above designations are appropriate for labeling differing levels of a type of culture and society that might be called "natural." A natural culture is one that is owned by a given society, usually speaking a single language and that is passed on through that language to those born into the society. But the term culture may also be legitimately applied in a kind of "horizontal" way to common patterns exhibited by certain categories of people in many societies. For example, it has been observed that poor people of many societies structure their lives in very similar ways and develop similar strategies for coping with their poverty even within quite different cultures. This led to the coining of the term *culture of poverty* by Oscar Lewis (1959). Similarly, we can observe *cultures of drug addicts*, *deaf people*, *urban gangs*, *athletes*, *factory workers* and any number of other life situations that impose conditions similar enough to require the development of similar coping strategies.

Cultures and Subcultures

A society may be made up of a smaller or a larger number of people. In general, the larger the number of people, the more complex will be the cultural structures they produce and live by. For example, a large population will typically develop more specialization than is necessary in a smaller population. Whereas in smaller societies any given head of a family may serve as a leader in political, economic, religious and social matters, in larger societies, there are likely to be specialists in each of these areas.

Larger societies will also develop more subgroupings. These subgroupings are usually referred to as *subcultures*. Since, however, this term is usually employed to refer to the people in the subgroupings rather than to the structuring of such groups, it would be more precise to call them *subsocieties*.

A large population such as that of Anglo-American society, for example will contain such subcultures/subsocieties as those of youth, blue collar workers, white collar workers, farmers, even computer specialists, taxi drivers, clergy and any number of others.

In addition, it is common for national and multinational sociocultural entities to contain other societies (called "included societies") each with its own cultural structuring. In a country like Nigeria, for example, there are hundreds of distinct societies each with its own language and culture, all functioning as parts of a larger national society and culture. Likewise, in the United States, there are included societies speaking Spanish, Korean, various Chinese languages, Japanese, Tagalog, Cambodian, various American Indian languages and any number of other languages. In addition, there are communities of Blacks, American Indians and the second and third generations of many of the above language groups who speak English but retain a good bit of their non-Anglo sociocultural identity. These sometimes class as included societies, sometimes as subcultures/subsocieties within the larger society, depending on the degree of integration into the mainstream of American society.

More about Culture

With this background, let us turn to a series of additional characteristics of culture. Though each of these characteristics applies primarily to fully formed "natural" cultures, they apply also to a greater or lesser extent to the more limited types of culture discussed above.

1. Culture is *complex*. All cultures are complex (though some are more complex than others). Anthropologists have never yet discovered a simple culture. Some groups have a simple technology. Their material culture might even be called "primitive," though this is a poor word to use for their culture as a whole. For, no matter how simple their technology and material culture might be, their ways of

living, their customs, their perceptions of and responses to the reality around them are patterned in a complex way that often defies the attempts of outsiders to learn or even to understand them.

2. We also know that culture tends to show *more or less tight integration* around its worldview. The basic worldview assumptions provide the "glue" in terms of which people tie each of the various subsystems (see below) of culture to the worldview and also to each other. Thus, in addition to their relationship with worldview itself, within a cultural system politics is closely related to economics and both of these subsystems closely related to religion and social structure (e.g., family, social control) while all are tightly tied to language, artistic expression, and so on. Tighter integration of these internal parts of a culture tends to result in a more satisfied people. A breakdown of integration, then, usually increases a people's dissatisfaction and psychological stress (often leading to breakdown).

3. The culture of a people provides for them *a total design for living*. It is comprehensive, dealing with every aspect of life. A culture provides a given people with the means of answering the vast majority of the questions they feel are important regarding the human problems they face. Such questions are usually so well taken care of that the people may not be able to even articulate either questions or answers. They simply accept both answers and questions as their way of life.

Cultural answers are designed to cover all facets of life, whether routine things such as eating or dressing or less tangible things like how to decide when to plant or how to think about relational, judicial, philosophical or spiritual issues. One implication of this totality of cultural coverage is the fact that when we bring something like Christianity to a people, we should not be misled into thinking we can simply add it to their culture as if there were a void there that their culture wasn't filling. Rather, we are appealing to them to replace something that is already there. We're not coming to people who are not committed to anything. We're asking people to commit themselves to Christ in place of whatever other primary commitment they are taught to have. Their society has already answered for them what their supreme commitment is expected to be.

4. Culture is an *adaptive system* or, as mentioned above a *mechanism for coping*. It provides people with patterns and strategies by means of which they can adapt to the physical and social conditions around them. Cultural patterns show great adaptation to the geographical environment. That's why cultures in the tropics differ from those in snowy countries. If you're in a tropical area where you can grow food all year round, the cultural patterns show adaptation to that particular circumstance. If you're in a cold area where you can grow only during a very limited growing season that requires you to store food for the rest of the year, the cultural patterning is adapted to that.

Cultural patterns also show adaptation to social circumstances. If you're in a situation where you have been conquered by another people, your cultural perspectives are adapted to that circumstance. If you're in a situation where you're free from that oppression, your patterns are adapted to that circumstance. There is also cultural adaptation to biological givens. People of short stature will develop at least some cultural patterns that differ from those of taller peoples. People whose stomachs cannot digest sweet (i.e., non-sour) milk will adapt culturally to that fact.

5. But *no culture seems to be perfectly adequate* either to the realities of biology and environment or to the answering of all of the questions of a people. There are always areas of life that are not handled perfectly. Another way of saying this is that while a cultural system is designed to answer all of people's questions, it's apparently true that all peoples, of whatever culture, always have some questions left over that are not very well answered.

One of the important things to recognize about Christianity is that there are lots of ways of approaching people with our message. One of the best ways is to find the questions people are asking for which their culture is not providing answers. Perhaps the Christian perspective can provide answers for some of those questions. If they can see that the new approach answers some questions they have never before been able to answer, they may be attracted to it initially as a supplement to what they already understand. The local chief in our area of northeastern Nigeria once asked me if Christianity could provide the answer to a major question his people were asking. This question was based on the belief of his people that God had gone far away due to a bad mistake they had made in the past. So he asked me if I knew where God had gone and how they could get back in contact with him. We were able to make use of the felt need for an answer to this question to enhance the entrance of the gospel into that society.

6. Culture is *learned as if it were absolute and perfect.* Before we (or any other people) knew or even suspected the existence of alternative ways of life, we as children were indoctrinated into ours. We learned our customs unconsciously, before we had any ability to compare and evaluate them. So we often consider them the only possible approaches, the best and only right way. We thus developed an attitude called *ethnocentrism,* the belief that our customs are the best. Ethnocentrism is one of our worst enemies, since it leads us to impose our ways on others. It is, however, a disease both we and the people we go to suffer from, unless we or they have been intimidated by another people into believing our customs to be wrong. We will treat this problem in detail in chapter 5 (in Kraft 1996).

7. Culture *makes sense to those within it.* When we look from our own cultural perspective at other people's ways of doing things, many times they don't make sense to us. "Why do they do it that way?" we may ask. "We would discipline our children if they did that." From our point of view, based on our worldview assumptions, their custom may indeed seem illogical or at least ill advised. Yet, the more we learn about other cultures, the clearer it becomes that what people do tends to be consistent with the assumptions they start with. Just as we aim at consistency, so do they. But, since their assumptions, their starting points, differ from ours, naturally what they end up with will differ. Cultural behavior itself, though (whether theirs or ours) only really makes sense when you understand the underlying assumptions.

I often wonder how many of the things I did and said looked strange to the Nigerians of the area in which we worked. If their customs seemed strange from our point of view, ours must have looked doubly strange from theirs. I imagine them getting a lot of entertainment from their contacts with me. They didn't have television to entertain them. But they didn't need television as long as they had a white man around! I'll bet they just laughed and laughed at all the crazy things I did (just as we missionaries laughed at the things they did).

One serious mistake I made was to carry my small children on my shoulders. It made sense to me to carry them that way, especially if we were walking any great distance and wanted to go faster than their little legs would carry them. That custom didn't make sense to them, however, since in their world only corpses were carried on a person's shoulder!

I'm very thankful to my Nigerian colleagues for being bold enough to tell me about this mistake. I wonder, though, about the thousands of other times they didn't tell me what they thought and probably got the wrong impression, not about me only, but about Christianity. How are they going to know what Christ is like except by looking at me? And when they draw their conclusions from looking at me, how are they to know that they shouldn't trust their conclusions? Do they know and will they make allowances for the fact that my behavior is based on different assumptions than theirs? Any given set of customs makes sense to those who practice them but not necessarily to people of another culture whose behavior is based on other assumptions. Yet we all evaluate what we see others doing on the basis of our own cultural assumptions. Watch out!

8. Cultural practices are *based on group or "multi-personal" agreements*. A social group is made up of many persons (i.e., it is multi-personal) who unconsciously agree to govern themselves according to the group's cultural patterns. Influenced by the social pressure toward conformity to these patterns, then, they ordinarily behave similarly and make decisions according to those patterns. Homer Barnett (1953) called such group behavior "multi-individual." I prefer to call it *multi-personal*.

Everything underlying culture depends on people's agreements to do things in one way or another. Things people agree are right, are considered right. Things they agree are wrong, are considered wrong. Culture is based on those agreements. This fact has particular relevance to those who seek to initiate change in a culture. For a change of custom or belief is itself the result of an agreement to change. Such an agreement to change, for its part, is usually the result of individual agreements on the part of the members of the group to follow the lead of one or more prestigious members (opinion leaders) who have decided to change. That is, prestigious persons ordinarily suggest changes. Others follow, usually after a period of time devoted to consideration and discussion so that what appears eventually on the surface to be a group change has very definitely a multi-personal basis. Those (like Christians) who seek to encourage culture change need to study this process. We will devote several chapters to this subject later in the book.

9. Culture is *a legacy from the past*. The customs we practice were developed by past generations as they saw fit to deal with the problems of life. They, therefore, represent the learning our ancestors arrived at and saw fit to pass on to us. This fact provides cultural continuity from generation to generation. It also provides the present generation with wisdom from the past.

Often we can be proud of the cultural wisdom of our ancestors. Their ways of dealing with the multiplicity of life problems we face serve us quite nicely most of the time. Many of the techniques they developed have enabled us to thrive and even become great in certain areas of life. All we do is strongly influenced by and usually built on foundations developed and passed on to us by our forebears.

Some of what is passed on, however, seems to be either unnecessary or counterproductive. Many things that seem to no longer be useful are preserved in the transmission of a culture from one generation. The buttons on the sleeves of men's coats would be one illustration of this fact in American culture. The English spelling system is another. We will further discuss this factor in chapter 22 (in Kraft 1996).

In another area, however, the legacy of the past may present those of the present generation with even greater problems, especially in rapidly changing societies. For what is passed on to us by our parents is the culture adapted to the problems of previous generations. Thus, many of the answers we are taught are answers to questions that people were asking last generation or the generation before. And frequently we find certain portions of the last generation's patterns not fitting the current generation very well. This is what's happening in many rapidly changing situations. Here in America, for example, we have to learn how to conserve things like trees and water. Previous generations learned to exploit these things and to simply use them in their manufacturing. They didn't worry about the pollution or depletion of such resources. The possibility of a problem never occurred to them. The answers of the last generation in this area have become problems for us in this generation, and we must change our cultural habits.

10. Culture provides people with *a way to regulate their lives*. It provides people with patterns as to how to do things: when and how to eat, sleep, go to the toilet, laugh, cry, work, play. Our whole lives are regulated by what we are taught is appropriate in such areas and in nearly all else as well. We are provided, for example, with customs regulating our behavior when we meet someone, when we marry, when there's a death, when we worship. Usually quite unconsciously we obey certain rules when we stand, walk, or sit, when we communicate, even when we think. Whether we are with others or by ourselves, we regulate our behavior by the cultural patterns we have been taught.

11. *A culture may be pictured as a maze of roads and a description of the culture as a map of those roads*. As mentioned above, people ordinarily follow the roads (= practice the customs) but may, whenever they choose, create new ways to arrive at the same destinations. When people create new roads, others in the society may object and apply social pressure to attempt to get them back on the established path. Or, especially if the one who innovates is an opinion leader, others may like the new path better and imitate it themselves. In the latter case, a new cultural road is created which then becomes a part of the legacy passed on to the next generation. See chapter 24 for more on this subject.

A description of a culture, then, is, like a map, an abstract representation of the reality of that culture. Knowing the information concerning the cultural patterns enables one to get around in a society just as a road map enables one to get around when traveling. Insiders in the society, of course, learn the map while growing up and conduct their life's journey according to those patterns. Maps concerning when and how to eat, sleep, toilet, cry, work, play, think, reason, love, hate are all imprinted in their minds. Outsiders, then, if the cultural map is presented to them (in, for example, an ethnographic description of the cultural patterns) can learn to negotiate the maze of cultural pathways according to that map.

12. There is *conscious (or explicit) culture and unconscious (or implicit) culture*. Conscious culture includes the ways of behaving and thinking that people are aware of and usually can see and explain. Unconscious culture, on the other hand, consists of those patterns of behaving and thinking that lie below the level of a people's consciousness. This distinction is not the same as that between surface culture and deep culture (worldview), though a greater percentage of the latter will be in the unconscious category. For much surface level behavior is unconscious and a fair number of the deep level assumptions can be consciously articulated by a people.

If outsiders ask about those parts of a culture the people are conscious of, an insider can usually describe and explain the customs. These include cultural patterns that parents (and other elders) openly explain to children. Many customs, rituals and even assumptions fall into this category. More difficult to get at, both for insiders and for outsiders, is unconscious culture. This consists of unconscious habits, attitudes, assumptions, values, and the like that people learn largely by imitation and inference and seldom, if ever, discuss.

Not infrequently, insiders are so unaware of such customs that it takes a perceptive outsider to call them to their attention. And sometimes, when an unconscious custom is called to an insider's attention, the person will either deny that such a custom exists or give an inaccurate explanation of the reason for it. If, for example, someone asks a typical American why we are so competitive, we may answer (wrongly) that we are not competitive. Or we may explain that we are competitive in order to "get ahead." Though there is some truth in the latter explanation, it masks the fact that we follow an unconscious underlying assumption that it is right for people to get ahead even though it involves (carefully) overriding the interests of others. The real reason for our competitiveness, as for most of the rest of our customs is, however, that we have been taught to be this way. Rational (conscious) reasons for why a people eat, sleep, dress, speak and live in particular ways are almost always less accurate than is the simple explanation, "We do . . . this way because our parents/elders taught us to do it this way."

13. There is *ideal culture and actual culture*. Every people has its ideals. In American society, for example, we believe that all people are created equal. But an outside observer may notice that certain people in our society are regularly granted more privileges than others. The reason is, we don't live up to our ideal in this matter (as in many other areas of life). Instead, we live at another level called the "actual" (or "real") level. This level may fall slightly or greatly below the ideal level.

People regularly idealize their behavior when they attempt to describe it. Often the ideals they describe are seldom, if ever, practiced. It is probably a part of the effects of sin that we regularly live below our ideals while claiming to live according to them.

The need to distinguish between ideal and actual relates to this text and our attitude toward other people's cultures in an interesting way. If we are to respect other people's ways of life, it is important to try to understand the intent (the ideal) of the customs being discussed. For example, in dealing with the custom called polygamy (marriage of one man to more than one wife), we need to understand that it can be defended at an ideal level just as rationally as we would defend monogamy (see chapter 18 for the arguments). And occasionally it is practiced in a relatively ideal way. Usually, like monogamy, however, plural marriage is practiced at a subideal level. In comparison, then, ideal polygamy and ideal monogamy each (from a human point of view) can be quite satisfactory while actual (subideal) monogamy or polygamy can be very destructive.

In an attempt to get us to respect other people's cultures, I will frequently direct our attention to ideal expressions of their customs. In attempting to combat the tendency both of westerners and of westernized non-westerners to idealize western customs, then, I will frequently criticize the actual (subideal) expressions of western customs. Though I take these positions to make important points, we need always, in considering any given way of life, to pay attention both to the ideals and to the actual expressions of its customs. This is especially important when we compare one set of customs with another. It is unfair to compare the ideals of one society (e.g., ideal monogamy) with the actuals (e.g., subideal polygamy) of another.

The Subsystems of Culture

To conclude this chapter, I want to briefly present a diagram picturing what I am calling the *subsystems of culture*. These subsystems are seen as divisions of surface level culture and, as such, provide various behavioral expressions of worldview assumptions.

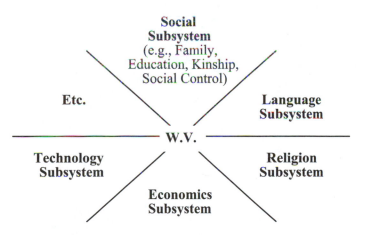

Figure 4.4 Typical subsystems within a culture

Concluding Remarks

I trust that this chapter has alerted the reader to such things as the nature, extent and importance of culture, the various ways in which the term culture is used and the relationships between culture and people. Culture is an extremely important factor in human life and, therefore, in any attempt to carry Christian witness to humans. I hope this chapter helps us see how crucial it is that cross-cultural witnesses take culture seriously.

If we are to reach people, we will have to reach them within their culture. We will do this either wisely or unwisely. It is hoped that by understanding more of what cultures are all about we can deal with them more wisely than might otherwise have been the case.

CHAPTER 5

AN ANTHROPOLOGICAL APOLOGETIC FOR THE HOMOGENEOUS UNIT PRINCIPLE IN MISSIOLOGY

Reprinted here with permission from
Occasional Bulletin of Missionary Research 2:121–126 (October 1978)

The "homogeneous unit principle" may be defined simply as the dual observation that (1) human beings show an overwhelming predisposition to band together with "their own kind" and that (2) God accepts this fact and works with it. McGavran introduced and incorporated the term into Church Growth Missiological Theory in 1955 and 1970. Wagner (1978b) and a forthcoming volume by A. R. Tippett based on a consultation sponsored by the Lausanne Theology and Education Committee, however, discuss and develop the concept in much greater detail. In spite of the fact that the principle seems to its proponents to be eminently reasonable and scripturally demonstrable (see Wagner 1978a), certain aspects of it are widely criticized in some quarters. I believe that the criticisms stem largely from misunderstandings inculcated by the conditioning of western culture.

There are several bases for misunderstanding the concept. Some see the concept as too mechanistic. Often they assume that for a group to be "homogeneous" there could be no internal diversity—everyone would have to be nearly a carbon copy of everyone else. Perhaps they are misled by their experience with the term "homogeneous" to assume that this principle advocates that some outside force reduces every member of such a group to sameness. On the contrary, the homogeneous unit (HU) principle simply recognizes that people who have learned via their sociocultural conditioning to prefer each other do, in fact, prefer to be together. It is another term for "society" or "group." The principle asserts, then, that God chooses to work with Jews as Jews and with Greeks as Greeks (1 Cor. 9:20–22). I seek in the first section below to discuss the principle and the variety of possible attitudes toward it.

Another source of misunderstanding stems from an inability or unwillingness of western (or westernized) Christians to distinguish properly between what we think God *should* do and the way the Scriptures show him to work. Many ethnocentrically hold God accountable to our doctrines of fairness and a melting-pot approach to sociocultural diversity. The temptation is to regard God's scripturally recorded acceptance of people as they are within their groups as but a temporary expedient, something that we can and should dispense with as unchristian. In support of this position it is common to pull Galatians 3:28 out of its context and to put it against the whole of the rest of Scripture to claim that God is in favor of a single Babel-type society. The Galatians 3 passage shows, rather, that God takes social diversity seriously while advocating a single transcultural allegiance to himself. In the second section below I attempt to point out certain of the western cultural values that lead people to this kind of misunderstanding.

A third source of misunderstanding comes, on the one hand, from fear and, on the other, from the American cultural tendency to blame impersonal structures rather than the personal users of those structures for whatever problems are associated with the structures. Americans place such faith in laws that they seem to fear that if there is no law against the misuse of such a principle as this one, it is inevitable that it will never be used well. In section three, below, I seek to deal with this objection.

A fourth source of misunderstanding lies in the American assumption that if Americans advocate employing the HU principle at all, they are, in fact, advocating that those groupings and the barriers between them be regarded as sacred and, therefore, never to be changed. This proneness to staticize as ideal any position advocated is an unfortunate occupational hazard readily fallen into by those influenced by western philosophy and theology. In the fourth section, below, I try to indicate that advocates of the HU principle see culture, culture change, and the influence of God in social processes more realistically. What we recommend as God's starting point is not, therefore, to be regarded as immutable and unchanging.

The Concept and Attitudes toward It

The homogeneous unit principle in missiology observes, first, that people cluster with those with whom they have something in common. The criteria that a people regard as basic to their "we-ness" form the overt focus of their homogeneity. Common language, culture, kinship, history, ritual, territory, time, and the like are typical criteria of sociocultural homogeneity. The HU principle observes, further, that in both the Bible and subsequent history, God seems to start his work with people where they are—within their sociocultural, spatial, and temporal homogeneity.

I find it difficult as an anthropologist to be against such a principle if it is well formulated. Poorly formulated concepts such as the mechanistic misunderstanding cited above that deny what we understand to be basic principles of human interaction are, of course, a different matter. Whenever groups of people get together they can interact effectively only because they have a very high degree of homogeneity. They need to have a common language and culture, to meet in the same time frame, to meet in the same place, to share the commonality of a particular frame of reference, to have the leisure, the health, the finances, and whatever else is required. From an anthropological perspective, if there is no homogeneity, there is no groupness. It is possible to have collections of people without homogeneity but not possible to have *groups* without homogeneity.

From this point of view, all groups *do* operate in terms of sociocultural homogeneity whether or not they like to define it in that way. Disliking homogeneity is, therefore, like disliking one's sex or one's nationality or one's language and culture or one's age or the time period in which one lives. We can argue about the definition of homogeneity, the components of homogeneity, the use of homogeneity, and several other issues with respect to it. But we cannot deny the necessity for homogeneity, and a rather high degree of homogeneity, if people are to interact effectively with each other. We might, in fact, suggest that the deeper the level of interaction, the greater the necessity for homogeneity.

There are several synonymous or nearly synonymous terms in use as labels for homogeneous units. I have mentioned the term "group." An ingroup is a group that defines its homogeneity at least partially with reference to other homogeneous units called outgroups. A society, often referred to as a culture, is a homogeneous unit functioning together in terms of a common language and culture.

The linguistic, cultural, and other criteria regarded as basic to the interaction of the members of a HU form a common structured "frame of reference" within which they operate. These frames of reference may be quite small, as with pairs of friends and families, or extremely large, as with multicultural and multinational groupings. The homogeneous units operating within such structured frames of reference will be correspondingly small or large. The larger the grouping, however, the smaller the number of criteria of homogeneity, the smaller the areas of interaction and the more fragile the frame of reference within which the homogeneity is expressed. The smaller the grouping, the greater the possibility (whether or not actualized) of tight-knit comprehensive homogeneity. Given human diversity and creativity, though, uniformity is never in view in the HU principle.

Cultural and linguistic criteria are basic to homogeneity. There are, however, a number of cross-cutting factors that interact with and subdivide culturally defined HUs. Among these may be listed geographical criteria, associational criteria, social class criteria, sexual criteria, temporal criteria, age criteria, health criteria, and religious- or worldview-commitment criteria. And this list is not, of course, exhaustive. The importance of any of these cross-cutting criteria may at given times be significantly greater than even culture and language criteria, however. The fact that a person is female, for example, immediately puts her into a kind of homogeneity with every other female in the world that, in certain ways, links her more closely with women of other societies and languages than with men of her own culture and language. Likewise, a common commitment to Christianity puts all Christians in an ingroup with those of other societies and languages who share their commitment. In terms of this criterion, then, we identify a homogeneity that transcends the ordinary cultural criteria for homogeneity. In spite of this fact, though, we must be aware of the problems involved in assuming too high a degree of homogeneity on the basis of a single shared factor. The more shared factors or criteria between the members of a group, the higher the degree of homogeneity. Further research is needed to identify and evaluate more precisely the variety and types of HU criteria.

The problem is not whether or not we agree to homogeneity, or even whether we agree to HU churches, but whether we *like* the homogeneity we see all around us. Homogeneity is a fact. The question is: What is our attitude toward it? It may be helpful here to provide a typology of attitudes toward cultural diversity and homogeneity:

1. *The Melting Pot Attitude.* This attitude holds that diversity (i.e., many HUs in the same nation) is bad. We should, therefore, stamp out such diversity. We should "integrate" the diverse HUs into cultural sameness, working for larger and larger HUs in the nation and the church.

2. *The Laissez-Faire Attitude.* This attitude holds that having many HUs is bad and must be overcome. The way to overcome them, however, is simply to leave them alone and let cultural processes have their way. Eventually, then, our nation and/or church will be a single HU.

3. *The Tourist Attitude.* The tourist takes the attitude that diversity is interesting and quaint. We are not, therefore, to do anything about it except to observe the differences and, perhaps, to thank God that we are not strange the way they are.

4. *The Reactionary Attitude.* This attitude glories in the multiplicity of HUs and seeks to preserve them. Those who glorify "primitivity" tend to fit into this category, as do many anthropologists who see their research laboratories disappearing if traditional cultures disappear.

5. *The Realist Attitude.* This attitude holds that HUs exist and will always exist. We must, therefore, learn to work in terms of HUs whether or not we approve of everything that HUs are used for. The realist cannot be unaware of the fact that homogeneity can be used badly. The realist also observes that the larger the grouping, the less likely the majority of its members will share a high number of homogeneity-creating factors. The realist, in applying this insight to biblical interpretation, recognizes that God seems to have worked *with,* rather than against, homogeneity throughout the Scriptures.

This presentation assumes the realist attitude. I assume that human beings are now and will continue to be organized in HUs. If, then, people find themselves against one type or usage of homogeneity, they can only recommend another type or usage. If they find themselves against one basis for homogeneity, they can only recommend another basis.

As Christians we are, of course, strongly committed to Christianity as the most important basis for homogeneity. But we find it absolutely necessary to ask ourselves the question: What relationship does the Christian basis for homogeneity bear to the homogeneity that already exists? If we observe that people are organized into culturally homogeneous groupings, what is the relationship of Christian criteria for homogeneity to cultural criteria for homogeneity? Is Christianity to provide another set of cultural criteria in terms of which people form themselves into a competing culture they label Christian? Or is Christianity a factor that can be added to any culture that, while bringing about changes in the culture, does not destroy all of the cultural criteria for homogeneity that existed before Christianity was introduced?

I see this matter as parallel to Jesus' teaching concerning the kingdom of God. Many of Jesus' followers saw the kingdom as a new cultural *form,* designed to compete with the kingdom of Rome. This would pit a Christian HU against a Roman HU in a battle for political power. I believe Jesus saw his kingdom in a different light, however. I believe he saw Christianity as a seed or yeast that exists and works within any and every HU. Christianity is to bring about change and transformation of existing HUs, but not to do away with them. This, I believe, is the point of Galatians 3:28 where Paul points to the fact that different HUs can and should place greater emphasis on the Christian criterion for homogeneity than on ethnic, sexual, or bondage criteria. None of these other criteria is, however, directly opposed.

Ethnocentrism and Homogeneous Units

As Euroamericans we live in societies where the majority opinion seems to be that cultural or linguistic diversity is bad or, at best, to be barely tolerated. The people we live among, at least those in power, deny that HUs are a good thing. Many, perhaps most, still hold to the "melting-pot philosophy" that I have cited above. Or perhaps they are in the "laissez-faire" group. These two groups want to see diversity done away with and differ only with respect to the strategy. Ours is a society that seeks to "integrate" minority groups in order to avoid the embarrassment of having them around. Ours is a society noted overseas for its cultural imperialism predicated often on the belief in the superiority of our culture and the inferiority of other approaches to life. Ours is the society that has gone around the world establishing schools and churches aimed at converting the peoples of the world to our way of life. We who write and read this are strongly influenced by these ideas.

As Euroamericans we live in societies where it is widely believed that "bigness is betterness." Westerners tend to strive for bigger numbers of people in organizations like nations, businesses, and churches. Ours is a mass society. It is also a mechanized society where large quantities of material items are dealt with at a time. We have a worldwide perspective that sees people as if they were mechanical things to be grouped together in large numbers. One visiting anthropologist has observed that Americans classify human beings into scenery, machinery, and persons (Smalley 1958). If bigness is betterness, there is little or no place for groups that happen to be small. Since this kind of thinking is endemic in our society, we can assume that we too are infected by it.

As Euroamericans we live in societies in which it is believed that we can control social processes as we have been able to control technological processes. In a discussion concerning HUs, one might, therefore, expect to hear a question such as: "Should we allow HUs?" The assumption behind such a question would be that it is possible for some people to control the social factors that organize people into HUs. But do we have control over such factors? Many of our fellow westerners, of course, believe that there are evolutionary factors at work in social processes similar to those that have been observed in technological processes that will make certain social structures inevitable. They see human beings moving from primitive homogeneity toward "civilized" heterogeneity eventuating, probably, in a single worldwide society (presumably with us in charge). Whether or not these ideas are accurate, we are affected by them.

Furthermore, analogizing from our experience with large social structures and technological processes, we tend to assume that there should be the same general rules for everybody and that there is one right way for everyone to do any given thing. Our criteria, then, for the "right way" are again often more appropriate for machines than for people. For example, it is often felt within our society that organizations of people should be *efficient.* That organization is best, we think, that works smoothest, most rapidly, and for the least cost. An organization ought, therefore, to be efficient no matter what happens to the people that are a part of it. Often, furthermore, we look at the members of an organization as if they were parts of a machine. People in leadership capacities, for example, are looked on as relatively undifferentiated. That is, they can be shuffled in or out of various positions without regard to personal and family considerations. They, like the parts of a machine, can be required to do whatever job is necessary whether or not it is fulfilling to them or well suited to their best abilities. It is recognized that there are differences between people but at the same time felt that these differences should not be emphasized. They should, rather, be overlooked, ignored, or stamped out. To the extent that such attitudes pervade our culture, we can assume that they also affect our own attitudes.

As Euroamerican Christians we are constantly linked with people who feel guilty over the fact that their denominations have grown largely within given ethnic and social groups (HUs). Probably under the influence of the general Euroamerican belief that ethnic homogeneity is bad, they see ethnic homogeneity in churches as something that needs to be stamped out. Often, therefore, Christians in such groups, especially those in leadership positions, try to compensate for the guilt they feel by turning against the homogeneity principle that was a major factor in making their groups strong. The desire for assimilation into the majority culture seems, at this point, to be more important to people of such denominations than the possibility of continued growth within their HU. Or perhaps the majority of the constituents of such denominations have already assimilated to the majority culture and therefore no longer see themselves as a distinct ethnic group. Either way, they are likely to be unaware of the sociocultural principles they have unwittingly used to become strong. They therefore react against them as majority-culture Americans do when such principles are pointed out to them. Many of us as readers and writer of this article have come from such backgrounds and are therefore influenced by such attitudes.

As Euroamericans we live in a society in which it is traditional for people (especially academics) to philosophize a lot about what *ought to be*, often at the expense of a realistic attitude toward what *is*. We philosophize that people *should* not be different and conclude that anything that allows/perpetuates differences is invalid and unchristian. Since people should not be different, our society concludes that they should all be the same—like us. "Like us" is defined as logical, "unlike us" is regarded as illogical. Those who are Christians, then, automatically interpret Christianity as concerned in a primary way for producing conformity to what we believe to be the ideal. People "should," if they are to be properly Christian, be democratic and capitalistic. Some in our society, of course, believe that individuals should be free to do their own thing. But even these tend to be conformist with respect to our governmental and economic forms. As simplistic as some of these views may sound to us, it is unlikely that we have escaped being influenced by them.

The point is that our attitude toward HUs is undoubtedly strongly influenced by the value system of the culture of which we are a part. Even those of us who seek to resist attitudes that are negative to HUs are likely to be influenced more than we realize by the ethnocentrism of the surrounding society. We are likely, for example, either not to be open enough to the HU principle, or to be reacting too strongly against traditional western values in an attempt to support the principle.

Anthropological insight makes us wary of the influence of the monocultural western values that form the basis for the attitudes above. The insights of anthropology help us to appreciate the diversity that we see in the world and to attempt to apply the Golden Rule at the cultural level as well as at the individual level. As Christians, influenced by the cross-cultural insights of anthropology, we seek, therefore, to grant to other groups the respect and acceptance that we want them to grant to us. The realistic acceptance of the potential rightness of other approaches to life is, at the cultural level, the equivalent of Christian acceptance of the validity of other individuals at the individual level. A cross-cultural perspective, informed by Christian love, enables us to refrain from evaluating our own HUs too highly and other HUs too lowly (see Rom. 12:3).

A cross-cultural perspective, furthermore, seeks to make generalizations concerning the peoples of the world on the basis of experience in *many* cultures. We seek in this way to restrain our inclinations to pontificate from a monocultural base concerning how it should be for everyone. In discussing HUs, therefore, we start from the recognition that people of all cultures organize themselves into groups on the basis of their feelings of homogeneity. If it is observed that at least certain of the people in western societies attempt to go against this principle, it must be asked how well it is working for westerners to stand against the tide of humanity as a whole. Usually, of course, we find that people who are against the HU principle are against it only in theory. In practice, they, like everyone else, operate in terms of the principle.

A Focus on the Usage of Homogeneity

It has become important within anthropology (since Linton 1936) to recognize distinctions between cultural forms, their functions, their meanings, and their usages. The *forms* of a culture are the observable parts of which the culture is made up. These may be material items such as axes, houses, and clothing. Or they may be nonmaterial customs and structures such as marriage ceremonies, family patterns, words, or groups. When we talk about a HU we are dealing with a cultural form that we observe in every culture.

Each cultural form serves one or more *functions* within the culture of which it is a part. Axes may function as implements for chopping wood and/or as status symbols showing the greater prestige of an ax owner, and/or as implements for hammering in a nail, and/or as decorations in the homes of tourists. Marriage ceremonies may function to legitimize the starting of a new family, to level off wealth, for those who have much money and, therefore, finance expensive weddings, to make people in the community feel that everything has been done properly, to help provide a livelihood for florists, organists, dressmakers, preachers, etc.

Each cultural form, then, is evaluated and perceived by the participants in a culture in terms of a variety of *meanings*. An ax may mean such things as food getting, danger, prestige, decoration, and the like to those who possess or observe it. A marriage ceremony, likewise, has a variety of meanings to those who participate in or observe such a ceremony. To the couple being married the ceremony may mean relief, frustration, expense, fear, and the like. The church janitor, on the other hand, may see wedding ceremonies as bothersome. A wide variety of other meanings may be attached to the same wedding ceremony by the various participants and observers.

In addition to cultural forms, their functions and meanings, there is the very important matter of how cultural forms are *used*. Indeed, the functions and meanings of a given cultural form are dependent on how it is used. People use axes in different ways. When a person uses an ax to chop down a tree, it has one set of meanings. When, however, a person hangs an ax on his wall as a decoration, it has a different set of meanings. Likewise with a wedding ceremony. If a family uses a wedding ceremony to display their wealth, it has one set of meanings to at least some of the participants. If, however, a less wealthy family struggles to provide their young people with a fancy wedding, it has quite a different set of meanings to those who are aware of what is going on. If an organist uses a wedding ceremony purely to increase his or her income, it has one set of meanings to that person. If, however, the organist participates in the ceremony totally out of love and regard for the participants, the ceremony has a different set of meanings for him or her.

When, therefore, we talk about HUs, it is of great importance that we distinguish which of these aspects of homogeneity we are talking about. If we say that HUs are bad, are we suggesting that the existence of HUs is bad in and of itself? That is, is the HU as a cultural *form* a bad thing? Or are we identifying some or all of the functions, meanings, and usages of HUs as bad? Or, on the other hand, if we say that HUs are good, are we talking about form, function, meaning, or usage? Not until we identify which aspect of the problem we are discussing can we properly deal with the matter of alternatives to those things that we identify as undesirable.

Suppose, for example, that we take the position that the cultural form called HU, ingroup, or subculture is always bad. What alternatives can we offer? Can we suggest that it would be better to dissolve every grouping of people who enjoy being together? If so, what would we dissolve it into? Can we suggest that bigger, more heterogeneous groupings are always better than homogeneous groupings? I think we rapidly find ourselves in quite untenable positions if we consider badness to lie within the HU form itself.

Among the functions that HUs serve within cultures is that of structuring societies into manageable groupings of people. Homogeneous groupings are usually small, friendly, and they operate fairly smoothly and equitably. Such groupings, by including those whom they do include, exclude others. In order for them to function as ingroups, therefore, it seems necessary for them to function also as producers of outgroups. For those within the HU, though, such a group functions to provide a sense of definition and of meaningfulness. That is, people within such a group tend to know who they are and to feel that their lives are more meaningful than if they did not belong to such a group. Can we identify such functions of HUs as totally bad? Or should we distinguish those functions that are likely to be bad from those functions that are likely to be good for the people involved?

With respect to meaning, likewise, we find people attaching quite a variety of meanings to homogeneity, some of which we would want to endorse heartily and some of which we would question. An ingroup provides a sense of belonging for those within it. We see such a meaning in Israel and in the church, as well as in the multiplicity of ingroups that have little or no connection with a commitment to God. Christians feel that by participating in such groups they are more effectively expressing their relationship to God and to his people than they would be able to if they were not a part of such groups. They (we) say, "These are 'our type of people.' This organization is ours, and it means more to us because it is ours than it would if it were someone else's." On the other hand—and we see this both in Israel and in the church as well as in other HUs—there is always the tendency toward exclusivity and snobbishness. For many of those within a HU, the existence of that particular ingroup means that they are better than other groups. For many, such groupings mean, "We are superior, they are inferior." In our assessment of HUs, I believe we will want to distinguish between the value of those meanings that are helpful and constructive in terms of the aims of Christianity and those meanings that are destructive.

The key thing in all of this is how people *use* the homogeneity of which they are a part. If a church HU communicates exclusivity and arrogance to another group, is it because homogeneity is bad in itself? Or is it because in this case those who participate in the church ingroup are using their homogeneity badly? True, there may be a long-standing reputation for exclusivity on the part of Christian churches that has to be dealt with by the present generation of Christians. But this reputation has been built up by particular kinds of *usage* of the homogeneity and needs to be overcome by means of a different usage. It is not inherent in homogeneity as a cultural form. Note, in contrast, the extremely positive effect that a HU has on one who is admitted to it and finds within it a sense of belonging, close friendship, and a matrix for healthy personal, social, and spiritual growth. Can we evaluate a HU used to meet such needs for some as totally bad, simply because it communicates exclusivity to others? Should we not continue to encourage the one usage while working diligently to improve the other?

Often, homogeneity is used in a kind of power game,[1] as a means to dominate other people. This I believe is a wrong use of ingroupness. HUs can, however, be

---

[1] It is disturbing to observe that many of those who voice the strongest opposition to the continued existence of ethnic diversity within given organizations are often those who stand to gain power for their own HU by crushing the felt identity of those belonging to other HUs. On the other hand, it is often those who are out of power—those who stand to gain most in the power game by gaining

used in such a way that they witness to other groups concerning the possibility of greater love and concern for people both within and outside the group. HUs can be used in such a way that they focus on the rejection of outgroups. Or they can be used in such a way that they focus on the acceptance of outgroups. I believe that Jesus, in the Parable of the Good Samaritan, was trying to transform the concept of the Jews of his day from the model of their HU as an outgroup-rejector to the model of their HU as an outgroup-acceptor (neighbor).

The point is that homogeneity may be good or bad, depending on *how it is used*. My suggestion is that, in keeping with the aims of Christian growth, we should take a position that attempts to reinforce the strengths of homogeneity but to overcome the difficulties. Church congregations are intended to be HUs that give highly important Christian meaning to those within them. But Christian groups are not intended to be exclusivistic. They are to live for themselves but not to live for themselves exclusively. They are commanded to live also for others without denying or minimizing the strengths of ingroupness. There needs, therefore, to be communication within the ingroup concerning a whole set of obligations to outgroups.

Christians are expected to grow in their experience of and relation to God and to their fellow Christians within the ingroup. Within this ingroup we are to experience and develop the security that we need in a relationship to God and to the other members of the ingroup. But we are also to learn a new definition of the concept "neighbor." We are, further, to learn a commitment to the cause for which Jesus gave his life. And these things that we learn in our HUs relate to the outgroups around us.

How to teach such things effectively within an ingroup is always problematic. It is clear, however, that one ineffective way of going about the process is to attempt to smash the homogeneity of the ingroup. For such attempts result in the smashing of the group's "selfhood"—their identity, the feelings of meaning and well-orderedness that they have based their lives on. This results in the kinds of insecurity that cripple people in all of their relationships and disable them for functioning effectively in their interactions with ingroup members and especially with the members of other groups. It reduces them, then, to a collection of demoralized individuals or subgroups, ripe for domination by an unscrupulous outgroup. They then either convert to the culture of the conquering outgroup or reconstitute themselves into one or more "underground" HUs awaiting their chance to reassert their selfhood as a fully functioning HU at a later date (see Tippett 1971). Such has been the plight of American blacks, Latin American Indians, and countless "Christianized" parts of tribal groups that, in the name of Christianity, have come to be dominated by a foreign culture at least as much as they have come to be indwelt by the living Christ.

recognition for their own HUs—who seem to be most in favor of recognizing and enshrining such diversity.

Culture Change and Homogeneous Units

The final anthropological insight that I would like to deal with concerns the relationship between culture change and homogeneity. Static views of culture (and of an anthropological perspective) give the impression that one who admits the validity of diverse groupings is locked in forever to endorsing the right for all of those groupings to continue to exist *as they are*. Informed missiologists, of course, assume no such thing. When we speak about accepting HUs as they are, we are speaking of a starting point only. We make no assumption that such groupings will or should continue to exist *as they now are* forever. Indeed, with anthropologists, we observe that every culture has always been and will continue to be in the process of change at all times. HUs that we now observe, therefore, are not now what they once were and will not continue to be what they now are—whether we like it or not.

We do not question the validity of change in HUs. We are, however, anxious that the changes that occur enhance the cause of Christ rather than retard it. We therefore seek to *work with what is to assist people to move* toward what we believe ought to be. This is what I have called *a realist attitude, not a laissez-faire attitude*. As part of this realist attitude I would like to point briefly to several important aspects of HU change.

The first thing to focus on is the fact that the *use* of homogeneity can be changed if need be. We have spoken above about the fact that homogeneity can be used wrongly. If we find, therefore, an unchristian exclusivism to characterize a given HU, I believe we have a Christian obligation to advocate change in the way that group is using its homogeneity. This is, I believe, what Jesus and Paul sought to do with Jewish homogeneity in the first century. They appealed for change from within the HU, not for the smashing of the unit. Even when they gave up on certain HUs it was to turn to other HUs, not to deny the validity of homogeneity.

In seeking to advocate change in the usage of homogeneity, however, it is crucial for the advocate to understand his or her position vis-a-vis the members of the HU. Homer Barnett (1953) presents what I believe to be the most helpful perspective in this regard. He points out that there are two kinds of advocate of change—those who advocate change in a HU of which they are a part and those who advocate change in someone else's HU. The rules are different for outsiders who advocate change from those for insiders who advocate and can actually effect ("innovate") changes within the ingroup. The bringing about of the changes is, however, always the task of cultural insiders that Barnett calls "innovators." These are persons within the HU who are convinced by the advocate that given changes need to be made and who then make those changes. Learning how to advocate Christian change effectively within HUs, especially if one is an outsider, is a critical matter for further research. See Barnett (1953), Tippett (1973), and Kraft (1979b) for further treatments.

That change can be brought about in the forms of HUs is abundantly clear from the number of cases in the United States where assimilation and integration have taken place. Many ethnic groups (especially those from northern Europe) that operated in the first generation in their native language and a modified version of their European culture have, by the third or fourth generation, become "mainstream" WASPs. In many cases the present American HU is made up entirely of the descendants of the original European HUs. But in many cases there has been a considerable amount of realignment. There are even HUs that are interracial as the result of realignments of previously monoracial HUs. The fact that there isn't more of this should not surprise us nearly so much as the fact that there is some of it.

Nevertheless, I believe we all feel that within each Christian HU there should be growth in understanding the implications of the functional oneness in Christ of all Christian HUs that exerts pressure against the exclusivistic usage of homogeneity. This, in turn, should lead to formal realignments in Christian HUs. It is very problematic, however, to know when and how to exert pressure for change in this regard, and when and how simply to accept what is, without pressuring for change. It is obvious that a laissez-faire approach is usually ineffective as a technique for directing change—though, since cultures are always changing, we cannot assume that a laissez-faire approach will result in no change at all. Again the rules will differ for insiders and outsiders.

I have alluded above to the criteria in terms of which homogeneity is defined. Just what those criteria are and how important each is are important matters for further research. It seems clear, however, that social factors are much more important to homogeneity than, for example, geographical factors. Yet Americans continually speak of churches serving "their communities" while defining community in a geographical way. The problem is that our model for church often assumes that the geographical and sociological factors that in rural areas combined to create homogeneity continue to operate in combination. In many urban situations, especially, this is no longer the case. Thus, when a church building is located in a geographical area where people of more than one cultural group live, it is often expected that that church ought to be composed of those people. Proximity of geographical location does not, however, necessarily mean communityness. The chances are that the "community" served by that particular congregation does not live very close to the church geographically.

With effort, however, such a congregation might find it possible to produce new HUs consisting of people in the church and people in the geographical proximity. One of the least effective ways of doing this appears to be simply to invite people from the neighborhood into the existing HU. A more effective way would be to plant new HU churches in the area that will relate to each other but not be dominated by any of the others (e.g., the Temple Baptist Church of Los Angeles). In relating to each other, probably over a period of time, there can and should be reconstituting of HUs from original HUs that no longer feel the need to remain distinct from each other. This can be best accomplished, however, if each HU starts out in its relationships with the other HUs secure in its standing as a valid entity in its own right. Any threat of domination by one or more of the other HUs is likely to affect adversely the possibility of a given HU voluntarily entering into the reconstitution of HUs with other groups.

I believe we have data in the Scriptures that can be analyzed to assist us in developing a Christian approach to these issues. But much more research needs to be done. Jesus, for example, seems to have accepted the woman taken in adultery without exerting pressure for change, though he pressured the Pharisees continually. Paul, in writing to Philemon, accepted the institution of slavery. Was his appeal to Philemon to accept Onesimus back "as a brother" as well as "as a slave" (v. 16), an application of pressure for change in the institution of slavery? And what are the implications for a Christian approach to culture change of Jesus' refusal to "take up the sword" to defend himself and his cause against his enemies? He seems to have led his disciples to pressure for change peaceably, via persuasion, rather than via violence. What should we learn from these and other portions of Scripture concerning our approaches to HU change?

Summary

I have attempted in this chapter to shine an "anthropological searchlight" on several issues in the HU principle debate. In particular, I have sought to zero in on four aspects of the debate where anthropological insight can be particularly helpful. We need, first, to delineate the concept carefully. The matter of ethnocentrism in dealing with this issue must be a continuing concern of all of us. The distinction between HUs as forms and the use that is made of them is of critical importance. And the place and nature of change in HUs, though needing greater study and development, is likewise crucial to the whole debate.

CHAPTER 6

RECEPTOR-ORIENTED ETHICS IN CROSS-CULTURAL INTERVENTION

Reprinted here with permission from
Transformation 8:20–25 (January-March 1991)

Christians working cross-culturally to bring about change in other societies desire to conduct their interventions ethically. What seems ethical and endorsed by God from the donor's point of view, however, may not be perceived as ethical in terms of the cultural values of the receptors. The nature of this problem is discussed and guidelines suggested to assist us in recognizing and overcoming the problem. The primary guideline is the application of the Golden Rule in terms of the culturally conditioned perception of the receptors.

As Christians, we are committed to assisting people. We are also committed to showing love. Yet, though often the social disruption caused by those in Christian ministries is less than that caused by such groups as traders, colonial governments, U.S. AID, Peace Corps and the like, a disturbing amount has resulted from many quite well intentioned efforts at helping people of other societies.

The primary concern of this chapter is to speak to those groups who seek to intervene in other societies in the name of Christ. Such groups include missionaries, relief organizations, evangelistic teams and a variety of others who go for longer or shorter periods of time into cross-cultural situations. This is a preliminary exploration into the subject, aimed not so much at answering as at airing and discussing what I believe to be a question of great importance to the target audience.

Christians are committed to abiding by ethical standards approved by God. And we are often quite certain that we understand what those standards are. Often, however, we have not pondered the implications for our ministries of the anthropological fact that there are in different societies different definitions of ethicality. Instead, we tend to identify our own culturally conditioned understandings of what is and is not ethical with what we believe to be God's standard.

Three Illustrative Cases

Case 1: A few years ago, newspapers in the USA were filled with a discussion of a contract between a North American company (Lockheed Aircraft) and the Japanese government that involved, apparently, the giving of sizable sums of money by Lockheed to the Japanese negotiators in order to secure the contract. From the Japanese point of view this was expected, ethical behavior. From the North American point of view such payments are labeled "kickbacks" and "bribes" and considered unethical.

Case 2: A North American family living in a rural area of Africa hired a young boy to assist the wife with the housework. From the North American family's point of view, the boy was simply hired to do a job and he had none of the rights of a family member. In his society, however, persons of his age group are regularly "borrowed" by other families to assist with the work. On such occasions, though, they are treated more like family members than like hirelings. They frequently both eat and sleep with the family they help. In addition, they are entitled to appropriate a reasonable amount of any surplus goods the family may possess.

The young man in question, therefore, though he did not eat and sleep in the American family's home, did on occasion take from the home bits of food, a pair of socks, a spoon or fork, a child's toy or other things he considered to be "extra." When accused by the family of "thievery," he was amazed and contended that he had done no wrong.

Case 3: Representatives of a North American relief agency visit a non-Western country and observe that children who are orphaned soon after birth are not taken care of and usually soon die. Out of compassion for these unfortunate children, they take up residence in the country and start an orphanage. Though they observe that these children are not accepted into normal social life even after they have grown up, the members of the organization firmly believe they are doing the right thing by "saving the lives of these infants." Their definition of life is, however, purely biological (in contrast to the more sociological understanding of life of their hosts) and they tend not to take seriously the sociological rejection, amounting to "sociological death" that these "rescued" ones experience.

The Setting

In an excellent chapter on this topic, George Foster (1973) notes that the belief that we should help those less fortunate than we is deeply embedded in the consciences of Americans and other Westerners. But we seldom ask questions such as "Why are we doing this?" or "What right have we to assume that our efforts to help others will be really helpful?" We simply go out and help them as best we can.

"Yet very genuine moral and ethical problems arise in every instance in which attempts are made to change the way of living of others" (Foster 1973:246).

We have, for example, been able to extend the life expectancy of peoples around the world through improvement of medical services. We have assumed that the aim of bettering health and lengthening biological life is sufficient to entitle us to export western techniques to other societies.

"Yet failure, until very recently, to integrate birth control with death control has produced a population problem far more threatening to man's future than unchecked disease . . . [raising the question] 'Will four billion undernourished people be more desirable than two billion undernourished people?'" (Foster 1973:247).

Both within and outside of Christian circles the western reverence for biological life has ordinarily gone unquestioned as a basis for intercultural intervention.

Other basic assumptions stemming from western worldviews have also been prevalent (again, both within and outside of Christian circles). Among them is the assumption that western societies have learned how to make "progress" happen and that such insight is suitable for export. Large numbers of those who work cross-culturally share with perhaps the majority of North Americans the belief that "in their heart of hearts" all peoples really want to live and be like us.

"Poverty, coupled with poor health, primitive agriculture producing insufficient food, and limited education—these, it was argued, were the conditions that inhibited peoples in most of the rest of the world from making the progress they desired toward the American way of life . . . [It was believed] that developing nations had neither the technical skills nor the financial means to lick poverty, disease, malnutrition, and ignorance" (Foster 1973:248–249).

The answer seemed simple, whether from the point of view of Christians or (especially after World War II) of western governments: send people with technological skills to provide education, medicine, agricultural insight and the like. The justification was on humanitarian grounds for both Christians and non-Christians—as defined in terms of western worldview assumptions. We assumed, furthermore, that all peoples would see the value of our efforts and praise and be loyal to us (and, for Christians, to our God) because of them.

But, Foster points out, "professional aid looks very different to the recipient than to the donor" (1973:254). He asks, "What does an offer of technical aid imply to potential recipients? It implies many things . . . Above all it says, in essence, 'if you people will learn to do more things the way we do them, you will be better off.' This is not a very flattering approach" (1973:253).

The same might be said of "spiritual aid." Whether in technical or spiritual areas, traditional peoples may be wrong. This is often the case. But, and this is often overlooked, they may also be very right in many areas. Furthermore, we may be right or we may be dead wrong in recommending a change—especially when their custom fits their life situation (whether technical or spiritual) better than our custom does.

As Foster notes with regard to technological matters: "It is wrong to assume that a method, because it is modern, scientific and western, is better than a traditional one" (1973:254). Again, we may assert the same thing with regard to spiritual matters and contend, with Foster, that "until we are sure they are wrong on a particular point, it is unwise *and morally wrong* to try to 'improve' them" (1973:254, emphasis mine).

But morally wrong according to whose definition of morality?

One perspective comes from an old woman in a Central African village: "You Europeans think you have everything to teach us. You tell us we eat the wrong food, treat our babies the wrong way, give our sick people the wrong medicine; you are always telling us we are wrong. Yet, if we had always done the wrong things, we should all he dead. And you see we are not" (Read 1955:7).

Questions of right and wrong are ethical questions. The answers to such questions are, however, deeply influenced by the cultural matrices in which people live.

Presuppositions

Before embarking on the discussion of our topic, I would like to state at least certain of my presuppositions:

As a committed Christian, I assume the existence and importance of God. I also assume that God cares for humans and that he has certain ethical ideals that he expects humans to aim for.

I hold to a "critical realism" epistemology (see Barbour 1974 and Kuhn 1970) that postulates what may be referred to as two levels of reality:

a) There is the "REAL" or objective item or fact. This "big R reality" consists of what actually exists or happens as seen by the only totally objective being, God. Though humans are often able to see this REAL, they always interpret it and therefore can seldom, if ever, be sure their perceptions correspond with what is actually there. The REAL may be material (e.g., physical objects), spiritual (e.g., what is actually happening in the spiritual realm), social (e.g., interactional events), psychological (e.g., the psychological facts of a given person's make-up), or any other event or thing.

b) There is also the "real" or subjective human perception/interpretation of the REAL. This "small r reality" consists of the pictures in human minds of things that exist or happen, plus, of course, any pictures that may be purely creations of human imagination. "Small r reality" is perceived reality, the product of human interpretation. It is on the basis of this reality that humans operate. Even the "big R reality" of God's ideal ethical standards revealed in the Bible goes through this process of interpretation. We cannot, therefore, necessarily be certain that we understand God's ideals accurately.

I also hold to the doctrine of cultural relativity which I prefer to call "cultural validity" or "cultural adequacy" (see Kraft 1979b and 1983). I assume that every cultural life way is valid, at least in the sense that if a culture survives, it does so because it is valid/adequate enough to enable those who live by it to survive. That is, there is no surviving culture that is totally "bad." It is not assumed (with the "absolute" relativists), however, that *everything* in any given culture is "good," satisfying, "functional," helpful and useful to those within the society and, therefore, not needing improvement. Nor is it assumed that any culture is totally "good" or God-ordained.

I stand, therefore, in favor both of cultural continuity and of certain kinds of intervention by certain outsiders for the purpose of improving a people's way of life. What is done in cross-cultural intervention, how it is done and who it is done by are, however, crucial questions for me, even if I am in general agreement with the aims and purposes of those who intervene.

Three Sets of Ethical Standards

This position yields two levels of ethical standards:

Transcultural Ethical Standards. We might also refer to these as "big E" ETHICS. These are the moral standards built into the universe by God which, if lived up to, enable the peoples of the world to experience whatever God intends for them. I will tentatively postulate this to include a more meaningful and fulfilling life. *Transcultural Morals*, then, are the guidelines for correct behavior established by God. Discerning what these ethical and moral ideals are, however, is quite another matter from merely postulating that they exist.

Culture-specific ethical standards. These are the "small e" moral ideals (principles, standards, values) of *a* society that the members of that society are taught and expected to live up to. *Culture-specific morals* are the guidelines for right/correct behavior generally accepted, approved and sanctioned by a social group.

Thus we contend that there is a REAL (ETHICAL) above and beyond the cultural (perceptual) real (ethical). The problem is, of course, that if such a REAL exists, humans can only see it through their cultural (perceptual) lenses. We are, therefore, guessing at what that REAL might be. The fact of cultural limitations and distortions, however, makes the question of how to discover that REAL a very large one.

I will here postulate three sets of ideals (ethics) to consider in any cross-cultural encounter: 1) that of the potential donors and their culture, 2) that of the receptors and their culture and 3) the transcultural. A triangle diagram can be used to illustrate the relationships between these.

Transculturally
Ethical

Donor-culture   Receptor-culture
Ethics   Ethics

Worldview Assumptions: The Basis for Ethical Judgments

The underlying reason for differing understandings of ethicality lies in differences in the "deep level" of culture, here called worldview. Worldview is defined as the structuring of the deep-level assumptions basic to cultural behavior. These are taught and acted upon, though seldom proven, and provide the perspective through which a society views reality. Many of these assumptions concern what exists, how it got here and what the nature of it is. Others concern "things or acts [that] are good and to be sought after, or bad and to he rejected" (Hoebel 1972). Such assumptions, called values, are the ones in terms of which we make evaluations. These we learn as children along with the rest of our worldview assumptions. They become the basis in terms of which we make ethical judgments.

Worldview assumptions give rise to what I have called "interpretational reflexes" (Kraft 1979b:26, 1983:131–134). That is, we ordinarily interpret what is or happens "reflexively," habitually and without thinking. And as we interpret we judge, and evaluate the rightness or wrongness, the goodness or badness of the thing or event.

Ethical judgments are thus a form of interpretation. They are based on worldview assumptions and made automatically as a part of our interpretational reflexes.

Receptors and Meaning

Communication theory alerts us to the fact that though messages pass between humans meanings do not. "Meanings are in people," not in the messages themselves (Berlo 1960:175). Meanings are *attached* to message symbols by the users of those symbols, they are not inherent in the symbols themselves.

One implication of this fact is that the meanings understood by the receptors of a given message are likely to be at least slightly different from the meanings intended by the communicator of the message. Yet it is the receptor, as the "end point" of the communicational process who plays the crucial part in determining whatever the outcome ("the meaning") of the interaction will be.

The attachment of meaning is a form of interpretation. And, as noted above, interpretation is always accompanied by evaluation of the goodness or badness, the rightness or wrongness (i.e., the ethicality) of an interaction.

Such evaluation is, of course, made from the perspective of the evaluators within their frame of reference. When communicator and receptor come from different cultural frames of reference, then, it is virtually certain that the meanings of speech and behavior will be interpreted and evaluated differently by each participant.

What may seem quite good or right (i.e., ethical) from the communicator's point of view, may be interpreted as unethical from the receptor's perspective.

What Receptors Have a Right to Expect

A key to this approach is to attempt to look at things from the point of view of the "receptors." This I call a "receptor orientation." I define such an orientation as an attitude on the part of those who communicate messages (both via words and behavior) that is primarily concerned to do whatever may be necessary to enable the receivers of the messages to understand their intentions as clearly as possible within the receivers' frame(s) of reference (Kraft 1983:23).

Though I assert that everyone's culture is valid/adequate, it is clear that none are perfect and beyond the need for improvement. Furthermore, cultural structures are regularly misused, especially by those in power. Most anthropologists and most Christians agree, then, that it is valid to advocate culture change that results in improvement in a people's way of life. Believing this and knowing just what needs to be changed and how and how fast the change is best brought about are, however, quite different things.

Nevertheless, we can, with Elvin Hatch (and, I think, Jesus) assert that "human well-being" is a value that transcends every culture (1983:134), relating to a level of human beingness that is deeper than culture. Though defining just what this means as a transcultural value poses numerous problems, Hatch advances two principles in this direction, and I will add a third. Hatch suggests:

> 1. It is good to treat people well . . . We can judge that human sacrifice, torture and political repression are wrong, whether they occur in our society or some other. Similarly, it is wrong for a person, to whatever society he or she may belong, to be indifferent toward the suffering of others . . . (Furthermore, we may judge it to be wrong when some members of a society deliberately and forcefully interfere in the affairs of other people (1983:135).

> 2. People ought to enjoy a reasonable level of material existence: we may judge that poverty, malnutrition, material discomfort, human suffering and the like are bad (1983:135).

While agreeing with these, I would add:

> 3. People ought to be free from spiritual oppression. Spiritual oppression is real because evil spiritual beings are real and actively oppress people in physical, psychological, material and relational ways (1 Pet. 3:5).

Thus we are aiming beyond the validity of specific cultural matrices toward what we might assume those cultural structures ought to be providing for their peoples: genuine quality of life in spiritual, relational, personal and material areas.

Problems to Contend With

The Problem of Interpretation by Insiders. Since interpretations and evaluations are grounded in worldview assumptions, cultural insiders can be expected both to understand and to judge the activities of an outsider wholly from their own point of view. Outsiders, then, must be prepared to have their motivations and intentions evaluated purely on the basis of the insider's perception of their overt behavior. Their means, seen from the perspective of the insider's worldview, therefore, become the basis on which their ends are understood.

The Problem of Cultural Goals/Ideals. People are conditioned to have certain expectations. Many of these seem to be rooted in basic human needs. Others seem to be socioculturally constructed. Humans are conditioned, then, to expect their society to provide for the meeting of all of these "needs." Freedom from want or lack (as defined by the society) in such areas is a very important ideal of any people.

People are conditioned to expect satisfaction of biological needs such as those for food, housing, safety, health and the like, of psychological needs such as meaning, communication, "love and belongingness" relationships with other humans (Maslow 1970), esteem, security and structure, and of spiritual needs such as a positive and beneficial relationship with benign supernatural beings and powers and protection from evil supernatural beings and powers.

The Problem of Interference of Donor Culture Goals and Ideals. As with those who are receiving, so with those giving—all activities are likely to be understood and evaluated according to home culture reflexes. Donor culture participants will from the best of motives, therefore, regularly attempt to provide such things as fit in with the goals and ideals of their own society.

Westerners regularly assume that people of other societies want the same things we want, including material prosperity, individualism, comfortable housing, schooling, clothing, rapid and effortless transportation, physical health, long life, "equality" of women (by our definition), even our religion. Furthermore, we assume (others are willing to pay the same social price that we pay. Thus, we assume, that others will (should) value individual rights over group concerns, material prosperity and creature comforts over family and group solidarity, easy mobility over isolation, mass information-oriented indoctrination in schools over individualized, person-oriented training at home, impersonal, naturalistic medical procedures over personal, supernaturalistic procedures, women who are "free" (by western definitions) like men, over women who are secure, our religion over their religion, and so on.

Most of the things we seek to provide, therefore, fall into the category we define as "good" in terms of our values and aims, Whether the receptors also consider them good, and how many other good things they are willing to sacrifice are serious questions that need to be faced realistically by those who would help people of other societies.

Toward a Solution

A belief in the validity of every culture predisposes us to take seriously the goals and aspirations of each people. If so, the place to start in determining which of the potential interventions might be appropriate would be with a serious attempt to ascertain just what those social ideals might be. But here we are faced with several problems. Among them are:

The conservativeness of cultural structures. There is plenty of evidence that many of the cultural structures that people have been taught are not well suited to handle today's problems. Though they may have served well in the past, they are today unsatisfactory and disappointing. Especially in rapidly changing situations, cultural structures never seem to be up to date. Thus, there is no assurance that it is a good idea even from the insider's point of view to prop up or to build on these structures.

Even without the complications of rapid social change, *there may often be latent dissatisfactions among the people with certain official ways in which their lives are structured by their cultures.* It is not possible to believe (with the older functionalists) that the relationship between a people and their cultural structures is always agreeable. Often people who appear to be quite satisfied with a given approach to life are in reality quite ready to give that up when they become aware of the possibility of an alternative approach.

Even should the desires of a people be carefully researched, what does the researcher do when different segments of a society come up with conflicting ideals? Furthermore, given the pervasiveness of self-interest on the part of those consulted, a characteristic that can be expected to skew all information obtained through interviews, how does one arrive at a proper basis for intervention even after one has carefully researched the situation? It is one thing to be able to look back at mostly bad examples of outside intervention and to analyze what went wrong. It is quite another thing to plan beforehand and to carry out an intervention that will not result in similar mistakes.

Another set of problems relates to the fact that a large number (perhaps most) of past interventions, no matter how sincere the agents have been, seem to have caused enough social disruption to make one question whether the benefits are sufficient to offset it. This raises the question of just how good anyone is at cultural manipulation in a positive direction.

Principles for Intervention

To the extent that the goals of a people can be ascertained, let me suggest a few candidates for transculturally ethical principles of intervention in another society along with a suggestion of some of the difficulties in their application.

1. *Golden Rule.* I propose that, whether on a religious or a non-religious basis, the Golden Role be regarded as a transculturally ethical principle of intervention. We are to treat others as we would ourselves like to be treated were we in their position. This means we are to seek to understand, respect and relate to a people and their way of life in the same way that we would like them to understand, respect and relate to us and our way of life if the tables were turned. It also means that we need to find out from them how they would like to be treated, what their (not our) definition of understanding, respect and love is and to treat them that way.

2. *Person/Group Orientation.* This principle recommends a primary concern for persons (as organized in groups) and what I will call "person factors" that lie at a level deeper than culture. For at this deepest level, "people are more alike than cultures" (Goldschmidt 1966:134).

Person factors would include such things as the quest for well-being in relational, material and spiritual areas. Such a quest and the expectations surrounding it are, to be sure, all culturally defined. But the universality of the quest for these things (and perhaps others) would seem to indicate that it is rooted in basic human-beingness, rather than simply in culture.

This emphasis is in contrast to a primarily structural emphasis, such as that to preserve a culture simply because cultures are believed to be good in and of themselves. The question to ask, then, is not "what can be done to preserve the culture?" but, "what will provide the greatest good for the person/group?" I believe that it is unethical in the transcultural sense for change agents to put any goals ahead of those that will seek the greatest benefit for person/groups.

3. *Ethnic Cohesion.* Any intervention in another society should give careful attention to helping the people to maintain what Tippett (1987) calls their "ethnic cohesion"—a combination of pride in one's cultural heritage and determination to survive no matter what. Its presence keeps a people struggling to maintain their sociocultural existence even in the presence of great pressure to change. The breaking of such cohesion results in demoralization and the loss of the will to continue living as a viable social entity.

Even though we are to focus on person/group over cultural structures as such, it is clear that persons/groups require both effective sociocultural structuring and a measure of pride in their way of life. Cultural breakdown leads to psychological breakdown and can easily proceed to a loss of ethnic cohesion which, unless followed by revitalization (Wallace 1956), moves into personal and Social disintegration. I believe it is unethical in the transcultural sense for an advocate of change to seek change that will result in a loss of ethnic cohesion.

One problem is, of course, the difficulty of knowing when and how what one advocates damages such cohesion. Another is the fact that for many of the peoples of the world, much damage has already been done. Widespread personal demoralization is an indication that ethnic cohesion is in danger. Sympathetic understanding and genuine personal caring may, therefore, be the best we can do to help stem the tide in at least some of the people.

4. *Involve Receptors.* A receptor orientation requires that any decisions relating to the future of the receiving people 1) be made with their permission and 2) involve

their participation both in the decisions themselves and in their implementation. People are to be treated as people, not as things. They are to be respected and consulted, not simply dominated, even when the power of the change agents is considerable. I believe it is unethical in the transcultural sense to attempt to change people without involving them in the decision making process.

Problems arise not only when the power differential is great but also when there is a significant differential in expertise. For example, western advocates of change have found that patience, personal friendship and a willingness to demonstrate changes within the receptors' categories have been more effective in winning over nonwestern receptors than assertions of their own expertise.

5. *Refrain from Use of Power*. Whether it is the power of political relationships or of wealth or simply of cultural prestige, Westerners are easily tempted to use power and prestige to achieve what they believe to be worthy ends in somebody else's territory. I believe this to be unethical in the transcultural sense, even if the goals seem justified.

A major problem in this area is the fact that as Westerners with an egalitarian perspective we often fail to perceive ourselves as more powerful than those we work among. It is very easy for us to miss or misunderstand the significance of, for example, rapid agreement from the receptor group to what was intended as merely a suggestion. Westerners must learn to perceive such situations as characterized by unequal power relationships and to lean over backwards to attempt to compensate. One effective cross-cultural worker suggests that in such situations, the change agent should never offer only one alternative but, rather, offer three or, at the very least, two alternatives, making it necessary for the receivers to choose or to come up with their own solutions (Loewen 1975).

Summary

This has been an attempt to discuss ethical issues in intercultural intervention with a focus on how the receptors perceive such interventions. We have concluded with an attempt to formulate five principles that may be ethical in a transcultural sense.

CHAPTER 7

ANTHROPOLOGICAL
PERSPECTIVES
ON AMERICAN WOMEN'S ISSUES

A revision of an unpublished paper originally used in a
1972 class at Fuller entitled, "God, Culture and Women"

Many American women are hurting and they may not know why. I would like in what follows to apply the insights of anthropology done from a Christian perspective to the understanding and, hopefully, the solution of some of the things that make women hurt.

When we hurt we tend to lash out at anything and everything that we think might be causing it. And our ability to hit tends to be best with those closest to us. For this reason we often lash out at and hit our husbands, or the nearest man, whether or not they are at fault.

It is my contention, however, that (in spite of much popular opinion) the reason why women in our society hurt is very seldom either men in general or any given man or men. Rather, we men are just as much the victims of the real culprit—society—as women are. And most of us men are hurting just as much or more than women are. Others are hurting too (e.g., blacks, youth, aged) and for many of the same reasons.

As with race and even youth and age, sex is a biological given. The definition of our sexual roles, states, positions, personal worth, etc. is, however, cultural, produced by the society into which we have been born rather than by our biological heritage. And the hurt is related to the cultural definitions and assignments made on the basis of sex, rather than to the mere biological facts.

How can I as a Christian anthropologist help? My purpose here is to (1) help us understand the nature and function of culture (2) indicate God's attitude toward culture, (3) provide insight into our own culture, and (4) suggest some practical ways of working out this problem.

The Nature and Function of Culture

Kluckhohn defines culture as "the total life way of a people, the social legacy the individual acquires from his group" (1949:20).

> Culture regulates our life at every turn. From the moment we are born until we die there is, whether we are conscious of it or not, constant pressure upon us to follow certain types of behavior that other men have created for us. Some paths we follow willingly, others we follow because we know no other way, still others we deviate from or go back to most unwillingly. Mothers of small children know how unnaturally most of this comes to us—how little regard we have, until we are "culturalized," for the "proper" place, time, and manner for certain acts such as eating, excreting, sleeping, getting dirty, and making loud noises. But by more or less adhering to a system of related designs for carrying out all the acts of living, a group of men and women feel themselves linked together by a powerful chain of sentiments. Ruth Benedict gave an almost complete definition of the concept when she said, "Culture is that which binds men together" (1949:27).

Every aspect of our life is affected by our culture. We are totally immersed in it. There is not one thing that we do, say or think that escapes its influence. Eating, drinking, sleeping, walking, talking are all culturally conditioned. The way we think, what we are aware of, what we ignore, what we regard as important, what we value and all interpersonal relationships are pervasively affected and conditioned by our culture.

There are many different arrangements of culture. We've been exposed to the fact that in other cultures they eat differently, sleep differently, marry differently, reason differently. And all of these different ways of doing things are equally valid for the people who live by them. But not for us—we must live according to our culture.

L. J. Luzbetak says that cultural patterns are like "the rules of a game. Although all players observe the same rules, no two players play exactly alike" (1963:114). That is, just like those who make up the rules of a game, our society sets up for us a series of guidelines in terms of which we must operate. These rules allow us a considerable amount of leeway, but they also show us the limits of this leeway. Have you ever tried to play a game without knowing the rules? You make a move and somebody says, "No, you can't do that." "Why?" "It's against the rules." This is very frustrating.

The rules are arbitrary to be sure—*but necessary*. Rules are different for every game. They are not the same for Monopoly as for Scrabble. Not the same for Bridge as for Pinochle. *What* the rules are is not particularly important but *that* there be rules is extremely important and *that everybody agree* to them is likewise important. Otherwise somebody gets cheated.

Margaret Mead has shown that to some extent such things as sex roles can be changed around from society to society. This is very interesting, and some have deduced from it that since the rules change from culture to culture, rules don't count.

The really significant thing she has shown, however, is not that rules don't count, but just how much they do count. Nobody reasons for games that since the rules change from game to game, we can choose any set of rules we want to play any game we're playing. We cannot live by the rules of another culture unless our society agrees to them. We have to live by our rules, they by theirs.

Now the purpose of the game rules and of culture is to regulate the activity, to keep it organized. Rules see to it that all of the routine, trivial decisions are made and the participants, therefore, are freed to apply their creative energies to making the more important decisions. The rules define the area of freedom within which a participant can operate and they keep him or her from trespassing on another player's territory.

In cards the rules tell what order the players play in, They make sure there are no arguments by making everyone agree that the order is fixed. Rules answer the question: "How much is a permissible bid?" Here a *range is allowed* though it demands some thought. But everyone knows that the rules fix the total possible points and they dare not go over that total. When one bids, she or he also knows something about the chance factor. And this knowledge serves as an informal rule that everyone knows and agrees to be limited by.

The type of rules is also very important. Some rules allow for a large amount of individual choice while others are highly regulative (i.e., restrict individual choice considerably). Games, for example, may be labeled easy or difficult according to the relative proportion of regulation to freedom which they set up. That is, the stricter the regulations the less thinking the players have to do for themselves and the easier the game is. When, however, the rule regulation is decreased, the number of areas in which individual choice is necessary increases and the greater the complexity of the game. Note, for example, the simplicity of Slap Jack or Chinese Checkers versus the complexity of Monopoly or Chess.

Figure 7.1 Proportion of Regulation to Free Choice.

Thus a people regulate the life of its participants by means of cultural rules. These rules regulate human conduct. Such rules as don't kill, steal, commit adultery, etc., are fixed rules—no leeway. Do eat in certain ways, dress, marry, reproduce, etc., are relatively fixed, allowing some flexibility. Who cooks, who fixes the house, who tends the children at what times, who settles disputes are relatively fixed but differentiated by most peoples. That is, the society usually assigns such jobs in such a way that the rules differ depending on one's sex, age, abilities, station in life, etc.

Societies also have cultural rules to arrange and regulate interpersonal relationships. Ideally, the cultural rules will provide maximum of fairness for the greatest number of people. Societies are, however, never completely successful in their attempts to do such things as reduce exploitation of one by another or to seek to balance the good of the group with the rights of the individual.

By means of cultural rules, societies provide definition for individuals and groups. We all need to know where we stand. We need to be oriented to feel that we and events around us have meaning, and how they relate to the people and things around us. Culture provides us with our psychological and social security.

Cultural rules provide the social gravity that keeps us in contact with the reference points valued by our society. By means of these rules we are provided definitions of our relations to the things around us, e.g., the universe, plants animals, material objects. Cultural guidelines enable us to know, for example, whether our attitude toward our environment is to exploit it or to allow it to exploit us. They define our relations to other people, e.g., the relationship between superiors-inferiors, male-female, parent-child. They tell us to whom and how we should show respect. They define for us who are our in-groups and who our out-groups, who is friend and who is foe, who is "we" and who is "they" and how to treat each. They define our movements in social space, e.g., who is a baby, a child, an adult, an elder. They define for us such steps and the transitions between.

These cultural rules provide us with our real social security—especially at times when we are most vulnerable. They regulate life so that families come into existence to offer protection and security for babies, providing the setting in which a mother can safely produce and nurture the child. These guidelines, then, enable a young person to be educated into adult status and responsibility in the society. Then they provide a kind of map for the young person to follow in moving toward and into marriage and an occupation. In terms of these guidelines, a people provides for the protection of the group from outside foes that would threaten it. Each society sets up guidelines that aim to prevent one part of the society from working against another by attempting to regulate competition among its people and institutions.

A society organizes life for its people around a given worldview, including a value system. Societies and their cultural structures may be likened to individuals, each with its own strengths and weaknesses, its unique insights and abilities and its peculiar idiosyncrasies and foibles.

Certain types of guidelines are present in all cultures. Among them are

1. Those providing for children, protection, education and opportunity to imitate proper adult models.

2. Those providing definition of the responsibilities, privileges and relations with others of various age categories.

3. Those providing definition of the responsibilities, privileges and relations with those of the opposite sex.

4. Those providing definition of various statuses and roles, how these are to be attained (i.e., by ascription or achievement) and the expectations attached to each.

5. Those providing individuals with a sense of personal worth.

Don't, therefore, downplay the influence of culture on yourself or anyone else. Some make statements like, "We live in a society that tells us things that aren't for real" implying that since such and such a thing is "just our culture," we needn't take it seriously. Don't believe it. *There is nothing more "real" than the influence of culture.* Culture is more "real" than biology, physical environment, psychology, race, intelligence, sex and all the rest, *because it is culture that provides the rules for how each of these is regarded, valued, channeled, focused upon and handled.* I will say more on this later.

But culture is not simply a one way street. True, we are molded in every way according to its guidelines. But we also influence it. Rules can be changed if groups agree to change them. I will also say more on this later.

God and Culture

God is in favor of culture. He created human beings with the capacity for culture. There is no human being who is not totally immersed in some culture. And it is impossible for humans to extricate themselves from culture. God knows that people cannot function without guidelines/rules/cultures. We need definition and limits that are well-defined.

God works in terms of culture (1 Cor. 9:19–22). He approached Hebrews in terms of their culture. He approached Greeks in terms of their culture. He starts where people are—in culture. He adopts our frame of reference as the medium for his interaction with us. He employs our language, our understanding, our cultural frame of reference. He does bring about changes in culture, but he always (1) starts there and (2) works even for change in terms of culture. Culture is simply a context, a channel, a vehicle that is available for the use of God, humans, or Satan.

God's people are always organized according to their culture. The Jews were organized as "God's People" according to the patterns already familiar to them from their culture. New Testament churches were organized and spoken to in terms of their cultures. The differences between God's people and others are not in cultural *forms*—these are the same for Christians and non-Christians. The differences are in the *functions* to which these forms are put. We Christians operate in the world (in terms of cultural forms) but not *of* it. That is, the functions, the motives, the use to which we put these cultural forms is different. We live in the same family structure, the same political structure, the same male-female roles, etc., that characterize the rest of our society, but with Christian motivations. For example, in Galatians 5, Paul recommends to Greco-Roman Christians the employment of Greco-Roman cultural forms to *Christian* ends (both with respect to husband-wife-children relations *and* with respect to slavery). Eventually through culture change, (influenced by Christianity) slavery was abolished. But God started where the people were, Christianizing the functions first. The forms of a culture can be changed later if necessary.

But, though God uses culture, we must recognize that Satan and people also use and affect culture. Not all change is for the good. This is true even in societies like our own in which Christianity has been influential. Many of the choices made by the groups within a society that influence culture change are not good decisions. Many such decisions bring about *imbalance* rather than balance and turn out to work *against* the best interests of the people within the society rather than for them.

But, in spite of this, God still chooses to use human culture.

Our Culture

Our customs are the products of a very specific cultural tradition called "Western Culture." Its roots are in Northern Europe, not in Greece. We participate in one or another of the American varieties of this cultural tradition, We are also a part of a specific subculture called Evangelical Christianity. We are pervasively affected by these cultural and subcultural traditions. There is nothing we do, say, or think that is not conditioned by this involvement. We may know that our cultural perspective is not the only possible one but we are bound by it, like it or not.

As an example of our total immersion in this cultural tradition, I would like us to note that in discussing what we call "women's liberation" we are operating in terms of a set of very specific, culturally inculcated assumptions that we assume to be valid only because our society conditions us to believe in their validity. As a matter of fact, the validity of certain aspects of these assumptions is very definitely challengeable, but not until we become aware of the culturally inculcated assumptions themselves.

For example, the term "Women's Liberation" (1) assumes the oppression of women and usually defines the oppressors as men, (2) assumes inequality between men and women, (3) assumes a particular definition of equality (= sameness), (4) assumes that individual freedom is more important than social security, (5) usually assumes that whatever is oppressing women does not oppress other people to the same extent.

"Potential of Women" (1) assumes that that potential should be evaluated in terms of a single set of criteria also applied to men, (2) assumes competition with men at all points, e.g., a single standard for I. Q. and other tests, an educational system requiring the same kind of performance of the same tasks, men and women competing in the same occupations.

"Freedom" (1) assumes that this is among the highest goods, (2) almost always means freedom *from* something (e.g., rules), seldom freedom *to* something (e.g., well orderedness of interpersonal relations), (3) assumes that restrictions, rules and especially role distinctions are at best necessary evils, never positive goods.

Such concepts are based on certain American values, usually held deeply by all of us Anglo-Americans that are very challengeable. Among them are that (1) freedom is more important than security. We see rules as oppressive and stifling, especially those that in any way curb our individualism and self-indulgence. We try to shun responsibility and to protect our children for as long as possible from having to face responsibility. To us individual rights are supreme. "Don't tell me what to do," we say. Note in this regard the problems in getting people concerned about ecology—we just don't want to be pushed around even if our lives depend on it.

(2) Equality to us means sameness or conformity. We interpret differences between people as connoting superiority or inferiority. We don't seem to be able to conceive of people being thoroughly different yet completely equal to each other. Why, then, in view of the solid research demonstrating that there are many major biologically-based differences between men and women, can't we have two scales of measurement: one for men, another for women. And two educational systems, one for each, producing first class men and first class women who relate to each other complementarily rather than competitively? We can't do it because our society won't allow it. We measure anything that we compare on a single scale from worst to best, inferior to superior, bad to good. Women, therefore, are compared with men in schools where the curriculum was designed to fit men's thinking and interests and in jobs outside the home which, again, have largely been designed for men. Men's standard is regarded as better because it allows and encourages more freedom (a men's value).

What should we do? We can either continue to fight the battle as at present—pitting women against men, and continue to destroy our society by blindly continuing to accept its misguided value-system. Or we can as men and women band together with each other to change the value system.

What about education or schooling which consists largely of the formal, information-based accumulation and passing on of facts? Education properly defined is the cultural process or totality of cultural processes by means of which a child is transformed into a fully-functioning member of a human society (see Mead 1964:162; Kraft 1996, ch. 17).

Our society has made several bad choices in this regard. (1) It ignores the fact that the true aim of education is effective participation in life rather than protection from life. It, rather, allows schools to function as prolongers of childhood, trains people to specialize out of effective participation in life, takes us out of the real world into a thought world. And it presents all this information over such a short period and in such isolation that we can't possibly use most of it before we forget it. (2) It seems to ignore the fact that education should be a life-long process. It crams what it identifies as education into one small part of our lives and leads us to focus primarily on teaching rather than learning, in seeming obliviousness of the fact that the object of education should be to produce good learners who will continue to learn long after they are out of school. (3) It gives the impression that real education is exclusively formal rather than primarily informal. Actually the reverse is the case in every society including our own. (4) It trains boys and girls to all be the same thing, teaching them to relate to each other as competitors rather than in a cooperative, complementary manner. It teaches both the same skills rather than distinct complementary skills. And these skills are often of very little relevance to the real problems we face in life outside of school. (5) It firmly sets us in the depersonalized mold of our society. At home we were more often treated as persons. In mass education schools we become impersonal "pupils," "students," "kids," "brats," etc., *not persons*. We compete for grades with other nonpersons and study under other nonpersons called "teachers" whom we only see and hear for brief periods of time and who often do not communicate themselves as persons but as information machines or computers. These are pitted in our minds against the persons in our lives—parents, relatives, friends. And these depersonalized "teacher things" win out. (6) It imbues us with a humanistic, naturalistic ideology or worldview that places humans squarely at the center of the universe and allows no room for God. Our society has allowed itself to become "profoundly irreligious" and has marshaled the schools in the name of separation of church and state to propagate its anti-faith. It has thereby ignored the fact that "a system of beliefs, profoundly felt, is unquestionably necessary to the survival of any society," not knowing perhaps that "the logical and symbolic expressions of the ultimate values of a civilization cannot arise directly from scientific investigators . . . (since) a mechanistic, materialistic 'science' hardly provides the orientations to the deeper problems of life that are essential for happy individuals and a healthy social order" (Kluckhohn 1949:190). (This is an anthropologist speaking.)

There are, in addition, several other values of our society that might be challenged, e.g., (1) change is progress, (2) youth is better than age and experience, (3) everybody can make it to the top, and (4) nobody needs anybody else—rugged individualism.

In many ways our society is badly ill. We said above that culture is like the rules for a game. If the rules are poorly defined or are contradictory the game goes badly. In our culture the rules are often indistinct or contradictory. Some questions frequently asked illustrate the kind of confusion engendered by indistinct or contradictory guidelines: (1) Shall I believe parent or teacher? (2) Shall I, a girl, fit into the mold the school is pushing me into (the same as it pushes boys into) or the one my mother is trying at home to help me to find? (3) Shall I plan on marriage, a career, or both? (4) I want to prove myself by having children but I don't want to have to raise them, I would rather work. (5) Shall I help my husband to achieve or try to "become something" myself? (6) Can I be proud of myself if I am *just* a housewife? Am I really fulfilling my potential if I stay home?

Our society tells women: (1) Be sexy but don't "sleep around" before marriage and don't get so excited about sex after marriage that you pose a threat to your husband. (2) You must get married but don't go after marriage openly and don't go to college simply to find a husband, (3) You must prepare for a career but marriage would be better. However, don't let marriage make you give up your career. (4) You must produce children but raising children isn't really fulfilling. And don't let your children make you give up your career. (5) Seek self-fulfillment directly, not jointly with or behind some man, even if it costs you your marriage, husband and children.

For women, the requirements are fairly well-defined: you need to develop sexiness, you need to prepare for a career, you need to get married, you need to prove yourself by having at least one child and seek self-fulfillment individually and directly, not through a husband. But the directions for achieving all of these things and how to balance them are always contradictory.

But men are getting a fouled-up message also. (1) Our society tells us "You are superior." But we notice that women get better grades and are better looking. (2) We are told, "Prove yourself." And it gives us several options. But we learn very little that will assure us success in proving ourselves. If we try for grades, many of us are fighting a losing battle—to girls. If we try to achieve in athletics, only a few of us make it. If we try to make it in music, we soon find out that very few are able to make a living in any of the entertainment fields. And as we aim at a career, we are soon confronted with the fact that is takes us so long to get the training that it seems we'll never arrive. Then, when we get into the career, we find ourselves often so depersonalized that it's difficult to maintain any semblance of self-respect. Our society tells us that sex is a legitimate area for proving ourselves, but Christianity makes it a "no-no," and anyway we have already learned that we can't win in anything that involves women. Then, when we get to be fathers and determine to really do well at that, we find that our careers don't allow us to be home enough

Neither the requirements nor the directions are clear for men. The rules are not clear for either men or women. And just when we think we've caught on, something changes. We don't know how we should relate to each other because this lack of clear direction leaves us with no consistent, satisfactory idea of who we are and who they are.

We are provided with very little security even at vulnerable times. During the very vulnerable childhood years, our parents, driven by our culture's values, are often more concerned about their own relationship and their careers than they are about us. At puberty, girls envy boys' freedom while boys envy girls' poise and good looks. How we are to reach adulthood and when we are to know we have arrived there is not defined. We have to fight our parents to gain independence. When we prepare for marriage, we are subject to any number of dating insecurities such as the intensive competition between boys and girls, girls and girls, boys and boys. Frequently as fellows, we have long since allowed ourselves to feel intimidated in our relationships with girls and often come to regard even very ordinary obligations as exploitive. And girls, too, come to look on very natural aspects of male-female relationships as exploitive (which, due frequently to cultural depersonalization, they often become). In marriage, then, we are required to learn how to cooperate with each other rather than to compete in spite of all our competitive conditioning. And even later in life, when we get established in a career most of us are still in imminent danger of being dumped.

Not everything about our society is bad, however. It does have many good points. The chief of these is the freedom, even encouragement to change things we don't like. And this is where I want to particularly zero in on trying to help us arrive at answers to our problems.

What Can We Do About the Situation?

First of all we must recognize that we are changers of culture as well as obeyers of it. We *are* culture bound but we have a higher commitment, a higher allegiance. Culture is always being changed and will continue to be changed whether or not we influence it. The only question is which direction it goes. Our society is *very* sick. But it does allow us the freedom to modify present rules and to work out new ones. We can accept the freedom our society gives us and use it to work at overcoming as many of the shortcomings as possible. And we can work at this as Christians, with a long-term perspective and with a commitment to ourselves and others for God's sake.

Secondly, then, we need to set about modifying the rules for ourselves, to set up our own subculture, as it were, to refuse to be driven blindly by our culture.

I would like to make the following suggestions for improving the situation:

(1) First, we should realize that the hurt you women feel is but part of the hurt we all are experiencing as our culture rips itself apart. It is not caused by men. The hurt may often be aided by men who in our frustration are lashing out and hitting those closest to us (just as women are). But this male "chauvinism" is not basically a cause but a symptom of the bigger problem (just like racism).

(2) We have to realize, though, that we are a part of our society. We can't escape. We've got to work with what we have. Your insecurities have been programmed into you and, therefore, you've got to take them seriously. But fight the insecurities and band together with others (including men) to fight them by developing security rather than by increasing insecurity.

(3) Thirdly, we need to recognize our built in need for culture, our need for rules. We should, therefore, not seek to escape the rules into some mythical realm of "absolute freedom." We should seek to use the mechanisms provided by our society rather than to let society use or drive us. We can change many things for ourselves, whether or not the changes we make go any further than that. And we can minimize at least the worst effects of much of the rest.

(4) We should aim at security by using our freedom to try to develop security— both personal security and group security. We need to take these steps in groups— husband and wife groups, singles groups, couples groups, groups of families, communes.

We need to work out better rules in an atmosphere of acceptance, love and honesty. We should face the hurts, the lack of meaning, the insecurities; face the unclarity in definition; face the reality of culturally-induced problems such as competitiveness, exploitiveness, loneliness; face our need for other people besides just our marriage partners. All of us need other close friends besides our mates. We are not the rugged, self-sufficient individuals our society says we are—neither is anyone else. If we face these things in groups we'll find that our problems are common, Then, again in groups, we can work on developing the solutions, the rules, the definitions, the security.

(5) And finally, we should aim at self-definition that encourages and builds up each other, not the kind that demoralizes or discourages our marriage partner (or others), not the kind that feeds on him, neglects his needs or tears him down in order to build up yourself and your own feelings of self-worth. Security in a mutually fulfilling relationship is much more satisfying in the long run than any attempt at individual fulfillment can ever be, even if such an attempt is successful. We need each other and can never be complete by ourselves. That relationship, therefore, is more valuable than anything we can ever attain as individuals *no matter what it costs us*. So work hard and determinedly at it.

Work to bring about a marriage and/or other social relationship that encourage distinctiveness with equal validity for each partner. Arrange with your husband

and/or a larger group to develop your differences so that you complement and complete each other rather than competing with each other as you've been taught to do. Define with your mate what you feel you need from him and from yourself to be fulfilled and satisfied as a First Class Woman (not a second class man) and for him to be fulfilled and satisfied as a First Class Man (not a second class man). Division of labor isn't bad in itself, but we need to work out and agree on the rules. But be willing and anxious to discuss and revise the rules as your needs change, (for they will).

Work for self-definition that allows appropriately different arrangements at different times in your lives. It may be very difficult for you to work while he "loafs" at school. You would so much rather have a baby. But your day will come, be patient. Help make him secure at this vulnerable time in his life and invite him to make you secure later when your more vulnerable time comes. He'll feel rewarded at both times. Later arrangements may be for you to be at home all the time or part time at home and part time in a job or full time in a job. But work it out together so that both of you are working toward definition and security according to agreed-upon rules.

Work toward self-definition that provides for security not only for you and your husband, but especially for your children. They are even more vulnerable than you are. Learn to be open, accepting, loving and security-providing for each other. Then invite—don't be driven to—children in to share this kind of life with you.

Singles—work toward self-definition that allows you to believe that a fulfilling career is just as valid as a fulfilling marriage, and infinitely better than a poor marriage. There are far worse tragedies than being unmarried (though your cultural conditioning will make it difficult for you to imagine any, and may, if you don't watch out, drive you into very vulnerable situations). But even if you don't marry, you still need close relationships with other people for completion, fulfillment and satisfactory self-definition. We all, whether married or unmarried, are lonely and need the closeness of other persons and of God to help us with this problem.

In summary, what I am suggesting is that each of us in cooperation with our mates and/or others with whom we are in close relationship involve ourselves in what might be called "ethnotherapy"—the attempt to bring greater health to our ailing culture, or at least those parts of it that most directly influence our lives. We can, I believe, with the kind of insight I've been talking about and with God's help create for ourselves a more satisfying subculture. We should not, I feel, allow our concern for broader cultural inequities (as important as these are) to cause us to lose our personal battle. If you feel called to fight the women's lib battle, fight it in *cooperation with* men, not as if men were the cause of the problem. Band together with men to fight the bigger battle with them. Work for security. Work for full-fledged personhood but not in such a way that differences in roles and functions are downgraded. Difference does not have to mean inequality or oppression. Learn to be a full-fledged female person or male person—a person who feels fulfilled because you are filling a valid role as defined by the subculture that you are developing.

WORLDVIEW

CHAPTER 8

A PERSPECTIVE ON WORLDVIEW

Adapted with permission from
Anthropology for Christian Witness, chapter 4 (Orbis 1996)

Introduction

As individuals, a model or map of reality provides for us a patterning in terms of which we can chart our life's course. Such patternings are not, however, simply operative at the individual level. A whole group (society) may chart its course according to a single map of reality. That is, within a range of allowed variation, large numbers of people employ (largely in response to their training) a single perception of the REALITY around them. We call such a perception shared by a social group a worldview. And we see that worldview as the core of a culture, functioning, on the one hand, as 1) the grid in terms of which reality is perceived and, on the other, as 2) that which provides the guidelines for a people's behavioral response to that perception of reality.

Worldview Defined

I define worldview as the culturally structured assumptions, values and commitments/allegiances underlying a people's perception of reality and their responses to those perceptions (Kraft 1989:20). Worldview is *not separate* from culture. *It is included in culture* as the structuring of the deepest level presuppositions on the basis of which people live their lives. Like every other aspect of culture, worldview does not *do* anything. Any supposed power of worldview lies in the *habits* of people. People are the ones who do things. But worldview provides the cultural bases and part of the structuring for people's actions.

1. A worldview is *culturally structured.* That is, as a part of culture, it participates in the structuring of that culture and is not independent of it. Like culture, a worldview is a human product, resulting from the fact that humans are

culture-producing creatures. The material within a worldview is organized and structured according to principles that are themselves based on worldview assumptions.

2. A worldview *consists of assumptions*. Though I often list values and allegiances/commitments as if they were parallel to assumptions, the term assumptions covers the whole territory. That is, it is the assumptions underlying values and commitments that are in view as well as all other more general assumptions. In terms of such assumptions, we assign meaning and respond to the meanings we assign. In doing so, we follow the worldview patterns taught us as we do such things as interpreting, evaluating, explaining, committing ourselves, relating and adapting. We will deal more specifically with these facets of worldview below.

3. These assumptions, then, *underlie a people's perception of reality and their responses to it*. Worldview assumptions provide the structuring of perceived reality. We respond, then, not to God's REALITY (see chapter 2 in Kraft 1996) but to the reality we perceive, our interpretation of REALITY.

As with culture, we may speak of an individual worldview, a family worldview, a community worldview, subcultural, national and multinational worldviews. As with cultures, there will be increasing variety within the worldviews at each level in accord with the increasing number of people involved. Furthermore, it is possible to refer to the worldview assumptions of such transcultural groups as poor people, factory workers, agriculturalists, women, youth, the deaf, etc.

Worldview and Sociocultural Specialization

The concept of worldview is important to our understanding of culture. It is, however, only relatively recently that anthropologists have begun to use the term. Not long ago certain anthropologists began to focus, not so much on the vast assortment of different customs (as had been their primary concern) as on the assumptions underlying these customs that seemed to relate them coherently to each other. For a high percentage of the peoples that anthropologists have studied, a preponderance of these assumptions related to supernatural beings and powers. From a western point of view, then, "religion" seemed to be at the core of most non-western cultures.

Thus came about a tendency, still apparent in the writings of many anthropologists and nonspecialists alike, to confuse the core of a culture (worldview) with a people's religion. Increasingly, though, it is being recognized that even in "supernaturalistically oriented" societies there appear to be deep level, core assumptions that are not easily labeled "religious." Furthermore, as greater attention is being given to cultures (e.g., western) whose core assumptions are largely non- (even anti-) supernaturalistic, it is becoming obvious that the term religion as the designation for the core of culture is misleading.

It seems better, then, to use the term "worldview," introduced by Redfield (1953), to label the central assumptions, concepts, premises, and values to which the people of a sociocultural group commit themselves, whether or not those are supernaturalistic.

This approach leaves us with one major problem: how to explain the fact that many societies seem to be dominated by religious concepts and practices. As I will explain more fully in chapter 8 (in Kraft 1996), this fact is paralleled by the fact that many other societies (e.g., many western peoples) seem to be dominated as much by economic concepts and practices as others seem to be by religion. Others (e.g., traditional Chinese) seem to be dominated more by family concerns than by either religion or economics.

I explain each of these situations as *sociocultural specialization*. In any given society, as with any given individual, greater attention is given to certain things than to others. Just as individuals specialize, then, so do groups of individuals (societies). Certain peoples give more attention to religious matters, other peoples to economic matters, others to family. And the surface level behavior that a people specializes in will have a greater influence on the core assumptions, values and allegiances (worldview) than the behavior that they do not emphasize as much.

In terms of a subsystems diagram like that introduced at the end of the previous chapter, we may picture this fact as follows:

The differential emphases of a *supernaturalistically-oriented society* might be pictured thus (with the amount of space in each "piece of the pie" representing the amount of emphasis):

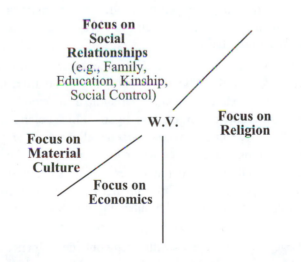

Figure 8.1 Differential emphases in a supernaturalistically-oriented society

The differential emphases of a society (e.g., western) *focused primarily on economics and material culture* might be pictured thus:

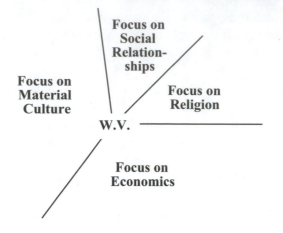

Figure 8.2 Differential emphases in a naturalistically-oriented society

As illustrated, the primary concerns of a people dominate the surface level of their culture. These same areas, then, will influence the worldview more than will the other subsystems. In supernaturalistic cultures we say that the religious subsystem influences the worldview more than, say, the economics or the concern for the material world or some other aspect of the culture as a whole. In western societies, though, we would say that subsystems dealing with economics and the control of the material world influence the worldview more than the religious subsystem. Such differences in focus suggest that we may characterize different societies as centered around a supernaturalistically-oriented worldview or a materialistically-oriented worldview or a social relationship-oriented worldview, or a worldview that emphasizes some other orientation.

Worldview assumptions, values, and allegiances (commitments) vary little from member to member and from subgroup to subgroup of smaller, more tightly knit societies. There is, however, considerable variation from member to member and from subgroup to subgroup of larger, less tightly knit societies, such as that of America. Though there is, apparently, always some allowed range of variation at the worldview level, that range tends to be wider in proportion to the size of a society and the intensity of contact with other societies. Again, smaller societies with little contact with other groups tend to exhibit a smaller range of allowed variation, while larger societies with greater contact with outside groups will show a wider range of variation.

Indeed, in large, diverse societies with strong outside influences, the tendency is for their people to experience a good bit of conflict at the worldview level between competing assumptions, allegiances and values. Such competition results in many people in such societies assimilating at least an important portion of one or more worldviews in addition to the one they learned as children. These whole or parts of worldviews, then, are often only partially reconciled with each other, leading to a situation where person or group apply one worldview perspective in one set of circumstances and another, at least partially contradictory, set of assumptions in other circumstances. Western Christians commonly experience such "worldview split personality" at any point where they need to decide whether to interpret an event from a naturalistic perspective or in terms of Christian supernaturalistic values.

To illustrate, picture an American Christian driving along a highway and narrowly avoiding an accident. How does she/he react? The naturalistic American worldview into which we have been trained will push us to respond with some such statement as, "Boy, was I lucky!" Our Christian perspective, which we have probably only partly assimilated, however, brings to our attention the fact that God is involved in every such event to protect us from harm (Rom. 8:28). An appropriate reflexive response stemming from that assumption, then, would be something like, "Thank you, God."

Such differences in our automatic (habitual) response to such a situation come from competing worldview assumptions within us. Some of us will have so integrated our lives around our Christian assumptions that we will automatically say, "Thank you, God. You saved me from that accident. You protected me," rather than "Boy, was I lucky!" But many of us will show less integration of our Christian values and sometimes go one way and sometimes the other. Such experiences bring to our attention the conflict between worldview assumptions going on within us.

Some internationals may even have parts of three or more sets of worldview assumptions competing within them—those they were brought up with, western assumptions taught them in western schools, and Christian assumptions (possibly infected by a western perspective). The situation can get quite complicated.

Characteristics of Worldviews

1. Worldview assumptions or premises are *not reasoned out, but assumed to be true without prior proof*. By definition, assumptions are simply accepted without the requirement that someone prove them. They are deeply imbedded in the structure of culture. The surface level customs serve as the behavioral acting out of these unconsciously accepted and agreed upon presuppositions. These assumptions are taught to each new generation so persuasively that they seem absolute and are seldom questioned. People then interpret their life experiences in terms of these assumptions and feel that they are proven.

To illustrate, let's look at *a people's definition of life*. Philosophically, we may ask, When does life begin? The answer for most of the peoples of the world is assumed rather than proved. People in one society grow up with the assumption that life begins at conception. Those in another society may assume another starting point before birth, or at birth, or at some point after birth. The Kamwe, like many peoples, made a distinction between the start of biological life and the start of human life. The latter started about a year and a half to two years after birth. For many peoples (including the Hebrews), life as a full-fledged human, as opposed to simple biological existence, starts at the naming of the child.

Assumptions concerning disease provide another example. Americans assume that disease is caused by germs. Recently when I "caught" a cold (or did the cold "catch" me?), I assumed what my American elders had taught me—that I came in contact with some germs that got into my system and caused the cold.

When I got to Nigeria, though, I came into contact with people whose parents taught them differently. These people learned that it is spirits, not germs, that cause disease. When we would discuss our differing points of view, they would contend that their theory handles the situation better because it explains that you got sick because a personal spirit chose to attack you and to leave me alone. The germ theory attempts to explain that aspect of disease in terms of the chance that the right (wrong?) germ came along at a time when the person's resistance was low. This doesn't make a very convincing explanation to a traditional Nigerian.

They, like I, had been taught theory as fact. We could argue with them that our theory is more "scientific" than theirs. But is it? What we often don't take into account is the fact that our science is based on the assumption that if there is any reality beyond the physical world, it is irrelevant when dealing with causation. This, however, is a *very* challengeable assumption, especially from a Christian perspective.

Any argument between those who espouse these different theories of disease is complicated by the fact that, in terms of a broader view of reality it is probable that neither theory is wrong, except when it is advanced as the whole truth. For it is entirely possible that a given disease may be caused ultimately by a spirit but that the spirit uses a germ to bring it about.

A third theory believed by many is that disease is caused by loss or damage to a person's soul. When a person is ill, they say that somebody has stolen the person's soul or that she/he has fallen and jarred the soul loose. To us westerners this seems like a very strange theory. But, like each of the other theories, it is taught convincingly, believed implicitly, and accepted as truth in each instance of illness (and of healing). They, like us, then, interpret whatever happens as proving their assumption. All worldviews are like this.

2. A people's worldview *provides them with a lens, model or map in terms of which REALITY is perceived and interpreted.* We talked in chapter 2 (in Kraft 1996) about lenses through which people look out at what goes on around them. Those lenses have a variety of components. It may be argued that the cultural (worldview) component is the most pervasive since it assures that most of the people in a society will understand and interpret most things in essentially the same way.

The vast majority of the assumptions we live with are not idiosyncratic. They are given to us by those who taught us our culture. Others of that generation taught others of our generation the same model of reality. We and all others of our generation in our society, then, learned to follow that map, to view through that lens habitually. And to the end of our days we follow most of the pathways of interpretation we were taught.

3. In terms of their worldview *a people organizes their life and experiences into an explanatory whole that they seldom (if ever) question unless some of its assumptions are challenged* by experiences that the people cannot interpret from within that framework.

When people become aware of such a challenge in areas considered very important, the result can often be widespread demoralization. Take, for example, the many peoples of the world (e.g., Anglo-Americans, many American Indian groups, the ancient Hebrews) who live(d) with the worldview assumption that they could not be defeated in war. When the unbelievable happened, they were forced either to change their assumption or to reinterpret the event in such a way that the defeat was not allowed to challenge the assumption. Many Americans have taken the latter course in interpreting the Vietnam war (which we did not win) as a "police action." Many American Indian groups, however, found themselves unable (or unwilling) either to change their assumption or to reinterpret. They, therefore, became demoralized (due to this plus other factors), and died out. The ancient Hebrews assumed they were "the People of God" (meaning to them that God would always protect them, regardless of how they related to him). They were able to survive by developing a broader understanding of the close relationship between their faithfulness to him and his assistance in war.

A second type of situation in which a people may question some portion of their worldview occurs when they become aware of alternative explanations or assumptions that both seem to work and cannot be explained away. Such a situation may occur either with or without outside pressure. This type of situation is widespread in non-western societies, enhanced by the pressure of western schools. Under such conditions, assumptions concerning agriculture, disease, God, the spirit world, and a myriad of other theories are being altered, replaced, or otherwise accommodated.

4. Of all the problems that occur when people of different societies come into contact with each other, *those arising from differences in worldview are the most difficult to deal with.* Since worldview is a matter of assumptions, it seldom occurs to the members of a social group that there may be people of other groups who do not share their assumptions.

This is a major reason why culture shock (better, "culture stress") is such a problem. If we are in another society, not only are they behaving on the basis of different assumptions than ours, they may not even understand why we are having a problem. We may be off balance because our assumptions aren't working, and we get no help because it never occurs to the people of the other society that we are having a problem.

In addition to culture stress problems, it is worldview differences that underlie most of the problems we face as we attempt to communicate Christianity cross-culturally. The gospel is intended to influence and change people at the deepest possible level—the worldview level. The changes brought about by Christianity should be basically changes in the worldview, changes in the basic assumptions. Worldview provides the guidelines in terms of which people assign meanings. It's these meanings that are to be influenced by Christianity.

Often the process goes afoul, however, since we tend to tangle up Christian assumptions with those of our own society, often quite unconsciously. In our attempts to discover and remedy such a problem we need to become conscious of which of our assumptions stem from our Christian commitment and which from our culture. It is one of the aims of this volume to assist us in this process. Another aim is to provide tools that will better enable us to learn and to work productively in terms of the worldview of those to whom we are called.

Functions of Worldview

In our attempt to understand worldview and the part it plays in the cultural life of a people, let's focus on the way people use worldview assumptions. Though, again, it is people using worldview, not worldview doing something by itself, we will label these *the functions of worldview*. To deal with these functions, let us return to the chart of personal behavior and cultural structuring presented in the chapter on culture.

	PERSONAL BEHAVING	**CULTURAL STRUCTURING**
S U R F A C E	*BEHAVING* *Habitual Behaving* Overt (Doing, Speaking, Emoting) Covert (Thinking, Feeling) *Creative Behaving* Overt (Doing, Speaking, Emoting) Covert (Thinking, Feeling)	*PATTERNS OF BEHAVIOR* Overt Customs that Pattern Doing, Speaking, Emoting, etc. Covert Customs that Pattern Thinking, Feeling, etc.
D E E P	*ASSUMING* (Usually Habitual, Often Creative) PRIMARY LEVEL ASSUMING 　Willing 　Emoting 　Reasoning 　Assuming Motivations 　Assuming Predispositions ASSIGNING MEANING 　Interpreting 　Evaluating RESPONDING TO ASSIGNED MEANINGS 　Explaining 　Committing/Pledging Allegiance 　Relating 　Adapting 　Seeking Psychological Reinforcement 　Striving toward Integration/Consistency	*PATTERNS OF WV ASSUMPTIONS* PATTERNS UNDERLYING PRIMARY BEHAVIOR 　Willing (Choosing) 　Emoting 　Reasoning 　Deciding Motivation 　Being Predisposed PATTERNS OF MEANING ASSIGNMENT 　Ways of Interpreting 　Ways of Evaluating/Validating PATTERNS OF RESPONSE TO MEANING 　Ways of Explaining 　Ways of Committing/Pledging Allegiance 　Ways of Relating 　Ways of Adapting 　Ways of Getting Psychological Reinforcement Ways of Integrating/Attaining Consistency

Figure 8.3 Surface and deep, personal and cultural

Focusing on the lower (deep level) portion of the chart, we will examine the categories portrayed there one by one, keeping in mind that it is always people who are the doers with the worldview patterns used as guidelines for their habitual behavior.

1. The first set of patterns provided by a worldview is that for the *structuring of deep, underlying personal characteristics*. We may call these "primary-level characteristics." Among them are willing, emoting, reasoning, motivation and predisposition.

a. *Patterning the way we use our wills*. We are taught the socially approved ways of choosing and deciding. Individualistic societies teach children to assert their wills individualistically. Group-oriented societies teach their children to use their willpower to conform to the group. "It is the one who wanders away from the group that gets in trouble," they are told.

b. *Patterning the use of emotions*. All societies structure the use of emotion. In few, if any, is it considered proper to express any emotion at any time. Though some allow great latitude in emotional expression, some are very repressive.

c. *Patterning logic and reason*. People in different societies reason differently. Westerners are known for what is called "linear logic." We tend to reason in a straight line. If such and such is true, then it follows that such and such is also true. We then tend to make rather sweeping generalizations on the basis either of logic or of a few experiences that we feel point in the direction of the generalization.

Many of the peoples of the world, however, reason "contextually." They see each event encased in a context that is different from any other context. The uniqueness of each context, then, makes each event unique and difficult to generalize from. In building a case for something they will tell story after story, in great detail, rather than making what we would consider logical point after logical point. The writer of the Book of Hebrews used a kind of contextual reasoning to make his points.

d. Worldview assumptions also *affect and pattern motivation*. What motivates people to behave in certain ways differs from society to society according to differential patterning at the worldview level. Though there are certain basic biologically-based motivaters (e.g., the need for food, water, sleep, sex, exercise), there are also socially inculcated wants (e.g., desire for prestige, wealth, comfort, freedom from trouble) that motivate people in powerful ways. Worldview assumptions govern both the motivators and the expected responses to them.

e. Even *predispositions are patterned by worldview*. Such attitudes as optimism versus pessimism are based on worldview assumptions and expressed differently from society to society. Though each of these attitudes will be found in every society, certain societies will teach their children in such a way that the vast majority of them will look on the positive side of things most of the time. Other societies teach their children to focus on the negative side.

2. The next two worldview functions (the patterning of interpreting and evaluating) relate to *the patterning of the assignment of meaning*. Assigning meaning is perhaps the most frequent activity human beings engage in. It is important to

recognize, as I detail in chapter 9 (in Kraft 1996) and in Kraft 1991a, meaning is assigned by people. Meaning is not inherent in the vehicles we use to convey it.

a. *Interpreting*. We have been taught how to interpret. For example, in the West it is common for us to interpret landscapes and flowers as beautiful. We interpret them that way in accord with the way we have been taught. In many societies, however, "beautiful" is not a word the people would use for landscapes and flowers. They have not been taught to assume such things are beautiful. With regard to beauty, Americans recognize that "beauty is in the eye of the beholder." That is, beauty is a matter of interpretation. The same is true for everything else in life.

The assignment of meaning is a matter of personal interpretation based on social agreements concerning how to interpret cultural forms. And these people agreements are, for the most part, quite predictable since they are based on the worldview structuring of assumptions that they have been taught. There's a sense in which all that we say and illustrate concerning worldview applies to this interpretation function. This being true, we will not further elaborate on this function here, allowing the following discussion to fill in additional details concerning it.

b. *Evaluating*. As we interpret, we also evaluate. Indeed, the evaluating, the "feeling" of the meaning is an extremely important part of the assignment of meaning. We are taught to feel differently about different words and other cultural items. When I say the word "dog," for example, not only do hearers think of a canine animal, they react positively, negatively or neutrally to that thought. People either like dogs (or a dog), dislike them or are neutral toward them. Whatever the evaluation, it becomes a part of the meaning they assign to the concept.

Evaluational assumptions provide the bases for judgments concerning what is good and what is not good. Typical areas in which these assumptions are applied are esthetics (e.g., judgments as to what is visually or aurally pleasing), ethics (e.g., judgments as to what is moral and what immoral), economics (e.g., judgments as to what ought to be more or less expensive), human character (e.g., judgments concerning proper versus improper or admirable versus criticizable conduct and/or character traits) and the like.

Most cross-cultural problems stem from differences in meaning assignment. Indeed, the examples of cross-cultural differences in understanding we have already given in this and the preceding chapters all relate to this area of worldview. When we go into another society, we are accountable for their assumptions, not ours. To the extent that we can assign meaning according to their, rather than our assumptions, to that extent we can understand and function properly within their world. Learning their language and culture, however, means learning their assumptions.

3. The next four worldview functions relate to *the patterning of how people respond to the meanings they assign*. These patterns include ways of explaining, pledging allegiance, relating and adapting.

a. *Patterning of explaining*. Explanatory assumptions concern the way things are or are supposed to be. They include basic assumptions concerning God (e.g., God exists, or God does not exist), concerning the universe (e.g., the universe is like a machine; the universe is like a person; the universe is predictable; the universe is capricious and unpredictable; the universe is controllable by humans; the universe is to be submitted to by humans; the universe is centered around the world; the universe is centered around the sun), concerning the nature of human beings (e.g., human nature is sinless, sinful, or neutral), and the like. The various explanations concerning disease that we have discussed also fit in here.

In addition to explanations concerning the origin and nature of the universe, we look to worldview assumptions for explanations concerning such things as how people, animals, plants and geographical phenomena got here and what we should expect of them. Areas covered by science, history, myth, legend, and the like fit in here. Whether such explanations can be proven or not is irrelevant. If they are assumed by a people, they are a part of their worldview.

b. *Patterns of pledging allegiance.* A worldview provides a map in terms of which people develop and prioritize allegiances. It thus enables us to sort out, arrange, and make differential commitments to the things we assume, value, and do. That is, we don't simply assume, believe, value, or relate to everything in the same way. We assume, believe, and relate with some degree of intensity, committing ourselves quite strongly to certain of our beliefs, values, and behaviors, but quite weakly to others. We are likely, for example, to be less strongly committed to the brand of toothpaste we use (even though we may use it because we believe it to be the best on the market) than we are to our parents (even though we may see faults in them).

How we have prioritized our allegiances becomes most obvious when we are forced to choose between them. Americans frequently have to prioritize allegiances in choosing between job and family, between self-interest and the best interests of loved ones (e.g., spouse, parents, children, friends), between self and community, and for Christians between God and any of these. For non-westerners the need to choose between allegiance to God and that to community is often excruciatingly difficult. Our real commitments are often most obvious when such choices are made unconsciously—as when during wartime most Christian citizens of a nation unconsciously agree to put allegiance to nation or tribe above an allegiance to their Christian brothers who are on the other side. The test of which are the highest allegiances is the question, Which of these commitments would one die for?

In general, the more intense the commitment of groups or individuals to an assumption, value, or practice, the less likely they are to change it. If, on the other hand, they become dissatisfied with the custom and/or discover an attractive alternative, the strength of their allegiance is likely to lessen, and they, therefore, become more open to the possibility of change.

c. *Patterns of relating.* A worldview provides assumptions concerning how people are to relate to one another. Perhaps most peoples (following their worldview) assume that it is good for people and groups within the society to relate cooperatively with each other. Working together, then, would be seen as good, and competing with each other as bad. People are taught according to worldview patterns how men should relate to women, how youth should relate to their elders, how people of low prestige should relate to those of higher prestige, how one occupational group should relate to another, how followers should relate to leaders and the like.

Relating to outsiders is a different matter for most peoples. A worldview structures assumptions concerning who is in our "in-group" and, therefore, to be treated as one of us and who is in our "out-group" and to be treated differently. Various out-groups, then, are to be ignored, treated with reserve or treated as enemies.

Even our relationships with animals, plants and other parts of the material universe are patterned by worldview assumptions. Are we to dominate the world around us or to submit to it? Relationships to any invisible beings and powers a people believes in are also patterned. Likewise with relationships to ideas, moral values and rules and regulations. Since we believe such and such, how should we behave? And if we don't behave as we are taught to, what will be the penalty? A society is in difficulty when the relationships between the various potentially competing groups within the society are not well-managed.

d. *Patterns of adapting.* We are not always able to handle everything that comes our way by following the guidelines of our worldview. So there are worldview assumptions concerning what to do when we perceive that things are not as we believe they ought to be. When this happens, we usually attempt to handle it without altering our assumptions. We try to interpret what we see in such a way that it is either conformed to our worldview or dismissed as unreal.

On occasion, however, either because of personal and/or group openness or because of the persistence of an uncongenial perception that we find ourselves unable to deny we may choose to make a change in some aspect of our worldview. For example, non-westerners under constant pressure from the teaching of western naturalistic interpretations of reality, may choose to replace part or all of their supernaturalistic assumptions with naturalistic ones. Or, under these kinds of pressure, persons and groups may attempt to retain two sets of mutually contradictory assumptions and thus to live their lives with the kind of worldview "split personality" spoken of at the beginning of this chapter.

In this regard our values and allegiances come strongly into play. We are committed so strongly to certain things that we would rather "fight than switch" if they are called into question. We may close our eyes to any other evidence to protect such assumptions. On the other hand, there are behaviors and assumptions that are not that important to us. So, if faced with evidence that change would be a good idea, we change.

If the challenges are too great and/or for some other reason the worldview assumptions are unable to handle the pressures for change, a people can lose confidence in their worldview. When this happens, and it is happening more and more in our day, there is breakdown at the worldview level commonly issuing in demoralization. Such demoralization is manifested in symptoms such as psychological, social, and moral breakdown and, unless it is checked and reversed, in cultural disintegration. See chapter 26 (in Kraft 1996) for more on people's reactions to such pressures.

4. Another function of worldview (not on the chart) is an *integrative function*. The fact that groups of people assume an incredibly large number of the same things provides a kind of glue holding a society together. People with a common worldview tend to apply the same principles and values in all areas of life. If, for example, their

worldview value in one area of life is (like Americans) individualism, they are likely to be individualistic in virtually all areas of life. Their life and culture are integrated around such a principle. If, on the other hand (like many non-western peoples), their worldview principle is communalism in one area of life, they are likely to practice communalism in virtually all areas of life. Likewise with other core values, such as freedom, hierarchy, male/female dominance, materialism, supernaturalism/naturalism, past/present/future time orientation, competitiveness, conformity, and the like.

Though such common assumptions push sociocultural life and structures toward integration, it is doubtful that any culture is or ever was perfectly integrated. Most seem to be integrated well enough that anything that is changed in the worldview automatically produces ramifications throughout the rest of the culture. This is because the whole of the culture is centered in the same worldview assumptions. The worldview, then, functions within culture much like a radio transmitter. Anything fed into it, whether normal operations or changed procedures, gets broadcast throughout the rest of the culture.

5. One further function will be mentioned. The fact that things seem to be in order at the worldview level enables people to relax psychologically. We can refer to this function as *providing psychological reinforcement*. On the basis of worldview assumptions, we know what to do in life when faced with normal and most abnormal situations. We usually have learned worldview assumptions that enable us to know what to do in transitions and crises, as well as in everyday life situations.

When we're trying to make a decision, for example, we work on the basis of the underlying assumptions we have been taught concerning how to go about decision-making. A baby is about to be born. Someone is to get married. Someone is ill. Someone has died. We have been taught to assume that it is proper to do thus and so. We do it and are psychologically at ease, because we have done the proper thing.

Often what is expected is a ritual. The ritual may be religious or secular, elaborate or simple. It may involve many people or only a single individual. Passage rituals such as those that commonly are prescribed at times such as birth, naming, puberty, marriage, retirement, and death are one kind. Crisis rituals such as those surrounding illness, accident, failure, and decision making may be similar to or dissimilar from passage rituals All of these and more are prescribed by a society and embedded in its worldview assumptions. And people feel satisfied when they conform to such assumptions.

Universals of Worldview

We may (largely following Kearney 1983) speak of six worldview universals. These are the areas of life with which every known worldview deals. We will simply outline these universals here. See Kraft 1989 for a more detailed presentation.

1. The first of these is *classification*. All peoples classify the reality they perceive around them according to the categories laid down for them in their

worldviews. Whether it's plants or animals, people or things, material objects or social categories, natural or supernatural entities, the visible or the invisible—all are labeled and put into categories together with other items and entities believed to be similar to them. These categories, then, are paralleled by other categories made up of other items and entities believed to be dissimilar from those in other categories.

2. A second area that all worldviews treat is that of *person/group*. The nature of the human universe and both its internal and external relationships needs to be understood in the same way by all the members of a society. A worldview provides this understanding. We are taught whether to see people primarily as individuals (as in America) or primarily as groups (as in many other societies). We are taught, then, whether people are expected to dominate the physical environment (as in western societies) or to submit to it (as in many non-western societies).

We are taught who is in-group and who out-group and how to treat each. We are taught the characteristics of good people and bad, of rich and poor, of leaders and followers, of wise and unwise, of respectable and not respectable. We are taught what is appropriate for men and what for women, what for adults and what for children, what for youth, what for parents, what for grandparents, what for various statuses and occupations. In short, whatever a society deems necessary for its members to know concerning people, their nature and behavior is codified in a society's worldview.

3. A third area addressed by every worldview is the matter of *causality*. The questions being answered under this label are questions of power or cause. What forces are at work in the universe? And what results do they bring about? Are the forces personal, impersonal, or both? The answers provided have names like God, gods, spirits, demons, luck, fate, mana, chance, cause and effect, political and economic structures, the power of persons, etc.

All questions of supernatural, natural or human causation fall into this category. As we have seen, many peoples focus greatly on supernatural causation. Other peoples virtually ignore the possibility of supernatural cause and focus almost entirely on human and natural causation.

4. *Time* is another worldview universal. All worldviews codify their society's concept of time. Daily, weekly, monthly, yearly, seasonal, and other cyclical entities are conceptualized. The passage of time is also noted, whether or not it is quantified into seconds, minutes, and hours, as in the West. Something is done about remembered events (e.g., myth, history), present events, and anticipated events (the future). But the systems may be quite different from each other.

Many peoples, for example, are more event-oriented than time-oriented. That is, they are more concerned with what happens than with how long it goes on. In the West, we set rather strict time limits on most of our activities. Whether or not the activity (e.g., church) is satisfying, then, we cut it off when the time is up. One wonders if God is pleased with the way we limit our time with him on Sunday mornings.

5. All worldviews, likewise, provide people with assumptions concerning *space*. Whether it's a matter of how to arrange buildings, how to structure the space within buildings, how to structure interpersonal standing space, sleeping space, eating

space, or how to conceive of and relate to geographical features or the universe as a whole, a people's worldview provides the rules.

Questions concerning the material universe, how it got here and how to arrange ourselves in relation to it are the subject of worldview assumptions of all peoples. But, as we would expect, the assumptions of each group will differ from those of others. Should we dominate nature or submit to it? Should we live in one place, or should we move around? Should we sleep all in one room, or should we sleep in separate rooms? These and millions of other questions regarding space and the material universe around us are answered in terms of worldview assumptions.

6. People, then, find it necessary to define the *relationships* between the various components of worldview and culture. Whether it is a matter of enabling people to relate time to space or classification to causality or space to persons and other relationships between categories or a matter of relating one kind of time to another (e.g., seasonal time to calendar time) or individuals to groups or one cause to another (e.g., God to spirits) within the various categories, a worldview provides the guidelines.

American Worldview (Middle Class)	Other Worldviews
Basic Assumptions	
1. Orderly universe	a. Capricious universe b. Different rules for different groups
2. Life analyzable in neat categories	a. Everything fuses into everything else
3. Natural and supernatural dichotomized	a. No distinction b. Dichotomized but psychological phenomena in the supernatural category
4. Linear time divided into neat segments	a. Cyclical (circular) time b. Spiraling time c. Time flows and can't be quantified
5. Can validly generalize about others from one's experience	a. Can't generalize. Experience always unique
6. Humans can understand truth	a. Humans can't understand truth
7. Human-centered universe	a. God- or spirit-centered universe b. Tribe or family centered c. Uncentered
8. Money/material the measure of value	a. Family relationships the measure b. Personal/family prestige the measure c. Spiritual power the measure
9. Unlimited good (i.e., wealth, power, prestige) available	a. Limited good available b. Amount of good getting less
10. Future orientation	a. Past orientation b. Present orientation
Etc.	
Values	
1. Competition good (need to "get ahead")	a. Competition evil b. Cooperation good (want everyone at same level)

American Worldview (Middle Class)	Other Worldviews
2. Change good (= "progress")	a. Change bad (= destruction of traditions) b. Change neither bad nor good
3. Individual good valued	a. Group good valued b. Individualism destructive
4. "51%" democracy	a. Consensus (100%) democracy b. Certain people "born to rule"
Allegiances	

1. Most frequent for men and career women
   1) self, 2) job, 3) family
2. Frequent for mothers
   1) family, 2) self
3. Christian varieties
   1) God, 2) self, 3) job, 4) family
   1) God, 2) family, 3) self, 4) job
	a. 1) family/clan, 2) job, 3) self
	b. 1) God/gods, 2) clan/family
	c. 1) ancestors/family, 2) self

Etc.	

Figure 8.4 Contrasting worldview emphases

Contrasting Worldviews

Though one needs to oversimplify to do so, it is helpful to present a chart like the above to point out in summary fashion some of the more distinct contrasts between American worldview assumptions and the assumptions of other peoples. In column two are listed several typical assumptions held by other peoples that contrast with American assumptions. Each letter (a, b, c) labels an assumption coming from a different worldview. The assumptions do not represent a single worldview.

Worldview and Culture Change

Solid culture change is a matter of changes in the worldview of a culture. Just as anything that affects the roots of a tree influences the fruit of the tree, so anything that affects a culture's worldview will affect the whole culture and, of course, the people that operate in terms of that culture. Jesus knew this. When he wanted to get across important points, he aimed at the worldview level. Someone asked, "Who is my neighbor?" So he told them a story and then asked who was being neighborly. He was leading them to reconsider and, hopefully, change a basic value down deep in their system. Paul and Philemon discussed a runaway slave. Paul said to Philemon,

"Accept your slave back, but recognize that now he is a Christian." Poor Philemon had to figure out on what basis he could accept a slave who was now a Christian. Onesimus was both a slave and a Christian brother. Paul was pressuring Philemon in the direction of a worldview change.

Jesus said,

You have heard that it was said, "Love your friends, hate your enemies." But now I tell you: love your enemies and pray for those who persecute you. . . . If anyone slaps you on the right cheek, let him slap your left cheek too" (Matt. 5:43, 44, 39 TEV).

Again the seeds were being planted for change at the deep worldview level.

When things are changed at a deep level, however, it frequently throws things off balance. And any disequilibrium or unbalance at the center of a culture tends to cause difficulty through the rest of the culture. We have spoken above of the demoralizing effect of defeat on a society that believes they cannot be defeated in war. Such a defeat causes disequilibrium at the deepest level.

Something even more bothersome to us, though, is the fact that the introduction of Christianity has sometimes resulted in unforeseen negative consequences, because it has threatened people at the deepest worldview level. The account by John Messenger (1959) referred to in chapter 2 (in Kraft 1996), plus several of the other examples given there, illustrate how well-meaning people can introduce apparently good changes that turn out to be culturally as well as spiritually damaging. Add to this the enormous damage (again both cultural and spiritual) that has been done through the influence of western schools introduced and run by missions, and you can understand that there are at least a few valid reasons (among the invalid ones) for certain anthropologists to be critical of missionary work.

In addition to the changes that flow from worldview throughout the culture, there are changes that flow the other way as well. Changes made (often in response to coercion) in peripheral customs lead people automatically to change the worldview assumption(s) that relate to that area of life. The requirement that Nigerian Christians reject polygamy and become monogamous led even Christians to certain undesirable worldview assumptions concerning the Christian God. Among these were: God is against the real leaders of Nigerian society, God is not in favor of women having help and companionship around the home, God wants men to be enslaved to a single wife (like whites seem to be), God favors divorce, social irresponsibility and even prostitution. None of these conclusions is irrational or far-fetched from their point of view. Undirected worldview change of this kind frequently results from a mandated change such as this one in a peripheral custom.

Similarly, people who, in the name of Christianity, change from indigenous medicine to western medicine often come to assume that God condemns their medicine and endorses western medicine. If they get deeply enough into secularized medicine, then, they may even conclude (as do most western medical personnel, including many Christians) that God is irrelevant to the healing process. People who in Christianizing change from task-centered work (i.e., one works to accomplish a task, then stops working) to time-intensive work (i.e., one works every day simply for the sake of working), often come to assume that God does not value their family and communal interactions and rituals, since these can no longer be maintained in the face of a daily work schedule. They will often assume that God wants them to be more oriented to money than to personal (family/clan) relationships. Changing from traditional or traditional types of religious rituals to western rituals often leads to worldview assumptions that regard western rituals as more powerful in a magical way than their own.

We will deal with worldview change in greater detail toward the end of the book (chapters 22–26, Kraft 1996). Suffice it to say here that cross-cultural witnesses would do well to learn as much as possible about this whole area.

Is There a Single Christian Worldview?

In concluding this chapter, I will briefly state my position with regard to whether or not there is a single Christian worldview. We have indicated in several ways that the coming of Christianity is intended to bring about change at the deepest level of a people's cultural assumptions. Helping people to develop those assumptions and the habitual behavior appropriate to them is a major concern of Christian growth.

In spite of this fact, I do not believe there is a single Christian worldview. If there were, Christians would need to have a single approach both to things like moral values and to things like time, space and categorization. There are those who speak of a Christian worldview (e.g., Sire 1976; Schaeffer 1976). They are not understanding, however, the all-encompassing nature of worldview in the anthropological sense. They are speaking of the influx of Christian assumptions, values and allegiances into a worldview as if that input constituted the whole worldview. It does not.

Christian Africans, Christian Asians, Christian Europeans and the multitude of committed Christians from the other societies of the world simply do not see most things the same way, in spite of their commitment to Christ. The question is, should they? My answer is, No. There will be certain very important similarities. But most of the differences in worldview, as in surface level cultural behavior, remain— unless, of course, in the process of becoming Christian, these people also change their culture. This latter is not, however, a Christian requirement.

Jesus had a worldview (see Kraft 1989, ch. 9). It consisted of his "Kingdom perspectives" integrated into his first century Hebrew worldview. Our task is to follow his example by integrating those same perspectives into our cultural worldview. We are, then, to assume Christian assumptions and to live habitually by them, each within his/her own cultural context, just as Jesus did within his context.

CHAPTER 9

WORLDVIEW IN INTERCULTURAL COMMUNICATION

Reprinted here with permission from
Intercultural and International Communication, Fred L. Casmir, ed.
Washington: University Press of America, 1978

Introduction

Commitment to a worldview or basic value system (often that labeled a religion or some surrogate religion such as atheism, science or a political persuasion) appears to be a cultural universal (Lessa and Vogt 1965:xi). If so, we may assume that the influence of such basic concepts within the minds of people is of high importance in the process of interpersonal, intergroup and intercultural communication. It is the aim of this chapter to probe these influences for the purpose of explicating the ways in which a worldview affects intercultural communication.

If, as many contend, worldview pervasively influences every area of life, our topic is a very broad one. We will, however, have space enough to deal with but three important facets of the matter. In the first place, it will be useful to deal briefly with the position and functions of worldview in culture. We will then attempt to discover what effects worldview influences have on intercultural communication in general. And, finally, we will probe the factors involved in attempts to communicate and win adherence to another worldview across a cultural boundary.

Worldview in Culture

Every social group has a worldview—a set of more or less systematized beliefs and values in terms of which that group evaluates and attaches meaning to the reality that surrounds it.[1] Groups will vary with regard to the degree to which they are

---

[1] See a good introductory text on anthropology for a discussion of this point. Hiebert 1976, Keesing and Keesing 1971, Bock 1968, and Beals and Hoijer 1965 are recommended.

conscious of or can make explicit their worldviews. But the presence of such an integrating core at the center of their perspective on reality has been observed for every social group from the simplest to the most complex and is assumed to be a universal.

Frequently, especially in nonwestern societies, we mistakenly label that worldview "religion." However, since a worldview consists of all of the basic assumptions in terms of which a people live their lives, many of the assumptions and values do not fit into what we ordinarily regard as religion. The worldview, then, consists of more assumptions than merely the religious ones. A religion, furthermore, consists of rituals and other behavior in addition to certain basic beliefs and values. These rituals and behavior are not a part of worldview. In addition, there are worldviews (or, rather, partial worldviews) such as communism, atheism or scientism that are antireligious.

It is a people's worldview more than any other aspect of their culture that affects communication. Thus its relevance here.

The worldview of a people serves a number of important functions. The first of these is an *explanatory* function. It provides for them explanations of how and why things got to be as they are and how and why they continue that way. The worldview embodies for a people, whether explicitly or implicitly, the basic assumptions concerning ultimate things on which they base their lives. If the worldview of a people conditions them to believe that the universe is operated by a number of invisible personal forces who are largely beyond human control, this will affect both their understanding of and their response to "reality." If, however, a people's worldview explains that the universe operates by means of a large number of impersonal, cause and effect operations that, if learned by people, can be employed by them to control the universe, the attitude of these people toward "reality" will be much different.

These ideas are customarily articulated in the mythology of a people. This mythology, however, takes a variety of forms from culture to culture. In a large number of cultures one would look to their fables, proverbs, riddles, songs and other forms of folklore for overt and covert indications of their worldview. In more complex societies one finds, in addition to the folklore, printed literature that often overtly philosophizes the mythology of the people's science, religion, politics, and the like. The portion of the worldview of which people are conscious is thus often more easily observable in the various subcultures within western (i.e., Euroamerican) culture than in preliterate societies.

The worldview of a people, secondly, serves an *evaluational* and *validating* function. The basic institutions, values and goals of a society find their sanctions in the worldview of their culture or subculture. And for most of the societies of the world the ultimate ground for these sanctions is supernatural. It is in their God or gods that most people understand their worldview and their culture as a whole to be rooted. And even when no external supernatural is postulated (as in communism and naturalistic American worldview) a sort of "internal supernatural" is generally present in the virtual deifying of such a concept as "the American way of life." Thus in our American worldview we find sanctions (supernatural or pseudo-supernatural) for such institutions as democratic government, a capitalistic economy, and monogamous marriage, for such values as scientism (with or without God), individual rights and freedoms and private property, and for such goals as world peace (on our terms), personal and national prosperity and a college education for everyone who wants one. As with regard to its explanatory function a people's worldview is not peripheral to but rather integral to every aspect of the life of a social group. All important and valued behavior, be it classified as economic, political, "scientific," social, educational or whatever is pervasively affected by the assumptions, beliefs, values, meanings and sanctions of the worldview of the group performing the behavior.

A third function served by the worldview of a group is to provide *psychological reinforcement* for that group. At points of anxiety or crisis in life it is to one's belief system that one turns for the encouragement to continue or the stimulus to take other action. Crisis times such as death, birth and illness, transition times such as puberty, marriage, planting and harvest, times of uncertainty, times of elation all tend to heighten anxiety or in some other way require adjustment between behavior and basic values. And each tends to be dealt with in a reinforcing way in accordance with the worldview of a society. Often this reinforcement takes the form of ritual or ceremony in which many people participate (e.g., funerals, harvest celebrations, initiation or graduation ceremonies). Frequently the worldview also requires individual reinforcement observances such as prayer, trance, scientific experimentation, or "thinking the matter through" for the purpose of squaring a prospective decision with one's core values. In such ways the worldview of a group provides security and support for the behavior of the group in a world that appears to be filled with capricious uncontrollable forces.

Fourth, the worldview of a social group serves an *integrating* function. It systematizes and orders for them their perceptions of reality into an overall design. In terms of this integrated and integrating perspective, then, a people conceptualizes what reality should be like and understands and interprets the multifarious events to which they are exposed. A people's worldview "establishes and validates basic premises about the world and man's place in it; and it relates the strivings and emotions of men to them" (Keesing and Keesing 1971:303).

Thus in its explanatory, evaluative, reinforcing and integrating functions worldview lies at the heart of a culture, bridging the gap between the "objective" reality outside of people's heads and the culturally agreed upon perception of that reality inside their heads. Worldview formulates for the members of a social group the conceptualizations in terms of which they perceive reality. It also filters out for them most glimpses of reality that do not conform to their beliefs concerning the way that reality should be. It provides for people

> ... a system of symbols which acts to establish powerful, pervasive, and long-lasting moods and motivations in men by formulating conceptions of a general order of existence and clothing these conceptions with such an aura of factuality that the moods and motivations seem uniquely realistic (Geertz 1966:4).

A group's worldview does not, however, completely determine the perception of all of its members at all times. Though there is characteristically a very high degree of conservatism to worldview conceptualization, there is change in this as well as all other areas of culture. People do, on occasion, perceive aspects of reality in ways that differ slightly (or even drastically) from the ways that their worldview has conditioned them to perceive of them. And such divergences in perception, especially if engaged in and reported by socially influential persons, may be accepted by other members of the social group. The result is worldview change.

Thus, over a period of time groups such as the ancient Jews moved from belief in many gods to a strong concept of monotheism. Likewise, have large segments of western society moved through Renaissance, Industrial Revolution and American Frontierism from a belief in the supremacy of the Judeo-Christian God to a belief in the actual or potential all-sufficiency of technological humanity.

There is, therefore, a fifth function of worldview that is of particular interest to us here, since it relates directly to the more disintegrative aspects of culture change. That function may be labeled *adaptational*. Wallace suggests that inherent in worldviews is the ability to reduce "internal structural contradictions" that occur in the process of culture change (Wallace 1966:27). We are taught as a part of our worldview how to devise means for resolving conflict and reducing cultural dissonance. That is, in circumstances of cultural distortion or disequilibrium we can find worldview assumptions by means of which we can reconcile hitherto apparently irreconcilable differences between the old understandings and any new ones that threaten to bring about social imbalance. These assumptions, then, enable us to adapt in order to bring our society back to equilibrium. If a society gets into such difficulty "it may be far easier to reinterpret values than to reorganize society" (Wallace 1966:29).

> Where mutually contradictory cognitions (including perceptions, knowledge, motives, values, and hopes) are entertained, the individual must act to reduce the dissonance. While, theoretically, he can do this by changing the real world in some respect, so as to modify the data coming in, he may also achieve the same effect by modifying his perceptions of self and of the real world in such a way that one horn of the dilemma is no longer recognized (1966:29).

In extreme cases this adaptation to changing perception calls for major replacement and what Wallace calls "revitalization" (dealt with later in this chapter). But short of such drastic "cultural surgery" the adaptational quality of worldviews is constantly in evidence in all sorts of culture change situations, whether these be mild or intensive.

The Effects of Worldview on Intercultural Communication

If a worldview is as central and integral to a cultural frame of reference as anthropological investigation would lead us to believe, it pervasively influences any attempt to communicate across cultural or subcultural boundaries. For it is the worldview of a culture or subculture that will specify which, if any, areas of the culture are closed to intercultural influence and which are open. And for those areas of culture specified as open, the worldview provides guidance as to just how open they are and on what conditions.

It is convenient to summarize a representative number of the worldview factors most affecting intercultural communication in the following chart. The stance taken by the worldview of a culture with respect to each of these factors and to groupings of them greatly influences the attitudes and behavior of the society with respect to ideas that come to it from the members of another social group. A discussion of the factors follows the chart.

Factors	Hindering Acceptance	Facilitating Acceptance
1. Basic Premises of Source and Receptor Cultures	Very Different	Very Similar
2. Attitude of Receptor(s) Toward Their Own Culture	Highly Positive	Very Negative
3. Attitude of Receptor(s) Toward Source Culture	Despised	Respected
4. Openness to New Ideas	Closed	Open
5. Pace of Present Change	Slow	Rapid
6. Borrowing Tradition	Rejection	Borrow Freely
7. Morale	Proud	Demoralized
8. Self-Sufficiency	Self-Sufficient	Doubting Self-Sufficiency
9. Security	Threatened	Secure
10. Flexibility	Resistant	Adaptive
11. Advocate	Non-Prestigious	Prestigious
12. Relation of Idea to Felt Needs	Perceived as Unrelated to Felt Needs	Perceived as Filling a Felt Need
13. Fit of Idea	Discontinuous with Present Worldview	Congruent with Present Worldview

Figure 9.1 Factors influencing intercultural acceptance or rejection of ideas

If (1) the basic premises on which the worldview of the receptor culture is based are similar to those of the communicator's culture the potential for acceptance, or at least of understanding, is increased. Understanding and acceptance are not, of course, the same thing. But, other things being equal, an increase in the ability to understand on the part of the receiving participant in an intercultural communication event will increase the possibility that he will be favorably disposed toward the idea. If, for example, one's worldview regards the addition of fertilizer to the soil as impermissible, tampering with an area of life that lies wholly within the province of God, it is unlikely that a simple recommendation that fertilizer be used will be either understood or accepted. If, however, both the recommender's worldview and that of the potential receptor accept the premise that such addition to the soil is legitimate, the arguments of the recommender are likely to be both understood and regarded as convincing.

If, though, even in spite of similar worldviews, such a recommendation were to come to the members of a social group whose (2) attitude toward their own culture was so positive that they believed that they had no need for suggestions from outside, the likelihood is that even good ideas would be rejected. Such was the case when attempts were made to innovate western (Christian) schools into the (Muslim) Hausa society of Northern Nigeria. The Hausas, even though they believed in and operated (Koranic) schools saw no need for what they regarded as inferior western schools promulgating an inferior western worldview. And today they find themselves competing at a disadvantage with their more thoroughly westernized countrymen of other tribes because their cultural pride led them to reject, while certain other tribes, manifesting perhaps a less positive attitude toward their own educational techniques, accepted educational innovation.

Likewise the (3) attitude of a group toward the source of would-be innovation affects the likelihood of acceptance. If a group despises the source, the likelihood of acceptance of ideas from that source is diminished—no matter how persuasively such ideas may be communicated.

Because of their worldviews certain societies are (4) more open to cross-culturally communicated ideas than others. Western societies in general have manifested a remarkable openness to such innovation. We believe in and expect to find good ideas coming to us from cultures and subcultures other than our own especially if we respect the source. Many peoples have, however, traditionally taken the opposite posture and have, because of their worldviews, been virtually closed to innovations advocated by outsiders.

In cultural dynamics (5) change tends to beget change. A culture that is changing rapidly tends to believe in change, and therefore, to readily accept recommendations for further change even if the recommenders are outsiders. If, further, (6) there is a tradition of borrowing in the society, the potential for acceptance is increased. If, however, the tradition is one of rejection, the potential for acceptance is decreased.

In our day, when the intensive impact of westernization is producing widespread cultural disruption the effect is frequently greater or lesser (7) demoralization on the part of the receptor people. Such demoralization constitutes a serious morale problem resulting, frequently, in both the questioning of the (8) self-sufficiency of the core values of the culture and a predisposition to experiment with innovative approaches to a restructuring of the worldview. People cannot live without "gods." And when the old gods are called into question, they will bend every effort to discover new gods—a new, more satisfying worldview.

A. L. Kroeber documents such a happening among the Kota of the Nilgiri plateau in South India (1948:503–508), while Anthony Wallace in a truly significant treatment points to such occurrences in literally thousands of societies throughout the course of history (Wallace 1956). In each case, cultural breakdown issuing in psychological demoralization and doubt of the sufficiency of the traditional answers to life problems has resulted in a conscious attempt on the part of certain members of the society to reformulate or accept from an outside source a more satisfying value system around which to reconstruct their culture. The roots of most of the world's religious movements from Christianity to nativistic religions, as well as political and economic movements are frequently, if not always, to be found in such revitalization of societies that were in some advanced state of self-doubt and demoralization. Societies in such a condition are peculiarly susceptible to intercultural communication of new worldview values.

Before this stage of cultural demoralization is reached, however there may be an almost opposite attitude toward worldview change. If a society feels (9) threatened rather than secure in the face of intensive outside pressures toward change, it may be less, rather than more receptive to intercultural communication of new values. Such is the case with many Latin American Indian tribal groupings whose reaction to even very worthy suggestions is usually to reject them without serious consideration due to their lack of socio-psychological security.

Such societies tend to develop (10) a highly resistant, rather than an adaptive attitude toward worldview change. American fundamentalism has been characterized by such an approach to issues such as evolution, biblical criticism, cultural relativity and many other new ideas. Rather than considering the possibility of revising their worldview to incorporate any truth in the new ideas, fundamentalists have characteristically built their walls higher and thicker to keep themselves and their children insulated from such "anti-Christian" concepts. The result, however, is frequently the opposite of their hopes. For, one way or another, many children of fundamentalists become exposed to such ideas and end up adopting them all uncritically in more or less total reaction against their fundamentalistic worldview. A more secure and adaptive worldview will characteristically examine even initially threatening concepts and accept at least those parts of the new concepts that are easily integratable into their value system.

With regard to the (11) person who advocates a given idea, much depends upon the prestige assigned to him by the potential receptor group. The worldview of a social group will lead it to expect worthy ideas from certain types of persons but not to expect them from others. If a people believes that the privilege of innovation belongs only to those of royal lineage, it may well require that even an outsider demonstrate his royal connections before his ideas will be taken seriously. Or, if a group expects to accept innovative ideas only from those who have demonstrated their abilities from within the cultural context of the potential receptor group, it is unlikely that a person who has not acquired such credentials will be taken seriously. For this reason certain Nigerian groups have been very resistant to accepting agricultural innovations even from Euroamericans (whose prestige is generally high) since they have never observed these "agricultural experts" to have actually grown a superior crop (or any crop) of guinea corn.

The (12) relationship of the proposed idea to an area of felt need in the society is clearly an important factor in its potential acceptance. All value systems have within them areas of inconsistency and/or inadequacy that are to a greater or lesser degree a part of the consciousness of the society. Wise intercultural communicators seek to discover the questions concerning reality that the people of the society regard as beyond their ability to answer. They then attempt to communicate their messages in such a way that the hearers perceive a relationship between that communication and questions they feel have been left unanswered or poorly answered by their present worldview.

Similarly, an idea is more likely to gain acceptance if it (13) is congruent with the receptor society's present worldview than if it is discontinuous with it. If the new can be built upon or grafted into the old rather than being introduced as unconnected or even in competition with it, the likelihood of acceptance is increased. In recognition of this fact, perceptive doctors, working among peoples whose concept of disease is that illness is always caused by personal forces, have learned to discuss germs as if they were personal rather than impersonal forces. Likewise, with respect to the acceptance or rejection of a "world religion" such as Christianity or Islam, the crucial issue is not the dedication of the advocate but whether or not the recommended changes in worldview can be fit into the conceptual framework of the receptor culture without completely remaking it.

These factors are not, of course, mutually exclusive. They frequently overlap or occur in association with each other. It is clear that a people with a highly positive (2) self-image may also be characterized by such things as lack of respect for other cultures (3), pride (7) and self-sufficiency (8). Or it might feel itself so secure (9) that it adopts a very adaptive (10) posture toward new ideas. Nor is the list exhaustive.

It should, however, be clear by now that such worldview-based factors as these pervasively affect both the process and the results of intercultural communication. No communication takes place in a vacuum. There are always worldview-based presuppositions, beliefs, understandings, and other concepts in the minds of the participants that pervade the presentation and the reception of the communication. The personal worldviews of two persons within the same social group will differ slightly, affecting the communication process in a variety of ways. The worldview differences between members of the same social group will, however, be very small in comparison to the differences in worldview between groups. Furthermore, the smaller the number of mutually accepted presuppositions, the greater the difficulty in communicating adequately and effectively between the groups.

Intercultural Communication
of Worldview

Ours is a day when the worldviews of group after group are being subjected to increasing pressure to change. Hundreds of the smaller, previously more isolated societies in the world are coming into intense contact with the naturalistic worldviews spawned within western cultures and are finding their previously satisfactory value systems unequal to the challenge. Western schools, western medicine, western philosophies of government, western economic systems, western individualism and western religion have combined to challenge traditional worldviews usually without adequately replacing them with new ones. And the result is, in the words of one Nigerian novelist, "things fall apart" (Achebe 1958).

For, as indicated above, a people's worldview provides for them the integrating core of their culture the "glue" that holds all the rest together. And when this core is challenged, called into question and/or held up to ridicule when it becomes obvious to the members of the society for which this ideology has provided a "place to feel at home" (Welbourn and Ogot 1966) that their perspective on reality is no longer adequate to cope with things as they are becoming, the society is in desperate shape. In the words of Clyde Kluckhohn, "a system of beliefs, profoundly felt is unquestionably necessary to the survival of any society" (1949:248), including our own.

And it is an ironic fact that the most serious challenging of the traditional worldview of a great many of the peoples of the world has come from a variety of western culture that anthropologists must characterize as "profoundly irreligious" (Kluckhohn 1949:248). For in place of a supernaturalistic worldview, we have adopted a naturalistic "scientism" in combination with a political philosophy that we call "democracy" and an economic philosophy that we call "capitalism." But the fact that we settle for these very shallow substitutes for a "profoundly felt" religion that would provide for our need for "symbolic, expressive and orientative" underpinnings demonstrates impoverishment at the core of our culture. For cross-cultural studies demonstrate that in order to survive

> every culture must define its ends as well as perfect its means. The logical and symbolic expressions of the ultimate values of a civilization cannot arise directly from scientific investigation ... A mechanistic, materialistic "science" hardly provides the orientations to the deeper problems of life that are essential for happy individuals and a healthy social order. Nor does a political philosophy such as "democracy." Men need tenets that ... are meaningful to the viscera and the aesthetic sensibilities. They must be symbolized in rites that gratify the heart, please the ear and eye, fulfill the hunger for drama (Kluckhohn 1949:248–249).

Such impoverishment seriously cripples a society. And this kind of crippling is a contemporary fact both in our own society and in other societies that, under western influences have abandoned major parts of their worldviews. In both situations the way is paved for the communication of new values. For as people become discouraged and demoralized, they lose their will to go on. And

> this process of deterioration can, if not checked, lead to the death of the society. Population may fall even to the point of extinction as a result of increasing death rates and decreasing birth rates; the society may be defeated in war, invaded, its population dispersed and its customs suppressed; factional disputes may nibble away areas and segments of the population (Wallace 1956:264–281).

Or there may be communicated to the disheartened society a new worldview, usually supernaturalistic in focus, around which the society rallies and rebuilds. Such "deliberate, conscious, organized efforts by members of a society to create a more satisfying culture" are termed by Wallace "revitalization movements" (Wallace 1956:279).

Thus, though many societies in history have deteriorated to the point of "cultural death," a large number have rebounded and revitalized—usually around newly developed or communicated religious ideas. Wallace holds that literally thousands of such occurrences have taken place in history, including a wide variety of nativistic, revivalistic, vitalistic, millenarian and messianic movements both outside of and within western societies. The origins of Christianity, Islam and possibly Buddhism, as well as of a large proportion of other religious phenomena, are theorized to have been in revitalization movements (1956:267, 279).

Social breakdown, therefore, provides a fertile setting for the communication of new worldview values (see factors 7, 8, and 12 on the Acceptance-Rejection Chart above). And the possibility of cultural revitalization holds out hope both to societies caught in the downward spiral toward destruction and to those who feel they have a worldview worth communicating. But how is a worldview communicated across cultures?

First of all it must be recognized, as Homer G. Barnett (1953) convincingly points out, (1) that all cultural change is at base the result of changes in ideas, (2) that all cultural changes are initiated by individuals, and (3) that, therefore, the laws of cultural change are psychological laws. "The fundamental condition is the desire or non-desire of a person or a group of persons" with respect to a given recommended change (1953:61).

Second, one must distinguish between the role in worldview change of the acceptor or innovator and that of the advocate of innovation. Though most change is recommended by persons within a society to others within the society, the advocate, the person who recommends a change, may come from outside—that is, from another society. The innovator, the person who actually effects the recommended change, however, is always an insider. It is therefore, the task of any outsider who advocates a change of worldview to convince someone(s) within the group of the desirability of a change. He must win that person or those persons over to his point of view. He must effectively and winsomely communicate his message to certain acceptors within the society who will first change their own ideas and then, hopefully, influence others within their group to change theirs.

To effectively advocate worldview change, it is necessary to employ some very basic principles of communication. Four of these will be dealt with here. They may be labeled: (1) the frame of reference principle, (2) the credibility principle, (3) the specificity principle and (4) the discovery principle (Kraft 1973d). These principles relate to each other in a kind of "nesting" manner thus:

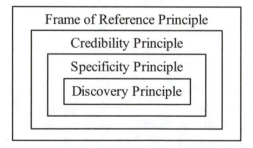

That is, if maximally effective intercultural communication is to take place, the advocate must employ first the frame of reference principle. Having established oneself in those terms, then, one is able to employ the credibility principle and only then the specificity and discovery principles.

The frame of reference principle simply suggests that for intercultural communication of basic concepts to take place the advocate and the potential receptor must share a common frame of reference. Interculturally, this sharing will involve primarily a common understanding of cultural and linguistic categories. The categories can be those of either party but with a different outcome depending on which party the categories belong to.

If the advocate demands that it be his or hers, rather than the hearer's frame of reference that provides the categories in terms of which the communication takes place, the approach may be labeled "extractionist." The attempt of the advocate, then, is to convert the receptor to her or his way of thinking—to teach the receptor to understand and look at reality in the same terms as those of the advocate. Factors 2 and 3 on the Acceptance-Rejection Chart are particularly influential whenever this approach is adopted. If, for example, the advocate's worldview holds that the physical environment is to be viewed as controllable by humans, while the receptor's worldview holds an opposite point of view, the extractionist approach attempts to convert the potential receptor to the advocate's position as pre- or co-requisite to any intercultural transaction. If, then, the culture of the advocate is highly regarded by the potential receptor, while the receptor's attitude toward his or her own culture is ambivalent or negative, the receptor may well agree to the advocate's demands and convert to the latter's worldview.

If, however, an "identificational" approach is taken, it is the *receptor's* frame of reference that is adopted as that in terms of which the communication takes place. In this approach the advocate becomes familiar with the worldview of the receptor and attempts to fit all communication to the categories and felt needs of that worldview. Factors 12 and 13 on the Acceptance-Rejection Chart particularly influence this approach to the communication of worldview values from one society to another. An advocate employing this approach in attempting to communicate an understanding of God as near and concerned might discover that the potential receptors feel that God has gone far away, having left us helpless and hopeless. The receptors may, however, feel very puzzled and concerned by this understanding of God. The identificational advocate, without denying the receptor's understanding, attempts to "fill in the blank" by communicating that part of his worldview that answers the receptor's felt need. By selecting those elements that most easily relate to the felt needs of the receptor society and that, therefore, most readily fit into their worldview, the advocate of worldview change seeks to lead the receptors into a value system that differs to some extent both from the worldview of the advocate and that of the receptor.

The aims of both identificationists and extractionists may be quite similar—to lead the receptors into a worldview that the advocate judges to be more satisfying than that previously held by the receptor. Extractionism, however, requires a high degree of indoctrination and a longish period of dependence of the receptor on indoctrination in order to be effective. For the frame of reference in terms of which the communication takes place must be carefully taught. Much Christian missionary effort has adopted this approach in spite of the fact that the major changes that this approach has effected in the worldviews of receptor peoples have proved to be counter to the specifically supernaturalistic aims of Christianity. That is, the intercultural advocates of Christianity have typically pressed people toward a scientific, naturalistic, secularistic worldview rather than a Christian supernaturalistic focus.

The identificational approach, however, seems to be more in keeping with the approach of the early Christians. Christ himself, working on an interpersonal though not on intercultural level, seemed to start with the felt needs of his potential receptors, adopting their frame of reference as that in terms of which he operated. The Apostle Paul, then, in keeping with his principle to be Jewish when attempting to communicate with Jews and Greek when attempting to communicate interculturally with Greeks, provides a prototypical example of an identificational approach (recorded in Acts 17:22–23). In speaking to a group of Athenian philosophers he says,

> Men of Athens! I see that in every way you are very religious. For as I walked through your city and looked at the places where you worship, I found also an altar on which is written, 'To an Unknown God.' That which you worship, then, even though you do not know it, is what I now proclaim to you (TEV).

Once the frame of reference is established, however, the remaining three principles come into play. Within any given frame of reference predictabilities with regard to expected roles develop which combine to produce stereotypes. An outsider advocating worldview change who simply conforms to stereotyped expectations operates at a low degree of credibility, since what she or he says and does is largely predictable in terms of the receptor's stereotype. If, however, what the communicator says and does is not predictable in terms of the stereotypic expectations of the potential receptors, the communication value of his message and his overall credibility is increased, provided it is within the frame of reference of the receptors. If, for example, the intercultural communicator of new worldview values is a missionary who simply conforms to the people's stereotype of what a missionary should act like, the communication value of his or her activity is slight. If, however, the missionary acts unpredictably in terms of the stereotype, while at the same time attempting to act intelligibly within the potential receptor's frame of reference, the person's credibility, the communication value of the message, and the potential for its acceptance are all increased. By thus identifying with the potential receptors of worldview change and acting credibly (i.e., unpredictably in terms of the stereotype), have hundreds of missionaries and others both endeared themselves to their hearers and effectively communicated their worldviews to people all over the world.

The third of these principles of effective intercultural communication of core values relates to the specificity to human experience with which the advocate presents the message. In general, the more specific a communication is to the real life of a receptor within her or his frame of reference, the greater the impact of the message. Yet human commonality is apparently such that even across cultural barriers interpersonal identification is possible at many points where human experience is quite similar. An intercultural communication phrased in terms specific to the receptor's culture is, of course, more readily grasped than one phrased in terms of generalizations, since real life or true to life accounts carry greater impact than generalizations. Even life-specific accounts of events in societies other than that of the receptor often carry great impact. This fact probably explains why, even after thousands of years, the casebook-like, life-specific accounts in the Bible and certain other religious books (e.g., *Pilgrim's Progress*) produce such an impact even upon peoples whose customs are widely different from those of the Bible characters. Perhaps it is at this life-specific level that, even though separated by great cultural differences, "people are more alike than cultures" (Goldschmidt 1966:134).

Though the first three of these principles all relate primarily to the activity of the advocate of worldview change, the fourth relates primarily to the potential receptor. This principle suggests that communicational effectiveness is heightened considerably if the receptor has the impression that the new information or insight has come to him via his or her own discovery, rather than as the result of being told something by an outsider. The able communicator, then, seeks to lead potential receptors to the discovery of both the substance and the value of the understandings he or she is trying to communicate rather than to simply provide for them "prefabricated" alternatives to their present understandings.

This principle does not mean that advocates of worldview change refrain from proclaiming their messages. On the contrary, they speak as persuasively as possible, employing the above-described principles as completely as possible but in a non-coercive manner. They recognize that the determinative role in the communication of worldview change is that of the acceptor rather than that of the advocate. It is the acceptor alone who can make the recommended changes in her or his own worldview. And everything depends upon the acceptor feeling that whatever change is made is on the basis of his or her own choice, rather than because of outside coercion. Discovery, then, is the process within the acceptor's mind by means of which she or he comes to understand the personal relevance of the communication and begins to apply the new insights to his or her own felt needs. Millions of members of tribal societies are in this way discovering for themselves the relevance for them of parts at least of the ideologies of world religions such as Islam and Christianity concerning which they receive communications from out-culture advocates. Such discovery not infrequently provides the kind of emotional potency necessary for the initiation of the revitalization movements referred to above and described by Wallace (1956).

Conclusion

In briefly surveying worldview factors in intercultural communication we first assessed the position and functions of worldview in culture. In this assessment we concluded that a people's worldview is central to their culture and that it serves at least five important functions for them. These functions have been labeled: explanatory, evaluational, reinforcing, integrating, and adaptive.

Second, we have dealt with a list of thirteen factors characteristic of worldviews that play important parts in the intercultural acceptance or rejection of new worldview values. These factors are listed in chart form above and need not be recapitulated here.

Lastly, we have turned our attention to how intercultural communication of worldview values is most effectively carried out. We noted first the widespread fact of such communication and the destructive consequences to societies who discover that the new values they are accepting are bankrupt, leading to demoralization and social disintegration rather than to the utopia they had hoped for. Such a process of disintegration is, however, frequently reversed by a religion-centered revitalization movement. Finally, we suggested four important principles of communication available to those who feel they possess worldview values that they would like to communicate interculturally. These principles have been labeled the frame of reference principle, the credibility principle, the specificity principle, and the discovery principle.

CHAPTER 10

WORLDVIEW AND BIBLE TRANSLATION

Reprinted here with permission in slightly revised form from
Notes on Anthropology and Intercultural Community Work
6/7:46–57 (June–September 1986)

Abstract: Every translator has a particular worldview. In the case of westerners, for example, there is a general denial of supernaturalistic interpretations. A clear understanding of cultural values and themes, including those of the biblical authors, is called for before translators unwittingly introduce culture change. The particular worldview concepts that should be studied are outlined.

Introduction

This chapter attempts to elucidate the concept of worldview with the expectation that this approach will help Bible translators. It will also provide a summary of my latest thinking on the subject.

Anyone who seeks to communicate cross-culturally is concerned with the influence of culture on the communication process. This requires that one probe considerably beneath the surface of culture into what may be termed "cultural deep structure" to discern what the rules are. That cultural deep structure is what anthropologists (and others) often call worldview.

Many scholars suggest that at the heart of everyone's culture is his or her religion. This makes sense only if religion is defined as covering a wide range of beliefs and assumptions beyond those that relate to supernatural beings and powers. For there are in all societies many other beliefs (e.g., those concerning family/social group, time, space and other aspects of the natural world, etc.) that are just as basic and pervasive as those concerning supernatural beings and powers. There are also many cultures (e.g., American) in which non/antisupernaturalism is a core belief.

Such facts have led anthropologists to introduce the term "world view" (following Redfield 1953) to label all of the basic assumptions by which a people live their lives. These may be supernaturalistic or naturalistic in the area of life

129

labeled by Westerners "religious," group-oriented or individualistic in what we call the social area, subsistence or market-oriented in what we refer to as economics, monarchical or democratic in that part of life we term political, etc.

There are many aspects of worldview that are changed when persons/groups come to Christ. The Christian message is directed to all of life and its aim has been hijacked if a person/group merely change(s) their religion. The vehicles most used by God in this process are human beings committed to him within a society, with the Bible in their language to serve as their guidebook.

Perspective and Definitions

A worldview is a social structuring of a people's *perceptions* of REALITY (where the "big R" reality is God's view). The human perspective is structured into another view, a perceptual view that I call "small r" reality. Thus, though we assert (in contrast to certain Indian philosophers and other absolute relativists) that there is an objective REALITY outside of our minds, we also assert that no human understands that "big R" reality absolutely (i.e., as God understands it). Humans are affected by such factors as limitedness, culture, experience, psychological idiosyncrasies and sin. All of these combine to form a lens (e.g., as used in a camera) through which we view REALITY:

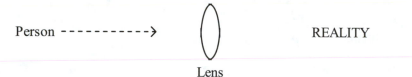

Person - - - - - - - - - - ->   REALITY

Lens

Our view is, however, a complex lens, made up of at least three component lenses: (1) What we believe to be possible; (2) What we actually experience; and (3) What of our experience we analyze (consciously or unconsciously). The latter yields our worldview (see Hiebert 1983):

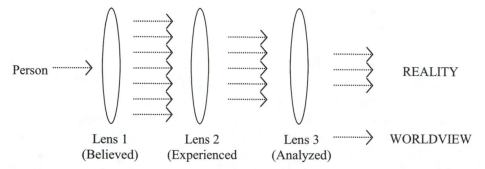

Person ·····>   REALITY

Lens 1   Lens 2   Lens 3   ·····>   WORLDVIEW
(Believed)   (Experienced)   (Analyzed)

Note that the number of things believed possible is greater than the number of things one experiences, which, in turn, is greater than the number of things analyzed. Thus, the worldview, based as it is on analysis, rather than on the totality of things possible, is always limited and partial. A worldview is focused on those things that attract a people's attention. Like the blind men examining the elephant, we picture what we perceive on the basis of our experience with other things. Though this process helps us to understand, it also partly misleads us. Nevertheless, any person or society survives only if they understand and relate effectively to the REALITY around them. So we assert that though humans cannot understand REALITY absolutely, if they are surviving, they are able to understand it *adequately* (i.e., well enough to survive).

We may define a worldview, then, as *the culturally patterned basic understandings (e.g., assumptions, presuppositions, beliefs, etc.) of REALITY by which the members of a society organize and live their lives.* Such understandings provide people both with a structured view of REALITY and with a perceptual map by which to relate to it. This definition is quite close to an ethnosemantic definition of culture (see Spradley 1979). Much of what we teach about culture is, therefore, applicable to the study of worldview. In my view culture, is divisible into surface behavior (cultural forms) and the deep-level assumptions, presuppositions, beliefs, etc., underlying that behavior:

SURFACE LEVEL—CUSTOMS
(Vehicles of Behavior)

DEEP LEVEL—WORLDVIEW
(Underlying Assumptions)

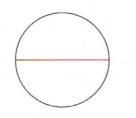

CULTURE A   CULTURE B

The term "worldview" may be applied to the overall structuring of the perspectives/understandings of individuals, societies (e.g., American) or groupings of societies (e.g., Western). The worldviews of various peoples often differ from each other precisely at those points that are of crucial importance in any attempt to communicate cross-culturally. Differing perceptions of how a human being should be defined, for example, can greatly frustrate a would-be cross-cultural communicator. So can differing understandings of the proper relationship between humans and nature, humans and God/gods, humans and material possessions, humans and other humans in the same in-group, humans and members of an out-group, and the like.

Of all the difficulties that occur in culture contact, those arising from differences in worldview are the most difficult to deal with. Since worldview is a matter of assumptions, it seldom occurs to a people that there may be others who do not share their assumptions or that some confusion they may be having in communicating with each other is due to differing basic assumptions. This is a major reason why culture stress/shock is such a problem. In another society, not only do people behave on the basis of different assumptions than ours, they may not even understand why we are having a problem.

Biblical interpretation is, likewise, strongly affected by such unconscious assumptions. For example, the more distant the worldview assumptions of the interpreters are from those of the biblical authors, the more likely they are to misinterpret the Scriptures. This is relevant to anyone using the Bible cross-culturally, and especially to Westerners, since Western worldviews are so different from those of the biblical peoples. One confirmation of this fact is that nonwestern peoples often can see the meaning of a biblical passage much more quickly and clearly than we can.

Internal Structuring of Worldviews

Worldviews are made up of at least three substructurings of assumptions, called "themes," "paradigms" and "models." A "theme" or "core value" (see Opler 1945, Spradley 1979 and 1980) is a "position, declared or implied, and usually controlling behavior or stimulating activity, which is tacitly approved or openly promoted in a society" (Opler 1945:198). In American worldview we can identify themes such as naturalistic scientism, individualism, democracy, freedom, equality, competition, youth orientation, frontier spirit, materialism, and the like. By way of contrast, M. Kraft (1978) has labeled three of the themes of the Kamwe (Higi) culture as supernaturalism, mountain orientation, and guinea-corn complex. Kluckhohn (1946) found the following themes in Navaho culture: All events are interrelated in an orderly universe; the universe is full of dangers; evil and good are complementary and always present; tradition and situation determine morality; family ties determine relationships; events are primary; and humans must submit to nature.

Related to such themes are thousands of semi-independent "picturings" of smaller segments of reality called "paradigms." These perspectives are the operative segments of a worldview and need both description and suggestions on how to encourage change in worldviews. We may, for example, speak of paradigms recommended in the Bible, such as God being actively involved in world affairs (versus a paradigm that sees no God, or one that pictures God as far away and uncaring). Another perspective accepts even outsiders as human beings, while a more common paradigm accepts insiders but regards outsiders as nonhumans. A further perspective pictures spirit beings such as angels and demons as alive and active, while another holds such beings to be fictitious.

Conversion to Christianity (or to any other ideology) thus becomes a paradigm shift" from one perspective to another, accompanied by the proper change in worldview-level allegiance. From this point of view, then, there is no "Christian culture," but only perspectives or paradigms recommended in Scripture. The reason why it doesn't make sense to speak of a "Christian worldview" is clear once we examine the wide variety of assumptions included in every worldview and see that most of these do not have to be changed much, if at all, in the process of becoming a Christian.

Within paradigms, then, are "models." These are picturings of still smaller, less complex portions of reality. Jesus' representation of his relationship to God in terms of the father-son analogy is a model. So are the pictures (metaphors) Jesus drew of himself as the Good Shepherd, the Bread of Life, the Lamb of God, and the like. Jesus' pictures of the Kingdom of God were also models designed to enable humans to better understand his view of reality.

In summary, then, any worldview is composed of various themes. Each theme is made up of several paradigms, each of which, in turn, is composed of a number of models.

Cultures differ from one another as to the proportion of attention given to each aspect of life on the surface level. For example, there are a number of cultures (e.g., African, Melanesian and Hebrew) in which Religion and Family are very important, while Material Technology receives less emphasis. In other cultures (e.g., American), Material Technology receives a lot of attention, while Religion and Family tend to be less important. In a third culture type these three aspects of life might receive equal emphasis.

Certain differences of focus at the worldview level that especially concern Christian witnesses may be highlighted by the following diagram:

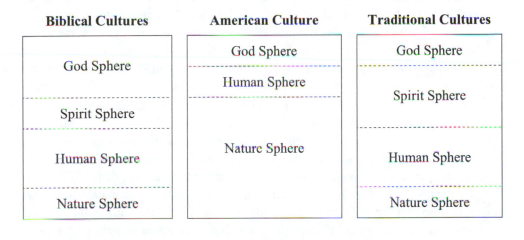

| Biblical Cultures | American Culture | Traditional Cultures |

Note that each of the culture types is divided into "spheres." These represent important relationships between the various types of beings believed to exist and either other beings or the natural environment. The chart relates the emphasis on each sphere to the dominant worldview of each of the culture types. If the biblical cultures are taken as ideal, a comparison between their proportions and those of the others indicates the areas in which cultural changes will need to be made. Note the advantage traditional peoples, who believe in the spirit world, have in interpreting those Scriptures that deal with this phenomenon. The need for greater attention to God is, however, approximately equal in American and traditional societies.

Some Implications of
Worldview Theory for Bible
Translation

Bible translators need to understand the pervasive influence of worldview in at least three areas: (1) Translators are products of their own society and, therefore, deeply influenced by the worldview of that society. (2) Translators should faithfully represent the meanings of the biblical authors, whose worldview assumptions were quite different from those of the translators. (3) Translators should faithfully represent the languages and cultures which are built on worldviews quite different from either their own or those of the biblical writers.

1. *Translators as products of their culture.* As Westerners, Americans are pervasively affected by the nonsupernaturalistic bias of their culture. This is bound to affect both the understanding and practice of Christianity and the handling of the supernatural Scriptures. The whole area of healing and the miraculous is a case in point. Even Christians (for worldview reasons) depend on naturalistic medicine rather than on prayer (with or without medicine) for healing. Thus we tend not to take Jesus seriously when he said we are to go into the world to do the works he did—and even more than he did (Jn. 14:12).

Our understandings are further affected by the influence of academic, rationalistic assumptions concerning life in general and Christianity in particular. One example is the expected impact of reasoning in the conversion process, often mediated via preaching and/or intellectually-oriented Bible study sessions. By way of contrast, the assumption of the biblical authors (and Jesus) seems to be that ministry events (e.g., what God did in relation to people, often by miraculous means) and word events (e.g., life-related stories and parables with God-inspired interpretations) are the vehicles through which God converts and teaches. Our focus on the importance of reading, as valuable as reading is, is based on worldview assumptions. Note in this regard our usual interpretation of the word "word" in the Scriptures as referring primarily to the written word, rather than (as it usually was intended) to God's spoken word (Is. 55:11).

There are, furthermore, assumptions that underlie the particular organization of which we are a part. As Foster (1973) has pointed out, the sending organization serves as the "donor culture." The assumptions of that donor culture, then, are crucial to the worldview of those supported by that organization. In the case of SIL/WBT the strategy of entering countries as academics, training programs that focus on linguistics, the lack of attention to church planting (so there's someone to use the Scriptures), the focus on the use of the vernacular, and the like, are based on fundamental assumptions. In addition, other assumptions arise from the culture of which an organization is a part, such as individualism, task specialization, the importance of literacy as the means of utilizing the Scriptures, a bias against the Old Testament, or even western interpretations of the Scriptures and Christian doctrine.

To effectively function as those who accurately mediate the written Word of God to those of other worldviews, the translator needs to be aware of these assumptions and, when necessary, to resist and change them. For, as we have pointed out, worldview assumptions strongly affect the way we interpret all of life.

2. *Understanding biblical worldviews*. The worldview assumptions underlying the Scriptures also need to be probed if the translator is to do his or her job well. These will invariably differ markedly from those of western translators and consultants. At this point, the study of anthropology, especially the study of worldview and worldview discovery procedures, is a crucial means of understanding the underlying assumptions of the authors of Scripture. Within anthropology an ethnosemantic approach is likely to be the most fruitful (see Spradley 1979, 1980). Such a perspective applied to biblical studies will enhance the task of interpretation so necessary to competent Bible translation.

Two mistakes often made by interpreters and translators of the New Testament are (1) to overestimate the underlying worldview similarities between Greek and English, and (2) to assume that the thought patterns (worldview) underlying the New Testament are Greek rather than predominantly Hebrew. This latter fact, when realized, ordinarily leads translators to recognize a close alignment between the worldview underlying the New Testament and that of most nonwestern receiving cultures.

For example, Western translators and consultants can capitalize on such things as parallels in pictorial thinking, or the fact that the thought underlying the word ordinarily translated "faith" is the Hebrew "faithfulness" rather than the Greek "intellectual belief." They may note the appeal to most traditional peoples of genealogies, or the fact that similarities between biblical and nonwestern worldviews often lead receptor peoples to see God more clearly in the Hebrew-oriented Scriptures rather than in portions of the New (e.g., Romans) that appeal most to Westerners (see C. Kraft 1979). Such helps to effective translation can be obtained through a worldview approach to the Scriptures.

3. *Understanding the target culture*. It is obvious that translators need to understand as much as possible of the receiving language and culture. The center of such a worldview involves a clear knowledge of the semantic characteristics of the language. All we have said about how to discover and analyze worldview applies here as well.

Conclusion

I trust that the foregoing has (1) convinced the reader of the importance of the study of worldview for translators; (2) provided both a perspective on and a method for analyzing worldview; and (3) at least pointed the reader in the direction of how to go about discovering and analyzing any given worldview.

ETHNOLINGUISTICS

CHAPTER 11

CHURCH PLANTERS AND ETHNOLINGUISTICS

Reprinted here with permission from
God, Man, and Church Growth.
A. R. Tippett, ed. Grand Rapids, MI: Eerdmans, 1973:226-249

Dr. McGavran is fond of saying that folk like to be with people of their own kind, and that people like to worship in their own language—the language of the heart. He has built into church growth theory the assumptions that rapid, solid church growth is most likely among linguistically and culturally homogeneous groups, and that the most effective form of cross-cultural communication is in terms of the language and cultural concepts of the target people. Furthermore he advocates the translation of Scripture into the "heart language" as a basic for Christian mission.

Ethnolinguistics frequently comes into focus in the study of helps and hindrances to church growth and in the training of missionaries. The linguistic dimensions of culture, or the cultural dimensions of language are relevant both to church planters and to the planted churches. Specific areas of ethnolinguistic study are: the relationship of a people's linguistic behavior to their overall conception of reality; the range of linguistic and cultural problems involved in cross-cultural preaching, Bible translation, missionary language learning, etc.; the use of specialized language or style (e.g., honorifics) for worship, prayer, singing, teaching, medicine, or for addressing persons of differing social status, sex, age, etc., or on special occasions; cultural attitudes towards one's own language, dialects and world languages; natural and directed change of language, particularly under the impact of religious diffusion, etc.

Effective church planters need to understand the differences between the system of logic of, say, Euroamerican society and that of non-western societies, lest they simply assume either that they can communicate effectively from the base of their own perception of reality, or that inability of the listeners to understand such communication is an indication of deficiency or inferiority on the part of the listeners and/or their society. The influence of a body of naive writing on the logic of other societies is still very much with us. Such writing uninfluenced by the insights of ethnolinguistics concerning the differences in cultural perception of reality, and the variety of equally valid logics developed on the basis of these differences, employed such now-discredited terms as "primitive mentality" and "prelogical thinking"

(Levy-Bruhl 1910, 1922, and comment by Bidney 1967:157–158). The church planter first has to accept the validity of cultural differences, to seek to understand and to work in terms of the system of logic of the receptor society.

Now let me outline ethnolinguistic methodology before developing a few areas for investigation. These areas are 1) The reality of perceptual differences between members of different language communities, 2) the need to take culturally-defined perceptual differences seriously in cross-cultural communication of the gospel, 3) the need to take culturally-defined perceptual differences seriously in Scripture translation and interpretation, 4) ethnolinguistics and the development of an indigenous Christian theology, and 5) Christianity and the conceptual transformation of language.

Ethnolinguistic Methodology

Ethnolinguistic method is a combination of approaches developed by such disciplines as linguistics, anthropology, semantics and folklore, with a few original techniques of its own. The greatest originality within the field has, however, related more to the conclusions arrived at than the methods employed. For example, in attempting to learn as much as possible concerning the worldview and value system of a given society, one might look first at any ethnographic and/or linguistic descriptions for clues as to which particular areas of grammar, mythology, vocabulary, folktales, proverbs, epithets, aphorisms, onomatology, slang and the like would be most likely to be fruitful.

A study of proverbs, for example, will prove fruitful since in most societies (especially, but not limited to, preliterate societies) proverbs play a prominent role in education and social control. Ethnolinguists collect and classify them according to themes. The particular emphases a society focuses on in the process of enculturating its children may be learned from such classifications. A plethora of proverbs recommending the patient acceptance of things as they are, in Hausa for example, shows that this society places a high value on that attitude.

Fables, mythology, epithets and other types of folklore may also be classified and ordinarily will reinforce the impressions gathered from the study of proverbs, their major difference being function rather than content. Mythology tends to be direct with respect to values. Fables tend to be less direct in stating both worldview and values, except for the proverb-like moral attached to them. Fables, however, illustrate the application or misapplication of the society's principles of conduct and drive the point home in a way that a simple statement cannot do.

Studies of vocabulary likewise point up such things as the value system of a culture. Cultural foci may be discovered by statistical listing of vocabulary items. For example, it is said that the Arabic language contains approximately 6000 terms for various kinds and parts of knives, indicating the high value of the knife in Arabic societies. Similar conclusions may be drawn from lists of things pertaining to camels among the Arabs, to snow among the Eskimos, and to technological, medical and scientific terms in Euroamerican languages.

Beyond this, ethnolinguists classify and analyze (using semantic techniques) the particulars of such cultural foci as indicated by vocabulary counting. They study the indigenous valuing of various terms and semantic categories (e.g., those valued or tabooed), and observe contrasts between semantic organization in different languages. For example, many societies identify but three primary colors while others may recognize up to eleven without becoming technical (Berlin and Kay 1969; Burling 1970). Specialized groups, especially occupational groups, develop many more precise distinctions (dyeing, weaving, etc.), using terms not known to the majority of people in their own society.

Through such semantic studies ethnolinguists are able to learn about culture-specific perceptual categories of varying relevance for cross-cultural communication. Perception of color, shape, heat and cold (which in Hausa is divided four ways, rather than two), for example, though important in cross-cultural communication are ordinarily not so crucial to missionaries and other advocates of culture change as are such things as the indigenous perception of the hierarchy of nonmaterial spirit forces and activities, or the indigenous habit of analogizing from material or concrete concepts to abstractions. Even so, the more the less crucial differences in perception are understood, the more intelligible and effective will be the cross-cultural communication.

An ethnolinguistic approach to grammar may also help to discover a people's worldview. For example, a given language specifies in its verbal inflection the kind of action (completed, continuing, potential) rather than the time (past, present, future) of the action. Noting this, we presume that the former society places a higher value on the nature of that action than on the time of it. In Hausa, for example, one uses the same completive construction for "I go" whether the context indicates that the going was in the past, the present or the future. The Hausa apparently see a greater similarity between these performances of "going" than do we in our time-conscious society. And this difference manifests itself in other areas of Hausa life as well confirming that it relates to their perception of reality and the values attached to it. Once a Nigerian who was to meet me at two o'clock did not arrive until five. When, then, I commented on what I considered to be unacceptable lateness, he incredulously replied, "But I have come." He interpreted our agreement in keeping with his own value system and focused on the "come" part of the action and could not fully understand why I was upset that he had not come earlier.

By these and similar techniques ethnolinguists probe the depths of the perceptual differences between peoples of differing cultures.

The Reality of Perceptual
Differences Between Members of
Different Language Communities

The American anthropologist and linguist, Edward Sapir, was among the first to focus attention on the reality and depth of the perceptual differences underlying the linguistic differences between peoples of different linguistic communities. In a now famous quote, he wrote in 1929:

> the "real world" is to a large extent unconsciously built up on the language habits of the group. No two languages are ever sufficiently similar to be considered as representing the same social reality. The worlds in which different societies live are distinct worlds, not merely the same world with different labels attached (1929:209).

This challenges the assumption of many monolingual Americans that languages are simple, different but equivalent codes applied by different peoples to the same reality, and that the major problem in becoming fluent in another language is merely learning to substitute the vocabulary of the new code for the old.

Sapir, Whorf and their followers have established the fact that each language provides and defines for its users a particular form of logic, a mold for the thought of its users, a peculiar frame of reference different from the speakers of any other language (Henle 1958:1, summarizing Whorf). Even more indicative of the differences between the worldviews of the members of different linguistic communities, however, are the contrasts between their grammatical categories. In contrasting Hopi with "Standard Average European" (SAE), for example, Whorf lists five points of grammatical divergence representing major broad areas of conceptual noncompatibility between the cultural perspectives of the two linguistic groups—plurality and numeration, physical quality, phases of cycles, temporal forms of verbs and the expression of duration and intensity. Speakers of SAE languages tend to see the world in terms of things, the things themselves built up of a formless stuff given a determinate form. Nonspatial entities are conceived of by spatial metaphor (Henle 1958:15).

On the other hand, the Hopi seem

> to have analyzed reality largely in terms of events (or better "eventing"). referred to in two ways: objective and subjective. Objectively, and only if perceptible physical experience, events are expressed mainly as outlines, colors, movements, and other perspective reports. Subjectively, for both the physical and non-physical, events are considered the expression of invisible intensity factors, on which depend their stability and persistence, or their fugitiveness and proclivities (Whorf 1941, Carroll 1958:147).

On the basis of the comparison of world views underlying Hopi and SAE grammatical categories, Whorf concludes that "Concepts of 'time' and 'matter' are not given in substantially the same form by experience to all men, but depend on the nature of the language or languages through the use of which they have been developed" (Whorf 1941, Carroll 1956:158).

The Need to Take Culturally-Defined Perceptual Differences Seriously in Communicating the Gospel Cross-Culturally

If culturally-defined perceptual differences between peoples of different societies are real and deep, communicators of the gospel must take them seriously. E. A. Nida points out the important role the experience of the hearer plays in the "hearing" of the message. "The way in which the receptor 'decodes' the message has as much effect upon its meaning as the way in which the source 'encodes' it" (1960:1, 34). The cross-cultural communicator must be asking continually "What are the hearers hearing?" This ethnolinguistic problem is of particular concern to missionaries since the eternal destiny of human beings is at stake.

If the speaker (missionary) and hearer (potential convert) are of different cultures the potential for miscommunication is great. The greater the difference between the cultures of the interactants, the greater the probability of misunderstanding. In northeast Nigeria, for example, the well-meaning missionary who presents Jesus as the Good Shepherd may discover to his chagrin that people have understood that Jesus never grew up or, worse, had something wrong with him, since in their society only young boys or the mentally incompetent tend sheep. And such nonidentity of the meanings attached to similar forms is a frequent cause of cross-cultural miscommunication.

The book of Acts records several other examples. In the healing of the cripple at Lystra (Acts 14:8–18), the action of Paul and Barnabas was intended to say "God is concerned with alleviating the suffering of the cripple." But the people interpreted the event in terms of their own frame of reference, and assumed that since only gods could heal, these men were "gods in the likeness of men," and proceeded to worship Paul and Barnabas. At Athens (17:18) the response of the philosophers, "He seems to be setting forth new gods" was a judgment based on their own cultural background. Fortunately, in each case Paul got the kind of feedback he needed to see that his message was misunderstood, and he was able to adjust or simplify it so that at least he was better understood.

Contemporary examples can be multiplied endlessly. A young Liberian, a product of western missionary schooling gave me his understanding of John 3:16 as follows: "God so loves Europeans that he accepts as Christian an African who turns his back on his own customs and becomes converted to western culture." Of course no missionary had ever said such a thing. But the total effect of his understanding of the missionary message and operation was this distorted form. Unfortunately, nothing was done to remedy the misperception until it was too late, for this man had concluded that Christianity was a purely western religion and had rejected it.

Within their own cultural framework the missionaries had spoken accurately, but this young man was receiving their word in his own conceptual framework. Let me tabulate what was said and heard:

WHAT WAS SAID	WHAT WAS HEARD
1. Christ is the way to a right relationship with the one True God.	1. They bring a foreign religion competing with our indigenous religion for my allegiance.
2. Accept Jesus Christ and you will have God's power.	2. Convert to western culture and I shall have God's power.
3. God is concerned about your health.	3. God endorses western medicine and condemns African medicine.
4. God wants you to be better educated in order to better know and serve him.	4. If I go to school, I can become a God-blessed, powerful European.
5. Follow Christ to have real life.	5. Follow Christ to be a European.

These and many other misconceptions came pouring forth from this man. The real tragedy lay, not only in the misconceptions, but the fact that they went uncorrected, because the missionaries neither took his culturally conditioned perception seriously, nor solicited the feedback that could have led to their correction (Acts 14:14).

The effective cross-cultural communicator must work within the culturally-defined frame of reference that permits proper communication and, if need be, the correction of miscommunication.

The Need to Take Culturally-Defined Perceptual Differences Seriously in Scripture Translation and Interpretation

Another crucial area is the translation and interpretation of the Bible. This involves the missionary, not in two, but three or four cultural frameworks. The Bible records God's revelation as it was perceived in Hebrew, Aramaic, and Greek language and culture. Our own perception of this revelation, however, is pervasively affected by our Euroamerican culture. Then we are called to translate and interpret the revelation into appropriate linguistic and cultural forms of still another culture.

Translators and interpreters must "be constantly aware of the contrast in the entire range of culture represented by" the source and target languages (Nida 1945:194). They must constantly be on their guard against interference from their own linguistic and cultural backgrounds. For example, through English we understand New Testament injunctions to continuing trust (such as Jn. 3:16) as a "once-for-all" action that many of us have experienced. Thus we translate faith as an act at a single point of time rather than a continuing commitment.

The Hausa language possesses a "continuative aspect" similar to the Greek "present tense," but the translation does not employ the continuative. It uses the Hausa equivalent for the Greek aorist, giving the popular English meaning rather than the Greek. Thus, the translator or interpreter can go astray if they strive for formal rather than cultural equivalence. Striving for literalness rather than functional equivalence has produced many misleading translations, both in the great historical versions and the missionary translations.

Ethnolinguistic insight into the nature of language, cultural conditioning and cross-cultural communication has led to a new understanding of what "correctness" in translation is really about. "Correctness must be determined by the extent to which the average reader for which a translation is intended will be likely to understand it correctly" (Nida and Taber 1969:1), rather than by some literalistic criteria, perhaps because of respect for the Scriptures, that focus more on the forms of the original text than on the meanings to be conveyed to the hearers. But biblical languages (and cultures) must be seen to be human (rather than some special creation of God), though treated reverently. "The writers of the biblical books expected to be understood" and are not well-translated, however motivated, if the original meaning is obscured (1969:7–8).

An ethnolinguistic approach to Bible translation and interpretation, therefore, paves the way for greater intelligibility of the message and consequently for a lower degree of dependence upon outsiders such as the missionary for its interpretation. This is good for church growth since it enables young churches to move rapidly toward indigeneity.

Ethnolinguistics and the Development of Indigenous Christian Theology: A Case Study from Africa

Among the pressing concerns of indigenous Christianity is the need to develop Christian theology framed in terms of the indigenous worldview, rather than in terms of the categories of the West. Given the dual facts of 1) the vast perceptual differences between cultures, and 2) that God has chosen to reveal himself within the cultural context, the result is and will continue to be a variety of culturally-conditioned understandings of theology (such as those of the West, of India, Latin America, Africa, etc.) none of which should be regarded as absolute, but all of which can contribute to a less culture-bound understanding of the supracultural God and his workings. Since God seeks to interact with human beings of each society in terms maximally comprehensible to them, we may assume he is in favor of the development of theological understandings within each society that will facilitate this end. Missionaries, therefore, should encourage the contextualization of theology, so that peoples of every society may have, what Welbourn terms "a place to feel at home" (Welbourn and Ogot 1966).

In Africa, at least, missionary endeavor has been focused primarily on western theologizing, that disregards the cultural factors underlying this process and tends to equate that theology with supracultural absolute models. Of the Baganda, John V. Taylor wrote that "missionaries preached from within the culture of the nineteenth-century Evangelical Protestantism—or nineteenth-century Roman Catholicism—while the Baganda heard from within the culture of the traditional African world view" (1958:253).

Welbourn says of the founder of an African independent church, that Kivuli wanted a home, with rational structures and thought-forms within which he could conceptualize his Christian theology; yet he and his countrymen had been presented with an often irrelevant "prefabricated" theology, based upon the concerns and "rational structure" of another society in which the people could not feel at home. For this reason thousands have split off from missions in quest of relevant theology.

Yet the culturally sympathetic missionary can assist in this worthy goal (as indeed an increasing number are) by taking seriously the insights and methodology of ethnolinguistics. The African, John Mbiti, in a recent volume, *New Testament Eschatology in an African Background* (1971) demonstrates the value of this approach for coming to grips with both the problem of extricating Africans from the maze of western theology and that of attempting to develop an African theology to feel at home in.

Mbiti focuses primarily on an analysis of the Akamba understanding of time and history, and the implications of this for their perception of the message already delivered, and for the development of an Akamba African theology based on ethnolinguistic data from which he examines "the inner, more profound, question of what Christianity has meant in this African situation" (1971:23). In doing so he seeks:

(a) to see the conceptual background of the Akamba;

(b) to find what has been taught and received as the Christian Faith, and the methods employed in its propagation;

(c) to assess the impact of such teaching upon the people's total understanding;

(d) by bringing together both traditional concepts and the New Testament, to see what light is thrown by each on the other; and

(e) to draw some theological implications of the whole picture (1971:23).

Mbiti's method of presentation involves five steps: 1) "Analysis of Akamba traditional concepts related to eschatology;" 2) a theological presentation of the New Testament teaching on the subject under discussion; 3) the teaching of "the main evangelizing agent among the Akamba" on the subject; 4) a discussion of "how Akamba Christians may have understood (or misunderstood) the Christian teaching, and with what results or consequences;" and 5) the drawing of "conclusions and deductions, some of which are purely theological while others tend in the direction of practical issues of evangelization" (3–4), in this way he treats such topics as "Time, History and Eschatology of the Sacraments," "The Nearness of the Spirit

World" and "The Resurrection as Corporate Eschatology." At each point he compares and contrasts New Testament, Akamba and missionary concepts in an enlightening way.

Mbiti pleads for the right to develop an indigenous theology, and demonstrates the need for it, recommending ethnolinguistic methods in laying the foundations. Whether or not he has succeeded in this, he has certainly proved the need for an Akamba Christian theology, and pointed up areas of investigation within the language and culture, that will have to be probed in the development of such a theology. An indigenous Christian theology will be affected by both language and culture, but on the other hand "to introduce eternal realities into African thought is to introduce something not only new but revolutionary" (Mbiti 1969:182). However, it is all important just how this "revolution" is brought about, for

> The eschaton must invade the African world, not destroy or colonize, but to fulfill, to inject into its cosmology Christian realities. Africa has an Eschatology, but it has no teleology, and this is an area where Christian Eschatology can make a radical contribution to God's natural revelation in Africa. Eschatology without teleology is as empty as a house without furniture (1969:181).

Mbiti also recommends as another end where change is needed "the sacraments of Baptism and the Eucharist (which) present themselves clearly as areas where temporal and eternal realities meet, and the media through which the temporal may catch glimpses of the eternal" (1969:181). He goes on to suggest that Africa should discover the theology of the Sacraments "and apply it to the work of evangelization, for the ground is already prepared" (1969:182).

Mbiti's own language and culture are beginning a kind of linguistic and cultural transformation that the gospel itself brings about. In the following section we shall look back on the process of conceptual transformation that Mbiti seeks, as it has occurred first in Greek, and then in Fijian.

Christianity and the Conceptual Transformation of Language: A Case Study from Greek and Fijian

---

Another area for ethnolinguistic consideration is that which takes place in the language of a people under culture contact. Such culture contact stimulates expansion, redefinition and replacement of vocabulary and maybe even modifications in the grammar, besides changes in the conceptual categories of a language

English, for example, has had prolonged contact with French in a context where French has been regarded as the more prestigious language. This culture contact with its prestige factor and the English predisposition to borrow has resulted in the large number of French words and even certain grammatical features in English. But borrowing is only one of the methods by means of which a society changes its linguistic habits. The processes of expansion and replacement of vocabulary through borrowing are well understood. What is not so well understood, but of greater importance to church planting is the process of linguistic transformation that occurs when words and concepts already present in the society are redefined, or otherwise expanded in scope, to accommodate the "new wine" of the innovative influences. Typically, the forms of the words and concepts remain virtually the same, but the meanings attached to them, and the uses to which they are put, change in accordance with the requirements of the new concepts and situations introduced into the society.

This process is another normal feature of linguistic change and adaptation. A language, like a culture, is adapted to changes in the reality with which it deals. Meanings are changed in denotation and connotation. The English word "manufacture" (originally meaning "made by hand") was "transformed," via the Industrial Revolution and mass production, into a symbol implying large scale and mechanized production of consumer goods. The term "turnpike," originally a turnstile-like device to obstruct the enemy in a narrow passage during wartime, came to mean a device at the entrance of a toll road in a non-war situation. When these roads gained more focus on tolls, the term "turnpike" came to signify the road, even when no toll was required. "Education" was changed from "child rearing" to "formal schooling" (Mead 1964:164). Many other examples could be cited of conceptual transformations as a result of culture change.

Some of the most striking examples of linguistic transformation, however, have come from the introduction of Christianity into a culture. The Greek word *agapao* (and its derivatives), for example, was transformed from a word the "etymology (of which) is uncertain, and its meaning weak and variable," a word which lacked "the power or magic of *erao*" and "the warmth of *philein*" and often meant "no more than 'to be satisfied with something'" (Kittel 1964, I:36) into the distinctively Christian word for love that to Paul was "the only vital force which had a future in this aeon of death" (1964, I:51) and to John "the principle of the world of Christ which is being built up in the cosmic crisis of the present" (1964, I:52).

Likewise the translators of the Septuagint chose to transform the word *kurios* into the Greek equivalent of the Hebrew Yahweh rather than to employ *despotes*, which was also possible and perhaps more natural in terms of current usage" (Kittel 1965, III:1802). *Kurios* was not, apparently, at that time widely, if ever, employed with reference to God, or even to the Greek gods, meaning "Lord" merely with reference to one human being who held legal rights over another. Then, when presumably under the influence of the Septuagint, the process of transformation had gotten underway, "it was in common use only in certain places where it corresponded to native, non-Greek usage" (1965, III:1051). In these areas, however (especially in Egypt), the word came to be "particularly used in expression of a personal relationship of a man to a deity, whether in prayer, thanksgiving or vow, and as a correlate of *doulos* (slave) inasmuch as the man concerned describes as *kurios* the god under whose orders he stands" (1965, III:1052). Thus the way was paved for the use of the term with reference both to God and Father and to Christ with the implication of "the personal, legitimate and all-embracing sovereignity of God" (1965, III:1088) clearly stamped upon it.

Thus likewise was a word like *ekklesia* transformed from meaning simply "the lawful citizenship rights" (Tippett 1958:12) customarily "summoned and called together by the herald" (Kittel 1965, III:513), into the distinctive designation for the Church of Christ both in its local sense (1 Cor. 1:2) with regard to the Church Universal (1 Cor. 10:32), and later, with reference to "one of the household Churches (1 Cor. 16:19) which were springing up throughout the Graeco-Roman world" (Tippett 1958:14). And the same type of transformation took place for term after term, concept after concept in Greek as a result of the birth and development of Christianity in a cultural setting where Greek was the language employed.

But Greek was far from the only language within which this kind of semantic and conceptual transformation has been stimulated by Christianity. The introduction of Christianity into culture after culture in our own day (not infrequently combined with massive westernization) has resulted in strikingly similar linguistic adaptation in hundreds of the languages of the world. Wherever, for example, a Christian preacher or Bible translator has chosen to employ an indigenous rather than a borrowed term for God, for forgiveness, for love, for faith or for any of the distinctive concepts of Christianity, the process of Christianity-stimulated linguistic transformation has begun.

Thus, at least for Christians of the Kaka and Bulu tribes of southern Cameroun, the perhaps ill-chosen term Ndjamble which referred to an impersonal, mythical cosmic spider, is being invested with meaning-transforming denotations and connotations because of its adoption by the Christian church as the designation of the Christian God (see Reyburn 1957). This term was chosen, according to Reyburn, because "there is no better native term . . . and a foreign word would be lacking entirely in the few equivalences which do exist" (1957:192). Some translators in an attempt to avoid syncretism have, according to Nida, elected to employ a borrowed term for God on the assumption "that the native people will automatically come to understand by the borrowed word . . . exactly what we understand by the same term." This approach, however, is not usually successful since "in almost every case the native will immediately try to equate this new name of God with one of the gods of his own religious system" and may end up with some sort of understanding like that of the Aztecs, who equate Dios with the sun and the Virgin Mary with the moon, and consider Jesus the offspring of the two. "Before the translator realizes it, instead of being able to fill an empty word with the proper meaning, he has a name which has already been given a content from the pagan religion" (Nida 1947:205).

Much better is the approach that recognizes that "in terms of the native culture the Greek word *theos*, the Latin *deus*, and the Gothic *gutli* could hardly be termed exact equivalents to the concept of God as taught in the Bible." They were, however, generic terms rather than names of particular specific gods such as Zeus, Jupiter or Woden, each of which was associated with "a great deal of legend as to the individual peculiarities, excesses, and immoral actions of the particular gods." The generic terms, however, that "designated any important supernatural entity" were taken by the Christians and "by context and teaching made (to) apply to only one such entity (Nida 1947:206). Nida recommends that this "transformational" approach be that employed in similar situations in today's languages, and lists a series of questions that translators should ask concerning the indigenous term(s) they may be considering to represent basic Christian concepts.

Tippett (1958:27–55) details a number of different aspects of what I am calling the process of linguistic transformation as a result of the penetration of Christianity into Fiji culture and language. This penetration, having started in 1835, is of long enough duration for us to safely assume that the observed changes are of permanent significance. Among the large number of words taken over by Fiji Christianity from the pre-Christian religion were words for sacrifice, prayer, worship, atonement and offerings. Though the major transformation seems to be the Christian usage of words, it is clear from the derivations that the elaboration of these concepts within Fijian Christianity has involved considerable transformation. Though, for example, the concept of church was transformed to apply to the bringing together of men and women alike in common gathering, true to other patterns in the culture, to this day there is a segregation of the men and women within the gathering to their respective portions of the building.

A second type of transformation prominent in Fiji Christianity was the extension of the meanings of certain common words to expose Christian meanings. Among these are the verb "to pour out," formerly used of liquids only but within Christianity now applied also to the pouring out of the Holy Spirit, "a concept common in Fijian prayer to this day" (Tippett 1958:35). An apparently greater degree of transformation has taken place in the extension of the word originally denoting the extinguishing of a fire first to "wipe out" then to "erase" (as of a blackboard) and eventually to cover the concept of forgiveness. This latter extension of meaning provided for Fijian Christianity the long-sought solution for an adequate translation of such passages as "forgive us our sins" in the Lord's Prayer which, until about 35 years ago had been rather unsatisfactorily rendered, "Do not be angry with us on account of our sins." Incidental, though important, changes in meaning have taken place in the words for "human flesh," once a highly prized food now reduced to a term of abuse and that which once meant "a desire to eat human flesh" but now means "a desire to eat fish."

In certain cases it was felt important to produce new constructions to adequately represent the new concepts. These were of two types: word extensions (grammatical rather than semantic) and word combinations. Among the former is the word for missionary or minister that, though a term for priest was available, was wisely constructed from the Fiji verb "to send" resulting in a term parallel to the Greek *apostelo,* meaning (literally) "the one sent forth with an important message" (Tippett 1958:37). A similar type of construction has proven a worthy choice to translate the word "gospel" since it both incorporates the "good news" concept and avoids the possibility of confusion with indigenous tales and oral traditions.

Among the conceptual transformations brought about through word combinations, the outstanding example, according to Tippett, is the combination of the terms for "bad" and "habits" or "customs" to represent "the idea of sin as active and continuing evil" (1958:38). The transformation of the term meaning "bad" as an adjective but "war" as a noun has proceeded so far that an expression that once meant "the land is at war" has now come to mean "the land is evil," since "Christianity has changed an era of internal wars into an era of peace, and the meanings no longer needed have dropped out of use" (1958:38). The ramifications of the semantic transformation have enabled the construction of combinations such as those meaning "hating one another," "to slander" and "to cause another to sin" (1958:39). Similar transformations are illustrated for word combinations involving the Fijian word meaning "true." And since "basic concepts like evil . . . and true or truth . . . change all aspects of daily life . . . a shift in meaning or depth or tone in one of these key root words will ramify throughout all private and social life. Truly then it may be said that the Church by giving new meaning to words like sin, truth, right, honor and many others, has charged a secular vocabulary with a spiritual quality" (1958:40).

There were, in addition, "words from the old way of life which were taken by the Church and deliberately changed for use in a new way" (Tippett 1958:41). Among these were the term for God which, in spite of the fact that these people have been monotheistic for many years, must still occur preceded by specifiers such as "the" or "our" as symbols of the fact that the term once applied (without such modifiers) to the deities of Fijian pre-Christian polytheism. The term employed by Christians for "blessed" or "happy," further, is that once applied to the happiness believed to result from a form of snake god worship. Perhaps the most dramatic change of all, however, underlies the word presently employed for Christian singing which once designated the chants and dances performed before and after wars of revenge at the completion of which it was customary to torture, kill and prepare as food any prisoners taken.

As implied above, some of the conceptual transformations stimulated by Christianity required the introduction or production of completely new terminology. Some few of these terms were borrowed. Among such borrowings were names for unfamiliar fauna and flora, e.g., *sipi* (sheep), *ose* (horse), *sita* (cedar), names of foreign places and people and the names for certain of the completely new cultural elements introduced, e.g., *sakaremede* (sacraments), *papitaiso* (baptism), *same* (psalm), *tevoro* (devil) and *lotu* (church, Christianity—from Tonga). More frequently the label for the new concept was constructed from indigenous Fiji vocabulary items. In this way the Christians produced organizational terms such as minister (mentioned above), catechist, village. teacher, lay church officer, preacher; terms labeling aspects of their religious experience such as an "inquiry concerning the way of life," "piety" (meaning literally "habitually at prayer") and the term with accompanying proverb labeling the gospel as something so astonishing and exciting that "it had to be expounded far and wide, to be shared, to be communicated" (Tippett 1958:46); and "the terminology of a new ethic" including expressions based on the word for spirit such as evil-spirited (i.e., angry), covetous, true-spirited (i.e., generous), cool-spirited (i.e., unenthusiastic), hot-spirited (i.e., enthusiastic), pity-spirited (i.e., merciful), long-spirited (taking a long time to act), little-spirited (discouraged). Another set of constructions can now also be made with the word for behavior (generally signifying the effect in behavior of the bent of the person's spirit) and the word for the mind (signifying basic attitudes).

Certain grammatical constructions have also come to be employed in new contexts because of Christianity. Among these is a "reciprocalizing prefix" the use of which has enabled the construction of terms meaning to be the same good disposition towards one another: "to love one another," "to know one another," "to hate one another," "to help one another," "praying for one another" (i.e., interceding), "being well-disposed toward each other" (i.e., peace), and "mutual help." Similarly, a suffix or postposed word meaning "together" or "of the same kind" enabled constructions meaning of the same spirit, of the same mind, or the same behavior, or, when employed with verbs, pray together, weep together or sing together. "By means of such constructions Christianity was able to develop a sense of Christian relationship and also fortify her demands for the corporateness of the Church, and for this reason that number of combinations was greatly increased and the language enriched" (Tippett 1958:52).

In summary, Tippett lists nine important aspects of the contribution of the coming of Christianity to semantic transformation of the Fiji language. And the fact that this type of thing has happened and should happen again in multitudes of other languages makes this summary and the following conclusions highly relevant to church planters around the world. These points are:

1. The church took over the linguistic forms of the native people and found her doctrine and ethic expressible in the constructions and thought-forms of the people, and there followed great semantic development within the indigenous heart of the language.

2. Foreign borrowings were restricted deliberately.

3. Many words from the pre-Christian liturgies and sacrificial ritual were preserved because they contained basic elements of worship, not confined to one religion; but these were charged with new meaning as the indigenous theology was developed in the light of scripture translation and Christian experience. Many new combinations were developed.

4. In some cases these words were reinterpreted in the light of the new religion, but in others they were given completely new meaning.

5. Some significant choices had to be made between old words for use in the new. The choice between the word meaning "priest" and the construction meaning "the one sent forth with an important message" as the designation for minister or missionary, for instance, is seen to involve the nature of the church ministry—was it to be priestly or apostolic. The semantic study shows the Fijian Church captured the true apostolic concept, and this had social implications.

6. The church widened the Fijian lexicography by means of word-combination, and thereby assisted the development of an indigenous ethic and theology. The doctrinal potential of the language was discovered and exploited.

7. Both morphological devices and endemic thought forms were used for the development of this potential, and words were found for concepts like incarnation and transfiguration, but are nevertheless conditioned by the scripture narrative. There is real semantic development here.

8. The church is found to have developed her own original and unique terminology in three respects:

    a. arising from her constitution and organizational power.

    b. growing from her ever-widening religious experiences.

    c. arising from the demand for a terminology of Christian ethics.

9. By the reduction of the spoken language to written form, the translation of the Scriptures, composition of hymns, preparation of a catechism and the writing and printing of other books the church has standardized the language, and expanded its vocabulary so that it is quite adequate for the Christian experience of its members. Secular vocabulary has been charged with spiritual significance and the moral quality of many acts is indicated by the word root and morphology much more obviously than in English (Tippett 1958:53–55).

In conclusion, Tippett points to the similarity between the processes of ethnolinguistic change and development (what I have labeled linguistic "transformation") in Fiji and those we can trace in New Testament Greek. He refers to these processes as "a continuity of the forces and factors that operated in the Apostolic Church" (1958:57) and suggests that

> we have here a method of God's work with man. So much there is to glorify Him, which lies dormant in life, awaiting the right mind to discover it and give it to mankind. Nothing brings home this truth better than the study of biblical and ecclesiastical ethnolinguistics (1958:56–57).

He goes on to suggest that in these modern continuations of the Book of Acts (i.e., the young churches) we are able to observe and participate in something truly exciting and truly different from the experience of our "home" churches, for these churches

> are still in the testing period, they have not yet fully developed their theological and ethical potential, there are spiritual and linguistic resources they have yet to discover and exploit, there are experiments of faith going on that have yet to be consolidated and interpreted, and there are experiences being worked out which will ultimately be reflected in new terminology. In the Young Churches (I speak generally, not of Fiji in particular) we are today able to observe the apostolic mission in action, and the Faith that is being forged today in one place in the face of Communism, and in another in the face of Caesar-worship and Roman persecution, because it is both experiential and apostolic. The home Church is fortunate in being able to observe these movements in our time, and might well question herself about the nature of her theology (is it mere accumulated tradition, or growing from a vital experience?) and whether or not we have a clear concept of her apostolic mission, and again whether or not her ministry is a commission or a career. She may not be able to answer herself satisfactorily, but the questions should be asked and answered nevertheless. Again, looking forward, we should ask whether the old world of Westernism has a sufficiently apostolic religion to face and explore and control the . . . atomic age?

> The persecutions of Rome were overcome only in an apostolic faith, and likewise the forces of Druidism, and the same applies to the cannibalism and widow strangling and patricide of Fiji. It would seem that only a church with apostolic faith and commission is likely to survive Communism, and surely nothing less will be required for the control of or survival in the atomic era.

> History reveals how churches have developed and been sorely tested, Some have survived and some have been exterminated, Their experiences have been reflected in the literary records they have left, not merely narrative but in the very words they have selected to use. Historic periods of spiritual growth have always been likewise periods of semantic growth. We see this in the words of Jesus, of Paul, of Augustine, of Coverdale, and Tyndale, of Luther and Calvin, of Wesley, and of

Hunt and Hazelwood in Fiji. Furthermore, periods of real religious strength growing in experience are reflected in semantic growth in the indigenous vocabulary, by the discovery and development of terminology with strong apostolic affinities (Tippett 1958:57–59).

Conclusion

We have surveyed but a very few of the areas in which the perspectives of Ethnolinguistics can make solid contributions to various aspects of the planting and growth of the Christian church throughout the world. If missionaries and others engaged in the cross-cultural communication of the gospel approached their tasks naturally on the basis of these understandings, there would be no need for a study such as Ethnolinguistics to be a part of the training of church planters. The fact is, however, that it is precisely at the points where ethnolinguistic study can be of assistance that much of the insensitivity and misunderstanding that have unfortunately, characterized a number of missionaries have occurred.

If, for example, prospective church planters instinctively understood the depths of culturally-defined perceptual differences there would be no need to labor the point. Or if there were no (or even few) people of mission lands who had misperceived the message of Christianity to be advocating mere cultural substitution, it would not be necessary to point to examples like that of my misled Liberian friend—an example that we all would rather not believe is common—as if his misperception were widespread (which unfortunately it is). Nor is it pleasant to allude to the fact that the lack of ethnolinguistic understanding has often resulted in Scripture translations and approaches to theology that compound rather than clarify cross-cultural misperception. It is however pleasant to end this chapter with a case study demonstrating the constructiveness of an approach that apparently applied ethnolinguistically informed insight to the solution of the problems raised earlier in this chapter.

Both the negative and the positive illustrations, however, speak eloquently to the extremely high importance for missionaries (whose ultimate aim is the planting of rapidly-growing churches that are thoroughly contextualized) to be trained in the insights and methodology of the cross-discipline of Ethnolinguistics. This would permit them to 1) better translate or assist in effective translation of the Scriptures, 2) more intelligently and sympathetically assist and encourage the development of indigenous approaches to theology and 3) through all of this, function as catalysts in the process of linguistic and cultural transformation through the "inculturating" of supracultural Christianity deeply into the conceptual heart of culture after culture around the world.

CHAPTER 12

TOWARD AN ETHNOGRAPHY
OF HAUSA RIDDLING

Reprinted here from
the Northern Nigerian publication *Ba Shiru: Oral Narrative*
(A Journal of African Languages and Literature) 6:2:17–24 (1975)

This paper was stimulated by, first, my own interest in Hausa ethnolinguistics, and second, by a paper by Professor Lee Haring of Brooklyn College, presented at the African studies Association meetings in Philadelphia, in November 1972. The former—my interest in Hausa ethnolinguistics—has led me to study anthropologically a number of types of Hausa folklore, including fables, proverbs, epithets and now riddles. The Haring paper led me to ask a series of questions concerning the riddling process itself, the freedom or lack of freedom of the participants in the process, the fixity of answers, and the role of the riddler in Hausa society.

My own experience with Hausa and with Hausa riddling goes back to 1957 when I began to learn and to teach the language in Northern Nigeria. As a pleasant part of the learning and teaching process, I was able on occasion, to induce my language helpers to engage in the mock warfare that riddling becomes in Hausaland. The dialog goes something like this:

—One says, "Here it is, here it is here." (This is the formulaic sentence introducing a fable or a riddle).

—The reply is, "Let it come, let it pass by." Or, "Let it come so we can hear it."

—"Okay," the riddler answers, "my father is in the hut, his beard is outside."

The listeners ponder what the riddler could be alluding to. If they hesitate the riddler asks, "Do you give me the town?" The analogy is to the conquest of a town in warfare. The riddler is asking his listeners to acknowledge his ability in the mock warfare of riddling by surrendering to him a town.

If the listeners are stumped they will say, "Okay we give you a town." Then the riddler may say, "Okay, give Kano" (the largest city in Northern Nigeria). The listeners will likely refuse to "give" him such a prestigious prize, but will instead offer, say, Bauchi or another town of relatively lower prestige. They will eventually agree on a town of higher prestige than Bauchi but of less prestige than Kano, will laugh good naturedly over the whole process and the riddler will say, "Fire and smoke." That is, the "old man" inside the house represents the fire that frequently burns inside the grass-roofed houses of rural Hausaland. The smoke filters up through the grass roof and is likened to the old man's beard.

Then one of the listeners will give the formula:

—"Here it is, here it is here."

—"Let it come, let it pass by."

—"One path splits into two."

One of the listeners may reply, "A pair of pants." The riddler then says, "Okay, you've conquered the town." And so it goes.

On Knowing the Answer

In his paper surveying riddling with particular reference to Africa, Haring raises the question, "Is the person to whom the riddle is posed really expected to guess the answer?" Haring's answer is no. He says:

> Most Western-educated people assume that he is, but I believe he is not. African riddling is more like a catechism than a creative inquiry. Usually in African riddles the association of the question and answer (or precedent and sequent) is fixed by tradition and popular acceptance (1972:2).

Haring's point is that the overall cultural context in which riddling takes place demands that the answer be learned with the riddle. And he supports his contention fairly well, for the majority of the cases in which riddling takes place in the African contexts to which he alludes.

He states, for example, that in his recording of Akamba riddles, he:

> saw no hint that any invention was taking place. Rather the informants, a lively group of children and adolescents, took delight in sharing with me, the outsider, a body of material which they seemed to recognize as a distinct cultural product. While eager to display their knowledge they were neither competing nor guessing any answers (Haring 1972:3).

Haring scores Lyndon Harries for giving the impression that the riddler invents his riddles and poses them to his audience with the expectation that they will not be able to guess the answer (Harries 1971:377–393). But, says Haring:

> What of the situation in which an African poses a riddle to someone else which he has not invented himself? Surely this is the basic performance situation which many investigators have observed and recorded ... Simply by weight of probability, most African riddling must consist of the exchange of fixed pairs of questions and answers which have not been invented by the speakers but which they are remembering (1972:3).

Likewise, according to Haring and Maranda, a scholar of Finnish and Melanesian riddling, the listener is not expected to be creative in his answer. For even though, due to the "greater applicability and fertility of certain metaphors" a given "riddle image" could conceivably elicit several answers, it is not expected or usually allowed that the listener will invent an answer during the riddling session. Rather, according to Maranda:

> . . . both the image and the answer are coded, and . . . the main intellectual effort in a riddling situation consists of a quick scanning of the coded message to "discover" the answer rather than of an intellectual effort to "invent" a novel answer. In this sense, riddling is always closer to an academic test than to creative research (1971:196).

But Haring adds:

> . . . riddlers do not simply repeat traditional items; rather, having learned the rules of folkloric competence, which are analogous to the rules of linguistic competence, they perform riddles according to those rules. Correctness then means not exact repetition but conformity to folkloric rules which are implicitly understood by all members of the folk group (1972:6–7).

However, even when alternative answers are a possibility according to the rules, the riddler is likely to accept only the answer he has in mind at the time. As my latest Hausa language helper replied when I asked him about alternative answers, "The riddler will only accept the answer he has decided upon." He may admit, however (at least to himself), that another answer given by a listener is a good one and may on a future occasion hold his listeners accountable for the latter answer, rather than the one he expected on the first occasion.

However, according to Haring:

> The right answer is a password for admission to the group of those who know; one's ingenuity in devising alternatives may be commendable, but it doesn't guarantee entry. Only the right answer does. The catechumen may be able to think up better answers than the ones expected—but that won't get him confirmed (1972:8).

This point is supported and elaborated upon by John Messenger in his study of riddling among the Anang Ibibio of Nigeria. He states that riddling is not engaged in with the intent of "baffling an audience and stimulating its members to provide correct answers" but, rather, for the purpose of enjoyment that "derives from the sharing of (riddling) by members of a group (Messenger 1960:226). This is not a competitive thing, then, but a participatory thing engaged in primarily by those who know for their own enjoyment and for the indoctrination of those who don't know (primarily younger children) into the knowledge of those who know.

> Older children and adults know most of the existing *ntan*, and when one is invented, its originator divulges the appropriate reply along with the question or initial statement rather than asking for possible solutions (Messenger 1960:226).

When one gets to be a "knower" of the riddles, both the question and the answer parts, he passes, as if from one grade of school to another, from the status of "outsider" to that of "insider."

> Hearing the same riddles later in life, the riddler is reminded of childhood days and is reinforced in his sense of unity with the group. The Anang pattern prohibits the competitive or aggressive use of riddles but encourages their use to promote group solidarity (Haring 1972:10, after Messenger 1960:227).

Riddles as a Catechism for
Hausa Children

There is no doubt in my mind that Haring is right in seeing riddles as a part of the catechism that the uninitiated in Hausa society are expected to learn. And as I study the Hausa riddles with their fixed answers I find myself at innumerable points being introduced to characteristically Hausa perspectives on reality. Though in a sense, both the Hausa child and I come to the riddles as outsiders to a system, the Hausa child as he learns cannot be nearly as fascinated as I am, because he has no alternative perspective on reality to compare these analogies to. Nor can I be as thoroughly conditioned by the Hausa system as he is, since I have been indoctrinated first into another perspective on reality.

Here is a brief illustration of certain of the aspects of the Hausa catechism that come through riddling. I have reversed the order in which the riddle and its answer are given to focus on the thing learned rather than the way in which it is learned.

A. Body parts—a considerable number of riddles deal with the body.

1. Fingernails are seen as (a) a little bow behind an anthill (i.e., finger) (b) a lovely thing in a grove of trees.

2. Shadows are (a) my brother who travels with me but whom I can't hear moving (b) the one who accompanies a full moon.

3. An arm or a hand is a trusty slave in that he will protect me from whatever comes my way.

4. Teeth are (a) white roosters on a fence (the gums) (b) a stump hard to pull out.

5. Hair is my farm that grows up very quickly after I harvest it.

6. Ears are (a) my father who goes around the house, my mother who does the same thing, but they don't meet (b) something of mine that is older than my grandfather (c) my father's twins—he turns around but they don't meet each other.

7. A tongue has a sharpness greater than that of a sword.

8. The back is always with me, but I can't see it.

9. Mucus is something I always try to get to return, but it keeps showing itself.

10. Eyes are (a) like strangers but they refuse/hate strangers (b) my marsh that is always full of water (c) two stallions that are always running out of sight and then returning (d) tireless messengers: if you send them now, immediately they'll return (e) my boy who will not mind—he will not stay put (f) two good friends—no matter how rough the river they'll cross it.

B. Fauna and insects.

1. A dog—I've given it to you, why are you still staring at me.

2. A dog's nose—I washed my bowl clean and put it in the sun to dry, but it didn't dry.

3. Doves—the girls of our house don't go to the bush without clapping their hands.

4. A scorpion—God gave him a saddle but I won't mount it.

5. Guinea fowl— (a) crease after crease, the body cloth (given by) God (b) he has woven a speckled dish cover.

6. Chicken—my girlfriend who eats, wipes her mouth and says nobody gave her anything.

7. A blind horse—when they try to sell it everyone refuses to buy.

8. Harvester ants—a thousand cattle travel without raising any dust.

9. Butterfly—teacher open your book.

10. Hedgehog—a little ball in the midst of the corn.

C. Flora.

1. Cotton—I went to the bush, the bush laughed at me.

2. Shade of a palm tree—the one close to this shade will be bothered by the heat of the sun.

3. A tree stump or ant hill—the bush is full of the sound of movement in the grass but the big bull buffalo just lies there silently.

4. A pumpkin—the walk of a woman expecting twins.

5. Withered leaves—I went to the bush, the living things didn't welcome me, only the dead things.

D. Celestial bodies.

1. The moon and the stars—the cattle are lying down with the bull standing over them.

2. Stars—white food covering.

3. The firmament—a dye bowl (calabash) that can't have a lid.

4. Dark overcast—shade that hasn't the dye (i.e., no variation of color).

E. Miscellany.

1. The medicine man—they fear him even though his business is lying.

2. Hunger—a switch on the path that beats children and adults alike.

3. Home—no matter how many young my animal has, they will sleep inside it.

4. A needle and thread—my horse doesn't do well unless it has a tail.

5. A bucket—a small trader that trades in the nether world's market (i.e., down the well).

6. A water dipper—(a) a young girl at our house who is always bathing (b) my goat went to the nether world and returned pregnant.

7. A drum—(a) from afar I hear the voice of my friend (b) something cries out in the bush but has no intestines.

8. Bow and arrow—the harlot pretties herself but the men run away.

9. A mat door covering—you always stand close to the doorway but don't enter. Is this your mother's home?

10. A Fulani picks up palm nuts—a red thing fell, a red one picked it up.

11. Indigo dye—a lot of substance but inedible.

12. A type of sugar cane—a young girl with a full head of hair.

13. Three-stone cooking place—three by three, holding the town together.

14. A broom—I have one thousand cattle tied with a single rope.

15. Weaving—here a thread, there a thread with a pregnant woman between them.

16. Granaries—the girls in our home are very stout.

17. A measuring cup—the judge of the market.

18. Defecating—one goes on the run but returns proudly.

The Implications of the Haring Paper

I have quoted extensively from the Haring paper for two reasons: (1) I am in substantial agreement with his conclusion, though I feel that he has overstated his case a bit and (2) his treatment of riddling in its cultural context raises very interesting theoretical points. These center largely around the matter of whether a restricted type of human activity such as riddling is best viewed as an inhibitor or a facilitator of human freedom

One point that I feel Haring supports well is that the riddling process in Africa is a good bit more structured at every point (i.e., gives less room for creativity) than the casual observer might assume. He also does well to focus on the part riddling plays in the education or initiation of children into the knowledge of adult society. In this sense, riddling participates with other types of folklore in acquainting the young with important aspects of the worldview and value system of the society. Furthermore, this education takes place in an enjoyable manner and in a noncompetitive atmosphere—or, perhaps better, in an atmosphere where potential competitiveness is strictly controlled.

But into the treatment of riddling by Haring and his sources come hints of an expression of creativity and innovation in the riddling process that Haring doesn't seem to focus on. For, though he quotes John Blacking on Venda riddling as saying "I never encountered anyone who thought about the meaning of an unknown riddle and tried to reason out the answer" (Blacking 1961:5) he also quotes those who refer to riddles and their answers as inventable. Messenger, for example, in the quote cited above, refers to a riddle's "originator." Harries and another of Haring's major sources, Wimsatt (1954) also refer to invention of riddles.

Indeed, common sense alone would be enough to tell us that someone, somewhere must have invented the riddles that exist today even if they are now simply passed on from generation to generation as one category of initiation secrets. So riddles (with their answers) must have once been invented. But is the process of riddle creation still taking place? And is there room for creativity in the answer given to a riddle?

A Hausa Experiment

To test Haring's conclusions and to attempt to answer these questions for myself, I engaged in an experiment in riddling with my present Hausa language assistant, Mr. Abba Kano. I started by simply asking a few questions:

(1) Are Hausa riddles learned or created on the spot?—He replied that most Hausa riddles are learned with their fixed answers. However, riddlers may make up new riddles.

(2) Is the answer always fixed?—He replied that for most riddles the answer is more or less fixed, though for many there are more than one answer. The riddler, however, may choose the answer that he will accept on a given occasion and reject all others. He may even have two or more answers in mind and reject whichever one the respondent comes up with. However, all that a refusal to accept the first reply normally does is to delay the giving of the acceptable answer, since no penalty seemed to be attached to giving the wrong answer. Indeed, if the wrong answer was judged by the group to be very clever, the one who gave it would be complimented for his cleverness.

If the riddle is created by the riddler, he determines the answer but may be open to learning other answers from his audience. These he will not accept on that occasion but might demand in a subsequent riddling session, especially if he judges someone else's answer to be superior to his original answer.

My informant stated that the more traditional the riddle is, the more fixed its answer. There is considerably more leeway allowed for alternative answers to more contemporary riddles.

Then my informant and I tried telling a few riddles. He, of course, frequently stumped me. But I also stumped him a couple of times. Once, however, when I had presented him with a riddle that I considered pretty difficult, he thought for a while and then came up with the correct answer. Yet, to the best of his recollection he had never heard that riddle before. That is, hearing the riddle stimulated him to attempt to produce the correct answer while, apparently, something in the culturally inculcated worldview and the rules for riddling enabled him to guess the right answer.

His personal competence in this aspect of the culture was, therefore, an important factor in his ability to arrive at the correct answer through guessing. It was probably, furthermore, a function of his overall feelings of competence in his operation of his culture that he felt able to even attempt a guess. Perhaps if he were a young child and, therefore, less confident of his cultural competence he would not have ventured a guess but, on failing to remember an answer he knew to be correct, simply would have given up. I would like to suggest that, since a high percentage of the data to which Haring refers relates to either children or foreign observers, there may be a factor of cultural insecurity operative here that explains why there seemed to be so little creativity apparent in those situations.

A Hypothesis

Indeed, I would like to hypothesize that in riddling, as in most other areas of culture, creativity is not so much missing as it is regulated. That is, there are in riddling situations as in other situations those who innovate. There will ordinarily be persons who feel more rather than less secure in the riddling situation and who are looked to by at least same others in the society for innovation in at least this area of life. They may have achieved their position through a demonstration of their ability to innovate or they may have been designated to such a position by their society.

I would expect that an in-depth study of creativity in riddling in any given society would uncover the fact that there are various levels of innovators. There will be those who at the lowest level will test their innovations on only the least enculturated or least able riddlers in the society. And there will be successive levels in innovators up to those who are so confident of their ability and their acceptance as riddle innovators that they will not hesitate to innovate riddles and/or answers to riddles in any company.

Thus, though much of what Haring and his sources indicate concerning the fixity of the riddling process confirms rather than disproves what I have learned about riddling among Hausa children, it is not true of my experience with adults. For children are after all basically recipients of the culture rather than the creators of the culture. Riddles, therefore, come to them out of the past with all of the fixity of tradition that for all they know is centuries old. Thus also comes such cultural data to foreign anthropologists or folklorists who, in spite of their sophistication in their own culture, come to another culture's folklore as a child comes—to a fixed body of already established data that they must first master before they even dream of adding to or otherwise altering it.

My suggestion is, therefore, that just as the erroneous view that riddling in African societies is a competitive and entirely creative game was due to the imperfect understanding of the situation by outside analysts so is a view that sees riddling as completely devoid of creativity. As the first pitfall was fallen into by those outsiders who did not analyze the situation closely enough, the latter may perhaps be the error of those who, though they still could not see the situation in its entirety, analyzed it too closely—or at least too rigidly. The corrective lies rather in seeing in this, as in every other aspect of culture, both the sometimes very strict guidelines that channel the human activity and also the areas for expression and creativity within these guidelines that societies allow and even compel some of their members to make use of.

As I see it, an adequate ethnography of riddling will have to specify both the restrictions under which the game is played and the allowances made for individual expression, variation and innovation. And we must assume from the fact that any given culture is continually being changed that there is some scope for variation in each. Where, however, the indoctrinational function of a cultural element such as riddling is most in focus, we can assume that the expressive and creative opportunities that that cultural element provides will be minimized. Societies simply don't want those whom they are indoctrinating (e.g., their children) to learn the system wrong. But play the same game with culturally secure adults and the opportunities for creativity come more into focus. To use Haring's analogy of the parallelism between riddling and the catechetical situation: while it is true that a young person is not encouraged (or even allowed) to alter the theology, there are those whose business it is to do just that—to innovate, to alter, to improve the existing to better meet the needs of the present and of the future.

It is by these designated innovators that some thoroughly updated examples of the Hausa folklore catechism have come about such as the proverb: "Perhaps" is what keeps the European from telling a lie. Or the epithet: As impossible as the Kano railway station. Or the riddle: There I am perfectly healthy, but I don't talk or move—my photograph.

Thus on the several occasions when I have observed adult Hausa speakers riddling there were a good many attempts to guess the answer and a good many compliments for those who guessed wrong but well. When, however, I became a participant in the process in an attempt to learn how to riddle, the attitude of my teachers changed completely. The flexibility was all gone and the catechetical character of the riddling process came much more into focus.

CHAPTER 13

AN ETHNOLINGUISTIC STUDY
OF HAUSA EPITHETS

Reprinted here with permission from
Studies in African Linguistics 6:135–146 (November 1976)

Introduction

It has been my privilege to be a student and colleague of William E. Welmers for some twenty-one years now. Two aspects of the scholarly example set by Professor Welmers that are particularly meaningful to me are, 1) the fact that in his study of language he never loses sight of the broader cultural context in which both linguistic structure and language events participate, and 2) the fact that he has never allowed his pursuit of linguistic theory to rob him of his interest in language data. As one whose linguistic interests are primarily applicational (rather than theoretical) and holistic (rather than particularistic) in terms of the relationships between language and other aspects of culture, I greatly appreciate these focuses.

The following is not intended to be profound. It is an old-fashioned data paper focusing on an interesting facet of Hausa speech behavior. This data exhibits one of the myriad ways that a society's value system is expressed via stylized linguistic utterance. In it I seek to classify and analyze, at least in a preliminary way, over five hundred of the seven hundred or more utterances labeled "epithet" by R. C. Abraham (1949, 1962). My purpose is to gain insight into Hausa values and general perception of life by discovering such things as what aspects of life Hausas have chosen to "epithetize," which things get the greatest amount of attention, and what is said about the various things so singled-out by Hausas.

I am working with a corpus that was collected a generation ago. The collection was a good one for its day and the collector a perceptive student of Hausa language and culture But there have been many changes during the intervening decades and it is unlikely that even such a conservative aspect of culture as this type of stylized speech has remained unaffected. I would expect a check of the present scene to reveal that a large number of new epithets have come into existence during this time and that a fair (though smaller) number of those recorded by Abraham have been lost. If this is true, the majority of those dealt with here are still in use. If the percentage of loss is actually greater, this corpus is still likely to be fairly representative.

Another consideration is the fact that stylized utterances preserve the values of previous generations. Like the majority of cultural patterns, they fit the past better than the present. The conclusions drawn concerning values and worldview from a study such as this are, therefore, more representative of some past time than they are of the present and would have to be tested against more current data before they could be considered as indicative of today's values.

I present all examples in (sometimes rough) English translation.

The Epithet in Hausa

An English understanding of epithets focuses (according to *The Random House Unabridged Dictionary*) on two types of utterance: 1) a word or phrase by which a person or thing is known that purportedly describes an actual or attributed quality of that person or thing (e.g., "Richard the Lionhearted"; "Jack the Ripper"), and 2) a characterizing word or phrase so firmly associated with a person or thing that it may be used in place of the ordinary designation (e.g., "man's best friend" for dog; "king of the beasts" for lion). Hausa employs epithets in both of these ways and, apparently, in several other ways as well. Several characteristics of Hausa epithets may be distinguished.

Epithets are used largely in informal conversation and often for the purpose of *spicing up the interaction*. In Hausa society, as in many other societies, a great deal of respect is accorded to those who are clever in verbalization. The frequent use of epithets is a preferred form of verbal cleverness for many. It is clever when the chief is mentioned to inject into the conversation the epithet, "eat, then take off your clothes" (i.e., he has an easy life), or to refer to a miserly person as "a balsam tree" (i.e., felt to be greedy because it doesn't shed its leaves). It keeps conversation lively when a person is described as wearing "dirt sweepers" (i.e., oversize trousers that drag on the ground), or when a kind of cheap perfume is referred to as "one whiff" or breakable earthenware as "fall and you die."

Hausa epithets often resemble *truncated proverbs*. There is, for example, a proverb that states that "night is evil's cloak." One epithet for nighttime is, therefore "cloak of evil."

Hausa epithets are applied to a much wider range of persons, things and actions than is true of English epithets. They are thus, much more often heard in Hausa than in English. A worthless person, for example, may be referred to as "a nose without a hole in it," or it might be said of an indecisive person, "the market is over and he's still wandering around." Beer may be called "pagan's milk," or a stronger kind of drink as "knee-killer." A lame excuse may be referred to as "running into the house to escape smallpox," lying as "producing flowers but no fruit," and pretending to sleep as "the kind of insomnia that is pleasanter than sleep" (because of what you can hear).

Hausa epithets are often phrased as *statements to the person, thing, or action that they refer to*. A train may be referred to as "you don't covet anyone's path, no one should covet yours," one's smile to hide pain by the statement, "you hurt more than crying," a busybody by "I heard your drumming and came over."

A number of Hausa epithets have been *reduced to mere nicknames* or simply alternative, now meaningless, designations of their referents. Any man named Àli-, for example, may alternatively be called Gargà or any Ha-ru-nà called Gìnsau. A chief has a variety of such nicknames, a man's penis is called *gò-di-*, and a chief's counselor, *tùkurà*.

Many Hausa epithets *involve a play on words*. The rainy season (*dà-muna-*) for example, may be referred to as *dà- ma- na- yi* "if I had only done it." A Hausa person (*bàhaushè-*) may be referred to as *mài ban haushi-* "one who causes irritation." A train may onomatopoetically be referred to as *fasà fushi-, kashè kudi-* said over and over again in imitation of the noise that the train makes. The meaning, which in this case is not as important as the sound of the words, is "vent (your) anger, spend (your) money."

Hausa epithets are *frequently accompanied by a brief explanation* of the sense in which they are intended. Gruel, a disliked food, is called "waster of three things" with the appended explanation that these are flour, water, and wood. Farming is called "stooping over" and explained as "you aren't begging, it's the one who refuses to stoop who becomes the beggar." Water may be called "chief" and the explanation appended "it doesn't stay anywhere without spreading out."

Hausa epithets, like much Hausa verbalization, are *frequently very "earthy"* (from an American point of view). Overmastering desire, for example, is referred to as "that which takes a man to bed naked," doing wickedness is referred to as "pissing on hard ground" (i.e., it will splash back on you), a common person is labeled "one who defecates on the ground," the supreme example of a mixture of good and bad things happening at the same time is when one begins excreting just at the point of sexual climax, and benefiting from coincidence is epithetized by referring to the "urinating of a mother carrying a child on her back" (since no one can tell if the urine is coming from the mother or the child).

A comparison of epithets dealing with the same subject reveals that Hausas, like other peoples, often carry with them *conflicting attitudes toward various aspects of their experience*. A chief, for example, is labeled by one epithet as "an antidote," by another "a thwarter of disputing," but in two others as "a snake" and "what a bad smell." Warfare is characterized on the one hand as "the food of a real man," and on the other as "the result of underhandedness." Sometimes the ambivalence is expressed in a single epithet as in one of those for a judge, "a bowl of sweetness and bitterness."

Though for the vast majority of the epithets studied, there is only a single epithet for any given aspect of Hausa experience, *many of the areas of life of most concern to Hausas are referred to by two or more epithets*. Thirty-six epithets were found for chiefs, for example, eight each for misers and hot-tempered persons, and seven each for trains and uselessness. There are many examples of two or three epithets being applied to a single aspect of experience. A tentative conclusion would be that Hausas either are or have been in the past more interested in these multiple-epithet areas than in single-epithet areas.

Epithets often manifest high *perceptiveness*. Though the focus of this kind of study is often on the differences between peoples of different cultures, it is interesting to note that, due no doubt to pervasive similarities in human beings, even those of a society as distant as ours is from Hausa can be impressed with the depth of Hausa perceptiveness. In this category, in addition to several of those already cited, we may put that for an underhanded person, "a dog who bites without barking," a two-faced person, "the voice of an hourglass drum" (it constantly changes its sound), that of a person or thing whose value is unknown, "a pregnant woman" (one never knows whether she will bring forth good or bad, joy or sorrow), that of a leather loincloth, "massager," and that of a rooster, "you reveal the home to the passerby and then need to be killed to feed him."

Classification of Hausa Epithets

1. *People*. Five hundred twenty-one examples of Hausa epithets were classified. Just under seventy percent of these (360 examples) focused on people. Within this grouping the following subcategories seem to be important.

    1.1. *Simple nicknames* (20 examples). Many of the most common names have an epithet that automatically goes with them. Thus, anyone named Àli– is automatically nicknamed "one with an elephant harpoon," À–madù "causer of horses to jump up and run away," and Hawà (Eve), "Friday" (considered a lucky day).

    1.2. *Occupations* (77 examples). General occupations are labeled by epithets such as, "governor's cattle" (a porter), "daybreaker" (the muezzin), "worthless person with a big turban" (a teacher). But officials get the most attention (70 of the 77 examples). A judge is called a "forgetter of friendship," a mounted attendant of a chief a "maker of a way through a crowd," a chief (36 examples) such things as "white and black," "a large yam" (it must be eaten very carefully), "preventer of farming" and "even in someone else's house you are more important than he is." Other officials are known as "a large needle for sewing the world together," "bachelor elephant," and "far-sighted but bad-tempered."

    1.3. *Special categories of people*. These are characterized by 36 of the most interesting of the epithets. Among the *tribal* epithets are "young dog" (Tuareg), "slave of yams" (Igbo), "one shave, one word" (Angas), "cause a quarrel but you have already run" (Fulani). There are 14 examples characterizing various kinds of *women*: "your whole body is pleasant" (young girl), "guinea corn that has spoiled before ripening" (an unmarried non-virgin), "a rag in which disease is wrapped for carrying" or "one who leaves contraceptive medicine on the bed" (a prostitute), "causer of anger" (a co-wife), "ridden by her child and by her husband too" (a nursing mother), "Mother, give the baby your breast" (maternal aunt). *Stepchildren* are regarded as unappreciative, thus "giving you meat is a thankless task." A *grandchild* is seen as "a maker poor of your grandparents," a *child* inseparable from his mother as "a tick," a child born long after the previous child as "savings of God," a child born late in his or her mother's life has it said of him or her, "food at night is better than sleeping hungry" (i.e., going barren), and of a young child it is said, "God protects you from drought" (since no matter how dry things get he has his mother's breast).

1.4. *Personal characteristics.* These make up the largest person category (173 examples). Among the *positively valued* characteristics (45 examples) are the following: an important person, may be referred to as a "grinding stone" (too big to carry in one's pocket), an influential person, as "a horse" (too powerful to be killed by the farmer whose crops he damages), or as "an elephant's buttocks" (crushes any grass it is dragged over), a great man as "an elephant's back" (covered with flies and birds benefitting from him), a generous person as "a crow" (raises someone else's child as his own) or as "a funeral bier" (it carries everyone eventually), a persevering person as "a hut" (though it storms, the hut just stands and takes it), and a father as "a protective wall" (protecting his children like a city wall protects the city).

The epithets give much attention to *negatively valued* characteristics of human beings (103 examples). Among these are the likening of an evil person to "a thorn" (it doesn't distinguish between people), a headstrong person to "a chicken" (pays no attention when told to shoo), a persistent person to "a baby" (he doesn't know the meaning of "no"), a quarrelsome person to "palm fronds" (prickly front, prickly back), a miser to "spoiled guinea corn with no gravy to boot," or to "tamarind fruit that has dried on the tree yet refuses to fall," a hot-tempered person to "a small pot" (things cooked in it boil quickly) or to "a crow turning over and over" (one sees both white and black), a mischief maker to "a war drum" (stirs up people to war "lest we die"), a sponger to "a cattle egret" (depends on cattle for its food), a hypocrite to "an adze" (its sharpness is on the inside), a Don Juan to "a billy goat" (seeks to get himself a brother by copulating with his own mother), a bachelor to "a Malmo tree" (its base/genitals always leak), a scatterbrained person to "a hyena's feast" (no organization), a gossiper to "a bush shrike" (you tell the news before you're asked to), and a person who looks deceptively mild to "a muslin cloth hobbling a horse's feet" (it's soft but it cuts). In addition, it is said of a malicious person that he "would even sell his lame wife's donkey (on which she rides) at the very time they have to flee," and of an indecisive person, "the market finishes, he's still wandering around."

A disappointing person may be called "a broad, shallow body of water" (looks good, but there's no depth), a novice "an ebony walking stick" (very brittle), an easygoing person "a fig tree" (it has no thorns), a destitute person a "drummer for naked people" (who are so poor they can't pay him), and of a man slow to ejaculate when copulating "one who leaves hair on the bed." Of an old man it is said, "he has to depend on stealth" (in place of strength), of a deaf person, "your messenger is a clod of dirt" (he doesn't respond to a call, only when he feels a clod of dirt hit him), and of a nobody, "if he's here we have gravy, if he's not here we still have gravy" (i.e., he makes no difference).

2. *Food and drink.* A second, much smaller, grouping of epithets concerns food and drink (only 18 examples). Of gruel (which is disliked as a substitute for regular food) it is said, "with gruel in your stomach, you sleep hungry," old cassava is called, "Stop! Eat me and you die!" Yams are known as "southerners' food," meat as "lion's food," palm wine that which "drives a boy crazy," and a certain kind of strong tobacco as "the dazer."

3. *Clothing, jewelry, or perfume.* There are in the corpus nine examples of epithets used for clothing, jewelry, or perfume. One kind of cap is called "a firefly," and another, "just right for everyone's head." Of a waistcoat it is said, "you don't even cover the belly button, yet you cost more than a large gown." A kind of small bangle is known as "the preventer of a co-wife's sleep," and metal bracelets or anklets as "we all, the chief's children."

4. *Material objects and implements.* These showed up 30 times in the corpus. A train is called, "scissors through the bush" or "crazy thing from Europe," an arrow, "the cause of covering one's stomach," a gun, "a large drum" (leads to fighting), a fire, "a butcher's mare" (whoever jumps on will jump off first) or "preventer of a person putting his hand down," or, when fire is used for felling trees, "a red axe that keeps chopping even at night." One kind of axe is called "a work finisher," a needle, "preventer of borrowing," and a fishhook, "a fisherman's slave" with the explanation "God is good to you giving you fish, but then you catch in your master's back."

5. *Nonmaterial things.* These also receive attention (18 examples). Study is called "hinderer of work," a loathed thing "a pack rat" (catching you is useless, letting you go is useless), an insuperable task "making a leper untie a donkey," a cock's crow at midnight "the remover of a bachelor's expectation" (i.e., it has gotten too late either to expect or to seek a sex partner), distant drumming "farting while standing up," and the extra nights that a husband is allowed to spend with a new bride "the bride's whip" (with it she gets the advantage over the other wives by depriving them of their normal rotation with their husband).

6. *States or conditions of life.* These are also epithetized (25 examples). A dilemma is likened to "a bachelor at weaning time," foolhardiness is "a blind man turning his head to get a second look" or "a bright eye that can't see," necessity to the fact that "even an old anus must work," restlessness or uneasiness to "the first copulation on marriage day," and hunger to "a sharp, steel tool for cutting out the pulp of a gourd."

7. *Activities.* Thirty epithets in the corpus refer to activities. Helping is called "the chaser away of fighting," warfare "a chief's farming," making a bad thing worse "an old woman giving birth" (the baby is already lying down, the mother too, becomes an invalid), buying on credit "the causer of illness," breaking one's word "Yoruba dickering" (after you accept his offer, he offers less), and marketing "God's communal labor party" or "God's food bowl."

8. *Natural phenomena.* These are the focus of 21 epithets. A storm may be referred to as "the breaker up of a communal labor party" or as "a ruin of wealth," the rainy season as "giver of profit" though the wettest part of the rainy season is called "preventer of work." The morning star may be called "night archer" or "father of stars," night "the hider of secrets" or "the limiter of a stranger's

wanderings," and early morning "the hindquarters of a hedgehog" (black and white mixed).

9.   *Animals*. Animals are epithetized as well (36 examples). Vultures are known as "men who wait for what they expect will come along," the lizard as "rustler of grass roof," the lion as "chief of the bush," the jackal as "professor of the bush," the hedgehog as "thorny animal," the ground squirrel as "the person with only one home is foolish," a flea as "preventer of sleep," driver ants as "expeller of the head of the house," a calf as "broken knees," a camel as "travel slowly, sleep far away," a large ram as "don't eat your own food until you have eaten up your master's," and dog as "you have no hut of your own, yet you fight to protect the home."

10. *Plants and plant products*. There are 26 examples citing plants and plant products (except food plants). Of the yellow poppy it is said, "you refuse God's water," and of the tobacco blossom, "in the mouth the flower is better than the tobacco." Among trees, the hairy thorn apple is called, "drive a boy crazy," the shrub *kirni* – "the killer of poison" (a brew from it is supposed to ward off poison). Of the palm tree it is said. "resting places are not set up at your base" (because they provide no shade), and of the twining fig tree, "get close to you and you kill" (it twines around and kills other trees). A kind of weed is called, "taker of a farm from a lazy person," and a hard rooted plant "a breaker of hoes."

11. *Places*. Finally, there are ten examples of epithets for places. Each major city has at least one major epithet, such as, "ruler over the land" (Daura), "entrance hut for those going out to see the world" (Zaria), "tobacco that enters one's heart" (Lagos—i.e., just as hard to give up as the smoking habit) "great Hausa one" (Kano) and "fodder grass visible from afar" (Katsina). Other places are known as "pregnant woman" (the world—i.e., no one knows what it will bring forth), "home of the fear of God" (the Koranic school), "a dog's heaven" (a small place in the midst of a crowd), and "a woman's drum" (her thigh—since women slap their thighs when they laugh).

Insight into Hausa Values and Worldview

As mentioned in the introduction, my interest is in what and how often subjects appear in the epithets and what is said about them. My assumption is that such information will, especially if used in conjunction with studies of other such materials (e.g., Kraft 1975), give insight into the structure and content of the psychocultral "deep structure" on which Hausa life is (or has in the recent past been) based.

If this assumption is correct we can, for example, tentatively conclude from studying epithets that either 1) Hausas are conditioned by their culture to show considerably more concern for people than for any other category of beings or objects, or that 2) Hausas consider epithetic expression to be more appropriately applied to people than to the other categories. Just under seventy percent (360) of the examples in this sample apply directly to people. In addition, thirty epithets relate to activities—nearly all of them people-activities—and twenty-five more to conditions or states that, again, are largely related to people. Personal characteristics are particularly stressed (173 examples), especially negative ones (103 examples). Of the various types of peoples in Hausa society, one would guess from the epithets that much attention is paid to chiefs (36 examples) and to officials in general (41 more).

Epithetic attention is much less on animals (36), natural phenomena (21), flora (26), miscellaneous material objects (57) and nonmaterial things (18).

It is intriguing to note how much attention is given to negatively valued personal characteristics. One might conclude that Hausa people have a jaundiced view of humanity. I think, however, that another explanation is more likely. I suspect that epithets, like riddles (see Kraft 1975), proverbs and fables, are important means of enculturating children into the approved values of the culture and then of maintaining social control. Undoubtedly many more would go astray from approved behavior if it weren't that they feared the nickname or other negative label that such straying would win them. Ridicule is a powerful force for social control even when it is stylized, particularly if it is phrased in a clever and catchy way.

The message of the society through the epithets would seem to be *don't be a person who is* evil, cantankerous, contrary, headstrong, treacherous, untrustworthy, two-faced, deceitful, mischievous, a slacker, a sponger, a wastrel, a spendthrift, a bachelor, etc. But above all, don't be a miser or hot-tempered. There is specific disdain shown for immoral women and bachelors, for certain kinds of chiefs and other officials, and for members of other tribes. In addition, there are warnings against persistence, co-wives, philandering, hypocrisy, indecision and disorganization. Uselessness in any area of life is ridiculed. Thus, no person wants to risk being referred to as "a nose without a hole in it."

On the other hand, the society says through the epithets *do be a person who is* persevering, helpful, dogged, silent, protective of one's children, etc. But, above all, be generous, liberal with possessions and helpful to others. How nice it would be to be known some day as "an elephant's back" (covered with flies and birds benefiting from him)!

Not all epithetic material is, however, didactic. Much is simply descriptive of what is, rather than recommending what ought to be. But this, too, tends to be clever, perceptive and, frequently, revealing of a perspective on reality that would not have occurred to us. There is, furthermore, plenty of evidence of the kind of culture that has produced these epithets. There are frequent allusions to material objects, social structure, political organization, flora and fauna, etc. There is even evidence of impact of culture change in the attention given in this corpus to railroad trains (7 examples). Undoubtedly, an updated collection would show much more such evidence.

A cursory comparison of the findings of this study with other folkloric materials that I am working on shows a general similarity between these emphases and those of proverbs, fables and, to a lesser extent, riddles. Such things as the focus on generosity and the other positive traits, the condemnation of greed, temper, etc., and the concern about chiefs and other officials are quite predictable from exposure to Hausa fables. Many of the people-traits specified in the epithets are generalized into animal stereotypes in the fables. Proverbs seem to fall somewhere in between the fables and epithets with respect to their focus on both chiefs and animals. The same kind of earthiness noted in the epithets is evident in fables and proverbs, as is the same deep insight into people and life. Hausa values seem to be, on the whole, more clearly stated in epithets and proverbs than in fables. One thing I was surprised to find almost completely absent from this corpus of epithets is the rather frequent reference to God and supernatural beings that is found in the fables and, to a lesser extent, in the proverbs.

But cultural interpretations, especially of stylized materials such a epithets, proverbs, riddles and fables, should never be made in isolation from what is known of the culture from more direct anthropological observation. Thus, this study is not intended to call into question any of the conclusions solidly based on anthropological fieldwork. But neither should the overall understanding that we seek of a culture be denied the input of ethnolinguistic research. It is hoped that this study may contribute something of value to that overall understanding of Hausa culture that we seek.

COMMUNICATION

CHAPTER 14

THE NEW WINE OF INDEPENDENCE

Reprinted here with permission from
World Vision Magazine 15:7–9 (February 1971)

We had packed and closed last suitcase. We called the porter, had someone call a cab for us and checked out of the hotel. The date was July 29, 1966. My family and I were in Geneva, Switzerland, about to board a Swiss Air jet to complete our trip to Nigeria. At the airport I went to the counter and handed the agent my ticket. She seemed rather surprised and puzzled. Finally she told me Nigeria was in turmoil that day. The military leader had been assassinated. The second coup that year had taken place, and no planes were landing in Nigeria until further notice.

What should we do? We had worked hard to earn the privilege of returning to Nigeria. But does one take a wife and four children into such a situation—into such uncertainty? Or does one turn around and go back home?

As we waited several more days in Geneva we wondered: what does all this mean? We wondered four days later as we finally boarded the plane and headed for the unknown. We wondered as we disembarked at Lagos, Nigeria, and noticed the soldiers with their machine guns all around us. We wondered several times during that year in Nigeria—is it worth the risk to work in Africa during these times of great and rapid upheaval? For these are times of continual upset, times of turmoil, times when the old familiar rules of operation do not work anymore. We wondered what all of this could mean to us as individuals and to the work of Christ in Africa.

These are truly unsettled times for Africa and for the work of Christ there. These are times when the new wine of independence is bursting the old colonial wineskins. These are times when the church of Jesus Christ in Africa is being forced to rethink its position. Perhaps it is this rethinking that God is seeking to stimulate.

In the days of colonial empires it seemed the natural thing for missions to pattern themselves after the colonialists. We already dressed like them, acted like them, talked like them, and in most other ways appeared like them. We frequently seemed to have just as high an opinion of our own culture and just as low an opinion of the cultures of the Africans as did the colonialists. Furthermore, we built houses as did the colonialists, established schools and hospitals as they did and hired laborers for the same tasks. We traveled as they did, learned the African languages as poorly as they did and, all in all, impressed Africans more with the similarities between us and the colonialists than with the differences between us.

But now the situation is changed. The new wine of independence has burst the old colonialist wineskins, and the colonialists have left most of the countries of Africa. However, missionaries have remained, confident in the belief that whatever might have been the attitude of the colonialists, the work of missions in Africa is not finished. And many Africans have been glad the missionaries stayed because they have learned over the years that there are in fact differences between missionaries and colonialists. Yet the temptation on the part of missions to continue their operations in terms of the "time-honored" methods developed in the days when missionaries and colonialists worked hand in hand has often been too strong to resist. Many Africans are proclaiming loudly that this is a new day and should be characterized by new approaches. Time-honored methods are no longer enough; old wineskins are no longer adequate to contain the fermenting new wine.

Many missions have become confused and are running from the situation. "Turn the church over to the nationals," they say, "let them solve their own problems." And to such missions frequently "in indigenization" becomes merely a mask for irresponsibility. But is this what the situation in modern Africa is intended to mean to the church today?

Some other missions have simply moved from the front of the room to the back of the room. Instead of continuing to direct the church from the front, they now pull strings from the back, and the indigenous church in these areas is really just a puppet church.

Some missions have refused to change at all. They still build their mission stations, establish churches, schools and hospitals patterned after the old colonial days. And in these missions whether overtly or covertly, it is the foreign missionary who still calls all the shots—in God's name.

There is a growing recognition, however, that today's new wine demands new wineskins—that the turmoil in modern Africa must be taken seriously by Christian missions. Many are coming to realize the model approach to Christian missionary work in Africa should not be the colonial conqueror's approach that demanded allegiance because of the power and prestige of Western culture and the white of their skins. Many are realizing that our model ought to be that of the Son of God who humbled himself to become man in order to win (not demand) a hearing in a world of men.

Can it be that this is what God is trying to get across to us? I believe that it is. I believe that the meaning of the present turmoil for the Christian church in Africa is to drive us back to a reconsideration of just what we are doing in Africa. Turmoil could force us to compare what we are doing as against the example of Christ who came into the world not as a *master* but as a *servant*, not as God but as man. I think the great cultural prestige with which we entered Africa predisposed Africans to receive the Christian message gladly because of our prestige rather than because of the truth of the message. This great prestige and the great response which it has occasioned have kept many missions from really evaluating their work until the current state of turmoil descended upon us. It is difficult to question this kind of success unless we are forced to do so.

Let me illustrate from my own experience some contrasts between the old colonialist approach and what might be called the "incarnational approach." I was sitting with a missionary one day in his lovely home. I asked, "Don't you feel guilty to have such a fine home?" He answered, "No, of course not, the Africans expect us to live this way." And he was absolutely right! The Africans expected us to play God—to lord it over them, to live in mansions, to boss them around. They felt themselves to be inferior and us to be superior. The colonialists had taught them this. And they expected us to fit right into this pattern.

Imagine the surprise of the Nigerians when we packed up our belongings, locked up our home and went seven miles into the bush to live with a Nigerian family in a Nigerian home for a couple of weeks. After we had been there a few days the head of the house asked me, "Now, just why have you come?" He continued, "Why, if I had a nice house like you have I wouldn't even step outside, much less come way out here to live! No other missionary does this, how come you do?" He was genuinely puzzled. But at the same time God was breaking through to him in much the same way that he broke through to all mankind in Jesus who moved out of his heavenly home to live in the world with men.

Then there was the time when some of the Nigerian church leaders asked me to preach. They were working out the monthly preaching schedule and they asked if I would speak twice a month. I said, "No." They asked "Three times a month?" I said, "Not even once." They said, "How come? Every other missionary we've known agrees to preach regularly, why won't you?" "You can preach yourselves," I replied, "and I refuse to compete with you. I'm here to help, not to compete or show off. I only want to do things you cannot do for yourselves."

They didn't understand then, but later they came to realize that I meant to treat them as equals, not as inferiors. I meant to treat them as those who could know and serve God in their own way, not as people who had to conform to my way.

On another occasion the leaders came to me to ask me to translate some songs for them. I said, "What kind of songs?" They said, "Christian songs like they have at the other churches of this area." I asked, "Must Christian songs have Western tunes? Can't God be glorified through your music?" Then I asked, "What do your people who have never heard the Christian message say about God when they hear Western hymn tunes put to Nigerian words?" They replied, "That this God is a White man's God." I asked, "Do you believe he's only the White Man's God?" "No," they answered, "he's our God as well." So they began producing Christian hymns using their own music and their own words in order to show that the Christian God is their God as well.

Some time later a national evangelist returned from a preaching tour and told me, "Mr. Kraft, the most amazing thing happened to us while we were in the village of Himakay. No one has ever preached there before, and we began a preaching service by singing some of our Christian songs. All of a sudden the chief stopped us, saying, 'Where did you learn all of these songs?' I said that we sing them all the time in our church down in the valley. He replied, 'Why our young girls have been singing these songs for months. Who is Jesus Christ, anyway?'" And the gospel spread very rapidly throughout that whole area because these church leaders had followed the pattern of a God who was willing to enter their life, rather than that of a mission which proclaimed a "White Man's God" through Western hymns.

"Fear God, fear the White Man" is an old proverb in this part of Africa. And it means that the White Man is to be respected and treated like God. You do not contradict or oppose God, or a White Man. You are not impolite to God, or to a White Man. Nor do you ever accuse either God or a White Man of having made a mistake. Doing so would break all the rules of Nigerian courtesy. But one day in a church meeting one of the church leaders got up and told me off! I had made a mistake, so he told me off in no uncertain terms. His people were so embarrassed they nearly pulled his clothes off trying to get him to sit down. But he had learned to live by a new set of rules that recognized I am just a human being and not God. He had gotten to know me well enough to know that I respected him and his opinion and that if I made a mistake I would be willing to make it right. He knew that if he pointed out my mistake to me I would be grateful to him rather than being angry at him. He did not feel free to talk that way to a missionary whom he equated with God, but he was free to speak that way to a missionary whom he knew as a human being.

In these ways the new wine is bursting the old wineskins in this part of Africa, forcing us to be honest in our approach to missionary work. These Africans are respectable fellow human beings. And we are but men—fallible, sinful, human—not God. Neither are their customs necessarily inferior to ours—just different—since our culture is no more endorsed by God than theirs, and their culture is just as usable a vehicle of God's grace as is ours.

The new situation in Africa is forcing us to go as witnesses, not as spiritual colonialists. It is forcing us to win a hearing, not to demand it merely because our skin is white and our culture is prestigious. The new situation is saying to us that we must first prove ourselves to be worthwhile persons before the Africans will feel inclined to listen to anything we have to say about God. We have been placed in this new role because the new wine could not be contained in the old wineskins.

Africa is saying to the church and missions today: "Send us a new breed of missionaries. Send us those who will model themselves after Christ, not after the colonialists. Send us those who will respect us as people and approach us as equals, not inferiors. Send us those who think enough of us to learn our language and our culture and to help us understand Christianity in terms of our life and customs, not as a technique for converting us to Western culture.

"We are as proud of ourselves as you are of yourselves—of our life and culture, of our past, present and future. And we invite you of the West to share in our life but not to dominate it. And we invite only those who will share without dominating."

These are very exciting and tremendously challenging days for Africa. The meaning I see for the church and missions may be expressed in a paraphrase of the question certain Greeks asked the disciple Phillip long ago: "Sir, we have seen and heard and talked to you long enough. Now, may we please see Jesus?" (Jn. 12:21).

The day of missions is not over in Africa but the day of the kind of missions we have known for so long may well be. The day of the missionary is not over in Africa. But the day when it was considered sufficient for a missionary merely to have a call and a knowledge of the Bible is gone.

Today's missionary to Africa needs to be more highly trained in cultural studies than in theological. He must be trained to the point where he realizes that he knows virtually nothing of the cultural world of the people he seeks to reach. He must be trained to the point where he will sit and listen to and learn from the people he seeks to reach. He must be conditioned to realize that the texts for his vocal witness to these people must come, as Christ's did, from their life and experience, not from his own. He must meet them where they are, not demand that they meet him where he is.

I sat with a Nigerian chief some ten years ago and asked him what his people believed about God before the missionary came. He told me:

"Once god was near. He and his son lived with us and walked and talked and ate and slept in our homes. All was well in those days. No one lied or cheated or stole or ran off with another man's wife. But then one day god and his son chanced to eat in the home of a family who did not take care to clean their dishes properly. God's son ate from a dirty dish, got sick, and died. God left in a huff! And we haven't heard from him since. At planting time, at harvest time, at times of illness and tragedy, we prepare the best kind of food we can prepare and the best kind of drink we can prepare, and offer it to god at one of our altars. But we don't know if he still listens or if he cares. He seems to have left us helpless and hopeless and to grant us no reply to our petitions." Then the chief turned to me and asked, "White Man, do you know where god has gone?"

This question is still being asked today by Africans and others. Where has God gone?

And in these same exciting but demanding times God, too, is still asking, "Whom shall I send? Who will go to show the people in ways they will understand that I am still within reach?"

CHAPTER 15

WHAT YOU HEARD IS
NOT WHAT I MEANT

Reprinted here with permission from
World Vision Magazine 13(4):10–12 (1969)

The young man from Liberia looked at me in disbelief. Nobody had ever told him that he could remain one hundred percent African and still be accepted by God—on the basis of faith alone.

He thought the main aim of Christian missions was to make a European out of him. He could not conceive of someone being totally African and yet a Christian. He had heard the message of Christ and accepted it (and, as far as I could tell, accepted it sincerely), but as a part of his overall conversion to western culture.

What he heard was something different from what was intended. Some miscommunication had caused him to understand John 3:16 something as follows: "God so loves Europeans that he accepts as Christian any African who turns his back on his own customs and becomes converted to western culture."

And I have heard essentially the same thing from enough other Africans to know that his interpretation of the Christian message is far from unique. What they have heard is not what we meant. We say one thing, they hear another.

And the really important thing in the communication process is not what is said but what the listener hears.

We have all experienced the difficulties of trying to communicate something to another person. One person says or does something. The listener or observer hears or understands something completely different. This is the kind of situation that the apostle Paul and his co-worker Barnabas found themselves in when they healed the crippled man at Lystra. They were saying by healing the man that "God is concerned with alleviating the suffering of a crippled man." What the people heard was that "the gods had come in human form"—and they began to worship Paul and Barnabas.

This was the ordinary type of communication problem experienced by anyone who tries to talk to someone else. But this problem was compounded by a language and culture problem of rather large proportions (just as are many of the misunderstandings that occur between missionaries and Nigerians). From the point of view of the people of Lystra, only the gods (not men) could heal a cripple. If Paul and Barnabas were gods they must be worshipped. The thing the people understood was quite different from what Paul and Barnabas intended. Fortunately, Paul and Barnabas got the benefit of some feedback. They found out what the people understood and were therefore able to take steps to straighten out the miscommunication.

Not always, though, in a land such as Nigeria, where the people do their utmost to keep from offending us, do we get the feedback we need to correct our communication mistakes. The Nigerians around us are true to their culture's value-system which demands that they quietly accept—without criticism or any attempt to influence—every decision made by a "social superior." They refuse to tell us when we make mistakes or when we are being misinterpreted. Thus we are often unsure of the kind of impression our words and works are making.

Some feedback is coming, however. A southern Nigerian invited my wife and me and three missionary candidates to share a meal with him. Before the meal he prayed, "Lord, help these men to realize that it is not *they* who are taking you to Africa, but you who are taking *them*."

When we asked what he had in mind when he prayed that way, he explained:

When missionaries first came to my country, they spoke of the God who created the world as if he were a different God from the one we already knew about. We listened and compared what we heard and read in the Bible about this God and discovered that he is the very same God we had always known about. We received many new insights from the missionaries and especially we heard that we could come to know God personally through Jesus Christ. But everyone except the missionaries realized that your God is the same as our God.

In other words, our God had brought the missionaries to add to our understanding and commitment. The missionaries had not brought a new God with them. And this is what I would like these young people to realize before they go so that they don't waste so much effort trying to change our ways but devote themselves to building something worthwhile on the foundations that are already there.

We missionaries have steadfastly maintained that the God we serve and proclaim is not merely "the white man's God." But many understand our message as proclamation of this kind of God, because we place emphasis on the discontinuities between African society and "the" Christian way of life (which we often equate naively with our western way of life) rather than helping the African churches to build their Christianity solidly on African foundations.

A Sierra Leonean who was hired by his mission to write articles for various church publications was brought to the United States to study journalism in order to become more effective. He was also given opportunities to speak in home churches. He got along quite well for awhile—as long as he refrained from saying some critical things about the mission that he knew were keenly felt by his people. But as time went by he found it more and more difficult to keep from speaking up.

Finally he wrote to the mission officials explaining that he felt he had thus far been working for them with a muzzle on but his conscience would no longer permit him to remain quiet on certain issues which he felt were hindering the work of Christ among his people. He lost his scholarship—in spite of the fact that he had been remarkably open and aboveboard. He had been taught by the missionaries that "love does not insist on its own way; it is not irritable or resentful." But he discovered that even in working for Christian missions, "he who pays the piper calls the tune."

Another time I chanced to hear from a Nigerian Christian a proverb that I hadn't heard before: "Fear God, fear the white man." I asked this man if he had made this saying up or if it was a widely used proverb. He assured me it was one of their most important doctrines and that, if anything, the white man (who is close at hand and unpredictable) was considered more to be feared than God (who is far away and good).

His people had no other way to explain the European than to assume that he is very close to God and gets his tremendous ability, power and confidence directly from God. It is difficult, he said, for him to tell a white man when the latter makes a mistake. It is difficult for him to feel at home in the presence of a white man. He is afraid of white men and will believe anything we say (even if he knows it is wrong) and do anything we tell him to do—because to him and his people we are to be feared as much as or more than God himself.

And many missionaries seem to feel it is proper for them to fit this role and "play God" as they are expected to do. "But they *expect* us to live and act this way," they say, as if this justified it.

This attitude of putting the white man and God in the same category is similar to that of the people of Lystra who felt compelled to worship Paul and Barnabas. From the point of view of many Africans the things we do can only be done by God. We must be no less categorical than Paul and Barnabas in rejecting this kind of reverence. Yet we often allow ourselves to communicate the impression that we believe we are in the same category as God, that our word is his word, that our will is his will. What are we communicating about God? We, like Paul and Barnabas, dare not leave without getting this one straightened out!

A missionary in Cameroon left his mission compound and went to live in the village for a little while to learn the language and customs. He tried to discover what it was like to be inside their skins, to be a part of their world. He tried to learn their approach to life, their system of values, how to communicate the gospel in terms they would not misinterpret.

The people were amazed. "How come you are different from all the others?" they asked him. "We see Europeans rushing by on the road this way and rushing back that way, but they never stop here to spend time with us. We see Europeans trying to learn our language by inviting a schoolboy into their missions to teach them, but they never come here to find out what our life is really like. What makes you different? You are interested in us—in understanding our ways and language. Your God is the one we want to follow."

Many missionaries come thousands of miles to Africa to preach the gospel of Christ but never move the extra few feet off the mission compound, or out of the shell of western culture which enwraps them, in order to get close to those they hope to communicate with.

Many missionaries spend hour after dedicated hour studying the Scriptures in order to proclaim the "unsearchable riches of Christ," but hardly spend any time at all in studying and really getting to know and appreciate the customs and culture of the people. They make almost no attempt to enter the world of the people to whom they come. In their attempts to communicate the Christian message they resemble a broken electrical cord—plugged in well at one end but only live wires at the other end, able to carry the electricity far enough to create some confusion but not far enough to accomplish its purpose.

Many missionaries content themselves with not learning the language of the people they work among, or with learning it so poorly that every utterance is like a kick in the shins to the person being spoken to. (This is why so many Nigerians would rather speak English to us.)

Many missionaries give their lives to take Christ to people who live in a different world but succeed only in transplanting a portion of the western world to Africa—inviting Africans to join this world to find Christ.

Many mission boards require their candidates to be well prepared theologically and practically but do not even suggest, much less require, that their candidates take advantage of excellent insights into the thinking of non-western peoples and the workings of non-western societies available to them in the cultural anthropology courses offered by many American colleges and universities today. Nor, often, do they require their candidates to learn the linguistic techniques now being taught for mastering difficult non-western languages. These boards send their candidates thousands of miles without the ability to move those last few steps to genuinely plug themselves in at the other end.

What are we really communicating? Impressions of condemnation, or of genuine understanding, love and concern? An impression that God accepts only those who adopt our way of life, or that he accepts all who come to him in faith? An impression that we serve God or that we *are* God?

CHAPTER 16

WHAT IS GOD TRYING TO DO?

Reprinted here with permission from
Theology News and Notes 23:9–11 (March 1977)

As evangelicals our concern for and dedication to the Scriptures as the Word of God often leads us to neglect what I believe to be a very important question. We concern ourselves with the intent of God and of the original authors when we try to interpret individual passages. But have we come to a satisfactory answer concerning the overall intent of God in inspiring Scripture in the first place? What was/is he trying to do anyway?

Many people do not ask this question because they assume they know. It is obvious, isn't it, that God is trying to display his mighty power How impressive God is in using human language to convey divine truth. How majestic is the language of the Bible. How appropriate it is that God's Word be considered great literature. Many, in short, look at God's Word much as Moses must have looked at God on the mountain. Moses stood in awe of God. Even so we stand in awe of God's Word. We memorize it and thus hide it in our hearts. We are excited over the fact that that Word has been recorded and preserved and translated down through thousands of years. We are convinced that that Word must be translated into the thousands of contemporary languages in the world today. So we provide large sums of money to support those who dedicate themselves to translating God's Word. This we should do, but for what purpose?

Is God content with simply making an impression? Is his revealing of himself limited to spectaculars like the giving of the Law on the mount? Is he pleased when people simply admire him or tremble in his presence? If so, why did he become man? Why did he commit his revelation to human language rather than developing a divine language for it?

Years ago a vain king wished to produce a literary monument to himself. At the same time a threatened archbishop sought to find some way of preserving a dying church from the inroads being made in it by the vital Christianity of another denomination. These two got together to plan and carry out the production of a literary masterpiece which would at the same time be a monument to the king and an aid to the archbishop in his attempt to compete with the vital Christianity of 16th century Presbyterianism. They gathered a group of translators who would carry out their bidding and succeeded in producing what we have come to know as the *King James Version.*

The product that resulted from these efforts was and is very impressive. It was not a new translation so much as it was a revision of the *Bishop's Bible.* It was, therefore, an intra-language product rather than an inter-language product. It was specifically designed to alter the more pedantic language of the *Bishop's Bible* in the direction of literary excellence. The result was and is very impressive. But I have a question: Is this what God intended?

Nearly three centuries later another group of men concerned about the translation of the Bible got together. They found themselves reacting against translation procedures that had gotten so loose that they tended toward irresponsibility in conveying the intention of the original writings. Their concern was for accuracy in the translation of the Word of God. They expressed this concern by producing in extremely literal *English Revised Version* which was followed later by the *American Standard Version.* The scholarship and effort extended by these men are truly impressive. Their dedication to faithfulness is likewise impressive. Their product is a masterpiece of word-for-word literal correspondence to the original document. This version has been characterized as—Good Greek and Hebrew, but poor English. Very impressive, but is this what God intended?

Half a century later a similar group of scholars got together to produce a revision of the *American Standard Version* that would not be quite so clumsy in its phraseology nor so archaic in its language. Their product, the *Revised Standard Version,* is another masterpiece of scholarly endeavor and a distinct improvement over the *American Standard* and *King James Versions* in its updating of the language. It is an impressive translation, especially of the Old Testament. Those whose concern is for the literalness of the representation in English of the Hebrew and Greek originals are often quite impressed with the *Revised Standard Version.* But no one would ever mistake it for an original production in English. Very impressive, but is this what God intends?

Does God Understand Radar?

J. B. Phillips, as a pastor, became heir to the kind of impression that people got concerning God from the use of such translations. He found that his people were assuming that God is a foreigner or out of date or, perhaps, that he has a speech defect (e.g., he can't say "has" only "hath"). Once during the war, Phillips asked a group of young people if they would answer a question quickly, by giving the first thing that came to their minds. They agreed, so he said:

> Do you think God understands Radar? They all said "no" and then, of course, roared with laughter at how ridiculous the answer was! But the "snap answer" showed me what I suspected—that at the back of their minds there was an idea of

> God as an old gentleman who lived in the past and was rather bewildered by modern progress.[1]

They had gotten the impression, largely from the Bible translations that they continually heard, that God was at least 300 years behind the times. They heard archaic language when the Bible was read, when prayers were offered, and at other places in the church ritual. Could a God who spoke like that possibly understand the latest technological developments?

Phillips, perceiving that such an impression was not the one that God intended, endeavored to produce a translation that does not content itself with making a good impression on the hearers. He sought to produce a translation that would communicate as effectively in today's language as the original word of God communicated in the original languages. In order to succeed in this, he suggests, a translation

> must not sound like a translation at all. If it is skillfully done, and we are not previously informed, we should be quite unaware that it is a translation, even though the work we are reading is far distant from us in both time and place.[2]

Phillips' aim was quite different from the aims of King James and the Archbishop of Canterbury who sought to produce from God's Word a literary masterpiece that would unite the 17th Century Anglican Church. Phillips' aims were likewise different from those of the literal translators of the American *Standard Version* and Revised Standard Version. They sought to simply transfer into English the word forms and grammatical patterns of the original languages in the belief that such a half translation by and for scholars could adequately convey God's intention. Literal translations are like bridges built only halfway across rivers. The one who seeks to use them must on his own get from the opposite bank to the point where the bridge ends. For they are in "Translator's English—that horrible mixture of ancient and modern which has never been spoken or written in any country at any time."[3] Phillips' aim was rather "to produce in the hearts and minds of [contemporary] readers an effect equivalent to that produced by the author upon his original readers."[4] That is, Phillips understood that God intended to communicate, not simply to impress his readers.

Such a purpose on the part of God seems to be inherent in the fact that in the original languages, especially in Greek, it was not the literary language that God chose to become the vehicle of his message but the slangy, common people's language. There is, I believe, a message to us in this concerning the kind of Bible translation that is in English most like the originals were in Hebrew and Greek. Could it be that we have allowed ourselves to be misled into believing that archaic or literal translations that merely impress people are good translations? Isn't it more in keeping with the spirit and form of the original documents to use translations that convey the original meanings in such a way that people don't feel that the language

---

[1] J. B. Phillips, *Plain Christianity* (London: Epworth, 1954), 65.

[2] J. B. Phillips, "Translator's Foreword" in *The New Testament in Modern English* (London: Geoffrey Bles, 1958), ix.

[3] Phillips 1954, p. 47.

[4] Phillips 1958, p. ix.

is strange? Doesn't God seek to impress by communicating rather than to make a good impression at the expense of communication?

That Man Is Not Talking
to Anyone

A translation, like any other vehicle of communication, is subject to certain rules of effectiveness. If a translation is to communicate it must communicate *to* someone. Effective communication does not happen when words are simply flung out into the air. Utterances need to be *aimed* if they are to achieve their desired goal. We have, however, often assumed that God's Word is above and beyond the ordinary rules of communication.

How glibly we often quote Isaiah 55:11 to justify some poorly conceived, inadequate attempt at communication of God's message on our part. God has said that his Word will not return to him void. But is this because there is some magic in the Word that makes it impervious to the rules of human communication? Or, is there a difference between God's Word "flung out" without reference to the principles of effective communication and God's Word effectively communicated?

John V. Taylor points up the difference between simply speaking and speaking *to* by recalling a discussion between himself and his son. He says,

> When my son decided to give up on the church he said to me, "Father that man is saying all of the right things, but he is not saying them to anybody. He does not know where I am, and it would never occur to him to ask."[5]

Communication specialists point to the fact that effective communication must be "receptor-oriented." That is, in order to be effective it needs to be presented in a way that is acceptable to and appreciated by those to whom it is directed. If the communication is in another language or in an unappreciated style of their own language, it will not he effective in communicating the intention of the communicator. This principle applies just as much to translation as it does to any other form of communication. A Bible translation that is in some language other than the one in which the receptors ordinarily function communicates something other than the communicator intended.

If the language in which the communication is phrased is a literary, formalistic kind of language, the communication will be indelibly affected by this fact. If the language is a technical kind of language, or an archaic kind of language, the communication will be affected by these facts. Such attitudes as snobbishness, unconcern, foreignness and the like are often communicated more through the style of language used than through the words spoken. If the language conveys to a given set of receptors that the message is directed primarily to someone else rather than to them, even the message that God gave his life to make relevant to common people will come across to them as a message directed to someone else.

---

[5] Unpublished lecture delivered at Fuller Theological Seminary in 1971.

The same is true of translations. A translation must be directed *to* some group or it risks the possibility of missing every group. If a translation is in a language that is maximally intelligible only to those who have a seminary education (as in the case of literal translations), those who have not had such schooling will often feel that God's message is directed to someone other than themselves.

In spite of Isaiah 55:11, much human experience would seem to indicate that even God's Word when not communicated properly does "return void." Even God's Word, apparently, needs to be made specific if it is to have its intended impact (see Jn. 1:14). Contemporary Bible translators recognize this fact and give their lives to produce translations that will have the kind of communicational impact on today's hearers that the originals had on the original hearers.

God Speaks My Language

The ultimate test of translation, then, is in the *impact* it makes upon those who hear it. It may be sufficient for a piece of great literature to make a great impression on the hearer. But this is not a high enough standard for the Word of God. God seeks to influence people's thinking and behavior. He seeks to communicate love and to elicit love in response. At times, as on Mount Sinai or on the Mount of Transfiguration, he does seek to impress people. But overall he is not content with simply making a good impression. His primary method seems to be through "still small voices" (1 Kg. 19:12), where people become aware of the message without ever noticing the vehicle through which that message comes.

It was like this in the Incarnation as well. Those who were looking for God to appear in spectacular form were often disappointed in Jesus because he ordinarily looked and acted so unspectacularly. Likewise, many down through the centuries have been unimpressed with the kind of language and grammar in which the biblical message was originally couched. Translators have often assumed that people could not respect God's Word if it were translated into a common, sometimes even ungrammatical and crude style of English equivalent to that of Koine Greek. So they have, in translation, attempted to rectify the situation by translating into "respectable" English. Such translators have produced Bible translations in elevated language and proper grammar. But in so doing they have diverted their own and their hearers' attention from the message to the form of the language in which the message is contained. This is similar to paying more attention to the riverbanks than to the water for the sake of which those banks exist.

But for those translators of God's Word who line themselves up with the communicative purpose and method of God the ultimate compliment is reserved. They alone hear the excitement in the voices of those who first realize that God can, after all, speak their language.

"Didn't our hearts burn within us?" asked the disciples on the road to Emmaus (Lk. 24:32). This is the response of those who first hear God speaking their own language. This is the response of those who hear God speaking to them, not simply above them or in their vicinity. The task of translation is the task of communication. As communication must be receptor-oriented if it is to elicit the intended response, so translation must be receptor-oriented.

Fortunately, it is now becoming more and more possible to obtain translations that genuinely communicate in English. For many years we have supported Bible translators overseas to produce for the speakers of other languages translations that communicate far better than the English translations that we use in our churches. Now, at long last, we are getting translations in English as good as those in use in many of the smaller languages overseas.

Can pastors any longer be content to use translations that give radically wrong impressions about God? Can we refuse to use the best, most highly communicative translations simply because we as Bible students have learned in seminary to understand (more or less) the literal translation? People are dying for lack of a God made specific. Can we be content to allow this to happen?

Correctness of a translation does not rest in its literalness or in the impression that it makes upon people. Correctness, rather, lies in the equivalence between the message understood by the receptors and the original intent of the authors of Scripture. This equivalence depends to no small degree on the ease with which the message flows through the linguistic vehicles that are the home territory of the receptors. A primary result of such equivalence, then, is an equivalence of involvement on the part of contemporary hearers in the cause for which the original hearers gave their all (Nida and Taber 1969:173).

The message is difficult and demanding—we can do nothing about this. The linguistic and cultural forms through which that message flowed to the original hearers, however, were not strange or foreign to them. Nor should they be to contemporary hearers. Translations that are "dynamically equivalent" to the originals are not the latest heresy but the latest hope for a dying world to hear once again the message of God in intelligible form. Most of what pastors give their lives for—to reincarnate God's message of life in a contemporary world—is compromised by antique Bible translations and antique ritual and hymnology. If there is heresy in Bible translations in use today it is more in those that communicate that God is out-of-date, foreign, stammering and irrelevant than in those that present him as living and contemporary.

God risked misunderstanding by becoming human enough to be intelligible to humans. He risked misunderstanding by committing his Word to living languages. The result was a movement that "turned the world upside down" (Acts 17:6). Jerome gave himself to translating God's Word into "vulgar" (common people's) Latin so that Latin speaking people could participate in the livingness of the Christian movement. When the church refused to translate and adapt the Vulgate to new situations, two things happened: (1) people came to revere the *form* of God's Word more than to obey its message (which they could no longer understand), and (2) the church turned from living communication to the preservation of dead ritual.

Luther, then, like Jerome, gave himself to producing a "dynamic equivalence" translation of God's Word in German. There was a spurt of life as Germans began to hear God speaking their language. But soon, through the same failure to adapt to new linguistic and cultural situations, reverence for the Word and church ritual replaced intelligent understanding of and obedience to God's message. And the church in Germany passed from a contemporary experience of life with God to the mummifying of past life.

The same process has happened throughout Europe, the Near East and much of America. But we have the opportunity to choose more wisely today—if we will. We can choose for ourselves and for our congregations Bible translations that communicate God's message more like the originals. We are not locked into the use of impressive but misleading translations like *King James Version, American Standard Version* and *Revised Standard Version.* We have *Phillips* translation, *Today's English Version, New English Bible, Living Bible* and others to prove to us and to those we lead that, after all, God can even speak English!

CHAPTER 17

THE INCARNATION, GOD'S MODEL FOR CROSS-CULTURAL COMMUNICATION

A slightly revised version of two articles originally published in *Evangelical Missions Quarterly* 9:205-216 and 277-284 (Summer and Fall 1973), as "God's Model for Cross-Cultural Communication — The Incarnation," and "The Incarnation, Cross-Cultural Communication and Communication Theory." Reprinted here with permission.

What is your communications batting average? If you act the way the nationals think you would act, then you can be pretty sure your average is about zero. How can this be? Isn't this our role? Aren't we supposed to live up to the expectations of the nationals in a consistent, predictable manner? In this, one of the most perceptive anthropological articles written in regard to missions, Charles Kraft challenges the stereotype. He forces us to reconsider that which we have previously assumed and taken for granted. His supreme example for rethinking the missionary role is Jesus Christ, for in Jesus "the stereotyped God broke out of the stereotype."

Roles and Stereotyping

A major problem for today's missionaries who seek to communicate the gospel in terms of the culture of the society to which they go is that of the role they should assume. To the unreflective, perhaps, this will not appear to be a problem, since he or she may assume that it will suffice for them to simply fit into the assigned role of "missionary." Perhaps, however, they would not be so unconcerned if they understood how adversely the simple assumption of such a role can affect the message they seek to communicate.

In many mission lands the nationals see very little difference between the role of "missionary" and that of "colonial government administrator" or that of "western businessman," or even that of "foreign tourist," since there often seems to be so little basic difference between the major attitudes, activities and concerns of the one and those of the other. True, the missionary talks about religion, while the others are more concerned with government or business or simply sightseeing. But beyond this there often seems to be very little to disturb the impression of sameness so convincingly evoked by the similarities in housing, clothing, traveling modes, linguistic ability (or, often, inability), concern for schools, hospitals and other institutional innovations from western culture and the like. Nor, often, is a distinction between "missionary" and "colonialist" or its modern synonym "imperialist" evident enough to the nationals to lead them to exonerate missionaries from the accusation that they are in league with the colonialists in their imperialistic designs. Indeed, "spiritual imperialist" is one of the more recent epithets felt by many to be appropriate as an alternative designation of the missionary.

A further confusion frequently arises in the minds of the peoples of mission lands with regard to the appropriate prestige to assign to the role "missionary." It was my experience that the Nigerians among whom I worked assigned such a high prestige to the missionary role that we were virtually regarded as fitting into the "God" category rather than into the "human being" category. From their point of view, beings are assignable to but one of two categories which may be labeled "human" and "supernatural." Human beings were easily assignable by analogy to themselves—that is, any stranger coming into their midst was simply observed and, if he acted more or less like they did, he was unthinkingly assigned to the "human being" category. But they had a big problem with the assignment of westerners to that category, since so many of the things with which we are associated in their minds have not traditionally been associated with their category "human being," but, rather, with their category "supernatural."

Who but supernatural beings, for example, could possess magic powerful enough to produce automobiles, trains, airplanes, radios, western medicines, monstrous buildings, engines for grinding grain, fertilizers, western cloth and clothing, sewing machines, paved roads, fantastic bridges across uncrossable rivers, self-propelled boats, etc.? How could these beings fit into their category "human being?" They must belong in the "God" category with the rest of the incomprehensible, superhuman, supernatural beings. So, these Nigerians said, "Fear God, fear the white man." They assigned westerners, including missionaries, to the "God" category—an assignment that, in the case of missionaries, is continually reinforced in their minds by the fact that we constantly both speak of God as if we are on intimate terms with him, and frequently act, to their way of thinking, both capriciously and with a confidence considered unwarranted by human beings, i.e., like God acts.

This type of stereotyping is perhaps the most disturbing thing about simply being assigned to a role such as missionary, since it allows the people to whom we go to understand us and our presence in their midst wholly in terms of whatever their stereotype of a missionary might be. That is, we become in their eyes well nigh absolutely predictable, isolated from effective contact with them and depersonalized. In the case of the Nigerian situation referred to above (which is not at all uncommon, especially in rural areas, the world over), this meant that missionaries were not expected to operate by the same rules that human beings operate by. They were not considered to be restricted by the same limitations that human beings are restricted by nor could they be approached in a manner appropriate to human beings. That is, at each of these points (and many others) the analogy in their minds as they sought to think about or interrelate with missionaries was not to be a human to human analogy but a human to God analogy. In other parts of the world, and especially in urban areas, the specifics of the stereotype may vary but the people will often generate a similarly well-defined set of predictabilities resulting in a similarly isolating and depersonalizing definition of the position and activities of the missionary.

A Stereotyped God Breaks Out

That is a situation similar to that which God faced in his relationships with the Jewish people over the years. In spite of his association with them and his constant working in human affairs both within and outside of the Jewish nation, he had come to be regarded as predictable, isolated from meaningful interpersonal contact with all but a very few human beings, and more or less depersonalized. But then "in the fullness of time" God did something about the situation.

In Jesus, the stereotyped God broke out of the stereotype. Though he was God and had every right to remain God; though he was above humanity and powerful and majestic and worshipable, and had every right to remain that way; though he had every right to accept the stereotype, to remain within it accepting the assigned status, the prescribed role, the assured respect that the stereotype provided for him, Jesus turned his back on all of this, refusing any longer to cling to his rights as God. He laid aside both his rightful position and power and became a human being for the purpose of coming to live among us (see Phil. 2:6-7 and Jn. 1:14). He broke out of the stereotype so that we could actually see, hear and touch him as he dwelt, not above or apart from us, but truly *among us.*

To many people of that day (and this) God was regarded as very impressive. His power, majesty and "otherness" made quite an impression on people. You might say that God had developed a very good reputation and lots of respect, but few of his creatures knew him well. He had many admirers but few friends. Much of what he said and did was subject to the same kind of suspicion with which we regard the words and deeds of the very rich or the very powerful—especially if their wealth or power has been inherited rather than earned.

"How could the Kennedys or the Rockefellers understand what I have to go through?" we ask, "since they have always had the wealth and/or the power to insulate themselves from these things. They could never understand my desires, my wants, my needs," we assume, "since they, without a struggle, were already in possession of the things that I am working so hard to attain."

And so, just as we suspect that such people don't really understand us, likewise humans had come to feel that God, being so far "out of it" with respect to the problems and difficulties of the human scene, could not possibly understand what "human beingness" is really like. Those who questioned God's ability to really understand were likely also to question whether he really cared. And if he didn't really care about us, why should we care about living up to what was called "God's standard?"

So humans assigned to God a status and a role (or non-role in relation to human beings). We fitted God into a stereotype that effectively insulated us from active concern about God or our relationship with God—a stereotype that kept God securely at arm's length and allowed us to go about our business with little or no concern about God. This was often as true of the professional religionists of that day (as it is of ours) as it was of the majority of the rest of the people.

But then God in Jesus broke out of that assigned status and role, rejecting the stereotype to which he had a right, and he incarnated himself. He became a real human being *among us*—a learner, a sharer, a participant in the affairs of men—no longer simply God *above us*. Nor did he then merely content himself to do God-type things *near us*. He spent approximately thirty-three years truly among us—seen, heard, touched, living as a human being among human beings and perceived by those around him as a human being. He learned, therefore, as the book of Hebrews contends, how to sympathize with human beings by allowing himself to be subjected to the temptations and sufferings of human beings (see Heb. 2:10, 17, 18; 4:15; 5:8, and elsewhere).

"Preposterous!" said the religious leaders of that day, "You can't expect us to believe a thing like that!" For they had studied the Scriptures and were sure they knew exactly how the Messiah would come. He would, they seemed to expect, be above ordinary men, he would associate with religious, good people, he would assume political power, he would demand that people follow him, and so forth.

"Mere mythology," say the religious experts of our own day, who find in the incarnation but another attempt on the part of human beings to deify ourselves. Jesus, an amazing man, yes, but incarnate God? Certainly not, they say.

And, we must admit, it was a rather incredible thing to do. What a terrible risk Jesus took in thus making himself vulnerable, able to be talked back to, able to be criticized by humans, able to be tempted. But in this process of rejecting the assigned status he had a right to retain, he put himself in the position to *win* (rather than demand—as he had a right to) our respect, to *earn* (rather than to simply assume) our admiration and allegiance on the basis of what he did. He became a man among us. And in the process, we discovered that God is even more impressive than our doctrine had told us he is. This discovery was doubly meaningful because it was based not simply on knowledge *about* God, but on experience *with* him.

How Does This Apply to Our Ministries?

But how does all of this apply to us as missionaries? We attempt to cross cultural barriers, to enter into the frame of reference of other peoples for the sake of confronting them with the message of Christ. But how do we go about it? And when we carry out our calling , what is their response? Do we simply allow them to fit us into their stereotype of what a missionary should be, whatever that stereotype may be, and, if that stereotype is a bad one, end up with zero communication?

How would the people we work with fill in the following blank: "The missionary acts like ____"? In many situations the predictable filler of that blank would be something like "colonial government administrator," or "foreign businessman," or, in the area of Nigeria where I worked, the statement might well be predicted as, "The missionary acts like God!"

As mentioned above, many people of mission lands may well feel that there are more reasons than the missionary's attitude to identify him or her with God. The stereotype would seem to them to fit very well for a variety of reasons as they evaluate the situation from within their frame of reference—a frame of reference into which the missionary may not have penetrated if, indeed, she or he is even aware of it. From the nationals' point of view there may well be a whole series of further predictable statements as well, such as: "The missionary lords it over us," "The missionary shouts at us," "The missionary lives separate from us," "The missionary only makes real friends of people with western schooling." These are statements of expectation as well as of prediction, since they simply define for the people various aspects of the way in which they expect the missionary to act. But by this very fact the communication value of the acts and words that allow such statements to stand as accurate descriptions is close to zero—unless, of course, it is the desire of the missionary to communicate this kind of information.

Becoming a Real Human Being

But suppose someone says something like this about a missionary: "This missionary acts like a real human being!" What a lot of information that kind of a statement often carries—because the person of a mission land who makes that kind of statement is defining "real human being" in terms of whatever is appropriate to that concept from within *his or her* cultural frame of reference. Now, the missionary who is interpreted as acting like God by the national may very well have been conforming to her or his own definition of what it is to act like a real human being. But what from within the missionary's frame of reference looks like humanness may to the national look like "Godness." Thus, if to the national the missionary looks human, there has been a major breakthrough involving the establishing of a beachhead within the national's frame of reference. There has been a breaking of the stereotype by overcoming the predictability barrier, making possible life-changing discovery on the part of the national.

The elements involved in establishing "humanness" within someone else's cultural frame of reference will vary from the quite trivial to the quite all-encompassing. A missionary who, for example, never betrays the slightest doubt about anything (especially about things that the national may assume are absolutely unknowable) may well be interpreted as acting like God—that is, our very certainty may prove detrimental to us at times. Note that the Apostle Paul chooses to be weak to the weak in order to win them (1 Cor. 9:19–22). Furthermore, a missionary who never has or admits to a health problem, or a security problem, or a moral (including thoughts) problem, or who never admits to nationals that he has made a mistake, may well appear to them to fit more properly in the supernatural category than in the human being category. On another level, I once had a Nigerian say to me, "Why, we never knew how you missionaries go to the bathroom—or even *that you* go to the bathroom!" In this regard it was a very positive factor in the understanding of a certain number of the young people in our area when, at a camp, I bathed with them.

One very important feature in the attempts of several missionaries that I know of to establish themselves as real human beings within another cultural frame of reference has been their willingness to participate with nationals in their recreational activities. In our part of the world this meant participating in a variety of play activities performed to the beat of the drum and commonly referred to (though to some extent misleadingly) as dancing. When the people could make statements like, "The missionary dances with us," they found it very difficult to maintain their stereotype of the missionary as God. Many of these people weren't quite sure what the missionary was paid to do, but they were reasonably sure that whatever it was, it wasn't to dance! The amount of information conveyed, therefore, when this strange person does an unexpected thing like participating with them at play is extremely high. When the missionary acts differently than their stereotype calls for her or him to act, the people are forced either to regard him or her as an exception to their stereotype, or to modify or abandon the stereotype. If the missionary's activity consistently contradicts the stereotype in the direction of their definition of humanness (there are other directions in which such reinterpretation could go as well), the kind of human-to-human basis for communication that the incarnation employs is established.

God, and We, Have a Choice of Roles

To summarize thus far, God had a choice of roles in his approach to us. He could have remained as God in heaven, or even come to earth as God, and retained the respect and prestige that is his right as God. He would have continued to have admirers but not friends. The risks would have been far fewer, but the real impact very low because the predictability would have been so high. But God chose not to go that route, choosing rather to become a human being within the frame of reference of human beings, so that, in spite of the tremendous risk involved, he might earn the respect of and, therefore, the right to be listened to by human beings. Likewise we as missionaries may choose to remain as gods above or as gods in the midst of the people we work among. Or we may seek to follow God's example and establish a beachhead within the frame of reference of the people to whom God has called us—a beachhead of "human beingness" according to their definition.

Soon after a young missionary had taken charge of a mission station in Africa he was sitting, chatting with the son of the local chief on the porch of the mission home. After some time the chief's son looked up at the missionary and asked, "How long have we been here?" The missionary calculated the time and said, "About three quarters of an hour." The chief's son then asked, "Do you know how long I would have been here if your predecessor were still here?" The missionary (lying) answered, "No." "Five minutes," the chief's son replied. "Your predecessor would have come to the door when I called and asked me, 'What do you want?' I would have stated my business, gotten my answer, and been off again in about five minutes! Just look," he continued, "here we've been sitting here for three quarters of an hour and I didn't even notice that the time was passing!"

The previous missionary had only made one major blunder. He had acted in a way perfectly intelligible from within *his* cultural framework. He had stepped outside to meet the chief's son, he had undoubtedly extended to the African a few common greetings, and then he had gotten right to the point so as not to waste too much time by asking very politely but directly what the man wanted. The African, however, was interpreting all of these things from within his own frame of reference—a frame of reference that regards a direct question such as "What do you want?" no matter how politely asked in that context, as an extreme breach of etiquette, about equivalent to a punch in the mouth. In the African's society, it is the prerogative of the one who comes to state his business in his own good time, and a matter of common courtesy for the person visited to wait until his visitor gets ready to bring up the matter that brought him. However, the chief's son had come to expect such breaches of etiquette on the part of missionaries, and this expectation had become a part of his stereotype of missionaries. It was not the actions of the earlier missionary that startled him, it was the fact that the newcomer was willing to sit and chat with him and never to ask what brought him—from his point of view, that the second missionary treated him like a human being—that caused him to sit up and take notice. That which he, in terms of his frame of reference, could define as courtesy was in this situation the unpredictable and led to a new discovery on the part of this chief's son.

A university student once came to a professor's office to ask some minor question about a course she was taking from him. He invited her to sit down and they began to talk about various things. This went on for some time, then she seemed to lose track of the conversation for a moment. Finally she broke in with something like, "Gee, you don't act like a professor! You know," she continued, "since I've come to this university no professor has ever spent more than ten minutes with me. And nobody has ever shown the interest in me that you've been showing." A poor lost student had finally found someone among the gods of that situation who had broken the stereotype and, at least for that hour or so, had begun to relate to her in terms of her definition of humanness.

Straight out of Bible college, a young man I know accepted a call to a small New England church. Soon after assuming that pastorate he also took a job in a factory. His deacons called him on the carpet for this, admitting that they weren't paying him the highest salary in the world but insisting that they expected him to devote all of his time to the work of the church. "Oh," he replied, "it's not for the sake of the money that I took the job in the factory. In fact," he continued, "the church is welcome to whatever I earn. It's just that to this point I've spent all my time in school, yet I'm expected to minister to people who spend from 9 to 5 every day in the factory. If I'm going to minister effectively to these people, I've got to find out what it's like to be in their shoes."

This is one of the most constructive approaches to the ministry I've ever seen. Though the pastor and his people were members of the same culture, he was able to recognize that in major ways they were operating within different frames of reference—he within an academic frame of reference, they within a quite different framework strongly influenced by their involvement in factory work. In this and other ways he was able to break through the stereotype that the church people had of a pastor, and to increase dramatically the effectiveness both of his preaching and of his overall relationship with the people.

Each of these illustrations points to the effectiveness for communication of putting oneself within the hearer's frame of reference, just as Jesus did. Jesus not only came, *he became*. He not only traversed the infinite distance between heaven and earth to get close to us, he also covered those last couple of feet that separate person from person, to identify with us in the human condition in which we were immersed.

I asked a missionary one time if he didn't feel a bit guilty about having fixed up his house so nicely. He had not only made the house comfortable by American standards, but had added a touch of luxury to it here and there. "No," he replied, "the Nigerians expect us to live this way." He was absolutely right. But the communication value of his living condition, since his actions were completely predictable, was zero. Another missionary locked up his comfortable mission home for a few weeks and moved his family and a few necessities seven miles out into the African bush to live in an African compound. He hadn't been there very long when his African host asked, "What in the world have you come for? Why," he continued, "if I had a home like yours, I wouldn't even poke my nose outside the door, much less come way out here to live." This missionary had put himself within the African's frame of reference. By acting so unpredictably he succeeded in eliciting some very interesting questions and comments on the part of his host. One day the African came to him and said, "I know why you don't like our food. We don't like yours either!" The practice had been for each to offer the other a portion of their food whenever it was mealtime. This sharing had resulted in quite a significant discovery on the part of the African to whom, up to this point, the missionary had been not only distant, isolated and unknown, but also a source of envy.

The African, for example, may well have envied him his food as well as his home. But when the missionary began to operate within the African's frame of reference, a new kind of understanding of the missionary and everything about him began to break through. This experience was doubly good, for the same sort of insight concerning what it is like to be inside the skin of an African was breaking through to the missionary as well—thus enabling him to communicate more effectively from within the African's frame of reference. In another, similar experiment in living in an African village, the missionary was told, "We want to follow your God, not that of the (other) missionaries!"

God became a human being—so must we. God broke through the isolating stereotype—so must we. Those close to Jesus discovered that this one who had invited them to get close to him, who had earned their respect and undying admiration and yet had called them "friends," could actually have *demanded* all of this. Even though he was God, it was as a full fledged man, from within the human frame of reference, that he demonstrated it. So must we demonstrate God's message from within the human frame of reference—in hopes that the result of our ministry can be the same kind of amazed yet transforming response that John records as the result of Jesus' ministry when he says (paraphrasing 1 Jn. 1:1–3):

> This man came along, an impressive teacher, and I and several others became his students. For three years we lived together. We walked together, talked together, ate together, slept together. We both listened to his teaching and watched closely how he lived. And what an impression he made on us! For as we lived together we began to realize that this was no ordinary man—that when he spoke of God as his Father he spoke from firsthand experience . . . for this man living among us was God himself! This man whom we called "Teacher," to whom we listened, with whom we lived—we discovered that he is the God who created the universe, but who chose to come in human form to live with us, his creatures, to demonstrate what he is like to us in a way that we could not misunderstand. And this discovery has so impressed us that we'll never be the same again!

Four Principles for Breaking Stereotypes

As suggested above, unaware missionaries may easily find themselves assigned by the people to whom they go to a role and status that is quite damaging to the task of communicating Christ cross-culturally. They may, for example, discover that their actions and words are being interpreted by the people in quite a different way than they intend, simply because they do not come across to them as real flesh and blood human beings according to *their* definition of human beingness.

For the cultural world of the people to whom we go is different, operating as it does on the basis of a completely different set of expectations and definitions. They assign outsiders positions (or nonpositions) within their society according to culturally-defined stereotypes that may be very difficult to get beyond (especially if the missionary is unaware of the damage done to his or her efforts at communication by a failure to break out of the isolation imposed by the stereotype).

Our Lord, however, was active with respect to such stereotyping. He did not simply fit into the expectations of the people to whom he ministered. He broke through the stereotype, choosing a role that enabled people to understand him within their cultural frame of reference. In the process, he demonstrated the validity of several of the basic principles to which the modern study of communication theory points. The explication of these principles can be very helpful to the missionary who seeks to "fill Jesus' shoes" in some cultural world other than that in which she or he grew up. For in many ways the activity of God in Christ in crossing the border between the supracultural and the cultural[1] is similar to what the missionary goes through when crossing from one cultural world to another.

There are at least four principles of communication theory discernable from Jesus' approach to communication that are applicable to our approach. These are illustrated in the previous article. The aim here is to make them more explicit, with the hope that by becoming more conscious of these principles missionaries may more effectively apply them in their ministries. In summary form these principles are: (1) For information to be conveyed accurately both the giver and the receiver of the information must operate within the same frame of reference; (2) Within a frame of reference, the greater the predictability of allowable segments of the message, the smaller the impact of that message and, conversely, the lower the predictability the greater the impact of the message; (3) The greater the specificity of the form in which the material is presented, the greater the impact; and (4) Something discovered by the receptor of the message has greater impact than something presented in predigested, generalized form by the communicator.[2]

Principle One: Frame of Reference

With regard to principle number one, the frame of reference may be as small as a single linguistic context, a given technical jargon such as that of a given science or that of children of a given age, or it may be as all-encompassing as all of human life. Significant intermediate points between these extremes are the frame of reference of a whole language or that of a whole culture. People attempting to communicate with each other on the basis of differing frames of reference, for example, find that very little, if any, of the intended information gets across in undistorted form.

If they speak different languages to each other (unless both are bilingual—in which case their bilingualism defines for them their frame of reference), or operate on the basis of different worldview assumptions, the communication will at least be seriously distorted, if not completely obstructed. This principle may be diagrammed as follows:

---

1 The term "supracultural" (first called "superculture" by WIlliam A. Smalley) designates the realm above and beyond culture where the absolute God exists. Since cultural systems are relative but God is absolute it seems important to employ such a term when referring to God's relation to culture. The fact that the Son left the supracultural realm of God and crossed the border between that realm and a cultural realm is the point being made here, since such a crossing is similar to the crossing from one culture into another.

2 See E. A. Nida, *Message and Mission* (Harper and Row, 1960, reprinted William Carey Library, 1972, revised 1990) for another treatment of some of these factors. Pages 72–75 are especially relevant.

SITUATION I
effective communication impossible

Frame of Reference A   Frame of Reference B

"a" seeks to communicate with "b" by   "b" never hears "a," because the Frame
speaking entirely in terms of Frame of   of Reference in terms of which the
Reference A   message is phrased is beyond the
                                              comprehension of "b" immersed as he is
                                              in Frame of Reference B

SITUATION II
effective communication possible

"a" seeks to communicate with "b" by   "b" hears "a" because "a" phrases his
establishing a basis for communication   message in terms of Frame of Reference
within Frame of Reference B   B

If, for example, God simply spoke a "heavenly language" rather than a human language, operating within his own frame of reference rather than in that of his hearers, the message would not get across, since the communicator and the receptor would be operating in different frames of reference. For this reason, God has chosen to operate within the linguistic frame of reference of the human receptors of his message. In his ultimate communication, however, he chose the more comprehensive total cultural frame of reference of the Jewish people to operate in the person of Jesus Christ.

Principle Two: Predictability

The second principle of communication theory employed by God in Christ relates to the predictability of the message. Within the linguistic frame of reference known as the English language, for example, if one says, "He winked his ____ ," or, "He shrugged his ____," the impact of (technically, the information value of) the word "eye" in the completed first statement, or the word "shoulder" in the second is exactly zero, since no other fillers of these blanks are allowable and, therefore, each is totally predictable in these contexts (frames of reference).[3] If, for example, as

---

[3] Note that this principle specifies unpredictability of elements within a frame of reference. That is, the frame of reference remains constant (i.e., predictable). The only unpredictable thing is which item or type of item among several possible alternatives will be employed in a given part of the frame of reference. If, for example, a statement such as that which follows were made, the nonsense word would convey very little information, since it is not an allowable word in the English language frame of reference: "I saw an oquap." The little information that it does convey is related to the fact that the unfamiliar term occurs in a place in the utterance that would enable one to say, "If 'oquap' is definable it will be a noun," and the spelling of the strange word is such that one can say, "This is a permissible sequence of sounds in English." That is, the little information that might be attributed to the strange word comes not from the word itself but from the frame of reference determined allowabilities that it exhibits.

someone says, "He winked his eye" some noise blots out the last word, nothing is lost, since "eye" is predictable in that context—the impact of that word symbol in that context is, therefore, nil.

In statements such as, "The ___ barked," or, "He smacked his ___," the predictability of the words that may fill the blanks is high but not quite 100 percent since, were a word spoken in each of the above blanks blotted out by some noise, one could not be sure whether it was a dog, a seal or a baboon that barked, or whether the latter person smacked his lips or his child. The information value of the words that fill the blank in either of these statements is, therefore, slightly higher than that of the fillers in the above paragraph, since its predictability is lower. This principle may be diagrammed thus:

PREDICTABILITY

| High | _____ | Low |
| Low | _____ | High |

IMPACT
(INFORMATION
VALUE)

Note that any movement along the above line toward, e.g., greater predictability is at the same time a movement toward a lessening of the impact of the message.

Now, with regard to God's approach to humans, the stereotyped (i.e., predictable) understanding of God will result in the completion of the following statements in highly predictable terms: "If God came to earth he would come as a ____," or, "He would associate with ____ people," or, "He would go to ____ places." The Pharisees, for example, thinking in terms of the stereotype, expected the Messiah to come as a king, to associate only with good people, and to go only to religiously respectable places. These were the predictable answers, and had Jesus acted according to these expectations he might well have been accepted by the Pharisees. But the very predictability of his message, had he lived it in these terms, would have meant that the communicational impact of his life would have been only slightly above the zero level.

But note the far greater communication value of filling the above blanks with unpredictable terms—terms that did not and still do not conform to the stereotype that most people have developed with regard to God. Suppose, for example, someone said, "When God came to earth he came as a peasant," or, "God associated with prostitutes and crooked tax collectors," or, "God went to a raucous wedding feast." These statements really make an impact (even today) because they are so unpredictable, so out of line with the stereotype. They sound like headlines (which are produced with the same technique in mind). They make you perk up your ears.

Principle Three: Specificity

The third communication principle employed by Jesus concerns the specificity of the form in which the message is presented. A communication presented in terms of the actions, attitudes and activities of real life, for example, makes a greater impact (i.e., has greater communication value) than a strictly verbal message. Even if the communication be verbal, a greater impact is made by specific, detailed descriptions of real life, or even illustrative parables describing true-to-life events, than by generalizations or abstract propositions concerning those events.[4] For this reason Jesus, living truly among human beings and teaching in terms of life-specific parables and miracles, communicated infinitely more to us concerning God than would all of the theological abstractions, no matter how true, that could be developed concerning God's interest in humans. Jesus not only taught truth, he presented it in such a way that it came across to his hearers and observers with impact. The fact that the life of Christ has been recorded and transmitted to us in biographical, casebook fashion rather than in abstract theological textbook fashion makes available to us even at this distance in time and culture a large degree of that communicational impact of his life and teaching in first century Palestine.

Principle Four: Discovery

The fourth of these principles of communication theory relates primarily to the manner in which the receptor is made aware of the message. In our society we are constantly besieged by predigested information, often presented in "one-way conversations" such as lectures, books and even so-called discussions. Much of the effect of all of this is to rob us of the opportunity of discovery. We are very privileged to read and hear of the discoveries of others, but often we have not been allowed to really discover much on our own. It is in the process of discovery, rather than in the simple hearing of the report of someone else's discovery presented in predigested form, that the deepest, most abiding kind of learning takes place. It is for this reason, I am sure, that God's written Word is presented to us in experience-oriented casebook fashion rather than as a predigested theology textbook.

This type of discovery-oriented learning is the kind that provides the basis for the educational systems of a majority of the world's societies. Education that makes much use of such things as proverbs, fables, parables and similar types of stylized recountings of the experience and accumulated wisdom of the community tends to be discovery-oriented. This kind of educational process is dependent upon learners deducing (discovering) what in the materials presented is of value to them and in what way it may be applicable to their lives.

---

[4] See chapter 2, "On Teaching by Parables" in R. C. Trench, *Notes on the Parables of our Lord* (various editions} for an interesting older treatment of this insight.

Jesus, working within a society whose educational system was learner- and discovery-oriented in this sense, taught from within this framework by means of living and verbal example. He employed familiar forms such as the discipleship teacher-student relationship and the parable as a primary model for the presentation of his material. He waited for discovery to take place. When, for example, John the Baptist inquired from prison about whether or not Jesus was the promised Messiah (a question raised in John's mind because Jesus did not fit the stereotype), the Master did not provide a predigested yes or no answer but, rather, told the messenger to simply report to John the "things you have seen and heard . . ." (Lk. 7:22), so that John could make his own discovery of the truth. Even at his trial before Pilate, Jesus answered the question, "Are you the King of the Jews?" by a return question—a question designed to probe and challenge Pilate to discovery. Jesus did not simply give an answer based on the information to be taught. He did not deny Pilate the opportunity of really confronting his own question and of possibly discovering real truth in the process.

We Should Imitate Jesus in Using These Principles

Jesus chose to operate in the cultural frame of reference of his hearers. He chose to become intelligible as a believable human being within *their* cultural context, rather than demanding that in some way they become a part of his frame of reference in order to receive his communication. The missionary seeking to truly communicate Christ will find that Jesus' way of choosing to operate within the cultural frame of reference of his hearers is a much more enlightened method of effective communication than the alternative approach employed by the Judaizers and some western mission agencies that requires the hearers to accommodate to the cultural frame of reference of the communicator.

Within that intelligible frame of reference, Jesus deliberately shunned the isolated, untouchable, nonparticipant religious expert stereotype that both the religious leaders and the people expected him to fit into. Missionaries, in allegiance to Christ's example, must likewise resist and reject such a stereotype, or see their efforts at effective cross-cultural communication of the gospel seriously compromised.

Jesus, furthermore, presented his message in a highly specific, non-generalized, even non-theological form. The message was both lived and illustrated in very specifically life-related fashion. Jesus seldom used Scripture texts as his starting point. He chose to base his communication on the life and interests of his hearers rather than on statements of the theological principles that may be derived from his teachings. Missionaries must imitate our Lord's approach by searching out, learning and employing the culturally appropriate forms of specific life-related communication available among the people to whom they are called.

Finally, our Lord encouraged and patiently waited for those around him to learn by discovery. "The kingdom is like such and such. It's up to you to discover how the analogy applies," he seems to be saying at many points, showing a high regard for our ability to discover eternal truth. "Observe me, spend time with me. Now who do you think I am?" "Reach forth your hand, Thomas, and draw your own conclusion." He lived close to people, always within reach of an inquirer's question or touch, seldom impatient except with those who knew better, always encouraging and patiently waiting for that life-transforming discovery of himself and of the truth of God that he sought to convey. Oh, that we might imitate him and communicate like he did!

CHAPTER 18

A COMMUNICATING GOD

Reprinted with permission from
Communicating the Gospel God's Way.
Pasadena, CA: William Carey Library, 1979:3–16

As one who specializes in communication and Bible translation I am increasingly fascinated by the communicational dimensions of the Word of God. I am, of course convinced that God knew what he was doing communicationally. I am, however, surprised that it has taken us so long to look at the Bible from this point of view. For generations, we who seek to communicate God's Word have looked to the Bible for our message. I am afraid, though, that we have seldom looked to the Bible for our method. I have become personally convinced that the inspiration of the Bible extends both to message and to method. My aim in this chapter, therefore, is to elucidate a scriptural method for getting God's message across that I dare to call "God's Model for Communication."

Though I will be talking about what I believe to be a method of approach that we see from cover to cover in the Bible, it might be helpful, by way of introduction, for me to point to a couple of Scripture verses which, if translated from a communicational point of view, lend support to the point I am trying to make. Look, for example, at Mark 16:15. It is, I think, allowable to translate this verse: "Go into all the world to communicate the Good News to all peoples." The word "preach" that is ordinarily used in English translations of this verse is only one way of communicating. Indeed, it is a form of communication that Jesus used very seldom. We are commanded by God not simply to monologue his Word but to communicate it as effectively as possible. A second illustrative verse is John 1:14. In this verse the Greek word *logos*, ordinarily translated "word" is employed. I believe it would not be doing the verse an injustice to suggest the following translation: "[God's] message became a human being to live among us." I will be alluding to other passages of Scripture as I go along but I wanted to point briefly to these verses at the beginning of my presentation to alert us to the fact that, in the first place, God is concerned about communication and that, in the second place, God's ultimate method of communication is via incarnation.

Now the problem I want to raise is: How can we follow God's example in our efforts to communicate his Good News? God has, of course, communicated very effectively. He has, furthermore, involved us in the contemporary phase of his communicational efforts. How then can we learn to involve ourselves in his work in his way? We do not believe that God simply overrules our humanity to make us into communicational robots. We believe that he leads us as we participate with him in such activities. We believe also that we need to do our best to learn how he wants us to conduct ourselves so that we may be of greater service to him. We may, therefore, analyze God's communicational activities as portrayed for us in the Scriptures in order to learn how he goes about his work so that we will know better how to go about our work for him.

Another way of putting this is to use a term that is increasingly coming into prominence in Bible translation theory. This term is "dynamic equivalence." Our aim communicationally is to perform in a way that is dynamically equivalent to God's communicational activity as portrayed in the Scripture. A dynamic equivalence Bible translation is a translation that has the kind of communicational impact on today's hearers that the original Scriptures had on the original hearers. Such translations as Phillips, Good News for Modern Man, and Living Bible have often had such an impact in contemporary English. If you can imagine yourself communicating the messages that God gives you as effectively as these translations communicate the Scriptural message, you will have a glimpse at least of what I am talking about as the goal of Christian communication.

Preliminary Observations Concerning God and His Communicative Activity

The first thing I would like to deal with in this regard is to suggest six preliminary observations concerning God's communication. I believe that these observations apply to all of Scripture. I also believe that if we seek to be Scriptural in our communicative activity, we will seek to imitate God in each of these areas.

1. In the first place, I would like to suggest that *God seeks to communicate, not simply to impress people*. You have all had the experience of sitting in church and hearing a soloist or an organist or even a preacher show off in front of you. You may have expected that they were going to communicate some message to you but, as they got into their performances, you began to realize that they were seeking only to impress you. They were of course communicating something, but that communication had more to do with their own ability than with anything they were talking, singing, or playing about. They seemed to be more interested in impressing people than in communicating with people. One basic principle of communication that is involved in such a situation is that *when a vehicle of communication calls attention to itself, the message is lost*. If, therefore, in a situation such as preaching, singing, or organ playing, we become more aware of the performer's ability to perform than of the message he or she is seeking to get across, then the situation becomes a performance rather than a communication.

What I'm suggesting is that God communicates not simply performs. Throughout the Bible he uses language that does not call attention to itself. He uses people who do not call attention to themselves. In fact, when, as in the case of King Saul, these people begin to call attention to themselves, they become unfit for God's service. Likewise with respect to Bible translation, where the beauty of the language calls such attention to itself that it obscures the message. The Scriptures in the original languages are fairly unimpressive from a literary point of view. Jesus, when he walked the earth was also, apparently, fairly unimpressive personally. But his message had great impact.

2. Second, *God wants to be understood not simply admired.* God, of course, is impressive and greatly to be admired. But there is a sense in which if we focus on merely admiring God, his ultimate purpose in interacting with human beings is thwarted. Some would seem to give the impression that God has an enormous ego that demands that people sit around admiring him at all times. This seems to be the way in which many define worship. Without denying the value for us of contemplating God's greatness and of worshipping him, however, I would like to suggest that his greater desire is that we understand and obey him. Though not infrequently what God says and does is difficult for us to understand, God's ultimate purpose

> is not "to mystify the truth" but to reveal it, not to hide verities behind historical accounts, hut to face man with the truth in any and all literary forms which they can understand (Nida 1960:223).

As pointed out above it is in order to be understood that God used human language. It is to be understood that he took on human shape, both in the incarnation and in the Old Testament theophanies (e.g., Gen. 18, Dan. 3:25). It is to be understood that God used dreams to reach those who believed in dreams and parables to reach those who had become accustomed to being taught through parables. On occasion God communicates through a spectacle (e.g., 1 Kg. 19:11–12). But the spectacle is not an end in itself, it is merely the means to the end of effective communication that God employs in order to be understood. Likewise with miracles. John points to this fact by constantly labeling Jesus' miracles "signs." They are intended to point beyond themselves, to communicate something, so that God's message can be understood. This is why Jesus ran from those who were only interested in the spectacle for its own sake, but spent countless hours with those who got at least part of the message. He sought to be understood, and responded to those who responded to what he was seeking to communicate.

3. In the third place, let us note that *God seeks response from his hearers not simply passive listening.* This is a corollary to God's desire to communicate and to be understood. Communication implies response. When God commands people he expects them to respond. God's promises to people typically require a response on their part. Proper response in turn, elicits further interaction between God and human beings. Indeed, God's interactions with human beings are characteristically in the form of dialogue, rather than monologue. The Bible, from beginning to end, represents God as seeking conversation with people. And such conversation demands responsiveness on the part of human beings. We are not simply to sit like bumps on logs listening to God without responding to him. To quote Nida again

The entire concept of the covenant of God with man is predicated upon two way communication, even though it is God who proposes and man who accepts. Of course, in Jesus Christ the "dialogue" of God with man is evident in all of its fullness, but the divine human conversation is eternal, for the end of man is for fellowship and communion with God himself, and for this the communication of "dialogue" is an indispensable and focal element (1960:225).

4. A fourth preliminary point is the suggestion that *God has revealed in the Scripture not only what to communicate, but how to communicate it*. I will not seek to elaborate this point at this time. I simply want to make the point explicit and to suggest that if what I have said above and what I will say below is true, this point is established.

5. My fifth preliminary point is to suggest that *God is receptor oriented*. In the communication process we have three basic elements: the communicator, the message and the receptor. Communicators, as they engage in the process of communication, may have their attention focused on any of the three elements. That is, they may focus so intently on themselves and what they are doing in the situation that they are virtually unaware of exactly what they are saying or of who they are attempting to say it to. Or they may be so focused in on what they are saying that they virtually forget both themselves and their receptors. Or, in the third place, they may so focus on their receptors, their concerns and the value of what they are saying to those receptors, that their concern for themselves and those aspects of the message that are not relevant to their hearers is diminished. This latter is what I mean by the term receptor oriented. Each of these approaches involves all three elements. They differ only with respect to which of the elements is in primary focus.

Communicators whose primary focus is on themselves tend to show off. Those who seek to impress people with their own abilities in order that they will admire them tend to fall into this trap. It may matter little to them whether people understand what they say or if they benefit from it. Their concern is to be admired. Communicators who are message centered, on the other hand, give great attention to the way the message is phrased. Their concern is for precise terminology and correct wording on the one hand, and for an elegantly constructed, well balanced presentation of the message on the other. Again, the concern is less for whether the receptors understand the message than for the formulation and presentation of that message. The tendency of such communicators will be to resort to technically precise language, whether or not such language is intelligible to their listeners, and to homiletically perfect organization, whether or not their listeners are most attracted to that kind of a message. Receptor oriented communicators, on the other hand, are careful to bend every effort to meet their receptors where they are. They will choose topics that relate directly to the felt needs of the receptors, they will choose methods of presentation that are appealing to them, they will use language that is maximally intelligible to them.

What I am suggesting is that God's communication shows that he is squarely in the latter position. He is primarily oriented toward getting his message into the minds and hearts of his receptors. That is, the methods chosen, the language employed, the topics dealt with, the places and times where he encounters human beings and all other factors indicate that God is receptor oriented. He does not, of course, always say what people like to hear. That is not required of one who is receptor oriented. The point is that whatever he says, whether it is pleasant or unpleasant, is presented in ways and via techniques that have maximum relevance to the receptors. They do not have to go somewhere else, learn someone else's language, or become something other than they already are as a precondition to hearing his message. Obedience to the message itself, of course, may require that they go somewhere else or become something else, but they are not required to make these adjustments before they can understand what God is saying to them. I will elaborate further on this point below.

6. In the sixth place, I'd like to suggest that *God's basic method of communication is incarnational*. Though the ultimate incarnation of God's communication was in Jesus Christ, God's method of using human beings to reach other human beings is also an incarnational method. In a real sense, everyone who is transformed by the power of God and genuinely lives her or his witness to Christ is an incarnation of God's message to human beings. It is not, I think, without significance that the early Christians at Antioch were called "little Christs," "Christians." God's witnesses are called by Paul "letters that have come from Christ," (2 Cor. 3:3). This is incarnational communication. And even the Bible, since it consists almost entirely of case studies of such incarnations of God's communications, may be seen as an incarnational document.

God's Approach: A Model
for Us to Imitate

I would now like to turn to ten characteristics of God's communication. In doing this I have in mind three primary aims: to describe at least certain of the characteristics of God's communicational activity, to point out how well these correspond with the insights of modern communication theory, and to suggest that each characteristic is something that we ought to imitate in our attempts to communicate on God's behalf. I make no apology for the fact that these characteristics frequently take us into territory already covered in the above list of preliminary observations. Those broader observations and these narrower characteristics are, after all, simply alternative ways of viewing the same territory.

1. The first characteristic to note is that *God communicates with impact*. Impact is that which makes an impression, that gets people up doing things in response to what has been communicated to them. To get an idea of the kind of impact that God's communication had on people, we might simply ask ourselves what it would take to get us to do some of the things that the people of Scripture did. What would it take to stimulate Abraham to leave home, country, family and all that was familiar to him? What was it that impelled Moses to stand up against Pharaoh? What transformed the prophets, or the disciples, or Paul? The Holy Spirit was involved to be sure. But they were human beings who responded to communicational stimuli just like we do. So our questions concern not whether or not the Holy Spirit was involved, but what kind of response they as human beings made to the

communicational techniques God employed with them. The point is that they received God's communication with the kind of impact that impelled them to things that the world might regard as strange.

Now, we have learned to think of communication as largely a matter of the transfer of information from communicator to receptor. We set up schools, we write books and articles, we preach sermons, in order to buy and sell information. When we go to school, read books or go to church, we are rather like the Athenians about whom it is recorded that they were primarily concerned with "talking or hearing about the latest novelty" (Acts 17:21). If we hear a lecture or a sermon or read a book that disappoints us we very often express our criticism by saying, "I didn't learn anything new." But the primary aim of God's communication, and hopefully of ours, is not simply to inform. It is to *stimulate* people to action. And when, via sermonizing, God's message is reduced to mere information about God rather than the passing on of stimulus from God, I wonder if we have not thwarted his purpose to some extent? The God who, through communicational channels, has had such an impact on our lives that we are in the process of transformation, desires that we communicate for him with a similar kind of impact. The characteristics by means of which he brings about that impact are delineated in the next nine points.

2. To create communicational impact, *God takes the initiative*. God does not simply sit there unconcerned. When Adam and Eve got into difficulty, God took the initiative and went to where they were to initiate the communication that would enable them to at least know how to get out of their situation. When he decided to destroy mankind, God initiated communication with Noah. Likewise with Abraham, Moses, and with person after person throughout Scripture. In Christ, God took the initiative that resulted both in his most significant communication and in salvation for humanity. We learn, therefore, that as communicators from God, the initiative lies with us.

3. When God seeks to communicate *he moves into the receptor's frame of reference*. I use the term "frame of reference" to designate the combination of things such as culture, language, space, time, etc., that make up the matrix within which the receptor operates. Each person operates within several frames of reference simultaneously. At one level, all of us are in our own frame of reference defined by those psychological, physiological and life history characteristics that make us uniquely different from every other individual in the world. At another level, however, we all share with many other people a language, a culture, a geographical area, a time frame, and many other similar characteristics. If, therefore, we are to be understood by our hearers, we will have to start by employing such definers of broader frames of reference as the same language, similar thought patterns, and the like and proceed to demonstrate a concern for the characteristics that define narrower frames of reference such as the personal interests and needs of the receptor.

Not infrequently, especially when communicators have some power over the receptors, they will designate their own frame of reference as that within which the communication must take place. They may, for example, use a technical type of language that they understand well but that loses their receptors. Professors and preachers often do just this when they use the jargon and thought patterns of the academic discipline they have studied when talking to people who are not normally a part of that frame of reference. Those who train for the ministry by going to seminary often get into the language and thought patterns of the seminary to such an extent that it may never occur to them that what they have learned needs translation into the language and thought patterns of their receptors if it is to have the desired impact on them. Many preachers, in fact, spend a large part of their ministries preaching to their homiletics professors. They have not learned that they need to use a different style to reach the people in their pews, so they simply continue to speak within the frame of reference they learned to use in seminary.

God, however, is not like that. he uses the language and thought patterns of those to whom he speaks. He could have constructed a heavenly language and required that we all learn that language in order to hear what he has to say to us. He has the power to do that. But he uses that power to *adapt* to us, to enter our frame of reference, rather than to *extract* us from our frame of reference into something that he has constructed. He has, apparently, no holy language, no holy culture, no sacred set of cultural and linguistic patterns that he endorses to the exclusion of all other patterns. He moves into the cultural and linguistic water in which we are immersed in order to make contact with us.

4. God's communication has great impact, furthermore, because *it is personal*. Unlike modern Americans, God refuses to mechanize communication. If he had asked our advice concerning how to win the world, we might well have suggested that he use microphones and loud speakers. Or, perhaps, we would have suggested that he write a book, or at least go on a lecture tour where he would be able to monologue with thousands of people at a time. But the God who could have done it any way he wanted turned away from such mass impersonal techniques to use human beings to reach other human beings and, ultimately, to become a human being himself. And as a human being he spent time with a small number of other human beings, running away from crowds in order to maximize the person-to-person nature of his interaction with that handful of disciples. We have much to learn from God's method at this point.

5. God's communication, then, is *interactional*. Note in your own experience the difference of impact between an impersonal, mass communication type of situation and a person-to-person interactional type of situation. I'm really impressed with how little Jesus monologued. And our misunderstanding of his approach to communication that leads us to recommend monologue preaching as if this were God's method disturbs me greatly. In the name of Jesus Christ who seldom monologued we recommend monologue preaching as the appropriate method of communication! It seems to me utterly inexcusable for our Bible translators to reduce the nearly thirty Greek words used in the New Testament for communication to two words in English: preach and proclaim. But this is what has been done in most of our English translations. If one term is to be used in English, that term should be "communicate," not preach or proclaim, both of which signify monologue presentation. I am afraid we have not imitated Jesus in church communication nearly so much as we have imitated the Greek love for oratory. Jesus seldom, if ever, monologued. He interacted.

6. A further characteristic of effective communication that God employs is that *he goes beyond the predictable and the stereotype* in his communicative efforts. It

seems that in all interaction, including communication, people either have or develop well defined expectations concerning other people. These expectations are defined in terms of such things as role relationships, age differences, linguistic and cultural factors and the like. On the basis of our previous experience with people in such categories, then, we develop stereotypes in terms of which we predict what is likely to happen when we interact with people who fit into a given category. When our prediction comes true—that is, when the person acts according to our expectations— the communicational impact of whatever that person says or does is very low. If, on the other hand, that person acts or speaks in a way that is unexpected in terms of the stereotype, the communicational impact is much greater. The principle may be stated as follows: if within a given frame of reference the information communicated is predictable, the impact of the communication will be low. If, however, within that frame of reference the information communicated is unpredictable, the impact of the communication will be high.

That's why, in Philippians 2:5–8, we see Jesus going through a two-step process. He could easily have become man, and, as man, simply announced that he was God. But reading between the lines of the passage, we see that as a human being he refused to demand the respect that he had a right to demand. He refused to use his title. Nobody was going to call him Reverend or Doctor. They did eventually call him Rabbi, but they learned to call him Rabbi on the basis of what he *earned*, rather than on the basis of what he demanded. And I think this is a critical difference. Jesus established his credibility, earned his respect, by what he did *within* the receptors' frame of reference. He called himself man (i.e., son of man) until they recognized him as God. And even when the disciples recognized that he was God, he forbade them to use that title for him. I believe he did not want others to use a title that he had not earned in interaction with them anymore than he wanted the disciples to. People have, of course, well defined stereotypes of God. If, for example, he had remained in his predictable glory or even, as a man, associated predictably with the powerful, the elite, the religiously safe people, the impact of what he sought to communicate would have been comparatively small. But he went beyond the predictable stereotypes at point after point and thereby increased enormously the impact of his communication. He went beyond the predictable to become a human being, and then even as a human being went beyond the predictable to become a commoner, and then as a commoner chose to associate with tax collectors and prostitutes, to go to such places as a raucous wedding feast and even to submit to a criminal's death.

As human beings, we too are boxed into stereotypes by those who interact with us. We are stereotyped according to our age group, whatever titles we possess, the kinds of people we associate with, the kinds of places we go to, etc. If we have a title such as Reverend or Doctor, if we fit into a category such as student or teacher, if we are male or if we are female, people will relate to us according to their expectations of the category by means of which they label us. And it is unlikely that they will pay much attention to the messages we seek to communicate as long as those messages are according to their expectations from a person in our category. If, for example, we are known to them as "Christians," and we say the kinds of things that they expect Christians to say, they may discount most or all of what we say. The impact of the communication will, however, be quite different if they find that we care for them more than they expect Christians to care for them or if we relate to them in a more genuine manner than they expect.

7. God's communication, then, *goes beyond generalities to become very specific to real life*. And such specificity increases the impact of these messages. Many general messages are, of course, quite true. The general message, "God is love," for example, is unquestionably true. But his love put in the form of such a general statement has very little communicational impact. His love put in the form of a specific Christian individual, ministering to the specific needs of someone in need, however, has great impact. Even in language, the difference in impact between the statement, "God loves everyone," and, "God loves me," is great. Note in this regard the great difference in impact between the statement of a major point in a sermon and a well chosen illustration of that point that applies it to the real life situation of the hearers.

Jesus frequently used true to life stories that we call parables to specifically relate his teachings to the lives of his hearers. When someone asked him, "Who is my neighbor?" he employed the parable of the Good Samaritan to make his teaching specific. When he sought to communicate truth concerning God as a loving Father, he told the story we know as the Parable of the Prodigal Son. He continually taught his disciples by dealing specifically with the life in which they were involved. He taught us all by ministering specifically to the needs of those around him. And the Bible that records these events is characterized by the specific life relatedness of a casebook. If God had communicated in our way, he might have written a theology textbook. Textbooks are noted for the large number of general and technical statements that they make concerning their subject matter. A casebook, however, is characterized by the kind of specificity to real life that the Bible is full of. The biblical accounts concern specific people in specific times and places with specific needs that are dealt with by means of specific interactions with God. God, in his communication, goes beyond the general to the specific. So should we.

8. God's communication *invites personal discovery*: The most impactful kind of learning is that that comes to us via discovery. In our western educational procedures, however, we seem to go largely against this principle. As a teacher, I'm supposed to predigest the material that I want to communicate to you and to simply dish it out for you in a form that requires little effort on your part. In school, we get predigested lectures followed by testing techniques designed to force us to get that material first into our notebooks, then from our notes into our heads. Our churches have been patterned after the lecture procedures of our classroom except that in church we give no exams. This means that church communication is largely ineffective, since it imitates the predigestion method of the schools but does not include the testing technique that is counted on to at least partially compensate for the lack of discovery involved in this kind of communication.

Note, for example, the difference between your ability to remember those things that someone simply tells you and your ability to remember those things that you discover on your own. Jesus specialized not in predigesting information in order to present it to his hearers in bite size chunks, but in leading his hearers to discovery. This is why his answers were so often in the form of questions. This is also why his hearers often found him to be difficult. When John the Baptist was in prison and sent his disciples to Jesus to ask if he was indeed the coming Messiah, Jesus did not give him a straight predigested answer. His answer was designed to lead John to a life transforming discovery. Likewise with Pilate when he asked Jesus if he was indeed the king of the Jews. Jesus seems to respect people too much to simply give them a predigested answer. I believe again, that the casebook format of the Bible is designed to lead us into impactful discovery learning that will transform our lives, rather than to simply increase our store of information concerning God.

9. A ninth characteristic of God's communicative activity is that *he invites the receptor to identify with himself*. In incarnation God identifies with the receptor. By so doing, however, he makes it possible for the receptor to complete what might be thought of as the communicational circle. That is, *when the communicator gets close enough to the receptor to identify with him or her, the receptor is able to identify, in turn, with the communicator*. As receptors, we seem to be able to understand messages best when we perceive that the communicator knows where we are. If communicators are able to get into our frame of reference, to establish their own personal credibility with us, to get to specific messages that show us they know where we are, then we will find our ability to relate to them and to their message greatly enhanced. When communicators relate to us in such a way that we can say, "I'm just like that," the impact of their messages on us is greatly increased. That is why it is so tragic when a preacher puts himself so high above his people that they can't identify with him. They may feel that he is not where they are and cannot understand them well enough to say anything helpful to them.

How, for example, do you respond when someone from the Kennedy family talks about poverty? We are likely to dismiss whatever they say on this subject on the assumption that they have never had to experience what they are talking about. On the other hand, how do we react when we hear a member of that same family talking about suffering and death? At this point we are likely to have quite a different attitude, since we know they have experienced great tragedy in these areas and have, therefore, earned their right to speak to us concerning them. Before God came to earth in Jesus Christ, how credible was anything he had to say concerning human life? It is all quite different now, however. For we know that Jesus lived and learned and suffered and died as one of us. Because, therefore, he identified with us, we can relate to him. We could not identify with a book or a loud speaker, only with a human being. When, therefore, he says, live as I have lived, suffer as I have suffered, give as I have given, we can follow him.

10. The tenth characteristic of God's communication is that he communicates with such impact that *people give themselves in commitment to his cause*. This is an indication of the ultimate in impactful communication. It is not difficult to communicate simple information. It is only slightly more difficult to communicate in such a way that receptors get excited about what they have heard. But to communicate in such a way that receptors leave what they are doing and commit themselves to the cause of the communicator, this is the ultimate indication of communicational impact. Jesus said to the disciples, "commit yourselves to me." And they did, even to the extent that they defied the whole Roman empire. That's impact. That's the kind of communicator God is. And it is his example that we need

to follow in our communicational effort—not to get people to follow us but to mediate God's communication in such a way that they will follow him.

CHAPTER 19

THE PLACE OF THE RECEPTOR
IN COMMUNICATION

Reprinted here with permission from
Theology, News and Notes 28(3):13–15, 23 (October 1981)

The more we learn about the communication process, the more we become aware of just how crucial the receiver of the communication is to that process. Whether we are attempting to deeply influence people or simply conveying information, the receiver of the communication has the final say over what the results will be. It thus behooves us to learn as much as we can about what is going on at the receiver's (receptor's) end when we attempt to communicate.

Receptors[1] are active, even when they seem to be "just sitting there." They interact actively in a transactional process in which the results are negotiated. There is nothing compelling receptors to interpret messages in the way intended by the communicator, though mutual trust and good will help a lot. Building that trust and good will (or at least not squandering it) becomes, therefore, an important part of any effective communicational interaction. And such building is more likely if we understand and take full account of who and where our receptors are. The following ten characteristics of receptors are presented to assist Christian communicators in getting across what they actually intend.

1. The first characteristic is the fact that *receptors have felt needs.* Apparently no human beings are completely satisfied with what and who they are. (And no cultural system or life-style appears to provide answers for all of life's questions.) Everyone has dissatisfactions and unanswered questions. Those at the conscious level are called "felt" or perceived needs. People seem to have a fairly strong drive to deal with and resolve needs of which they are conscious as long as they are not too deep-seated. Deep level needs are, however, ordinarily judged to be too difficult to deal with and, therefore, ignored.

Effective communicators look for and seek to deal with those needs that each given receptor both feels and is willing to discuss. Topics chosen for discussion or sermonizing in the early stages of a relationship should, therefore, be chosen with this recognition in mind. When a communicator proves effective in dealing with

---

[1] Though I am aware of valid theoretical and practical objections to the use of the term "receptor" for the one who receives and interprets communications, I find no less objectional term to use.

these needs, then, a receptor will ordinarily give permission for a deeper probe. At such a time needs felt at deeper levels can be uncovered and dealt with. This recognition and most of those that follow are evident in Jesus' ministry when that ministry is analyzed from a communicational perspective.

Felt needs are very personal, even those at the surface level. They are, furthermore, a matter of transaction and negotiation between receptor and communicator. That is, a given receptor will only allow a given communicator to deal directly with those needs deemed by the receptor as appropriate to their relationship. It is for this reason that public and mass communication techniques are such inadequate vehicles for either uncovering or dealing with felt needs—unless the receptors are desperate.

Felt needs are, however, the touchstones from which life-change can be recommended and accomplished. And the Christian message is designed to change life. It is of paramount importance, then, for Christian communicators to recognize the importance of felt needs and to employ those communicational techniques that will result in stimulating receptors to effectively deal with them.

2. *Receptors are parts of reference groups.* Receptors, like all other human beings, are not alone. Anyone considering a change of behavior will ask, "What will people think?" And the people that the receptor is concerned about are those often termed "significant others," who make up the person's "reference group." These are the people considered by that person to be most important and, therefore, most necessary to please.

All of us have reference groups consisting of relatives, friends, business associates, members of our social class, neighbors, church associates, etc. These may often be quite distant from us geographically and may even be a figment of our imagination. But they exist in our perceived reality and are strongly considered when we contemplate making a decision for change.

We are influenced by more than one reference group, sometimes in different directions and often at different times. Any change that we contemplate or carry out is, therefore, contemplated and/or carried out in relation to these groups. We may well turn away from a change in anticipation of a negative reaction by any of our reference groups. Or we may make the change and later have to decide whether to go back on the change or to leave the group.

Groups ordinarily allow their members considerable leeway in areas that the group considers trivial. Changes made in values, allegiances, beliefs and the like, considered by the group to be crucial to their well being, however, are a far different matter. Change in such areas will not ordinarily be allowed by the group unless the appeal is made to the opinion leaders of the group. They, then, may either lead the group to make the change or give permission to certain of the membership to make it. Wise communicators take such group phenomena into account and appeal to individuals and their groups accordingly.

3. *Receptors are already committed* both to their groups and to certain values and beliefs. When a Christian communicator appeals for initial or deeper commitment to Christ, he or she is inviting the receptor to move from one commitment to another commitment. It is likely, furthermore, that the communicator

is requesting change in the ultimate commitment of the receptor. A person may, for example, simultaneously be committed to self, family, occupation, one or more friends, God, one or more organizations, a hobby and a host of other material and nonmaterial things that he or she values. The question for Christians is, of course, "which commitment is the greatest?" A wise communicator must take seriously such commitments and seek to present a message in such a way that the receptor is attracted to the option of exchanging his or her present primary commitment for the one recommended by the communicator.

4. *Receptors are constantly interpreting.* All communication is bathed in the interpretations of the participants. Thus even such nonverbal things as the time and place of the interaction, the communicator's life, gestures, tone of voice, use of space, etc. and even the past experiences of the receptor all play very important parts in the way the receptor interprets the messages sent. For this reason, a given verbal message presented informally to an individual at home will be quite different from the "same" message presented formally in church from behind a pulpit.

Interpretation is clearly one of the most important activities engaged in by receptors. A communicator must, therefore, do his or her utmost to insure that everything presented in a message will be interpreted by the receptors in a way that enhances the intended meaning. Not infrequently factors of formality, impersonalness, insincerity, inappropriateness, and the like creep into the way a message is presented resulting in the discounting of the message by the interpreter/receptor. Effective communicators learn to control such factors.

5. The most important activity that receptors engage in is that of *constructing the meanings of the messages they receive.* Meanings do not lie in words or other symbols that we use but, rather, in the people that use them. Meaning is not transmitted from person to person but constructed by people on the basis of their interpretations of the words and other communicational symbols used. It is the people who interpret the words and symbols according to community agreements rather than the words and symbols themselves that determine what their meaning will be.

The attachment of meanings to the symbols employed in communication is a creative kind of activity that receptors perform in keeping with whatever motivations they deem to be appropriate. No matter what the message, the receptor is likely to interpret it in accordance with the way in which he or she relates to the communicator. Such relational characteristics as friendliness/unfriendliness, personalness/impersonal-ness, informality/formality, intergenerational or interclass affection/antipathy or any of a host of other factors become important building blocks from which receptors construct meanings.

6. *Receptors give or withhold permission to enter what might be termed their "communicational space."* Since communication is a transaction it proceeds at the permission of the transactors. Receptors may give or withhold permission totally or they may agree to listen to the communicator on certain subjects but not on others. Or the receptor may take a "wait and see" attitude until the communicator has finished before deciding if or what to accept.

It is as if people have a certain "range of tolerance" for people and messages the they encounter. Any message that is to be permitted to enter a receptor's mind must fit through the opening provided by that range. Such factors as the credibility of the communicator, the maturity of the receptor, the potential threat of the message, the acceptability of the language use, the place and time of the interaction and even the mood of the receptor greatly affect the receptor's tolerance for a message. "I have much more to tell you, but now it would be too much for you to bear" (Jn. 16:12), Jesus told the disciples. Apparently either maturity or circumstances (or both) affected their range of tolerance at that point and Jesus was wise enough not to push matters beyond his hearers' limits. The first priority of any communicator is to win and retain permission to enter the receptor's "communicational space."

7. *Receptors are constantly evaluating everything that goes on.* As with interpretation, the receptors' evaluation extends to every aspect of the communicational interaction, whether personal, situational, grammatical, whether internal or external to themselves. A receptor asks such questions as, "Is this communicator worth listening to?" "Is this message of value to me?" "Is there congruence between the communicator, message, setting, language, etc.?" "Does the communicator know what he or she is talking about?" "If I accept this message, what will it cost me?" The answers to such questions, even more than the content of the message, form the basis for the receptor's response.

8. *Receptors attempt to maintain their equilibrium.* Many receptors find receiving certain kinds of communication so threatening that they develop elaborate strategies to minimize the risk. For many, almost any change, especially in religious areas, is perceived as a threat to their equilibrium. Thus they will reject almost any kind of communication that seems to require change. They will act as if they have all the facts necessary on that subject and either "tune out" when the subject is raised, or provide themselves with a store of counter arguments, each prefaced with "yes, but. . ." Others will simply ignore or forget anything that, if taken seriously, would require change and, therefore, threaten their equilibrium. Such receptors feel compelled to somehow stem the flow of what they consider to be equilibrium-disturbing messages.

The matter of equilibrium is closely related both to felt needs and to the relationship of the receptor to his or her reference group. For it is the felt needs that often seem to demand change while it is the person's relationship with his or her reference group that provides the major symbols of equilibrium. The primary question that arises is, "what will accepting the recommended change cost personally, socially, economically, etc.?" For most people the desire to maintain a known, though perhaps flawed, equilibrium seems usually to outweigh the desire to move toward an unknown, though perhaps attractive change. Ordinarily only the most desperate and the most psychologically secure are likely to seriously consider a message that appeals for radical change.

9. *Receptors produce feedback.* We use the term "feedback" to label the messages sent by receptors to communicators. Feedback is the reversal of the flow of messages so that the receptor becomes the communicator. It can serve all the purposes that any communication serves, though it is often limited to the use of nonverbal techniques. Via feedback, receptors often encourage the communicator or ask for some kind of adjustment in the presentation.

Feedback, like all communication, is subject to the rule that says the meaning is the creation of the receptor (in this case, the communicator). Communicators may or may not, however, even give permission for certain kinds of feedback to enter their perception. For they too are attempting to maintain their equilibrium. And radical suggestions for change are especially unwelcome when a communicator is working from a prepared text. Wise communicators, however, are constantly on the lookout for even disturbing kinds of feedback and always ready to make adjustments in order to keep their presentations from simply becoming performances.

10. Lastly, *receptors decide what to do with the messages they receive.* They decide such things as whether to accept or reject, remember or forget, pay attention or ignore, treat now or deal with later. Often, however, conscious decisions such as that to remember the message are interfered with by the presentation of a "glut" of other messages so that the result is that the receptor forgets.

If the response is to accept the message, such acceptance may be partial, total or conditional. Partial acceptance involves the receptor in the activity of discriminating between those parts he or she wishes to reject. Total acceptance does not involve such discriminations. Conditional acceptance, then, sets up conditions which, if met, will result in the receptor's acceptance of the message, but if not met will result in the receptor's rejection of the message. Complementary to acceptance is, of course, rejection. Rejection, too, may be partial, total or conditional.

In these and other ways the receptor of communication has at least as much to do with the outcome of that communication as the communicator does. Indeed, it is likely that the receptors actually have more control over the outcome of communicational events than communicators do. For this reason it is crucial that those who would be effective communicators learn and make good use of this kind of information concerning those who will have so much to say about what they attempt to get across.

CHAPTER 20

THE POWER OF LIFE INVOLVEMENT

Reprinted here with permission from
Communicating the Gospel God's Way.
Pasadena, CA: William Carey Library, 1979:43–60

Introduction

The topic that I want to deal with in this chapter is something that will, on the one hand, serve as an illustration of a number of things that I've already said and on the other hand, as a probe into some new areas that are important to us as Christian communicators. I'd like to suggest as texts Matthew 4:19 and John 10:11–15. In Matthew 4:19 (and Mk. 2:14; Lk. 5:27, etc.), Jesus says, "Come along with me." The word "follow" in many Semitic and related languages implies "come along with" or even, "commit yourself to." It is not the kind of thing that one would say to a dog to get it to follow. It is a matter of commitment. I would then like to pick out of the passage in John 10, particularly verses 11–15, the implication that not only would the Good Shepherd die for the sheep, but that the Good Shepherd would also *live* for the sheep. I think that is strongly implied in the whole section.

A few years ago I began to ask myself about the communicational *means* that we use to bring about the ends that we desire. I asked things like, what are we trying to bring about through church services? I concluded that we are trying to bring about behavioral change. That is, we want people who are so solidly influenced by our message that their behavior is radically affected. Whether it is the behavior of people who have not yet committed themselves to Christ, or the behavior of those who have already started on the road, our aim is to try to deepen and broaden their commitment.

I further asked, what kind of communication methodology is appropriate for trying to bring about that type of behavioral change? And, if monologue is not the best method for appealing for behavioral change, what is it good for? In grappling with these questions I began to develop a typology of approaches to communication in which I try to summarize several elements of three approaches to communication.

The first approach is the monologue approach. The second is the dialog or discussion approach. The third approach is what I label "life involvement." The following chart outlines the items I discuss below.

A Typology of Approaches to Communication

Characteristic	Approach I *(Monologue)*	Approach II *(Dialog)*	Approach III *(Life Involvement)*
1. Method of Presentation	Monologue/Lecture	Dialog/Discussion	Life Involvement
2. Appropriate Type of Message	General Messages	Specific to Thinking Behavior	Specific to Total Behavior
3. Appropriate Audience	Large Groups	Small Groups	Individuals or Very Small Groups
4. Time Required for Given Amount of Information	Small Amount	Medium Amount	Large Amount
5. Formality of Situation	Formal Dominant	Informal Prominent	Informal Dominant
6. Character of Communicator	Reputation Important	Personality Characteristics Important	Total Behavior Important
7. Focus of Participant	Source Dominant-Message	Message Prominent (Source-Receptor)	Receptor Prominent (Source-Message)
8. Activity of Receptor	Passive—Merely Listens	Considerable Mental Activity	Total Life Involvement
9. Consciousness of Main Message	High (Both Source and Receptor)	Medium	Low (Perhaps Contradictory Verbal Message
10. Reinforcement and Retention	Low	Medium	High
11. Feedback and Adjustment	Little Opportunity	Considerable Opportunity	Maximum Opportunity
12. Discovery by Receptor	Little—Message Predigested	Considerable Discovery	Maximum Opportunity for Discovery
13. Type of Identification	Source Identifies Primarily with Message	Reciprocal Identification with Each Other's Ideas	Reciprocal Source-Receptor Identification on Personal Level over All of Life
14. Impact on Receptor	Low—Unless Felt Need Met	Potential High on Thinking	Maximum on Total Behavior
15. Appropriate Aim of Approach	Increase Knowledge	Influence Thinking	Influence Total Behavior

1. In the above typology the first characteristic to deal with is the *method of presentation*. We all know what *monologue* is. We experience this form of communication as the almost exclusive method used in sermons and lectures. *Dialog or discussion*, on the other hand, is more frequently employed in situations like Sunday School classes, Bible studies or other smaller group experiences. Many situations that look like dialog situations are, of course, merely opportunities for a leader to monologue. The leader may or may not allow serious discussion type interaction on the part of the others in the group. Such a situation would fall under the monologue column rather than under the dialog/discussion column.

The third method of presentation, here termed *life involvement*, may not be as readily understandable as the first two, however. What I am thinking of here is a long term association between communicator and receptors in a variety of life situations, many of which might be quite informal and not highly dependent upon verbalization as the only means of communication. Discipleship and apprenticeship are examples of this kind of communicational method. In discipleship the teacher spends long periods of time with his disciples in a wide variety of life activity. Jesus and his disciples were together twenty-four hours a day for three years. In apprenticeship, an apprentice spends long periods of time with his teacher in a variety of work related activities.

Another illustration of life involvement communication is the family. As we grow up within our family we are life involved with our parents, with our siblings and not infrequently with a variety of other relatives, neighbors and friends. We may or may not like everything about the way we have learned to live from such life involvement, but the fact is that we have learned our lessons well. We have become very much like those with whom we have associated.

The question that I am asking concerning the method of presentation is, if we seek to bring about genuine solid, deep, behavioral change in the people to whom we try to communicate the Christian message, can it be effectively done via monologue? Jesus seldom, if ever, monologued. Is it possible he rejected this method of communication because he considered it inadequate for the purposes that he had in mind? Did he, on the other hand, choose life involvement as his method because he knew that this was the only adequate method for accomplishing his purpose? If so, could it be that we have been misled into depending heavily upon a method that the church has learned more from Greek orators than from Jesus?

2. In the second place I would like to ask, *what type of message is appropriate* to each method of presentation? Though we may note that solid behavior change seldom results from monologue presentations, we also observe that much of value can be accomplished. Perhaps, then, the problem is not so much that one method is appropriate in all contexts while the other method is never appropriate, as it is that we learn to use each method in the context in which each is most appropriate. Indeed, suppose you have a general message about which there is some urgency such as, "Your house is on fire." It would, I think, be poor advice to suggest that such a message be presented via dialog or life involvement! Monologue is the proper method for that kind of message. Likewise for a general message such as "Two and two are four." Unless you are in the initial stages of teaching someone basic addition it is unlikely that a communicator would take the time involved to dialog that

message either. News broadcasts and other presentations of a purely informational nature are also effectively presented via monologue.

If, however, your aim is to affect your receptors at a deeper level than simply the information level, it is likely that monologue will not adequately serve your purpose, unless, of course, what you present via monologue connects strongly with one or more of the felt needs of your receptors. In that case, as I have pointed out, nearly any method will work because the receptor is so anxious for the material presented that he will accept it and appropriate it no matter what form it comes in. But for situations that go beyond the mere presentation of information to receptors who do not have a strong felt need for the message, some other approach is likely to be necessary if our aim is to bring about some change in the receptor.

For this purpose we can recommend dialog as an appropriate way to seek to bring about change in the receptors' thinking behavior. Dialog, of course, is a type of life involvement. It is, however, very often quite limited with respect to time, place and the extent of the areas within the lives of the participants over which involvement takes place. But for wrestling with differences in the thinking of the participants, dialog might be quite adequate. If, however, the aim of the message is to affect the receptors' total behavior, the depth and breadth of the change brought about is quite dependent upon the ability of the receptor first to realize what is being recommended and then to imitate it. And this involves what psychologists call "modeling." Though it is possible for receptors to imagine Christian models or, on occasion, to be able to recall previous experiences with such models, the most effective modeling comes from live involvement between the communicator and the receptors. In the preceding chapters I have already dealt with many of the aspects of a life involvement approach to communicating Christianity. This is, I believe, merely another way of talking about an incarnational methodology.

3. These methods differ with respect to the *appropriate size of audience*. With very large audiences, monologue is perhaps the only possibility. It usually does not work very well to attempt to dialog with a large group. And life involvement with very many is completely out. To some extent, of course, we are life involved even when we monologue with a large group. But this is in a very minimal way and the few things receptors learn from such life involvement with lecturers center largely around getting used to the lecturer's style, mannerisms, facial and vocal expression and the like. The general rule, then, is large groups for monologue, smaller groups for dialog, and still smaller groups for life involvement.

Could Jesus have operated in a life involvement way with more than twelve disciples? Probably not. In fact, even with dialog the numbers involved cannot be very large. Notice what happens to Sunday School classes when the attendance grows beyond, say, twenty-five to thirty. If the class continues to use a dialog format, the number on the roll may continue to rise but the attendance will usually level off at about twenty-five to thirty at most. This seems to be the optimum number for dialog in our society. If the number attending the class gets to be much larger than this, the teacher will ordinarily change to a monologue method. Almost invariable, when there are large Sunday School classes, they are conducted on a monologue basis. We don't seem to be able to handle discussion with more than a small number of people. And with apprenticeship or discipleship, the number that can be handled is even smaller.

4. Our fourth consideration is to ask the question, given a certain amount of material to be gotten across, *how much time would each method require*? In a monologue format, it does not take very much time to present a fairly large amount of information. Note, however, that is it merely information, rather than something that is likely to have a greater impact on the receptor, that is being presented. I believe that our attachment to preaching and lecturing has affected Christianity enormously at this point. By using a monologue format so exclusively, we have come to treat Christian communication as primarily the passing of large amounts of information from communicators to receptors. We have come to focus primarily on information that we should know in order to be Christians rather than on learning a life that is to be lived. I believe this is a serious distortion of the Christian message. The amount of crucial information involved in Christianity is, I believe, quite small. The amount of Christian behavior demanded in response to that information is, however, quite large. We have, however, given ourselves to a methodology that emphasizes the lesser of the two ingredients.

Be that as it may, it is clear that a monologue method is better at presenting large amounts of information, while a life involvement method is better at applying smaller amounts of information to larger areas of behavior. Dialog, then, fits somewhere in between. The amount of information that can be presented in a given amount of time via dialog is not very great, especially when compared with monologue. But it is certainly greater than is possible with life involvement.

5. The fifth consideration is a matter of *the formality of the situation*. Though not all monologue situations are extremely formal, they tend to be more formal than either dialog or life involvement. Life involvement situations, on the other hand, tend to be considerably less formal than either of the other two. Dialog/discussion situations fall somewhere in between. I will not go into further detail concerning the formality of communicational situations, except to suggest that formality affects communicational impact by defining the social distance between communicator and receptors. If that social distance is perceived by the receptors to be great, that fact will affect the kind and nature of the messages at every point. Likewise, if the social distance is perceived to be small and the relationship between the communicator and receptors perceived to be intimate.

6. In the sixth place, I would like to raise the matter of the *perceived character of the communicator*. In general, the greater the social distance entailed in the communicational situation, the more important the reputation of the communicator is to that situation. When deciding whether or not to attend a lecture, we are greatly concerned with whether that person has the credentials, the reputation to enable him to deal with the topic in a helpful way. Advertisements for lectures, therefore, focus strongly on the credentials of the lecturer. In such formalized situations, there is little opportunity for the receptors to assess for themselves the overall credibility of the communicator, except as he deals with that subject in that situation. It is highly desirable, therefore, that the trust level of the audience already be high before the communicator makes his presentation.

In dialog, and especially in life involvement situations, there is much more opportunity for receptors to make their own assessment of the communicator's ability. Though it is still desirable for the communicator to be perceived as credible and trustworthy going into the communicational situation, there is much more opportunity for receptors to modify their original opinions of the communicator in more intimate communicational situations. Often, for example, receptors go away from a lecture situation with essentially the same attitude toward the speaker with which they started. In more intimate situations, however, receptors are often much more impressed with the communicator, both with respect to his subject matter and with respect to himself/herself as a person. On the other hand, students exposed to teachers over small periods of time in classroom situations are often quite impressed with their teachers as long as their exposure is limited to those formalized situations. If, however, a student gets to know his teacher in other areas of life, he may discover some things about that teacher that cause him to revise his opinion downward, even to the point is discounting the validity of the things communicated by the teacher in the classroom. This of course, quite often works the other way as well, especially with respect to teachers who might not be particularly effective in formalized classroom situations who happen to be outstanding persons overall.

7. In monologue situations, furthermore, the *focus of the participants* is squarely on the source, with the message also in focus but to a lesser extent. Receptors are much less in focus. The chairs are set up in such a way that everyone faces the communicator. All eyes are on the front of the room. It is expected that people will sit quietly and take all of their cues from the speaker rather than from anyone or anything else in the room

In a dialog situation, on the other hand, there is often an attempt to arrange the furniture in a circle, down playing the importance of the leader to some extent. The discussion, then, will focus on grappling with the subject by means of a lively interchange between leader and receptors. Thus the message comes into greater prominence as do the receptors, while the prominence of the communicator diminishes a bit in comparison to his prominence in a monologue situation. In life involvement, then, it is the needs of the receptors that come strongly into focus. The activity of the communicator and the nature of the messages are bent to the meeting of the particular needs of the receptors. In Jesus' case, though he was in complete control at all times, the choice of the subjects with which he dealt and the manner in terms of which he dealt with them shows a strong primary focus on meeting the needs of his followers.

8. As I have pointed out in chapter eighteen, *receptors are not inactive*. In a monologue situation, however, receptors tend to be considerably less active than in discussion and life involvement situations. When we listen to lectures or sermons, we basically just sit there. Things are going on in our minds and, at least in classroom situations, we may be taking notes. But our activity is often the more mechanical activity of simply ingesting the material as it is presented, rather than the more demanding activity of considering the material in relation to our total life experience with a view toward incorporating it into our lives. It is that kind of activity, however, that discussion and life involvement communication forces us into. This is why many people dislike more intimate communicational situations

where they will be forced to answer questions or in other ways to indicate the kind of deep level interaction with the material that is going on within their minds and hearts. They consider such a process too threatening to be comfortable.

9. Given the fact that in every communicational situation there is a multiplicity of messages being sent, we ask, in the ninth place, *what the level of consciousness of the main message might be in each of these approaches to communication*. In a monologue situation, of course, the intention of the communicator is that the main message will be strongly in focus. And, unless he/she acts in such a way as to distract from the main message, or unless something else distracting happens while he is presenting that message it is likely that that message will be in primary focus. If, however, the communicator breaks some rules by, say, standing too close to certain of the members of his audience, or by belching during the course of his presentation or by wandering around the room during the presentation, it will be these strange things rather than the main message that will be remembered.

In discussion situations, and particularly in life involvement situations, however, the messages communicated regularly go far beyond the main message. Messages concerning the openness of the communicator, his kindness, his patience, his ability to deal with problems that he may not have anticipated, his ability to integrate the things about which he speaks into his own life, and similar messages are often strongly communicated along with the main message. Indeed, for many of the receptors the way in which the communication is dealt with becomes a more important message than the primary topic itself. Not infrequently, then, these additional messages, technically known as "paramessages," cancel out much or all of the main message. This leads, then, to responses such as, "Your life speaks so loudly, I can't hear what you're saying."

In life involvement, it is often the tone of voice or the timing of the message that indicates to the receptor that the most important message is not the one being verbalized. Often, for example, a sharp or angry response has more to do with the communicator's discomfort than with the receptor's needs. Such a situation is indicated, for example, by the reported response of a bright child when her mother told her to go to bed. Her response was, "Mommy, how come when you get tired, I have to go to bed?" The mother might well have felt that she was communicating only the "go to bed" message. But the perceptive child picked up a paramessage that was probably more accurate as an explanation of the situation than the message that the mother wanted to be in focus. In life involvement, then, what is communicated goes far beyond what might be regarded as the main message.

10. Learning is highly dependent upon what is termed "reinforcement." That is, messages that we hear once and never again tend to be crowded out by messages that we hear over and over again in a variety of ways and applied to a variety of contexts. Our tenth point is, therefore, a consideration of the *opportunity for reinforcement* and the consequent likelihood that the receptor will retain the messages presented via each of these approaches. The monologue approach, of course, due to such factors as the generality of the messages, the large amounts of information involved, and the small amount of interpersonal contact between communicator and receptors, provides little opportunity for the messages to be reinforced and is, therefore, likely to result in low retention on the part of the receptor. Dialog provides considerably

more opportunity for reinforcement and, therefore, much more likelihood of retention. Life involvement, then, is especially adapted to provide large amounts of reinforcement and to result in correspondingly large amounts of retention. Note, for example, what happens to reinforcement and retention when, after a lecture, the audience engages in a lively discussion with the communicator concerning certain of his points. The communicator, then, has opportunity to illustrate, to explain, and to apply certain of his points much more fully. Receptors will typically respond to such a situation by indicating that they now have a much higher level of understanding than they obtained from the lecture. If, then, a certain few of those who listened to the lecture and participated in the discussion are able to spend long periods of informal time with the lecturer, perhaps even living with him for awhile, his ability to reinforce his message and their ability to retain are increased enormously. Pastors should know that the ability of their hearers to retain messages presented in their sermons is substantially increased by visitation and other informal techniques designed to increase a life involvement relationship between themselves and their hearers.

11. *Feedback and the opportunity of the communicator to adjust his message* on the basis of it is of great importance in the process of communication. There is, of course, little opportunity for feedback in a monologue situation, more opportunity in a discussion situation and a maximum opportunity in a life involvement situation. An audience who perceives that the communicator has chosen the wrong message in a monologue situation may, therefore, have little opportunity to let him know in hopes that he might adjust. In a life involvement situation, on the other hand, there is maximum opportunity for the hearers to get such a message back to the communicator and a high likelihood that if the communicator does not make the proper adjustments, his audience will leave him. Indeed, the formal nature of most monologue situations is often the only thing that keeps the audience from completely dissipating.

12. All of this has great implications for the *amount of discovery learning* that the receptors may engage in. As I have suggested above, discovery learning is the most impactful kind and the kind that Jesus employed. Monologue, of course, emphasizes the predigestion of the message at the expense of discovery on the part of the receptors. Life involvement, on the other hand, specializes in leading the receptors to discovery. Discussion is somewhere between these two extremes. In dialog and life involvement situations especially, and to a lesser extent in response to certain sermons and lectures, we find people saying, 'Wow, I haven't thought of that before." Such comments are an indication of discovery learning. We find the disciples making comments like that throughout their experience with Jesus.

13. The *primary type of identificational process* is the thirteenth characteristic in our typology. In a monologue approach it seems as though the source attempts to identify primarily with his/her message and perhaps to a lesser extent with the receptors. In dialog, on the other hand, the identification seems to be more reciprocal between communicator and receptor, though often primarily at the idea level. Life involvement, then involves reciprocal identification between source and receptor at a highly personal level and over the whole of their lives. In terms of what I have said above, concerning the importance of the receptors may be to identify with the

communicator, it is easy to see the superiority of dialog and life involvement as communicational techniques. I will suggest below certain modifications that can be made in monologue presentations to overcome the more disastrous possibilities of that approach in this regard.

14. All of this leads to an *assessment of the communicational impact* on receptors of communication employing each of these approaches. The impact via monologue is likely to Ice quite low unless one or both of the following situations exist: (a) The felt needs of the receptors for the material being presented are high, or (b) the communicator makes the kind of adjustments in his presentation that I speak about below. Dialog communication, on the other hand, has high potential for impact at least on people's thinking behavior. Life involvement, then, has the potential for maximum impact on the total behavior of the receptors.

In employing sermons, lectures, or the kind of written medium that I am employing here, we count on at least certain members of our audiences coming to the situation with a need for what we are presenting. Our ability to communicate effectively to them, then, is highly dependent upon our ability to guess where their felt needs lie. Sometimes, of course, we guess very well. On other occasions, however, our guesses may be quite wide of the mark. Certain communicators, furthermore, seem to be either unconcerned or unable to guess well at any time. Others, happily, seem to be able to regularly transcend the probability factors in their ability to communicate effectively via monologue. Some of the reasons for this may lie in the factors that I discuss below.

15. I ask, therefore, as point fifteen, what the *appropriate expectation* should be in our use of these three approaches. It seems that if our aim is simply to increase the knowledge of the receptors, that monologue is the appropriate method. If, however, we seek to solidly influence the thinking of our receptors, we should use a dialog/discussion method. Influencing total behavior, however, demands much more total life involvement than either of the other methods affords. As I have mentioned before, monologue can be effectively used much like a display in a store window, to alert people to the good things that await them once they get beyond that display. Monologue is also good at bringing people to make decisions that they have been considering for a long time. Monologue can, furthermore, be usefully employed to support people in decisions that they have already made. This is probably the major function that sermonizing serves in our churches and over the mass media. Studies of the use of sermons via radio and television point out, however, that very few people who do not already agree with the communicator either listen to the presentation or have their opinions affected by them. And those who do have their opinions changed via mass media are almost always those whose felt needs predispose them to be positive toward the kind of change there advocated. Even then, however, the durability of the opinion change is highly dependent upon the continued reinforcement of a group of like-minded people. This is one of the primary functions of the church within Christianity. Monologue does, however, enable us to present large amounts of information in a relatively efficient way. The church's overdependence on monologue has, however, as I have indicated above, led us into what I regard as a serious heresy, the heresy of regarding Christian orthodoxy as primarily a matter of correct thinking, rather than a matter of correct behavior. This

has, I believe, even led many evangelicals to unconsciously advocate a kind of "salvation by knowledge" doctrine in place of what Scripture teaches—salvation by faithfulness.

Dialog, too, can be a primarily intellectual knowledge kind of thing. Even though the method may be superior communicationally, if the content is purely cognitive, we may still have botched the message that we are called to communicate. With life involvement, however, it is much more difficult to present a purely cognitive message, since the overall message presented via this means relates so thoroughly to all of life. This method, therefore, provides a considerable corrective to the intellectualizing of the Christian message, provided our example is a properly Christian one. The contrast I am getting at between the kinds of messages via these methods was nicely pointed out to me by an African who said, "You Euroamericans are primarily concerned with intellectual heresy. We Africans are more concerned with interpersonal heresy." I think what he was getting at is at the heart of the Scriptural message—that the real Christian message lies in the behavior of the messenger rather than in his words. Christians who behave as Christians relate in Christian ways to other people, whether or not these people agree with them intellectually. Euroamerican Christianity, however, has turned so completely to a concern for knowledge, information and doctrine, that it frequently occurs that we defend our doctrine at the expense of relating to even fellow Christians in a Christian way. It is my feeling, therefore, that even a discussion of the communicational techniques that we employ should lead us into a critical evaluation of the actual message that our receptors perceive us to be advocating.

What if One Is Limited to Monologue?

Having considered all of these things with respect to the ideal way to communicate the message to which we are committed, I began to ask myself if there is anything that we can do to increase the effectiveness of our communication in situations where monologue is the only method available to us. That is, suppose I find myself in a church situation or even a classroom situation, or even worse in a situation where I must attempt to communicate via writing, can I make any adjustments that will increase the impact of my communication while minimizing the less desirable characteristics of the medium that I employ? The answer that I came to was that there is indeed much that can be done to bring our audiences to experience more of the kind of impact that characterizes dialog and life involvement communication, even when we are limited to monologue presentations. Though, for example, monologue interaction does not permit a high degree of life involvement between communicator and receptors, it is possible to increase the amount of such involvement and thereby to increase the communicational impact.

I have suggested that the above chart of approaches to communication presents us with a kind of scale with monologue at one end of the scale and life involvement at the other end. If, therefore, we look at certain of the items on that chart, we will discover that at least certain of the characteristics of dialog and life involvement can be approximated in a monologue situation. If this is done, then, at least certain of the numbers of our audiences may be able to fill in the gaps and by imagining themselves in a full life involvement situation with us to get beyond the more crippling effects of formalized monologue.

If, for example, at point 2 on the chart, the communicator refrains from presenting simply general messages and makes his messages more specific to the actual lives of his receptors, he is likely to increase the impact of his presentation. This will, of course, mean that he will need to take more time in his presentations, dealing with a smaller amount of material (see point 4) rather than the smaller amount of time dealing with larger amounts of material that often characterizes monologue presentations. He will illustrate his points more fully and, in keeping with point 6 and much of the material presented in chapters one and two concerning identification, let his receptors hear considerably more about his own personal experience than is often done in monologue.

This will, of course, involve the reduction of the formality of the situation (point 5). Even though the method of presentation is monologic, the speaker may come across more as one who is conducting a conversation, one who is participating with his hearers not only in verbalizing, but even in other areas of life. He may, as is frequently the case in conversations, reduce his material to a single point which he wraps in true to life illustrations, many of which relate to his own personal experience. I have been exposed to one preacher who did this extremely well. He never had more than one point but he illustrated it in a variety of ways and from a variety of perspectives. Because those illustrations bring about a kind of pseudo-life involvement, we found it very easy to get wrapped up in what the speaker was communicating and to get beyond such superficial characteristics of the communicational situation as the speaker's reputation and his focus on his message (point 7). I remember feeling frequently that I and I alone was in focus. I, furthermore, found myself getting much more involved (point 8) in the application of what the speaker was saying to my own experience and the integration of his perspectives into my perspective. Jesus, of course, did this very well when he used true to life stories that we call parables.

Now, we should be warned that not all decrease of formality and increase of the personalness of the communicator automatically increases the impact of communication. Often such breaking of the rules can be taken quite badly by the receptors. Say, for example, the communicator stands on the pulpit rather than standing behind it. His receptors might take this quite badly. Or, for example, suppose the communicator is not careful about the personal things that he reveals concerning himself. He might in public reveal intimate details that are considered quite inappropriate in public and thereby seriously hinder the communication. Or, suppose he is perceived to be showing off his ability to tell clever stories rather than enhancing his message by means of these stories. His communication is likely to be seriously hindered thereby or, at least, the message that is actually communicated may be something quite different from the message that he supposedly intended. If a communicator is psychologically insecure, for example, he may latch onto some of the techniques that I am recommending as means of enhancing his own prestige rather than enhancing the communication of the message.

A further adaptation that can often be made is to increase the effectiveness of the feedback and adjustment process (point 11). Some speakers are quite effective in raising questions that the audience is generally concerned with. A speaker may say, for example, something like, "You are probably asking concerning this subject such and such a question." If he has hit on a question that his audience actually is asking, they will say to themselves, "Sure enough, I am asking that question. I wonder what he is going to say about it." So the involvement of the receptor is increased (point 8) by the communicator's setting up of a fictitious though realistic feedback situation. Or, the communicator might elicit actual feedback by asking a question that the audience will answer. This technique may be less feasible in a preaching situation, particularly on Sunday morning. However, not infrequently it is possible to raise questions that the audience can answer with a nod of the head or a shake of the head rather than verbally. Often, furthermore, it is possible for a communicator to develop a sensitivity to the feedback that his hearers send via the expressions on their faces or other gestures to such an extent that he can respond by adjusting his message on the spot. Some communicators even plant people in the audience to provide such feedback for them. Pastors wives are often good at this.

In monologue situations we may also increase the possibility of discovery (point 12). Sometimes it is a good idea for us to ask questions that we don't even intend to answer directly. In this way we may stimulate people to think about these questions and to go out and grapple with them on their own. Jesus very often did this. Sometimes, furthermore, he would answer a question with another question. Even this might be possible in certain monologue presentations. Often via a series of monologue presentations it may be possible to lead people into discovery of a new perspective. Questions relating to the adequacy of the old perspective and pointed illustrations demonstrating the greater adequacy of the new perspective can play an important part in leading people to this kind of discovery.

These techniques, and probably several others that I have not mentioned, can do much to bring about the right kind of identification between the receptor and the communicator (point 13). As I have pointed out in chapters one and two, communicational impact is directly related to the ability of the receptor to identify with the source. As I have mentioned, self-exposure on the part of the communicator is often crucial to bringing about such "reverse identification." When people in the audience can say, "He may be a preacher (or teacher, etc.), but he is just like me," the potential impact of even monologue communication can be increased enormously. Or, if a significant number of those in the audience have entered into life involvement experiences with the communicator (even, for example, on the golf course), the effectiveness of material presented via monologue can be enhanced. When the communicator is known as a human being, rather than simply a reputation (point 6), even monologue communication can be very effective because it then becomes a part of a total life involvement.

In summary, it has been my intent in this and the preceding chapters to advocate incarnational, life involvement communication as the right way to go for Christian communicators. I have attempted to develop this point from the perspective of communication theory, on the one hand, and from the example of God through Christ on the other. I have generalized to a considerable extent in order to cover a large amount of material in a fairly short presentation. I have, furthermore, employed a technique that is more like those techniques that I do not recommend than it is like those that I do recommend. I have, for the sake of getting some of these ideas across to a wider audience, employed techniques that I recognized to be less effective than techniques that would involve person to person life involvement between myself and you as the receptors. Nevertheless, I am in hopes that the felt needs that exist within you will make it possible for at least some of this material to be useful to you.

THEOLOGY

AN ANTHROPOLOGICAL APPROACH TO THEOLOGY

CHAPTER 21

CULTURAL ANTHROPOLOGY: ITS MEANING FOR CHRISTIAN THEOLOGY

Reprinted here with permission from
Theology Today 41:390-400 (1985)

The academic discipline we know as Christian theology is a part of culture. It is amenable, therefore, to analysis from an anthropological or cross-cultural point of view. It is, furthermore, a discipline that has frequently incorporated the insights and perspectives of other disciplines. Though cultural anthropology, like theology, is but a human discipline and can claim no corner on truth, it is not unlikely that some of the insights developed by anthropologists might be found helpful for theologians.

It is the intent of this article, in a far too brief and largely undocumented manner, to survey the kinds of issues that come to the mind of at least one anthropologist with a Christian commitment as he ponders this topic.

This essay is in two parts: (1) How Christian theology looks to an anthropologist, and (2) help that might be available to theologians from anthropology. Though the total discipline called "anthropology" also includes physical anthropology, archeology and linguistics (in addition to cultural anthropology), the cross-cultural perspective on the basis of which the following comments are made is so pervasive within the discipline as a whole that I have taken the liberty of employing the general designators "anthropology" and "anthropologist," rather than the more specific forms "cultural anthropology/anthropologist."

I

Anthropologists attempt to analyze human behavior with a particular focus on the cultural influences on and cultural results of that behavior. Theologians are human beings influenced by and influencing other humans, all within cultural matrices. Both the history of theology and theologians and their current status and influence are of interest to at least some of us. From an anthropological perspective, several observations about theology may be offered.

(1) There seems to be an inappropriate degree of culture-boundness about Christian theology as it has been developed and is taught. An anthropologist would expect a certain amount of this from a discipline that has been produced within Western cultures and for Western audiences. Yet the scriptural data that theologians work with are not Western and the claims made by those documents embrace the two-thirds or more of the world that lies outside of the West. It would seem, therefore, that an approach less hampered by Western ethnocentrism would be indicated.

Though one could hardly fault early theologians who only did the best they could with approaches available to them, there are now sharper tools for dealing with the cultural and linguistic materials with which theologians spend their time. Whether it is in the application of one or another of the approaches of metaphysical philosophy, or in the use of historical perspectives infected with social evolutionism, or in the dependence upon philological perspectives that take little, if any, note of the plethora of insights into language that have come to us from the study of thousands of non-Western, non-literary languages, from an anthropologist's perspective the discipline seems not to have grown with the world.

Such a judgment is not, of course, entirely fair, since it results from holding one discipline accountable for expertise in the area of the other's primary interest. However, to the extent that this judgment is accurate, it is serious. For not only do the biblical and historical data with which theologians work come from other cultures, the world at our doorstep is increasingly multicultural in its makeup. And the problems it generates—problems to which theologians are expected to speak— are increasingly the result of relationships between peoples with differing cultural maps and agendas in their heads.

In addition, those outside the field of theology—even many committed Christians—are often finding what seem to them to be better answers to problems to which theologians have traditionally spoken from the application of the perspectives of anthropology and the other behavioral sciences (for example, psychology and sociology) than they are from theology.

(2) Part of the problem may, of course, lie in the overly academic nature of much theological thinking, writing, and teaching. Though academic anthropology is just as guilty of obfuscation as any discipline, a student of American culture easily recognizes that academic efforts that apparently bear such a tangential relationship to the life of the world around them are not being taken seriously by most people. Would such disciplines (including academic anthropology) even survive if our nations were not so wealthy? Or if schooling for its own sake had not become the religion of middleclass Western society? And given the constant claim of seminary graduates that theological study is largely irrelevant to any ministry other than the teaching of theology, would the teaching of theology survive in its present form if it were required to serve the needs of the marketplace?

An anthropologist studying contemporary Christian groupings would quickly point out that there are among ordinary people other types of theology—popular or "folk" theologies. These are the theologies that people actually live by. They tend not to be written (at least not by specialists writing in the academic jargon of the discipline) and seldom are systematized. They are, however, often more influential than academic theologies, tend to relate more obviously to "life issues" and proliferate most when Christian faith is most vigorous. They also tend to be more lived than analyzed (in contrast, often, to academic theologies). They thus deserve study and serious discussion in theological training institutions (if for no other reason than to help students to find correctives).

It might be questioned from an anthropologist's view of Western culture if academic theological teaching and writing (or that of other disciplines, including anthropology) are really of much value to any but those elite for whom they provide employment.

(3) It looks like many engaged in theological discussion and teaching have too great a tendency to equate their own perspective on the reality or truth they study with that reality itself. And this criticism does not only apply to the more conservative among us. Both conservative and liberal camps have their share of members who are closed to any views but their own and who insist that only their understandings are valid.

Anthropologists have learned that, though reality may ultimately be one, there are likely to be many equally valid understandings of that reality (with each understanding probably also at least partly invalid). They would observe that it is especially important in conceptual areas such as those primarily in focus in theological discussion that we lose our longstanding cultural and academic ties to positivism. Though our Christian convictions ordinarily lead us to assert that there is a Reality and that we actually see that Reality when we do theological study, we should also be careful to assert that we never see that Reality absolutely. God is always greater than our ability to understand.

If we believe in the sacredness of at least part of the data that we study, we should not allow ourselves or others to believe that the human understandings that we generate concerning that data are similarly sacred or inspired (even though we may believe them to be God-led). Again, this criticism would apply to many other disciplines as well. A good dose of Kuhn, Barbour, and others writing on the philosophy of science would help us all.[1]

(4) Anthropologists (and others) have recently become much more aware than formerly of the processes that are crucial to cultural behavior. It was once in vogue, even within anthropology, to describe cultures as a still photograph pictures life. Human life, however, is not reducible to still photograph representations, except at the expense of severe distortion. Theological discussion, as most of us have experienced it, however, seems to reflect this same tendency. Theologies are usually presented and passed on as final products to be adhered to or criticized as if they were timeless formulations, relevant once and for all for all peoples in all cultural contexts. The uniqueness of the cultural context, including such variables as the political, economic, social, and personal factors involved in the producing of the theology, while of great historical interest, is seldom analyzed with a view to

---

[1] Thomas S. Kuhn, *The Structure of Scientific Revolutions* (Chicago: The University of Chicago Press, 1970). Ian G. Barbour, *Myths, Models and Paradigms* (New York: Harper and Row, 1974).

learning what we need to know to engage in that same process today. Yet, as von Allmen helps us to understand, this would be a better aim of theological instruction than simply the passing on of ancient theological products.[2]

To illustrate, I have several times been involved in discussions designed to discover just who should be considered a "good" Lutheran (or Calvinist or theological heir of Thomas Aquinas or Paul or Jesus Christ). Should we consider one a good Lutheran who has studied well and subscribed to the theological "product" that Luther produced? Or should that label be applied to those who attempt to live and think in their cultural context in as equivalent a fashion as possible to the way Luther might live and think if alive today? Would Luther want his followers simply to accept his *product,* or would he want them to follow his example by imitating in their times and contexts the *process* by means of which he attempted to interact with and speak to the issues of his day?

A discipline that seeks to speak relevantly to its own day (if that is what theology seeks) will need to give primary attention to the process by means of which theological products have come into existence in the past with a view to understanding and teaching the implications of that process for contemporary theological efforts.

II

If the above observations are of any merit, an anthropological perspective could be of help to theology in further analyzing and discovering answers to the problems, as well as in identifying them. Indeed, since most of the things I have said above are likely to be well known even to those not anthropologically trained, the analytical and problem-solving capabilities of anthropology in these areas are likely to be of more interest to theologians than the fact that an anthropological perspective can help identify them.

(1) The first area in which anthropological insight could be of help to theology would be where anthropology is strongest—the understanding of culture. Any discipline that seeks to deal with human beings needs the sharpest insights possible into the nature and workings of that within which humans "live and move and have their being"—culture. Theologians need to know as much as possible about such things as the patterning, integrating, and channeling influence of culture on every aspect of human thinking and behavior. The wide differences in peoples' perceptions of and responses to those perceptions of reality caused by their cultures (including subcultures) and worldviews should be of particular interest and profit to theologians.

Such insight can be helpful to theologians in at least three important areas: (a) by enabling them to understand better the biblical and other documents written in other cultural matrices, (b) by enabling them to apply theological insights to

---

[2] Daniel von Allmen, "The Birth of Theology," *International Review of Mission* 44 (1975) 37-55.

contemporary peoples within their cultural and subcultural matrices, and (c) by enabling them to understand and compensate for the kinds of influence that their own culture has on their perceptual and interpretational efforts. My reading of theologians shows them better at treating ancient documents in their cultural contexts than at recognizing and compensating for their own culturally-conditioned interpretational reflexes.

Bultmann and his followers, for example, were good at the former, but seem to have fallen for the myth of European cultural superiority even while attempting to unmyth the biblical materials. An anthropological perspective would have enabled them to see strengths and weaknesses, truth and error in their own culture as well as in biblical cultures. In spite of the cultural theory concerning the existence of demons and spirits that we Euroamericans have been taught in the learning of our culture, we do *not* know that our theory is superior to that of biblical peoples (and most of the rest of our contemporary world). Even though most anthropologists are at least as naturalistic as most theologians, the cross-cultural nature of the discipline can at least alert us to the fact that *both* understandings are cultural theories developed by people to explain certain data. Even "scientific" explanations are cultural theories. And our theory is not necessarily better than theirs simply because it is ours.

The appearance of books by Gottwald, Malina, Rogerson, and Wolff is indeed encouraging, at least with respect to the application of anthropological insight to the interpretation of the biblical world.[3] Perhaps at last we can get beyond the mere recognition of "something out there" that H. Richard Niebuhr documents for a number of theologians or the naive philosophizing about culture that Tillich pursued.[4]

(2) A related way in which anthropology can be helpful for theology is by providing a broader understanding of language, especially as it relates to culture. Much insight into the workings of language has come from the study of non-Western languages, many of them more similar linguistically and/or culturally to Hebrew than to European languages on which philological understandings of language are based. It is unfortunate that many of the misunderstandings and limitations of the traditional European approach to analyzing languages (that is, philology) are still crippling many, even two decades after Barr.[5]

Language is made up of thoughts, not merely words and syntax. And thoughts are cultural things. Meanings are felt, not simply reasoned. And feelings are both culturally conditioned and seldom derivable with any degree of accuracy from written records. Experience with contemporary cultures and languages more similar than those of Europe to biblical cultures and languages can provide clearer windows into many scriptural meanings than most learned theologians can provide—as many missionaries who have worked in such languages and cultures frequently attest.

---

[3] Norman K. Gottwald, *The Tribes of Yahweh* (Maryknoll, NY: Orbis Books, 1979). Bruce J. Malina, *The New Testament World* (Atlanta: John Knox Press, 1981). J. W. Rogerson, *Anthropology and the Old Testament* (London: Basil Blackwell, 1978). Hans Walter Wolff, *Anthropology of the Old Testament* (London: SCM Press, 1974).

[4] H. Richard Niebuhr, *Christ and Culture* (New York: Harper and Row, 1951). Paul Tillich, *Theology of Culture*. ed. Robert C. Kimball (New York: Oxford University Press, 1959).

[5] James Barr, *The Semantics of Biblical Language* (London: Oxford University Press, 1961).

Learning to "feel with" the biblical authors, as one would do in learning to function in a contemporary language, could be an important enhancement of current exegetical procedures and largely replace the rigorous (and impersonal) "decipherment" approach that is usually taken to materials in ancient languages.

It is anachronistic that many church leaders who have supposedly been trained theologically still perpetuate fallacies such as the following: (a) biblical languages are qualitatively different from other languages; (b) biblical texts should be analyzed as if they were written as technical, scientific treatises; (c) words are the focal points of language; (d) we cannot interpret scriptural language the way we interpret ordinary language; (e) the meanings of biblical words are accurately discovered by tracing their etymologies; and (f) literal translations more faithfully convey the original meanings than other types of translations.[6]

(3) As important as the process of translation is to many aspects of theological practice and teaching, my impression is that theologians tend to be behind the times in their understanding and application of contemporary insight into the translation process. The application of anthropological (including linguistic) insight has brought about a revolution in this field. Theologians, for example, tend to endorse literal Bible translations without recognizing what professional translators recognize, namely that "a literal translation of the words of the Bible can be tragically misleading.[7] This is true because the meanings underlying the linguistic forms of the biblical materials are firmly rooted in the cultures in which those peoples participate. A translation that does not make enough of that culture explicit in the receiving language to enable contemporary readers to understand without the necessity of special study of the original cultures is, therefore, only of value to those who have done such study.

Those who do not have the ability to interpret the English words as if they were part of the original cultural context ordinarily assume that words and constructions were intended to convey meanings that come to their minds when they hear them in English. Thus, the reflex interpretation by an English speaker of such a sentence as "the wicked will not stand in the judgment" (Ps. 1:5 RSV) would likely be something like "the wicked will not be judged"—a meaning quite different from what a Hebrew would have gotten from the same construction. The reference to the tax collector "beating his breast" in Luke 18:13 (RSV) is likewise misinterpreted as indicating self-congratulation. And the frequent phrase in Amos, chapter 1, "for three transgressions and for four," is incorrectly understood by speakers of English to refer to three or four transgressions, rather than "repeatedly." And what English speaker could be expected to guess that "cleanness of teeth" in Amos 4:6 had nothing to do with dental hygiene but, rather, is a Hebrew way of referring to famine? The list of such completely misleading renderings in the literal translations is virtually endless.

Bible translators have to deal with cultural, linguistic, and theological (including hermeneutical) issues all at the same time. The theological enterprise would profit greatly (as some theologians have already learned) by drinking deeply at the wells

---

[6] Eugene A. Nida and Charles R. Taber, *The Theory and Practice of Translation* (Leiden: Brill, 1969).

[7] Eugene A. Nida, *The Book of a Thousand Tongues* (London: United Bible Societies, 1972).

provided by the several hundred practicing Bible translators and translation theorists with doctoral degrees or similar academic credentials. These tend to cluster in organizations like The United Bible Societies (including the American Bible Society) and Wycliffe Bible Translators. They frequently write up their insights in publications such as *The Bible Translator*.

(4) Theologians can learn from anthropology how to deal more precisely with the relationships between the surface level forms of culture and the deep level meanings that those forms convey. Cultural forms (such as customs, words, ceremonies, behaviors, material objects, etc.) are important for what they mean to people (that is, how they are interpreted by people), not in and of themselves. Though the distinction between form and content is well known outside of anthropology, it is not uncommon for those without specific input from anthropology or linguistics to regard surface level customs as the essence of culture. They often feel that if these are described, the major portion of the culture (or ritual, ceremony, or other expression of culture) has been adequately treated. This is, however, far from the case. For it is the *meanings,* rooted in the basic assumptions concerning reality called worldview, that form the essence of human culture and the basis for human behavior.

The forms of culture are the vehicles or containers for the expression and transmission of the meanings that lie beneath the surface of culture. Theologians have often correctly seen (and anthropologists have often not made explicit) that most of the meanings expressed via cultural forms have their roots in common human need and experience. Which cultural forms express which deep level meanings, however, differs widely from culture to culture. There is, therefore, much more similarity between Old Testament and New Testament peoples at the deep level than on the surface. For cultural forms are assigned their meanings by the people who use them on the basis of their employment within a specific cultural experience. There are, apparently, no cultural (including linguistic) forms that automatically carry the same meanings in all cultures, or even in any two cultures.

The same form will always change meaning when borrowed from one culture to another, or even when passed on from one generation to the next within the same culture. Thus, cultural practices (sacrifices, temple, rituals) endorsed by God in one generation are condemned in a later generation—because the meaning had changed from an acceptable meaning to an unacceptable one. Whether in biblical times or in the present, the way to preserve the original meanings is to discover and employ forms in the new culture or new generation (that is, new generational subculture) that are interpreted by the new group as expressing meanings equivalent to the original meanings. To transmit and preserve deep level meaning, surface level cultural forms need to be changed. This principle is clear in the Scriptures to those who have become aware of it (whether with or without anthropological input).

The application of such a principle makes it possible for those who believe the Bible to be normative to define and apply that normativity in a principled way. With respect to such issues as the role of women in church leadership, for example, this principle enables us to note that at least certain of the forms that the scriptural authors recommended as meaning propriety in their cultural contexts convey in our contexts meanings of suppression and denial of the right to exercise God-given gifts.

This being the case, the primary question ceases to be, "How can we maintain the forms (for example, the role relationships) that are commanded in the New Testament?" We recognize, rather, that these commands, as all commands in Scripture, are couched in culture-specific forms and that these forms (like all forms in culture) are designed to convey meanings. It is the meanings, then, not (as the Pharisees believed) the forms of Scripture that are normative for today. The questions we are to ask, therefore, are, "What are the meanings that the scriptural authors intended to get across? What cultural forms in our culture will adequately express those meanings?" Such a principle provides an antidote to Pharisaism. It can also enable those theologians who seek to retain a belief in the authority and applicability of biblical teachings in contemporary contexts to embrace many of the insights of liberal and secular scholarship without abandoning a high view of scriptural inspiration.

(5) The question of the contextualization of theology suggests another anthropological perspective that can be helpful. If, as anthropologists contend, no form has the same meaning in two different cultural contexts, no theological system can either. If, therefore, a given theological system is passed from one society to another or from one generation to another, it can be expected that the meaning to the new group will be different. First of all, it is not likely to be seen as "ours" by the receiving group. Secondly, it is not likely to be seen as speaking to the issues they are concerned with. Since it was developed in a different place, time, and culture (a different context) by people whose experience and problems were different, its relevance will be limited to those issues where there is a convergence of experience and concern between these receivers and the originators of the theological system.

What becomes evident from such considerations is that all theologies are contextualized by those who develop them for the context within which they function. They are, therefore, to a greater or lesser extent, at least partially unsuited for any other context. Theology is not to be seen, then, as a single once-for-all thing, but as a variety of specific, focused theologies, springing from specific needs, incorporating specific insights and speaking to specific situations. There will be a large degree of common concern between Christian theologies based on the Bible, since the primary data are the same for all. But such interpretational things as the underlying assumptions, the matters focused on, which teachings are emphasized, and the ways in which they are derived and related to life may legitimately differ as widely as the cultural contexts and the individual theologians differ.

(6) Theologians need anthropological input concerning the processes of culture. Understanding of cultural structures (forms) must be balanced with understanding of the processes in which those structures participate and that result in the changing of the structures. People engage in culturally structured processes that result in such things as support, maintenance, communication, education, social control, and adaptation to the new. Christianity is intensely interested in such processes, especially as they relate to communication, conversion, and spiritual growth. Theologians, like most academics, have ordinarily been more concerned with conceptualization than with communication. Their findings are, therefore, widely ignored by the people involved in such processes, not because the conceptualizations are inaccurate or lacking potential value, but simply because they are unintelligible

to nonspecialists in the way they are articulated. In this and several other areas, insight into the circumstances under which, and the processes by means of which, people change their ideas ought to be known and utilized by theologians with a degree of preciseness not ordinarily available within the discipline.

Concern for crumbling family structures, for example, stimulates many to talk of the need for a "theology of the family." And some have put their minds to developing such—but usually without any but an idealized philosophical understanding of what a healthy family might look like. More concrete understandings are abundantly available from studying the family cross-culturally. Family structuring and dynamics are cultural things, and both the processes that lead to family illness and those that lead to family health are cultural processes that should be studied and understood to inform theological approaches to them.

The church, likewise, is primarily a Christian use of cultural processes of grouping. Other cultural processes lie behind such things as conversion, nurture, education, expressing concern, faithing, even sinning. Theologizing concerning these areas should give more attention to a much greater range of valid cultural and individual expression of the processes involved than is ordinarily true.

Students in my courses on conversion and the church frequently express their amazement and enthusiasm over the valuable difference they experience between a cross-culturally informed treatment of these topics and the more traditional mono-cultural treatments they have been exposed to in traditional theology classes and books. They are often startled to discover that once one has been exposed to what is termed the theology of any of these doctrines, one has come to understand only a very small fraction of even the scriptural treatment of the doctrine. A high percentage of what we need to know about the church, for example, is more susceptible to discovery through anthropological methodology than through theological methodology—though one cannot deny the value of traditional theological insight into the nature of the church.

(7) Anthropology can also be of assistance to theologians by pointing to another way to do research. Though the empiricist approach to dealing with what we perceive as reality has serious pitfalls of its own, a reasonable infusion of people-oriented (not merely statistics-oriented) empiricism into theological method would be of considerable help in balancing the tendency to focus too exclusively on what "ought to be" with solid attention to what "actually happens."

Anthropologists learned long ago that if we seek to learn about people, we need to study *people,* not just books about people (often written by those who simply read books themselves). Learning to observe perceptively and also to participate with people in order to get the "feel" of their behavior have been the hallmarks of anthropological field method for many years. Much theological writing concerning people suffers from a lack of insight that could be derived from "hands on" experience with people outside of the academic ghettos within which many theologians seem to be imprisoned.

Too many of the concepts of theology seem to be based on generalizations that, though they may have been applicable to some situations somewhere in the past, are not specifically applicable to many, if any, of today's variety of situations. Understandings of shame and guilt, conscience, the relationships of faith to psychological and spiritual well-being, the interaction between meaning and experience, and the kind of blockage of communication that occurs due to certain types of experience could be cited as examples of the kinds of things that theologians need to study empirically.

I have suggested above the need to study the family cross-culturally to arrive at insights to help in dealing with the serious problems that face contemporary American families. The "participant-observation" method is the way to get the data for such an approach. This is, likewise, the method to be used to discover better approaches to church life, conversion, and the other areas mentioned in which our ability to deal effectively with them is hampered by our lack of proper understanding of what is really going on at the human level.

III

As I have pointed out above, anthropology is no new messiah. It is a fallible, human discipline like theology. Indeed, another article might helpfully be written on the assistance that anthropology might gain from theology. But theology has a tradition of incorporating into its stream insights and methodologies developed by other disciplines. I would like to see such incorporation of the insights and methodologies of cultural anthropology. I believe we all would profit from such an effort. Though it is not uncommon to find persons on theological faculties with sociological or psychological training, it is rare to find those with the broader, cross-cultural perspectives of anthropology (except among those teaching missions). I would hope that the benefits of such input would lead to an improvement of this situation in the years to come.

CHAPTER 22

CAN ANTHROPOLOGICAL INSIGHT ASSIST EVANGELICAL THEOLOGY?

Reprinted here with permission from
Christian Scholars Review 7:165–202 (1977)

Personal Introduction

Academically I am labeled an anthropological linguist. By convention, therefore, I should stick to my own specialization and not meddle in somebody else's specialty. But that convention causes me problems.

For I am also an evangelical Christian, dedicated to both the relevance of the Christian gospel and the usefulness of analytical thinking (theologizing) concerning the gospel. I speak from within an evangelical theological institution, but as one whose primary specialization and experience provide me with a perspective not ordinarily included in such institutions. My academic specialization, the fact that I have served as a missionary (in Nigeria) and my present vocation as a trainer of cross-cultural communicators of the gospel, all lead me to be intensely concerned with both the clear understanding and the clear communication of theological truths.

It is this concern that leads me to be greatly disturbed by the state of contemporary evangelical theology and of the institutions that teach it. I am disturbed by the impression of irrelevance that many people associate with theology and theological institutions. I am bothered by the fact that many perceptive graduates of evangelical seminaries who go into pastorates are claiming that one of the first things they must do is to forget most of what they have learned in seminary and to begin their education all over again. I am also concerned that the less perceptive graduates seem to feel that it is an adequate fulfillment of their ministry simply to dish out from the pulpit what they have learned in seminary, whether or not their people have a need for such material.

Furthermore, it has been my experience (shared by a majority of the missionaries who are my students) that the theological training we received in seminary has not served us well in cross-cultural contexts. I ask, "Why?" And in attempting an answer I am forced to transgress the sacred border between my discipline and that called theology.

The decision to transgress in this way, however, immediately raises two serious problems. Phrased as questions these may be recorded as, 1) How can one function competently in an area in which he is not an expert? and 2) How can one point out "motes" in the eye of another discipline without seeming to be unaware of the "beams" in the eye of his own specialization?

With respect to the first problem, it is unlikely that a "meddler" like myself could function competently as a theologian—if by this is meant that to be a theologian one must handle the same data in the same way that theologians do. If, however, it were possible to "do theology" according to different rules, such "meddling" could perhaps prove helpful in the overall attempt to gain greater insight into God and his works. In what follows I will, in fact, be trying to gain theologically relevant insight by applying perspectives that are not (at least in my experience) ordinarily employed by traditional evangelical theologians. In doing this my aim is primarily to seek theological insight that is more relevant to cultural and subcultural contexts in which available theological formulations do not seem to convey the meanings they were intended to convey. If I can trust my own experience and that of my missionary students and colleagues, such cultural and subcultural contexts exist in abundance both overseas and, increasingly, among a variety of subcultural groups at home.

I am encouraged to meddle (or, perhaps better, experiment) in this way not only by felt needs deriving from my own and my students' experience, but also by expressions of felt need for such experimentation on the part of theologians themselves. In a recent issue of *Christianity and Crisis* (May 12, 1975)[1] twelve theologians responded to the question, "What Ever Happened to Theology?" Few of them considered their discipline "alive and well." Among their comments were, "I believe that the demise of such systematic theology . . . has been in preparation since the Enlightenment" (Ruether 1975:109); "The entire paradigm of consciousness that has governed the line of Western culture and its reflection in theology has lost its credibility" (1975:110); theology "has largely become . . . simply a pawn in the socio-cultural process" (Kaufman 1975: 111); theology "has tried to prolong its existence when the conditions that gave it birth and made it possible have entered their decline and demise" (Bonino 1975:112); "Theology has, for many of us, lost its roots in experience. . . [it] has become at best an interpretive overlay that does not contradict what we *already* know. . . [it] is boring" (Christ 1975:113); "The decline of theology can . . . be understood as a result of the widening gap between the beliefs nurtured in the Church and the dominant culture of our time" (Cobb 1975:117).

It is indeed unfortunate that such statements can be made concerning a discipline that traces its roots to the efforts of Paul the Apostle to present the gospel in as relevant a fashion as possible to people with a Greek worldview and thought patterns.[2] Apparently somewhere along the line the theology that Paul's hearers

---

[1] *Christianity and Crisis* 35:106-120 (1975).

[2] For a helpful presentation of the way Paul went about contextualizing Christian theology in his day with applications for our day, see von Allmen 1975.

perceived as either transforming or upsetting has come in our day to be identified more with the needs of Paul's day than with those of our day.

Such expressions of felt need from within the discipline embolden sympathetic outsiders like myself at least to offer suggestions and to point in new directions. We may perhaps even be able to work toward the development of new models or paradigms or to be one example of the kind of activity that Harvey Cox speaks of when he says, "Theology is being done today—in curious places, under unusual sponsorship, by unauthorized persons, unnoticed by those who read only the right journals" (1975:115).

I mean for what follows to be constructive rather than destructive, even though it might be possible to construe some of my remarks as unsympathetic. I have great respect for theology and theologians and am deeply disturbed when theological insight is ignored, misapplied or judged to be irrelevant. I do, however, feel that there are certain aspects of traditional evangelical theologies that need to be looked at critically from a cross-cultural perspective (see below). At times such critical evaluation by an outsider may bring into play the kind of defensiveness that is the response of any in-group that feels either actually or potentially vulnerable to outside attack (even though often the matters raised by the outsider may be hotly debated by insiders). I will risk this in hopes that those within theology who read this may be interested enough to restrain their defensiveness.

With respect to the second of the above-noted problems inherent in this kind of transgression of disciplinary borders, outsiders to my discipline should be aware of the fact that as a Christian I must "break ranks" with and become critical of my fellow anthropologist in at least one major area. Anthropology has been developed within western culture at a time when taking God and religion seriously is no longer in vogue. It is, therefore, committed to a methodology (empiricism) that normally denies the existence of that which is postulated to be outside the limits of sense perception. Anthropology as normally done thus allows itself to be bound by the anti-supernaturalistic bias of the culture within which it operates. Such culture-boundness is particularly disturbing in a discipline that prides itself in pointing out the culture-boundness of other perspectives.

I, of course, reject this anti-supernaturalistic bias. I believe, however, that it is just as possible to employ anthropological perspectives and methodology with underlying Christian assumptions as with underlying naturalistic, non-Christian assumptions. This I will try to do. For my Christian assumptions are basic for me and, in my frame of reference, replace the competing assumptions on which anthropology is ordinarily built.

I believe that much of what I perceive to have happened to evangelical theology is understandable in terms of natural processes that affect all academic disciplines (including anthropology) and the Institutions devoted to their perpetuation. I believe it can be shown that academic disciplines tend to go through a cycle that starts with some new perception of reality that is embraced by enough influential people to give them their start. They then proceed through stages in which they win adherents because of the attractiveness of the new approach into stages where those involved in perpetuating the discipline become more and more concerned with theorizing and less and less concerned with the practical applications of their insights.[3] Thence they turn to a primary concern for the perpetuation of the discipline, whether or not it is perceived as relevant by those outside of the institutions that are set up to preserve it. Evangelical theology is regarded by many to have reached the latter stage.

In the case of theology, I think there is an additional problem as well—that is the tendency of many within and outside of the discipline to regard as sacred the discipline (no matter how fallible it may be) that deals with sacred subject matter. Combine then a primary concern with theoretical rather than practical matters, with the impression that the way one thinks about these matters is sacred, and you get both the possibility of great "out-of-touchness" and the refusal of many (both insiders and outsiders) to challenge the discipline.

My desire here is to apply insights from a younger discipline (anthropology/ linguistics).[4] In so doing, I will seek to develop a series of challenging perceptions that will 1) suggest certain modifications in theological thinking, and 2) increase the possibility that when one attempts to communicate theological content, what he says will be perceived as relevant by lion-theologians.

There are, of course, several varieties of theology. Evangelicals frequently mention a distinction between systematic theology (with both liberal and conservative varieties) and biblical theology. In addition to these and certainly more important than either are a wide variety of popularizations of theology. We might, for purposes of this presentation, lump all of the latter into a category called "folk" or "pop" theology. By this designation I mean specifically to label and call attention to theology as it is understood by interested non-theologians. It is with theology at this level that I am most concerned, since I believe that even accurate theological insight poorly communicated and incorrectly perceived is likely to be at least as misleading as bad theology. Such concern for theology at the popular level, however, leads me inevitably to a concern for academic theologizing, since it is largely due to misperception and miscommunication at that level that distortions at the folk level have come into being.

As anthropology and evangelical theology are ordinarily done, they seem usually to either ignore or show antagonism toward each other. There are, I think, certain factors that can be pointed out that help us considerably in explaining why this is true. Each of these factors developed as a result of processes that we now describe as a part of history. The factors continue to exist, however, as sometimes radically different subjects of focus within the two disciplines or, better, within the separate academic streams of which these two disciplines are parts.

The treatment that follow will start with a somewhat oversimplified highlighting of these issues. We will then proceed to the meddlesome critique of evangelical theology promised above and follow that with a series of suggestions concerning the kind of assistance that I believe an anthropological or cross-cultural perspective can provide toward the improvement of evangelical theologizing.

---

[3] See James 1968 for a discussion of this process within philosophy.

[4] I note that Miller (1975:4-6) optimistically predicts the soon incorporation into theological curricula of many of the things that I here recommend.

Issues Raising Actual or
Potential Antagonism Between
Theology and Anthropology

Actual or potential antagonism between evangelical theologians and anthropologists may arise over several issues. Perhaps the foremost issue is the one mentioned above—the fact that anthropology (and its sister behavioral sciences, psychology and sociology) as ordinarily operated proceed from *naturalistic*, rather than *supernaturalistic* worldview assumptions. That is, they are ordinarily characterized by an assumption that either God does not exist or that he is irrelevant to the interests of scientific investigation: To evangelicals, then, the behavioral sciences look too man- and human science-centered. These emphases are, I believe, perceived by many thinking evangelicals as utterly incompatible with the apparently God-centered orientation of traditional evangelical theology.

Indeed, given the compulsion that western culture seems to have toward polarization, it is likely that the religious fervor with which many behavioral scientists operate their discipline is at least partly explainable on the assumption that they have chosen a man- and science-oriented "religion" (their discipline) in place of a God-centered religion.[5] Certainly many of the advocates of the behavioral sciences have attempted to promote their cause at the expense of supernaturalistic religion (e.g., Freud, Skinner). Such a fact has led William James to contend that the supreme commandment of what he calls "scientism" is, "Thou shalt not be a theist" (1904:131).

The fact that theological liberals often have virtually abandoned a supernaturalistic perspective in favor of a man-centered concern (often that of sociology) has also frequently turned evangelicals against the behavioral sciences. Man-centeredness with its concomitant emphasis on cultural, social, and psychological relativities has appeared antithetical to a discipline that attempts to focus on God and God-given absolutes.

A further threatening feature of anthropology and the other behavioral sciences is their popularity. Our culture is changing and the new concerns of our culture are at least as much mirrored in the behavioral sciences as produced by them. Anthropology, thus, addresses itself to much more contemporary concerns and in much more contemporary ways than those disciplines (like theology) that are the products of previous varieties of western culture. And this fact has important implications for the way in which anthropological answers are perceived by non-theologians. Often they are evaluated by laymen as more relevant than theological concerns and answers. Perhaps this is the reason why one seminary president has

---

[5] I think it can be demonstrated that many of the most avid devotees of the behavioral sciences are those who have been brought up under the strong influence of Christian or Jewish theology but have reacted against that influence. Often these have not lost their concern for the kind of problems that theology deals with, but they have changed their assumptions concerning how to best arrive at those answers. Often, too, they have retained an evangelistic zeal in their commitment to the new worldview.

stated, "The greatest challenges to evangelical Christianity are coming from the behavioral sciences" (Hubbard n.d.).[6]

But in the face of such challenges, do we do well to hole up in our present positions no matter how irrelevant they may seem to the world around us? Can the understandings of evangelical theologies be regarded as absolute and timeless just because they are understandings of a revelation from the absolute God? Or are theological interpretations to be treated as man-made, like the interpretation of any other man-made discipline?

Certainly we must recognize the man-madeness and consequent fallibility of every academic discipline. There is no essential superiority of "The Queen of the Sciences" (theology) over any other discipline, even though we may contend that the scriptural data that theologians work with is more sacred than the data ordinarily treated by other disciplines. But, as informed theologians know, the assumption of sacredness is in assumptions about the data, not in the perspective from which that data are analyzed. This fact opens the possibility that that sacred data may fruitfully be analyzed from the perspectives of other man-made disciplines than theology.

Is it right that evangelicals should feel threatened by the concepts, the focuses, the insights of the behavioral sciences? Is the evident polarization of the concerns of evangelical theology and of the behavioral sciences a necessary concomitant of the incompatibility of evangelical faith with naturalistic scientism? Or is it simply an artifact of the inability of either theology or the behavioral sciences to overcome the pressure of western culture to push persons and disciplines to absolutize their specialized insights? One could, for example, infer that in areas of concern to both theology and the behavioral sciences such as the following, it was reaction to the unreasonableness of absolutizing the theological extreme that "drove" behavioral scientists to the opposite extreme. Though there is a fair measure of variation within each discipline, the variations tend to cluster around the pole preferred by the discipline.

1. The first problem is that of where to look for ultimate authority. To theologians, God has traditionally been the source of ultimate authority. But, due I believe to the tendency of western culture to absolutize one or the other of two alternatives, evangelical theologians have often exalted God's authority at the expense of any respectable position for man. Anthropologists, for their part, have been just as guilty of polarization as theologians, and have, in reaction, turned completely to man as the source of authority. This is, of course, in keeping with the naturalistic humanistic worldview that the behavioral sciences espouse.

Is it possible for an evangelical Christian theologian to develop a perspective that neither denies God nor denies man—a perspective that holds to the ultimate authority of God, without denying either the importance of the delegation of certain authority to man or the fact that on occasion God limits himself to that human authority? The Psalmist asked, "What is man?," and concluded that we are "but little less than God" (Ps. 8:4-5). Jesus became a man and trusted man (in spite of many good reasons for mistrust) to carry on his work after him. Perhaps the insights of the

---

[6] Verbal comment by David Hubbard, President of Fuller Theological Seminary.

Science of Man (anthropology) can assist us to develop a higher doctrine of man—a view more in keeping with that of Jesus and the Scriptures.

2. The second problem is the related problem of how to arrive at truth. Evangelical theology has focused on revelation from God as the source of at least the most important truths, whereas anthropology looks to scientific discovery via empirical research as the source of truth. To evangelical theologians truth tends to be primarily a cognitive, propositional kind of thing, derived from faithful interpretation of the once-for-all revelation given in the Scriptures. For anthropology, on the other hand, a never-ending process of sense perception leading to theory building, testing and modification is seen as the key to finding truth.

And yet both disciplines are bound by the same human limitations and operate according to the same dynamics, whether overtly or covertly. The processes of conceptualization and perception (see below) are the same—only the starting assumptions, some of the data and, of course, the conclusions differ. There is much room for and much to be gained from an approach that takes seriously both divine revelation and the human discovery processes by means of which that revelation is made vital to us. We can be helped also by becoming more aware of the fact that there exist at the human level many perceptions of most truths that are apparently, equally valid (or invalid).

3. A third problem of concern to both disciplines is that of determinism and free will. Theologians have seen human beings as circumscribed by God. And those who have gone to the determinist extreme have seen them as absolutely determined by God. In reaction against such divine determinism, other theologians have focused on human freedom. Both groups of theologians have, however, tended to deal rather imprecisely with the circumscribing, sometimes determining, nature of culture. Anthropology has, of course, ignored the possibility of divine limitation and focused in on the interaction between man and culture.

Is it not, however, necessary to recognize both the limitations placed upon us by God and those of the culture in which we exist? It makes no sense, in the face of a mass of anthropological data concerning culture's influences on man, to deal, as evangelical theology characteristically does, with man and God with only imprecise, passing reference to culture. Anthropology's strength at this point is in an area of one of evangelical theology's greatest weaknesses. For (as discussed below) culture not only circumscribes humanity, it provides the milieu within which human beings and God interact. And anthropology is the discipline that has devoted the most attention to the development of an understanding of culture.

4. A fourth concern pertains to the matter of absolutes and relativities. Evangelical theologians have felt it important that their theologies be firmly based upon and give strong witness to theological absolutes. Evangelical theologians have, therefore, tended to regard divinely endorsed absolutes as the proper major focus of their study. Anthropologists, in reaction, have made the culturally relative aspects of human existence their focus.

If evangelical theology is to be credible, though, great care must be taken lest, in addition to truly divine absolutes, certain culturally variable features also be identified as absolute. Evangelical theologians have often been suspected even by their sympathizers of regarding at least certain culturally variable truths as though they were absolute. Anthropologists and others with a relativistic bias have, of course, been quick to criticize Christians for regarding as absolute certain aspects of western culture. And many Christians have been forced to admit the validity of at least certain of these contentions.

In such a crucial area as this, evangelical theology cannot afford to ignore criticism. We must by all means take the criticisms seriously. But we must also make ourselves expert in dealing with the whole matter of how to interpret and apply our source of information concerning absolutes (the Scriptures) in such a way that whatever interpretations we make are cross-culturally valid rather than ethnocentric. Evangelical theology badly needs the insights of anthropology at this point.

5. The final problem that I will mention is the problem of imperfection. To evangelical theologians, the immediate cause of evil is in human nature corrupted by the fall. Satan is, of course, seen as the ultimate source of the rebellion against God in which man participates. Anthropologists have, however, tended to go to an opposite extreme and taken a positive view of human nature. Evil, therefore, has largely been seen as a function of imperfect sociocultural systems rather than of imperfect people.[7]

Again, though we cannot agree that human nature is uncorrupted, there is so much to learn from the anthropological perspective concerning the outworking of evil in sociocultural systems that we dare not ignore their insights. For evangelical theology needs to deal in an informed way both with the evil in human beings and with its outworking in sociocultural systems.

These are but a few of the major issues on which evangelical theologians and anthropologists tend to take radically different positions. But, as I seek to hint above and to develop more fully below (and in a forthcoming book), it must be questioned whether the polarization that has occurred is necessary or healthy. For in so many areas the concerns of the two disciplines seem more complementary than mutually exclusive, once the tendency to polarize completely at one extreme or the other is overcome. And the call becomes one for greater cross-fertilization and balance in dealing with each of these fundamental issues and a myriad of other issues, some of which are treated below.

One could wish for greater balance within each discipline. And it is not impossible that such will someday come about. There is an encouraging increase in the willingness of at least certain anthropologists to take seriously theological phenomena that previously would have been dismissed as the product of Judeo-Christian mythology (see Goldschmidt 1966:134–138). But this paper is directed to those who can work toward greater balance within evangelical theology.

---

[7] Goldschmidt shows what might be considered a mediating position, however, in *Comparative Functionalism* (1966:134–138).

Limitations of Evangelical Theology

Again taking cognizance of my position as an outsider and of the need for self-criticism on the part of anthropologists, I will here venture to suggest five limitations of evangelical theological perspectives as I have experienced them.

1. The first of the limitations that I would point to is that Christian theology as we know it seems to be unaware of its culture-boundness within western culture. Western theologians, working totally within the context of western culture, have raised and sought to answer only those questions that occurred to them as a part of their participation within western culture. For this they could not be faulted. The more influential of these theologians have recorded their answers in volumes that have tended to become the models for their followers—volumes that have given attention to only that selection of topics that for cultural reasons interested their authors. This process is, of course, a natural one but it has imposed serious limitations on those of us who seek to use their theological insights in an increasingly pluralistic world. The major limitation is that many of the most pressing questions that we have to face today (such as the questions raised by cultural diversity) have not been fully dealt with by traditional theologians.

We observe in Scripture, for example, that God works within various cultures for his purposes. Can we infer that any culture is equally usable by God? If so, on what conditions? We understand that God accepted Hebrews who continued to believe in many gods but who elevated Jehovah to the top of their pantheon.[8] Will he accept people today who do no more than make that same change (provided they also commit themselves to God in faith)? What is the relationship between knowledge about Christ and faith in God without reference to knowledge about Christ? Could people today be saved by means of such faith as they have been in the past? If so, under what circumstances? And what about natural revelation, demon possession, religious pluralism, cultural concomitants of conversion, Christian maturation, churchness and the like? Western theologians have not, of course, been completely silent on such issues, but the perspectives of western culture have been too limiting to allow the breadth of insight often needed by cross-cultural communicators of Christianity. Often, indeed, the perspectives have been too limiting to enable Christians to develop satisfying answers to the problems of contemporary western cultures.

Furthermore, our western values have led us to expect both a single right answer to every question and the superiority of answers developed by western academicians to the answers developed by the members of any other culture, or by non-academicians within our own culture. Thus we are often ill-prepared to accept the possibility that there might be more than one equally valid approach to our understanding of many issues, depending on one's cultural (or subcultural)

---

[8] See the detailed article by Kautzsch entitled "Religion of Israel" (1904:612–634) for one treatment of this subject.

perspective. It is entirely possible, for example, that many of the so-called heresies that we deal with in church history were no more wrong than the positions that were adopted and called orthodox by the group in power. Just possibly, the latter were adopted more often because they were culturally appropriate to the group in power than because they were more true than the rejected positions. Rejected positions, on the other hand, were often the understandings of groups that were not respected by the group in power. They were thus dubbed "heresies" not primarily because they were less correct understandings, but because they were understandings developed from the perspectives of other (non-respected) cultures or subcultures. It is likely that in many cases neither the "orthodox" understanding nor the "heretical" one is completely right or completely wrong. But each meaningfully mediated some valid portion of the truth to the people of the culture or subculture within which the insight was generated.[9]

It is likewise difficult for us to accept the possibility that those dealing with theological data from another cultural perspective may be in a better position to develop more scriptural positions on many issues than are our experts from within western culture. People of other cultures may, for example, be better able to understand the existence and nature of evil spirits than we can. For our culture denies us the possibility of interpreting any of the events of life as involving the activity of spirit beings. We would thus be hard put to recognize the activity of spirits if we saw it. Our culture would lead us to interpret such activity in other ways. If the problem was disease, we would blame it on germs. If there were a calamity actually caused by evil spirits, we could only attribute it to "chance" allowed by God.

2. A second, related, limitation of traditional theology is our over-attachment to those parts of the Scriptures that are couched in thought forms culturally closest to western culture. Since our culture holds to an evolutionary view of history that places western culture at the top and all other cultures inferior to ours, we have, I believe, tended to evaluate those portions of the Scriptures that most display Greek ways of thinking as of greater importance than those portions couched in Hebrew and Aramaic thought forms. This has led to positions on inspiration that claim to accept the inspiration of the whole of the Bible, but actually adopt but a partial canon for purposes of theologizing, preaching and witness. It is natural that for cultural reasons western theologians prefer the writings of Paul to, for example, the writings of James and Peter in the New Testament and all of the Old Testament.[10] But it is a serious limitation nonetheless, since, on the one hand, it robs us of more than half of the revelation and, on the other hand, denies to us the compulsion we should feel to provide people today with those portions of the Word that will reveal God to them most clearly.

Since the New Testament records the events in which Jesus was actually involved, and the Pauline epistles formulate understandings of these events in terms most amenable to us, our tendency is often to relegate the Old Testament to the position of an interesting historical prelude to the really significant materials. In so doing we fail to see that God can often speak more clearly through the Old

---

[9] See Robert A. Kraft (1975:47–49) for a treatment of certain aspects of this subject.

[10] Note in this regard Luther's oft referred-to characterization of the Book of James as, "a right strawy epistle."

Testament and the Hebraic parts of the New Testament to people whose cultures are similar to Old Testament cultures. If, then, our choice is to translate or preach only from those portions that speak most clearly to us, we deny them parts of the inspired Word that they need most. This fact came vividly to me in Northern Nigeria as I began to realize that the church leaders with whom I was studying Romans did not share my enthusiasm for that book. When, however, we studied the Gospels and the Old Testament, their enthusiasm and understanding was frequently much greater than mine. For their culture gave them a better basis than mine gave me for seeing God and his message in terms of Hebrew and Aramaic cultural and linguistic forms.

The problem I am underlining here is not the fact that different portions of Scripture speak more effectively to people of different cultures—though I believe that this is an important and often ignored fact. The larger problem is that we have allowed our ethnocentrism to so affect our use of the Scriptures that we often ignore important parts of what God wants to reveal to us because they are presented in the two-thirds of the Bible that is couched in Hebrew and Aramaic thought patterns. And then we deny those portions of Scripture to peoples of other cultures who see God's message as indistinctly through our favorite portions as we do through those portions that speak most clearly to them. I believe, for example, that it is this limitation of evangelical theology that has resulted in the fact that Wycliffe Bible Translators have not to date produced a complete Old Testament translation in any of the hundreds of languages in which they work.[11]

3. A third limitation of traditional theology is that it has been so thoroughly academic. A priority has been put on thinking in an academically respectable way rather than on the practicality of the insights to real life. Such an emphasis has generated a view of the Bible that often portrays it more as a textbook on theology than as a down-to-earth guide-book for life. Such emphases have, I believe, tended to brand theology as an elitist activity, done by specialists who are provided with the leisure to spend most of their time reading and writing heavy books. As I have pointed out above, it is very easy for such elitist activity to lose touch with the concerns of common people, or even of many of the elite non-theologians who attend evangelical churches.

Not infrequently, one of the effects of theological study on young ministers is to provide them with a way of thinking and speaking that requires laymen to undergo rather extensive adjustment simply to understand the minister. This is because the seminarian has ordinarily received training that fits him better to teach in an academic institution than to relate to the real life needs of people outside of such institutions.[12] He has learned the dialect of the seminary and learned to use that dialect to talk about things that are of interest to people within the seminary. He has learned to please his professors and to imitate their approaches to the materials that they by virtue of their employment have been given the leisure to study. And often, even when he leaves the seminary and takes charge of a church, he preaches and

---

[11] I have, however recently heard that the first complete Old Testament is now nearing completion. Many Wycliffe Translators have translated selected portions of the Old Testament.

[12] Unfortunately, these statements all too often apply to the training received in Christian college and Bible schools as well.

carries on his church activities more as if to win the approval of his teachers than to communicate effectively to his audience.

If the seminarian has the ability to apply imaginatively the concerns of such intellectuals to the life of the parish, things may come but well. Or, if he has had the good fortune to be taught by professors who have resisted the pressures of academic life toward isolation from the concerns of the rest of mankind, both he and his flock may be able to transcend the problems caused by the lack of fit between the concerns of seminaries and the needs of laymen. The academic concerns of the seminary are, however, seldom the major concerns of more than a small percentage of the people in the pews, not to mention those outside the church, to whom the minister is expected to communicate. The layman's impression that theology and theologians are by definition irrelevant is often strongly felt and constantly reinforced by the academic nature of what he hears from those trained in or otherwise representing theological institutions.

4. A fourth limiting factor, akin to number three, is that theology has normally been done almost entirely from the point of view of traditional metaphysical philosophy. This fact has locked theology into both the strengths and the weaknesses of philosophical attempts to describe ultimate reality. It has obscured the fact that theologizing can and should be done from a variety of perspectives other than philosophical perspectives. The philosophical predisposition of those who have done theology has led to the highlighting of the more philosophical portions of the Bible mentioned above. There has also been an almost exclusive concern with the questions that philosophically-oriented minds have been asking, to the exclusion of questions asked by others but not by philosophers. But the greatest problem stemming from this bond between evangelical theology and metaphysical philosophy may be the static of the latter perspective.

For, as William James pointed out some time ago, metaphysical philosophy has long since lost its concern for what he calls "the perceptual order" of things experienced in real life. In place of the perceptual order, philosophers have constructed a series of "conceptual orders . . . all abstracted and generalized from long forgotten perceptual instances, from which they have as it were flowed out" (1911:51–52). And the relationships between the concepts in these abstract worlds are static.

> Nothing happens in the worlds of logic mathematics or moral and aesthetic preference. The static nature of the relations in these worlds . . . gives to the propositions that express them [an] "eternal" character (James 1911:68).

But life is not experienced as static. Thus the static nature of the relationship articulated in such propositions does not, as many assume, prove their eternal truth value but, rather, the lack of fit between that kind of truth and real life. The propositions may well articulate eternal truths, but giving people the impression that such truths are most properly packaged in abstract philosophical terms Is seriously misleading. For the God of the Scriptures is the God of dynamic life, not of static philosophical propositions. He who said "I am . . . the truth" (Jn. 14:6) is on the side of the Spirit who gives life, not of the general principle that kills (2 Cor. 3:6).

As mentioned above, much of value has come from the long association between theology and philosophy. Many of the best minds in western culture have thought and written on a wide variety of useful topics, and we would be much the poorer today had they not done their work. Yet one has the nagging feeling that there must have been more people down through the ages asking questions like, "How do I live truth?" than "How do I think about truth?" Were the behavioral concerns as unimportant and the cognitive concerns as important to the general populace as they seem to have been to the theologians? Or is it just in our day that behavioral concerns have come to the fore?

5. A fifth limitation is the tendency to focus on God and his ideals to the virtual exclusion of a focus on human beings and what their understandings of and relationship to God are at the actual level. In their treatment of scriptural teaching concerning humanity, for example, evangelical theologians have tended to represent God as more concerned with what human beings ought to be and in condemnation of what actually is than as one who is genuinely pro-human being. Evangelical theology has, in general, attempted to be God-centered rather than, like the Scriptures, interaction-centered (interaction between God and man and between man and man). In the process, understandings of God and his will are focused upon, while people and their part in the interaction are often slighted, ignored or even negated. Thus one of the weakest parts of evangelical theology is its treatment of human beings.

Are we as evangelicals perhaps afraid that if we regard man highly we are only be able to do so by lowering our concept of God? Jesus did not ignore God's ideals for people (e.g., Matt. 5), yet he accepted people (even some quite unlikely people like the adulteress, Matthew and Zacchaeus) pretty much as they were. He treated Peter kindly after his denial (Jn. 21:15–19) and, when he ascended, turned the whole work of the Kingdom over to him and the other disciples. Jesus seems to have had a higher regard for human beings than evangelicals often do. He also seems to have allowed for a range of acceptability between where he is willing to start with humans and the ideal (but probably humanly unattainable) standards that he sets for us to aim at.

Evangelical theology likewise focuses on ideal understandings of the person and work of Christ (resulting often in a Christology that emphasizes Jesus' deity at the expense of his humanity), of the requirements for salvation, of the belief system required to be considered orthodox, of the kinds of moral behavior required of Christians, and the like, Yet in real life, if we are growing, we experience movement from barely acceptable beliefs and behaviors toward more ideal concepts and habits, But lack of teaching concerning this process in favor of the constant stressing of the ideals, as if the latter only were acceptable, often results in guilt complexes that cripple sincere Christians.

We need to study seriously the range of acceptable variation allowed by God in man's response to him. From the Scriptures we learn that God's ideal concerning man's understanding of him is monotheistic. He allowed, however, a lesser understanding (henotheism) among the early Hebrews (see the Ten Commandments and the Book of Jonah).

With respect to marriage, though God's ideal would seem to be loving monogamy, he has accepted polygamy and Greek monogamy in which the ideal was that the wife not be noticed either for bad or for good. With respect to adultery, murder and the other commandments, God accepted the Hebrew definition of these practices as his starting point.

We need to study and to teach not only God's ideals, but God's starting points, for the latter are as much in scriptural focus as the former. Furthermore, they are as relevant today as the former, both in non-western cultural situations and in our attempts to reach those who have adopted life styles within our own culture that traditional evangelicalism regards as less than ideal.

In each of the problem areas discussed in the first section of this paper, evangelical theology seems to exalt God and his ideals at the expense of a parallel focus on human beings and the actual levels at which God works with us. But by ignoring or downplaying a respectful doctrine of man, has not our doctrine of the God who gave himself to redeem man also suffered? Is God so lacking in intelligence or good sense that he paid the price he did for no more than our theology says he got when he redeemed man? Perhaps at least some of the marvelous things that anthropologists, psychologists and others are discovering about this being that God created and redeemed can help us increase our respect for both man and God who became a man and invited us into his inner circle (Jn. 15:15).

Though we dare not go to the anthropologist's extreme by replacing God with man, much of anthropological insight can, I believe, be built upon or grafted into an evangelical Christian perspective. It is my desire below to suggest several areas in which this can be done if evangelical theologizing is to attain the kind of balance that will enable it to perform the vital function that God has called it to perform in today's world.

Further limitations of evangelical theology could be listed, some of which are implicit in the discussion that follows, but to no useful purpose. For our aim is not to condemn evangelical theology, but to assist in attaining a more balanced perspective on and a more relevant approach to certain areas (such as these) where insight from anthropology can be helpful.

I would like to point, therefore, to several emphases of anthropology (including anthropological linguistics), some of which are shared by other disciplines, that I feel point up insights that could usefully be incorporated into evangelical theology. These relate largely to culture (including language) and man. They would most strongly affect the conceptualization of many aspects of theology. This in turn would have important ramifications for the communication of theology. At least one area of theological methodology would also be affected—that concerning the study of human beings.

I do not wish to be interpreted as contending that there has never been a concern for any of these matters within theology.[13] On the contrary, there has been and still is intense concern by many people at many of the points that I will focus on. But the isolation between the disciplines has been such that the much sharper perspectives of

---

[13] Indeed, it is refreshing to read an occasional book like Ramm's (1961) where the author shows that he has been influenced by the writings of Christian anthropological linguists such as Eugene A. Nida to say some of the same things that I am trying to say.

anthropology in the areas of its specialization have. not ordinarily been noticed, much less accepted, by evangelical theologians.[14]

I have, perhaps rather arbitrarily, arranged my suggestions in three categories: 1) general areas, 2) conceptual areas and, 3) methodology.

General Areas in Which an Anthropological Perspective Can Help

1. Evangelical theologians, it seems to me, need to emphasize more clearly and consistently the distinction between data and analytical perspective. It seems to be an irresistible temptation to many popularizers of theology (including preachers) to give the impression that both the data (often biblical) and their understanding of the meaning of that data are sacred. This is a serious error since it obscures the fact that though they, or (for fairness' sake) let me say we, may strongly contend for the divine inspiration of the scriptural data, we should equally strongly recognize the human fallibility of the interpreters and of the discipline (theology) that they represent.

Within anthropology (as within many other disciplines), it is coming increasingly into vogue to identify both the database for one's observations and generalizations and the theoretical model in terms of which those observations and generalizations are being made. I would like to see theologians (especially at the popular level and in the pulpit) show more overt awareness of the conceptual models that they employ, of the variety of equally valid models that could be employed and especially of the cultural limitations of all models, including traditional, time-honored ones. It is, for example, increasingly damaging to our cause for the students of biblical theologians to represent themselves as operating without presuppositions as they attempt to apply to urban America insights generated within theological models developed to deal with the concerns of academic theologians in sixteenth century Europe (Calvinism, Lutheranism), eighteenth century England (Wesleyanism) or even nineteenth century rural America, We all operate according to one or another model (often referred to as a worldview or set of assumptions) at all times, Frequently, however, these models, in terms of which we interpret whatever data come to us, are not at the conscious level. In ignorance of the diversity of possible models available to us from other cultures and subcultures (such as academic disciplines), we frequently regard our own, or our favorite theologian's perspective, as so natural to humanity as a whole that it contains little or no bias.

The tendency for evangelicals to regard historical perseverance as an appropriate substitute for contemporary relevance appears to be a rather common

---

[14] Liberals, too, have largely neglected anthropology, though many of them have come to certain of the insights with which I am concerned via sociology. Sociology, however, has often lacked the cross cultural and holistic emphases of anthropology, including the focus on language, that is so important to this discussion.

pitfall. It seems to be so much easier highly to value and avidly to study the products of respected theologians of the past than to study and imitate the processes that they went through to produce theology relevant to their times (when it was relevant). We claim to believe that God is alive and in continuous interaction with human beings today on the basis of the same principles that guided his interactions with people in the past. But we often act as if he died when the canon was closed (or when the last volume of *Calvin's Institutes* or the *Works of Luther* was completed)—as if he and those whom he led have completed all the revealing and theologizing that is worth doing, leaving us to study the residue.

But if, as Jesus contended, God's illuminating activity is a continuing process (Jn. 16:13), surely the reciprocal human activity of interpreting or theologizing in terms of new models is also a continuing process. And we need to learn to do under the leading of God for our day what the apostles, prophets and the best of the theologians did for theirs. We should not simply consume their products and naively exalt their models as if the latter were as God-ordained for our day as they were for theirs. For the revealed message that flowed through those models needs to flow through models that are at least as relevant to the people of our day as those models were for those days.

The point is that we need to learn to make an overt distinction, even at the popular level, between the data that we regard as sacred and the human, fallible ways in which we (as well as other interpreters) handle that data. Many of our hearers have learned to make such a distinction and are not attracted by presentations that ignore the need to distinguish data from perspective. In so distinguishing, I believe we can both enhance the credibility of theological endeavor and encourage the development of a greater diversity of approaches to theology to answer questions raised and needs felt by a greater variety of people. There should be, for example, in a culture as strongly influenced by the insights of psychology as ours, several theological approaches that are built upon psychological models and perspectives. So-called "Relational Theology" is attempting to do this at the popular level. These efforts should, I believe, both be taken seriously and imitated by academic theologians— though as one of many equally valid modes of theologizing, rather than as another candidate for the title of "the one right way to theologize."

2. A second general area where anthropological perspectives can assist us is in relation to the increasing "in-vogueness" of behavioral science's concepts and terminology and the increasing "out-of-vogueness" of the language and concepts of metaphysical philosophy.[15] I have mentioned this problem above and dealt briefly with the need consciously to recognize and switch models. The point here is that since anthropological models and terminology are on the in-vogue side of the ledger, we can learn from them how to conceptualize and present theological truth in a style that is perceived by contemporary Americans as both relevant and "with it."

We should not be satisfied with the kind of "groundhogism" practiced by many evangelical theologians and preachers when some important issue is brought to their

---

[15] Note, for example, the preponderance of psychologically, sociologically and (to a lesser extent) anthropologically oriented books over those with a philosophical perspective on the non-fiction best seller lists. Note also the widespread popular use of behavioral science jargon and concepts in fiction, news reporting and in everyday speech.

attention by naturalistic behavioral scientists. Such persons simply pop up to critique what they understand of the treatment of the issue and then retreat into the safety of the accustomed hole without ever really dealing with the issue. Often it is not the real issue that we see at all, but some shadow that we ourselves cast. Such has been the approach of many to such books as *Future Shock* and *Open Marriage* (not to mention the plethora of psychological and sociological books that attract theologian's attention from time to time). We surface just long enough to cast a shadow out of the past over such presentations of contemporary issues without ever taking seriously either the concerns that have made such books best sellers or the perspective from which they are written. Many with this mind set applaud Francis Schaeffer when he represents God as unable to work with contemporary man unless he returns to the thought patterns (the models) of medieval philosophy.[16]

But God is not so limited—any more than he was limited to Hebrew models when the target audience was Gentile (see Acts for many examples) or to Roman Catholic models when the target audience was Northern European (at the time of the Reformation). Nor is he limited to the models of contemporary theology when the target audience has different concerns and different assumptions. Merely condemning and turning away from issues such as relativity neither settles them nor keeps people from asking about them (except at church). Such an approach merely increases the perception of irrelevance that many already attach to theology.

Evangelical theologians need to learn to approach their concerns and to state their conclusions in ways that do not demand the extraction of those they seek to reach (whether laymen or students of theology) from their familiar frames of reference, I believe there is a direct relationship between the out-of-vogueness of theological thinking and such facts as the high diversion rate to other occupations of those planning on going into pastoral work who attend seminary,[17] the frequently-given impression that theologizing is only for experts, and the inability of many pastors to communicate much of what they learn in seminary in such a way that they get laymen excited over what they do attempt to communicate. Evangelical theology needs to learn to translate its concepts into the language and conceptual frame of reference of people of today.[18]

As mentioned above, Relational Theology is making a worthy attempt in this direction, using psychological concepts and terminology. I am, however, disturbed on the one hand by a certain lack of confidence on the part of the relational

---

[16] See for one of many examples, Schaeffer 1968:168–70, where his total conception of truth is philosophical. He, in the name of the Christ who represented truth as personal (Jn. 14:6), demands allegiance to this philosophical understanding of truth as preconditional to salvation (1968:143, 168). His contention that Christianity proceeds from and requires belief in certain truths is, of course, valid and important. But his parallel contention that the only appropriate understanding and expression of these truths is in terms of philosophic propositions to which non-Christians must be converted before they can know the personal truth, Christ, is surely overdrawn.

[17] I have heard that a Ph.D. dissertation by Gordon Cochrane (now of Seattle Pacific College) done at the University of Southern California in 1965 in sociology deals with this topic. I have not seen the dissertation

[18] Thomas Oden discovered in his teaching of theology to students at Drew University that teaching theology in the language of psychology was more effective than teaching it in traditional theological language. He concluded that the language of psychology is more the idiom even of theological students than the language of theology. See Oden 1974.

theologians that what they are doing is really theology (perhaps they feel that since it is relevant, it cannot be properly labeled theology) and on the other hand by the reluctance of traditional theologians to take them seriously. But the vogue has changed, and evangelical theologians gain nothing and risk losing everything if they arrogantly refuse to respond to such changes in the world around us.

3. A third general area where anthropology can be of assistance is in our attempts to compensate for the culture-boundness within western culture of the interpretational and communicational mechanisms of evangelical theology (see limitation #1 above). Scriptural data are presented to us via the forms of other cultures. And witness to peoples of the world's diverse cultures and subcultures must take place in terms comprehensible within those cultures and subcultures. We, the interpreters and communicators, are, furthermore, pervasively affected in every way by our own cultural perspectives. It is not enough to understand (as many evangelicals do) *that* the Word must be interpreted in its cultural context and communicated in terms relevant to the cultural context of the receptors. We need to learn *how* to do both in such a way that there is a minimum of interference and even obstruction in both processes from our own cultural biases.

Assumptions such as those often held either explicitly or (more frequently) implicitly concerning the overall superiority (or Christianness) of our culture, the greater accuracy of our perception of reality, the superiority of our approaches to, e.g., education, government, economics, religion, and the like, simply cannot be maintained except in ignorance of anthropological insight. Our culture is but one fallible culture among others, with glaring weaknesses as well as impressive strengths. Biblical cultures are, likewise, totally human when seen in cross-cultural perspective. Every culture is also, however, respectable and usable by God. Anthropological techniques are, therefore, valid and needed by evangelical theology for discovering and counteracting ethnocentrism, for interpreting sympathetically and with balance within the cultural context, and for effectively transferring meanings (rather than merely the forms) from one culture to another. See below for more detailed treatments of such issues.

The tendency mentioned above to identify the revelation of God with our own culture-bound understanding of that revelation is a function of our ethnocentrism. It is unlikely that any human perception of any part of the revelation is totally correct. Many understandings, even those of persons and cultures that our tradition refuses to respect, are, however, just as likely as ours to be valid and to result in the communication of at least part of what God intended often that part that best meets the felt needs of the receptors who focus on it. We need anthropology's powerful insights concerning the pervasiveness of our culture's influence on us to assist us in counteracting this temptation to evaluate our understandings too highly and other people's understandings too lowly.

4. A fourth general area relates to the need to develop approaches to theology that start from the questions that concern ordinary people, rather than from those that are of vital concern only to academicians (see limitation #3 above). Academicians belong to particular subcultures that have perfectly valid needs and interests. But as in all subcultures. a great many of these needs and interests are specific to the kinds of life experience peculiar to that subculture alone. If, therefore, theologizing is done

only by academicians, it will continue to relate rather specifically to their concerns, rather than to those of the members of other subculture—unless it is done by academicians who learn to study other groups of people where they are and to deal theologically with their concerns as well.

Discussions concerning such things as the number of angels that can sit on the head of a pin have become proverbial as illustrations of this kind of irrelevance. But only slightly less damaging to the cause of theological relevance are the amounts of energy invested in theorizing over the intricacies of eschatology, the habit of regularly theologizing people back to the first century (when all the great things happened), rather than of focusing on understanding and applying those revealed meanings to today's concerns, the practice of pressing the meanings of the words and phrases of Scripture far beyond the common sense limits of linguistic usage, and the constantly given impression (intensified by the unintelligibility of literal Bible translations) that only those highly trained in theological schools can get at the truth that an uncooperative God has mischievously hidden in his Word.

Meanwhile, even well-taught Christians often give up hope of finding help in the Scriptures on their own, since only experts can be expected to do that. And we all struggle with a here and now that doesn't seem to match very much in either Scripture or theological theorizing. We often seem to be asking pressing questions that theologians don't seem to care about, and listening to their answers to questions that we don't care about. I recently had the traumatic experience of sitting through a typical evangelical sermon in which the preacher followed a model commonly recommended in evangelical seminaries. He spoke expositorily from a passage of Scripture which he felt raised four "important" questions. As I listened, I tried my best to imagine any human being anywhere (outside of a theological institution) who might ever ask any of those questions. I could imagine none,

How different (and more like Jesus' example) would be an approach that started from a solid anthropological study of people's frustrations with respect to loneliness, meaninglessness, and other felt needs. It could then proceed to develop experimental cultural forms to deal with the relationship between these needs and the answers stemming from a relationship to Christ. This is what the Christians in the first century did when they developed the practice of appointing deacons to meet the needs of the widows (Acts 6). One function of culturally aware theologians in such a procedure would be to lead the way in discovering the scriptural meanings applicable to the problems, and in discovering appropriate contemporary cultural forms to express those meanings (see below for a discussion of cultural forms and meanings). Such effort would, I believe, be of greater theological (and practical) significance than the publication of the world's thousandth commentary on the Gospel of John, designed to give one more generation of Christians the impression that Christianity is more concerned with the first century than with the twentieth, or of another "definitive" set of speculations concerning biblical prophecy, designed to assist people with their loneliness problem by diverting their attention from it. Anthropological techniques for studying people and their cultures (see below) can fruitfully be employed by evangelical theologians to bring us into greater and more effective contact with contemporary people and their concerns.

Conceptual Areas in Which an Anthropological Perspective Can Help

In addition to, and stemming from these general areas are several areas where anthropological input can, I believe, assist evangelical theologians in revising, updating and balancing their approach to many of the important concepts with which they must work. As mentioned above, anthropology has developed in rather total isolation from and in an antagonistic relationship to evangelical theology. Yet the areas in which anthropologists have specialized are of constant concern to theology. Theologians cannot operate their discipline without dealing in major ways with several cultures and several languages. They are constantly faced with the necessity to translate, to interpret events and concepts within their cultural contexts and to communicate meanings originally expressed in one culture to those whose life is lived in another. These are all areas in which anthropologists (including linguists) have developed a great deal of expertise.

Yet evangelical theologians and, with one area of exception, evangelicals in general have not generally availed themselves of anthropological insight. The one area of exception is with respect to Bible translation, where hundreds of evangelicals, few of whom have even minimal theological credentials, have learned to incorporate linguistic and, to a lesser extent, broader anthropological insight into the process of translating the Bible into non-western languages. But in order to accomplish this, organizations like Wycliffe Bible Translators have been forced to set up their own training programs to compensate for the fact that Bible schools and theological seminaries have not ordinarily provided the needed perspective even when they have strongly emphasized the teaching of Greek and Hebrew.

Anthropological generalizations concerning human beings and culture are developed on the basis of cross-cultural comparison and contrast. No generalization concerning human nature is regarded as acceptable that is based (as such generalizations by theologians typically are) on experience in only a few, often closely related, cultures. An anthropological perspective is also characterized by an attempt to study and describe people and cultures *as they are* rather than in terms of some set of ideals as to what they should be. Anthropologists study all aspects of people, not simply some selection of certain human ideas. And their study is conducted on the basis of the investigator's attempt to so understand life from their point of view that he can participate to some extent with them in their perspective and, if they are a living people, in their behavior.

It is my conviction that an anthropological cross-cultural perspective on theological data can lead us to much valuable insight that we were not aware of before, particularly with respect to culture and incorporation into theological curricula, research and writing of anthropologically-informed treatments of such concepts as the following could make the approaches to many aspects of theological subject matter both more precise and more relevant to the concerns of people today.

1. Evangelical theology needs a better understanding of culture in general. Many contend that anthropology's greatest contribution is its development of the culture concept. Culture may be defined as

> the integrated system of learned behavior patterns which are characteristic of the members of a society and which are not the result of biological inheritance (Hoebel 1972:5).

For centuries it has been recognized that human beings are strongly affected by something that is real but not biologically or environmentally determined. This "something" has become the focal point of anthropological investigation and central to the anthropological perspective advocated here. Culture has been found to be "transmitted and maintained solely through communication and learning" (Hoebel 1972:5), rather than inherited genetically or imposed by the environment—though both genetic and environmental factors interact with culture. Culture is, furthermore, patterned, integrated and all-pervasive-patterning, integrating and channeling every aspect of a person's thinking and behavior. Though human beings are constantly modifying their cultures (usually in quite minor ways) no one ever escapes his culture. One's culture strongly influences everything one perceives, thinks and does. It interprets and structures for us all aspects of life (including biological and environmental givens) so that we never see reality except as interpreted for us by our culture. Thus culture is more real to us than even biology and physical environment.

But cultures differ. Each culture imposes or patterns a different perception of reality upon its members. The variety of equally workable perceptions of reality seems to be very great. The resultant cultural understandings vary widely from each other at many points. Perceptions of major aspects of reality that do not work are either abandoned by the culture or result in its destruction. Thus, those cultures that survive do so because they are close enough to reality, on the one hand, to keep from breaking down and, on the other, to keep convincing their members of the validity of their understandings of how to relate to that reality.

Given the fact that human culture is the milieu within which God communicates with man and in terms of which man responds to God, theologians need as precise an understanding of culture as possible. If we were teaching fishing, we would spend a considerable amount of time dealing with the characteristics of the water in which the fish are found. But, like fish require water, human beings require culture if they are to live. There are characteristics of running water, of still water, of muddy water, or polluted water that fishermen must know if they are to be expert. Furthermore, fishermen cannot expect to catch fish if they cast their lines or throw their nets away from, rather than into the fishes' habitat, or shallowly if the fish are deep water fish, or deeply if the fish are shallow water fish, or without reference to swiftly moving currents that affect the fish, or using bait that the fish are not interested in. And, should it be the desire of the teacher of fishermen (as with the theologian) to teach his students how to catch and care for the fish alive, a host of additional problems are encountered. For keeping fish alive and enabling them to continue growing requires that their relationship to water, preferably the same kind of water they have grown accustomed to, be kept intact.

If fishermen would study the characteristics and influences of water this thoroughly, how much more should we study the characteristics and influences of culture. For any interaction with human beings within culture—whether the interaction be between man and man or between God and man. Cultural and subcultural currents differ, as do the nature and strength of their effect on the human "fish" that are pervasively influenced by them. Furthermore, people swim at different depths within their cultures and respond to different baits. And they often prefer to die (at least psychologically or sociologically) rather than to adapt when moved from one cultural water to another.

Aptness in theologizing and in ministering demands that we get beyond the mere recognition of "something out there" that Niebuhr documents for a number of theologians (see Niebuhr 1951) or the naive philosophizing about culture that Tillich engages in (see Tillich 1959). These authors document well, I think, the need for the more precise input of anthropologically-informed concepts.

The kinds of cultural influence on human beings need much more detailed treatment in theological curricula when doctrines relating to humans are considered. The fact of man's cultural involvement is, however, also crucial to our understanding of God and of the process of divine-human interaction that is central to both the biblical revelation and to our own Christian experience. Evangelical theologians need to begin to probe the multitude of scriptural illustrations of such interactions from an anthropological point of view to discover what there is for us to learn concerning their nature and variety. For the data on which Christian theology is based took place within human cultures that are foreign to us, and the applications of theology are to be made within contemporary human cultures. God chose human cultural frames of reference as the milieu for his interactions with man. Many examples of these divine-human interactions are recorded in case history fashion in the Scriptures and could, if they were analyzed from an anthropologically-informed perspective, yield valuable insights concerning the way God desires to use culture in our own day.

Such probing would raise and deal with questions such as: How and when does God limit himself to human culture and language? How and when does he transcend human culture and language? How and when does he use them differently than they would ordinarily be used? What kinds of culture-bound human perception and response are acceptable to God and under what conditions? What is the relationship between the total inspiration of the Bible and the fact that it is also one hundred percent cultural? May a culture today that, like the Hebrews, practices blood sacrifice, continue that sacrificial system within Christianity? Likewise, is the God who accepted Hebrews and Greeks with definitions of marriage, adultery, sexual roles, family structures, etc. radically different from what we have learned to call Christian, willing to accept as valid starting points some or all of the current varieties of practice in these areas prominent in certain American subcultures?

Our understanding of church history could be greatly sharpened by the input of anthropological insight. Cultural matters have always been dealt with as a part of the study of history. But again there has often been less preciseness than is now available to us from anthropology and ethnohistory. It could be very useful, for example, for contemporary students to see that in former times (as in the present) the primary reasons for church splits and theological controversies have been cultural rather than theological. For too long we have been encouraged to believe that the Protestant

Reformation was primarily a matter of doctrinal differences between Luther and the Roman Catholic Church. And yet the historical data, analyzed anthropologically, show the Reformation to be centered around whether the Catholic Church will allow Christianity to be indigenized in Germany or whether Germans must continue to subscribe to a foreign (Roman) Christianity. This was, of course, the same issue as that between Paul and the Judaizers that came to a head in the Jerusalem Council (Acts 15). The fact that cultural factors were of major importance In so many of the early doctrinal controversies as well as in more recent splits makes this aspect of church history very amenable to more culturally-precise investigation. Such investigation makes more clear than ever before just how similar are the attitudes and events of days gone by to those of the present.

The application of anthropological perspectives to the analysis of historical data both outside of and within the Scriptures can assist students in better understanding just how human and culturally-conditioned is the process of theologizing. They can also learn that theologizing is but one way of abstracting from reality. From a cross-cultural perspective the functions of ritual, ceremonial, stones of remembrance, storytelling and the like in Hebrew culture were similar to the functions of theologizing (i.e., philosophizing about the things of God) in Greek culture. The fact that we prefer to abstract from reality by theologizing, therefore, does not in any way mean that people of all cultures and subcultures need to go this route. The means of abstracting for ritual-oriented cultures (such as Hebrew culture) and subcultures may more appropriately be ritual behavior than philosophical thinking. The Hebrews (and similar cultures and subcultures today) should not be seen as inferior merely because they preferred ritual expression to philosophical expression. With respect to either ritual or philosophical expression, anthropological input can make clearer than ever before the fact that theologizing has been and is most appropriately done with specific reference to the concerns and needs of the audience addressed, rather than as a quest for a single set of once-for-all formulations of truth.

More specific aspects of a sharpened understanding of culture (including language) are dealt with below.

2. Evangelical theology needs a better understanding of language in general. Flowing from and overlapping with the focus on culture dealt with above and below is the need for greater understanding of language and its processes. Language is an important part of culture, mirroring it, influencing it and being influenced by culture at every point. Thus, all that we say about language or culture applies to some extent to the other as well. And many aspects of the patterns and processes of culture are illustrated most clearly from language.

Evangelical theology needs to employ the sharpest available understandings of language, since the scriptural data we work with are reported in human languages other than our own. Understandings and techniques developed by the science of linguistics on the basis of wide experience with a large variety of diverse human languages, however, carry us much farther than the understandings of the more limited discipline of philology that has been traditionally looked to by theologians. For the latter is based almost entirely upon understandings of language developed from experience with western languages only (with a nod in the direction of Semitics). And often these understandings are derived from philosophical notions of what language should be like, rather than from observation of what languages actually are.[19]

It is both unfortunate and anachronistic that such fallacies concerning language as the following are still very much alive in theological thinking (especially at the popular level): that there is something qualitatively different about biblical languages from other languages,[20] that words are the focal points of language, that due to inspiration we cannot interpret scriptural language the way we interpret ordinary language, that the meanings of biblical words are to be determined by tracing their etymologies (e.g., the mistranslation "debts"—rather than sins—in the Lord's Prayer, Mt. 6:12), that the original meanings of Scripture are most faithfully conveyed via literal translation, and many similar fallacies. The fact is, of course, that the more we learn about the similarities and differences between the world's 5000–6000 languages, the more human the biblical languages look. And the more it looks as though God limited himself to human language rather than creating for his use languages with special suprahuman characteristics.[21]

Theologians need to learn to deal much more knowledgeably and to communicate to non-theologians much more effectively concerning such vital areas as: a) the closeness of the relationship between language and culture and the implications of this bond for semantic interpretation, b) the implications of linguistic focus for understanding the strengths and limitations of each language and the people whose perception is shaped by it with respect to stating and perceiving each aspect of the revelation, and c) the problems and principles of effective meaning to meaning (as opposed to form to form) translation (see point 3 below). With respect to these areas there is, however, already a large amount of insight available to theologians. Due to the efforts of the Bible Societies and The Wycliffe Bible Translators, there is available today a wealth of application of linguistic and anthropological insight to the understanding of the problems and processes of Bible translation and interpretation.[22] Wycliffe alone has approximately 100 of their translators who have pursued their specialty to the Ph.D. level. All of their work is relevant and vital to theology, but to date has been almost totally ignored by evangelical theologians.[23]

For example, evangelicals widely hold to concepts of translation that exalt such translations as the (New) American Standard Version and the Revised Standard Version, while demeaning such translations as Phillips' *New Testament in Modern English* and the *Living Bible*. These latter are commonly (often slightingly) referred to as "paraphrases," as if there was something inherently inferior about the process

---

[19] See Barr 1961 for a critique of philosophical understandings of language and Nida 1972b, for a brief contrasting of philology and linguistics plus much of additional value for our topic.

[20] Nida states that there is no basis for "the often claimed sublimity of Hebrew idioms or the elegance of Greek grammar. Chinese is far more flexible in idiomatic structure than Hebrew, and Zulu is formally a more precise language than Greek" (1960:49).

[21] See the various writings of L. Wittgenstein for an enlightened perspective on language from within philosophy.

[22] See the list of relevant works at the end of this chapter.

[23] See, for example, the review of nine English translations of the Bible by eight "experts" in *Eternity* (1974:27–31), for some surprisingly nonexpert opinions by theologians concerning what constitutes a good translation. Disturbingly, none of the hundreds of evangelicals (many with Ph.D.s) who are devoting their lives to Bible translating—the real experts on Bible translation was included in that group.

by means of which they came into existence. Yet it is these so-called paraphrases, rather than the literal translations, that are in English most like what the original documents were in Greek and Hebrew. The original Scriptures gave the original hearers the impression that God could effectively and expertly use their languages. Our literal translations communicate just the opposite to English readers and hearers. Many of the readers and hearers of literal translations quite subtly develop the impression that God did not intend to be understood. Nor can they quite believe that God used really down-to-earth, common people's language in past times, since they have been biased against hearing or studying his Word in that kind of language today. The impression given is often that you can never really understand God unless you learn enough Greek to be able to understand the "Greekized" English of the literal translations.

Evangelical theologians need to learn that from the perspective of those most informed on language and culture the best English translations are "dynamic equivalence" translations—those that produce a response in unindoctrinated English hearers essentially equivalent to that produced in the original hearers. Any translation, therefore, that requires a person to learn another language (such as Greek) or a weird dialect of his own language that is never spoken by anyone (such as the dialect of the American Standard or Revised Standard Versions) is a poor translation. This is not because the translators did not understand the original languages—they usually understood them very well—but because they didn't know enough about language in general and the requirements of the translation process in particular. They have gone back into the past, but have produced "translations" that require that the reader join them in the past. They did not develop the kind of insight and expertise in translation that Phillips and Taylor have achieved to enable them to produce translations that are both reasonably faithful to the originals and speak today as God originally spoke.

Such translators have learned that "a literal translation of the words of the Bible can be tragically misleading" (Nida 1972a:xi). For literal translations lead people into the easy assumption that those words and constructions were intended to convey the meanings that come to the hearer's mind when he hears them in his own language. Yet a sentence such as "the wicked will not stand in the judgment" was not intended to mean (as it would in normal English) that the wicked will not be judged. Nor should "to smite the breast" mean to congratulate oneself (in Tarzan fashion). Likewise, "for three transgressions and for four" in Amos should not be understood (as in English) to refer to three or four transgressions. It means what English would mean by "repeatedly" and should be translated that way. "Cleanness of teeth" in Amos 4:6, too, has nothing to do with what that phrase is understood to mean in English. For the author is talking about famine, not dental hygiene. The list of such completely misleading renderings in the literal translations is virtually endless.

> Increasingly, therefore, Bible translators have not been content merely to match words or phrases. They have insisted that one must determine as precisely as possible what the receptors of a translation will understand by a particular expression, and only when it is thus likely to be correctly understood can one say that the translation is a faithful rendering of the original message (Nida 1972a:xi).

There is hardly an area of the interpretation and communication of the Christian message that the Bible translator is not forced to deal with. Furthermore, students who attempt to, identify with Bible translators and the writers of the New Testament in putting God's Word into another language, or even into another dialect of their own language, frequently experience a participation with the Spirit of God beyond that experienced in other contexts.[24] I am aware of the fact that many seminary and Bible school courses already require students to do a good bit of translation. This is all to the good, since all that would be needed to transform those exercises into the broader-ranging and deeper experience alluded to here would be to introduce instruction to enable the students to perform those exercises more expertly and more profitably. The major changes that such instruction would bring about would be in areas such as the greater appreciation of the cross-cultural nature of the task, the greater understanding of the necessity for and the implications of translating from meaning to meaning, rather than from form to form (see below), the greater recognition of the necessity for paraphrase in translation, the increased appreciation of the responsibility of the translator to translate all the way (not just part of the way) into the language of a given target audience, and the recognition of the principle that translational accuracy is a matter of the similarity between the impact of the translation on today's receptors to the impact of the original on the original receptors.

Courses dealing with Bible translation from this perspective could take us a long way toward understanding aspects of language and linguistic usage where traditional theology has misled us. Just the realization, for example, that a good paraphrase is more true to the original than a literal translation can give great insight into both the demands of contemporary communication and translation and the process by means of which the gospel events that took place in Aramaic got recorded in Greek and ultimately in English. The process of translation is both so important in itself and so similar to the processes of communicating and effective theologizing that if the introduction of up-to-date courses in translation theory was the only change made in a theological curriculum, much of what I am suggesting would be well underway.[25]

The application of contemporary linguistics to more effective language teaching methodology is, of course, another badly needed input from this source. I will not deal with this application in detail here. I would, however, like to recommend that theological training institutions take seriously the experiments of Dr. Donald Larson of Bethel College in teaching biblical Greek as a spoken language and of Dr. H. A. Gleason, Jr. of the University of Toronto in rather totally revising the approach to the analysis and teaching of Hebrew.[26]

3. The distinction between cultural (including linguistic) forms and their meanings is another anthropological understanding that evangelical theology can

---

[24] Phillips speaks helpfully of such an experience in his "Translator's Forward" (1958). This statement should be required reading for all who seek to translate.

[25] If the implications of the message of the Bible translation focus are correctly perceived, there will be other areas of the theological curriculum affected as well. We can, for example, learn that churches are to be as dynamically equivalent in their cultures as Bible translations are in their languages (see Kraft 1973b:39–57). Likewise, we should study, teach and develop the implications of dynamic equivalence communication, theologizing, conversion, etc.

[26] Both unpublished.

profit from. Among the more specific areas where anthropological insight can contribute is by keeping constantly before us the fact that cultural forms are important for what they mean to people, not in and of themselves. By cultural forms we mean the more obvious, often visible or audible parts of culture such as words, ceremonies, behaviors, material objects, etc. We are most aware of these formal aspects of a culture and can frequently describe in great detail the forms of behavior that make up, for example, a wedding ceremony, a greeting sequence or a church service. Non-specialists, in fact, often regard the forms of such customs as the essence of culture, feeling that if one has described the customs he has described the culture.

This is, however, far from the case. For the forms of culture are but vehicles or containers for the expression and transmission of meanings that lie beneath the surface of culture. Most of the meanings expressed via cultural forms have their roots in common human concerns and thus are quite similar from culture to culture. But which cultural forms express which meanings differs widely from culture to culture. For cultural forms are assigned their meanings on the basis of their participation in a specific cultural context. There are no cultural forms that bear the same meanings in every culture.[27] The same form, therefore (even supposedly "Christian" forms such as preaching, baptism, hymns, etc.), if borrowed into another culture or subculture will always have a different meaning in the new culture than it had in the original culture. Thus if in translation or Christianization the original forms are preserved, the original meanings will be lost. In order to preserve the original meanings it is necessary to discover and employ forms in the receptor culture that express meanings equivalent to the original meanings. To preserve the meanings, then, the cultural forms must be changed (see Nida and Taber 1969:5).

Since cultural forms derive their meanings entirely from their participation within a cultural context, the attempt to discover the appropriate meanings of every linguistic and cultural form employed in Scripture must proceed via an analysis of the original cultural forms within their total cultural context. To communicate those meanings, then, one must "reinculturate" those same meanings in contemporary forms in their contemporary cultural context. What is being suggested is not essentially different from the traditional theological principle of "interpreting in context." What an anthropological orientation can add, though, is a) the constant recognition that that context is always the broad cultural context, not simply the literary context of the paragraph or book in which a given passage of Scripture occurs, and b) a greater understanding of how to deal with the transfer of scriptural meanings into another culture in such a way that the meanings perceived by today's receptors are essentially equivalent to those perceived by the original receptors.

Evangelicals have often seemed to be characterized by a preoccupation with the cultural forms of Christianity. We have tended to study the Scriptures on the one hand and to perpetuate the church on the other on the apparent assumption that the bond between the forms employed in the original expressions of Christianity and the correctness of the meanings thereby expressed is a permanent thing. If we can only discover the original way in which the church baptized, or conducted the communion

---

[27] See Nida 1960, chapter 4 for an elucidation of this principle.

service, or proclaimed the Word, or organized itself, we feel, we will have settled the problem of how we should do these things. This kind of assumption is, of course, very damaging because the same cultural forms never mean the same thing to people of different cultures or subcultures. If, therefore, the same forms are retained from culture to culture, or even from generation to generation, the meanings will always be perceived differently by the receptors than they were by the originators.

There is, in fact, a direct relationship between the foreignness of imposed cultural forms and the tendency of many to regard the forms as *sacred in themselves* and to miss the intended meanings. Note in this regard the tendency of many to consider water baptism (according to their denominational mode), the elements of the communion service, and monologue preaching as sacred in and of themselves, rather than to focus on the fact that those forms were employed in the original cultural setting not because in themselves they possessed some sacred quality but because through them it was possible to appropriately express with a minimum of interference the meanings God and his people wished to convey. To be true to those meanings, then, we will need to ask, What forms in our cultural setting adequately convey the meanings that those forms were meant to convey? Then, after having determined the original meanings and discovered appropriate contemporary cultural forms, we must begin to employ the new, more effective forms.

The application of such form-meaning insight could easily resolve the contemporary debate over the appropriate roles of women in Christianity. The first step would be to discover what Paul's commands such as those against women taking places of prominence in public meant in that culture. On the assumption that God intends those meanings to be conveyed to Christians in our culture today, we would ask, What equivalent forms in our culture convey those meanings? We could then work out equivalent rules for our day. And even if we experienced some difficulty with developing forms today that convey those same meanings, we can at least understand and teach why it is counter to the intent of Scripture to simply imitate the forms that Paul commanded Greeks to employ. It is the content (the meanings) of Scripture, not the cultural forms that is normative. Since those forms that meant propriety in Paul's context mean suppression and denial of the right to exercise spiritual gifts in our context, it is unscriptural (and Pharisaic) to simply impose them.

A clearer, more principled understanding of cultural forms and meanings in their contexts should make it possible for theologians to get beyond at least three common pitfalls: a) that a high percentage of the cultural forms recorded in the Bible are transcultural (i.e., convey the same meanings in every culture), b) that anything of importance in the Scriptures can be adequately interpreted as one would understand it if it had occurred in our culture (e.g. "the clear meaning" of Scripture), and c) that interpretation is basically a matter of moving directly from the original forms to contemporary forms. Such fallacies have often led (especially at the popular level) to principles of scriptural interpretation that label those passages recommending forms that our tradition considers unimportant as "cultural" (e.g., that women should cover their heads and keep silent in public, or that people should not eat pork) while forms that our tradition considers important (e.g., monogamy) are labeled as binding on everyone at every time.

A sharpened understanding of the way meanings are determined and communicated would give us the means of arriving at a more consistent hermeneutic. Such an approach would in every case seek the meanings behind the cultural forms, would seek some God-given meaning behind every set of scriptural forms, and would endeavor to move from the original meanings to equivalent contemporary meanings and thence to contemporary forms, rather than simply from form to form. These meanings would be expressed in contemporary cultural forms that differ from the original cultural forms to whatever extent is necessary to assure that they carry an impact in today's context as equivalent as possible to the impact of the original forms in their context.

Since none of the basic scriptural data on which we depend occurred within any contemporary culture, such a cross-cultural perspective on form and meaning is necessary at every level of interpretation and application of the Scriptures. The Greeks were not simply "primitive Americans," as many seem ethnocentrically to assume. They were not even closely related biologically or culturally to our northern European ancestors. So we cannot trust our own culture-bound reflexes to enable us to understand the meanings intended by the biblical authors. For they were expressed entirely through the culture-bound linguistic and cultural forms of their languages and cultures. There are, as stated above, no cultural symbols with universal meanings. And Christianity is much more than a system designed to perpetuate a selection of sacred ancient cultural forms. We need the greater preciseness of anthropological techniques for dealing more effectively with such cultural matters.

4. Evangelical theology needs anthropological insight to assist it in sorting out what is absolute from what is relative. Implied in the above discussion are two basic principles that enable us to deal more effectively with this issue: a) that God works within and in terms of human culture rather than against it, and b) that it is the meanings of Christianity that are absolute, rather than the cultural forms through which those meanings are expressed.

Anthropology some time ago began to recognize the pervasive ethnocentrism of western culture that has led us to evaluate all other cultures according to criteria that we value and thus to find them all inferior to our culture. We typically select those customs and culture patterns that we specialize in and measure other cultures according to how close they come to meeting our standards. We, for example, tend to grade down other cultures that have not achieved materially, medically, literarily, etc. We fail to note, however, that there are other areas in which they excel but we do not. Among the latter for many cultures are the solid family and social structures that they have but we do not, the greater satisfaction and fulfillment in life that they feel, the less traumatic path to adulthood, etc. While we have built skyscrapers and let our social structures crumble, other cultures have often built solid social structures to the neglect of excessive emphasis on material accomplishment.

This ethnocentrism is as much a part of western theological thinking as of the thinking of the rest of the populace. It often shows itself in our lack of interest in and respect for the understandings of theological matters generated by peoples of other cultures and subcultures. Many evangelicals (especially theologians) take a dim view of the attempts of those outside of the western theological tradition to do theology, as if theology can only be properly done from the "superior" perspective developed by them. Those from other cultures and subcultures are not highly enough educated, they say—meaning (as the Jewish leaders meant when they said the same thing about Peter and John-Acts 4:13) that they have not been educated in the theologian's way. They might be very well educated by other standards (as were the disciples) and very able to discern and apply theological insight from their own perspective.

To combat our ethnocentrism and to enable us to focus more fairly on the strengths of other cultures, anthropology has developed a doctrine called "cultural relativism." Theologians, like everyone else, need a good dose of this doctrine to help us to be more Christian in our acceptance of other approaches to life, and less vain in our evaluation of our own approach. Cultural relativism advocates the kind of respect for other cultures that Christianity advocates for other individuals. It is the equivalent on the cultural level of the Golden Rule. It recommends that, rather than moralizing about the good or the bad in another culture (on the basis of standards developed totally from within our own culture), one should accept the validity of that culture whether or not our own values predispose us to approve of the behavior encouraged by that culture. For that culture meets the needs of its people relatively well, just as our culture meets our needs relatively well.

Cultural relativity holds that all cultures are relatively equal to each other, each with its strengths and its weaknesses, but each worthy of respect. None, not even ours, is to be regarded as absolutely superior to any other, though there may be areas in any given culture where in terms of certain criteria the given culture may excel many or all others.

Some anthropologists in reaction against western cultural ethnocentrism have gone to an extreme that might be labeled "absolute cultural relativism." Such a position holds that there is no basis on which to evaluate cultural behavior from outside of the culture in question. Christians, of course, cannot go to such an extreme. We cannot simply live and let live without every attempting to influence anyone else in the direction of Christian values. For we believe that there are absolute standards that apply to all cultures and all people.

Our position, however, if it is to be scriptural, must be what Nida calls that of "relative cultural relativism" (1954:50). This position does not deny the presence of absolutes, but relates all absolutes to God who stands outside of culture, rather than to any cultural expression or system, be it American, Greek or Hebrew. Nida points out that the Bible

> clearly recognizes that different cultures have different standards and that these differences are recognized by God as having different values. The relativism of the Bible is relative to three principal factors: (1) the endowment and opportunities of people, (2) the extent *of* revelation, and (3) the cultural patterns of the society in question (1954:50).

The Parable of the Talents (Mt. 25:14–30) teaches the relativity of the endowment and opportunities of people. Jesus' statements in Matthew 5 changing Old Testament ideals to principles, such as "love your enemies" (Mt. 5:44), hate equals murder (Mt. 5:21-22), lust equals adultery (Mt. 5:27-28), etc., show a relativity in the extent of revelation. God's willingness to work with customs such as slavery (Lev. 25:39–46), polygamy (2 Sam. 12:7, 8) and many others in the Old Testament that he does not endorse in the New Testament, plus Paul's statement that he attempted to be a Jew to Jews and a Gentile to Gentiles (1 Cor. 9:20–22), show biblical relativism with respect to cultural patterns.

Biblical Christianity requires such cultural relativism lest we absolutize the forms of any culture (even a biblical culture). It "clearly establishes

> the principle of relative relativism, which permits growth, adaptation, and freedom, under the Lordship of Jesus Christ . . . The Christian position is not one of static conformance to dead rules. but of dynamic obedience to a living God (Nida 1954:52).

Such a position, informed by the insights of anthropology with respect to culture, should be a cornerstone of evangelical theology.

God is absolute. And the principles (the meanings, the content) of Christianity that we exegete from the Scriptures make up our understanding of the transculturally valid message from the absolute God committed to us. But it is the meanings, not the cultural forms through which those meanings flow, that are transcultural, valid for people of every culture at all times. It is the meaning "church" that is to be communicated and expressed in the forms of the receptor culture, not the forms that may be appropriate in another culture. Likewise, the meanings faith, conversion, love, fellowship, theology (if appropriate), etc. are to be fit to the appropriate cultural forms of whatever culture they are expressed in. The meanings are constant, the forms variable (relative) from culture to culture. Evangelical theology needs to be able to handle these concepts expertly if it is to adequately meet today's challenges.

5. Evangelical theology needs greater understanding of the processes of culture. I have spoken above of culture mainly in terms of its forms and patterns. But cultural systems channel people in terms of a great many processes as well—processes that result in support. maintenance and social control of and education into the existing system, but also in adaptation and change of that system. Christianity is intensely interested in the change processes and these must be studied much more carefully and precisely than the conceptual tools so far available to theologians will allow. But the relationship of the change processes to the processes of stabilization must also be known, since they have a critical bearing on the circumstances under which the advocates of Christianity will be allowed to employ the change mechanisms for Christian ends.

What, for example, should Christianity do about the crumbling of family structures in western societies under the impact of such forces as the school system, occupational mobility, the constant propaganda to the effect that a woman cannot fulfill herself by "simply" devoting herself to raising children, etc.? With little informed understanding of what healthy family structures look like—understanding abundantly available from studying the family cross-culturally-culture-bound theologians plow on, publishing books full of references to the writings of equally culture-bound theologians of former days, rather than to the anthropological materials. Family structure is a cultural thing, and both the processes that lead to family illness and those that lead to family health are cultural processes—processes that can be studied and employed by Christians for Christian ends.

The church, likewise, is primarily a matter of God making use of cultural relationships and processes. So are the processes of conversion, nurture, maturation, witnessing, communicating verbally and nonverbally, expressing affection, and the like. Courses on Christian doctrines such as faith, conversion, the church, salvation and the like should regularly include attention to a much greater range of valid cultural expression of the processes involved than is currently recognized. Students in my courses on conversion and indigeneity (the church) frequently express their amazement and enthusiasm over the valuable difference they experience between a cross-culturally informed treatment of these topics and the more traditional monocultural theological treatments they experienced in their theology classes. It is often quite a shock to these students to discover that once one has been exposed to what is termed the theology of any of these doctrines, one has come to understand only a very small fraction of even the scriptural treatment of the doctrine. A high percentage of what we need to know about the church, for example, is more susceptible to discovery via anthropological methodology than via theological methodology—though I would certainly not want to deny the value of traditional theological insight into the nature of the church.

Theological focus has often been almost entirely on the products of such processes. We often talk about the point of conversion without much understanding of the cultural processes that God employs to bring the person to that point. Likewise, with respect to Christian maturity, we tend to recommend behavior that ought to characterize a mature Christian without helping him to understand the processes via which one comes to maturity. In theology also, our primary concern is for that which theologians have produced, rather than with learning to imitate the process that a theologian must go through to produce a theology that genuinely speaks to the people of his generation. Learning to study the processes that the authors of Scripture went through could enable us to be imitators of them, not simply admirers of them and consumers of their products. Processes of communication, culture change, worldview change, church planting and organization and the like can also be brought into sharper focus by employing the perspectives of anthropology in the task of theologizing.

Greater anthropological understanding of these and other cultural processes can enable us to work better with them for God. We can also learn to measure and thus to predict more accurately such matters as receptivity, indigeneity, the probable appropriateness of innovations, the behavioral (as opposed to the merely intellectual) impact of Christian teaching, and the like. The fact that religious movements have often served to revitalize demoralized, disintegrating cultures has already been documented (Wallace 1956:264–281). We should be learning how and where this information can be put to work for Christianity. The antidote to the naive imposition of unity on the church at any cost to powerless minorities is already available to us. All we need do is to study and implement such sociocultural insights as the need to be greatly concerned for cultural homogeneity (see McGavran 1970). The church, hopefully led by its theologians, needs to get its feet on the ground on such issues. And much material on these subjects is already available if we will but look in the right places for it.

In these and many other conceptual areas, anthropological input can be of great benefit to evangelical theology. Though I have here dealt indirectly rather than directly with them, a longer treatment might give additional focus to such important conceptual areas as the doctrine of man, culture and the Bible, culture and hermeneutics, etc. I attempt to deal at length with such matters in a forthcoming book.[28]

Anthropological Methodology for Studying People Can Help

In addition to the assistance evangelical theology can obtain from an anthropological perspective in conceptualization, there is help in learning how to learn about man in culture. Anthropological insight into how to study people in other ways than simply by reading books could assist evangelical theology to overcome at least some of its propensity toward the overly academic. Anthropologists have specialized in studying people about whom no books have been written. In spite of the many studies of people that have been written, most of those even within western culture with whom we must deal have not been written about. We need to know how to learn about them and the involvements that influence them. Anthropological method can greatly help in meeting this need.

We need to learn how to find out where people are by studying people. If, as maintained above, God starts where people are, and if this is to be a model for us, then theologians need the tools to enable them to study man as he is, in each diverse situation, for the purpose of determining what specific approaches each situation demands.[29] The "participant-observation" field method of anthropology is particularly useful for this purpose in that it enables academicians to study people directly. Too many of the concepts of theology seem to be based on generalizations that, though they may have been applicable to some situations somewhere in the past, are not specifically applicable to many, if any, of today's variety of situations. Understandings of shame and guilt, conscience, the relationships of faith to psychological and spiritual well-being, the interaction between meaning and experience and the kind of blockage of communication that occurs due to certain types of experience, and the like could be cited as examples of the kinds of things that theologians need to study empirically.

I have suggested above the need to study the family cross-culturally to arrive at insights that would be helpful in our attempts to deal with the serious problems that face contemporary American families. This kind of method is the way to get at the data we need for such an approach. This is likewise the way to get the data needed to develop more effective approaches to churchness, conversion and the large number of other areas mentioned above in which our ability to deal effectively with them is hampered by our lack of proper understanding of what is really going on at the human level. The fact is that in many parts of the world Christians of other cultures are doing a more effective job of expressing many aspects of Christianity than we

---

[28] Since published as *Christianity in Culture* (1979a).

[29] See several of the publications of Thielicke for one theologian's attempt to meet this need. See especially 1965 and 1962.

are. We should study their approaches, study our situations anthropologically and apply the insight we learn from such an approach to the betterment of this part of God's Kingdom.

Many Christian groups in communally-oriented societies have indigenous models after which they can pattern their churches that are more like what God must have intended than any of the prominent western varieties of church in that they seem to lend themselves more to the expression of the Christian meanings that churches are intended to express than our forms often do. Many cultures with a supernaturalistic worldview, even though it may not be Christian, are already closer to what appears to be a biblical Christian interpretation of life than many Euroamerican Christians. For they automatically see God's hand in every event, whereas we perceive everything in terms of a strongly naturalistic bias. As participant-observers who know how to learn from people in these kinds of cultural situations, as well as in the many more typically American situations that surround us, theologians could assist their discipline enormously. Such study should at least become a standard preparation for the planting of new churches especially in segments of society other than the academic subculture in which the prospective church planters have probably been trained.

The inclusion in theological curricula of coursework and fieldwork employing anthropological field methodology would be a complete innovation. But it would, I predict, be as helpful as it is innovative. Students need, as contended above, to learn how to learn about people from studying people. We have specialized in teaching them how to learn from books, but they need to learn how to get beyond books. Field experience in another culture or subculture (e.g., Black, Chicano, etc.) after an appropriate period of study of anthropological techniques would be a valuable requirement.

By first studying how, and then by putting the principles into practice, theological students could learn a bit at least of how to perceive life from another cultural or subcultural perspective. This would bring greater awareness of the variety of subcultural differences in perception to be faced in each "typical" congregation. It should, then, lead the student to give greater attention to preparing his messages and doing his theologizing with the needs and perceptions of his hearers more firmly in mind than would otherwise be true.

Such study and fieldwork would teach how to discern the actual leadership patterns in a given community. This would put him in a better position to discover the actual (as opposed to the apparent or theoretical) patterns in any given congregation. Decision-making patterns, likewise, would be an important subject to study in such fieldwork, as would patterns of grouping. Applications of this kind of learning to ministry in a local congregation would help pastors greatly in their quest to develop appropriate approaches to decision-making (whether for conversion or in church government) and organizational patterning at the local level. There is much of this nature beneath the surface of our culture that we think we know but often don't, that would be most effectively brought to students' attention by exposing them to the study of these things in a different culture or subculture.

Conclusion

If any of these suggestions is valid and taken seriously by evangelical theologians, consideration will have to be given to the kinds of alterations that would be necessitated in theological training and research. Some of these changes could be initiated simply by adding new courses to the curricula of theological training institutions. It is, however, important that such courses be taught by people with training in both theology and anthropology plus, if possible, experience in communicating the gospel cross-culturally. For the insights focused on in these courses become most apparent to both teacher and students when dealt with from a cross-cultural perspective by one whose perception of the problems and the needs of the receptors has been sensitized by such experience.

I would hope that, in addition to new courses, many of the applications of anthropological insight here recommended can be incorporated at numerous points in courses that already exist. As suggested above, I believe that insight into the requirements of effective Bible translation can and should be an important part of exegesis courses where students are required to produce their own translations. The cultural processes involved in conversion and Christian maturation should be brought sharply into focus in every course that deals with these matters. The importance of being hearer-oriented and the implications of such an orientation should be stressed in a variety of classes whether the subject matter is biblical (for God demonstrates a hearer-orientation throughout Scripture), homiletical (for we need to present the message in terms of the needs and interests of our hearers) or theological (for we need to produce theologies that scratch people where they itch).

Many of the areas that need to be dealt with require a good bit of further research and publication by evangelicals. A good start has been made in the application of anthropological insight to missionary work and to Bible translation, and many of the resultant publications should be required reading for all theological students and their professors,[30] even though the immediate purpose of those publications was to assist people to work outside of Euroamerica. But we need much more research and writing that focuses anthropological insight more specifically on the concerns of effectively communicating and articulating Christianity to Euroamericans. For we are today in the strange position, with respect to an activity such as Bible translating, of investing enormous resources in sending out Bible translators to provide better translations for peoples of other cultures than evangelicals will ordinarily accept for their own use in English. In this area at least, where much of the theoretical groundwork has already been done and published, we should be equipping pastors and teachers at least to keep up with what is being done by Bible translators and other effective communicators overseas.

Indeed, it may be that we should look to such Bible translating to provide us with the new model for theologizing that we seek. For, as Sundkler has pointed out, good theology is really good translation—translation that communicates to today's

---

[30] See the listing of such works at the end of this chapter.

common people as effectively as Paul's theologizing communicated to the common people who spoke the slang Koine Greek of the first century. Good theology, he says,

> is an ever-renewed re-interpretation to new generations and peoples of the given Gospel, a re-interpretation of the will and the way of the one Christ in a dialogue with new thought forms and culture patterns (1960:281).

Unfortunately, to many common people today, evangelical theology sounds as foreign to their real concerns as the language of the King James Version sounds in comparison to their daily language. And I'm afraid it will remain so to the extent to which it continues to be produced by those more oriented toward the study of the past concerns of western academicians than to the study of the present concerns of real live people. I have hereby tried to suggest some of the ways that I believe anthropological insight and methodology can fruitfully be employed by evangelical theologians to bring them into greater and more effective contact with contemporary people and their concerns, and then to communicate their insights more effectively to those people.

A Representative List of Publications Applying Anthropological Insight to Missionary Work and to Bible Translation:

1. Books and Articles

Beekman, J., and J. Callow, *Translating the Word of God*. Grand Rapids, MI: Zondervan, 1974.

Bratcher, R., and E. A. Nida, *Translator's Handbook on the Gospel of Mark*. Leiden: Brill (for United Bible Societies), 1961.

Fueter, P. D., "Communicating the Bible," *International Review of Mission* 60:437-51 (1971).

Hulst, A. R., *Old Testament Translation Problems*. Leiden: Brill (for the United Bible Societies), 1960.

Loewen, J., *Culture and Human Values*. Pasadena, CA: William Carey Library, 1965.

Luzbetak, L., *The Church and Cultures*. Techny, IL: Divine Word Publications, 1963.

Mayers, M., *Christianity Confronts Culture*. Grand Rapids, MI: Eerdmans, 1974.

McGavran, D., *Understanding Church Growth*. Grand Rapids, MI: Eerdmans, 1970.

Newman, B., and E. A. Nida, *A Translator's Handbook on the Acts of the Apostles*. London: United Bible Societies, 1972.

Nida, E. A., *Bible Translating*. New York: American Bible Society, 1947.

-----*Customs and Cultures*. New York: Harper and Row, 1954 (reprinted William Carey Library, 1975).

-----*Message and Mission*. New York: Harper and Row, 1960 (revised edition William Carey Library, 1990).

-----*Toward a Science of Translating*. Leiden: Brill, 1964.

-----"Implications of Contemporary Linguistics for Biblical Scholarship," *Journal of Biblical Literature* 91:73-89 (1972). Reprinted in Nida, E. A., *Language Structure and Translation.* Stanford: Stanford University Press, 1975, pp. 248-70.

Nida, E. A., and C. Taber, *The Theory and Practice of Translation.* Leiden: Brill, 1969.

Reiling, J., and J. Swellengrebel, *A Translator's Handbook on the Gospel of Luke.* Leiden: Brill (for the United Bible Societies), 1971.

Smalley, W., *Readings in Missionary Anthropology.* Pasadena, CA: William Carey Library, 1972.

Tippett, A., *Verdict Theology in Missionary Theory.* Pasadena, CA: William Carey Library, 1973.

-----(ed), *God, Man and Church Growth.* Grand Rapids, MI: Eerdmans, 1973.

Wonderly, W., *Bible Translations for Popular Use.* London: United Bible Societies, 1968.

2. Journals

The Bible Translator. United Bible Societies, London, 1950-Present.

A large number of helpful exegetical articles, reviews of major Bible translations and the like appear regularly in this journal.

Missiology. American Society of Missiology, 1973-Present.

This journal is a continuation and expansion of *Practical Anthropology.* It contains a variety of articles relating to the cross-cultural communication and application of the gospel.

Practical Anthropology. 1953-1972.

This journal was dedicated to the application of anthropological insight to the communication of the gospel. It contains a large number of articles of high relevance to the topic of this article. Among the most useful are those by members of the American Bible Society Translations Department, E. A. Nida, W. A. Smalley (longtime editor of *Practical Anthropology*), W. D. Reyburn and J. A. Loewen.

CHAPTER 23

AN ANTHROPOLOGIST'S APPROACH TO THEOLOGY

Reprinted here with permission from the book *After Therapy What?* (1974:136-159) published by C.C. Thomas and containing the lectures of Thomas Oden presented to the Fuller School of Psychology and the responses by Fuller faculty members

Introduction

I would first like to express my appreciation to the organizing committee for inviting me to participate in the Oden lectures and discussions. I found myself strongly identifying with Professor Oden in pursuit of answers to a complex of problems relating to the contemporary need within western society for understanding and expressions of Christianity that will he perceived as relevant. This is a major preoccupation of those of us primarily concerned with the communication of Christianity to peoples of nonwestern societies. It is, therefore, a challenge and privilege to relate some of the insights of my primary disciplinary specialty, anthropology, to certain of the concerns expressed by Professor Oden.

It is a growing impression of mine that the western cultural philosophic-theological frame of reference in which theology as we know it has been studied, understood and proclaimed is no longer adequate as the sole framework for theological expression. There are at least two reasons for this: (1) our understanding of life has forced us outside the limits that philosophy has traditionally defined for itself; and (2) since a primary purpose for gaining theological understanding is to develop greater effectiveness in the communication of Christian truth, such communication should he phrased and lived in terms demonstrably relevant to today's people, most of whom are not thinking in terms of a philosophico-theological frame of reference. Where the intellectual action really is for western people today, as Oden points out, is in terms of the concepts provided by the behavioral sciences. It is, therefore, in this direction that western theology must turn in order both to gain new understandings and to be perceived of as relevant to contemporary westerners.

It is not by accident that Oden's theological students no longer "dig the language of the church" but find it "easy and native . . . to get inside the language

281

frame of psychology" (Oden 1974c:45). Our society has changed, for both better and worse, and theology and the church have not kept up at the level where the eternal verities of theology either do or do not get across to people—at the level of perceived relevance, where people recognize that what is being recommended relates directly to the needs they feel and, therefore, is worth grabbing. Theology *is* relevant only in a potential sense. If it is not perceived as relevant by those who need it, all of its great potential is wasted. For relevance is as relevance is perceived.

That theology was meant to be perceived as relevant both in conceptualization and in communication I deduce from the fact that God has consistently chosen to employ human tools, a human frame of reference, as the vehicle of his interaction with us. The theological concepts in terms of which God communicates himself are human concepts—out of the language and culture of those with whom he interacts. And this is still true even after a period of time when, in the process of God's employment of human concepts, these concepts are transformed into something greater than they were when the process first started. They are still human concepts even when employed by God. And the process of God's self-revelation in terms of these concepts is only effective when it involves both a sending God and a receiving human being. In fact, communication science tells us, the way in which the receptor decodes the message is at least as important as, if not more important than, the way in which the sender encodes the message (Nida 1960:34). That is, what the hearer hears is at least as important as what the potential communicator says. Thus, when the would-be communicator discovers that the message is not getting through clearly to the hearers, it is incumbent upon the would-be communicator to adjust the manner in which he or she attempts to communicate so that the message is properly perceived at the other end.

I think, therefore, if my contention is true that modern westerners are more in tune with the conceptual framework of the behavioral sciences than with what has become a more and more isolated philosophic-historic-theological manner of conceptualization, God would have us give serious attention to the attempt to conceptualize and express theological truth in terms of the constructs of the behavioral sciences. This I regard as one of the more important of my own preoccupations. It was, therefore, with a great deal of excitement that I read, listened to, and interacted with Professor Oden.

I must confess, though, that I often did not completely understand either what Oden was driving at or why he seemed to be having such difficulty making his point. I attribute this difficulty in understanding to one of two reasons: (1) my own unpreparedness with regard to specialized concepts and jargon of psychology; or (2) Oden's inability at points to completely free himself from either the philosophical frame of reference of western theologizing or the intellectual faddism in which western theology has too often indulged itself. The first of these problems (i.e., my own lack of acquaintance with psychological concepts and jargon) does not concern me greatly, though I would beg the indulgence of the reader at those points where my deficits in this regard become disturbing to her or him. At the second point, however, I think Oden, with a more relevant behavioral scientific frame of reference already in his grasp, did not help his argument by continually reverting to formulations of theological truth expressed in terms of the philosophical frame of reference—truths that can and should he reexamined without apology in terms of the new perspective and phrased unashamedly in the language and concepts of the behavioral sciences which Oden has discovered to be the linguistic home territory of his students (Oden 1974c:45).

But in spite of these concerns, I found myself experiencing at many points an exciting identification with either Oden's aims or his approach, or both, and it is in that spirit, perhaps to be equated with what he termed an "ecumenism of spirit," that I offer the following remarks.

The Perspective: Beyond Dialogue

I would like to comment on Professor Oden's presentations from a perspective that I would recommend for a contemporary approach to theology. It is not fully anthropological, though I consider myself an anthropologist, nor does it conform to the philosophical perspective of western theology, though in my own nontraditional sense I would also claim to be a theologian. The perspective is, rather, one I have tentatively labeled "Christian Ethnotheology"—a perspective that attempts to examine and interpret theological data from a point of view that not only takes God and humans seriously, as traditional theology does, hut also takes culture, society and psychology seriously, as the behavioral sciences do. The aim of this approach is not to compromise traditional theology, but to rechannel it in such a way as to increase its relevance to real life.

This is simply an attempt at translation, predicated on the assumption that the linguistic and conceptual frame of reference of modern, westerners has, as Oden points out, changed. This approach seeks to resist the tendency of any of the source disciplines to absolutize its own particular concerns or to press its own particular predilections if the findings of another discipline prove contradictory. It, rather, attempts to reconcile the contradictory findings in the conviction that in reality truth is one and that, therefore, a given insight is not to be rejected simply because it has been arrived at by psychologists rather than by theologians. I will suggest below certain modifications in our theology that I believe psychology and/or anthropology are calling us to consider.

Where, however, the insights of two or more disciplines are largely complementary rather than contradictory, Christian Ethnotheology seeks to integrate both into a single frame of reference. Thus it finds it possible to accept most of what western theology has to say about the character and power of God and the fact of human sinfulness and to unite these insights with those of the behavioral sciences. Diagrammatically such concerns and the primary sources of information about them may be expressed as follows:

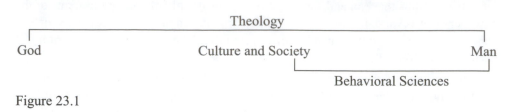

Figure 23.1

Christian Ethnotheology, then, looks to traditional theology for information concerning the absolute God and transcultural truths concerning humanity. It specifically accepts the existence of the personal, omnipotent, omniscient, omnipresent, triune, transcendent, self-revealing God of Judeo-Christianity. It further accepts the remainder of the cardinal doctrines of Christian theology (generalized) concerning, for example, the fallenness of man, his need for redemption, God's concern for and activity (revelational and otherwise) toward the meeting of that need, the primacy of human faith-response to God in the salvation process, the activity of the Holy Spirit in revealing (and/or illuminating) and in the leading of Christians (individuals and groups) toward spiritual maturity, the need for groupness in human response to God (e.g., the Hebrew nation, the church), the primacy of the Incarnation and of the Bible in God's revelation to us, etc. Christian Ethnotheology does not, however, feel bound in every case to interpretations or formulations of these doctrines in purely western cultural conceptualization or in philosophico-theological terms.

This integrating approach looks unashamedly to disciplines such as anthropology, sociology and psychology for greater insight into matters of human limitation, perception, and potential. The fact that human perception is not only pervasively influenced by sin and finiteness (as traditional theology states) but is also pervasively influenced by culture, subculture, and individual psychology is an important contribution of the behavioral sciences to ethnotheology.

This approach, then, is an attempt to go beyond the mere dialoguing between two (or more) disciplines that Oden discusses to the more important matter of actually facilitating the communication of theological truth. That is, the real aim cannot simply be that the representatives of the disciplines talk *to each other* (and, probably, fight with each other) but, rather, that someone begins to employ whatever insights God permits us to the carrying out of the real task before us: the mediation of God to humanity. And for this purpose the question that Professor Oden found so difficult to deal with as to the difference (if any) between believing and unbelieving therapists fades into insignificance behind the greater concern: How do we as believers maximize the employment of whatever cultural, disciplinary, theoretical or other channels that are available to us to mediate God to humans.

And at this point a distinction focused on by anthropology is helpful. The key terms ordinarily used are *form* and *function*, though the latter may be looked at from several perspectives, including objective social and/or psychological function, internal perceived meaning (of individuals or groups) and the use to which a thing is put. Theology, the church, psychotherapy or an axe, for example, each have distinct forms in terms of which they may be described. These forms have various properties that may be very much in focus both in the minds of the users of the forms and of the recipients related to whatever use is made of them. But this use of the forms, their meanings and the overall part they play in the cultural and psychological frame of reference of the user are labeled *function* and regarded as quite distinct from the form.

The same is true of disciplines such as theology or psychotherapy or of institutions such as the church or the family. In setting up such disciplines or institutions there must first be a determination of the intended function and then the choice of the appropriate form(s) to employ in order to serve the desired function. In the case of an already existing form, numerous questions must continually be asked. Is this form serving the desired function, or has it somehow ceased to serve that function? Has its perceived meaning changed over the years as the meanings of word forms in language are continually changed, as people add new connotations and drop some of their previous connotations? For one of the disturbing things about cultural forms (whether they be institutions or words) is that as culture is changed, the meanings attached to these cultural forms change. And this gives rise to a very interesting principle of translation and "transculturation" of cultural institutions from culture to culture or from a previous to a present stage of the same culture: it is frequently necessary to alter or update the form of a concept or an institution in order to preserve its intended meaning (Nida and Taber 1969:5).

This, I believe, is the same truth that Oden quotes Cardinal Newman as pointing to by suggesting that "it is only through change . . . only through the living process of constant rebirth and reappropriation of the Christian tradition that the church can be the same" (Oden 1974b:92). Perhaps, though, had Newman's frame of reference had available to it such a dynamic concept of behavioral science as the form-function dichotomy, he would not have had to resort to the static photographic analogy to make his point. For such a model has to account for any new interpretation of truth in terms of a discovery of something already stored in the forms themselves rather than in terms of a dynamic, living, Spirit-led, continual updating of the cultural wineskins in recognition of the fact that the wine of Christianity refuses to stop fermenting, for God's Spirit is still guiding his church into new truth (Jn. 16:13). It is the behavioral sciences that provide us with this more dynamic model and, I suppose, it is a function of my own involvement in a behavioral science frame of reference that I had difficulty understanding why Professor Oden or anyone else could get so excited about Newman's exposition, except for the fact that he arrived at this insight so long ago.

Contemporary western theology, set in the philosophic-theological mold, is a form of theologizing that may once have communicated the intended meaning. But it has long since ceased to do so (at least to the unbrainwashed). If we take as the true purpose of theology what Oden claims it to be: "to put to work human language in an attempt to point to how God has made himself known in history" (1974c:67) or "to make self-consistent and intelligible the life of faith in the Christian community" in ultimate accountability to the reality to which Scripture points, viz. the judgment, grace and care of God in and for the whole of history" (1974b:81), then certain changes are warranted. And I believe that it is somewhere in this area that the purpose of theologizing lies. For theology, like the Word and acts of God that form its database, is intended to effectively communicate God to humans. It must, therefore, give just as much attention to the adequacy with which its message is getting across as it gives to the accuracy of its understandings of the revelation.

With regard to psychotherapy the situation does not appear to be quite the same, at least on the surface. The language, concepts and overall frame of reference of psychotherapy are, as Oden points out, eminently "in," even with theological students, leading to the temptation on the part of both client and therapist to expect more of this form than it can deliver. Yet psychotherapy, like theology, is but a form that can be put to any of a number of functions, only some of which can be regarded as appropriate from a Christian perspective. That is, psychotherapy functioning as a substitute for God, rather than employed to mediate him, must be regarded as an inappropriate use of the psychotherapeutic form by those whose dedication to Christianity predisposes them to see all of life and labor as instruments to be employed to God's glory.

Thus, whether or not God is active in psychotherapy as administered by an unbeliever is an interesting but irrelevant question (although I would claim that the answer must be positive since—"incognito Christ" or not—my understanding of the Bible is that God is constantly at work in all that goes on in the world). The only relevant question for me is this regard is how well the primary and specific Christian objective is being realized. For the end of psychotherapy for the Christian psychotherapist cannot simply be the bringing about of psychological health—health that, in the absence of a relationship with the eternal God, can only serve to make more bearable the life on earth that precedes the person's ultimate estrangement from God. For health and life themselves are but means, not ends. Christian psychotherapists must be concerned with at least specifying the Christian tenets to which they have committed themselves if they are not to be acting unconcernedly vis-a-vis their clients who, like they, need ultimate as well as penultimate answers. But for this purpose Christian psychotherapists need to hear from a theology that not only talks about what Christian objectives are, and how to live and speak convincingly concerning them, but talks in such a way that what it says is perceived as relevant by Christian psychotherapists.

We can make genuine progress in relating theology and the behavioral sciences, if only we will stop regarding Christian theologizing as the sacred preserve of those still enmeshed in the philosophico-theological matrix and begin to experiment with more contemporary formulations of the same truths—not, of course, neglecting to consult with and elicit the assistance of traditional theologians. For many of them are likewise unhappy about the current state of affairs and are as anxious to experiment as any of us. But we must get beyond mere dialogue.

Mediating God's Love and Concern across Interpersonal Boundaries

Of the numerous subjects discussed by Professor Oden I would like to comment on several that connect in some way with my own thinking relative to the development of the ethnotheological understanding of the God-human interaction briefly outlined above. These areas gravitate around the central theme of how to mediate God's love and concern across boundaries—boundaries that are ultimately interpersonal but that may intermediately be interdisciplinary, intercultural, or between God and humans.

Oden speaks much about empathy (1966:1–17) and likens it to the Incarnation. I accept this analogy and, in fact, seek, below, to make even greater use of the analogy that he does. Oden's struggle to understand the human ability to empathize in terms of such philosophico-theological constructs as Barth's "incognito Christ," however, bothers me since I feel that it is based on the perpetuation of an overly negative, western theological evaluation of human potential to which such approaches as psychotherapy give the lie. Why not, rather, take seriously the observation of psychology (and of a great deal of other social scientific investigation and popular experience) that human beings possess the ability to partially enter into the experience of other human beings, and then modify our theological understanding of what constitutes basic humanness?

I would contend that since truth is one, insights into the nature and potential of human beings derived from western psychology are at least as likely to be valid as are those of western theology, provided only that they do not conflict with the clear teachings of Scripture (an evaluation just as difficult for theologians to make as for Spirit-led psychologists). I cannot, therefore, regard as acceptable the hypothesis (apparently held by Oden) that one of the effects of the Fall was the total eradication of the ability to empathize with other human beings and also, to an extent, with God, especially in the light of (1) the findings of the behavioral sciences, and (2) the Incarnation.

The effective crossing of barriers, however, involves a number of principles pointed to by various of the behavioral sciences as present in effective human to human relationships, and all employed by God in the Incarnation. Those to be dealt with here are (1) the necessity for the initiator of the communication/therapy process to adopt the frame of reference of the receptor/client in order to make effective contact with him or her; (2) the responsibility of the receptor/client to determine what her or his response will be; (3) the greater effectiveness of the communication/therapy process if the primary type of learning that takes place is by means of discovery on the part of the receptor/client; and (4) the need for some sort of permanent therapeutic community for the receptor/client to fit into if the process initiated between the potential helper and the helped is to continue. It is probably no longer possible to categorically identify each of these insights with but a single social science. Personally, however, I identify the third with learning or education theory and the fourth with a combination of anthropological insight and reflection on what the church is intended to be (i.e., an ethnotheological insight).

The Receptor/Client's Frame of Reference

With respect to the first principle, it seems axiomatic that potential helpers must know where those they seek to help are before they can assist them. But they must go much further than simply knowing: they must make the effort to genuinely enter into the experience of those persons—into their cultural and psychological frame of reference—in a way that is acceptable and intelligible to them if the barrier(s) between them are to be effectively crossed. For as mentioned above, how the hearer understands the communication is every bit as important as and probably more important than the way the potential communicator attempts to get the message across (Nida 1960:34). And this principle applies whether the potential helper is a psychologist working within the same culture as the client, a missionary working across cultures, or the Son of God crossing from the supracultural into culture.

But this crossing has several complicating factors to it in addition to the major psychological and cultural ones on which we have already focused. Chief among these factors are those surrounding the role adopted by the potential helper and the stereotype of the helper held by the potential recipient of the help. It is at this point that I feel Oden's remarks concerning the inadequacy of the doctor-patient model for the therapist are particularly well-taken. For, it seems, it is not until potential helpers, be they therapists, missionaries, preachers, professors or God, are perceived by the one in need of assistance as fully human (i.e., fully within that person's frame of reference) that the setting for true assistance has been attained. "You don't seem like a university professor," one young student once remarked as we chatted in my university office. This was an indication we had reached that stage in our relationship where she could relate to me as a *human being,* not simply in terms of her stereotype of a professor.

Likewise, I read between the lines of the prologue to the First Epistle of John a large degree of amazement at a God who broke through the stereotype, turned his back on an assigned prestige and a prescribed role in favor of a position *within* the frame of reference of those, like John, whom he sought to reach—a position in which he was forced to *earn* as an intelligible equal, rather than to *demand* as a largely unintelligible superior, any respect accorded him. And this type of stereotype-smashing both communicates and genuinely helps.

No, I would say, therapists do not help their therapy by imitating the doctor-patient model, and the best indication that we have of this is the fact that when God—who presumably could have employed any model he chose but who, we can assume, chose the most effective—sought to really help, he employed a model that put him fully within the frame of reference of those he came to assist. And the really redemptive part of the process was what those close to him got to know about him because he allowed them to get close. As John says, they saw and heard and *touched* him. Apparently the helping relationship, both as employed by God and as defined by at least some psychotherapists, is most effective when helpers gets beyond whatever the stereotype is of their role and allow themselves to be perceived by the receptors as human, vulnerable, touchable and, therefore, credible.

Our understanding of why breaking out of the "doctor" or "God" stereotype facilitates genuine communication, and thus therapy, is furthered by the insights of a relatively recent field of study known as Information Theory. Two of the major tenets of this perspective are: (1) The less expected the action or word is, the greater the amount of information it conveys; and (2) the more specifically a matter is presented) the greater the amount of information conveyed. A doctor (or God) is expected to fit into a particular stereotype. If the doctor breaks out of it, he or she communicates more than if she or he stays within it. If, in addition, that person *specifically* reveals him or herself to the one he or she is trying to assist, the potential for more effective communication and assistance is greatly increased. The Gospels are full of illustrations both of Jesus' unpredictability and of the specificity of the real life stories and experiences in terms of which he communicated eternal truths.

It should, however, be noted that in order to cross a stereotype barrier the helper (whether therapist, missionary, preacher, professor, doctor or Son of God) must first have legitimate title to the prestige and other accouterments that the stereotype assigns. If the therapist has not come, through or apart from (and sometimes in spite of) training, both to personal wholeness and to an understanding of how to assist others toward wholeness, she or he will not be well-advised to risk the position assigned by the stereotype for the sake of a position that requires that person to *earn* (rather than to demand) whatever prestige he or she attains in each new interpersonal encounter. For an unqualified person or one who lacks the personal security to take such a risk, the professionalism allowed by the stereotype provides a ready refuge from reality. That is, one cannot turn his back on a position that one has not already attained. Nor could Jesus turn his back on his "Godness" for the purpose of truly identifying with humans, as Philippians 2 states that he did, if he did not have a rightful claim to retain his position as God.

This insight, I believe, has something to say both to the problem that Professor Oden raised with regard to the acceptance or rejection of the doctor-patient model and also to the concomitant problem that Professor Oden labeled professionalism. It would seem advisable for prospective therapists to get professional credentials and, in the process, come to psychological wholeness themselves as a necessary precondition to their adopting an incarnational approach to therapy. Only then will they have the credentials that will enable them to effectively communicate by (at least at times) turning their backs on that which they have the right to have ascribed to them by their clients—professionalism and psychological health—and genuinely sharing themselves, even their specific hang-ups, with their clients. Jesus gave *himself*, shared *himself* and *won* the admiration and allegiance that he had a right to demand. And this set the stage for a truly therapeutic relationship.

The Responsibility of
Receptors/Clients to
Determine Their Response

But whether or not the openness, acceptance, and self-sharing of the communicator/therapist will result in therapy for the receptor/client is up to the receptor. If the process of barrier crossing is to be anything but an academic exercise, it must involve not only the *offer* of self on the part of the communicator but the *acceptance* of that offer on the part of the receptor. And this positive response is no less important to the therapeutic process than the offer itself, as innumerable psychologists, missionaries and others who seek to cross interpersonal barriers of one kind or another for the purpose of bringing about change can testify.

Thus it is that the best situation for effective interpersonal barrier crossing involves both the demonstration of relevance (i.e., empathy) on the part of the communicator and the feeling of need for whatever the communicator has to offer on the part of the receptor. If, then, the felt need, there already or stimulated by the communicator, is for behavioral change, the change itself can be accomplished only by the recipient of the message, never by the communicator/therapist. The anthropologist H. G. Barnett (1953), strongly influenced by a psychological perspective on social change, distinguishes at this point between the function of an advocate and that of an innovator. The advocate of change may come either from outside a society or from within. An innovator, however—the one who actually effects the change—must always be an insider since the locus of culture change is within the society, whether the new idea is produced by the insider or suggested by an outsider. It is only the insider who can take the new idea in whole or in part and integrate it into the culture of which he or she is a part in such a way that from henceforth that innovation forms a part of the structure of that culture.

On the psychological level therapists can analyze, understand, empathize, and identify with the client, but ultimately their part of the operation is limited by the fact that they cannot actually effect the required changes in the client's psychological structure. They can only advocate, recommend, persuade, and plead for such change. Any actual changes—any innovations—must be made by the client her or himself.

Professor Oden, of course, recognizes this fact when he states that "the real healing competencies reside in the ordinary people in the group, not in the professional therapeutic agent" (Oden 1974a:10). They could reside nowhere else. But what Oden seems to ignore in stressing his concept of laicization is the fact that, though people possess great potential for a variety of things, much of this potential is not actualized due to lack of stimulus. Thus, though any therapeutic behavioral change takes place within the client and *may* result from response to the fairly weak stimulus of an untrained friend, in many cases the stimulus must be greater than can be provided by one whose imagination and experience have not been expanded through training. That such behavioral change is often most effectively carried out in the context of groupness is undeniable (see below). But such change is not always, as Oden implies, because of the therapy applied by the group but, rather, because the group provides the *support* needed by the individual while she or he effects the recommended therapy.

Note, however, the attribution of responsibility to the receptor of the therapy—a point on which certain theological positions are weak. The behavioral sciences demonstrate, I believe, that human beings are capable (even without the Holy Spirit's aid) of positive change for the better. It is, therefore, incumbent upon us to accept this evidence and to modify our theological understandings accordingly. A theological understanding of humans that regards them as essentially passive in either the determination of their response to God or in the effecting of positive behavioral change after conversion must, I believe, in response to the findings of the behavioral sciences, be abandoned. Certainly a theological view of humans more consonant with that of the behavioral sciences would enable Oden to escape some of what seems to me to be unwarranted dependence upon the concept of the incognito Christ to explain our ability to help ourselves.

The Greater Effectiveness of the Communication/Therapy Process If the Receptor/Client Learns by Discovery

The third of the principles that contribute to effective interpersonal barrier-crossing relates to the means by which the potential acceptor comes to new insight and understanding. In our day of mass dissemination of predigested information, it is easy to overlook the significance of the fact that the value to the learner of the material learned is usually directly proportionate to the degree of discovery-learning involved in the learning process. Predigested information has its value, but its influence on the learner is seldom either as deep or as pervasive as that of insights that the learner feels he or she has discovered himself.

"Keith, I didn't know you were a Christian," said a secretary to Keith Miller on one occasion as continued association with and observation of him bore fruit in discovery learning. "You are the Christ, the Son of the living God," said Peter long ago in expression of a similar discovery encouraged by a teacher who respected the intelligence of the people he sought to help to such an extent that he taught in terms of real and true-to-life analogies that challenged his hearers to *discover* truth and thus to learn how to learn. This he did in preference to a method that would have predigested truth into theological propositions and taught his hearers to depend upon their teacher rather than to think for themselves. This latter approach might well have resulted in a greater uniformity of theological understanding but only at the expense of (1) a lower degree of real learning, since the discovery element would have been lessened considerably; and (2) the demonstration of a much lower estimate of humans on the part of the Son of God.

Again this insight of behavioral science and the observation that Jesus sought to stimulate discovery-learning speak eloquently for the revision upward of our theological estimate of humans. Both Jesus and the behavioral sciences seem to evaluate us and our potential more highly than western theologies do.

If persons of faith, functioning as therapists, genuinely share themselves in integrated Christian wholeness with their clients, they invite discovery on the part of those clients of the source of their integrated wholeness. Witness is, of course, far more than a verbal and cognitive thing, but person to person, boundary-crossing sharing does not stop short of verbalizing even cognitive understandings when interaction with the client and the possibility of thereby leading him or her to discovery invite it. But even then it is my opinion that the type of verbalization employed should, after Jesus' example, be in the form of meaningful linguistic and conceptual forms that stimulate further inquiry and further discovery, rather than in those that hinder or squelch discovery. Often a retreat to what appears to the hearer to be authoritative theological propositions results in the latter.

The discovery approach to arriving at truth is but the focus of a longer process of experiential growth that I see as involving at least the following stages. These apply whether the experience under consideration is ordinary learning or something more special like Christian conversion or one of the multitude of similar learnings in the process of psychospiritual maturation. Since Professor Oden specifically asked me to comment on my understanding of this process, and since I feel this tangent is germane both to the matter of interpersonal boundary crossing and to the task of Christian psychotherapy, I will briefly outline it here. The stages,[1] arranged in two cycles, are (as I see them):

Cycle   Expanding   Peak   (Tentative)
I: Stimulus→ Awareness→ Encounter→ Discovery→ Decision→ Experience→ Incorporation
                                                                            (→)

Cycle
II: Feedback→ Adjustment→ Final Incorporation

Figure 23.2

The stimulus may be anything, informational or otherwise, that breaks through to the learner from any source (such as therapy, preaching, personal experience) whether external or internal to the learner. This stimulus is reflected upon by learners, producing an expansion of their awareness and an encounter with it in which they are forced to deal with it either positively, negatively or evasively. Though even a rejection of the demands of the new awareness may result in discovery of some kind, acceptance of it is more likely to issue in the kind of discovery that produces a decision and a revitalized peak in the learners' experience. This is often followed by at least a tentative attempt to incorporate the discovery into their frame of reference. In this attempt at incorporation, however, they may be only partially successful, or that may only partially incorporate due to a variety of factors. These factors often center around what turns out to be an incorrect or incomplete understanding of either the nature or the implications of the stimulus. And when this happens at this point or at any of the others in the cycle, most potentially useful

---

[1] My scheme is an elaboration of that suggested in Tippett 1969.

learning simply gets lost because we are not ready for it, we forget it, or it is displaced by some other learning.

Having completed this first cycle, learners may, if they are fortunate, be able to begin a second cycle by obtaining assistance in the form of sympathetic feedback, preferably from the source of the original stimulus, if that source be human (e.g., therapist, teacher, preacher, etc.). On this basis, then, learners make whatever adjustments may be required prior to the final incorporation and integration of the learning into their life.

As I have said, such discovery-learning typically takes place at innumerable times in a person's life and he or she may label one of these times as her or his "Christian conversion." But this discovery and peak experience may not he perceived as differing in kind from other such learnings—only in content. Nor need it always differ in intensity from other such learnings. Indeed, it is the experience of most of us who were converted early in life that there have been many peak experiences subsequent to that which we label the conversion experience that have in most ways been both more meaningful to us and more life-changing.

The aim of such a learning process, whether stimulated by therapy, teaching, interpersonal relationships, or whatever, is of course, maturity. Two points of particular importance for theology are, it seems to me: (1) that maturation whether psychological, intellectual or spiritual is always a process. One never arrives at the point where one can be regarded as mature in any but a relative sense; and (2) though many of the stages in the Christian conversion and maturation process can also be assigned distinct theological labels (such as the "wooing of the Spirit," "illumination," "redemption" and "sanctification") designed to enable us to focus on the activity of God in the process, this in no way obviates our right to describe and come to understand the whole process from the standpoint of human perception of what is transpiring. For there is no greater sanctity to one set of terms or concepts over the other, even though the one approach claims to view the process from God's perspective while the other views it from the human end. Indeed, it is only as we analyze the process in terms of our human perception that many of us gain the insights we need to effectively advocate such Christian innovation on the part of others across interpersonal barriers between us and them.

The Need for a Therapeutic Community

But it is in the fourth point, the need for a therapeutic community, that all this really comes together. Professor Oden spoke wistfully of his desire to see the therapeutic process become self-perpetuating through the activity of those thus brought to wholeness in the society of which they are a part, a society that will seek "stability, continuity, a sustained, viable self-understanding and an understanding of the wholeness of the historical process" (Oden 1974b:24). Oden seeks, in short, a permanent therapeutic community. For humans are a cultural beings and seem to function best when they are parts of a group affording security.

When, as the Leightons (Leighton 1959), and Hughes (Hughes 1960) and others have shown, groupness breaks down and cultural disintegration takes place, psychological problems increase. An important part, therefore, of the therapeutic process, if the wholeness is to endure, must be the building once again of integrated cultural matrices within which the processes leading toward psychological wholeness can be continued and encouraged. A proper aim of psychotherapy, then, is "ethnotherapy"—the reintegration and revitalization of groups.

This is a powerful concept, often considered to be beyond the reach of psychology proper, but again with a theological analog—the church. Oden reaches out for such a concept when he describes clients as "searching for intimacy, for community: looking for some way of putting it all together, of integrating their lives into some cohesive unity" (1974a:39), and suggests that what such expressions indicate is that today's clients expect through psychotherapy to be led into genuine community in which are achieved "relationships of intimacy and trust which they find missing in ordinary social transactions" (1974a:38–39). He suggests, however, that the expectations aroused by modern psychotherapy are often more than it can deliver in this regard and asks, "How are we to care for persons who have experienced seriously all that effective psychotherapy can do, and still find themselves struggling?" (1974a:35).

Oden's solution envisions the secularization of the therapeutic process as therapeutically helped persons reach out to help others in need. But, I feel, following an unfortunate technological choice on the part of certain theologians, he misses (as they missed) the real significance of what is being called for. For, if I read correctly between the lines, what the secularizing theologians are really expressing is not a need for the secularization of Christianity but for the revitalization of a disintegrating society through the deprofessionalization and deinstitutionalization of Christianity. But they, like Freud, are not free to see society as a positive thing since as we learn our western values, we learn to regard social structuring as "repressive" (Oden 1974b:27) and so feel compelled to look elsewhere for answers. But what they (and, I believe, Oden, when he speaks of the deprofessionalization of psychotherapy) are really hinting at is the need for social revitalization. But they all, in their culturally inculcated, anti-social-structure mentality seem to miss the important point that dissatisfaction with the present type of leaders does not warrant the contention that leaders are unnecessary, much less demonstrate that things would be better without leaders. What Oden (and the secularizationists) haltingly call for, I believe, is a movement with leaders who are psychologically and spiritually healthy, aware and contemporary in their approach. Such leadership seems to be all too rarely found within traditional Christianity.

In recommending a real solution, however, we would do well to look at a very significant study by the anthropologist Anthony F. C. Wallace entitled "Revitalization Movements" (1956:264–281). In this study the author points to a process of cultural change through which many societies go, and from which many societies never recover. This process involves a progression from what Wallace terms a "steady state" through a state of "individual stress" into a "period of cultural distortion." The steady state is a state of maximum integration and well-roundedness for the society and for a high percentage of the individuals within the society. It is a time in which the society (which may be a whole culture or any definable social group within it) fulfills for the vast majority of its people a maximum of the security, regulation, personal and group definition, and overall organization of life that a well functioning society is intended to provide for its participants, with a minimum of the stress that characterizes a malfunctioning society.

As time goes by and the culture changes, however, he describes a tendency toward the decreasing efficiency of "certain reduction techniques" resulting in a "continuous diminution in its efficiency in satisfying needs." This Wallace terms a "period of increased individual stress" which in turn issues in a "period of cultural distortion" in which some members of the society are able to function reasonably well while others are driven to "psychodynamically regressive innovations."

> The regressive response empirically exhibits itself in increasing incidence of such things as alcoholism, extreme passivity and indolence, the development of highly ambivalent dependency relationships, intragroup violence, disregard of kinship and sexual mores, irresponsibility in public officials, states of depression and self-reproach, and probably a variety of psychosomatic and neurotic disorders. . . .
>
> In this phase, the culture is internally distorted: the elements are not harmoniously related but are mutually inconsistent and interfering. For this reason alone, stress continues to rise. "Regressive" behavior, as defined by the society, will arouse considerable guilt and hence increase the stress level or at least maintain it at a high point: and the general process of piecemeal cultural substitution will multiply situations of mutual conflict and misunderstanding, which in turn increase the stress-level again (Wallace 1956:269–270).

As such a process continues, driving people to the breaking point, not infrequently disillusionment, demoralization and social deterioration of the kind we see all around us set in, leading to the disintegration of the society. As happened with many of the American Indian societies, people may lose the will to go on, and then they begin to stop reproducing themselves. Or a society may be defeated in war and its customs suppressed either through assimilation or dispersion, resulting in the extinction of the society.

Or, says Wallace, the whole process may move in another direction entirely into a state which he calls a "period of revitalization, a state that he sees as a rather frequently occurring but "special kind of culture change phenomenon." A revitalization movement, says Wallace, "is defined as a deliberate, organized, conscious effort by members of a society to construct a more satisfying culture" (1956:265). This reconstruction which, he claims, has happened literally thousands of times in documented human history, typically involves the "innovation of whole cultural systems, or at least substantial portions of such systems" (1956:264), systems that tend to be religious in character.

It is, I believe, this type of ethnotherapeutic revitalization that our rapidly disintegrating society is calling for and that the Christian church once again brought into touch with reality and recalled to true groupness must speak. The institutional church, to the extent that it has contributed to the production of social and individual stress—including guilt, self-reproach and general lack of harmony and consistency in behavioral expectations—has, of course, joined in the intensification of the problem. But essential Christianity, whether expressed in the institutional church, in Christ-motivated psychotherapy or in any other cultural institution could again provide the kind of revitalization spark that it produced in a similar social situation in the first century. But it would need to be presented in such a way that it would answer questions that people are concerned about now, e.g., questions about interpersonal relationships and groupness and the expression and experiencing of love and acceptance.

The Christian groupness here envisioned as an agency of social revitalization is, however, more than a temporary thing—more than an occasional or weekly get together, be it for church or for group therapy. Such groups would he characterized by the kind of permanence, mutual commitment and functional interrelationships that are the hallmark of well-integrated social groups operating in Wallace's steady state. In such a society the kind of psychotherapeutic laicization of which Oden speaks is a reality, for people meet each other's needs before they grow into psychological illnesses, within the confines of a naturally accepting, committed, caring and permanent group, and without either the expectation of ostracization if one deviates a bit from the group norms or the necessity of being forced to go to a stranger for counsel.

The kind of group here recommended is specifically not oriented toward two-sphere thinking of either the church versus outside society or the encounter group versus outside society types. It does not indulge itself in escape from existing cultural patterns but specifically dedicates itself to the transformation of them—the kind of transformation that Christianity originally brought about when it turned certain sectors of the Greco-Roman world upside down *from within.* This kind of community takes existing cultural forms and invests them with Christian meanings, starting consciously with the transformation/revitalization process. This kind of community is already developing in many parts of the world, including Africa, where God has taught many of us what the church was meant to be. For, returning from such exposure to true, well-integrated groupness we begin to see afresh in the pages of the New Testament a dynamic *community* experimenting with what Christian groupness meant in Greco-Roman society. We see there not a community that has already become perfect but one which, in the words of John V. Taylor, "is manifestly alive and moving and becoming. If there is a falling back into sin, it is known to friends, challenged and forgiven: the partially blind have others' eyes to guide them forward: the timid draw on others' courage, the stale are renewed by others' inspiration" (Taylor 1963:131). Such a church community we need today.

Groups such as these should probably start (as both Israel and the church started) as small face to face groups of persons well on their way toward psychological, sociological and spiritual wholeness, people dedicated totally to carrying out both within and outside of the group the functions and meanings of Christianity in whatever cultural forms they carry over from their previous society or develop anew. Effective face to face groups in our culture seldom number more than thirty, although, over a period of years, they could get much larger through biological growth. I find the kind of self-perpetuating therapy that Oden calls for, difficult to conceive of apart from such groups. The fact that members of numerous, small, well-integrated societies in all parts of the world betray little if any serious psychological dysfunction testifies to the fact that the result Oden seeks lies in this direction.

Such groups could orient themselves either existentially or eschatologically or with some measure of each depending on the felt needs of the members of the given group. The point at issue should not be the fulfilling of the American cultural imperative to arrive at a single "best" outlook on life, but to select from these and perhaps other options offered by Christianity those that turn on the members of the group. Diversity in the forms of conceptualization and expression of Christianity should, however, always be allowed, accepted and encouraged in recognition of the fact that the cohesion of the group is predicated not on sameness of cultural, especially cognitive, forms but on commitment to Christian functions. For it is only the functions and meanings of life that may he labeled "Christian" since any of the forms—even religious, theological and psychotherapeutic forms—are equally operable by Christian and non-Christian. It is the use to which these forms are put, the motives of those who employ them, and the content or meaning with which they are invested that may properly be labeled Christian or non-Christian—a point that Jesus came back to again and again in his dealings with the Pharisees.

Now, since my concern here is the effective crossing of interpersonal boundaries, let me make more explicit the part that I see real, integrated, psychologically healthy groupness playing in this process:

1. The major function of such a group/church would be to provide a permanent, well-functioning sociocultural matrix in which psychological and spiritual health can be experienced and can grow.

2. The groups would need to be small enough to be face to face, integrated enough to provide a maximum of security (defined as low stress) for each member, especially at times of high vulnerability (such as at natural and unnatural times of crisis), but open enough to allow for and encourage individual and subgroup diversity in an atmosphere of trust.

3. The groups should be permanent, living together, spending considerable time together, and dynamically moving together along the path of growth to maturity.

4. But just as the members of the group should come to see themselves as living not only for themselves but also for the group, so each group, in fulfillment of its life with and for Christ, needs to see itself as living for the sake of other persons and groups as well as for itself. And one result of this self-image will be the dedication of such groups to the establishment of other such groups that function in such a way that they are genuinely Christian and genuinely therapeutic whether or not they bear much formal resemblance either to what we now know as churches or to any present-day therapy group.

Conclusion

In conclusion, I would like to say again that I have been greatly stimulated by the Oden lectures. I wish to express my gratitude both to Professor Oden and to the organizing committee for the opportunity to participate. I sincerely hope that the reactions that these lectures and discussions have stimulated in me are as valuable to my readers as they have been to me.

HERMENEUTICS

CHAPTER 24

INTERPRETING IN CULTURAL CONTEXT

Reprinted here with permission from the
Journal of the Evangelical Theological Society 21:357-367 (1978)

At the start of this paper I would like to briefly introduce myself. First of all I am an evangelical Christian, committed to God through Jesus Christ as revealed in the written Word. I have been trained in an evangelical college and seminary and now, as a professor in an evangelical seminary, I endeavor to maintain in all that I do a commitment to the authority of the Scriptures as interpreted from an evangelical perspective. I am, furthermore, a missionary and trainer of missionaries. I am thus committed to the communication of the revealed message of God to the ends of the earth. Additionally I am an anthropologist, linguist and communicologist. From these disciplinary involvements I am committed to studying and analyzing the Word and the communication of God's message from a Christ-centered, cross-cultural perspective.

An evangelical anthropologist should have something to say about culture and the Bible, and I feel that my evangelical commitment to the inspired Word of God and my attempts to integrate that commitment with my academic disciplines enable me to at least take a stab at certain of the cultural issues that affect our attempts to interpret the Bible. Many, however, consider the disciplines that I represent to be basically antagonistic to an evangelical commitment. I do not find them so. Indeed, I feel that my involvement in cultural, linguistic and communicational studies has deepened and strengthened my commitment to God's inspired Word. I find that these perspectives continually illumine for me the Scriptural message for which I have given my life. For the Bible is a cross-cultural book, and to interpret it properly we need the sharpest tools available to enable us to deal reverently—and yet precisely— with the inspired message that comes to us in cultural forms that are not our own.

The matter of interpretation in culture is a weighty concern. For the Word has come to us via the forms of Hebrew, Aramaic and Greek cultures. We are immersed in a culture far different from any of these. We cannot, therefore, always trust our culturally-conditioned reflexes to give us the proper interpretation of Scripture. We trust the Holy Spirit to keep us from going too far astray in our interpretations. Yet we are often puzzled that God's Spirit does not lead us all to the same answer concerning every issue.

In this paper I have selected four areas where insight into the influences of culture can assist us in our understanding of how the Scriptures are to be interpreted. Underlying my discussion is an assumption that I have examined in another place.[1] This assumption is that God communicates via culture and language in essentially the same way that human beings do. If this is true, the insights into culture and language provided by my disciplines are going to be very helpful with respect to our understanding of what it means to interpret the Bible in context.

Evangelical biblical theologians have for some time focused on the need to interpret the Bible in context. The context that has been largely in view has been that of the whole Bible. "The Bible is its own best interpreter" is a statement that is often made to emphasize the importance of this context. Without denying the necessity to focus strongly on the whole Bible as context, evangelical biblical theologians have also been coming to recognize more and more the importance of the individual cultural context in which each portion of the Bible has been written. Largely through the input of the grammatico-historical method, evangelical scholars have begun to pay more and more attention to the interrelationships between the ways in which things are stated in Scripture and the ways in which things were stated in the wider cultural context in which the people and events recorded in Scripture participated. When it comes to the analysis of such cultural contexts, however, it is likely that contemporary disciplines such as anthropology and linguistics, dedicated as they are to a primary focus on these issues, may be able to provide us with sharper tools for analysis than the disciplines of history and philology have provided.[2] On this assumption, I am attempting to develop an approach that may be labeled culturo-linguistic (or, better, ethnolinguistic) as a contemporary evangelical modification and amplification of the grammatico-historical method. This method depends greatly on the pioneering insights of Bible translation theorists such as Eugene Nida and John Beekman, who have for some time now been forced to wrestle with the cultural and linguistic dimensions of the Bible at a deeper level than most theologians have felt to be necessary.

The basic difference here centers around the matter of whether the interpreter has two or more than two cultural contexts in view. If he only considers the biblical cultural context and his own cultural context (the latter usually being that of the academic interpreter), the problems (and the insights) are significantly less than if the interpreter must, in addition to these two contexts, consider a third cultural context into which he must intelligibly render the message. In the latter case the interpreter is forced to develop what may be called a "cross-cultural perspective" as opposed to a "mono-cultural perspective" on the problems of biblical interpretation. A mono-cultural perspective may assume, as many historically oriented interpreters do, that when one attempts to move the biblical message from the biblical cultures into Euroamerican language and culture he is moving from less adequate cultures and languages into more adequate cultures and languages. This was one of the mistakes that Bultmann made. A cross-cultural perspective, however, is one that has learned that all cultures and languages, like all varieties of human being, are potentially

---

[1] C. H. Kraft, *Christianity in Culture* (Maryknoll, NY: Orbis, 1979a).

[2] E. A. Nida, "Implications of Contemporary Linguistics for Biblical Scholarship," *JBL* 91 (1971) 73–89.

adequate vehicles for the communication of the biblical message. It is not, therefore, quite so prone to be ethnocentric in its approach to the relationship between the messages and the cultural context in which they are presented. Though I will not be able to develop the implications of these statements in this presentation,[3] there often seems to be a large gap in understanding between those who have experience with only one receptor culture (their own) and those who have experience with many receptor cultures. The latter are, I believe, usually in a much better position to understand and interpret the relationships between the message and its cultural context. It is this kind of insight that I see as the basic difference between what I am calling the ethnolinguistic approach to biblical interpretation and the grammatico-historical approach. To illustrate this approach I would like to focus on four specific areas, each of which has its contribution to make to a deepened evangelical understanding of the relationship of culture to biblical interpretation. These areas are (1) the definition of meaning, (2) communication within a range, (3) culture and interpretational reflexes, and (4) levels of abstraction in interpretation.

Definition of Meaning

The first of these areas, and in many senses the most basic, has to do with how meanings are arrived at. By "meaning" I do not mean the same thing as "message." Meaning is, from this point of view, that which the receiver of a message constructs within his head and responds to. We know, of course, that there is often a wide discrepancy between the meanings that the communicator seeks to get across and those meanings that the receptor understands. The process seems to be one in which the communicator has certain meanings in his mind that he encodes in cultural symbols (primarily linguistic symbols) and transmits in the form of a message to one or more receptors. The receptors, for their part, decode the message in their heads and thereby derive the meanings on the basis of which they act.

Culture provides the matrix in terms of which such meanings are both encoded by communicators and decoded by receptors. The symbols used for the transmission of such meanings are all defined and interpreted culturally. We may say, therefore, that words and all other cultural symbols derive their meanings only from their participation in the cultural context of which they are a part. There are, apparently, no symbols that mean exactly the same thing in all cultures and few, if any, that mean exactly the same thing in two or more cultures.

The crucial thing in the transmission of messages via such culturally defined symbols is the extent of agreement between the communicator and the receptor concerning what the cultural symbols signify. If the communicator and the receptor have been taught by means of their participation in the same culture that such-and-such a word has such-and-such a meaning, the degree of difficulty that they experience in understanding each other will be minimal. If, however, communicator and receptor have been taught different meanings for the same word, the degree of

---

[3] Cf. further C. H. Kraft, *Christianity in Culture*.

difficulty will be large. We may say that common agreements concerning cultural and linguistic symbols minimize the difficulty of communication between participants in a communicational event, while lack of such agreements makes difficult or even blocks communication. The same can be said for interpretation of materials such as the biblical materials. The fact that we who live in Euroamerican culture attempt to interpret the Bible, none of which was spoken or written in Euroamerican culture, raises great difficulty for us. For we are unlikely to share with the original authors many, if any, of the agreements concerning the meanings of the concepts that they use, since our cultural conditioning is so different from theirs.

Communication within a Range

Considerations of how cultural symbols convey meanings lead to the recognition that all communication (including interpretation) is approximate. I believe we can state boldly that no receiver of a message ever understands exactly what the communicator intends even when both communicator and receiver participate in the same culture. The lack of correspondence between intent and interpretation is even greater, of course, when there is a culture gap and/or a time gap between the communicator and his receptor(s).

In ordinary communicational interaction we attempt to compensate for this fact in two ways. (1) The communicator attempts to elicit "feedback" from the receptors to see how well they are getting his message. If he finds out that they are not understanding him well, he adjusts his message by rephrasing, providing additional information, explaining more elaborately, and so forth, in order to bring about greater correspondence between his intent and the receptors' understanding. Such was the process that Paul and Barnabas went through in Acts 14 when the people of Lystra interpreted their healing as the act of gods and began to worship them. Paul and Barnabas, through feedback, discovered their miscommunication and took steps to straighten it out. (2) The second method of compensation in communication is the fact that human beings settle for approximate understandings of what they seek to communicate, as long as they are reasonably close to what is intended. We make a statement and the receptor restates in his own words roughly what we intend and we settle for that.

In interpreting the Scriptures we are, of course, cut off from the possibility of asking the original authors to clarify their meanings for us. So the first of these techniques for compensating for communicational impreciseness is not available to us. The fact that messages can be interpreted within a range is, however, of great significance to our attempts to understand the Bible from within another culture. For I believe that the Holy Spirit, as he assists us in interpreting his Word, works in terms of such an allowable range.

At one level, of course, the God-allowed range of acceptable interpretation is very narrow. The fact that God exists, that Jesus is the Mediator between God and man, that human beings are sinful, and soon, are either assumed or continually asserted by Scripture. These matters are not debatable, at least at that deep level. At another more surface level, though, there is—even within Scripture—a range of allowable understanding that is culturally conditioned. This fact raises the hope that additional interpretations developed by God-led people within contemporary cultures may also fall within the range allowed by Scripture.

Though the existence of God is not debatable (Heb. 11:6), we see in Scripture a range of understandings of him allowed. Likewise with sin, the understanding of the nature of man (one, two or three parts), understandings of the spirit world, and so forth. The problem is, of course, to determine which contemporary understandings of these things fit within the Scripturally-allowed range and which fall outside. Within the allowed range fall both the intent of the author and the intent of God, but these are not always the same. In prophetic utterances, for example, the human author was often unaware of the later use God would make of those utterances.

Accuracy of interpretation is, therefore, a matter of coming to understand what is said or written within an allowable range.

Culture and Interpretational Reflexes

This recognition, coupled with the recognition of how meanings are arrived at, leads to our next point: the consideration of our ability to accurately interpret the Scriptures. The major problem here stems from the fact that those who agree on large areas of cultural experience seldom discuss these areas of agreement. What everyone in a given situation assumes is not mentioned.

The Hebrew people, for example, assumed that God exists. They did not, therefore, attempt to prove his existence. Jesus assumed that his hearers understood what a mustard bush and its seeds looked like, that those who sowed seed scattered them around broadcast, that sheep could be led by the shepherd, and so on.

The interpretational reflexes of Jesus' hearers were conditioned by the same culture as his were. They therefore did not need explanation of the assumptions and agreements underlying the things that Jesus said and did. Our interpretational reflexes are, however, conditioned by quite a different culture. We are therefore subject to several pitfalls that accompany the cross-cultural transmission of materials such as that in the Scriptures.

We may, for example, not understand major portions of what is going on at all, since we do not know the cultural agreements. In the story of the woman at the well, for example, we are likely to entirely miss the significance of such things as Jesus' going through Samaria, his talking to a woman, the fact that the woman was at the well at midday, the necessity that she go back to get her supposed husband before she could make a decision, and so forth. For us to understand such things we need large doses of explanation by those who study the cultural background. We cannot simply trust our culturally-conditioned interpretational reflexes. For the Scriptures are specific to the cultural settings of the original events. Sheep, mustard seeds and bushes, broadcast sowing, levirate marriage and many other aspects of the life of biblical cultures fit into this category.

A much bigger problem of interpretation lies in those areas where the Scriptures use cultural symbols that are familiar to us but for which our cultural agreements are different. We are tempted to simply interpret according to what seems to be the "plain meaning" as if we could get the proper meaning of Scripture as we would from a document originally written in English. It is to avoid this pitfall that many translation theorists are now contending that a faithful translation of the Scriptures must involve enough interpretation to protect the reader from being seriously misled at points such as these. Our interpretational reflexes tell us, for example, that a fox is sly and cunning. So, when Jesus refers to Herod as a fox (Lk. 13:32) we misinterpret the symbol to mean sly when, in fact, on the basis of the Hebrew cultural agreement it was intended to signify treachery. Our cultural reflexes tell us that plural marriage is primarily a sexual matter, though in nonwestern cultures it seldom is. Our cultural reflexes tell us that Jesus was impolite to his mother when he addressed her the way he did in the temple and at the wedding feast. Our culturally-conditioned interpretational reflexes lead us to understand "the faith once for all delivered to the saints" (Jude 3) to be a system of doctrine rather than a relationship to God. The culturally-conditioned interpretational reflexes of the Nigerians I worked among misled them into thinking that Psalm 23 presented Jesus as insane, since in their culture only young boys and insane men tend sheep. The interpretational reflexes of the Sawi of New Guinea misled them into admiring the treacherous Judas even more than Jesus and those of the Chinese into regarding positively the dragon of the book of Revelation.

The point is that for cultural reasons we who are not a part of the biblical cultures cannot trust our interpretational reflexes to give us the meanings that the original authors intended. What to us are the "plain meanings" are almost certain to be the wrong meanings unless the statements are very general (see below). We must, therefore, engage in exegesis to discover what the original utterances meant to those whose interpretational reflexes were the same as those of the authors.

With respect to interpretational reflexes there seem to be four principles:

1. If the culture of the original is at any given point very similar to ours, our reflexes are going to serve us fairly well. In these instances the interpretational principle that says that "the plain meaning is the true meaning" is a good principle. Such a situation is rarely the case between Euroamerican culture and the Hebrew and Aramaic portions of Scripture. Certain Greek customs do, however, seem to be similar enough to Euroamerican customs that our interpretational reflexes will give us the correct meaning. I think in this regard of the language of the race track that Paul uses in Philippians 3. The same may be true of the language of economics that Paul uses earlier in that same chapter. The amount of biblical material where there is such close cultural similarity to our agreements is, however, distressingly small. And the fact that we cannot trust our interpretational reflexes in most places means that we can never be sure of them unless we have independent evidence that this is a place where their custom is close to ours.

2. If the Scriptural statement is a cultural universal, however, our interpretational reflexes will enable us to get close to the intended meaning. Statements such

as those in the Ten Commandments that exist, as far as we know, in every one of the world's cultures are easy to interpret relatively accurately. There is a slight problem in the fact that each culture defines murder, adultery, and so on, in its own way. But the fact that such commands occur in all cultures means that these statements are elevated out of the most difficult interpretational category-that of the culturally specific. Other parts of Scripture such as those dealing with eating together, such injunctions as "love your neighbor," and many of the proverbs of Scripture are also in the cultural universal category.

3. Similarly, if a Scriptural statement relates to experiences that are common to all mankind our culturally-conditioned interpretational reflexes can be of considerable help. When the Scriptures say "go," "come," "trust," "be patient," and the like, they are dealing with experiences that are common to all human beings and therefore readily interpretable. Likewise with respect to illness and death, childbirth and rearing, obtaining and preparing food, and the like.

4. But as indicated above, much of the biblical material is presented in cultural forms that are very specific to cultural practices quite different from ours. These materials, because of their specificity to the cultural agreements of the original hearers, communicated with maximum impact to them. This is, I believe, a major part of the genius of God and of his Word-that he speaks specifically to people where they are and in terms of the culture in which they are immersed. This fact does, however, enormously complicate the task of the one immersed in another culture who seeks to interpret the Scriptures.

The fact that our interpretational reflexes are so limited when dealing with biblical materials argues strongly for the application of the sharpest tools available to the study of the cultural matrices through which God revealed his Word. The harnessing of the perspectives of anthropology and linguistics to this end of the interpretational task (as well as to the communication end) could be a real boon to the evangelical exegete. One important result of such harnessing is the development of faithful dynamic-equivalence translations and highly interpretive "transculturations" of God's Word. These aim to communicate God's message as specifically as possible in today's languages and cultures so that the members of these cultures will be able to trust their interpretational reflexes when they study the Scriptures.

Levels of Abstraction in Interpretation

The fact that so much of the biblical material is presented in a form that is specific to the biblical cultures but distant in its forms from our cultural matrix presents us with the major problem in our search to discover a principled way of interpretation. And yet, as I have endeavored to point out, not all the Scriptural material is at this culturally specific, distant-from-us level. What we find is, rather, a mixture of materials, some of which require a great deal of expert exegesis and some of which are readily interpretable even by twentieth-century American laymen. We need, therefore, an approach to interpretation that will sort out which is which.

I came to feel this need deeply as a result of the question directed to me by one of the Nigerian church leaders whom I was assisting. He pointed out to me that the Bible commands both that we not steal and that we not allow women to pray with their heads uncovered. He then asked, "Why is it that you missionaries teach us that we are to obey the one command and to ignore the other?" I do not feel that I was able to give him a very good answer at that time. But I have been able, I believe, to get closer to a satisfying approach since then.

My suggestion is that we recognize that when people speak they continually mix levels of abstraction. In this presentation I have mixed general statements with very specific illustrations. The Bible does the same. The statement, "God is love," and the statement, "The Lord is my shepherd," say much the same thing. But one is at a general level of abstraction, while the other is rather specific to Hebrew culture.

With respect to the head-covering versus the "do not steal" commands, likewise, we have statements at two different levels of abstraction. "Do not steal" is a general command that occurs in every culture. Analysis of the meaning of this command from culture to culture yields slight culturally-conditioned alternative understandings within a fairly narrow range.

With respect to the head-covering command, however, analysis of the meaning of the custom in its cultural context does not simply lead to an alternative understanding of the same command. It leads, rather, to a meaning that demands expression via a different cultural form if it is to be understood in English. In the Greek culture of that day, apparently, the cultural form "female praying in public without head covering" would have been interpreted to mean that "this female is immoral" or, at least, that "she is not showing proper respect to men (see commentaries on 1 Cor. 11:10-12). Since that meaning was not consonant with the witness that Christians ought to make, Paul commands against the use of the head-uncovered symbol in favor of its opposite, the head-covered symbol. For only this latter symbol conveyed the proper Christian meaning in that culture-that Christian women were not immoral and/or were properly subject to their men. The theological truth, then—a truth just as relevant today as in the first century—is that Christian women should not behave in such a way that people judge them to be "out of line" (whether morally or with respect to authority).[4]

Such cross-cultural analysis shows that in comparing the two commands we are not comparing sames. The commands are given at different levels of abstraction-that is, the relative importance of the specific cultural context to the meaning of the utterances differs. Those utterances that relate most specifically to their particular cultural contexts are here termed "at a lower level of abstraction." Those utterances in which the specific context is less important to the meaning and which, therefore, relate to pancultural human commonality are termed "at a higher level of abstraction." That the stealing command is at a higher level of abstraction is evident from the fact that it does not refer to a specific cultural act but to a category of

---

[4] See R. C. Sproul, "Controversy at Culture Gap," *Eternity* 27 (1976) 13–15, 40, for a useful discussion of this issue.

cultural behavior. The command is general rather than specific. Note, by way of contrast, the specificity of the tenth command. That command is at a lower level of abstraction (like the head-covering command) in that it specifies the proscribed cultural acts rather than (until the final phrase) generalizing them into an overall principle as we do when we refer to that command as the command against "coveteousness" in general. Note the wording: "Do not desire another man's house; do not desire his wife, his slaves, his cattle, his donkeys, or anything else that he owns" (Ex. 20:17 TEV*)*.

The head-covering command is at this more specific level, where the particular cultural context is very important to the meaning. A corresponding specific stealing command would be something like this: "Do not take your neighbor's donkey without his permission." A head-covering command at the same level of generality as the stealing command would be something like this: "Do not appear out of line with respect to immorality or authority." Thus we see a specific cultural form/symbol level with context contributing relatively more to the meaning, and a deeper "general principle" level in which the context contributes relatively less. "Seesaw" diagrams illustrating these two possibilities are as follows:

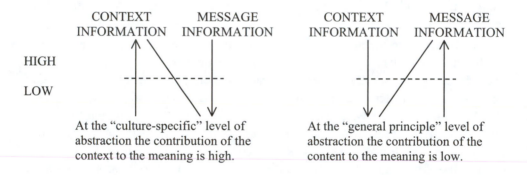

There seems in Scripture to be yet a deeper level of abstraction, however. This is made explicit by Jesus when he summarizes the teaching of the law and the prophets in two statements:

> "Love the Lord your God with all your heart, with all your soul, and with all your mind." This is the greatest and the moat important commandment. The second most important commandment is like it: "Love your neighbor as you love your-self." The whole law of Moses and the teachings of the prophets depend on these two commandments (Matt. 22:37-40; cf. Deut. 6:5; Mark 12:29–31; Luke 10:27 TEV).

In such a three-level scheme there are occasional problems with respect to which of the levels to assign certain of the general statements of Scripture. We may, however, advance the following chart as a step in the direction of developing this model more precisely. Note that a complete chart would show (even more than this one does) the fact that there are fewer categories at the basic ideal level, more at the general principle level and an enormous number at the specific cultural form level.

1. BASIC IDEAL LEVEL	2. GENERAL PRINCIPLE LEVEL	3. SPECIFIC CULTURAL FORM/SYMBOL LEVEL

← — — — — More General ⟷ More Specific — — — —
→

A. Love your neighbor as you love yourself (Matt. 22:39)	1. Do not steal (Ex. 20:17)	a. Do not take your neighbor's donkey (Hebrew)
		b. Do not take your employer's money (U.S.A.)
	2. Do not covet	a. Do not desire another man's house . . . (Ex. 20:17)
		b. Same for U.S.A.
	3. Be free from partiality (1 Tim. 5:21; Jas. 3:17)	a. Treat Gentiles/blacks/ women as human beings
		b. Rebuke whoever needs it (1 Tim. 5:20)
B. Love the Lord your God with all your heart . . . (Matt. 22:37)	1. Worship no God but me (Ex. 20:3)	a. Do not bow down to any idol or worship it (Ex. 20:5)
		b. Do not pledge primary allegiance to material wealth (U.S.A.)
	2. Seek by all means to save people (1 Cor. 9:22)	a. Live as a Jew to win Jews (1 Cor. 9:20)
		b. Live as Gentile to win Gentiles (1 Cor. 9:21)
		c. Live as an African to win Africans
C. Everything must be done in a proper and orderly way (1 Cor. 14:40)	1. Leaders should be beyond reproach (1 Tim. 3:2; Tit. 1:6)	a. They must be self-controlled, etc. (1 Tim. 3:2)
	2. Christian women should not appear out of line	a. They should cover their heads when praying in Greek culture (1 Cor. 11:10)
		b. They should not wear their clothes too tight (U.S.A.)
	3. Christians should live according to the rules of the culture (as long as they do not conflict with Christian principles)	a. Women should learn in silence in Greek culture (1 Tim. 2:11)
		b. Women may speak up in mixed groups in U.S.A.

1. BASIC IDEAL LEVEL	2. GENERAL PRINCIPLE LEVEL	3. SPECIFIC CULTURAL FORM/SYMBOL LEVEL
		c. Pay the government what belongs to it (Matt. 22:21)
		d. Obey governmental authorities (Rom. 13:1)
		e. Wives, submit to your husbands in Greek and many segments of U.S.A. culture (Eph. 5:22; Col. 3:18; etc.)

D. Other ideals?

In such expositions as the Ten Commandments (especially as Jesus summarizes them in Matt. 22:37–40), the Sermon on the mount, the listing of the fruits of the Spirit (Gal. 5:22–23) and the many similar statements, the Scriptures seem to come closest to a clear statement of a portion of the supracultural will of God for man's conduct. The reason for the apparent clarity of these portions is that they are phrased at a level of abstraction that largely extricates them from specific application to the original cultures in which they were uttered. As one moves from specific cultural applications of supracultural truth (as with the head-covering command) back toward the most general statements of the truth, however, the statements require less understanding of the original cultural context to be accurately understood. They therefore have ore immediate (though general) meaning to us in another culture. The "plain meaning" principle is therefore often adequate for interpreting information presented at this deeper level of abstraction.

Note, however, that the effectiveness of the communicational impact is a matter of cultural perception. For the original hearers, it was presentations of supracultural truth in terms of specific applications (abstraction level three) that communicated most effectively. For us, likewise, it would be specific applications of Scriptural generalizations that most effectively communicate. But since the Scriptures were written in terms of cultures other than ours, we are denied inscripturated applications of supracultural truth in our culture. The general statements, therefore, make more sense to us than the specific cultural forms through which these principles were applied in biblical cultures. And the more specific applications in the Scriptures are often the most confusing to us.

Throughout the Scriptures we are provided with glimpses of supracultural truth, clothed in specific events taking place within specific cultures at specific times. Frequently, as with statements at the general principle or basic ideal level, we get the impression that we are looking at such truth with a minimum of cultural conditioning. More frequently, however, we are exposed to supracultural truth applied in a specific situation in a specific biblical culture. The record of this, then, comes to us only in translation, so that we see such truth as "puzzling reflections in a mirror" (1 Cor. 13:12 Phillips). Among these "reflections" William Smalley feels that those parts of Scripture which give us evaluations of human motives and emotions, human attitudes and personalities, give us the deepest insight into God's ultimate will, and that to understand the revelation in terms of God's will for our behavior we will have to learn to look behind the cultural façade to see as much as we can of what the Word indicates about those questions. The cultural examples given us are thereby not lost. They provide most valuable examples of the way in which God's will was performed in another cultural setting to help us see how we may perform it in ours.[5]

In this way it is possible for Christians to learn something of supracultural truth even though this, like all human knowledge, is perceived by us in terms of the cultural grid in which we operate. Though often puzzling and never total or absolute, such knowledge is adequate for God's purposes-the salvation and spiritual growth of all who give themselves to him in faith.[6] We may, then, under the leading of the Spirit come to know something of how he desires us to live out these truths in terms of our cultural forms.

Conclusion

I have attempted to raise four closely interdependent issues that relate to the matter of Scriptural interpretation on which my fields (anthropology, linguistics and communicology) cast some light. I am hopeful that these considerations will make some contribution and/or stimulate my readers to greater insight into faithful Scriptural interpretation in culture.

---

[5] W. A. Smalley, "Culture and Superculture," *Practical Anthropology* 2 (1955) 58–71.
[6] A. B. Mickelsen, *Interpreting the Bible* (Grand Bapids: Feidmans, 1963) 353.

CHAPTER 25

SUPRACULTURAL MEANINGS
VIA CULTURAL FORMS

Reprinted here with permission in slightly edited form from
D. K. McKim, ed., *A Guide to Contemporary Hermeneutics* (1986).
That chapter was taken from my *Christianity in Culture*, chapter 7

In an early attempt to deal with God and culture from what I am labeling a Christian ethnotheological position, William A. Smalley and Marie Fetzer (now Reyburn) coined the terms *superculture* and *supercultural* to refer to God's transcendent relationship to culture (Smalley and Fetzer 1950). Smalley later developed this concept in the pages of the journal *Practical Anthropology* in an article entitled "Culture and Superculture" (1955). His article was prompted by a letter published in that journal the previous year, the author of which betrayed a high degree of confusion as to just what roles theology and anthropology should play in our attempts to discover what is absolute and what is relative.

The author of the letter contended that "one should not establish an episcopal church government simply because the society is characterized by strong kings and subordinate lords" since "the question of church government is not an anthropological but a theological one."[1] Rather, the missionary should go into the situation convinced through a study of theology "that either the congregational or the episcopal or some other form of church government is the kind Jesus Christ meant for every society, all over the world and at all times." He continues,

> this procedure-first the theological and then the anthropological-must be applied to a myriad of problems . . . such as theft, polygamy, premarital sexual relations, lying, lay and/or clerical marriages, etc. . . . An anthropologist *describes* but a Christian *prescribe'*. He believes that God has revealed a system which is *absolutely* right, valid for every society during every epoch (italics mine).

The writer of that letter was seeking to dichotomize the theological and the anthropological evaluations of the situation. He says, "it is one thing to be a Christian and another to be an anthropologist." One may look at the situation anthropologically, he contends, only in order to obtain information about the customs

---

[1] Since the author of the letter has now totally changed his views, I think it best to refrain from referring to him by name. The position he espoused is so common and well articulated, however, that it is helpful to cite the letter directly.

of the people one seeks to reach. One should have already made up one's mind on the theological issues. Thus, in applying his theological conclusions to the indigenous situation, the writer says, "I must 'play God' and 'prescribe' the system that God has revealed to me through my study of theology as "absolutely right, valid for every society during every epoch."

The writer is undoubtedly right when he says, "The anthropology minded Christian missionary . . . *must not be so enchanted by his science* that *he fails to pursue the consummation of his goal:* the establishment of a truly Christian but, nevertheless, indigenous Church" (italics mine).

The author's desire to discover absolute models before approaching the indigenous system and his feeling that it is to theology that we should turn for understanding of these models are likewise commendable. Unfortunately, his position appears deficient at two crucial points: (1) he does not see the contradiction between the imposition from outside of an "absolutely right" system that will be the same in cultural form (not merely in function or meaning) "for every society during every epoch" and the necessity that a truly indigenous church spring from the employment by Christianity of indigenous cultural forms, and (2) he fails to take account of the extreme limitation that the monoculturalness of most Western theology imposes upon its ability to deal with these issues in a cross-culturally valid way.

What cross-cultural witnesses need is not a continuation of the current dichotomization of the theological and the anthropological perspectives but a single perspective in which the insights of each specialization are taken seriously *at the same level.* For both are human-made disciplines (in spite of the sacredness of the subject matter of the one). And both disciplines suffer from the kind of myopia that all specialization leads to. For when we specialize *into* anything we automatically specialize *out* of everything else. In attempting to understand this or any other aspect of the relationships between Christianity and culture, therefore, we cannot afford to be "enchanted" with either discipline. For each discipline is too limited by itself to handle the specialization of the other adequately. Our model 4b postulates that *theology (as well as anthropology) is human-made and culture-bound.* Our theology, therefore, must be informed by anthropology and our anthropology informed by theology.

From an anthropologically informed theology, then, we propose model 4c: *Christianness lies primarily in the "supracultural"* (see below) *functions and meanings* expressed in culture rather than in the mere forms of any given culture. What God desires is not a single *form* of church government "absolutely right, valid for every society and during every epoch," but the employment of the large number of diverse cultural forms of government with a single *function*—to glorify God by facilitating the smooth, well-ordered, and in-culturally intelligible operation of the organizations that bear his name.

To assume that this point of view endorses an abandonment of theological absolutes (or constants) is to miss' the point in the other direction. Yet this is a natural overreaction, since theological understandings (especially at the popular level) have so often focused strongly on particular cultural *forms* such as the wording of creeds, the modes (rather than the meanings) of baptism and the Lord's Supper, the supposed sacredness of monologic preaching, the merits of one or another form of church government, refraining from smoking and drinking, and the like-as if these were absolute understandings of God's absolute models. Seldom have arguments over such matters dealt with anything but the *forms* of belief or practice.

Neither the Reformation nor any subsequent church split, for example, has centered around *whether* the church should be governed (i.e., the necessity or non-necessity of the governing function). That churches *should be* governed has always been assumed, since Christian things are to be done "decently and in order" (1 Cor. 14:40). Church splits have, rather, focused on the *type* of church government-a matter of form, not of function. Nor have arguments concerning doctrine generally focused on whether or not, for example, God has provided for human redemption, inspired the Scriptures, invited human beings to respond in faith, worked in history, or the like. They have nearly always dealt with the forms these doctrines should take. They have ordinarily centered on theories of how they are to be understood and formulated rather than on the fact that God has provided for these very important functions.

An anthropologically informed approach, however, identifies as the constants of Christianity the functions and meanings behind such forms rather than any given set of doctrinal or behavioral forms. It would leave the cultural forms in which these constant functions are expressed largely negotiable in terms of the cultural matrix of those with whom God is dealing at the time. In what follows, then, I will argue that it is the *meaning conveyed* by a particular doctrine (e.g., consumption of alcoholic beverages, baptism) that is of primary concern of God. There is, I believe, no absoluteness to the human formulation of the doctrine, the historical accuracy of the way in which the ritual is performed, or the rigidity with which one abides by one's behavioral rules.

This is the point at which Jesus scored the Pharisees. For they, in their strict adherence to the forms of their orthodox doctrines, rituals, and behavior, had ignored the fact that these forms had changed their meanings. The way they used the forms had come to signify oppression rather than concern, self-interest rather than divine interest, rejection rather than acceptance, God against human beings rather than God with them. That is, as the culture changed, the meanings of the forms that once adequately conveyed God's message changed, along with the rest of the culture. And those whose responsibility it was to see to it that the message of God continued to be understood became primarily concerned with perpetuating and elaborating on the cultural forms in which the message came to them. They became legalistic concerning the traditional forms. But according to Jesus, godliness lies in the motives behind the meanings conveyed by the forms of belief and behavior, not simply in adherence to the beliefs and practices as traditionally observed. The beliefs and practices are simply the cultural vehicles (the forms) through which God-motivated concern, interest, and acceptance are to be expressed. And these forms must be continually watched and altered to make sure that they are fulfilling their proper function--the transmission of the eternal message of God. As culture changes, these forms of belief and behavior must be updated in order to preserve the eternal message.

Perhaps it is this focus on function and meaning rather than on cultural form that led John to refer to Christ as the *logos,* the expression of God (Jn. 1:1 JBP). Perhaps more clearly than with other cultural forms, linguistic forms such as words are seen to be important only insofar as their function is important. In John's prologue, Christ the Word, the Expression of God, is presented functioning as creator and sustainer, as the light of the world, and, latterly, as a human embodiment of God. The focus is continually on his functioning on behalf of God, on his expressing God with respect to the human context. The form that he took to communicate these functions is mentioned but never elaborated upon because it is so subsidiary to his function of expressing God.

This is not to deny the importance of cultural forms-whether they be words, rituals, behavior, beliefs, or the physical body in which the Son of God lived on earth. The forms are extremely important because only through the forms does the communication take place. Even though it may be said that the water is more important to a river than the riverbed in which it flows, it is still the riverbed that determines what the destination of the water will be (except in a flood). So it is that the forms (like the riverbed) through which the meanings of language and culture flow determine the destination of those meanings. In communication, however, as in irrigating a garden, it is of crucial importance that would-be communicators (or irrigators) choose the proper channel (set of forms). They must then direct their message (water) into that channel rather than into another one if they are to reach those whom they seek to reach. Intelligent irrigators do not choose last year's channels simply because they have become attached to them, having learned to regard them reverently because the channels served them so well last year. Rather, they decide where they want the water to go and adapt last year's channels or create new ones to reach this year's crops. Even so, the effective communicator (human or God) chooses, adapts, or creates cultural forms (channels) specifically appropriate to the task of getting his or her meaning (the "water") across to the present hearers. In this way the forms he or she chooses are very important, but only as means, never as ends in themselves.

The Supracultural and the Cultural (Model 4d)

In the development of an ethnotheological understanding of the relationship between God and culture, Smalley's reply to the letter mentioned previously was a truly significant contribution. I will here build upon that approach, though with two major and several minor modifications. The first of these is to change Smalley's term *supercultural* to *supracultural* and to reject noun forms such as *superculture* or *supraculture* as unusable.[2] Since I contend that there is no such thing as an absolute

---

[2] Smalley's original term *supercultural* was developed by analogy with supernatural. Perhaps because of such widespread terms as *superman, superbowl, superstar,* and the like, the prefix super- makes a word to which it is appended particularly prone to be used as a noun. The use of the prefix supra- is

set of cultural forms, terms such as *super-culture* or *supraculture* that would seem to imply the existence of some sort of absolute cultural structure (i.e., some set of absolute cultural forms) are so misleading that they must be abandoned.

The adjective *supracultural,* however, serves a very useful purpose in signifying the transcendence of God with respect to culture. That is, God, being completely unbound by any culture (except as he chooses to operate within or in terms of culture) is supracultural (i.e., above and outside culture). Likewise, any absolute principles or functions proceeding from God's nature, attributes, or activities may be labeled *supracultural.* For they, too, transcend and are not bound by any specific culture, except when they are expressed within a culture.

The second major modification of Smalley's scheme, though noted here, will not be developed in detail here. It divides the outside-of-culture realm (the supracultural) into two compartments in order to show the place of angels, demons, and Satan in relationship to God, human beings, and culture. And this leads to a distinction between *supracultural* and *absolute* that Smalley did not seem to envision. That is, though God is supracultural, standing outside culture, so are angels, demons, and Satan. The latter, however, are not absolute, as God is. Smalley dealt with only two categories—the cultural, which is relative (i.e., nonabsolute) and the supracultural, which is absolute. The present treatment, however, assumes three categories: the supracultural absolute God, the supracultural non-absolute beings (angels, demons, Satan), and the relative cultural context (see Figure 25.1).

As Smalley states (in a rather Pauline sentence),

> The whole question might well be phrased in the following form: Granted that there is a God above and beyond all human culture, that He has revealed Himself to man in several cultural forms (notably the Holy Scriptures and the life of His Son, lived as a man partaking fully of the life of a particular human culture), and that He has taken an active interest in parts of man's cultural behavior through time, proscribing and prescribing at various times and places; granted also that moat (if not all) culture has developed through time by natural processes of development in different times and places, that particular forms in one place may have a completely different meaning in terms of function than what nearly identical forms do in another place, that God has at various historical periods proscribed certain forms of behavior which he has not proscribed at other times, that He has emphasized as highly desirable certain forms of behavior which He has not prescribed at other times, and that the heavy emotional attachment which people normally have for the familiar pattern (i.e., ethnocentrism) colors and distorts judgment; granted all this, what in human experience is God's absolute, unchanging, permanent will, and what is His will for particular times and places, and what is neutral? (1955:59).

---

not nearly so likely to result in a noun. I understand that Smalley himself now prefers the term *supracultural.*

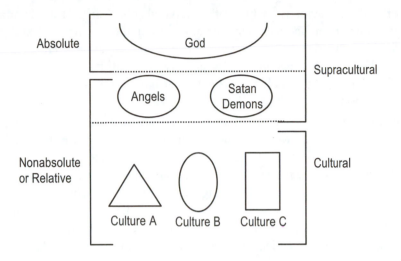

Figure 25.1 The cultural, supracultural, absolute, and relative.

In approaching an answer to this question, E. A. Nida states categorically that "the only absolute in Christianity is the triune God" (1954:282). If finite, limited humans are involved, Nida continues, the thing under consideration must of necessity be limited and therefore relative. Nida is clearly correct with respect to God as the only absolute *being* in the universe. Christian theology has always strongly asserted this. One might contend, in fact, that if the universe and all in it has been created, it is logically impossible to have more than one absolute related to it. Only that One who has brought the universe into being and who stands outside it can be said to be unlimited by it (as far as we know). All else that we know is somehow limited by the universe or, in the case of angels, demons, and Satan, by God directly, and is therefore relative to either or both God and the universe. For relativity is simply "the state of being dependent for existence on or determined in nature, value or quality by relation to something else."

One might qualify Nida's categorical statement by suggesting that the absolute God has, in his manifold activities, manifested attributes and operated in terms of principles that are constant. These also look like absolutes from our vantage point. Smalley suggests, therefore, that the concept of the triune God as the only absolute in Christianity be interpreted as "specifically including His attributes, His nature, and His ultimate, over-all will which is part of His nature and which stems from His nature." Other aspects of God's interaction with human beings such as "his immediate will for specific people and specific events" and any other outworking of his will in human affairs "must of necessity be relative to human finiteness, human limitations, human differences of personality, language and culture" (1955:59-60).

The designation "supracultural and absolute," then, will be employed here for "God himself, His nature, attributes and character, for the moral principles which stem from what He is (but not for particular acts of behavior which may attempt to fulfill those principles), for His plan and total will" (Smalley 1955:59-60). This designation may not by definition be applied to any cultural behavior, even if that behavior is "prescribed or proscribed by God for a given time or place, or for all time" or if the behavior is "a kind of 'relative absolute' in that a Christian is not allowed a choice in his particular situation, [for] the behavior is still cultural" (1955:59-60). Christian behavior, therefore, and the specific interactions between God and humans that resulted in it are always cultural, even though God is supracultural and the principles on which the behavior is based are constants of the human condition.

But can we know these principles and can we trust our understanding of God and his will? That is, can we know supracultural truth? The answer is "Yes," because of God's revelation of himself. But our understanding can never be absolute or infallible, since it is only partial. Our culture-bound perspectives allow us to see even revealed truth only "like the dim image in a mirror" (1 Cor. 13:12 TEV). The Christian does, however, "know something, at least, of the nature of the [supracultural], but does not know all, and what he does know is colored by the cultural screen through which he must know anything he does know" (Smalley 1955:60).

The writer of the letter raises another difficult question. He suggests the possibility that this view of God may portray him as extremely fickle, since he seems always to be "changing the arithmetic so that poor Jack [can] understand it." Can it be that the God whom Scripture contends is "the same yesterday, today and forever" (Heb. 13:8) has such a variety of standards that we cannot, through the study of the Scriptures, ascertain a trustworthy answer to any problem of Christian belief or behavior?

The answer to such queries lies in a redefinition of our understanding of God's consistency. I believe the Scriptures show God to be marvelously consistent, operating always in terms of the same principles. But one of these principles (a constant) is that he adapts his approach to human beings to the cultural, sociological, and psychological limitations in which humans exist. The apostle Paul, following God's principle, endeavored to be a Hebrew to Hebrews and a Greek to Greeks (1 Cor. 9:19-23). God did not deal with Moses as if he were a Greek or with the Athenians (Acts 17) as if they were Hebrews. A culturally perceptive understanding of the Scriptures leads to the conviction that

> one of the supreme characteristics of God's grace to man [is] the fact that God changed the arithmetic repeatedly so that Jack could understand it. The very fact that the Revelation came through language, a finite cultural medium, limits the Revelation, and limitation is a change. The fact that Revelation came through the life of Jesus Christ
>
> . . . living out a typical world culture modifies the Revelation, for it gives it the cast and hue of a particular finite culture at a particular period of time.
>
> When Jesus said, "Ye have heard that it hath been said by them of old time . . . but I say unto you God was changing the arithmetic so that Jack could know more about it than Jack's grandparents knew. All church history records the changes in the cultural super-structure of Christianity. This does not mean that the [supracultural) has changed. The [supracultural] is God, His personality, His over-all will, His principles. The cultural manifestations of the [supracultural) change, and are relative to the particular situation (Smalley 1955:61-62).

We see, therefore, that what from one point of view looks like inconsistency on God's part is actually the outworking of a greater consistency. For God in his mercy has decided consistently to adapt his approach to human beings in their cultural contexts. Many, however (with the author of the letter cited above), will find such a view threatening. Among these will be closed conservatives who regard their particular culturally conditioned understandings of God's revelation as well-nigh absolute and their culturally molded behavior in response to his revelation as the only behavior acceptable to God. Such persons, under the tutelage of ethnocentric theological traditions, fail to make the distinction between the inspiration of the scriptural data and the fallibility of their understanding of God and his works. They therefore look on any deviation from their understandings as a deviation from orthodoxy.[3]

The perspective presented here is not a deviation from orthodoxy. It is, rather, an attempt to modify the understanding and expression of orthodoxy in such a way that (1) it will be more useful to cross-cultural witnesses and (2) it will not have to be abandoned by anyone who recognizes that a good bit of the insight of the behavioral sciences into the relativities of human existence simply cannot be dismissed. From this point of view we are forced to recognize "that much of what [certain ethnocentric theologies have) decreed to be absolute is not, that much theological difference of view arises out of the ethnocentrism of theologians and their followers, and that God is not culture-bound" (Smalley 1955:69). For the human-made discipline known as theology has developed into "the philosophical study of almost anything identified with Christianity," including in a major way the behavior of humans and God within the cultural milieu. Theologies, therefore, concern themselves with culture-but often without the preciseness that anthropological study has developed in this area (Smalley 1955:62). Since theological study is (largely for historical reasons) often limited in its understanding of culture, its insights need to be supplemented with the insights into culture of other human-made disciplines such as anthropology. Only then can theological understandings of the relationships between supracultural truth and culture-bound expressions of that truth be both maximally useful to cross-cultural witnesses and relevant and attractive to contemporary Westerners, who often know more about culture than do those trained in traditional conservative theology.

Biblical Cultural Relativism
Model (4e)

As we have suggested elsewhere (Kraft 1979a:81-99), we cannot go all the way with those anthropologists (a decreasing number, by the way) who might he labeled "absolute cultural relativists." We can sympathize with the motivation to combat the evolutionary hypothesis of cultural development that, by evaluating all cultures by

---

[3] See Harold Lindsell, *The Battle for the Bible* (Grand Rapids: Zondervan, 1976), and Francis Schaeffer, *How Should We Then Live?* (Old Tappan, NJ: Revell, 1976).

European technological criteria, ethnocentrically saw our culture as superior to all others. And I believe we must continue to oppose such a misinformed point of view whenever we find it (especially among Christians). But the proper alternative is not absolute relativism if by this we mean that it is never permissible to evaluate cultural behavior. For Christians (and, indeed, non-Christians) are never completely neutral toward cultural behavior, whether their own or that of others. We constantly monitor and evaluate the behavior of our-selves and of others.

The difficulty is that too often when we evaluate the behavior of others we do not first seek to understand the behavior from the point of view of that person and of that culture (i.e., in its cultural context). We simply judge the behavior as if it were a part of our own system. Yet the meaning of that behavior is derived entirely from within the other's system, never from ours or from some "cosmic pool" of universal meanings. And when we evaluate our own behavior we frequently ignore the fact that our actions make sense only within the total pattern of life in which we are involved. We cannot assume that the behavior which we hold so dear and which we may feel to be so superior can simply be grafted into someone else's culture as it is and prove to. be superior within that system.

We must adopt a sufficiently relativistic stance to help us toward understanding and appreciation (rather than judgmental condemnation) of another's activity within that person's cultural system. But we must reject emphatically the absolute relativism that simply says, "Live and let live without ever attempting to influence anyone else in the direction of one's own values since there are no absolute standards and, therefore, his system is just as good as ours."[4]

Rather, as Christians we may find helpful a model or perspective that Nida calls "relative cultural relativism" (1954:50). This model asserts the presence of absolutes (supracultural truths) but relates them all to God, who stands outside of culture, rather than to any cultural expression, description, or exemplification of a God-human relationship (be it American, Greek, or Hebrew). Nida and other Christian ethnotheologians see this "biblical cultural relativism" as "an obligatory feature of our incarnational religion," asserting that "without it we would either absolutize human institutions" (as ethnocentric positions do) or, going to the opposite extreme (as absolute relativists do), we would "relativize God" (Nida 1954:282). In his excellent discussion of this topic, Nida points out that the Bible

> clearly recognizes that different cultures have different standards and that these differences are recognized by God as having different values. The relativism of the Bible is relative to three principal factors: (1) the endowment and opportunities of people, (2) the extent of revelation, and (3) the cultural patterns of the society in question (1954:50).

1. God conditions his expectations of human beings, in the first place, by making allowance for differences in the endowment and opportunities of the people with whom he is dealing. In the parable of the Talents (Matt. 25:14-30) and again in the parable of the Pounds (Lk. 19:12-27), Jesus teaches a modified relativism. For in God's interaction with people, "rewards and judgment are relative to people's

---

[4] For illustrations of certain disturbing results of this kind of principle, see Donald A. McGavran, *The Clash between Christianity and Cultures* (Washington: Canon Press, 1974), 2–6.

endowments, for the one who receives five talents and gains five additional talents receives not only the commendation of his master but an additional talent," the one taken from the servant who refused to use (and risk) that which was entrusted to him (Nida 1954:50). Likewise, the one to whom two talents were given was commended because he also had used what he had to gain more. Though the main point of the passage has to do with the importance of people using what is given them for the sake of their master, it is clear that the parable also implies (a) that there is relativity (i.e., difference) in what each human being starts with, (b) that God therefore expects relatively more from those who have started with relatively more, and (c) that his judgment of people is relative both to what they have been given and to what they do with it:

This is not an absolute relativity, since the principle in terms of which the master makes his judgments is constant and universally applicable. Note that the servant who received relatively less than the others was not condemned because he started with less, nor even because he finished with less (these are both relative), but because he refused to operate by a supracultural principle of accountability. This principle is articulated clearly in Luke 12:48: "The man to whom much is given, of him much is required; the man to whom more is given, of him much more is required" (TEV). Thus we are here dealing with a relative relativity rather than with absolute relativity, which would allow no standard of evaluation whatsoever.

2. In the second place (and partially overlapping with the first), we see in the Bible a relativism with respect to the extent of the revelational information available to given culture-bound human beings. Jesus points clearly to this fact time and time again when he compares his superior revelation of God to previous (Old Testament) revelations of God. To the Hebrews of Moses' time God allowed and even endorsed their cultural principle of "an eye for an eye and a tooth for a tooth" (Lev. 24:20). But Jesus spoke differently to Moses' descendants who, several hundred years later, had an understanding of God based on the accumulation of considerably more revealed information than was available to their ancestors. To them he said:

> You have heard that it was said, "An eye for an eye, and a tooth for a tooth." But now I tell you: do not take revenge on someone who does you wrong. If anyone slaps you on the right cheek, let him slap your left cheek too (Matt. 5:38-39 TEV).

When Jesus "changed the arithmetic" from "retaliate" to "love your enemies" (Matt. 5:44), his hearers and all of us who have come after them (i.e., who are "informationally A.D.") (see Kraft 1969:239-257) became accountable for a higher standard than was expected of the Hebrews of Moses' day. This higher standard is also illustrated in the matter of murder (i.e., hate now equals murder—Matt. 5:21-22) and with reference to adultery (i.e., lust equals adultery—Matt. 5:27-28). Perhaps the lowest revelational standard available to people is that referred to by Paul in Romans 2:14-16:

> When Gentiles who do not possess the law carry out its precepts by the light of nature [culture?), then, although they have no law, they are their own law, for they display the effect of the law inscribed on their hearts. Their conscience is called as witness, and their own thoughts argue the case on either side, against them or even for them, on the day when God judges the secrets of human hearts through Christ Jesus. So my gospel declares (NEB).

It is clear, then, that human accountability before God is relative to the extent of revelation that human beings have received. And we end up with respect to revelation at the same point at which we ended vis-à-vis endowment, at a degree of accountability determined according to a supraculturally controlled given that differs from person to person and from group to group. Thus,

> the servant who knew his master's wishes, yet made no attempt to carry them out, will be flogged severely. But one who did not know them and earned a beating will be flogged less severely. Where a man has been given much, much will be expected of him; and the more a man has had entrusted to him the more he will be required to repay (Lk. 12:47-48 NEB).

3. A third aspect of biblical relativism (again partially overlapping with the other two) is the fact that God takes into account the cultures of the peoples with whom he deals. That is, God conditions his expectations for each society to take account of the cultural patterns in terms of which their lives are lived. True, God works with people for culture change. But he starts by accepting and even endorsing customs practiced by Old Testament peoples that he condemns or at least does not endorse in his dealings with Greco-Roman peoples. God's approach, then, is relative to the human cultures of the Bible. We assume that he deals with contemporary cultures in terms of the same principle.[5]

Leviticus 25:39-46, for example, sanctions the enslaving of Gentiles by Jews (though not of Jews by Jews). This was undoubtedly the prevalent custom. But God chose to work *with* it on the surface, while at the same time advocating other principles that would eventually do away with the custom. It seems to have died out by New Testament times. He seems to have chosen to refrain from making a big issue of such nonideal customs, probably to keep from diverting attention from more important aspects of his interaction with the Hebrews. He treated polygamy (see 2 Sam. 12:7-8) including levirate marriage (Deut. 25:5-6), trial by ordeal (Num. 5:1-28), and numerous other Hebrew customs similarly. In dealing with divorce, Jesus makes explicit the reason why God chose to allow and endorse such less-than-ideal customs—it was because of the "hardness of their hearts" or, as the New English Bible translates it, "because their minds were closed" (Mark 10:5) and God was patient (2 Pet. 3:9).

The most significant New Testament indication of biblical endorsement of a relativistic attitude toward culture, however, lies in Paul's statement that he attempted to be "all things to all men." This statement is buttressed by several illustrations of his application of this principle. In 1 Corinthians 9:19-22, for example, he indicates his movement back and forth over the cultural barrier separating Jews from Greeks:

> To Jews I became like a Jew, to win Jews; as they are subject to the Law of Moses, I put myself under that law to win them, although I am not myself subject to it. To win Gentiles, who are outside the Law, I made myself like one of them, although I am not in truth outside God's law, being under the law of Christ . . . Indeed, I have become everything in turn to men of every sort, so that in one way or another I may save some (NEB).

---

[5] For a good contemporary illustration of this approach, see G. Linwood Barney, The Meo—An Incipient Church," *Practical Anthropology* 4 (1957): 31-50.

This principle of approaching each situation in terms of its own special cultural circumstances is a constant supracultural principle of God's interaction with people. The principle therefore, is not relative, but its application in the relative context of human culture illustrates once again the correctness of the "biblical relativity" understanding of God's approach to people. Both the supracultural principle and this understanding of biblical relativity enable us to explain a large number of apparent discrepancies in the working of God in the human context. The relative application of God's supracultural principle explains, for example, how Paul could object strenuously to Peter's compromising in a Gentile context under pressure from the Judaizers (Gal. 2:11-14). Yet, later, he himself, when in a wholly Jewish context, went through Hebrew rites of purification to demonstrate to them that he had not abandoned Judaism (Acts 21:20-26). Likewise, Paul could circumcise Timothy, who had a Greek father but a Jewish mother, in order to give him an "in" with the Jews (Acts 16:3), yet not compel Titus, whose parentage allowed him no such "in" with the Jews, to go the same route (Gal. 2:3).

Nida helpfully summarizes this perspective by stating,

> biblical relativism is not a matter of inconsistency but a recognition of the different cultural factors which influence standards and actions. While the Koran attempts to fix for all time the behavior of Muslims, *the Bible clearly establishes the principle* of *relative relativism, which permits growth, adaptation, and freedom, under the Lordship of Jesus Christ.* The Bible presents realistically the facts of culture and the plan of God, by which He continues to work in the hearts of men "till we all come in the unity of the faith, and of the knowledge of the Son of God, unto a perfect man, unto the measure of the stature of the fullness of Christ" (Eph. 4:13). *The Christian position is not one of static conformance to dead rules, but of dynamic obedience to a living God* (1954:52, emphasis mine).

Far from being a threat to a Christian perspective (even a conservative one), the development of an understanding of biblical cultural relativism should be regarded as a part of the leading "into all truth" (Jn. 16:13), which is one of the important functions of the Holy Spirit today.

Adequate, though Never Absolute, Human Perception of Supracultural Truth (Model 5a)

Perhaps the most basic problem in this whole area is the reliability of our perception of supracultural truth. Can we trust what we think we understand? If sincere specialists such as theologians are not exempt from cultural limitations in their understandings of supracultural truth, where does that leave the rest of us? Furthermore, if we adopt the position here advocated and open ourselves up to the validity of a diversity of culturally conditioned interpretations, can we be certain that any supracultural truth will survive at all? The answers lie in (1) coming to better understand how the Holy Spirit goes about leading culture-bound human beings "into all truth" and (2) accepting the sufficiency of an adequate, though nonabsolute, understanding of supracultural truth.

The Spirit leads "into all truth" via the human perception of those to whom he speaks. Since the channel is culture-bound human perception, the receptors do not understand supracultural truth absolutely. Indeed, we are limited by at least five factors:

1. The limitations of the revelations (including "illuminations"). God has seen fit to reveal only certain things concerning himself, his plans, and his purposes. That which he has not yet revealed we cannot know.

2. Our finiteness. We are limited in our understanding of even that which has been revealed. We all study the same Scriptures, but there are a multitude of differing interpretations of the meaning of much of what is there revealed.

3. Our sinfulness. Our perception and ability to understand and respond to God's revelation is, like every other aspect of our lives, affected at every point by sin. For this reason our motives are never completely pure nor our vision completely lucid.

4. Our cultural conditioning. The fact that we are totally immersed in a given culture conditions us to perceive all of reality, including God's revelation, in terms of that culture.

5. Our individual psychological and experiential conditioning. Even within shared cultural boundaries, the life experience of every individual is unique. This likewise conditions one's perception of the revelation.

The assumption here is that supracultural truth exists (with God) above and beyond any cultural perception or expressions of it. God reveals to us glimpses of this truth via the human languages and cultures of the Scriptures. Our perception of the various aspects of this truth may be barely acceptable to God at the start but may, during the course of our maturing as Christians, develop into a much more ideal understanding. This may eventually approach, though never quite reach, the supracultural ideal that lies outside culture and therefore beyond our grasp.

As receptors who are limited in these ways, we interpret the Word and other (e.g., experiential) data at our disposal in terms of culturally organized models that incorporate and exhibit these limitations. Though we are not totally unable to see beyond what such cultural structuring channels us into, our tendency is to gravitate toward and most readily understand those portions of supracultural truth that connect most closely with life as we already perceive it. How the faces of Africans light up as they hear that God endorsed levirate (Deut. 25:10), polygamous (2 Sam. 12:7-9), arranged marriages (Gen. 24:50-51; 34:1-12) and many other customs similar to theirs. But none of these Hebrew perceptions of God excited Luther, for German culture is related to and has been influenced by Greek culture. So it was those portions of Scripture couched in Greek thought patterns that caught Luther's attention. The Spirit, then, spoke most clearly to Luther via those portions.

In the original revelation of biblical materials, God also worked in terms of culturally conditioned human perception. For each biblical writing participates completely in the context to which it is addressed. And the topics treated are dealt with, under the leading of the Spirit, in categories culturally and linguistically appropriate to the way a particular culturally and psychologically conditioned participant perceives of that situation and its needs.

It is not at all strange that large portions of the New Testament are phrased in terms of *Greek* conceptual categories (rather than in supracultural categories). For God wanted his message contextualized within the human frame of reference in such a way that it would be maximally intelligible to those within that frame of reference. So he led Paul and others to write about those things that they noticed and perceived to be important both to God and to their hearers. There are many questions that we twentieth-century Euroamericans wish Paul had written about (e.g., race relations, the place of women, the relative importance of evangelism, and "social action"). But he, in his cultural setting, did not see the importance of providing a word from God on such issues. God will have to provide that word through people today whom he leads to be as concerned about these issues as Paul was about the issues he faced.

Nor is it strange that the writings of the Old Testament and those portions of the New Testament written to Hebrews show other authors dealing under the leading of God with other issues. Apparently it has always been God's plan to lead people via their concerns. What might be considered surprising is that so many very specific issues in both the Old Testament and the New Testament are of such wide general relevance to peoples of many other cultures, and are dealt with within Hebrew and Greek cultural matrices in such a way that people today can benefit from the scriptural treatments. Beyond the divine factors involved, we can point to two human conditions that God has exploited. The first is the high degree of basic similarity between peoples of different cultures. So much of the Bible deals with basic issues of life that its relevance is assured at this level. The second of the human conditions is the great similarity between the cultures of the Bible and contemporary cultures. This is especially true of Hebrew culture throughout most of the world and of Greek culture and European cultures. Most of the Bible is couched in Hebrew thought patterns. Though those portions of the Scriptures are often less compelling for Europeans, the Spirit frequently speaks clearly through them to other peoples of the world.

The Scriptures are like the ocean and supracultural truth like the icebergs that float in it. Many icebergs show at least a bit of themselves above the surface, though some lie entirely beneath the surface. Much of God's revelation of himself in the Scriptures is at least partially visible to nearly anyone who is willing to see it— though belief must precede "seeing" (Jn. 5:39). But much lies beneath the surface, visible only to those who search to discover what supracultural truth lies beneath the specific cultural applications in Scripture.

"Plain Meaning" and "Interpretational Reflexes"

Searching beneath the surface involves the process of interpretation (technically called *hermeneutics)*. The fact that we are in a different culture from that in which the original events occurred causes problems, for our perception and our interpretation are affected by that different culture. We learn as part of our cultural conditioning a set of "interpretational reflexes"—a set of habits in terms of which we automatically interpret whatever happens. We don't think things through before we interpret in these ways. Our responses are reflexive in the same way that most of our muscular responses are reflexive. We need to develop hermeneutical techniques for getting beyond these reflexive interpretations into as dose an approximation as possible to the perception of the original participants. What follows is but a preliminary presentation of an approach to biblical interpretation.

Those unaware of the pervasive influence of their own culture on their interpretations often slip unconsciously into the assumption that arriving at most supracultural truth is simply a matter of accepting the "dear" or "plain meanings" of Scripture. A typical statement of this view says, "The plain meaning of the Bible is the true meaning (McGavran 1974:65). Harold Lindsell condemns those who disagree with his point of view by accusing them of developing "interpretations of Scripture *at variance with the plain reading* of the texts" (1976:39, emphasis mine).

A plain-meaning position assumes that our interpretation corresponds with that of the authors of Scripture. There is, however, a major problem here, stemming from the fact that those who agree on large areas of cultural experience seldom discuss (or make explicit in other ways) these areas of agreement. What everyone in a given context assumes (i.e., agrees on) is not mentioned. People conditioned by the same culture agree on, and therefore seldom if ever discuss, thousands of interpretationally (hermeneutically) significant understandings and perspectives. Hebrews, for example, assumed that God exists. The author of Genesis, as a Hebrew writing to other Hebrews, did not have to prove God's existence. Jesus could rightfully assume that his hearers understood what a mustard bush and its seeds looked like, that those who sowed seeds scattered them "broadcast" (rather than, say, putting each seed in a separate hole), that sheep could be *led* (rather than driven) by a shepherd, and so on.

The interpretational reflexes of Jesus' hearers were conditioned by the same culture as his were, and so they did not need explanation of the assumptions and agreements underlying his words and actions. Our interpretational reflexes are conditioned by quite a different culture. Thus we are likely to find that any given portion of Scripture falls into one or the other of the following categories characteristic of any communicational situation that involves the crossing of a cultural border.

1. We, as readers, may not understand major portions of what is going on at all, since we don't know the cultural agreements. In the story of the Woman at the Well, for example, we are likely to miss entirely the significance of such things as Jesus' going through Samaria, his talking to a woman, the fact that the woman was at the well at midday, the necessity that she go back to get her supposed husband before she could make a decision, and so on. For us to understand such things we need large doses of explanation by those who study the cultural background. We cannot simply trust our culturally conditioned interpretational reflexes. For the Scriptures are specific to the cultural settings of the original events. Sheep, mustard seeds and bushes, broadcast sowing, levirate marriage, and many other aspects of the life of biblical cultures fit into this category.

2. A much bigger problem of interpretation lies in those areas where the Scriptures use cultural symbols that are familiar to us but for which our cultural agreements are different. We are tempted to interpret according to what seems to be the "plain meaning," as if we could get the proper meaning of Scripture as we would from a document originally written in English. To avoid this pitfall, many translation theorists are now contending that a faithful translation of the Scriptures must involve enough interpretation to protect the reader from being seriously misled at points such as these. Our interpretational reflexes tell us, for example, that a fox is sly and cunning. So, when Jesus refers to Herod as a fox (Lk. 13:32), we misinterpret the symbol to mean sly when, in fact, on the basis of the Hebrew cultural agreement, it was intended to signify treachery. Our cultural reflexes tell us that plural marriage is primarily a sexual matter, though in non-Western cultures it seldom is. Our cultural reflexes tell us that Jesus was impolite to his mother when he addressed her the way he did in the temple and at the wedding feast. Our culturally conditioned interpretational reflexes lead us to understand "the faith once for all delivered to the saints" (Jude 3) to be a system of doctrine rather than a relationship to God, and the "by faith" of Hebrews 11 to signify something somewhat less than behavioral obedience (faith = faithfulness or obedience in Hebrew categories). The culturally conditioned interpretational reflexes of the Nigerians I worked among misled them into thinking that Psalm 23 presented Jesus as Insane, since in their culture only young boys and insane men tend sheep. The interpretational reflexes of the Sawi of New Guinea misled them into admiring the treacherous Judas even more than Jesus (Richardson 1974), and those of the Chinese to regarding positively the dragon of Revelation.

The point is that, for cultural reasons, we who are not a part of the biblical cultures cannot trust our interpretational reflexes to give us the meanings that the original authors intended. What are to us the "plain meanings" are almost certain to be the wrong meanings unless the statements are very general. Therefore, we must engage in exegesis to discover what the original utterances meant to those whose interpretational reflexes were the same as those of the authors.

With respect to interpretational reflexes, there seem to be four principles:

1. If the culture of the original is at any given point very similar to ours, our reflexes are going to serve us fairly well. In these instances the interpretational principle that says "the plain meaning is the true meaning" is a valid principle. Such a situation is rarely the case between Euroamerican culture and the Hebrew and Aramaic portions of the Scripture. Certain Greek customs do, however, seem to be similar enough to Euroamerican customs that our interpretational reflexes will give us the correct meaning. I think in this regard of the language of the track meet that Paul uses in Philippians 3. The same may be true of the language of economics that Paul uses earlier in that same chapter. The amount of biblical material where there is such close cultural similarity to our agreements is, however, distressingly small, and the fact that we cannot trust our interpretational reflexes in most places means that we can never be sure them unless we have independent evidence that this is a place where their custom is close to ours.

2. If the scriptural statement is a cultural universal, however, our interpretational reflexes will enable us to get close to the intended meaning. Statements that exist, as

far as we know, in every one of the world's cultures (e.g., the concepts in the Ten Commandments) are easy to interpret relatively accurately. There is a slight problem in the fact that each culture defines murder, adultery, and so on in its own way. But the fact that such commands occur in all cultures means that these statements are elevated out of the most difficult interpretational category--that of the culturally specific. Other parts of Scripture, such as those dealing with eating together, injunctions like "Love your neighbor," and many of the proverbs, are also in the cultural-universal category.

3. Similarly, if a scriptural statement relates to experiences that are common to all humankind, our culturally conditioned interpretational reflexes can be of considerable help. When the Scriptures say "go," "come," trust," "be patient," and the like, they are dealing with experiences that are common to all human beings and readily interpretable. Likewise with respect to illness and death, childbirth and rearing, obtaining and preparing food, and the like.

4. But, as indicated above, much of the biblical material is presented in cultural forms that are very specific to cultural practices quite different from ours. Because of their specificity to the cultural agreements of the original hearers, these materials communicated with maximum impact to them. This is a major part of the genius of God and of his Word—that he speaks specifically to people where they are and in terms of the culture in which they are immersed. At the same time, this fact enormously complicates the task of the person immersed in another culture who seeks to interpret the Scriptures.

The fact that our interpretational reflexes are so limited when dealing with biblical materials argues strongly for the application of the sharpest tools available to the study of the cultural matrices through which God revealed his Word. The harnessing of the perspectives of anthropology and linguistics to this end of the interpretational task (as well as to the communication end) could be a real boon to the exegete. One important result of such harnessing is the development of faithful dynamic equivalence translations and highly interpretive "transculturations" of God's Word (see Kraft 1979a:261-290). These aim to communicate God's message as specifically as possible in today's languages and cultures so that the members of these societies will be able to trust their interpretational reflexes when they study the Scriptures.

Beyond Grammatico-Historical to Ethnolinguistic Interpretation (Model 5b)

The statement of model 5b does not differ in essence from the ordinary hermeneutical principle of biblical theology that states that biblical passages are to be interpreted in their original contexts.[6] The method employed is often referred to by some such label as "the grammatico-historical method."[7]

The hermeneutical concern is for "extracting" or decoding from biblical texts the meanings that their authors encoded in those texts. The problem of biblical hermeneutics is thus the same problem as that faced by the receptor of any message in any context. It is therefore likely that the insights of contemporary studies into the nature of the ethnolinguistic setting in which communication takes place and into the nature and process of communication itself will be most helpful. Such insights enable us to go beyond the grammatico-historical model as previously developed to at least two points: (1) the extent to which the linguistic (grammatical) and cultural (historical) facts are taken into account, and (2) the attempt to focus both on the central biblical message in the original linguistic and cultural vehicles (as that approach does) and on certain other important aspects of supracultural truth— especially those related to the processes God uses to convey that truth.

This approach attempts to see more deeply into language and culture both at the biblical end and with respect to their influence on the interpreter himself. We may refer to this approach as "ethnolinguistic" (i.e., "culturo-linguistic") hermeneutics or even as "ethnohermeneutics."[8] The "context" of which we speak is not simply the literary or even the linguistic context in which an utterance occurs;[9] *it is the total cultural context* (including both literary and extraliterary components). And we focus not only on the central message of the Scriptures as expressed in the original linguistic and cultural vehicles (as important as that is), but also on the total process by means of which God seeks to communicate that and numerous other messages (both then and now) via language and culture. This approach, in keeping with the aims of biblical theology, emphasizes the pervasive importance of the cultural context but adds considerations of process to those related to the product (the Scriptures).

At this point it is important to define, in at least a preliminary way, several of the key concepts that will be employed below. The complex relationships between information, message, context, and meaning will be in primary focus. By *information* we designate the raw materials from which messages and meanings are constructed. A *message* consists of the structuring of a body of information in a way appropriate to the ethnolinguistic context within which it is transmitted. The *context* is the structured and structuring matrix within which and according to the rules of which information is organized into messages that may then be reliably encoded, trans-

---

[6] See, for example, Bernard Ramm, *Protestant Biblical Interpretation,* 3d rev. ed. (Grand Rapids: Baker Book, 1970), 138ff. For a critique of certain of the methods of interpretation traditionally used by biblical theologians, see James Barr, *The Semantics of Biblical Language* (London: Oxford University Press, 1961).

[7] See Ramm, *Protestant Biblical Interpretation,* p.114; A. Berkeley Mickelsen, *Interpreting the Bible* (Grand Rapids: Eerdmans, 1963), 159; and Daniel P. Fuller, "Hermeneutics," unpublished syllabus in use at Fuller Theological Seminary, Pasadena, California, in 1969, chapter 11.

[8] I am indebted to Mr. Phillip Leung, a Chinese student at the School of World Mission, 1976–1978, for suggesting this term.

[9] For an elaboration of this point, see Ramm, *Protestant Biblical Interpretation,* pp. 138-39; and Nida, *Toward a Science of Translating* (Leiden: E. J. Brill, 1964), and "Implications of Contemporary Linguistics for Biblical Scholarship," *Journal of Biblical Literature* 91(1971): 73-89.

mitted, and decoded to provide people with meanings. *Meaning* is the structuring of information in the minds of persons. It is frequently encoded into messages that are transmitted by communicators to receptors who decode the messages and, under the stimulus of those messages, restructure meanings in their own minds.

The fact seems to be that messages and, by implication, the information they contain require structured contexts in order to be interpretable (i.e., to be transformed into meanings in the mind of the receptor of the message). As Edward T. Hall states, "Information taken out of context is meaningless and cannot be reliably interpreted. . . . [The] separation of information from context, as though the two were unrelated, is an artifact of Western science and Western thought" (1974:21). And, as David Hunter and Mary Ann Foley suggest, "information, context, and meaning are inseparably and dynamically linked to one another" (1976:45). Figure 25.2, similar to one provided by Hunter and Foley (1976:46), is an attempt to depict this dynamic relationship.

If this perspective is correct, there is no possibility of a message (a structured body of information) making sense (i.e., taking on meaning) to a receptor without participating in *some* context. Two questions arise, however: (1) Which is the essential context, that of the originator of the communication, or that of the receptor? and (2) In the interaction between the message and the context, what does each contribute to the resultant meaning?

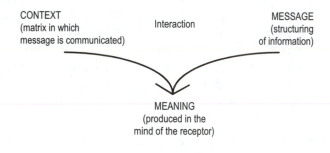

Figure 25.2 The dynamic relationship between context, message, and meaning. Read: In a given situation information is structured into a Message and communicated within a Context to produce signals that a receptor transforms into Meanings.

Model 5b holds that it is the interaction between the message and the *original* context that determines the correct meaning—the meaning that the interpreter seeks to ferret out. As discussed above, the biblical interpreter is hindered in this process by interpretational reflexes conditioned to derive meanings immediately from messages interacting with a different cultural context. Such an interpreter, to transcend this disability, needs to probe to discover the answer to the second question.

The context contributes that part of the meaning deriving from the culture-specific nature of an event. A certain amount of information implicit in the context is a part of this contribution. The fact that a given event occurred in the first century rather than in the twentieth, in Palestine rather than in America, and in Hebrew culture rather than in American culture is extremely significant to the meanings of that event at every point. The context must, therefore, be taken as seriously and analyzed as thoroughly as the message if the meaning of the message is to be understood either for its own time or for ours. The fallacy of the plain-meaning concept lies in the fact that it advocates simply extracting the message as if it would mean the same in interaction with a contemporary context *in that same form.* Such extracted messages "cannot be reliably interpreted" (Hall 1974:21).

Nida points in this regard to the unsatisfactory way in which words are traditionally dealt with by biblical scholars. He points to three fallacies (we shall cite only two of these) that stem from certain deficiencies in the philological and historical models commonly employed by such scholars:

> In the first place, there has been the tendency to regard the "true meaning" of a word as somehow related to some central core of meaning which is said to exist, either implicitly or explicitly, in each of the different meanings of such a word or lexical unit. It is from this central core of meaning that all the different meanings are supposed to be derivable (1971:84).

Words are, therefore, regarded by many as *bearing meaning* independently of their contexts. But words, like all information-bearing vehicles within culture, derive their meanings from their interaction with the contexts in which they participate. Nida goes on:

> In the second place, a common mistake has been to regard the presumed historical development of meaning as reflecting the "true meaning" of a word. The so-called etymology of a word is supposed to contain the key to the proper understanding of all its meanings (1971:85).

The historical development of a word or other cultural form is occasionally relevant to its meaning in the same way that a person's genealogy is occasionally relevant to his or her "meaning" (the nature of his or her participation) in a given context. But again, it is the relevance of this aspect of the cultural form to and in interaction with the context in which it occurs that determines its meaning. *A cultural form does not have inherent meaning, only perceived meaning, and this is context-specific.* "Valid lexicography must depend in the ultimate analysis upon patterns of co-occurrence in actual discourse," in actual situations.[10]

As an example of the kind of contextual analysis here recommended, we may choose two scriptural commands that ought to be treated the same according to the plain-meaning dictum (though in practice they seldom are). The problem is how to explain the difference between the command against stealing (Ex. 20:15) and the command that a woman cover (veil) her head when praying in public (1 Cor. 11:10). In America I have heard the one strongly advocated as it stands, while the other is explained away as "merely cultural." This approach is very unsatisfactory. The problem of the differential interpretation of these commands was vividly brought home to me by one of the Nigerian church leaders whom I was assisting. He pointed out to me that the Bible commands both that we not steal and that we not allow women to pray with their heads uncovered. He then asked why we missionaries

---

[10] Nida, "Implications of Contemporary Linguistics for Biblical Scholarship" (1971:85). For further elaboration of this point see *Christianity in Culture* (Kraft 1979a:34–59).

teach that the one command be obeyed and the other ignored. Are we using a different Bible?

The fact is that both commands are expressed in cultural terms—that is, via cultural and linguistic forms or symbols. So both are cultural messages. But, since nothing in the Bible is "merely" cultural, we need to look beyond each command to discover how the word and custom symbols were understood by the authors and those to whom they were originally written. That is, we need to look for the supracultural meaning in each by getting beyond our own cultural conditioning (with its "plain meanings") to the interpretation of each within its original cultural context.

At this point we are in danger of being put off by the fact that our culture has a rule against stealing. We may, therefore, simply employ our interpretational reflexes and assume that we know what the command against stealing meant in its Hebrew context on the basis of what similar word symbols mean in our culture. We are wrong, however, since no cultural symbols have exactly the same meanings in any two cultures, owing to the differences in the contexts with which the symbols interact. Yet, since those words do have a meaning in our culture and that meaning is consonant with Christianity, most accept the meaning assigned to those words (that message) in our culture as the plain meaning of Scripture. They see no need to go into Hebrew culture to discover their original meaning.

With respect to the headcovering command, however, many take an opposite point of view and appear to some to be "explaining" the command. Since those word symbols and the whole context in which they occur have no plain meaning that seems to bear Christian truth in our culture, most American Christians feel compelled to study the Greek cultural background to discover the original meaning. Some groups, of course, are consistent at this point and interpret the headcovering command in terms of the meaning of those word forms within our culture. These groups make their women wear headcoverings.

We infer that the stealing command already existed in Hebrew culture (as, from cross-cultural data, we learn it does in every culture). It had specific reference, however, only to what the Hebrews of that time considered to be the unwarranted appropriation of certain of those things considered to be the property of another. In that kind of strongly kinship-oriented society it is unlikely that it would be considered stealing if a person appropriated his brother's goods without asking. Nor is it likely that a starving person who "helped himself" to someone else's food could be accused of stealing (see Matt. 12:1-4).

By interpreting in terms of the Hebrew cultural context, we find this command to differ only slightly from our own cultural understanding of it. This fact illustrates that, due to human commonality, meanings derived from the interaction of certain (general) messages with any cultural context are appropriate even in quite diverse cultures. The relative importance of context and message, however, varies from situation to situation. In situations such as this where the significance of the context in the determination of the meaning is less, the possibility is increased for transferring the message from one cultural situation to another in roughly its original form with *most* (never all) of its meaning intact. Truly "propositional" statements in

Scripture such as "God is love" illustrate this point.[11] For this reason, even plain-meaning interpretations are fairly accurate for such statements.

When, however, the contribution to the meaning of implicit contextual information is high (as, for example, with the genealogies or the headcovering issue), it is necessary to interpret at a much deeper level of abstraction (see model 5c below) to ferret out the more general transferable meanings. Ethnolinguistic insight into the cultural and linguistic factors involved is especially valuable at this point. For there is much more meaning that God seeks to communicate through his Word than the surface level, context-specific messages so often in focus.

As for the headcovering command, analysis of the meaning of the custom in its cultural context does not lead simply to an alternative understanding of the same command. It leads, rather, to a *meaning* that demands *expression via a different cultural form* if it is to be understood in English. In the Greek culture of that day, apparently, the cultural form "female praying in public without headcovering" would have been interpreted to mean "this female is immoral," or, at least "she is not showing proper respect to men" (see commentaries on 1 Cor. 11:10-12). Since that meaning was not consonant with the witness that Christians ought to make, Paul commands against the use of the head-uncovered symbol in favor of its opposite, the head-covered symbol. For only this latter symbol conveyed the proper Christian meaning in that culture—that Christian women were not immoral and were properly subject to their men. The theological truth then—a truth just as relevant today as in the first century—is that Christian women should not behave in such a way that people judge them to be "out of line" (whether morally or with respect authority).[12]

Differing Levels of Abstraction (Model 5c)

Such cross-cultural analysis of the two passages shows that in comparing the two commands we are not comparing sames. For the commands are given at different levels of abstraction. That is, the relative importance of the specific cultural context to the meaning of the utterances differs. Those utterances that relate most specifically to their particular cultural contexts are at what is here termed the "surface" or "cultural-specific" level of abstraction. For correct understanding (interpretation) these depend greatly on implicit in formation embedded in the context with which the given custom interacts. Those utterances in which the specific context is less important to the meaning, and which, therefore, relate to pancultural human commonality, are at what may be termed a "deeper" or "general-principle" level of abstraction. These utterances are not so dependent on information implicit to

---

[11] For an enlightened discussion of the pros and eons of using the term *proposition* as a designation for that which God has revealed, see Ronald H. Nash, "Truth By Any Other Name," *Christianity Today* 22 (1977): 15–17, 19.

[12] For a useful discussion of this issue, see Robert C. Sproul, "Controversy at Culture Gap," *Eternity* 27(1976): 13-15, 40.

their original contexts for Interpretation. That the stealing command is at a deeper level of abstraction is evident from the fact that it does not refer to a specific cultural act but to a *category* of cultural behavior. The command is general rather than specific. Note, by way of contrast, the specificity of the tenth command. That command is at the surface level of abstraction (like the headcovering command) in that it specifies the proscribed cultural *acts* rather than (until the final phrase) generalizing them into an *overall principle* as we do when we refer to that command as a general command against "covetousness." Note the wording:

> Do not desire another man's house; do not desire his wife, his slaves, his cattle, his donkeys, or anything else that he owns (Ex. 20:17 TEV).

The headcovering command is at this more specific level, where the embedded information in that particular cultural context is very important to the meaning. A corresponding specific stealing command would be something like "Don't take your neighbor's donkey without his permission." A headcovering command at the same level of generality as the stealing command would be something like "Don't appear out of line with respect to immorality or authority." Thus we see a specific cultural form/symbol level with the original context contributing relatively more to the meaning, and a deeper general-principle level in which the original context contributes relatively less. These two possibilities are illustrated in Figure 25.3.

There seems, however, to be a yet deeper level of abstraction in Scripture. This is made explicit by Jesus when he summarizes the teaching of the law and the prophets in two statements:

> "Love the Lord your God with all your heart, with all your soul, and with all your mind." This is the greatest and the most important commandment. The second most important commandment is like it:

> "Love your neighbor as you love yourself." The whole Law of Moses and the teachings of the prophets depend on these two commandments (Matt. 22:37-40 TEV; cf Deut. 6:5; Mark 12:2931; Luke 10:27).

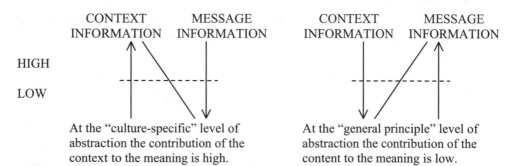

Figure 25.3 "Seesaw" diagrams illustrating the relationship between the context-message interaction concept and the levels of abstraction concept.

These three levels correspond to some extent with the three levels charted in Figure 25.4: the level of specific customs, the level of worldview values, and the deep level of human universals. The universals apply to every person in every culture at all times. These may be regarded as transcultural or even supracultural ideals. The general principles (such as the Ten Commandments) seem, likewise, to apply universally. If these are seen as corresponding with the cultural worldview level, it is with the recognition that values such as these occur in the worldviews of every culture. At the level of specific custom, though, there is a considerable range of diversity expressive of the general principles.

There are occasional problems as to which of the levels to assign certain of the general statements of Scripture. We may advance Figure 25.5 as a step in the direction of developing this model more precisely. Note that a complete chart would show (even more than this one does) the fact that there are fewer categories at the Basic Ideal Level, more at the General Principle Level, and an enormous number at the Specific Cultural Form/Symbol Level.

In such expositions as the Ten Commandments (especially as Jesus summarizes them in Matt. 22:37-40), the Sermon on the Mount, the listing of the fruits of the Spirit (Gal. 5:22-23), and many similar statements, the Scriptures seem to us to come closest to a clear statement of a portion of the supracultural will of God for human conduct. The reason for the apparent clarity of these portions is that they are phrased at a level of abstraction that largely extricates them from specific application to the original cultures in which they were uttered. As one moves from specific cultural applications of supracultural truth (as with the headcovering command) back toward the most general statements of the truth, the statements require less understanding of the original cultural context to be accurately understood. They have more immediate (though general) meaning to us in another culture. The plain-meaning principle is therefore often adequate for interpreting information presented at this deeper level of abstraction.

Note, however, that the effectiveness of the communication is a matter of cultural perception. For the original hearers, it was presentations of supracultural truth in terms of specific applications (abstraction level 3) that communicated most effectively. For us, likewise, specific applications of scriptural generalizations would most effectively communicate. But, since the Scriptures were written in terms of cultures other than ours, we are denied enscripturated applications of supracultural truth in our culture. The general statements, therefore, make more sense to us than the specific cultural forms through which these principles were applied in biblical cultures. And the more specific applications in the Scriptures are often the most confusing to us.

\ Customs A\	\ Customs B\	/ Customs C\	/ Customs D /	/ Customs E /
Worldview A\	Worldview B\	Worldview C\	Worldview D /	Worldview E/

	UNIVERSAL	CULTURAL	FUNCTIONS	
Obtaining and maintaining biological necessities — food, shelter, health, sex, air, excretion	Obtaining and maintaining psychological necessities — meaning in life, personal security, a measure of freedom	Obtaining and maintaining socio-cultural necessities — language, family, education, social control	Obtaining and maintaining spiritual necessities — mythology, ritual	
Food, shelter, air, sex, excretion, health	Meaning, maintenance of individual psyche	Communication, provide for children, transmission of culture, maintenance of social system	Understanding of and relationships to supracultural beings and factors	
BIOLOGICAL	PSYCHOLOGICAL	SOCIO-CULTURAL	SPIRITUAL	
	UNIVERSAL HUMAN NEEDS			

Figure 25.4 Human commonality and cultural diversity.

1. BASIC IDEAL LEVEL	*2. GENERAL PRINCIPLE LEVEL*	*3. SPECIFIC CULTURAL FORM/SYMBOL LEVEL*
← — — — — More General ←——→ More Specific — — — — →		
A. Love your neighbor as you love yourself (Matt. 22:39)	1. Do not steal (Ex. 20:17)	a. Do not take your neighbor's donkey (Hebrew)
		b. Do not take your employer's money (U.S.A.)
	2. Do not covet	a. Do not desire another man's house . . . (Ex. 20:17)
		b. Same for U.S.A.
	3. Be free from partiality (1 Tim. 5:21; Jas. 3:17)	a. Treat Gentiles/blacks/ women as human beings
		b. Rebuke whoever needs it (1 Tim. 5:20)
B. Love the Lord your God with all your heart . . . (Matt. 22:37)	1. Worship no God but me (Ex. 20:3)	a. Do not bow down to any idol or worship it (Ex. 20:5)
		b. Do not pledge primary allegiance to material wealth (U.S.A.)
	2. Seek by all means to save people (1 Cor. 9:22)	a. Live as a Jew to win Jews (1 Cor. 9:20)

1. BASIC IDEAL LEVEL	2. GENERAL PRINCIPLE LEVEL	3. SPECIFIC CULTURAL FORM/SYMBOL LEVEL
		b. Live as Gentile to win Gentiles (1 Cor. 9:21)
		c. Live as an African to win Africans
C. Everything must be done in a proper and orderly way (1 Cor. 14:40)	1. Leaders should be beyond reproach (1 Tim. 3:2; Tit. 1:6)	a. They must be self-controlled, etc. (1 Tim. 3:2)
	2. Christian women should not appear out of line	a. They should cover their heads when praying in Greek culture (1 Cor. 11:10)
		b. They should not wear their clothes too tight (U.S.A.)
	3. Christians should live according to the rules of the culture (as long as they do not conflict with Christian principles)	a. Women should learn in silence in Greek culture (1 Tim. 2:11)
		b. Women may speak up in mixed groups in U.S.A.
		c. Pay the government what belongs to it (Matt. 22:21)
		d. Obey governmental authorities (Rom. 13:1)
		e. Wives, submit to your husbands in Greek and many segments of U.S.A. culture (Eph. 5:22; Col. 3:18; etc.)

D. Other ideals?

Figure 25.5 Illustrative chart of differing levels of abstraction model (5c).

Throughout the Scriptures we are provided with glimpses of the supracultural, clothed in specific events taking place within specific cultures at specific times. Frequently, as with statements at the general-principle or basic-ideal level, we get the impression that we are looking at supracultural truth with a minimum of cultural conditioning. More frequently, however, we are exposed to supracultural truth applied in a specific situation. in a specific biblical culture. The record of this comes to us only in translation, so that we see such truth as "puzzling reflections in a mirror" (1 Cor. 13:12 JBP). Among these "reflections," Smalley feels that

> those parts of Scripture which give us evaluations of human motives and emotions, human attitudes and personalities, give us the deepest insight into God's ultimate will, and that to understand the revelation in terms of God's will for our behavior we will have to learn to look behind the cultural facade to see as much as we can of what the Word indicates about those questions. The cultural examples given us are thereby not lost. They provide most valuable examples of the way in which God's will was performed in another cultural setting to help us see how we may perform it in ours (1955:66).

In this way it is possible for Christians to learn something of supracultural truth even though this, like all human knowledge, is perceived by us in terms of the cultural grid in which we operate. Though often puzzling and never total or absolute, such knowledge is adequate for God's purposes-the salvation and spiritual growth of all who give themselves to him in faith (see Mickelsen 1963:353). We may then, under the leading of the Spirit, come to know something of how the Spirit desires us to live out these truths in terms of our cultural forms.

"Two Culture Dialogic" Interpretation (Model 5d)

As amply indicated in the foregoing, we are dealing with both the interpreter's culture and the ethnolinguistics of the biblical contexts when we interpret. Any model of hermeneutics that ignores the influence of the interpreter's culture on that person's attempts to understand the Scriptures is seriously deficient. Many who seek to employ grammatico-historical methodology are severely hampered by a failure to grasp the full significance of the culture-boundness, of themselves and of their methodology.

The plain-meaning approach, though providing reasonably accurate interpretations at the most general levels of abstraction is flawed by its simplistic approach to the original contexts. In reaction against that approach the grammatico-historical approach digs deeply into the original contexts. But it tends to overestimate the possibility of objectivity on the part of the contemporary scholarly interpreter. We have attempted, by means of the application of anthropological, linguistic, and communicational insights, to increase our ability to maximize the strengths of these approaches (especially the latter) while minimizing their deficiencies. It remains to deal explicitly with the dialogical nature of the interaction between the messages of Scripture in their contexts and the concerns of the interpreters in their contexts.

A concern for the contextualization of biblical messages is a concern that scriptural meanings get all the way across what might be pictured as a "hermeneutical bridge" into the real-life contexts of ordinary people. In a perceptive article dealing with hermeneutics from the perspective of one deeply committed to the contextualization of Christianity, C. René Padilla says,

> hermeneutics has to do with a dialogue between Scripture and a contemporary culture. Its purpose is to transpose the biblical message from its original context into a particular twentieth-century situation. Its basic assumption is that the God who spoke in the past and whose Word was recorded in the Bible continues to speak today in Scripture (1978:11).

If interpretation is done naively, as in the plain-meaning approach, meaningful dialogue between past revelation and present need is often prevented, owing to a premature application of hastily and superficially derived meanings. Scholarly approaches to interpretation, on the other hand, have prevented such dialogue by considering the biblical message in its original context in such a way that its meanings remain "in a world which is definitely not our world." A balanced approach takes both contexts seriously and gives both due weight. "The aim is that the horizon of the receptor culture is merged with the horizon of the text in such a way that the message proclaimed in the receptor culture may be a dynamic equivalent of the message proclaimed in the original context" (Padilla 1978:5-6).

The hermeneutical process, then, involves a dynamic interaction or dialogue between an interpreter deeply enmeshed in his or her own culture and worldview (including theological biases) and the Scriptures. The interpreter has needs, some of which he or she formulates into questions, "asking" these questions of the Scriptures and finding certain of them answered. Other questions remain unanswered, since "there is a large number of topics on which Scripture says nothing or very little" (Padilla 1978:17). Still other questions are stimulated in the mind of the interpreter as a result of the person's interaction with Scripture. Meanwhile, in attempting to live life in a particular context, the interpreter's interaction with that context also stimulates new questions.

> The richer and deeper the questions brought by the interpreter from the receptor culture, the richer and deeper the answers provided by Scripture. It follows that without a good understanding of the moral issues involved in living in a particular situation there cannot be an adequate understanding of the relevance of the biblical message to that situation. Each new formulation of the questions based on a more refined understanding of the situation makes possible a reading of Scripture and consequently the discovery of new implications of its message. If it is true that Scripture illuminates life it is also true that life illuminates Scripture (Padilla 1978:17).

Hermeneutics is not, therefore, merely an academic game to be played by supposedly objective scholars. It is a dynamic process that properly demands deep subjective involvement on the part of Christian interpreters operating within the Christian community (which includes scholars) both with the Scriptures and with the life of the world around them in which they live. Hermeneutics is thus a kind of three-way conversation, proceeding according to the rules of communication (see Taber 1978), under the guidance of the Holy Spirit, issuing in what might be pictured as an upward "spiraling" of understanding of Scriptures, of self, of the world, and of the proper, God-guided interactions between the three at *this* time and in *this* setting. At the beginning of the "spiral" the interpreter goes with certain felt needs of the Scriptures under the guidance of God and with the assistance of the Christian community (in person or via published materials). Within the community, then, the interpreter moves from needs to Scripture, to application in the living of his or her life, to needs (some of which are newly perceived and at a deeper level), to Scripture (some of which he or she sees with "new eyes"), to deeper level application in the living of his or her life, and so on.

The life context with which the interpreter is interacting is critical to the whole process. If the life context to which the application's are made is merely an academic context, the nature of the insights derived from Scripture and their usability outside that context are vitally affected. This is what makes much of what goes on in academic institutions and scholarly writings unusable in life contexts other than the classroom. One of the damaging effects of such academicization of biblical interpretation has been the excessive informationalizing of revelation (see Kraft 1979a:169-193). Given the "down-to-earth" nature of the Scriptures, it is often the unschooled interpreter who can best interpret them, in spite of the difficulty that one may have in under-standing the more culture-specific passages. For the Scriptures are life-related, not merely "religious discourse. . . couched in technical language," as Western exegetes have tended to assume (see Taber 1978:12).

This dialogical approach to hermeneutics is more serious than previous approaches in the place it gives to the interpreter and the receptor group in their respective contexts. It does not assume either unbiased interpreters or the universality for all times and places of the answers arrived at by previous interpreters in their times and places. It places real people with real needs in real-life contexts at the center of the hermeneutical process. It questions the ultimacy of academic, scholarly interpretation outside academic, scholarly contexts. Dialogical hermeneutics. draws its concern for context from the Bible itself. And it recognizes in the multi-leveled character of biblical context the multi-leveled character of context in the process of understanding itself. What was that original context addressed by Jesus Christ when he called, "Repent, for the kingdom of heaven is at hand" (Matt. 4:17)? What was that context to which Matthew spoke as interpreter of Jesus when he used the words, "kingdom of heaven"? How was it different from the context of Mark who summarizes the same message of Jesus in terms of the "kingdom of God" (Mark 1:15)? What was the context Paul addressed as the re-encoder of the kingdom message at Rome, transposing "preaching the kingdom of God" into "teaching concerning the Lord Jesus Christ" (Acts 28:23, 31)?

> A process of this kind can be liberating as the man of God wrestles with biblical context, his own, and those to whom he speaks and before whom he lives. Charles Taber writes that such an appeal to Scripture "can free indigenous theology from the bondage of Western categories and methodologies."[13]

The concern for the importance of the contexts of interpreter and receptor must not diminish our concern for Scriptures as our "tether" and "yardstick." For the hermeneutical process is an interactional process with the Bible as the necessary point with which all else is to interact.

---

[13] Harvie M. Conn, "Contextualization: A New Dimension For Cross-Cultural Hermeneutic," *Evangelical Missions Quarterly* 14 (1978): 45. Conn's citation of Taber is taken from "The Limits of Indigenization in Theology," *Missiology* 6 (1978): 71.

CONTEXTUALIZATION

CONTEXTUALIZATION OF THEOLOGY

CHAPTER 26

WHAT IS THE CONTEXTUALIZATION OF THEOLOGY?

Reprinted here with permission from
Evangelical Missions Quarterly 14:311-36 (1978)

Introduction

For many the term "theology" has about it an aura of irrelevance. It conjures up in the mind the seemingly endless history of bickering between those in favor of one set of interpretations of the Bible and Christian experience with those who hold another set of interpretations. Many have become so impatient with theological arguing that they attempt to ignore the whole subject. Others are so convinced that their theology is identical with biblical teaching that they dismiss any thoughts on the subject that are not generated by their favorite theologians.

In mission lands, however, where the church is young, the development of theological understandings that are appropriate to the linguistic and cultural contexts in which the young churches exist is of high relevance. Young Christians in these parts of the world are often engaged in a life or death struggle with anti-Christian belief systems that are more like those encountered by biblical peoples than like those abroad in the western world today. The development of theological understandings of biblical Christianity that will enable these people to stand against pagan thought systems is, therefore, of great importance.

The concept "contextualization of theology" is a technical label for this vital process. It is the purpose of this article to deal with some of the foundational issues with respect to the development of theologies that are truly biblical and truly relevant to the cultural context of non-western peoples around the world.

What Is Contextualization?

Theologizing always involves interpretation. As evangelicals we believe that the basis for Christian theologizing should always be the Bible. Any interpretation of the Bible is a form of theologizing. This means that theologizing is done in sermons, in hymns, in poems, in discussions, in art and in many other ways.

All human interpretation is done from the point of view of the interpreter. Human interpreters are never free of bias. A given Christian theology is, therefore, an interpretation of Christianity from a particular point of view. No theology is absolute. of the theologian is Spirit-led, however, the theological perspective that he develops will fall within a range of variation allowed by the Scriptures The differences between the theological understandings of Spirit-led interpreters correspond to the differences between their understandings of reality.

At least certain liberals use the term "contextualization of theology" in a different sense than is intended here. To them the biblical materials are but one example of religious thinking. From their point of view, therefore, understandings of God can be just as validly developed on the basis of the materials presented in some other holy book or some body of oral traditions. That is not the position advocated here. When we speak of the contextualization of theology, we speak of the interpretation of the Christian Bible alone. We recognize, however, that the wider the cultural differences between interpreters of the Bible, the greater will be the differences in the resulting interpretations, especially with respect to peripheral issues. From our point of view, all theologizing must be within the range of biblical allowability or it cannot be considered Christian.

Evangelicals believe that the Bible must be interpreted in its original context. Evangelical scholars devote their time and energy to understanding the original linguistic and cultural contexts in which God revealed himself to the original authors and in which they recorded his revelation. But the task of interpretation is not complete when the original materials are understood by the scholar. The message that God communicated in those ancient times and places must be interpreted in such a way that it is properly understood and responded to by contemporary people in contemporary times and places. This is the aspect of biblical interpretation that is referred to as contextualization.

Contextualization Is Biblical

The contextualization of Christianity is part and parcel of the New Testament record. This is the process that Paul and Peter and John and the other Apostles were involved in as they sought to take the Christian message that had come to them in Aramaic language and culture and to communicate it to those who spoke Greek. In order to contextualize Christianity for Greek speakers, the Apostles gave themselves to the expression of Christian truth in the thought patterns of those to whom they spoke. Indigenous words and concepts were used (and transformed in their usage) to deal with such topics as God, church, sin, conversion, repentance, initiation, "word" (*logos*) and most other areas of Christian life and practice.

The early Greek churches were in danger of being dominated by Hebrew theology, just as many non-western churches today are in danger of being dominated by western theologies. God, however, led the Apostle Paul and others to struggle against the Hebrew Christians to develop a contextualized Christian theology for those who spoke Greek. In order to do this, Paul had to fight a running battle with many of the Hebrew church leaders who felt that it was the job of Christian preachers to simply impose Hebrew theological concepts on new converts (see Acts 15). These conservative Hebrews were, as Daniel von Allmen points out, the heretics against whom Paul fights for the right for Greek-speaking Christians to have the gospel contextualized in their language and culture (von Allmen 1975:49).

We conclude from such passages as Acts 10 and 15 that it is the intent of God that biblical Christianity be "reincarnated" in every language and culture at every point in history. Evangelicals believe that God has something to say to every people at every time and in every place God intends that his message be just as relevant to people in today's cultural context as it was to those in the original cultural context. We believe, therefore, that it is biblical to devote ourselves to the contextualization of biblical theology.

Contextualization Is a Process

Some might feel that the intensive investigations of generations of western theologians must surely have produced by now a once for all set of theological understandings that can simply be passed on from culture to culture. Those of us who have been involved in contextualizing Christian theology in non-western cultures have not, however, found this position to be entirely accurate. The pressing questions addressed by western theologians (particularly academic theologians) are very often quite different from the questions being asked by village Africans, Asians and Latin Americans. Our experience underlines the validity of the statement made by von Allmen when he suggests that

> Any authentic theology must start ever anew from the focal point of the faith, which is the confession of the Lord Jesus Christ who died and was raised for us; and it must be built or re-built (whether in Africa or in Europe) in a way which is both faithful to the inner thrust of the Christian revelation and also in harmony with the mentality of the person who formulates it. There is no short cut to be found by simply adapting an existing theology to contemporary or local taste (1975:50).

The contextualization of Christian theology is, therefore, not simply the passing on of a "product" that has been developed once for all in Europe or America. It is, rather, the imitating of the process that the early apostles went through. Since the materials from which the theologizing is done are the same biblical materials the essential message will be the same. The formulation of that message and the relative prominence of many of the issues addressed will, however, differ from culture to culture. New Testament teaching concerning the superiority of the power of Christ to that of evil spirits is, for example, a much more prominent part of contextualized African theology than of American theology.

Because of such differences in cultural focus, it is imperative that Christians within every culture be encouraged to contextualize Christian theology within their cultures. Such contextualization should be done in such a way that their people perceive the gospel to be excitingly relevant to the problems that they struggle with. There are, of course, similar basic problems (e.g., the problem of sin) for peoples of all cultures. But the way those problems manifest themselves differ from culture to culture. Christian theologies should address themselves to even those common problems in culturally appropriate ways today just as the earliest theologians did in New Testament times. We ought, therefore, to assist people living at the frontiers of Christianity

> to uncover the forces that govern the making of their theology, in order that they may ... be guided by the same dynamism as they set about creating a contemporary theology whether it be in Africa or in Europe (von Allmen 1975:51).

Pre-formulated theology that is merely passed from one cultural context to another, rather than being developed within that context, is frequently judged as irrelevant whether in Euroamerica or in Asia or Africa. In America, theology perceived by the hearers as mere academic philosophizing is often judged to be irrelevant, not on its own merits, but simply because the hearer judges the framework in terms of which the theology is proclaimed to be irrelevant to him. Christian truth must be recreated within the language and accompanying conceptual framework of the hearers if its true relevance is to be properly perceived by him. Theologizing, like all Christian communication must be directed *to* someone if it is to serve its purpose. It cannot simply be flung out into thin air. The idea of simply passing along to those in other cultural contexts prefabricated theology developed by western academics has no biblical support.

No Theology Is Absolute

As indicated above, theologizing is a human, fallible process. It follows then that no theology is perfect or absolute. We do not see the mind of God clearly but, rather, "as dim reflections in a mirror" (1 Cor. 13:12). Theologies then, are always to some extent individualized and ethnic. They are at best the Spirit-led perceptions of people and groups in contemporary contexts who, under the leading of God, have given themselves to interpreting God's word. Though not absolute, theologies become an important part of the repackaging of the Christian message as it moves from culture to culture and from subculture to subculture. If theologies are properly in tune with the surrounding cultures, they will manifest differences of focus, differences of understanding, and differences of expression proportionate to the differences between the cultures and subcultures in which they are involved. This is true even though there are two strong pulls toward uniformity—the fact that theologies in order to be Christian are based upon the biblical revelation, and the fact that beyond cultural differences human beings share an extensive common humanity. But such differences of focus, understanding and expression are necessary if the theologies are to be meaningful to those to whom they are directed.

Theologizing is meant to be relevant. It is tragic, therefore, when an inappropriate theological system is adopted by or imposed upon those of another culture or subculture. This error often results when 1) a given approach to theology is regarded as highly prestigious and/or 2) proponents of that theological system assume that the system is absolutely correct for all times and places and, therefore, relevant to all peoples and/or 3) the proponents have the power to impose their system on others. As missionaries and Christians who seek to present the Christian message in Christian ways, we need to be very careful that we do not engage in theological imperialism. The imposition of theologies that might be quite relevant in one cultural context on the people of another cultural context has often resulted in negative reactions to those theologies, to theologizing in general, or even to Christianity as a whole. Without an understanding of the need for contextualization of theology, many advocates of Christianity have offered to non-western peoples only varieties of theology that are preoccupied with the theological concerns of a former stage of western culture. The result for those churches that accept such theological imposition, is often that they are characterized by a high degree of foreignness even within their own cultural context. The result for those churches that reject such prefabricated theology, is that they often reject the essence of Christianity along with the objectionable features.

Contextualizing Christian Theology Is Very Risky

Any enthusiasm for the desirability of theological contextualization needs to be tempered by the recognition that there are great risks involved. The risk of syncretism is always present. But there are at least two paths that lead to syncretism. One is by making mistakes when adapting the Christian message to indigenous forms. Often people experiment with using words and customs to express Christian meaning, and it doesn't work well. Sometimes people are even irresponsible about their attempts to contextualize. The risk of making mistakes is always there.

The other way of bringing about syncretism is, however, a much greater threat. In New Testament times the Pharisees produced syncretism by refusing to adapt God's meanings to new cultural forms. Likewise, the Judaizers produced syncretism by being conservative and refusing to change the foreign (Hebrew) forms of Christianity. Later the Roman Catholic Church produced syncretism, and Luther had to reject it in order to recover a measure of Christianity. The same thing has happened to denomination after denomination since that time because they have refused to contextualize the message of God for their times and places. And God has had to continually raise up new denominations to correct the syncretisms produced by the domination of rigid orthodoxies.

The greatest risk of syncretism today, as in Jesus' day comes not from those who are attempting to discover ways of expressing Christianity in non-western cultures (though there is great risk there). It comes, rather, from those who try, like the Pharisees and Judaizers, to preserve the foreign expressions of God's message. When foreign forms of Christianity are kept, the meanings change, and often become unchristian. We must be careful that we don't take what the Master has given us (i.e., Christian theology in western clothing) and try to simply preserve it like the unprofitable servant in the Parable of the Talents. Because he sought to preserve his talent, refusing to risk and invest it, he lost it. It is, I believe, less Scriptural to attempt to preserve western theologies in non-western cultures than it is to follow the Apostle Paul's example in attempting, under the guidance of the Spirit, to contextualize the Christian message in every culture.

The risk of syncretism is, however, always present. This fact should not be ignored or taken lightly. The fact that there is great risk should not, however, induce those of us who work with younger churches to resort to theological domination. The sin of theological domination is every bit as bad as the risk of theological error.

Conclusion

What is the contextualization of theology? This is what happens whenever the given gospel, the message of Christ, is reinterpreted in new cultural contexts in ways equivalent to the ways in which Paul and the other Apostles interpreted it from Aramaic into Greek thought patterns. Contextualization of theology must be biblically based if it is to be Christian. It may take place in a number of different ways—such as via sermons, hymns, poems, discussions, art and many other ways. Contextualizing Christian theology is risky, but is not as likely to lead to syncretism as is the preservation of antique forms of theologizing and the importation of these forms into contexts in which they are not appropriate. No theology is an absolute representation of the mind of God. Appropriate contextualization, produced by Spirit-led interpreters of God's word, present the Christian message within a biblically allowed range of variation in such a way that today's peoples will respond to Christ as those in the first century did. The contextualization of Christian theology is an essential process in the effective communication of the gospel.

CHAPTER 27

THEOLOGY AND THEOLOGIES

Following are two articles worked into one and reprinted with permission from *Theology, News and Notes* 18(2):4-6, 9 (June 1972) and 18(3):17-20 (October 1972)

"Black Theology," "Latin American Theology," "African Theology," "Street Culture Theology!"—what is all this? Isn't theology theology? There can't be more than one theology unless the others are based on something other than God's revealed Word and, therefore, wrong, can there? Or can there?

One of the distinct benefits of living and working outside of one's own culture, as a foreign missionary does, is that he learns so much about his own culture, his own frame of reference, his own way of doing and looking at things. One of the things he becomes aware of is that people of other cultures actually perceive reality differently than he does. He comes to recognize the deep truth of the famous statement of the anthropologist Edward Sapir that people of different cultures, speaking different languages are not simply attaching different linguistic labels to elements of the same real world but are actually operating in terms of *different realities*. That is, reality at the perceptual level is culturally and subculturally defined rather than a function of biology or environment. And this is just as true of our culture as it is of the cultures of Asia, Africa or Latin America—our own perception of reality is pervasively affected by our culture and even by such subcultural perceptual frameworks as an academic discipline or an occupational or residential social grouping.

In an absolute sense Reality and Truth remain one. But it is a fact of life that perceptions of that Reality and Truth differ greatly from culture to culture, from subculture to subculture within each culture and even from individual to individual within a given subculture. And this fact gives rise to considerable discussion as to which perception of Reality is the right one—a discussion that is usually answered fairly easily (though inaccurately) by each participant: "Why, the right perception of reality is my own, of course."

And yet we as individuals, if we are reflective, are forced to recognize concerning our own perceptions, 1) that as we grow and mature our understandings of Reality change, and 2) that sympathetic attempts to understand and enter into the points of view of other human beings inevitably result in our own enrichment and growth. For me, then, which perception of reality is/was the right one? Is it the one I have now? Or is it the next one that I'll develop? Or am I still like a child totally dependent upon someone else's decipherment to guide me through the maze?

"Christian theology," says F. R. Tennant

> ... sets forth the contents and implications of the revelation of Christ. It consists of a systematic exposition of doctrine and of the course of its development ..., the historical, critical and exegetical study of the Bible and the history of the church, its institutions, etc. Thus theology is a science, or a group of connected sciences, that, on the one hand, is in touch with general philosophy ... and, on the other hand, is more or less isolable in that it deals with the deliverances of distinctively religious experience and its pre-eminent manifestations.[1]

Theology as we know it, then, is a disciplinary perspective on or perception of Reality. It is the product of a specific historical process within western culture, and this history includes a specific deep and abiding relationship between western theology and western philosophy. And this relationship between theological inquiry and the very vital and leisureful culture of western Europe on the one hand and the vitality of the discipline of western philosophy on the other, has resulted in a large body of extremely insightful perceptions of the portion of Reality revealed to man by God in and through the Christian Scriptures. But this body of perceptions cannot be exhaustive for at least three reasons: 1) the perceptions have been generated almost totally from within a single culture (and this in spite of the fact that the source materials were recorded in terms of very different cultures—Hebrew and Greek); 2) the perceptions have been generated almost totally within but a single academic discipline within that culture; and 3) even within this strictly limited frame of reference understandings differ, change and develop—i.e., they are never absolute understandings even though they are attempts to understand the Absolute.

With regard to the fact that theology as we know it has been generated almost totally from within a single culture, this fact is not raised here as a criticism but as a point that must be kept in mind in discussing Theology versus theologies. For if we are tempted to absolutize the perceptions of our culture-bound understandings of the revelation of God, a revelation none of which either took place within western European culture or was recorded in a western European language,[2] we are culturally taking a position equivalent to that of the individual who regards none but his own understandings of Truth to be absolutely correct. We accuse such an individual of egocentrism, label such a view on the cultural level ethnocentrism and find, I believe, that Jesus' discussion of the mote and the beam applies both at the individual and the cultural level. This cultural limitedness does not, however, obviate the value of the perceptions of absolute Truth thus gained for those immersed in western culture. It merely means that we must recognize that *any* monocultural perspective on Truth, even revealed truth, whether this perspective be that of

---

[1] F. R. Tennant, "Theology" in *Encyclopedia Britannica*, vol. 22 (Chicago, IL: Encyclopedia Britannica, 1962), 61B.

[2] Linguistic classification doesn't use the term "western European languages." If it did, though, it is clear that Greek would stand outside of such a grouping since the Greek languages stand by themselves within Indo-European, showing neither an alignment with the I-E languages groupings to the east of the Greek languages or with those groupings to the west and northwest of it that one would ordinarily regard as western European (e.g., Romance, Germanic). Hebrew and Aramaic, or course, belong to a completely different family from I-E, recently named Afroasiatic.

Hebrew, Greek or western culture, though extremely valuable, cannot be complete any more than the single perspective of any given individual can be.

And the same can be said concerning the perspective of a single academic discipline such as philosophy. Such a discipline has clearly focused in on certain things by specializing in its own perspective (as cultures and individuals also have), but, as a byproduct of this specialization, it has become unable to see other things clearly, if at all. Just as individuals not only gain things by becoming right handed but also lose the potential to do certain things with their left hands, so disciplines and cultures both gain and lose by specializing.

We are aware, however, that even within a single culture a single discipline the perception of Truth is anything but monolithic. The history of western theology is full of individual and group differences. often labeled "heresies" if they don't seem to square with the perceptions of one's own group(or the group in power). But such differences often stimulate reactions and both the original differences/deviations and the reactions are studied by succeeding groups. Thus the original differences, the reactions and subsequent study of them, all provide learning experiences for those involved, which are defined by them as deepenings in their understandings of Christian Truth.

Theologizing, then, may he seen to be a process taking place at the perceptual level—a process which is indebted to diversity of perspective and of approach, a process that is helped when the participants in the process are granted the freedom to dissent and to pursue the discovery of Truth in terms of their own frame of reference. Theologizing is thus seen to be a dynamic, discovery process rather than a passive acceptance of a doctrine "once for all delivered." It proceeds according to the rules of (Spirit-led) human interaction (both with men and with God) rather than by means of simple indoctrination. And this is true at the perceptual (human) level even though we are dealing with the divine revelation of a portion of absolute Truth. Theology, then, must always be seen as the result of the dynamic process of human theologizing rather than confused with the change less, absolute divine model which remains in the mind of God (and thus beyond our reach in any total sense) even though he has seen to it that an adequate (for his purposes) amount of insight into that absolute Truth has been revealed to us in terms of certain Spirit-led perceptions of that Truth recorded by the authors of Holy Scripture.

But theology is not only perceived, it is also transmitted. And when transmitted it is "reperceived" by the hearer in terms of *his* psychological, subcultural (including disciplinary and/or other group) and cultural frame of reference. And at this point it must be perceived by the hearer as relevant or it will be judged by him to be irrelevant. Theology perceived by a layman or by a member of another discipline as mere philosophizing, therefore, is often judged to be irrelevant not on its own merits, but simply because the hearer judges the philosophic framework in terms of which the theology is proclaimed to be irrelevant to him. That is, theology must be translated into the language and accompanying conceptual framework of the hearer if its true relevance is to be properly perceived by him.

It is for this reason that the missiologist Bengt Sundkler states that

Theology is, in the last resort, translation. It is an ever-renewed re-interpretation to new generations and peoples of the given Gospel, a re-interpretation of the will and the way of the one Christ in a dialogue with new thought-forms and culture patterns . . . Theology, in essence, is to understand the fact of Christ.[3]

Thus it is that in theologizing as in preaching what the hearer hears is of greater significance to the way in which he perceives the message than what the speaker or writer says. It is incumbent, therefore, for the would-be communicator to phrase his theology or his preaching in terms of the frame of reference of his hearers. And a large portion of the blame if the hearer perceives theology or preaching to be irrelevant falls squarely on the shoulders of the would-be communicator.

Culture and subculture, therefore, pervasively affect theologizing, both in the understanding of God's revelation and in the communication of these understandings. If, then, Christian theology as we know it in western philosophic garb is to be of value (i.e., perceived as relevant) to Latin Americans, to Asians, to Africans, it must be "transculturated" into the concepts and language framework in terms of which they operate. If, likewise, theology is to be of value to psychologists, to sociologists, to chemists, it must be "transdisciplinated" out of its present western philosophico-historical mold into the conceptual and linguistic frame of reference of these disciplines. if, further, theology is to be perceived as relevant by factory workers, by farmers, by engineers, by youth, by hippies, by blacks, by women's libbers, it must be translated into the terms and concepts meaningful to each group. And the responsibility for this lies on the would-be communicator—on the theologian or the preacher. For too long have we simply paraded an unintelligible static theology before our public in the conviction that there is nothing more relevant than theology, without considering the fact that relevance is as relevance is perceived.

The process of transculturation is not really new. It is the process employed by every good exegete as he seeks to understand materials that happened thousands of years ago and then to present them in such a way that the real issues of that situation are understood by today's hearer within his cultural and subcultural frame of reference in an equivalently meaningful way so as to evoke in him an equivalent response. The matter is, however, very serious today, since there is ample evidence both within and outside the western world to indicate that Christian theology is very often either misperceived or perceived as irrelevant, not because theology is irrelevant or even often because people are unconcerned but simply because it has been presented in terms meaningful only within the would-be communicator's frame of reference. The following diagram may be helpful in indicating what is involved in transculturating or transdisciplinating from one frame of reference to another:

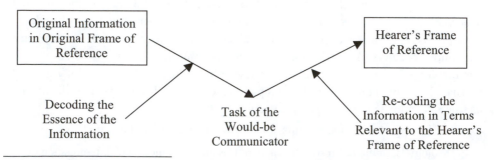

---

[3] Bengt Sundlkler, *The Christian Ministry in Africa*. (London: SCM Press, 1960), 281.

But more than relevance must be perceived by the receptor of the theologizing. It must be understood that the task of theologizing is the privilege and the responsibility of every man and of *every* group and that the Christian world is seriously deprived as long as it continues to allow theologizing to remain the private preserve of but a single discipline within a single culture. For we need the theologizing of Africans, of Asians, of Latin Americans; of psychologists, of sociologists, of chemists; of factory workers, of farmers, of engineers, of youth, of hippies, of blacks, of women's libbers, of these and a vast number of other cultural, subcultural, disciplinary and occupational groups, if we are ever to come to a better balanced understanding of God's Truth, for this Truth transcends the capacity of any single individual or group or discipline or culture to grasp fully even that portion of it that has been revealed to us. Every individual, group, discipline and culture has much to offer the rest by way of insight and specialized understanding.

A. R. Tippett, for example, testifies that it was his experience as a missionary to the Fiji people rather than his study of western theology or his experience in western churches that taught him most of what he understands to be a sound doctrine of the church.[4] A western cultural perspective, focused as it is on individuality, seems peculiarly blind to a large number of important aspects of this doctrine which, among other things, recognizes the human need for well-integrated groupness. This need Fijian culture seems to have long provided for though western behavioral scientists are just now coming to assert it. Likewise, many of us who have served in Africa can point to a heightening of our understanding of and respect for the Old Testament (even the genealogies) as a fully valid, fully inspired and still usable record of divine-human interaction, because of our exposure to cultures which are much more similar to Hebrew than to western culture.

Similarly, a recent visiting lecturer at Fuller could point to the fact that he has learned how difficult theology phrased in the language and concepts of traditional theology (i.e., the philosophico-historical frame of reference) is for even his theology students to understand, though, apparently, theology phrased in the language of psychology gets across to them very well. Apparently, he says, "psychology is their home territory linguistically."[5] Theology, therefore, if it is to be perceived as relevant by these students and by a significant proportion of the rest of America's student generation, must be translated into the linguistic and conceptual framework of the behavioral sciences—for this is where these students are. For them there ought to be a behavioral sciences-based theology rather than simply a philosophy-based theology. And if there is not such a discipline today Christian psychologists, sociologists, anthropologists and others with both behavioral science and theological credentials should he encouraged to develop one.

What is here being advocated, then, is first a recognition of certain facts with regard to the limitedness of the cultural and disciplinary perspective of what is presently known as theology—a limitedness that affects both the understanding and the transmission—of Christian theological truths—and, secondly, the need for the development (in some cases the continuing of a development already started) of a

---

[4] A. R. Tippett, private conversation.

[5] T. R. Oden, lecture entitled "Beyond Normalcy" delivered at Fuller Theological Seminary, January 3, 1972 (transcription pp. 9–10)

diversity of cultural, subcultural and disciplinary approaches to the study and presentation of theological truth. We have always recognized, of course, that truth of one kind or another is discoverable from within the framework of a multiplicity of disciplines and cultures. But we must recognize that much of this truth is of high relevance both in the understanding and the communication of God and his works. The breadth and depth of theological truth available to us in the revelation of God is simply not attainable by or containable in a single culture or a single discipline.

What is being proposed may be diagrammed as below:

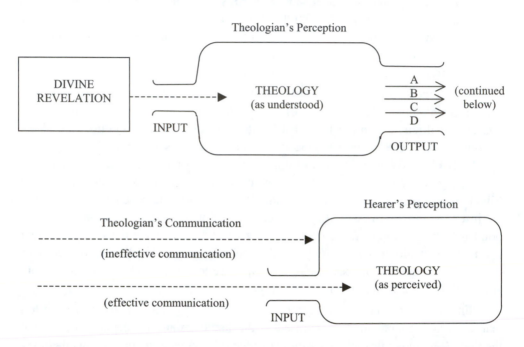

Interpretations: The theologian seeks to understand and communicate "the contents and implications" of divine revelation. These contents and implications come to him via a given perspective which he has learned through some combination of instruction and self-teaching (Input). He seeks to communicate his understanding to a given hearer—a hearer whose particular involvement in the cultural, subcultural and psychological realities of his experience have defined for him a frame of reference with a particular Input Channel which must be employed by the theologian if he wishes to be understood correctly by his hearer. If, however, the theologian simply attempts to convey the information in the same terms in which it has been conveyed to him (Output A), he will not be understood well by any except hearers tuned in to his frame of reference. He must, therefore, develop several possible Outputs to that he can choose the appropriate one to reach the prospective hearer. It should be the hearer's frame of reference (Input) that determines which of the communicator's Outputs is chosen. The process of reformulation of the information to be presented in terms of the hearer's frame of reference is that here termed transculturation. This diagram fits each of the levels (i.e., cultural, subcultural—including disciplinary, occupational, social grouping—or psychological) in focus in the above presentation.

Another approach to the communication problem is for the would-be communicator to attempt to indoctrinate his hearers into his frame of reference. This is, unfortunately, the approach taken by may theologians and preachers who steadfastly refuse to budge from the presentation of theology in almost wholly philosophical terms which they have come to regard as sacred, unlike their Lord who adopted the linguistic and cultural frame of reference of his hearers. Many missionaries likewise insists that their converts convert not only to Christ but to a western cultural understanding and verbalizing of Christian theology. Jesus' approach, however, was to phrase theological truth in terms of whatever conceptual framework was appropriate to his hearers—employing parables with the masses and Scripture with the Pharisees and Satan. Paul articulated the same approach when he stated that he sought to be a Jew to Jews and a Greek to Greeks.

Part II

In "Theology and Theologies I," I attempted to point to the difference between absolute Reality and human culturally conditioned understandings of that Reality. The Reality (God) exists outside of any culture while human beings are always bound by cultural, subcultural (including disciplinary) and psychological conditioning to perceive and interpret what we see of Reality in ways appropriate to these conditionings. The Absolute, therefore, is not perceived absolutely by culture-bound human beings.

It is, however, possible to perceive God *adequately* because he has revealed himself to man within man's cultural context. Furthermore, he has guided certain men to record their perceptions of experience with him and guided his people to preserve and pass on certain of these records for the benefit of other people, most of whom participate in quite different cultural, subcultural and psychological frames of reference than those whose perceptions have been preserved. And because 1) beyond the diversity of human frames of reference human beings participate in a pervasive common humanity, 2) the perceptions recorded in the Scriptures focus on the same unchanging God and 3) God's Spirit is active in guiding men into God's truth, the study of this inspired Casebook yields understandings adequate for human salvation and sanctification.

It is this study that has traditionally been labeled "Theology." Since, however, theological inquiry, being human and, therefore, culture-bound, yields culturally conditioned differences of perception, it seems proper to speak of "theologies" at this perceptual level. We will reserve the term 'Theology" for the absolute theological Reality that lies outside of culture in the mind of God himself, only knowable to human beings in adequate, though not absolute glimpses as through a dirty window (1 Cor. 13:12).

The object of theologies, then, is to come to ever more adequate, accurate, understandable (by the group in focus) and communicable perceptions of the glimpses of God's absolute Theology embedded in the inspired Casebook. But, since perception differs so from culture to culture (and even from subculture to subculture and discipline to discipline), understandings perfectly satisfactory for one group are frequently perceived as somewhat less than satisfactory by another.

Witness a recent change that has taken place in our own culture from a predominant concern for quantity of life (i.e., everlastingness) to a much greater concern for the quality of life (i.e., in terms of meaningfulness). Unfortunately (for modern Americans) the Greek cultural focus was also on quantity of life, leading to a comparatively greater use in the New Testament of expressions translated "eternal life" or "everlasting life" than of expressions like "abundant life." And allegiance to such a fact has kept many American Christians from recognizing that theologically it is just as appropriate to speak of Christ as offering "real" or "meaningful" life as to speak of the quantitative aspects of this life. But, since it is incumbent upon theologies that they be flexible and adaptive to the realities of the frame of reference in which they are developed and to which they seek to communicate, we do not do justice to the revelation if we cling to theological expressions appropriate in other cultures or at other times in our own culture in preference to an equally valid and much more relevant expression of the glimpse of absolute Theology involved.

Absolute supracultural Theology is not synonymous with the theology which John Calvin developed to meet the needs (as he perceived them) of sixteenth century Geneva, or with that developed by John Wesley to meet the needs (as he perceived them) of eighteenth century England, or of any of the prominent twentieth century theologians as they struggle to understand the revelation in relation to twentieth century Switzerland, Germany, England or America. These are all theologies—valuable as expressions of particular perceptions of God's Truth but not synonymous with it. These are all (at least insofar as they are true both to the inspired revelation and the surrounding cultural context) attempts to translate and transculturate the Truth of God into linguistic and cultural frame of reference of the people for whom these theologies were developed. They have no inherent claim to perpetuity except and unless people of other times and other cultures discover them (or parts of them) to be of value in their contexts as well.

Theologies, then, become a part (and an important part) of the necessary repackaging of the Christian message as it moves from culture to culture and from subculture to subculture. If theologies are properly in tune with the surrounding cultures, they will manifest differences of focus, differences of understanding and differences of expression proportionate to the differences between the cultures and subcultures in which they are involved, even though there are two strong pulls toward uniformity—the fact that theologies in order to be Christian are based upon the biblical revelation, and the fact that beyond cultural differences human beings share an extensive common humanity. But such differences of focus, understanding and expression are necessary if the theologies are to be meaningful to the consumers of these theologies.

It is tragic, therefore, when because of the prestige of a given approach to theology or a misassessment of its relevance to another group on the part of proponents who have the power to impose it on others, a given theological system (or creed based thereon) is adopted by or imposed upon those of another culture or subculture. The result is frequently an impression of such irrelevance that both the recommended theology and the quest for relevant understandings is abandoned—often with all other commitment to Christianity as well. Such is too often the case today due to the increasing divergence between the concerns and expressions of philosophical modes of thought in which much theology is still couched and the concerns of contemporary Americans. Or the situation may be more like that of many Christian churches in non-western cultures where the only approaches to theology offered to them are preoccupied with certain theological concerns of (often a former stage of) western culture. They are then forced to choose between theological domination by these approaches to theology and rebellion against the proponents of these theologies with concomitant loss of all the other valuable assistance that these churches have available to them by continuing their friendly association with western missions.

If, however, we could both understand the pressing need for the development of home-grown, culturally relevant theologies which freely borrow from, but are not dominated by, foreign models and encourage Christians everywhere in dependence upon the Holy Spirit to theologize freely, the Christian church would be much the richer. To date, though, the attitude has often been more one of repression of theological diversity, especially outside of western culture. And we of the west, as well as those of other cultures, are being denied theological insight because of this lack of positive regard and respect for the perspectives of those other cultures. For, as John V. Taylor states concerning Africa:

> Christ has been presented as the answer to the questions a white man would ask, the solution to the needs that Western man would feel, the Saviour of the world of the European world-view, the object of the adoration and prayer of historic Christendom. But if Christ were to appear as the answer to the questions that Africans are asking, what would he look like? If he came into the world of African cosmology to redeem Man as Africans understand him, would he be recognizable to the rest of the Church Universal? And if Africa offered him the praises and petitions of her total, uninhibited humanity, would they be acceptable?[6]

To an African, for example, a Christian theology that can offer no more than an impersonal western medical approach to disease is not only culturally unacceptable but Scripturally inaccurate. Africans, unlike theologians bound by a western cultural worldview, know that illness is not usually caused by mere germs. And when they study the Scriptures they find abundant confirmation of their point of view and abundant disconfirmation of the theological understandings of the west.

The African expects that anyone speaking for God will automatically concern himself with healing and exorcism. If, then, the man of God attempting to communicate Christ in traditional Africa will not or cannot address himself effectively to the illness problem, he can expect to make little if any real impact on African worldviews with his inadequate proclamation of Christian truth For he has failed to follow the example of Christ who, dealing with a people with similar expectations in this regard, combined in himself what we of the overspecialized west regard as two different tasks—the ministry of proclamation and that of healing. In

---

[6] John V. Taylor, *The Primal Vision: Christian Presence Amid African Religion* (London: SCM, 1963), 24.

this and other matters of Christian proclamation in non-western cultures, all with important theological ramifications, it is, in fact,

> an ironical thing that the West, which is most concerned with the spread of Christianity in the world today, and which is financially best able to undertake the task of worldwide evangelism, is culturally the least suited for its task because of the way in which it has specialized itself to a point where it is very difficult for it to have an adequate understanding of other peoples.[7]

So we continue to send out doctors who by training (or lack of it) and interest are very ill-prepared to conceive of or employ their skills (even if they are allowed to learn the language) in such a way as to reap maximum benefit. They do not realize that, from the African point of view, they alone among the missionaries effectively demonstrate their close contact with God by healing physical illness. And we compound the error by continuing to train and send pastors and evangelists with no knowledge of medicine who, from the African point of view, can "talk a good game" but give no convincing demonstration of their close relationship to God. High on the list of reasons why six thousand or more African independent movements have broken away from missionary Christianity is the fact that the mission churches, preoccupied with the concerns of western theologies, did not pay adequate attention to matters of health and illness[8]—matters which are to the African highly theological.

Thus the Christ that we present is only the partial Christ we have perceived from studying the Scriptures from within our cultural frame of reference. We present, therefore, only the part of God's revelation focused upon by our culturally and disciplinarily bound theologians and other expositors as providing answers to the questions in their (and our) minds. Other questions, often of prime concern to the members of another culture, have not been posed by us at all. Or, as is the case with the relationship between faith and healing, the question may have been posed but seldom taken seriously—except by Pentecostalism (which because it deals positively with this particular issue is being mightily used of God in Africa, Latin America and elsewhere).

For to Africans and multitudes of others throughout the world there may be nothing clearer in all of God's Word than the fact that God (not merely medicine) heals physical—as well as spiritual illness—unless it be the fact that God deals effectively with evil spirits. But again western theology, at least as practiced, is virtually silent or even negative toward the existence of such spirits. Likewise, the theological treatments (if any) of western Christianity regarding man in his group relationships, the spirits of the departed, the significance of ritual—including traditional naming and initiation ceremonies as well as baptism and the Lord's Supper, the place of celebration (including dance) in Christian life and worship, etc., are less than satisfying to Africans. For, from our point of view, we have specialized many of these concerns into the realm of the secular and, therefore, beyond the purview of theological consideration. But to the African, who, in spite of the

---

[7] William A. Smalley, "Cultural Implications of an Indigenous Church," *Practical Anthropology* 5(1958), 51-65.

[8] See David Barrett, *Schism and Renewal* (London: Oxford, 1968) concerning African independent churches and their reasons for breaking with traditional Christianity.

onslaughts of westernization, is still in possession of a more integrated perspective on life, these are theological issues.

Thus it is refreshing to note the recent emergence of several sincere attempts to apply African insight and perspective to the interpretation of the Bible and of theologically generalized Christian truth based on the Bible. It is, unfortunately, not without significance that this growing freedom on the part of Africans comes hand in hand with the very rapid development of African independent churches and other movements toward indigenization of Christianity in Africa. But it is a matter for rejoicing nonetheless for at least two reasons: 1) At last there is hope that African Christianity will begin to hear Christ addressing himself to a larger number of "the questions that Africans are asking," and 2) At last we of the western world will be able to have our own theological horizons broadened by being exposed to the insight of African perceptions of Christian truth.

In *New Testament Eschatology in an African Background*,[9] John S. Mbiti, the man emerging as Africa's leading theologian, struggles with the meaning of Christian eschatology to a people (his people—the Akamba) with a virtually two-dimensional concept of time (no distant future) and the implications for the Akamba worldview of the acceptance of the Christian hope. Mbiti is no mean theologian even by western standards, and thus is anything but limited to African perspectives in his treatment. Nor does he completely reject western understandings, though he finds them partial and incomplete providing only "the solution to the needs that Western man would feel." Rather, on the basis of a deep study of the Scriptures and of western interpretations plus the assumption of the potential validity of perspectives on Time other than the western past, present, future lineal concept, he concludes that the New Testament—especially those portions directed primarily to Jewish readers—can very well be interpreted from within an African culture without the prior necessity (often naively required by traditional approaches) of the African adopting a non-African concept of time.

Specifically, he sees the Hebrew two-dimensional division of time into "This Age" and "The Age to Come" united in the Incarnation into a single time-transcending, present Kingdom of God which, though looking forward to the *Parousia*, does not require a three-dimensional concept of Time as prerequisite to understanding it. An understanding of Christian eschatology may, therefore, be legitimately approached from an African two-dimensional background (even though not corresponding exactly to the two Hebrew dimensions). One result, however, of building Christian eschatology upon an African conception of time will be the invasion of the African worldview by the Christian *eschaton*, producing perhaps for the first time an African teleology. An approach to such an African-based Christian eschatology and the consequent development of an African teleology have, however, been hindered to date, Mbiti contends, by an excessive overlay of western cultural interpretations of the Scriptures to which Africans have been required to subscribe. Now, fortunately, after more than a hundred years of missionary effort in Africa, theologians like Mbiti who take seriously both Christ and African culture are beginning to emerge. He and others making similar attempts may from time to time

---

[9] London: Oxford, 1971.

err as they sail such uncharted seas—making mistakes that will be as African as the insights. But Africans now know that they can and must look directly to the Holy Spirit for their leading, and this bodes well for the future of theology in Africa.

In another volume entitled, *Biblical Revelation and African Beliefs*, Mbiti joins seven other Africans in dealing with theological issues of special relevance to Africa. The volume is the result of a consultation of African theologians which became

> an expression of a deep longing that the churches of Africa might have an opportunity of thinking together of the Christian faith which had come to them . . . through missionaries of a different cultural background who . . . could not fully appreciate the reactions of their converts to their faith in the light of their own traditional beliefs and practices.[10]

In the belief that "the urgent predicament of the Church in Africa today is that of the apparent foreignness of Christianity,"[11] these African scholars set themselves the task of discovering "in what way the Christian faith could best be presented, interpreted and inculcated in Africa so that Africans will hear God in Jesus Christ addressing himself immediately to them in their own native situation and particular circumstances."[12]

Dr. Raimo Harjula of Lutheran Theological College, Tanzania, in an unpublished paper entitled "Towards a Theologia Africana" defines Christian theology as "the critical reflection on, articulation and translation of God's self-disclosure, especially in Jesus Christ, in and for a given historical and cultural context."[13] Theology is, from this point of view, a functional, dynamic, relevant thing described by Bengt Sundkler

> as an ever-renewed re-interpretation to the new generations and peoples of the given Gospel, a re-presentation of the will and the way of the one Christ in a dialogue with new thought-forms and culture patterns. . . . Theology . . . is to understand the fact of Christ; theology in Africa has to interpret this Christ in terms that are relevant and essential to African existence.[14]

Just as in Acts 2 it is recorded that the Christian witness went forth in the various languages of the hearers, so must Christian theology be heard by Africans (and others) embodied in their own conceptual categories. For though "the Gospel is absolute . . . its framework and embodiment . . . are something relative which vary according to the historical and cultural context."[15]

An armchair European theologian like Barth, for example, can perhaps be excused for being pessimistic with respect to the value of "natural religion" if one understands his theologizing as at best designed to handle issues of concern to western theologians at a particular point in time. African Christians, however, cannot afford the luxury of such pessimism. They must provide intelligible yet Christian answers concerning what in the old ways is compatible and what is incompatible

---

[10] Kwesi Dickson and Paul Ellingworth, eds. (London: Lutterworth, 1969), vii.

[11] Ibid., 13.

[12] Ibid., 16.

[13] Harjula (Tanzania: Lutheran Theological College, n.d.), 1.

[14] *The Christian Ministry in Africa* (London: SCM Press, 1960), 211.

[15] Harjula, 4.

with Christianity. They must develop what Henri Maurier calls "A Theology of Paganism"—an understanding of "the meaning of paganisms in the history of salvation."[16] In what sense (if any) can it be maintained that "the grace of God has never deserted mankind and that, even among the pagans, some men have responded to it"?[17] Perhaps Maurier has the answer in the distinction that he makes between pagan man continually in search of God and the various non-Christian religious systems which imperfect man has created as an expression of this search. But these expressions inevitably consist of complexes of truth and error and constitute at best imperfect means and at worst obstacles to man in his search.[18] But whether or not this approach be deemed helpful to Africans (and others), there is no doubt that it attempts to deal with an issue of critical importance to Theologia Africana.

Critical also are a host of related issues of but academic importance to western theologians, such as the question of the identity or non-identity of a given tribal deity with the Christian God—or even of the son of a tribal deity and the Son of God (as among the Yala of Southeastern Nigeria). Further, "how is the Christian understanding of Creation and the 'Fall' related to the hundreds of African myths of Creation and the Supreme Being's 'departing' or 'going faraway' due to man's misdeed or misbehaviour?"[19] And what about ancestor veneration? Are those who honor their ancestors breaking the first commandment ("no other gods") or obeying the fifth ("honor your father and your mother")? And does Jesus' preaching "to the spirits in prison" (1 Pet. 3:19) hold out any hope for the salvation of Africa's ancestors? Such issues as these, as well as those related to health and spirits, can be virtually ignored by western theologians, but they are live and pressing issues in the minds and hearts of Africans. Many will turn sadly from Christ because they hear only solutions to the needs felt by western man. African theologians cannot ignore such issues.

Nor can Indian theologians ignore the equivalent issues in Indian culture as they press themselves upon the consciousness of Indian Christians. For to India as to Africa, Latin America, Oceania and other areas missionized from the West, Christianity

> has been like a pot-plant transplanted into a garden. At first it grew in its imported soil [but often someone forgot to break the pot. As time passed the roots grew large and shattered the pot from within, often to the dismay of the gardener, so that now the gardener no longer has] to bring the water of the Word from a distant source, for the plant has struck its own deep tap-root to the perennial springs. It grows larger and more luxuriant than it ever did in its bleak northern home....The western confessions have indeed been channels for bringing the Water of Life, but they are not the only ones and the Indian Church must...develop its own confessions [which will provide for the Indian churches an] understanding of the deepest Christian insights into the very nature and being of God, Christ, man and the world, and their expression in Indian language which can be understood and so accepted.[20]

---

[16] *The Other Covenant: A Theology of Paganism* (New York: Newman Press, 1968), xi.

[17] Ibid., xii.

[18] Ibid.

[19] Harjula, 7.

[20] R. H. S. Boyd, *An Introduction to Indian Theology* (Madras, 1969), 259–260.

But the Indian, African or other developer of an indigenous theology must feel himself free of the obligation to conform to the theological maxims of another culture. He may or may not have studied western theology. His guidelines, however, do not lie there but, rather, in his own Spirit-led understanding of the Scriptures and of their applicability to his own cultural world. If his theology is to be a culturally relevant expression of supracultural Theology he

> must not keep looking over his shoulder to see if he is in step with Aquinas or Calvin or Barth; rather he must 'look unto Jesus;' the hope of glory who is present in his Church.... As he does so, basing himself firmly in the Christian [Scriptures] and using all the resources of thought and terminology which are available to him, the inner, underlying Truth of the Christian faith will make itself plain.[21]

So likewise should the western theologian demand and make use of such freedom from theological expressions bound to history and culture of past times and circumstances within western societies. For, if Sundkler is right that theology is meant to be "an ever-renewed re-interpretation to . . . new generations and peoples of the given Gospel, a re-presentation of the will and the way of the one Christ in a dialogue with new thought-forms and culture patterns,"[22] this necessity for constant renewal applies just as much to the movement from generation to generation within a single society as it does to movement from culture to culture. Thus, contemporary western theologizing must not hide its head in the sand of an increasingly irrelevant philosophical disciplinary frame of reference, ignoring pressing theological problems raised by the Behavioral Sciences such as the relationship between what is absolute and what is relative. The apathy of contemporary Christians toward what western society knows as Christian theology and toward preaching based thereon provides in a more familiar context the same kind of protest against a message that promises so much but gets expressed so irrelevantly that we have alluded to above as prominent in Africa, India and other missionized areas of the world. And this protest has in both areas (the west and the "third world") issued in a lively surge toward independency which must be regarded as promising, since it will result in theological experimentation as well, with its promise of new and renewed theological insight.

"Theology and theologies." Absolute, supracultural Theology exists—outside of culture and beyond the grasp of finite, sinful human beings. But God has provided revelation of himself within the human cultural context—much of which, including detailed records of his supreme revelation in Jesus Christ, has been recorded and preserved in the Christian Scriptures. To the understanding of this revelation a variety of Spirit-led human beings apply a variety of culturally, psychologically, disciplinarily and otherwise-conditioned perceptions and develop theologies appropriate to their own insights and experiences and, hopefully, instructive to others with both similar and dissimilar backgrounds. If, as certain absolutistic theologies contend, God simply "did theology" *through* man, all Spirit-led theologies and theologians would come out with the same answers on all issues. Differences in theologies, then, would have to be explained wholly in terms of the entrance of the sin factor. More is involved, however, than simply the sin factor (though I would not

---

[21] Ibid., 261.
[22] Sundkler, 211.

want to be interpreted as denying the pervasiveness of sin in human experience)—there are sincere culturally and otherwise-conditioned differences in perception that have to be regarded as the primary factors influencing differences in theological understanding. Since the sin factor is more or less constant for everyone whatever his culture.

But in spite of both sin and culture, apparently, God chooses to work in partnership *with* (not simply *through*) man in theologizing (as in all other areas of life) and is concerned not so much with conformity, or even with the absolute correctness of the conclusions reached, as with their appropriateness to a given individual or group at the particular stage of Christian development at which he/they find themselves. If this be true we may assume that God is in favor of the development of theologies which not only derive from his revelation of himself in the Scriptures but which show a maximum of relevance to the situation out of which and for which they are developed.

CHAPTER 28

TOWARD A CHRISTIAN ETHNOTHEOLOGY

Reprinted here with permission from A. R. Tippett, ed.
God, Man and Church Growth. Grand Rapids, MI: Eerdmans, 1973:109–126

Among the significant accomplishments of Donald McGavran is the establishment of the missionary research and teaching institution at Fuller Theological Seminary.

Dr. McGavran early saw that what has come to be called "church growth theory" would lean heavily upon the disciplines of theology and anthropology. Thus competence in both disciplines came to be a prerequisite for faculty members at SWM-ICG and a major goal for those being trained. However, it is neither advisable nor possible for us to keep the disciplines separated or even to label our course offerings one or the other. In training for mission, when we deal with man in culture—ordinarily an anthropological topic—we cannot do so without reference to insights derived from theology. Nor can we usefully treat the relationship between God and man—a theological topic—without reference to an anthropological understanding of the place of culture in human experience. We have just not been able to keep the disciplines distinct. Nor has it been possible for us to make use of the totality of either discipline.

At certain points we have found it necessary to recognize a fundamental incompatibility between certain of the tenets of the two disciplines as well as a certain lack of relevance to our concerns with respect to some of the goals and subject matter of each discipline.

The original intention to "harness" anthropology and theology to the missionary task, as McGavran is fond of phrasing it, foundered to some extent on the twin rocks of general incompatibility and lack of total relevance. It has thus become a necessary part of the thinking of the SWM-ICG faculty to develop a theoretical perspective that is at once properly integrative and properly discriminating with respect to the disciplines of theology and anthropology. The purpose of this paper is to outline the dimensions of the undertaking.

The Name of the Proposed
Discipline

Ours is a day when reaction to the increasing specialization of certain major disciplines and their consequent isolation from each other has led to the initiation of a number of interdisciplinary approaches to areas of study which, due to the fact that they lie at the periphery of more than one of the established disciplines, have often been neglected. Thus, with the developing of the widespread interest in the non-Western world (and wealth and leisure to pursue it) a number of "cross-disciplines" have sprung up between areas of study heretofore specializing on a single aspect of Western culture and the relevant part of cultural anthropology. There are now, for example, areas of study known as ethnohistory, ethnomusicology, ethnolinguistics, ethnopsychology, ethnobotany and the like which attempt to study their subject matter from either a cross-cultural or a non-Western perspective.

Thus we may conceive of a cross-discipline, labeled *Christian ethnotheology*, that takes both Christian theology and anthropology seriously while devoting itself to an Interpretive approach to the study of God, man and divine-human interaction. From theology such a discipline would draw understandings of eternal (absolute) truths relating each of the areas it treats. From anthropology it would draw cultural (relative) truths and perceptions concerning these areas. Such a discipline would have both a theoretical and a practical component, the latter of which might consist largely of the "harnessing" both of anthropology and of theology for the purpose of bringing about more effective cross-cultural communication of the gospel of Jesus Christ.

Note that this proposal is for a specifically *Christian ethnotheology*, based pointedly on a wedding of *Christian* theology with anthropology. There are other theologies which might form the theological component of a more broadly conceived discipline. And it might be that at some point the proponents of these theologies would want to develop such a study. The aim here, however, is not that more broadly conceived discipline but one that is of specific relevance to those who take Christianity seriously.

However, Christian ethnotheology would not simply serve as a handmaiden of missions. It would as well serve the needs of any person or group who sought to retain belief in an absolute God (as anthropology does not) and a responsible yet culture-bound man (concepts on which theology is generally weak). Within Christian ethnotheology, for example, the pressing problem of what is absolute and what is relative in human experience can be worked out. And any insights into this problem would be of much wider relevance than simply to missionary work. One (perhaps the) major application of Christian ethnotheology, however, would be to Christian missions.

The study of Christian ethnotheology is not new, however. The proposed label is the main innovation. The informal development of such a discipline has been underway at least since the early fifties, notably through the efforts of E. A. Nida, W. A. Smalley, W. D. Reyburn, J. A. Loewen and others associated with the

American Bible Society (Translation Department). The journal *Practical Anthropology* has been perhaps the major participant. Books such as Nida's *Customs and Cultures* (1954) and especially *Message and Mission* (1960), Luzbetak's *The Church and Cultures* (1963), McGavran's *Bridges of God* (1955), and *Understanding Church Growth* (1970) have played an important part as well. Furthermore, the studies going on in such institutions as the Kennedy School of Missions (now unfortunately defunct), the Anthropology Department of Wheaton College, Jaffray School of Missions, SWM-ICG and elsewhere has to a great extent fallen into this category.

Not all students are able to achieve integration of the various elements or the necessary balance between the relativism of anthropology and the absolutism of theology. Many, going to the theological extreme, have absolutized some western cultural approach to Christianity and sought to convert people to that particular expression of Christianity. Others, however, led to the opposite extreme by an guarded exposure to anthropology, have virtually relativized the essentials of Christianity, as if Christianity were but one of the myriad of cultural expressions of religion. Certainly the need for a balanced, integrating approach to the subject matter of theology and anthropology is urgent.

Why Can This Not be Done as a Part of the Study of Theology?

Ideally it should be possible to treat Christian ethnotheology as a subdiscipline of theology. Indeed, it is hoped that the not too distant future the administrators of theological institutions will see the great urgency for the kind of serious approach to such problems as that of absolutivity versus relativity that is to be a major focus of Christian ethnotheology. But at present, it appears, Evangelical Theology at least is more concerned with defending its basic tenets an with developing them.

Christian ethnotheology would, for example, examine all the basic formulations of Christian theology to determine just which of these formulations represent eternal Truth and may, therefore, be presented to the Christians of another culture (or subculture) as essential parts of Christianity, and which represent discussible theories or interpretations of such Truth, and therefore should be regarded in a cross-cultural situation as the attempts of the Christians of a given culture to come to an understanding of eternal Truth. A disturbingly high percentage of the formulations of western theology seems to fit into the latter category. As the theologian F. R. Tennant admits:

> . . . the doctrine of Original Sin is not contained in the Old Testament and the only unmistakable presentation of it that can be found in the New does not appear to have been the starting-point for the first framers of the ecclesiastical doctrine. Tertullian set out from stoic psychology, Origen from the institution of infant baptism and also from the myth of Plato concerning the fall of the soul from the celestial sphere into earthly life (1962:22, 63).

Thus Christian ethnotheology would attempt to distinguish carefully what in Christian doctrine is supracultural revelation from God, (defined below) and what is the cultural "enclothing" of this revelation in terms meaningful either to those who originally received the revelation or to those in another culture (e.g., ours) to whom it has been transmitted in the Bible and interpreted by theologians. In so seeking to understand the message it would be necessary to divest the theological interpretation of such modifications as the pervasive influence of Greek philosophy on western theology and the tendency to absolutize certain elements of western culture by attributing them (often wrongly) to Christian influence on our culture.

The study of Christian theology has a long and venerable history within western culture. Western theology however, has become so specialized in approaching reality from a single valuable and necessary (philosophical) perspective that it seems unable at present to adequately tackle certain problems which have only recently begun to attract our attention. Typically, for example, western theology is apt at describing eternal verities, such as the attributes of God, the sinfulness of man and the faith-remedy for man's plight. However, it is not nearly so able to deal with questions such as: What is the permissible range of valid human perception of God? Or, what is the permissible range of valid human response to God? Or even, what changes in behavior are preconditional to a relationship with God? Nor is western theology very helpful in providing Christians with a principled approach as to which of the commands of Scripture speak most significantly to a twentieth century American. What, for example, is the principle by means of which one decides that the Old Testament injunction against stealing is to be strictly obeyed but the New Testament command that women cover their heads when praying (1 Cor. 11:5, 10, 12) may be ignored?

When both the students of theology and those to whom they seek to communicate Christian truth share a degree of cultural homogeneity and experience many such questions do not seem pressing. When one attempts to proclaim the gospel message relevantly to those of another culture, however, one is faced with these and myriads of unexpected questions that our theology has not taught us to deal with. How, for example, does one explain the difference between the stealing and head covering commands to an African who has come to understand that since the Bible is God's Word its commands are to be obeyed, yet observes that not a single missionary woman covers her head when praying? One such African once said to me, "You missionaries live by a different Bible than the one you give us!" Likewise, is the permissible range of valid human perception of and response to God wide enough to allow those of mission lands to identify with the Christian God and to respond to him in their own way. Or must Christianity set up a competing system, which presents God in terms only of our Christian perception of him, advocates response to him after our patterns, and recommends or requires behavioral changes in them that make them behave more like us?

The strengths of our theology lie in the fact that it has been developed especially to deal with the problems in western culture, and to do so in a way that we regard as appropriate. Thus since our culture demands it, western theology is absolutistic—we demand that there be only one right way to do or think about a thing. There can be no such thing as differing, but equally valid theologies, systems church organization, patterns of witness and preaching, understandings of moral behavior, etc. Our culture tells us there is only one right way—the rest are heretical. This absolutism is applied not only to doctrines which are clearly expressions of absolute Truth (such as the that God created the universe) but, frequently, also to the much more discussible matter as to exactly how God what he did. We often reason, for example, that since God could have created the universe in seven literal days, therefore, he must have done it that way.

Furthermore, western theology tends to be monocultural in its perspective—often looking at the biblical cultures (especially Greek culture) as direct antecedents of our own and interpreting biblical events as if they form a part of a historical and cultural continuum which has over thousands of years at last progressed to the pinnacle on which our "Christian (or nearly Christian) culture" stands. In keeping with our western philosophy of history, many westerners see our culture as the product of such cultural development, denying our real cultural roots among the illiterate pagan tribes of western Europe in favor of a much more flattering (and recorded) Greek (and sometimes even Hebrew) ancestry.

Western theology, furthermore, springing as it has from Greek philosophy, has adopted almost entirely philosophical models of thought. As F. R. Tennant has said, "the very terms and conceptions . . . into which the relatively undefined traditional beliefs of the early Church . . . (were cast) were supplied by Creek philosophy" (1962:22, 63). Theology has therefore focused mainly upon thought, reason and the propositionalization of Christian truth and experience. And this is all well and good as long as one is living within the culture which feels that philosophical abstraction is the appropriate mode to apply to theologizing. But there are other methods of abstracting from experience (ritualizing, for example, is a very common method in many cultures as it was among the Hebrews) and there are many other forms of philosophy than the one(s) we know.

Under the influence of philosophy, theology has often taken a negative attitude toward what it has understood to be culture—usually on the basis of an incorrect identification of culture with "the world" which, according to certain Scriptures, is a source of stumbling to the Christian. Nor does it take a positive attitude toward more informed (often anthropological) treatments of culture since they tend to start from a relativistic position unacceptable to theology. Thus, unless western theology shows a greater flexibility, it would seem that the creation of a new discipline integrating theology and anthropology is called for.

Why Not Simply Look to Anthropology for Ethnotheological Insight?

If it is true that western theology would be unreceptive to the spawning of Christian ethnotheology it is perhaps doubly true that anthropology as we know it does not provide a friendly atmosphere for its development, for much anthropology completely relativizes God and theology. In spite of indications of a certain wistfulness on the part of some anthropologists for some sort of standard of measurement between cultures, anthropology has by and large turned from any possibility of dealing with absolutes.

Christian ethnotheology in the hands of anthropology, therefore, would be reduced to a mere study of competing equally valid approaches to the understanding of the supernatural. It would thus be indistinguishable from studies such as comparative mythology or "primitive" religion. This is not what is intended here. Christian ethnotheology would seek to avoid relativizing God every bit as much as to avoid absolutizing culture.

Furthermore, anthropology as it has developed within its own form of increasingly naturalistic western culture itself betrays its own form of culture-boundness in that it refuses even to consider the possible existence of absolutes (other than "universals") either within or outside of culture. Christian ethnotheology believes in absolutes—not as western theology proposes perhaps, but far more than anthropology admits.

Contributions of Theology and Anthropology to Christian Ethnotheology

Christian ethnotheology needs both disciplines—the one to inform it concerning absolutes, the other to deal with culture, man and even God at the level of human perception. statements of each discipline, however, will have to be evaluated in the light of the other. The ethnotheological conclusion then, may side with either, both, or neither of the source disciplines. For example:

Theological Understanding	Anthropological Understanding	Ethnotheological Understanding
1. God created man.	People of each culture create their own god(s) as an idealization of themselves.	God created man. Man perceives God in terms meaningful in his culture. This human perception will always be influenced by culture and sin.
2. God reveals himself to man.	Man thinks he receives communication from a supernatural source.	God reveals himself to man in terms appropriate to man's cultural perception.

Theological Understanding	**Anthropological Understanding**	**Ethnotheological Understanding**
3. Christianity absolutely valid (tends to define Christianity in western philosophic terms)	Christianity but one of many valid cultural expressions of religion (sees no absolute model. only cultural expressions of Christianity)	Supracultural Christianity absolutely valid. Must be distinguished from its cultural expressions and transmitted apart from them.
4. Western culture more Christian than other cultures.	All cultures valid and relatively comparable to each other in terms of their ability to cope with reality.	All cultures usable by God as vehicles for his interaction with man.
5. Man pervasively sinful and needing redemption.	Man the product of his culture.	Culture the vehicle of Satan as well as of God. Man and culture pervasively sinful and needing redemption.

It may appear from the above chart that Christian ethnotheology leans more heavily on theology than upon anthropology. This is to some extent true, especially with regard to basic theological tenets such as 1, 2, 3, and 5 above. However, it should be noted that in every case above the statement of ethnotheological understanding involves a mention of the place of culture in the understanding. And, since theology virtually ignores culture; this is a contribution from anthropology. The areas of concern of the two disciplines may be diagrammed as follows:

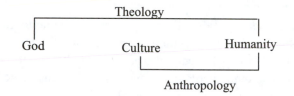

Or alternatively, we may see theology dealing with man encircled by God, anthropology with man encircled by culture, but Christian ethnotheology as treating all three thus:

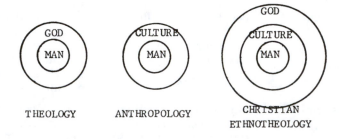

Theology, as it were, reduces the place of culture to insignificance (mainly, of course, due to historical reasons). Anthropology, on the other hand, refuses to consider an absolute God. Hence the need for a more balanced approach.

The Cultural and the
Supracultural

One of the major quests of Christian ethnotheology will the understanding of what in Christianity is absolute, supracultural and valid for any church at any time, and that which is cultural, relative, and valid for a single culture only. God of course, is supracultural. He stands outside of culture and is not bound by culture unless he chooses to be bound by it. Man however, is immersed in culture and unable to escape his culture-boundness.

God however, from outside of culture reveals himself to man in terms meaningful to culture-bound humanity and elicits from at least certain men responses acceptable to himself. He indwells certain human beings, leading them act within the cultural context on his behalf and even once became a human participant within a culture himself. And some of his interactions with men have been recorded—interactions which happened in particular cultures and were recorded in particular languages and collected in case-book fashion in a Book which in translated form has come down to us.

And it is this document preeminently that provides for us both the demonstration that God chooses to meet man where lie is culturally and the source from which we seek to discern that which is supracultural—which was only relevant to the original participants in the interaction. Likewise we learn from an ethnotheological approach to the Bible something of what God is willing to start with, with respect to human perception of himself and supracultural Truth.

One approach to this aspect of ethnotheological investigation would be to seek to fill out the following incomplete illustrative chart. Note that in the left hand column are listed certain supracultural truths, while the larger right hand column is divided into two parts labeled "less ideal" (at the far right) and "more ideal." This is to show the possibility of differential perception of supracultural truth within the cultural context and of the possibility of movement from a less ideal to a more ideal (i.e., more close approximation to the supracultural model) understanding of the mind of God in each matter. Note however, the line between cultural perception and supracultural is uncrossable (at least this side of heaven).

Supracultural Truth *(The Mind of God)*	*Cultural Perception of Supracultural Truth*	
Absolute Truth	Growth in Relative Understanding	
	More Ideal Understanding ←———————	Less Ideal Understanding
The Great Cardinal Doctrines of Scripture		
God exists	Close, Personal	Distant, Impersonal

Supracultural Truth (The Mind of God)	Cultural Perception of Supracultural Truth		
God interacts with man	Direct and warm	Direct but cool	Indirect, Judgmental
Man created in God's image	Understanding implications		
God accepts man on a basis of faith	Well-nigh total commitment		Small, kernel faith
Don't steal	Coveting equals stealing	From anyone	From ingroup
Don't commit adultery	Lust equals adultery	With anyone	With married person

Cultural Relativism in Ethnotheological Perspective

One of the most important tasks of Christian ethnology (and a primary reason why this discipline is of wider relevance than simply to Christian missions) is to deal with the matter of the doctrine of cultural relativity from an informed Christian point of view. I would like by of illustration to outline the method in which the suggested discipline would deal with this issue.

Cultural relativism is a doctrine developed by anthropology which, maintains that "each culture may be evaluated in its own terms" and therefore, "it is objectively impossible 'to distinguish worldwide levels of cultural progress'" (Beals and Hoijer 1965:720). That is, cultures are to be regarded not as assignable to some level of overall superiority or inferiority to other cultures, but rather as more or less equal to each other overall and of equal validity to their own members. Each culture therefore, is valid for those immersed in it but not for those of another culture.

"Cultural relativism," said Melville Herskovits, one of its most active advocates,

> is a philosophy which, in recognizing the values set up by every society to guide its own life, lays stress on the dignity inherent in every body of custom, and on the need for tolerance of conventions though they may differ from one's own, instead of underscoring differences from absolute norms . . . the relativistic point of view brings into relief the validity of every set of norms for the people whose lives are guided by them, and the values these represent.

"The very core of cultural relativism," he continues, "is the discipline that comes of respect for differences—of mutual respect" (Herskovits 1951:77).

This doctrine is therefore, on the cultural level, what personal acceptance is on the individual level. It recommends that, rather than moralizing about the good or bad in the given culture (or in the given individual), the proper attitude to take has nothing to do with whether or not one approves of the behavior of that culture (or individual). Nor does it imply any change or desire for change of the evaluator's behavior in the direction of the cultural (or individual) behavior being considered, it simply means that one should take seriously, respect and accept the culture (or the individual's behavior) as in some overall sense valid for those immersed in it.

The previously prevalent attitude (against which this doctrine developed) was that of the cultural evolutionists who, strongly influenced by the traditional ethnocentrism of western culture, and the attempts of scholars to apply Darwinism to social theory, "saw individual cultures mainly as illustrative of particular stages in a world-wide evolutionary sequence" (Beals and Hoijer 1965:720) with our so-called "civilized" (European) cultures at the top and the technically less developed cultures arranged in descending order down to the most "primitive." This ethnocentrism was developed in the crucible of a society which tends "to arrange objects on a single scale of value from best to worst, biggest to smallest, cheapest to most expensive, etc." (Mead 1947:113)—a society which insists on evaluating all other perspectives toward life either as black or white, good or bad, superior or inferior. Since "judgments are based on experience, and experience is interpreted by each individual in terms of his enculturation" (Herskovits 1948:78), cultural difference is interpreted by Euroamericans as cultural inferiority.

> In a culture where absolute values are stressed, the relativism of a world that encompasses many ways of living will be difficult to comprehend. Rather, it will offer a field-day for value-judgments based on the degree to which a given body of customs resembles or differs from those of Euro-American culture (Herskovits 1948:78).

However, while much of the western world holds (at least nominally) the relativistic viewpoint, the western church (reinforced by monocultural theology) and the rest of the population retain the evolutionary position. Often the western church has falsely equated cultural and moral relativism, rejecting the former on the presupposition that any relativism is a threat to Christianity and/or the Euroamerican way of life. Furthermore, much of western Christianity associates a supposed superiority of western culture to western Christianity, and this has led to the diffusion of the evolutionary, ethnocentric view of the cultures of mankind.

Yet Christian applied anthropologists, studying the cross-cultural operations of the church, have considered what Nida calls a position of "relative cultural relativism." This position does not deny the presence of absolutes but relates all absolutes to God, who stands outside of culture, rather than to any cultural expression, description or exemplification of a God-man relationship (be it American, Greek or Hebrew). "The only absolute in Christianity," says Nida in what may be an overstatement, "is the triune God. Anything which involves man, who is finite and limited, must of necessity be limited, and hence relative" (Nida 1954:282).

Nida and other Christian ethnotheologians see a "biblical cultural relativism" as "an obligatory feature of our incarnational religion," asserting that "without it we would either absolutize human institutions" (as theologians often do) or, going to the other extreme (as anthropologists often do), "we would relativize God" (Nida 1954:282). This biblical relativism maintains that the absolute God in his interaction with man takes into account the relativity of the human situation in least three respects. His expectation with regard to human beings is conditioned and therefore relative with respect to: 1) The endowment and opportunities of people (Mt. 25:14–

30; Lk. 12:48). 2) The extent of revelation (Rom. 2:14; cf. Lev. 24:20; Deut. 23:6 and Mt. 5:38-39, 44). 3) The cultural patterns of society (e.g., the Old Testament sanctions slavery (Lev. 25:39–46), trial by ordeal (Num. 5), polygamy (2 Sam. 12:7-8) and divorce (Deut. 24:1–4). None of these were sanctioned in the New Testament, while divorce was challenged (Mt. 5:31–32, Mk. 10:2–12). Paul sought to be "all things to all men" culturally (1 Cor. 9:20–21). (Also contrast Gal. 2:11–16 with Acts 21:24, and Acts 16:3 with Gal. 2:3.)

"Biblical relativism" Nida continues:

> is not a matter of inconsistency, but a recognition of the different cultural factors which influence standards and actions. While the Koran attempts to fix for all time the behavior of Muslims, the Bible clearly establishes the principle of relative relativism, which permits growth, adaptation and freedom, under the Lordship of Jesus Christ . . . The Christian position is not one of static conformance to dead rules, but of dynamic obedience to a living God (1954:52).

However, many persons (Christians and non-Christians) assume that if cultures are relative, the proclamation of Christianity across cultural boundaries is invalid. "What right have we to change their culture?" they ask, "They are happy as they are." These questions imply two false assumptions, 1) that the primary aim of cross-cultural proclamation is to destroy culture patterns, and 2) that Rousseau's "happy savage" exists.

While one could not contend that everything done cross-culturally in the name of Christianity had avoided culture change In some way or other, or that it had not often led to physical hardship; nevertheless ethnotheologians would challenge both the above assumptions. Beyond the fact of the wide diversity in cultures, there are other facts of commonality that need to be focused on. Some of these, though long implicit in theology of the human condition, are now receiving attention from certain anthropologists. These commonalities provide Christian ethnotheology with an anthropological as well as a theological base for cross-cultural communication of the supra-cultural gospel, without the necessity of culture change as a presupposition.

The respected anthropologist, Walter Goldschmidt of UCLA, for example, states that "people are more alike than cultures . . . There is" he continues, "a good deal of evidence that, for instance, the average Zuni and the average Kwakluti man behave a good deal more like each other than the normative patterns of the two cultures are alike." He suggests that this recognition be interpreted not merely as "an expression of the limitations of culture," but as an insight into "the nature of man *to which culture must adapt*" (Goldschmidt 1966:134–135, italics mine). Relativity, therefore, though applying to cultures does not apply to basic man.

Goldschmidt then goes on to specify a series of generalizations concerning cross-cultural human similarity which suggest (among other things) that they may be universals: 1) the presence of deep dissatisfaction, selfishness, exploitiveness and conflict in every culture and 2) a longing for escape from all of this into "some kind of symbolic eternity." Furthermore, he asserts the presence of communal groupings which involve individuals in patterns of activity in which they share with other persons is not (as Montague and others have suggested) to be interpreted as indicating "that man is . . . fundamentally a loving creature," but rather, as dictating that humanity needs institutional devices "to preserve society against the essential self-interest of the human individual" (1966:136).

An Integrated View of God, Culture and Man

By drawing insights from both theology and anthropology Christian ethnotheology may arrive at conclusions concerning both the relativity of culture and the essential oneness of mankind, including his lostness in sin—in spite of the cultural differences in perceptions and expressions of this sinfulness. Drawing from theology alone our discipline may arrive at conclusions regarding God's provision for man's need and the supracultural condition (i.e., faith) for meeting that need. We then turn to anthropology for the techniques of cross-cultural communication of this supracultural message in terms meaningful within the hearer's culture. Basic to the employment of these techniques is the understanding derived from anthropology that the hearer's culture is valid and logical and must be taken seriously by the communicator. Furthermore understanding derived from a culture-conscious interpretation of the Bible, that a supracultural God is willing and anxious to accept any culture without pre-condition) as a vehicle of his interaction with culture-bound man is an axiom of ethnotheology.

On a basis of these and other insights arrived at through the study of Christian ethnotheology the matrix can be developed that will issue in the kind of integrated approach to God, culture and man that has been tabulated below.

Christian Ethnotheology

GOD	CULTURE	MAN
A. God Exists Outside of Culture Supracultural-Transcendent	Cultural Diversity a Fact	Basic Human Similarity a Fact
B. God Ordains Culture - To Restrain Human Self-Interest - To Channel Human Potential - As Areas for His Interaction with Man	Functional Relative Validity of Culture Each Culture More or Less Adequate Reflects Man's Organizational Ability	Human Total Involvement in Culture
C. God Provides Ultimate Meaning for Man	Culture Always Lopsided Reflects Man's Sinfulness	An Individual's Culture Can Never Provide Complete Satisfaction

Theological Understanding	Anthropological Understanding	Ethnotheological Understanding
D. God Desires to Answer Man's Problem No Matter How He Perceives It	Each Society Defines Its Own 'Hang-ups'	An Individual's Perception of the Problems and Their Answers Are Culturally Determined
E. God Seeks Man	The Ultimate Answer to Cultural Lopsidedness Comes from Outside Culture	An Individual's Perception of the Supracultural Is in Terms of His Own Culture
F. God Will Be Found by Those Who Diligently Seek Him (Hebrews 11:6)	Cultural Lopsidedness Challenges People to Seek God	An Individual's Search Is Culturally Channeled
G. Missionaries Are to Serve Both as Discoverers of the Culturally-Expressed Need for God and as Proclaimers of the Answer	Culture Contact Is Often an Instrument for Stimulating this Search	The Individual's Perspective May Be Broadened, His Discomfort Increased and/or His Search Ended

EXAMPLES OF
CONTEXTUALIZATION

CHAPTER 29

CONTEXTUALIZING COMMUNICATION

Reprinted here with permission from Dean S. Gilliland, ed.
The Word Among Us. Dallas, TX: Word, 1989:121–138

It's any Sunday morning in almost any church in the world. The procedure is virtually identical no matter what country no matter what language the meeting is conducted in. The meeting starts with an introductory word followed by prayer, followed by a song consisting of words in the national language wedded more or less appropriately to a Western tune. After that come the reading of some passage of Scripture, another prayer, other songs, an offering, and an intellectual discourse, presented in monologue fashion concerning some topic suggested by the Scripture reading. A benediction or another prayer follows the sermon and people go home with little carryover of what they have heard and done into their daily lives.

In the remote area of northeastern Nigeria where I served as a missionary, one frequent response to such church meetings was the question, "Why does the Christian God not respect our old men?" I was told that any meeting in which the older men who led the village were not allowed to speak first was considered an insult to them and to the village as a whole.

I was also made aware of the fact that Western hymn tunes gave the impression that God endorsed Western music and condemned their traditional music. Furthermore, speaking intellectually rather than practically or pictorially in the sermons gave the impression that only those who went to Western schools and learned to think like white men would be able to understand what these messages were about and, therefore, be acceptable to God. And speaking about a God who used to do wonderful things but who is apparently powerless to do such things in the present provided very little reason for following Christ. People, therefore, found the primary attraction of Christianity to be in the things offered by Western culture, not in the things spoken of in the Bible.

But Africa is not the only place we can speak of. J. B. Phillips says an experience he had with a group of British youth during the Second World War helped propel him into doing a contextualized translation of the New Testament. In response to their experience of Christianity couched in antique language, antique buildings, antique forms of worship, and often led by antique people, these youth assumed that God was "an old gentleman who lived in the past and was rather bewildered by modern progress" (Phillips 1954:65). Many in the Western world would concur with these youth concerning such an impression of Christianity. They would say that it stems from the pervasive out-of-dateness and irrelevance that are by-products of the vehicles used to communicate Christian messages.

These few things are but the tip of the iceberg when we begin to consider the widespread impression that Christianity is irrelevant to the real lives of peoples. Who would ever guess from the way Christianity is presented that God is our contemporary?[1] Yet, in Jesus, God's desire to be understood as relevant and important to contemporary human life led him to so contextualize himself as a human being that he was not even recognized by most of the people of his day. He looked too human.

For the Incarnation is the ultimate contextualization of the Christian message, since with messages aimed at affecting life, "the person who communicates the . . . message is not only the vehicle of the message, but the major component of the message" (Kraft 1983:62). If such a message is not contextualized in human life, then, it ceases to be true to what God intended, and the message, as presented, becomes to some extent heretical.

This kind of contextualization, taught by Jesus through demonstration, was carried on by his disciples and articulated by Paul in 1 Corinthians 9:19–22. Our task as contemporary disciples of Jesus is, then, to live our lives in a way that is "dynamically equivalent"[2] to those of Jesus' first disciples. Yet our theological curricula, ostensibly designed to teach us to minister as Jesus and his first followers ministered, tend to ignore this dimension rather completely.

---

[1] Phillips was one of the most articulate early advocates in the traditional church world for what we are now calling contextualization. In each of his books (many based on talks broadcast over the radio) he contends for a perception of God and Christianity as relevant, contemporary and meaningful to moderns. A similar movement was going on within missionary thinking, with Eugene Nida and others associated with the American Bible Society leading the way. It is interesting that much of the impetus for the contextualization movement has come from those involved in Bible translation (e.g., Phillips, Nida, Smalley, Reyburn, Loewen, Taber, Kraft).

[2] The term "dynamic equivalence" was developed by Eugene Nida to designate an approach to Bible translation that gives primary attention to "the degree to which the receptors of the message in the receptor language respond to it in substantially the same manner as [did] the receptors in the source language" (Nida and Taber 1969:69). The best Bible translations in English (e.g., Good News Bible, Phillips) and in many other languages are produced in accordance with this theory. In Kraft 1979a I have expanded the use of this concept to speak of a "dynamically equivalent" Christianity in which churches, theologizing, conversion, cultural transformation, and other aspects of our understandings and expressions of the gospel messages approximate the understandings and expressions of those messages recommended in the Scriptures. Though the term *contextualization* is more widely used, my preference would be to describe a truly biblical contemporary expression of Christianity as dynamically equivalent to what the Scriptures indicate to be God's desire.

Communication as a Valid Theological Topic

Our God is a communicating God. His desire to communicate with his creatures is obvious from the very beginnings of human existence. He no sooner had created humans than he began to talk to them (Gen. 1:28–30). He who spoke the universe into being chose to speak to the highest of his created beings. For reasons I cannot claim to understand, he seems to have an incurable love affair with humans. And he works hard to communicate his concern.

In communicating to humans, then, he chooses to express himself in ways human beings can understand and respond to. His concern is to be understood, so he chooses ways that will be intelligible at our end of the process. Though his thoughts and ways are high above ours (Isa. 55:8-9), he chooses to limit himself to human vehicles when he relates to us.

This being true, it is unfortunate that communication is not more firmly established as a legitimate theological specialization.[3] For example, dealing with the deity of Christ is considered a "must" in every theological curriculum. But Jesus' favorite name for himself did not focus on his deity but on his humanity. He regularly referred to himself as "Son of Man," a designation intended to assert his relationship with humans.

If we see Jesus as a kind of bridge between God and humans, it is significant that Jesus so frequently emphasized the relationships at the human end of that bridge. For at this end the name of the game is communication. And, apart from his carrying out the plan of salvation, it was the communication of God's messages to humans to which he devoted his ministry. To neglect the communicational aspects of the activity of the triune God is, therefore, to miss a major part of what he did and said.

It is, therefore, highly appropriate in any treatment of the contextualization of biblical Christianity to address the contextualization of the communication of that message initiated by God for the sake of his errant creatures. At least three principles can be observed as basic to God's communicative activity (see Kraft 1979a, 1979b, 1983, as well as Nida 1960 and Hesselgrave 1978 for further elaboration of these points).

Our God Is a Relational God

God's communicational aim is not simply to inform. He desires a relationship with his creatures. They may philosophize about him or about that relationship. But

---

[3] Unfortunately, there seem to be very few attempts to deal with a theology of communication. Webber 1980; Kraft 1979a, 1979b, 1983; and Jorgensen 1986 are among the works that at least partly tackle the subject.

that philosophizing or theologizing is merely a by-product, never to be confused with his true aim: to relate and interact with humans.

And this relating is a living thing. He does not treat his people as "faceless." They are treated as genuinely alive within their contexts and it is the concern of a living, life-giving God to relate "life to life" with them. This is why mere words can only point to, never contain, the Christian message. This message is a "life" or "person" message and can only be adequately conveyed in and through life. That life and the relationship that feeds it can be spoken about; but it can only really be portrayed incarnationally—in human flesh.

It is theologically significant, therefore, that the medium must be life, not simply words. Words can convey information (e.g., a news broadcast). But only life can convey relationship. The fact that God is relational and the message incarnational must inform all of our efforts to communicate it to others (see Kraft 1983 for more on this subject).

Our God Is Self-Revealing

No one can coerce God into communicating. He communicates of his own free will. Furthermore, he is not passive. He chooses to reach out to make himself known to his creatures. Even though as humans we have continually distanced ourselves from him through rebellion, God has chosen to seek to make contact with us.

This pattern is first displayed in the Garden of Eden (Gen. 3). Adam had disobeyed God and, therefore, forfeited his right to God's favor. At that point, God could legitimately have called off the whole experiment. But the very evening of their disobedience we find God walking in the garden calling out to the man, "Where are you?" (Gen. 3:9).

As with Adam, so with us—God himself takes the initiative in the communication process. It is theologically noteworthy that he neither neglects us nor waits for us to seek him. As Jesus said, his purpose in coming is "to seek and to save the lost" (Lk. 19:10). God speaks; God acts. And in so doing he opens up the communicational channels by means of which we can be aware of and respond to him.

Our God Wants To Be Understood

He does nothing simply to perform or show off and is not content if people merely think well of him or admire him. Impressive church buildings, flowery language, and majestic music do not adequately represent his true nature. For he is in the business of communicating, not impressing.

As with any good communicator, he wants people to interpret what he says and does in such a way that they get his point and respond to it. For this to happen, he enters the frame of reference of those he seeks to reach, employing their languages, their cultures, their ways of life—and ultimately in Jesus—even human form to get his messages across.

Any theology of the Incarnation should, therefore, deal with the implications of such an approach to communication (see Nida 1960), for it both informs us concerning the nature of God and provides us with an inspired model for our own efforts to serve him.

God's way of working for relating, revealing, and being understood is to contextualize his messages within the language, culture, and thought forms of the people he seeks to reach.

The Contextual Nature of God's Communicational Activity

In seeking insight into the nature of God's communication, we look to the Bible as the source of basic understandings and to our experience for confirmation and reinforcement of what we find there. Though all interpretation is strongly influenced by experience, the inspired biblical record of certain of the past experiences of certain of the people of God is normative. We turn to the Bible, then, to measure and regulate even our own experiences.

When Paul speaks of living like a Jew to win Jews, like a Gentile to win Gentiles, and like the weak in faith to win the weak in faith (1 Cor. 9:20–22), he is making a statement concerning God's approach to communication. He presents God as a contextualizer, one who adapts his approach to the context of those he seeks to reach. We should not assume that the fact that God's message is the same for all peoples requires a single, simple approach to getting it across.

Rather, God practices what I have called "communicational love" (Kraft 1979a:23). His orientation is to do whatever is necessary to put the receptor at ease, at whatever expense to himself. This means that:

1. God *chooses human media* as those he will use to reach humans.[4] The rules of human communication require that people who wish to interact understandably must function within the same frame of reference. To interact, they will need to make use of symbols (such as words and gestures) to which they will attach agreed-upon meanings.[5] The frame of reference will define how the meanings are to be attached to the symbols used. In human experience, the primary frames of reference are cultural and, beyond culture, "human commonality" (see point 3 below).

---

[4] See Jorgensen 1986 for an excellent treatment of the church as God's primary medium of communication.

[5] As communication theorist Berlo asserts in a classic statement concerning the relationship of meaning to people, messages, and symbols, "meanings are in people not in messages. . . . The elements and structure of a language . . . are only symbols. . . . Meanings are not transmittable. . . . Only messages are transmittable, and meanings are not in the message, they are in the message-users" (Berlo 1960:175). See also Condon 1975 and Hiebert 1985 on symbols and meanings.

Presumably God could have required that humans interact with him in his own frame of reference. If this were the case, we would have to learn a special divine language and culture in order to relate to him. Though these would undoubtedly be more precise than human languages and cultures can be, the effort required to learn them would be enormous. And only after they were learned could any meaningful communication between Creator and creature take place.

Though human cultural vehicles (including language) are pitifully inadequate and imprecise as media for conveying God's messages, he has chosen to humble himself to use them. At all points in the Scriptures we see God's revelation in human life and thought. Indeed, this is true to such an extent that the greatest challenge for an exegete is to disentangle God's eternal truths from the cultural trappings (especially the worldview assumptions and values) in terms of which they are presented (see Kraft 1989 for more on this).

By way of contrast, it is often the human practice to require those of another language and culture to adapt to the frame of reference of the communicator. The latter has the power, as it were, to require people to move his or her way if they are to understand and relate. Note, for example, how often highly schooled persons (including preachers) require that those who listen to them understand their language and adapt to their customs as preconditions to relating to them. Preachers and those who have attended church for a long time are often so used to using the jargon of the theology classroom and of antique Bible translations that they are seldom understood by new converts.

God, however, is not like that. He speaks the language of the people he seeks to reach—even disrespected languages such as Galilean Aramaic (Jesus' language) and koine (common people's) Greek. And he uses even cultural practices such as those of the pagan society of which Abraham was a part and those of the pagan Greeks of the first century he chooses to adapt to his receptors rather than requiring them to adapt to him. He chooses to risk the impreciseness of the receptors' vehicles of communication in order to put the receptors at ease. This is communicational love. It is also communicational contextualization.

2. God *chooses to* appeal *to* needs *felt by humans at a level deeper* than *culture.* Though he uses the cultural context as the medium of his interaction with us concerning our felt needs, the most important of these needs lie deeper. So he contexts his messages even beyond the context of culture, in the deepest needs and longings of the human heart.[6]

Among these are the needs for forgiveness from sin, freedom from satanic oppression, and the security that can only come from a relationship with God. This is a kind of contextualization not ordinarily in view—into the depths of human need that cannot be satisfied through socio-cultural structuring and relationships. Though the scriptural message is presented in cultural terms, it concerns these deeper needs.

---

[6] The fact that in dealing with humans we need to deal with both the cultural and the deeper personal level argues for an approach to witness that combines the insights of anthropology with those of theology, as I have attempted to do in Kraft 1979a. Theological training seeks to enable people to deal with the deeper needs of humans but often without the ability to get at them through understanding the more visible, culturally defined felt needs in which anthropologists specialize.

People come into the world insecure, powerless, and to some extent, at the mercy of suprahuman powers. Feelings of inadequacy in the face of such a condition, then, plague us and cause us to cry out for assistance. Though human relationships and structures cushion the impact of such feelings to some extent, most people still seek more power and security for the living of life. A contextually oriented God chooses to address these subjects in terms intelligible at the deepest personal level.

Through offering covenantal relationships to humans, he addresses the security need. By means of such relationships he offers protection from evil spiritual forces and the assurance of favor with the Creator and Sustainer of the universe. He offers release from sin and freedom from bondage to any of Satan's schemes, such as poverty, captivity, blindness, or oppression (Lk. 4:18). He thus speaks contextually to the deepest felt needs of his creatures.

3. God's *preferred method of contextualization is incarnation.* He comes to where we are as persons in a way that is maximally within our context and intelligible to us—through other persons. He has from the beginning of human existence usually chosen this incarnational approach to reaching people. In Jesus, then, he produced the supreme example of incarnation. Since this is where people are, such an approach is contextually appropriate.

We may, therefore, call him "receptor-oriented." That is, like the best of human communicators, he makes it his primary concern to focus on the results of his communicational efforts at the receiving end. He will, then, do whatever is necessary to bring the receivers of the message to the point where they understand and respond to it. And this means incarnating the message in human flesh within the trappings of human contexts in order to reach those whose lives are lived within such limitations.

Both his message and his method remain the same from generation to generation (see Kraft 1979a:194–197, 227–235). The method is, however, to adapt the specifics of the message in such a way that the receptors understand it. He adapts his presentation to the context[7] and, beyond that, to the felt needs of those he seeks to reach. Thus, each receptor is approached on his or her own terms.

Within the human context, then, our God does not simply generalize concerning the topics he treats. His concern is specific both to the persons and to their needs. He interacts with specific people in the ways most appropriate to them concerning those topics he knows they most need. And he does it from within their life situations, from within their contexts.

4. *Our* God *does not depend simply on words to get his messages across.* His primary medium is life. He demonstrates in and through life what he recommends for life. His letters are in flesh (2 Cor. 3:2-3). In Jesus and through those who obey him, he uses his power to show his love, especially to the powerless and others victimized by satanic and human misuse of power.

What I have called "word messages" (Kraft 1983:58–63) simply convey information about their subject matter. They do not require a relationship to be effective. Nor does the acceptance of them necessarily require a life change. News

---

[7] See Hall 1976 and Kraft 1983 for important understandings concerning the use people make of their contexts in the ways they construct meaning.

broadcasts and answers to requests for information can be rendered in word messages. When one asks, "How much are 2 and 2?" a simple word answer suffices.

Words alone are not sufficient to adequately convey most of God's messages, however. What he offers needs to be lived by the communicator to be truly intelligible. For he offers a "person or life message," from the source of life, through the life of the communicator aimed to effect a life-change in the receptor. God's messages, therefore, require incarnation, a living out that may be spoken of in words but never limited to mere words. It moves from person to person via life rubbing against life to produce in the receptor a higher quality of life.

Love must be demonstrated if it is to be understood. So must righteousness, truth, faithfulness, acceptance, forgiveness, and all the rest of the treasures of Christianity. Jesus said, "I *am* the Way, the Truth and the Life" (Jn. 14:6 NIV, emphasis added). None of these comes via words alone. They are personal, relational, and life-related both in their expression and in their communication. God, therefore, contextualizes them in the lives of his people for all to see and respond to.

5. All of this implies that God *is also in favor of contextually appropriate extending media.* That is, though the basic medium of person messages is the human being himself, God is in favor of using appropriate secondary vehicles such as music, storytelling, public presentation (various kinds), poetry, ritual, dance, and the like. [8] He stands, however, against the imposition by a more powerful group on a less powerful group of their own vehicles as if only those vehicles were especially endorsed by him.

He would, therefore, stand against the contextual inappropriateness of the usual practice of imposing Western music,[9] ritual, and lecture forms on non-Western peoples as if these forms were sacred and to be adopted by everyone. God's method would be to see traditional cultural forms used to express a people's relationship with him and to communicate his messages to others.

Interference in God's Communicational Process

1. God's communicational process is, of course, interfered with at every point due to the Fall. Human sin of all types and especially our rebellion against God's sovereignty in our lives interfere at both the receptor's end and in the lives of God's human communicators. Satan, furthermore, does his best to confuse things at both ends of the process.

Whenever there is sin in the lives of God's people, God's process is interfered with. Likewise, when we turn to merely human means to attempt to accomplish

---

[8] See Klem 1982 for a particularly good presentation of both contemporary and scriptural bases for using indigenous methods of communication. Søgaard 1975, 1986; and Weber 1957 are also useful.

[9] For insight into contextualized communication of Christianity through music, see R. King 1982 and her forthcoming Ph.D. dissertation.

spiritual ends (Gal. 3:3). When, for example, we fail to wage God's battles in prayer, both the communicators' and the receptors' ends of the process are affected adversely. Satan cannot be defeated by merely human means. Nor can those who have not properly dealt with their sinfulness provide adequate channels for God's messages.

2. In addition, God's plan for contextualized witness is often rendered inoperable by those of his people who for one reason or another are perceived by the receptors as failing to live his messages. We are called to contextualize God's messages by living in such a way that his witness comes across accurately through our lives, whether or not we also speak for him. Often, however, quite unconsciously we are perceived as living for someone or something other than the Lord we claim to serve.

As humans, we will be observed by others. Our lives thus become witnesses to something. If our lives are lived in foreign, noncontextualized ways, they become witnesses to foreignness.[10] Or our behavior may easily be misinterpreted to be witnessing to something we never intended. We may, for example, be interpreted as greedy or arrogant or as misusing power when we are simply living according to our normal cultural patterns.

3. Interference comes from attempts to reduce the life message to a word or a ritual message. Much church communication consists simply of words and/or religious rituals concerning God and his objectives. But God never intended to introduce another religion. He came to bring life (Jn. 10:10), to contextualize a relationship between humans and himself in the very fabric of human existence. But humans often reduce his plan to mere religious rhetoric and ritual, thus frustrating God's communicational intent (see Kraft 1983; Hall 1976; Condon 1975 for treatments of different levels of language usage).

4. We often go about communicating without spiritual power. We imitate the Galatians whom Paul accused of starting by God's Spirit but then turning to human means (Gal. 3:3). Jesus told his followers to wait until they received the power of the Holy Spirit before they set out to witness (Acts 1:4, 8), because God's messages are not adequately portrayed without the demonstrations of spiritual power that always accompanied the words of Jesus and his apostles and that he promised would accompany his followers (Jn. 14: 12).[11] Nor are those messages as appealing as they should be to the majority of human receptors for whom the quest for greater spiritual power is primary in life.

In Jesus, God was contextualized as a God of great authority and power who always uses his power to express God's love to victims and his judgment to the victimizers. Any gospel without that power used in that way is not the true gospel of Jesus Christ.

---

[10] Illustrations of foreignness in approaches to the communication of the Christian message abound in books such as Smalley 1974, 1978; Nida 1954; Loewen 1975; and Luzbetak 1963/1975. Reading in such sources can greatly help the reader who is tempted to feel that the problem is not as serious as we seem to think it is.

[11] The contemporary movement, sometimes termed the "third wave" of the Holy Spirit, is an attempt to contextualize the use of the power Jesus has given his followers within an evangelical context. See Wimber 1986, 1987; Wagner 1988; Williams 1989; and Kraft 1989 for examples.

The wedding of spiritual salvation to material and secular power that characterizes so much of western Christianity is problematic in that, though it appears to be contextually relevant to certain segments of Western societies, in reality it is only true to part of God's revelation. Those segments of Christianity that use God's power for purposes other than to show his love are, however, equally to be questioned. For, though their use of spiritual power may be perceived as relevant, its use in a way God did not intend distorts his message.

5. The misuse of human prestige and power in the communication of God's messages is frequently an evidence of human interference in God's plan for contextualization of his messages. Those in power frequently impose on those not in power their own cultural forms, as if they were ordained by God to be used by all peoples everywhere. This is the problem behind the controversy dealt with in Acts 15 (see Kraft 1979a). The Jewish Christians assumed that God wanted Gentile converts to adopt Hebrew culture.

Westerners frequently err in this regard also. Whether consciously or unconsciously they often expect that God wants them to ignore the receptors' communicational vehicles and introduce such Western practices as reading, Western music, monologue preaching, church buildings, and even rationalistic theology and school-based training. Such vehicles were little used, if at all, throughout the Bible; instead, whatever vehicles were appropriate to the receptors were used.

Biblical peoples seemed to share with most of the peoples of the Two-Thirds World[12] the recognition that oral communication is far more relevant than written (see Klem 1982; Goody 1968; and Weber 1957); indigenous music is far more appropriate than Western; apprenticeship-type training is far more effective than school-based learning; [13] and discussion is far more sure than monologue (see Kraft 1979b, 1983), if one wants to get a point across. Jesus also seemed to know that working personally and in depth with a few leaders is more effective than trying to work more or less impersonally with groups of more than twelve.

Again, God is receptor-oriented in desiring that the primary vehicles of communication be those of the receptors, not those of the witnesses who bring the message. I doubt that he is totally against some use of reading and classrooms. But the wholesale introduction of these vehicles while almost totally ignoring most of the indigenous vehicles is surely against his will, especially since it contributes to the impression that he wants receptor peoples dominated by Western methods and techniques.

6. God's plan to contextualize his messages in every sociocultural context is often thwarted through what may be termed "overcontextualization" to the sociocultural assumptions and values of the receiving society. God seeks to adapt his messages, but not to have them "captured" by the worldview of the receptors. Thus, we see throughout the Scriptures a judging of the values and assumptions of biblical peoples even while their cultural vehicles are being used by God.

---

[12] Two-Thirds World is used in preference to the rather condescending term "Third World."

[13] This was recognized as long ago as Bruce 1898, but it is seldom taken seriously in theological circles even today.

The Jews had overcontextualized in their assumption that Yahweh belonged to them alone. And when Jews became Christians, many of them refused to allow Gentiles to come to Christ without also converting to Hebrew culture (Acts 15:1). These who overcontextualized in Hebrew culture but fought contextualization in Gentile cultures were soundly condemned by Paul (Gal. 1:6–2:21). This problem is, of course, tied to the question of power. Those with the power to admit or to keep others out of organizations supposedly endorsed by God tend to set their standards according to their own cultural norms rather than according to the intent of God.

In our day this has been a major problem with Western Christianity. On the basis of our cultural prestige and power, we, too, have imported into other cultural contexts Christian messages already overcontextualized in our own. Western Christianity unfortunately exhibits a high degree of overcontextualization to a series of quite unscriptural Western cultural assumptions and values—such as individualism, rationalism, secularism, and materialism (see Kraft 1989).

When such Christianity is exported to societies with worldviews differing greatly from Western worldviews, the misimpression is often given that God intends that all peoples everywhere accept Western brands of Christianity. Both the receptors and, frequently, those Westerners who carry God's messages often conclude that Western Christianity is the epitome of what God intended. Those in power, who earn their living in Christian ministry especially often fail to notice the vast difference between God's ideals as expressed in the Bible and the Christianity forged in the West.[14]

The God who, in the Scriptures, is seen as seeking to contextualize in Jewish ways for Jews and in Greek ways for Greeks (1 Cor. 9:20–21) is often seen as One who demands conversion to Western cultural forms as part of the price of a relationship with him. The cultural prestige and power of the West is frequently employed (often quite unconsciously) to propagate the heresy that God is not a contextualizer but, rather, One who seeks to impose Western cultural vehicles as the only adequate containers for Christianity. Biblical teaching on contextualization is thus obscured as we make the same mistake the Judaizers made in the first century.

7. But overcontextualization can happen even within societies that are virtually powerless to impose their understandings on other peoples. Through conversion followed by a lack of guidance into scriptural understandings of what Christianity ought to be, people can "nativize" their new allegiance. That is, they can accommodate it to all kinds of assumptions and values that should be judged and abandoned.[15] This form of overcontextualization can be just as dangerous and can interfere just as much in God's communicational process as the overcontextualization of the Christianity of the powerful.

---

[14] J. B. Phillips, in order to point up this difference, re-phrased the Beatitudes as believed by contemporary Westerners to extol the "pushers" "for they get on in the world," the hard-boiled for they don't let life hurt them, those who complain for they get their way, the blase for they don't need to worry over their sins, the slave drivers "for they get results," the knowledgeable for "they know their way around," and the troublemakers "for they make people take notice of them" (1954:19). Each Western "beatitude" is nearly the opposite of what Jesus recommended, yet the extent to which these have been incorporated into Western Christianity is frightening.

[15] Three articles by Tippett (1975) are especially helpful in understanding the problems of syncretism.

Nativization (often called *syncretism*) has occurred when, for example, the founder of a Christian movement is identified with the Third Person of the Trinity (see Bertsche 1966). It is also apparent when allegiance to pagan gods and spirits is continued, though they may now be called by different (supposedly Christian) names (see Madsen 1957 and Wonderly 1958), or when mushrooms or other hallucinogens become a crucial part of Christian worship (see Pike and Cowan 1959), or when God is understood as bound to obey our wishes whenever we use the proper words or rituals.

In any of these seven ways and, probably, in many others, the contextualizing essence of God's communicational strategy can be hindered and messages communicated that distort his very nature. He seeks to communicate his love and concern in ways that will be maximally understandable and relevant to the receptors. Human efforts, however, often obscure his intent and convey a distorted picture of who he is.

Learning to Contextualize

If contextualization is God's method, then, we need to learn how to carry out our efforts on his behalf by employing his method. Toward that end, I have attempted to identify some of the ways in which God contextualizes. We then looked at the kinds of interference that contribute to the frequent differences between our efforts and what God seems to intend.

I believe we can assert that God's ultimate intent in this area, as in many others, is shown in the life and ministry of Jesus (see Kraft 1979b, 1983). We should, therefore, pattern our communicative activity after his. To that end, the following points are offered:

1. Preliminary to any attempt to communicate, we need to be sure we are both presenting the correct message and employing the correct method. Jesus demonstrated that *working under the authority of and in dependence upon* God *is the starting point for both message and method.* In coming to earth, Jesus became a distinct being from God the Father. He refused, however, to work separately from the Father. Rather, he practiced an intimate, childlike dependence on the Father, stating, "the Son can do nothing on his own; he does only what he sees his Father doing" (Jn. 5:19 TEV), and "I can do nothing on my own authority . . . I am not trying to do what I want, but only what he who sent me wants" (Jn. 5:30 TEV).

Whatever we do, then, needs to spring from the same kind of dependence on God. It is not enough to connect well with the receptors of our messages. We must connect tightly with the proper Source of all we seek to do. So, establishing and maintaining our intimacy with and dependence upon God in the same ways Jesus did is our first order of business.

As Jesus regularly withdrew to be with the Father (Lk. 5:16), so should we. During these times, I doubt that Jesus did as much talking as he did listening. He cultivated intimacy and the ability to hear what the Father was saying. He then said only what the Father had instructed him to say (Jn. 8:26, 28) and did only what he saw the Father doing (Jn. 5:19). We need to cultivate the same kind of intimacy and to develop the same spiritual sharpness of hearing and seeing, if we are to do his works in his way.[16]

2. As *Jesus became Emmanuel, "God with humans," so must we become genuinely human to those we seek to reach.* The incarnational method is the supreme biblical method. And all that we do and teach needs to be biblical if we are to avoid communicating the wrong things. We need to live the Bible morally spiritually and communicationally. But such living out of the Bible needs to be in terms intelligible to our receptors. This requires a contextually interpretable lifestyle. That is, how we live our lives in the receptor context needs to be enough in their style for them to interpret it as consonant with biblical principles.[17]

Our spirituality must also be contextually interpretable. That is, what we do both in private and in public to express our relationship with God needs to make sense to them in terms of the only world they know. Often their standards for spirituality are higher, or at least different than ours. The privacy and lack of ritual and public expression of our spirituality then, though considered adequate by us, often makes our Christianity seem very secular to them.[18]

3. *A focus on living—especially spiritually meaningful living—according to their criteria provides the kind of witness at the deep personal level that* God *desires.* Beyond the cultural differences, people everywhere seek relationships, love, and enough power to handle life needs. God offers relationship through his own people within human contexts. If we are to serve him, we need to be present and intelligible within the life contexts of those he seeks to reach. This provides the basis for all person-level communication.

The love people seek can then be expressed by Christians, as long as it is done in their ways rather than according to foreign patterns. Western impersonal generosity, for example, seldom is understood as loving in person-to-person societies. Such relationship and love, then, provide the channel through which the power of God for guided human living is provided. People seek enough power to enable them to persevere in the face of both normal and abnormal challenges to their survival. Christians are often best understood in non-Western contexts when offering the spiritual power we have been authorized to use (Lk. 9:1-2).

---

[16] See the focus on intimacy with God as the source of Jesus' and our authority in Kraft 1989 and Wimber 1986, 1987.

[17] See articles by Reyburn (1978) and Loewen (1975) for excellent treatments of human identification in the receptors' context as the best we can do in aiming at incarnation.

[18] This is often true in societies such as those of India. Thannickal 1975 gives helpful insight from an Indian point of view.

Conclusion

If, then, we are to learn how to communicate God's messages in God's way we need to take account of at least the following points highlighted earlier:

1. Those at the receiving end of God's communicational activity are very important to him. He seeks to relate to them, reach out to redeem them, and to be understood by them. Those we seek to reach should be equally important to us. We should, therefore, imitate God's approach to them.

2. God seeks to employ appropriate sociocultural vehicles to reach those receptors. Those vehicles are the ones familiar to the receptors. God is, therefore, a contextualizer. We should, then, confidently imitate his approach.

3. God's appeal, however, is not to the concerns that lie closest to the surface of culture but to the deeply felt human needs that lie at the deepest levels of human life. Recognizing this, we should be concerned to learn to use cultural vehicles to get beyond purely cultural concerns.

4. God's messages need to be conveyed through life, not simply through words. Only life is an adequate conveyor of messages directed to the deepest levels of human experience. This kind of communication can be contextualized only through persons who live in other people's contexts as incarnationally as possible.

5. God's messages are to be accompanied by the works of God. God does not simply talk. He demonstrates. Thus he *shows* who he is and what the benefits of a relationship with him involve.

6. The messages communicated should be biblical, not merely the overcontextualized versions of God's messages in the forms of Western or any other culture. There should be no contrast in people's minds between what the Bible teaches and what those teach who claim to represent the God of the Bible.

7. The vehicles used should be contextually relevant, not simply imported from a more prestigious or powerful source. God can make use of whatever is present within the receiving society. He endorses no vehicles as the proper ones for all contexts.

CHAPTER 30

CHRISTIAN CONVERSION
OR CULTURAL CONVERSION?

Reprinted here with permission from
Practical Anthropology 10:179–187 (1963)

The Christian God is represented in the Bible and Christian doctrine as desirous of communicating himself to men.[1] We observe from the biblical record that this communication has taken into account the cultures in which men are wrapped. We gain the impression that God views the cultures of men as channels usable for interaction between himself and men.

God saw fit to reveal himself to the Hebrew people in terms of the Hebrew language and culture. The New Testament shows the same God beginning to reveal himself to the Greco-Roman world in terms of first century Greco-Roman language and culture. By analogy, then, we may assume that it is God's will, not simply accident, that the revelation of himself to 20th century Americans be in terms of 20th century American language and culture. And, on the basis of this assumption, we witness to the fact that God wishes to communicate with man, and recommend response to God in terms of 20th century American life.

At the risk, then, of the considerable oversimplification implicit in any attempt to represent God's approach to man diagrammatically, we may say that the following diagram pictures something of the nature of God's desire in communicating to man:

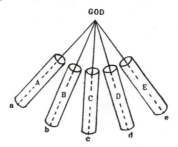

DIAGRAM 1. God desires to communicate with a given man through the channel

---

[1] I want to acknowledge my debt to and dependence upon the ideas and personal stimulation of Drs. Nida, Smalley, and Reyburn of the American Bible Society. So much of their thinking has (however imperfectly) become a part of my own that I find it quite impossible to properly identify the source of much of what I have to say. I will not, therefore, endeavor to provide extensive footnoting to their writings.

of the culture in which that man is immersed. Cylinders *A*, *B*, *C*, *D*, *E* represent specific cultures of men. Points *a*, *b*, *c*, *d*, *e* represent individuals within these cultures. Direct broken lines pass from God to individuals *a–e* through cultures *A–E* to represent the possibility of direct communication by God to e.g., individual *a* in terms of his own language and culture *A*. Culture *A* is the channel used by God to reach individual *a*. Culture *B* is the channel used by God to reach individual *b*, etc.

The tops of the above culture cylinders might be considered to represent specific cultures at their highest, most generalized level where each culture is most similar to every other culture (i.e., at a level where such statements can be made as every culture has language, religion, family, etc."). The bottoms of the cylinders, then, would represent cultures as they are actually worked out in the human context— where they are most dissimilar from each other. Statements made to describe cultures at this level would describe the particular type of language, religion, or family found in the culture under consideration. It is on the latter, lower level—where there is a maximum of diversity between cultures—that men live and that cross-cultural communication takes place.

Peter and Cornelius

God's revelation came to Peter in terms of Hebrew (Aramaic) culture. Peter was a Jew and, though a Christian, understood Christianity in the Hebrew cultural context and continued to live according to Hebrew patterns,[2] though, at times, making certain adaptations.[3] God's revelation had come to Peter and he had responded to it thus:

GOD

PETER

DIAGRAM 2. God had made contact with Peter as a member of the Hebrew culture of his day, evoking Peter's response in terms of the same culture. The arrows indicate that communication takes place In both directions between Peter and God, but all within a single cultural framework.

---

[2] Acts 10:15.
[3] Galatians 2:11–14.

But it was Peter's task[4] to carry the revelation which he received in Hebrew dress and to which he responded in Hebrew terms, to Cornelius, a Roman, a member of another culture. Diagrammatically, Peter's problem might be represented as follows:

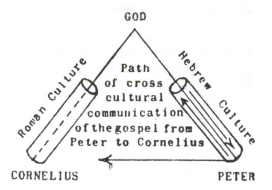

DIAGRAM 3. Peter, having established contact with God from within his own culture, seeks to communicate to Cornelius, wrapped in another culture, concerning his experience with God. For Cornelius, Roman culture is as yet but a potential vehicle of God's communication.

Peter could easily assume that only Hebrew culture was a suitable vehicle of God's communication and only a Hebrew type of response acceptable to God. To Peter, Roman culture and Roman people were alike unacceptable to God.

But God communicated to Peter (in a Hebrew way by commanding him in a vision to kill and eat animals which Peter considered unclean) the fact that at least one Roman person (hitherto regarded as "unclean" by Peter) was acceptable to God. Peter testifies to his new-found discovery saying, "I can now see that God is no respecter of persons, but that in every nation the man who reverences him and does what is right is acceptable to him!"[5]

The record goes on to indicate that a considerable number of Cornelius' "relations and intimate friends" responded to the message delivered by Peter and received from God the confirmation that they had been accepted by him, without the necessity of their first becoming Jews. That is, they received God's Holy Spirit into their lives and were baptized into the Christian fellowship without reference to matters of Hebrew custom and this in spite of the fact that Cornelius (and, presumably, many of his friends) are identified as "God-fearers"[6] and thus might well have been expected to become proselytes to Judaism.

A diagram of Cornelius' situation as a Christian would thus look like this:

---

[4] Acts 10.

[5] Acts 10:34, Phillips translation.

[6] Acts 10:2.

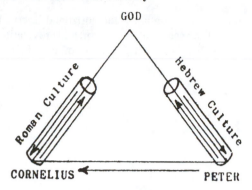

DIAGRAM 4. Peter, in contact with God within Hebrew culture, has communicated the possibility and terms of such contact with God to Cornelius across cultural boundaries. Cornelius. upon hearing the message, responds to God (not merely to Peter), whereupon contact is established between God and Cornelius without the necessity of a change of cultural allegiance on the part of the latter.

This is not to imply that the conversion of Cornelius, minus the necessity of prior allegiance to Judaism, means that his approach to God was therefore completely divested of all trace of Hebrew cultural elements. On the contrary, we must assume that Cornelius' response to and subsequent practice of Christianity embodied considerable assimilation of Hebrew Christian practice into his Roman Christian life. In this incident the influence of Hebrew culture on Christianity was not being removed (this must forever remain), but the necessity for each convert in embracing Christianity, to embrace likewise the culture in which Christianity was born.

However, it was necessary for Peter to experience the events recorded in Acts 10 to bring him to the correct view of conversion. Previously he (in common with, apparently, nearly all the Christian leaders except Paul) had assumed that conversion to Christianity implied conversion to Judaism, the Hebrew approach to God. God had made contact with Peter through this approach, and in terms of this God had accepted Peter's response. Rather naturally, the apostles regarded the culture into which God had come personally in Jesus Christ both as a particularly well-suited vehicle of God's self-manifestation, and (wrongly) as prescribing the only proper forms of human response to God.

Perhaps it was to be expected that they would assume man's response to God must retrace the path along which the revelation had come. Diagrammatically, their assumption would look thus:

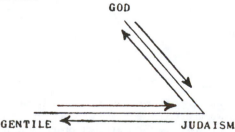

DIAGRAM 5. God's revelation has come first to the Jew and only thence, through Judaism, to Gentiles (following the outside arrows). Conversion of Gentiles

involves, therefore, first a conversion along the horizontal line to Judaism, then a response to God in terms of the same culture in which his revelation is couched. In other words, a Gentile must first become a Jew to become a Christian.

The Position of the Early Church

God, in Acts 10, leads Peter to repudiate this view of the nature of Christian conversion. In Acts 15 a gathering of the apostles and elders, provoked by some rather determined Judaizers,[7] came to the same decision. The apostolic church thus came to the position that Gentiles need not be required to become Jews to become Christians. Their official position may, therefore, be diagrammed as follows:

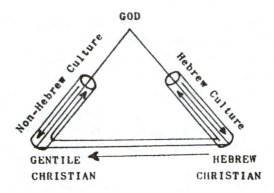

DIAGRAM 6. Though the communication of the gospel takes place cross-culturally from Hebrew Christian to Gentile (along the base of the triangle), the Gentile Christian establishes direct communication with God and God with him, employing his own culture as the channel rather than the (Hebrew) culture which provided the channel for the original revelation. That is, though the intermediate source of the Gentile's knowledge of the true way to God is a culture other than his own, his response to the supracultural God (the expression of his faith) will be in terms of his own Gentile culture. He, or his group of believers as a whole, may, however, retain certain minimal cultural evidences of the fact that Christianity was originally practiced by those of another culture and certain of its institutions (baptism, communion) developed therein (hence the inner arrow from Hebrew to non-Hebrew culture).

---

[7] W. D. Davies, in his *Christian Origins and Judaism* (London: Darton, Longman and Todd, 1962), says: "The New Testament would not seem to present us with a single fixed pattern of Church order which we are to regard as normative . . . , it is constantly evolving by adapting itself to ever-changing conditions that it may properly fulfill the . . . tasks committed to it" (p. 229). "Any Church order, therefore, which presumes to impose terms upon the sovereign freedom of Christ, which limits His activity to certain prescribed channels, episcopal or other, is a denial of His sovereignty" (p. 225).

Church History

Church history, however, provides illustrations of reversion to the type of presentation of the Christian message represented by Diagram 5, which demands primary allegiance to a particular cultural or subcultural approach to God as prerequisite to being regarded as Christian.

To some groups the idea that one must be converted to a particular philosophy or worldview (particular culture or subculture different from one's own) is obligatory if one is to be considered "Christian" by them. Such groups, especially those more inclined toward exclusiveness, commonly predicate their own *raison d'être* upon the truth of their particular theological or organizational position as opposed to all others. And, according to our terms of reference, their approach to the matter of conversion can be diagrammed as follows:

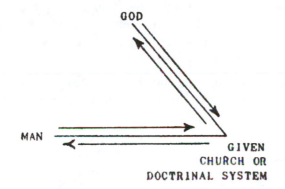

DIAGRAM 7. God reveals himself to man via a given church or doctrinal system and is approachable by man only via the same medium.

This kind of approach takes little cognizance of the possibility of God's using any but a single culture or subculture as a vehicle for his interaction with men. Each such view tends to identify its own approach to God with that of the first century and fails to make allowance for differences of approach based on difference of culture or subculture. Such a position may either ignore such differences completely, or consider the cultural factor irrelevant. It will tend to be absolutistic not only with reference to the claims of Christianity as a whole, but also with regard to its own particular cultural norms, and may even revert completely to the attitude of the Judaizers in considering both the type of Christianity espoused and its cultural or subcultural milieu as the products of divine-human interaction and, therefore, sacred.

The Present Situation in
Missionary Work

Unfortunately, many possessing such inadequate views with regard to culture in general and Western culture in particular, find their way into Christian missionary work. And these attitudes provide a primary hindrance to effective cross-cultural communication of the Christian message, since they generally lead to a definition of "conversion to Christianity" which is concerned primarily with purely cultural issues. That is, this type of attitude toward conversion aims more at promoting Western moral and spiritual ends than at the demonstration of the acceptability of any culture as a vehicle of God's interaction with man. Nor does it take proper cognizance of the fact that Western culture is but one such vehicle, and neither the original nor the only vehicle usable by God.

Thus much of modem missionary effort is, in effect, promoting an approach to Christianity more akin to that of the first century Judaizers than to that of Paul and Peter. It has merely substituted Western culture for Hebrew culture as the *sine qua non* for God's acceptance of man.

A diagram of the message presented by such missionaries would, therefore, be the same as diagrams 5 and 7 but with different labels, thus:

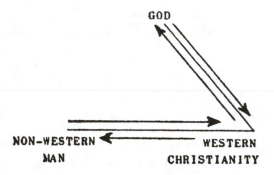

DIAGRAM 8. God's message has been proclaimed to non-Western man through the instrumentality of Western Christianity. The non-Western convert is urged to respond to God by embracing that Western-style Christianity. "Conversion to Christianity" is, therefore, defined as conversion to the particular Western system of Christianity presented. The non-Western man must first become Westernized to become a Christian.

Many Western missionaries fail to recognize the fact that Western culture is but one of many usable by God, even though Christianity has displaced, through long association, all previous religious systems in the West. This latter fact merely means that there are now two Christianities which the missionary must take into account. I will attempt to distinguish between them by spelling one with a small c and the other with a capital C.

The christianity of which we are most aware is really the adaptation of Christianity to Western cultural forms. Western christianity is (ideally) God in Christ made relevant to the members of Western culture. Thus it is characterized familiar forms of worship, music, organization, philosophy (theology), moral standards. This is the religious aspect of the culture of which we are a part.

The christianity of the first century which we see in the New Testament is the same Christianity but adapted to a different culture. Thus, for example, first century christianity accepted and regulated slavery, 20th century Western christianity cannot. First century christianity felt it necessary to speak against haircutting on the part of first century Christian women. Twentieth century Western christianity feels no such compulsion.

Christianity (capital C), on the other hand, is at once more than and less than its cultural manifestations. This Christianity is supracultural, absolute, universally applicable, yet only visible to finite, culture-bound mankind as expressed in culture—seen only dimly and partially, as in reflections.[8] Nevertheless, the glimpses are there—many, including that of God in human form, recorded in the Book, many apparent in the lives of modern-day Christians—glimpses of Reality beyond the cultural "real," glimpses of Truth beyond cultural truths, glimpses of God beyond man's understanding of him. Christianity (capital C) is more than christianity in the same way that God is more than man. It is less to the extent that cultural christianity necessarily accrues to itself nonessential cultural elements (details of organization and practice), as it is communicated to culture-bound men.

A missionary stands, as it were, committed to attempt to communicate Christianity on the basis of his best understanding of it as seen through the Western cultural christianity of his native land. His allegiance must be to God and to the supracultural Christianity to which he subscribes in spite of his culture-bound understanding of it and of God. His concept of conversion must therefore be conceived in terms of bringing about a relationship between the non-Western individual or group and the supracultural God and Christianity, rather than in purely cultural terms, if it is to square with the missionary's own commitment.

And such commitment to supracultural Christianity implies a like commitment to the conviction that non-Western converts must be allowed to develop their own particular type of cultural christianity—differing as much from Western christianity as their non-Western culture differs from Western culture. The missionary and his fellow Western Christians have demanded just such a right to adapt the supracultural message which came originally in Hebrew dress.

Present Approach in Africa

But a consideration of the present missionary situation leads us to question whether the present approach is actually designed to bring about the desired kind of conversion. In Africa, for example, the most effective means of bringing about conversion to Christianity is through mission schools. Missionaries were early

---

[8] 1 Corinthians 13:12.

impressed with the lack of education (in the Western sense of the word of formally organized, daily schools) in Africa. Accordingly, the establishment and management of schools became one of the major activities of many missions. As children attended these schools they were required to study at least the basic subjects taught in American (or European) schools—reading, writing, arithmetic, history (often European), geography—as well as Christianity (usually the Bible). In the process of such schooling it was found that a majority of the children embraced the religion of the white man along with his reading and writing.

A method of conversion as successful as the mission schools have been—in some areas, it is said, over 90 percent of the children in the schools become Christians—is seldom seriously questioned; especially if other benefits such as literacy, widened horizons, more adequate preparation to effectively participate in the modern world are considered important. Yet hereby missions are allowing a false understanding of the nature of conversion to Christianity to be communicated.

Without questioning the many very desirable cultural benefits which may assist the emerging Africans to participate in an increasingly Westernized world, it is to be expected that the presentation of Christianity primarily through the medium of Western schools would lead to an emphasis on cultural conversion rather than on true Christian conversion. We may expect that the religious teaching provided in the schools will be interpreted by the students as part and parcel of the same culture as is the reading, writing, and arithmetic, and accepted as merely such. And this appears to be the case for, in spite of wide-scale indigenization of mission-started churches, Christianity is regarded as much "the white man's religion" today as it ever was. Acceptance as church members thus comes to be regarded by Africans as a sort of school diploma, attainable by any one who can pass the necessary examination, and signifying a pledge of allegiance to the white man's way.

Other aspects of Western missionary activity in Africa often appear to confirm rather than offset the impression given by the schools. Hospitals, bent on displacing traditional African medicine and techniques for handling unseen evil forces, never require the Western doctors to understand the African's point of view, and so strongly support the position of the schools. The message of the mission hospitals is that the Christian God endorses only one approach to medicine and is determined to displace all that is African (without bothering to examine it) with that which is Western.

Western schools and Western medicine, as promoted by missionary organizations, have provided much of considerable value in the African context. But the degree of reliance which many missions place on these as methods of bringing about Christian conversion appears unwarranted. Such reliance appears, rather, to support the contention that Christian missions seek to be no more than advance bases for the spread of Western civilization.

Nor have more directly evangelistic efforts provided the necessary corrective to the situation, though it must be said that basic evangelistic work has shown far more promise as a means of relevant cross-cultural communication of the Christian message than most other aspects of missionary work, evangelistic effort has, however, too easily encouraged converts and potential converts to focus primary attention on cultural issues such as "Christian" (which always means Western) marriage, "Christian" attitudes toward adultery and other moral issues, and Western patterns of church government or full-time clergy. Many of the attitudes thus encouraged are based, missionaries claim, on the Bible. But too often the impression is given that the Bible can only be interpreted in Western ways.

Nevertheless, when the more personal witness demanded by undisguised evangelistic work is combined with a sincere appreciation of the people and an adequate command of their language, the true message of God is usually communicated. Here, at least in some sense, the missionary or native preacher is less able to demand—more compelled to win—his hearing. On this level it is less possible to merely ignore embarrassing problems of culture. It will be a sad thing, indeed, if the process of indigenization results in a lessening of such face-to-face, person-to-person contact between Western Christian and non-Western potential convert.

Need to Redefine Aims and Revamp Means

In Africa and in many other areas of the world there is need for a redefining of exactly what the aim of missionary endeavor is with regard to conversion. Missions have had and continue to have a major hand in the process of Westernization. They have in most cases exported Western culture at its best and have acted worthily as ambassadors of the culture (including its religious aspect) within which they have developed.

Missions and missionaries claim, however, to be ambassadors of God and of supracultural Christianity (capital C). They claim to be dedicated to bringing about Christian, not merely cultural conversion, on the part of their adherents. Their aim is not to Westernize but to bring about direct interaction between non-Western man and God, without the necessity of allegiance on the part of the convert to the culture of the missionary. Yet their methods appear to detract from rather than to contribute to the success of their aim. The type of conversion encouraged by the primary methods employed appears to be more cultural than Christian.

Perhaps it is not presumptuous to suggest that the present approach needs revamping and that the opportunity for change is still with us. The message of the Judaizers was repudiated by the first century church. Its 20th century counterpart must be repudiated by the 20th century church. The same freedom must be allowed to Africans and other non-Western converts to Christianity to develop non-Western styles of Christianity, as was allowed to our Roman and Greek forebears to develop non-Jewish types. Present missionary practice in Africa and in other non-Western areas of the world does not appear to be allowing such freedom or to be aiming at truly Christian conversion.

I fear that the heresy of the Judaizers is perpetuated every time a Western-originated rule forbids the baptism of a polygamist to whom God has vouchsafed his Spirit. The heresy combated by God through Peter's vision is allowed to continue unchecked wherever the impression is given that God demands literate membership, paid, Westernized clergy, nonindigenous hymn types and forms of worship, church government according to Robert's Rules of Order, or church discipline based on rules which contradict both biblical principles[9] and indigenous conscience.

The cultural dimension needs to be taken into account in modern missionary endeavor. Missionaries must come to understand and appreciate both the importance of each culture to those born into it and the usability of each as a vehicle of God's interaction with man. They must learn to refrain from regarding Western culture too highly or non-Western culture too lowly. Most of all they must take pains to see to it that the message communicated by the totality of the mission witness (in word and deed) appeals for truly Christian conversion, not merely conversion to a new cultural allegiance—no matter how profitable this might be in terms of other values.

---

[9] Such as those set forth in Matthew 7:1 and Romans 2:1ff. The Nigerians among whom I worked were strong on this point.

CHAPTER 31

LET'S BE CHRISTIAN ABOUT POLYGAMY[1]

Written in 1962, previously unpublished

The subject at hand is one concerning which I am deeply exercised. In three years of missionary experience in rural Northern Nigeria I found no subject alluded to more frequently by Nigerians as detrimental to the cause of Christ than the missionary position toward polygamists. I became convinced that their reasoning is sound and that ours is unsound. I became further convinced that their position needs support from the missionary's side of the fence.

Like Trevor Huddleston, who warns in his preface to *Naught for Your Comfort* against the attempt to appear unprejudiced when supporting a cause to which you've dedicated yourself, I will make no attempt to approach my subject in an unbiased manner. My experience with Nigerians who feel that God has rejected them because mission-founded churches won't accept them has left too deep an impression upon me. For they are unable to be heard in our world.

The Problem

The all but universal position of western-rooted Christian churches in Africa is that monogamy is the only form of marriage acceptable to God. Plural marriage is looked on, therefore, as contrary to God's will and, being contrary to God's will cannot be allowed in the churches. Men with more than one wife are, accordingly, not accepted into church membership in most churches.

Polygamy is equated by many present and probably the majority of past missionaries with open adultery or, at best, with legalized concubinage. Hence it is regarded as sinful, unacceptable to God, and sufficient reason for disqualifying a man for membership in God's church.

---

[1] In accordance with popular usage I am using the more general term "polygamy" to refer to what is more precisely labeled "polygyny" by anthropologists.

Polygamists who apply for church membership are advised to rid themselves of all but one of their wives before they can hope even to be considered. Thus the issue of one wife becomes of central concern to those charged with the tasks of churchmanship in Africa.

In recent years some few missions have boldly modified their position in such a way that a man with more than one wife may hold a sort of second-class membership in the church. And I have heard rumors, none documented, of one or two missions that allow full membership to polygamists.

But for the most part, the assumption seems to be that the polygamist must divorce all his wives but one before applying for church membership. In the case of a wife of a polygamous man, we may require that she leave him either to live alone or to remarry monogamously. We have strict rules to cut off from fellowship any Christian who takes a second wife.

We have equated plurality of wives with promiscuity and treated polygamists as adulterers. We have read our motives into their behavior and condemned, as if they are the same thing, both the promiscuity that, in their society as in ours, is extra-legal, and a legally sanctioned form of marriage as well. Yet the two are by no means the same thing. And our witness has been unnecessarily confused by our treatment.

The "problem of polygamy" is basically *our* problem, not theirs. Nor, if we can judge by the Scriptures, did it appear to be a major problem to God in the days when it was prevalent among the Jews.

This position of western-oriented churches in Africa (and in other parts of the world) has long been under attack on anthropological grounds. Anthropologists point out that polygamy is true marriage, legalized by the members of the societies in which it occurs and of which it forms an integral part, and not necessarily detrimental to the position of women in those societies in their pre-westernized state. Much has been convincingly written by anthropologists to carefully explain that economic and social, rather than moral or sexual factors are the true bases for such a custom. But missionaries, assuming that this is a moral issue concerning which anthropological insight cannot be trusted, rarely listen to what anthropologists have to say.

It is possible for the casual observer, the missionary who is primarily preoccupied with administrative matters, or one who for reasons of linguistic inability or short temper (or both) is not in close contact with African nationals, to spend considerable time in Africa without fully appreciating the gravity of the present situation. These limit themselves almost exclusively to contacts with Africans who have achieved positions of leadership in the church through rigid, unquestioning adherence to the rules, regulations and every whim of their "fathers in the faith"—the missionaries.

One mission administrator admitted to me that he had once been very concerned about the church's position on polygamy. He indicated, however, that his position had changed over the years until he now felt that "there's really no problem." I was interested to note from his subsequent remarks that the end of his real concern over the issue closely coincided with the time of his election to an administrative position in one of the mission schools! I was able to observe exactly this same course of events take place in the experience of one of my own contemporaries while we were serving together in Nigeria.

Yet another colleague had a more effective technique for insulating himself against this (and any other) problem of the Nigerians that he chose not to face. The Nigerian church leaders I worked with told me that the first time or two they tried to discuss the subject of polygamy with this missionary, they noted that his neck would begin to get red, indicating that he was getting angry. So they stopped mentioning the problem in his presence. The missionary deduced from this that polygamy wasn't really very important to the Nigerians!

Nevertheless, it is the experience of some of us who have sought to approach rural African missionary situations with an attitude of sympathetic concern for the problems and felt needs of the people, that nearly every extended discussion of whatever nature inevitably leads us into one or more facets of the polygamy problem.

A Discussion with Nigerian Church Leaders

At one point I asked a group of Nigerian church leaders with whom I had been working for two years, if the polygamy issue was really as important to them as they, and my own observation, seemed to indicate. Their reply it was, that led me to dedicate myself to do what I could to promote a more sensible attitude on the part of missionaries and their supporters toward plural marriage in the African context. The church leaders said: "Mr. Kraft, there is no single problem affecting missionary national Christian relationships or the relationships between African Christian and African non-Christian that causes us more concern than the missionary attitude toward polygamy."

They went on to explain how little basis they felt could be found in Scripture for the missionary attitude and how hypocritical they felt when preaching or teaching communicants on the subject. On the contrary, it was their conviction that the weight of the biblical references to plural marriage demonstrate unequivocally that God takes a very different view of such a custom than Whites do.

How could the African pastors be expected to refute the fanciful explanations their parishioners advance concerning the reasons behind the church structures if even the Bible to which the missionaries pointed for support actually provides no support for the position they must espouse? Common explanations of the thinking behind the church rules represented the missionaries as employing such marriage restrictions to keep Nigerians from attaining prosperity and thus becoming a threat to the missionaries' position, or to keep down the number of children to what the Whites considered a respectable number. Some even suggested that the real reason lay in the fact that White husbands are dominated by their wives and, therefore, forced by them to perpetuate their own misery in the guise of Christian doctrine. It was interesting to me to observe in this and in many other similar discussions with

Christian Africans both 1) the conviction that the mission attitude can only be based on western custom, not on biblical teaching and 2) the conviction that whatever else might be the case with regard to the relative merits of monogamy over polygamy, the fact that the missionaries would never consent to discuss the matter with them openly, indicated that the missionaries themselves felt their position was weak.

Yet, the primary concern of these Nigerian church leaders was for the disastrous effect of the missionary-initiated church position on their efforts to propagate the Christian message among their own people. It disturbed them deeply to be forced by powers beyond their control to promote what they considered an unreasonable dogma concerning a peripheral matter as if it were of the essence of the Christian message. They personally had experienced so much of permanent worth in their Christian faith that it hurt them deeply to see many of their most respected and thinking fellow-tribesmen turning away from Christianity without really giving it a try. Many, in fact, never even investigated the Christian option very thoroughly merely because they, as these leaders put it, "are too Christian" to send away wives and children toward whom they feel responsibility.

My friends could give me name after name of respected heads of families of their acquaintance who had personally communicated to them the fact that they were convinced of the superiority of Christianity. But, since the Christian God was so unreasonable, they saw no acceptable alternative but to turn to Islam or remain as they were. Indeed, these observed, the Christian God is only interested in women, children, misfits, those unable to obtain a second wife and those looking for favor in the missionaries' eyes.

My own experience with one of my language informants had shown a similar attitude on his part. He was a respected member of the community and had formerly belonged to a mission church and taught in a mission school. In spite of the fact that his formal connection with the mission had ended, he indicated to me that at heart he was still a Christian. Nevertheless, his present position as a pillar of the community demanded that he demonstrate his ability to function properly in the affairs of the elders by being able to adequately manage a home with more than one wife in it. And for this reason, being unable to align himself any longer with the Christian community, he had professed allegiance to Islam. "Christ is number one," he said, "but God is the same. Muhammad is second choice, and in my heart I still follow Christ, but I have two wives." My suspicion is that perhaps the primary reason for the reputed higher conversion ratio of Islam over Christianity in much of Africa is the manifest intransigence of the Christian churches regarding such peripheral issues as plural marriage.

The leaders were completely frustrated. The obvious inflexibility of the missionaries and their westernized African apprentices in this matter stifled their desire to discuss the matter intelligently with their leaders. The coldly impersonal church rulebook, blocked them from following their own consciences. Yet they were committed to proclaim as truth a message that contained this unreasonable position against polygamy as well as the many more important aspects of the Christian faith so badly needed by their people. Since the missionaries would not reason with them, they could counsel with no one but each other. Their only alternatives were either to continue in their frustration, preaching a gospel only half of which they found worthy of their complete dedication, or to quit. Several of them told me frankly that if they weren't so dependent upon their present church or mission salaries, they would have quit their jobs long ago, as Mr. Babi, the Headmaster of a nearby Senior Primary School actually did for similar reasons.

In short, my own experience with these and other Nigerian leaders and missionaries has led me to the conviction that the position of western-oriented churches against allowing full membership to individuals with more than one wife is wrong and cannot be supported either on practical or theological grounds. I feel, further, that the only correct basis for acceptance or rejection of potential communicants should be the scriptural one—a faith-commitment to Jesus Christ as Lord and Savior.

Four Areas of Embarrassment

I would like to rather briefly suggest several of the areas of embarrassment into which our present position has forced us.

1. First of all, let us consider what has happened to the missionary. With regard to the Scriptures, he is forced to exaggerate the importance of such references as the creation story (God created one wife for Adam) and Christ's statement concerning marriage (they two shall be one flesh) and to apply them in a situation that could not have been in the minds of the original authors. On the other hand, he must devise some view of the Bible that allows him to completely discount the validity of the Old Testament representation of God's attitude toward Hebrew polygamy, while maintaining the usefulness of the same Old Testament when it refers to other matters. Furthermore, some method must be found to interpret the references in the Pastoral Epistles (1 Tim. 3:2, 12; Tit. 1:6) that indicate that church leaders should be husbands of one wife in such a way that the natural implication is avoided that the New Testament allows ordinary church members to have more than one wife. (I will not dwell here on the fact that, since polygamy did not exist in Greco-Roman society, the likelihood is that these passages refer not to polygamy but, rather, to the practice of remarriage after the death of a man's first wife.) In any event, one of the effects of our position with regard to plural marriage and the church in Africa has been to force us into highly vulnerable and, I feel, quite untenable biblical interpretations.

2. The missionary, likewise, has been encouraged by his stand on this issue to continue in the naive failure to come to grips with cultural matters involved in the communication of the Gospel. While this may have been excusable in former generations due to the general lack of awareness of the depth of cultural differences, it is doubtful that anyone could seriously maintain that such failure is excusable in our day. By continually finding support for our western cultural norms in the Scriptures without recognizing the possibility that God can and does use any culture as a vehicle of his grace, we are found to perpetuate the attitude that only our culture is a fit vehicle for the working of God. In this particular issue we are found to be

pitting the supposed superiority of western marriage—an institution which, even according to our own standards, is a source of considerable embarrassment to thinking westerners—against a form of marriage that, if seriously examined would be found to possess considerable strength at just the points where our form is weakest. Our perpetuation of naiveness in this issue is a powerful deterrent to our ever learning to render to these people the respect that (according to our own standards) is their God-given due.

3. We have been forced, likewise, by our insistence that only monogamy can be permitted in the church, to espouse the doctrine that the end justifies the means, a doctrine that most of us would violently disclaim as a proper basis for Christian action. Our insistence that almost anything is preferable to plural marriage in the church leads us to justify divorce as the means of extricating oneself from a polygamous marriage. (It is interesting to note that we are here advocating divorce, which Jesus specifically condemned, as the means of getting out of a type of marriage that we condemn but Jesus never mentioned.) The feeling that in this case the end justifies the means leads us further to encourage the continuance of the complex of disciplinary functions piled on the church by former generations of missionaries. Such a focus on discipline makes it the primary function of the church leadership the ferreting out and punishment of those who transgress the church rules, especially those concerned with morals and marriage. The punishments for such offenses, then, usually involve such things as exclusion from communion, excommunication, loss of employment and other such penalties unsupportable from Scripture.

4. Though the effect of our attitude upon ourselves as missionaries has been grave, the effect on the emerging churches is, perhaps, even more serious since it might be questioned whether it will be possible for them to adequately extricate themselves from the shackles in which we have left them for many years to come. In the first place, they are forced, like the Pharisees, to give primary attention to the rules, regulations and canons of interpretation of the Scriptures that we have passed on to them in order to maintain the "purity of the church." That is, we have more or less canonized for them our procedures for running the church so that they will forever be able to maintain a white man's type of religion in an African context. And they are handcuffed perhaps as much out of respect for us as out of the lack of a feeling of freedom to follow their own consciences in matters of their faith.

Our intransigence with respect to polygamy results in several major problems. For example, matters of discipline become disproportionately important. Church "purity" is of more concern than is the relevance or irrelevance of the message. Discovering and punishing sin are more important than forgiving it. The necessity of properly indoctrinating potential propagators is such that rules are actually passed disallowing the right of new converts to witness concerning their Christian experience until they have been through a course that will insure that they will not give a polygamist the impression that God accepts him on the same basis as he would a man with only one wife. The church often takes on the proportions of an exclusive club of the westernized and those aspiring to become westernized bound together by the fact that they have given up (at least for the present) the idea of polygamy.

Results

The church, therefore, becomes most exclusive in the area where it should be most inclusive—in the area of its witness. Those with plural marriages or those who aspire to such, if informed, disqualify themselves from all hope of entering the Christian fold and never ask to be admitted. They look elsewhere to pledge their allegiance, often to Islam. This group usually includes the most important leaders of the African community.

The church leadership, then, tends to be made up of thoroughly indoctrinated but second-class men, drawn from the ranks of those who have gone through the mission schools but have not quite made the grade to become teachers. And their followers consist almost entirely of women, children and social misfits.

The heart of the problem leading to such a situation (though by no means the entirety of it) is the type of attitude particularly apparent with regard to polygamy. And any change in this attitude can result only from willingness on the part of those who are responsible for the attitude to initiate the change or through the recipients reacting strongly against it. Neither appears imminent at this point since those into whose hands the missionaries are passing their authority over church matters are almost exclusively those who have been most thoroughly indoctrinated with the attitude that such a prohibition as that against polygamists in the church is God-ordained. These have usually willingly or unwillingly, lived so long under the prohibition and had to argue so often in favor of the missionary attitude that any reversal of their position would entail severe loss of face for them. They are likewise most often dependent either directly or indirectly upon western or westernized sources for both financial and sociopsychological support. The church, under this type of leadership, and firmly committed to an antipolygamy position with all its concomitants, is still very much a puppet of its withdrawing parent and is, if anything, in more desperate shape than formerly when they were ruled openly by missionaries.

As noted above, one of the effects of these attitudes on the non-Christian African community is that most polygamists disqualify themselves, saving the churches the trouble of denying them membership. Another effect is to drive countless numbers to turn to Islam as a more congenial (though not, as commonly supposed, necessarily less demanding) allegiance. The non-Christian community is, further, the more strongly confirmed in the prevalent attitude that Christianity is merely the White Man's approach to God and, therefore, relevant in the African context only insofar as one aspires to emulate the Whites.

It is ironic that our opposition to allowing polygamists to obtain church membership, and the steps we take to assure that they don't, result in church membership for many who manifest quite unchristian attitudes. Such strictures, on the other hand, bring about the rejection of those with plural marriages who act in a far more Christian way toward their families by refusing to send away those women and children for whom they have, rightly or wrongly, accepted responsibility previous to their contact with Christianity. I know personally of a few polygamists who consider themselves Christians and actively do all in their power to promote the work of the church, while maintaining the position that their allegiance to truly Christian principles is the thing that keeps them from divorcing their wives and becoming church members.

From a practical point of view the effect of insistence upon the exclusion of polygamists from church membership has been disastrous. It has seriously compromised the attitudes and witness of both missionaries and national Christians and provided "proof" for the unbeliever that the religion brought by the missionaries, is, after all, merely the White Man's religion, the door to which is open only to pseudo-Whites.

Yet, I can't help feeling that the theological implications of our position are even more serious than these practical considerations. The present exclusion of polygamists from church membership is crippling the work of missions in Africa. This is a very serious consideration and sufficient in itself to cause us to rethink our position if we are at all so inclined. But to me the most pressing reasons for reconsideration lie in an examination of the theological distortions forced upon us by our present position.

Implications for Biblical Interpretation and Communication

1. I have already alluded to the fact that our position, if rationalized, demands considerable looseness in our principles of biblical interpretation, and have mentioned a few specific instance of such interpretation. But in these biblical references to marriage, I have not ruled out the possibility that some overall method of biblical interpretation that takes the fact of culture fully into account might, for example, make it possible to demonstrate that the Old Testament references to polygamy are irrelevant in the present situation.

As a matter of fact I feel that just such a possibility exists and allows us to refrain from advocating polygamy for America (but not for Africa) on the basis of such commands as that in Deuteronomy 25:5 (commanding a man to marry his deceased brother's wife). For the cultural setting of twentieth century U.S.A. is such that the following of such a command would bring about considerable distortion of both the message we seek to communicate and of the motives involved. Yet we refuse to apply the same principle of cultural relevance in the approach to the Scriptures that we employ and teach in Africa, since this would lead to the permission of marriage customs once permitted openly by God yet violently opposed by us—the guardians of God's work. Thus are we forced into utterly indefensible theological positions.

The most important of these theological distortions cluster around the implication that God can accept only monogamists. To me it is no mean thing for a man or an organization to assume the right to summarily deny access to the mercy of

God to a significant segment of those whom we ostensibly seek to reach. God says "Come … all." We say, "Only those who have disposed of their excess wives need apply." God says, "Whoever puts his trust in Christ has life." We say, "Believe and cast out all but one of your wives and you shall be saved."

Of small import is it that we never preach this Gospel in so many words. The exact words we use are far less important than the impression communicated by the totality of our witness. And this total impression involves a prejudgment on our part that God cannot accept those who are not married in the way we think they should be married. I submit that we are guilty in this of the gravest kind of theological distortion possible—the elevating of a human custom to a position equal to or of more importance than the requirements of God for entrance into what we fondly call "God's family."

2. A further, more pervasive result of our position is the diversion of focus from central matters, such as faith-allegiance to Christ, to peripheral matters, such as the replacement of traditional African morality by western morality the main symbol of which is the requirement of monogamy elevated to the position of an entrance requirement for church membership. The focus in the cross-cultural communication of the Gospel comes to be on the cultural, rather than on the supracultural elements. We focus on the necessity to change customs to accord with those of the bringers of the message, rather than on the overriding importance of responding to the God who, while residing outside of the cultural milieu himself, channels his appeal for people to respond to him through human cultures. The issue we make over polygamy makes it the more impossible for Africans to understand our message and motivation in any other sense than that we are primarily concerned with converting them to western customs as the way to God.

Africans see clearly that we feel that God has put his stamp of approval on only our culture, and that we feel that God is on our side in our passion to supplant African culture with our own. Yet the picture is often confused by the fact that what we say about God (as opposed to what we do concerning the matter of church membership) portrays the kind of God for whom African s have unconsciously sought all their lives. So does the information about God and Christ that they get from the Bible, and their own culturally-derived perception of what the relatively unknown but good God is like. These combine to produce a picture of the kind of God that they feel could satisfy his deepest longings and they are instinctively drawn to this kind of God. Their long unsatisfied hopes are raised, only to be dashed against the rock of other-cultural entrance requirements that they see to be inconsistent with the bright new, attractive revelation of God that have come to them from the same source.

They turn away sadly—not as the rich young man turned away from Christ because he found something wrong with his own attitudes, but, rather, as those who on a cold wintry night are forced to withdraw from an open door beyond which lies visible the warm, open hearth that their beings crave. They have been rebuffed by an unthinking hearthkeeper who only has room for women, children, and those who think so little of themselves that they sell out to the hearthkeeper for the sake of a bit of physical warmth. To such persons we, in God's name, have both denied God's mercy and diverted their attention from focusing on the God whom they seek, to focusing on the White Man who blocks the way.

Indefensible

It is my conviction that our actions and attitudes manifested in our opposition to allowing polygamists into full church membership necessarily imply a theological position that cannot be seriously defended as Christian. Somehow our exclusiveness doesn't square up with the universality of the invitation extended by the Scriptures. And when the church becomes more exclusive than God is, it's high time some adjustments be made.

Somehow our insistence on the meeting of certain cultural standards as prerequisite to church membership puts us on the wrong side, the pre-Christian side, of the argument concerning whether or not it was right to require circumcision of Christian converts (Acts 15). Somehow we seem to have missed the point of Peter's visions and subsequent action in accepting Cornelius on the basis of his expression of faith alone (Acts 10). And somehow we seem to be setting ourselves squarely against the God whom we claim to serve, by refusing to accept into membership all those whom the Spirit, who moves where he chooses to move, has succeeded in convicting and converting regardless of their marital status.

Nor are the best interests served of the One who sought to focus our attention on heart-motives. By so completely misinterpreting or, at best, ignoring motivation in our passion to do away with polygamy, our concern is invariably with the outward manifestation, the living of one man with more than one woman. Our condemnation is of the *form*, and our presentation of "God's teaching" in the matter deals solely with external, rather than heart things. Moreover, we are more than willing to overlook or represent God as anxious to forgive far more weighty matters of pride, greed, gluttony, etc.—*but no polygamist may come into or remain in the church,* no matter how repentant he may be, if he feels he is bound to fulfill his social obligations to those to whom he is legally married or whom he has legally borne!

Wuliki's Story

Wuliki is still a Christian. But he has been banished from the church. No church leader had taken the time to listen sympathetically to his story. He was simply asked whether or not he now had two wives and he had honestly answered, "yes." The missionary who asked him that question concluded that Wuliki had made his choice to turn away from Christianity. Wuliki, however, explained to me later that his action had been the culmination of months of intense soul-searching and prayer that led him to conclude that it was his Christian obligation to follow God rather than human rules at all costs.

He began his story by saying that he had been married according to the local custom some fifteen or more years before, to a woman who had turned out to be shiftless. The bride-price had been nearly all paid, as was the custom, and their marriage consummated. Within a short time, however, she had run off with another man. From that time until this, the efforts of Wuliki's family to bring about the return of the bride-price to make the separation a legal divorce had been unsuccessful. After a couple of years of separation, he had married another girl in full anticipation of the time when the bride-price expended for his previous wife would be returned and their divorce official.

In the meantime, Wuliki had become a Christian and a zealous witness to his fellow tribesmen concerning his new-found faith. His efforts on behalf of the Christian faith were such that the mission, which had not yet started work in his area, contacted him and volunteered to pay him a monthly salary for his efforts, in spite of the fact that he had not had the formal schooling ordinarily required by the mission for such a position. His position as evangelist with the mission continued thus for thirteen years. Then his first wife came back.

She and her family demanded that he take her back in lieu of repayment of the brideprice. His own family, unable as they were to bring about the return of the brideprice, considered this the best way out and regarded him as under obligation to take her back. To Wuliki it became a choice between fulfilling his obligations to his family, his former wife, her family and, in effect, the whole community to which he belonged, but forfeiting his position with the mission, or obeying the mission rule against plural marriage, sending away one of his wives and becoming a virtual outcast in his own community. The question to him was on which side of the issue God stood.

Wuliki eventually chose to maintain his ties with his community with the conviction that, in spite of loss of church membership, he could best serve God by remaining an African. As best I can judge from what I know of his situation, I am convinced that Wuliki made the right decision. But I will never be able to erase the scars left on my mind and heart from having worked in a situation where such a choice was forced unnecessarily upon Wuliki and upon thousands of others like him because we seek to present the Christian gospel in an unchristian way!

Let's Be Christian about Polygamy

Let's be Christian about polygamy. Our present position must be regarded as untenable—indefensible on either practical or theological grounds—standing squarely in the way of any adequate presentation of God's offer of mercy to every person on the basis of faith, not cultural reform. Even the admission that monogamy is the ideal form of marriage, the most Christian form, toward which a society in which God is at work will strive, cannot begin to justify the unchristian means that we employ to bring this change of custom about.

After a year of study in West Africa on behalf of the United Church of Christ, Rev. Chester Marcus of Cleveland, Ohio, was recently quoted as saying:

> Polygamy is all these people have known. When they come in contact with Christianity and believe it, they want to be a part of it, Yet they have a responsibility to their families—to several wives and children.

> It is asking too much to say that a man should abandon three of his four wives, especially when this relationship was entered in good faith.[2]

Our attitude in this regard has crippled the work of Christ in Africa for better than a hundred years now. It has provided a primary reason for the rapid advance of Islam. It has turned much of the nationalistic spirit not only against white missionaries, but against Christ and Christianity as well. And this has been a major reason for the development and antagonism of separatist movements, the truly indigenous churches of Africa.

Our intransigence in the matter has encouraged us in the error of concentrating nearly all our efforts on the development and indoctrinating of a westernized minority (what we fondly call "the church") rather than providing an imitatable example of responsible, relevant witness to the non-Christian majority. It has led us to devote ourselves uncritically to the attempt to bring about an end, monogamy, which God is recorded as having worked toward patiently, by advocating means that both show our lack of patience and belie our whole purpose in being in Africa. The Christian thing for us to do in the present situation is to repent of and renounce our former position and the irresponsibility that allows us now to sit quietly by watching "indigenized" churches struggle with a load which we found too great to bear. Ours is the mistake, ours is the responsibility for leading the way back to the Good News that God accepts people on the basis of faith alone, regardless of their cultural allegiance.

---

[2] Taken from an article in the Flint, Michigan *Journal*, Feb. 12, 1961.

CHAPTER 32

THE BEARING OF THE PASSAGES IN
1 TIMOTHY AND TITUS ON THE
MATTER OF CHURCH LEADERSHIP
IN POLYGAMOUS SOCIETIES

Written in 1971 (slightly revised 1999), previously unpublished

Introduction

I want to speak to the dilemma missionaries and churches in Africa (and other places) get into when they accept the enlightened position that those who come to Christ who have more than one wife are eligible for baptism but then go on to say that they are not eligible for church leadership. See, for example, Wold (1968:181-182) where he quotes the action of the Lutheran Church in Liberia with regard to the baptism of polygamists. This statement contains the following sentence: "We affirm, however, that in accordance with St. Paul's teaching (1 Tim. 3:2, 12) no such person, man or woman, shall be permitted to hold office in the Church or congregation or be engaged as a Christian worker."

We, the advocates of Church Growth Missiology, have a special problem if we advocate, on the one hand, 1) the baptism of believing polygamists but, on the other, 2) the exclusion of polygamists from church leadership positions[1], yet, with regard to patterns of conversion hold to the desirability of 3) multi-individual (group) conversions that bring whole families, clans and tribes into Christianity complete with polygamous members who are in leadership positions within their groups (often as concomitant to their plural marriages) and 4) the desirability of the continuance

---

[1] See D. A. McGavran, writing in the *Church Growth Bulletin* in March 1969 on the incorrect assumption that 1 Timothy 3:2, 12 and Titus 1:6 infer "that in the New Testament Church were men who had two or more wives [who were] men of sufficiently good standing that, but for Paul's counsel, they might have been chosen for deacons or elders." Having said this, however, he goes on to suggest that though "one-wifeness" and all of the other virtues listed are to be regarded as strongly desirable, none of them is to be regarded as absolute. He sums up his position as follows: "These three passages then support the position that believing polygamists out of non-Christian society may be baptized. (a) They strongly infer that in the Early Church there were husbands of two or more wives. (b) They may even indicate that in the choice of deacons and elders there was no absolute prohibition of men with two or more wives."

within the church of leadership patterns familiar to Christians and non-Christians alike because they are modeled upon the patterns of the society as a whole.

The bind shows up particularly in societies that require or expect plural marriage of their leaders. I worked in one such society (called Kamwe or Higi) where the close connection between polygamy and leadership was brought out in terms of the question, "How could we respect as a leader of our society anyone who had not first proven his ability to lead by the proper administration of a household with more than one wife in it?"

Throughout Africa, at least, the connection between polygamy and qualifications for leadership appears to be a close one in many societies (e.g., Sukuma, Shambala).[2]

The dilemma is this: our principles of advocating the acceptance of all who come to faith and our principle of advocating the incorporation into the Christian church of such indigenous social structures as leadership patterns conflict in societies such as those mentioned, if polygamous marriage is regarded as disqualifying one for church leadership.

This dilemma stems from an apparent conflict between our anthropology and our theology at the point where we attempt to understand God's willingness to accept believers on the basis of their faith alone and to work with them in terms of their social structure while holding firmly to the Bible as our guidebook. When the Bible makes clear statements, of course, there is no real problem (even though there are slight cultural differences in the understanding of what constitutes such things as stealing, murder, adultery, etc. Where, furthermore, the Bible presents us with enough examples that we can feel confident that our inferences line up with his will in a matter, there is no great problem (as in the matter of God's willingness to employ human culture as the medium for his interaction with man). But where an otherwise valid inference (e.g., that God wants to employ indigenous leadership patterns in the operation of the church) appears to contradict a direct statement such as "a bishop must be the husband of one wife" (1 Tim. 3:2), problems arise that demand a careful examination of both the general principle and the apparently contradictory statement.

What I would like to here suggest is that, on the basis of principles of biblical interpretation that I think we all agree to, it is actually possible for us to take a stand with regard to polygamists in positions of church leadership that does away with the bind we have apparently gotten ourselves into.

---

[2] E.g., the Sukuma: see Tanner 1967, where he states that leadership in Sukuma society is attained through a "combination of age, socially utilized wealth in the acquisition of connections, and intelligence" (p. 215) and at least infers the necessity of polygamous marriage to this end by linking status to plural marriage (p. 106 - "there is status in being the head of a polygamous household"). With regard to the Shambala, E. V. Winans writes that the Royal Chief's Council of advisors and functionaries are "drawn from the commoner clans" (p. 121), work closely with the chief and are consulted by him on nearly all decisions. These "are important and powerful men and are usually polygynous" (p. 122) since "the ideal familial pattern in Shambala terms is the compound polygynous family" (p. 32).

Principles of Interpretation

I believe there are very few contentions that can be more strongly inferred from the biblical record than that God chooses to interact with human beings within and in terms of their cultures. It is clear in both Old and New Testaments that God meets people within *their* cultures rather than, say, creating a new culture as a matrix for his interactions with people.

Whether or not this principle allows us today to advocate the acceptance of polygamous leadership in the church, however, is a question that requires more discussion. The following three principles of biblical interpretation should lead us to a more tenable position than that reported above:

1. First, I take very seriously the traditional evangelical theological stance that "The whole Bible is equally inspired." I deny, therefore, the strong impression we often give that the NT is more inspired than the OT, and so needs to be taken much more seriously even to the point of denying the authoritativeness of the OT for our day. The most satisfactory and consistent basis on which to understand the differences between the OT and the NT, I believe, is to commit ourselves to the equal inspiration of both and to see the major (though far from the only) differences between the testaments to be *cultural* rather than theological. Our problem in this regard is due partly to the respect we feel for the NT because it records and analyzes the centrality of Christ and the way in which God brought about our salvation through him. Our attitude is, however, even more affected by the cultural and linguistic distance between our culture and the cultures of the OT and the comparative closeness between our culture and those of the NT This factor leads to a much greater likelihood that we will understand and appreciate the NT but not understand and appreciate the ways in which God and his works are revealed in the OT If, though, as I believe, 1) the whole Bible is equally inspired and 2) the major differences between God's approach to Jews and his approach to Greeks and Romans are to be interpreted culturally rather than in terms of culture-bound western theological positions, we may assume that God has showed us in the OT how he desires us to behave when we deal with similar customs today. With regard to polygamy, then, we need to take God's patience with the custom in the OT as indicative of how he wishes us to regard it, unless there is specific new revelation given in the NT

2. The second inference I would draw stems from noting that the Scriptures show God condemning certain elements of culture (e.g., idolatry) while encouraging other elements (e.g., the patriarchal head of family approach to religious leadership), yet manifesting apparent neutrality toward others. Polygamy in OT times falls into the latter category. And even if polygamy is envisioned in the Timothy and Titus passages in the NT, the approach is to allow and, if necessary, to regulate the custom. It is significant, I think, that polygamy falls into the neutral and/or regulated category rather than into the proscribed category. It is also significant that the nature of God's regulation of polygamy in Hebrew society was not such that the practice of plural marriage by Israel's leaders was regarded as in any way prejudicial to their positions

as leaders. It probably, in fact, was regarded as a virtual requirement or at least a privilege of high office during much of Hebrew history.

I conclude from this that God adopts a similar "allow but regulate" attitude toward polygamy today. Therefore, unless there is in the NT some change in the teaching regarding this matter (such as the "You have heard it said...but I say to you..." passages) the fact that God not only allowed the Patriarchs, David and others to be in positions of leadership though polygamists (even to the extent that he adopts a positive stance toward the custom in reprimanding David concerning his affair with Bathsheba (see 2 Sam. 12:8)[3], is still of relevance in attempting to discern God's will in similar cultural situations today.

3. The third inference is that the biblical record is presented "situationally," as it were. That is, only problems that were live issues at the time of the events recorded are dealt with. The understanding, therefore, of any given passage is to be determined with reference not only to the biblical context but also to the cultural context in which the event took place or to which the statement applied. This principle means that specific biblical statements are *specifically* (as opposed to generally) applicable to present-day situations only when there is a correspondence or "fit" between the biblical cultural context and that of the present-day situation. Lacking such a correspondence the surest guide to action is the application of the *general* principle evident from the biblical record of God's activity throughout the Bible (especially if there appears to be a conflict between a given specific statement and a general biblical principle). This principle of interpretation and application has long been recognized and is stated as early as 1871 (though in slightly different vocabulary) by Bishop Alford in his commentary on 1 Timothy 3:2:

> How far such a prohibition is to be considered binding on us, now that the Christian life has entered into another and totally different phase, is of course an open question for the present Christian church at any time to deal with. It must be as a matter of course understood that regulations, in all lawful things, depend, even when made by an Apostle, on circumstances: and the superstitious observance of the letter in such cases is often pregnant with mischief to the people and cause of Christ (1871,:3:322)

I conclude, therefore, that unless the "husband of one wife" passages can be demonstrated to have been spoken to a situation comparable to that of the present-day Kamwe/Higi, Shambala, Sukuma, etc., the most appropriate guidelines we have for these situations are to be found either in general scriptural principles or perhaps in specific OT events.

Our treatment of this subject then revolves around two questions:

1. Is there a cultural correspondence between the NT context in which the statements in I Timothy and Titus were understood and cultural contexts such as those of the African tribes referred to above? If there is such a correspondence, it is clear that the position adopted by some churches, including the Lutheran Church in Liberia is the only justifiable position to take. This position allows polygamists to belong to the church but excludes them from leadership positions.

---

[3] Where God says to David through the prophet Nathan ". . . I gave you your master's house, and your master's wives into your bosom, and gave you the house of Israel and of Judah; and if this were too little, I would add to you as much more" (RSV).

2. If, however, there is a lack of correspondence between the two situations and, therefore, the need to approach the African problem on the basis of general scriptural principles rather than in terms of a direct command, what are the relevant principles?

Correspondence between First Century Greco-Roman Society and Twentieth Century African Society

With regard to the first question one is tempted to suggest that first century Greco-Roman society and contemporary Kamwe/Higi society are so different as to obviate any suggestion of a correspondence between them. And I believe this to be true. If, however, it were possible to demonstrate a "partial correspondence" between these societies at the point of plural marriage one could contend that a position such as that of the Lutherans is warranted.

It behooves us, therefore, to look at the Timothy and Titus passages expositorily in relation to the above discussion of principles and the information available to us concerning the existence of polygamous marriages in the early church and the society in which that church operated.

Context of the Timothy and Titus Passages

There are three cultures to be considered in our discussion: Roman, Greek and Jewish. The standard work dealing with family and marriage in biblical times is the monumental three volume study by Westermarck (1922). Our understanding of the cultural context will, therefore, based on that work plus commentaries and the *Encyclopedia Brittanica*.

With regard to Roman culture, the sources are unanimous that no polygamy occurred. All (including the *Brittanica* and the commentaries) agree with Westermarck that "Roman marriage was strictly monogamous" (1922, 3:49) and "...the only legitimate form of marriage in Greece." (1922, 3:48). E. F. Brown in the *Westminster Commentary*, adds, "polygamy...was forbidden by Roman law" (1917:24).

In Greek culture, as noted above, "...monogamy was the only recognized form of marriage in Greece" (Westermarck 1922, 3:48). Though "concubinage existed at Athens...it was well distinguished from marriage" (1922, 3:40). The commentaries and *Brittanica* agree.

In First Century Jewish society the situation is a bit different. Polygamy was still legitimate but, according to Westermarck, "in post-exilic times polygamy was a rare exception" (1922, 3:42). A. J. Maclean in Hastings' *Dictionary of the Apostolic Church*, then, states that "Among the Jews polygamy had greatly decreased since the time of the patriarchs, and at the commencement of the Christian era was little practiced...perhaps largely in consequence of Roman influence" (1916-18, 2:14). Josephus (c. 115 A.D.), referring to Herod and his sons, mentions that the custom sometimes occurred and Justin Martyr, writing likewise in the second century, speaks to Jews, saying, "It is better that ye follow God than that ye follow your unwise and blind leaders who still unchangingly allow each one of you to have as much as four or five wives" (Archambault quoted by Helander 1958:26). Helander comments: "this latter statement shows that the Christian Church during the second century disapproved of polygamy, but that this form of marriage then still existed amongst the Jews."

We see, then, that polygamy still existed among Jews, though it never existed among the Greeks or the Romans. It was, therefore, thoroughly disapproved of by the Greco-Roman church. This led at least one of their apologists, Justin, to use the fact that polygamy still occasionally occurred in Jewish society as an occasion to taunt the Jews. The fact that only this remark and the Josephus reference can be cited from the sizeable Christian literature of the first few centuries, however, seems to indicate that the disapproving first century church very rarely had to even face the issue in any of the societies in which it operated.

It is interesting, though, that the custom was not officially prohibited among the Jews until the tenth or eleventh century. This was at Worms in 1030 A.D., according to Epstein or in 950 at Mainz, according to K. Wilhelm of Stockholm (see Helander 1958:25-26; see also Westermarck 1922).

An interesting piece of evidence concerning demise of polygamy among Jews comes from the Septuagint, the 3rd century B.C. translation of the OT into Greek. These translators added the word "two" to the text of Genesis 2:24 so that it reads in Greek: "the *two* shall become one flesh," whereas the Hebrew reads simply: "they shall be one flesh." It was the Septuagint version, then, that was quoted by Paul in 1 Corinthians 6:16. So, since these were Jewish translators, we may conclude that a reasonably strong predisposition toward monogamy as the only legitimate form of marriage had developed in Jewish society already by the 3rd century B.C.

It is interesting to look to what Jesus said and didn't say. Polygamy was apparently a non-issue to him. He doesn't mention polygamy in his teaching concerning divorce (Mt. 5:32; 19:6, 9; Mk. 10:9, 11 ff.; Lk. 16:18). Furthermore, he quotes the Septuagint version of Genesis 2:24, with the word "two" in it (Mt. 19:5). In addition, he says nothing about the custom, neither condemning nor recommending it, when the Sadducees test him with regard to Levirate marriage (Mt. 22:23 ff.).

Geoffrey Parrinder, who published a book on our subject in 1958, states,

> Now it is very significant, and a point often overlooked, that there is no record of a question about whether a man might in any circumstances, take a second wife. If there had been any doubt at all about whether a serious-minded Jew could have several wives, we should very probably have some reference to it in the Gospels or the Epistles. This would certainly have been preserved by the early Christian communities, if the problem had ever arisen in their own moral life. The absence

of a negative command against polygamy in the New Testament, is, therefore, very significant, in exactly the opposite direction to that which is commonly and rashly assumed. It shows that the question no longer arose among the Jewish or Gentile communities to whom the gospel was addressed (1958:43).

In conclusion, Parrinder further points out,

> We have seen that the Jews also, by the time of Christ, had practically all become monogamists. Monogamy had come by itself, and was not disputed by the Rabbis. For Paul, therefore, or any early Christian writer, to permit, even by implication, polygamy to Gentile or to Jew would be to shock them (1958:51).

Exegesis of 1 Timothy 3:2, 12;
Titus 1:6

The passages in question are in the form of what were known as "ethical lists." These were lists that are found regularly in the writings of Greek-speaking Jews of the first century.

As Guthrie points out,

> With precise detail Paul proceeds to list the qualities required in an overseer. Easton, following Vogtle, has shown that parallel ethical lists were current in Greek circles designed for various occupations, e.g., king, general, midwife, etc. The qualities required for Christian rulers are strikingly similar in many particulars (1957:80).

Easton gives samples of four of these ethical lists—those for The King, The General, The Ruler and The Midwife. Such lists, says Easton,

> originated in Hellenism. In their simplest forms they were learned by children, the teacher adding explanations and comments suitable to the pupils' age ...

> Such lists were among the most serviceable of rhetoricians' common-places; whether couched in very general terms or arranged for themes of common occurrence, such as "The Ruler," "The Philosopher," "The Good Woman," "The Traitor," etc. And lists designed for one purpose were used for another ... (Easton 1948:197-198).

Of the lists given by Easton, the one most like those in Timothy and Titus is the one for "The Ruler." This list specifies that rulers should be "not accusable, *once married*, temperate, sober, well-ordered, hospitable, good teacher, no drunkard, no assaulter, mild, peaceable, no money lover, ruling his home" (1948:201, emphasis mine).

In the Timothy and Titus lists we find the requirement that bishops and deacons be "husbands of one wife." The question is, how to interpret this phrase, given the fact that polygamy did not occur in Greek or Roman society and had all but died out in Jewish society.

Several possible interpretations of the reference have been advanced. The one we have been dealing with is that it refers to polygamy. But, as we have seen, it is highly unlikely that Paul would have had polygamy in mind, since the custom didn't occur in Greco-Roman society and only very occasionally in Jewish society. Another possible interpretation is that the reference is to "digamy," the practice of a man remarrying after the death or divorce of his wife. More on this below. The possibility has also been raised that the statement is to be taken as a positive requirement of marriage, rather than a negative prohibition. The interpretation would then be, "a wifed man" or "a married man," as opposed to a single, unmarried man.

Which interpretation is chosen is pretty much irrelevant to the issue at hand, since the statement as it stands, if taken absolutely, prohibits any form of second marriage. Given this fact, our interest here is whether or not the passages imply the presence of polygamists in the churches.

A defining condition in this regard would seem to be the fact, agreed to by nearly all evangelical commentators, that these letters were written to speak to situations in Ephesus (Timothy) and Crete (Titus). Since the Christians in these places were predominantly Greek and Roman, it is extremely unlikely, then, that Paul has in mind the needs of Jewish converts. But even if he did have Jewish converts in mind, as we have seen, polygamy was such a dead issue among Jews that none of the other NT writings allude to it, even the Gospels, Acts, Hebrews, James and 1 and 2 Peter, books written with Jewish audiences in mind. Unless, therefore, it can be established from some new historical source that polygamy was a part of Greco-Roman life or of significantly greater prominence among Jews in Paul's day than in Christ's, I find it inconceivable that these verses are to be interpreted as assuming the presence of polygamists in these churches.

This being true, Parrinder concludes,

> The true explanation of these verses from the Pastoral Epistles seems almost certainly to be a prohibition of a second marriage, after either the death or the divorce of the first wife. So Professor Ryder Smith writes, "the phrase 'the husband of one wife,' found in the First Epistle to Timothy, both about bishops and deacons, cannot mean that these officers were to be monogamists while other Christians might be polygamists, for there were no polygamists even among the 'heathen.' The phrase probably means that a man who in his heathen days had been divorced and had married again—and who therefore had more than one 'wife' living—must not be appointed to church office" (1958:52).

J. H. Bernard also supports this interpretation in his comment on the phrase *mias gunaikos andra* in 1 Timothy 3:2:

> The sense is fixed by the parallel clause in ch. v. 9... *enos andros gune* which cannot possibly mean anything but a woman who has not remarried after the death or divorce of her husband. It excludes from ecclesiastical position those who have been married more than once. For ordinary Christians second marriages are not forbidden: see esp. Rom. vii.3: I Cor. vii.9 and 39; and I Tim. v.14. But they are forbidden to [church leaders] as it is all important that they should be [without reproach] (1906:52).

Bernard then adds as a footnote,

> Under the Pentateuchal law, the regulations about marriage were in like manner stricter for the priests than for the people; the priest was forbidden to marry a widow or a divorced woman (Lev. xxi. 14) (1906:52).

E. F. Brown (1917:24), likewise, concludes that the meaning of *husband of one wife* means having married, if at all, only once. "What is here forbidden is digamy under any circumstances" (White 1909/1951:111). Brown points to a number of other commentators, some quite old, who came to the same conclusion. He says,

> Liddon, Ellicott, Alford, Wace (Speaker's Comm.), Plummer (Expositors' Bible) and Bernard (Camb. Greek Test.) all decide that this is the only possible interpretation consistent with (i) the parallel expression 'wife of one husband' in ch. v.9...; (ii) the early Christian Fathers and Councils... (iii) the fact that the early Church had not to deal with polygamy, which was forbidden by Roman law...; (iv) the fact that even Roman Flamens, and other heathen priests, were not allowed to marry more than once... (1917:24).

To show some other, even contrary, positions, Brown notes that "Theodore of Mopsuesta argues against this view, but admits that it was the one taken by the Church..." He goes on to refer to the position of Jerome, whom he says was inconsistent, defending a Spanish bishop who had remarried but admitting that "a person twice married cannot be enrolled in the ranks of the clergy." Of more recent commentators, Brown cites Calvin, Bengel, and Luther as holding that "the text only forbids marriage after divorce," and Bishop John Wordsworth that "it enjoins at least one marriage upon all clergy" (1917:24).

Bishop Alford, as early as 1871, penned these words concerning the phrase "husband of one wife." Though he seems to overestimate the amount of polygamy among the Jews, he comes to the same conclusion as later commentators. These words, he says,

> have been supposed to prohibit either 1) simultaneous polygamy, or 2) successive polygamy. 1) has somewhat to be said for it. The custom of polygamy was then prevalent among the Jews...and might easily find its way into the Christian community.... But the objection to taking this meaning is, that the Apostle would hardly have specified that as a requisite for the episcopate or presbyteriate, which we know to have been fulfilled by all Christians whatever: no instance being adduced of polygamy being practised in the Christian church, and no exhortations to abstain from it... 2) ... the view that second marriages are prohibited to aspirants after the episcopate [is] the most probable meaning...[due to] the wide prevalence in the early Church of the idea that, although second marriages were not forbidden to Christians, abstinence from them was better than indulgence in them.... With regard to the Apostle's own command and permissions of this state... they do not come into account here, because they are confessedly (and expressly so in ch. v.14) for those whom it was not contemplated to admit into ecclesiastical office.... The view then which must I think be adopted, especially in presence of ch. v.9...is, that to candidates for the episcopate (presbytery) St. Paul forbids second marriage. He requires of them preeminent chastity, and abstinence from a license which is allowed to other Christians (1871, 3:321-322).

In summarizing the positions concerning the interpretation of these verses, Bernard states,

> Other interpretations of these disputed words are (a) that they forbid polygamy. But, although polygamy is said to have been not unknown among the Jews of the Apostolic age (Joseph. Antt. xvii.12; Just. Mart. Trypho 134), it was quite an exceptional thing; and it was never countenanced by Christians. Polygamy would not have been lawful for any Christian convert, whether from Judaism or from

heathendom; and, therefore, the special prohibition in the case of a bishop would have been without point. Such an interpretation is indeed absolutely excluded by the parallel clause *enos andros gune* of ch. v.9 (b) That they forbid any deviation from the ordinary laws of Christian purity of life. But this is not a satisfactory or precise interpretation of the words. (c) That the *episkopos must* be a married man, not a celibate. This would not only be inconsistent with I Cor. vii. 17, but does not represent the force of *mias*, the emphatic word in the sentence. No explanation is adequate save that which lies on the surface, viz. the *episkopos* must be married only once, if at all (1906:53).

What about the Cultural Fit?

Having sought to discover the author's intent in these passages, we come back to our original concern with the question, Do these passages have any relevance to the African situation described above? The points to make would seem to be the following:

1. It is clear that if polygamy was in Paul's mind at all it only applied to the Jewish communities.

2. It is clear, however, that whether or not polygamy is alluded to here, the proscription of any second marriage would have applied to any polygamists in the church. As Bernard points out "polygamy would not have been lawful for *any* Christian," and Alford, "no instance being adduced of polygamy being practiced in the Christian church."

3. It is clear also that whatever the situation vis-à-vis the prevalence of polygamy in Hebrew society at that time, it was not regarded as the ideal form of marriage (as in the African societies discussed above). Nor does it seem to have been associated with Jewish leadership in any way similar to that of the African societies in question. On this point, however, the silence of my sources, except for Josephus' negative reference to the Herods, makes it difficult to argue persuasively.

4. Even so, we may confidently conclude that there is no discernable fit between the sociocultural context to which these biblical passages were directed and that of the African peoples we are discussing.

What Then Are the Relevant Scriptural Guidelines for the African Situation?

Given the above conclusion, we will need to seek general guidelines rather than specific statements from Scripture to enable us to decide the proper approach to the African situation. In developing these guidelines, then, we will assume the inspiration and consequent applicability of the whole Bible.

The first of these guidelines involves observing from the Scriptures how God handled the problem when he faced it in Old Testament times. His approach was to accept the custom, not as his ideal, but also not as something to hold against his people. He was patient and focused on more central and important issues such as obedience and the effects of disobedience on the relationship between him and his people. I would suggest that we take God's attitude and approach toward the practice as our basic guideline. If we are patient, then, we may expect the eventual dying out of the practice, as it did in Hebrew society as a result of the long-term work of the Holy Spirit in that society.

With regard to the qualifications for leadership in the church, the real theme of these verses, I believe there is a supracultural principle here set forth that is completely relevant to the African situation. This principle is that *Christian leaders are to conduct themselves in a manner that is judged by Christians and non-Christians alike to be beyond reproach*. That is, it is the supracultural requirement of *irreproachability* on the part of Christian leaders that is here being advocated. The "one-wifeness" (whatever it means) is simply an appropriate culturally specific illustration, listed along with a series of other culturally specific illustrations of how this irreproachability was to be worked out in first century Greco-Roman society.

Though the listing of qualities given in these passages contains many items that will likely be found to be relevant among many (perhaps a majority) of the world's peoples, it is basically applicable in detail only to first century Greco-Roman society. That is, the forms here advocated by Paul as demonstrations of irreproachability are specific to the culture of that day, though the meaning (i.e., irreproachability as a requirement for Christian leadership) is supracultural.

On the basis of this principle, that irreproachability is required of Christian leaders, we will need to ask, What qualities in another society are required if their leaders are to be considered irreproachable? Will the list be the same as that in these passages? Or will differences in culture require that a different, parallel list be generated? I believe that another list of specifics needs to be produced—a list that details the qualities required by *that* society in demonstration of the irreproachability requirement.

We subconsciously generate one such item when we interpret for our society the headcovering passage (1 Cor. 11:2-16). Likewise, when we teach on the tenth commandment (Ex. 20:17). With respect to headcovering, we recognize that the real issue, the thing Paul was teaching about, is that Christian women are not to dress like immoral women. So we speak to our people of those items of dress appropriate to our society. With respect to the tenth commandment, we do not speak of coveting oxen or donkeys, we speak of other things, things appropriate to our cultural context. And the meaning of these Scriptures is gotten across *because of,* not in spite of, the fact that we have changed the specifics of these passages.

Given this important principle, the question arises, What do we recommend in a society that defines irreproachability in such a way as to demand the proper administration of a polygamous household? If we are to generate an appropriately scriptural list for such a people, should it not contain the requirement that a Christian leader be beyond reproach in the eyes of his fellows in this area of life as well as in others? That is, for the Christian leader in that society, polygamy and, more specifically, the proper administration of a polygamous household becomes a requirement. The rest of the list, then, would also be made up of socioculturally appropriate items, some of which might well be the same as those in the passages under consideration.

If the matter of plural wives, even for leaders, is handled in this way, however, it is clear that Scripture teaches that a man in this kind of marriage, as in all other kinds, needs to conduct himself in a manner that is beyond reproach in the relationship. We would, I believe, be more aligned with God's approach if we asked not how many wives a Christian man has, but how he treats them. That is, the Christian church should focus on requiring of its leaders in marriage as well as in every other area of life, the kind of socioculturally appropriate irreproachability taught in these passages without prescribing the form of the marriage (i.e., as between monogamy and polygamy).

There is a difference, easily demonstrated from Scripture and from our own lives, between where God is willing to start with people and the ideals he wishes that we strive toward. I do not question that loving monogamy is his ideal. He only created one Eve for Adam. In every society, then, this ideal is to be taught. But in every society, God's patience is also to be taught and practiced. He has shown us in the Old Testament how he wants us to handle polygamy, even among leaders. We should learn, then, from a proper understanding of the Timothy and Titus passages that they do not give us permission to support an imposition of our cultural ideal on leaders in place of the patience and acceptance of even subideal custom so evident in God's approach.

Conclusion

Interpretation of these passages in the light of their cultural context and culturally appropriate application of scriptural principles, therefore, supports rather than prohibits the appointment of otherwise qualified polygamists to positions of church leadership in societies that ordinarily expect or demand polygamous marriage of their leadership.

CHAPTER 33

DYNAMIC EQUIVALENCE CHURCHES:
AN ETHNOTHEOLOGICAL APPROACH
TO INDIGENEITY

Reprinted here with permission from
Missiology: An International Review 1:39-57 (1973)

Since the days of Henry Venn and Rufus Anderson the concept of *indigeneity* has been a missionary ideal, but what it means and how one measures it are not always clear. From these early theorists the *three-selfs* definition of indigeneity developed. Venn contended that the aim of his mission (Church Missionary Society) should be "the development of Native Churches, with a view to their ultimate settlement upon a self-supporting, self-governing and self-extending system" (Stock 1899, 2:83), and Anderson independently was making similar statements about the American Board of Commissioners of Foreign Missions (Strong 1910:167–168). This concept was farsighted for its time but was subsequently submerged by a long period of paternalism to be revived in our own century.

However it has often blinded its adherents to the fact that a self-governing church is not necessarily indigenous. Just "indoctrinate a few leaders in Western patterns of church government, and let them take over," Smalley points out, and you have "a Church governed in a slavishly foreign manner" (1958:52). Without denying the real advance in missionary theory that the three-self theory embodied, one must insist that not every church that governs, supports and propagates itself can be properly labeled "indigenous" except in a superficial, formal sense, for the three-self elements, even when present, "are essentially independent variables" (1958:51–52) rather than diagnostic criteria of indigeneity. They do not necessarily guarantee the quality of indigeneity, which lies in the manner in which the selfhood is expressed. Simple evaluation of the forms of government, support and propagation is inadequate. One has to look at the ways in which these cultural forms are operated and the meanings attached to them by both the church itself and the surrounding community.

> There is, for example, a church which is advertised by its founding mission as a great indigenous church, where its pastors are completely supported by the local church members, yet the mission behind the scenes pulls the strings and the church does its bidding like the puppets of the 'independent' iron curtain countries (Smalley 1958:59).

In other churches the power is no longer, directly or indirectly, in the hands of foreigners, but the nationals in power have been so indoctrinated in foreign ways (which they consider "Christian") that they resolutely perpetuate the foreign system in the name of Christ. In both situations the "indigeneity" is of outward form only—the essence, the content, the meanings conveyed and impressions given are all foreign.

Nor is "'indigeneity" necessarily the most appropriate label for the ideal toward which we strive, because something totally indigenous would in appearance, functioning and meaning be no different from the rest of the culture. Christianity is "always intrusive to a certain degree." There is "no such thing as an absolutely indigenous church in any culture" (Smalley 1959:137). Absolute indigeneity would so conform to the culture in every respect that it would not be Christian. Furthermore, it would be so predictable in terms of the indigenous culture that it would have no communication value (Kraft 1973b). A certain basic incompatibility exists between the terms "indigenous" and "Christian" unless we agree that by "indigenous Christian Church" we imply something less than absolute indigeneity.

What, then, is the ideal towards which we strive? Smalley defines an indigenous church as:

> a group of believers who live out their life, including their socialized Christian activity, in the patterns of the local society, and for whom any transformation of that society comes out of their felt needs under the guidance of the Holy Spirit and the Scriptures (1958:55).

With a slightly different focus, Tippett states:

> When the indigenous people of a community think of the Lord as their own, not a foreign Christ; when they do things as unto the Lord meeting the cultural needs around them, worshipping in patterns they understand; when their congregations function in participation in a body, which is structurally indigenous; then you have an indigenous Church (1969:136).

Just as in a good Bible translation, the readers, who are unaware of the fact that the Bible was originally written in other languages than their own, assume that it is an original production in their language; so should Christians feel that their church is an original institution within their own culture. The following discussion is an attempt to apply certain models, developed by Bible translation theorists, to the concept of the "indigenous Christian church."

Dynamic (Functional) Equivalence Versus Formal Correspondence

The traditional three-self concept is inadequate because it measures indigeneity purely with reference to a select few of the forms, without reference to the way in which these forms operate or function, or their meanings. A more appropriate model is now in vogue among informed Bible translators, who aim not for mere "formal correspondence" between the forms of the source and receptor languages as do literal translators (KJV, RSV and ASV). Such translators have a non-English (i.e., non-indigenous) flavor because the translators have not made sure that the English renderings are the functional equivalents (not merely the formal correspondents) of their Hebrew, Aramaic and Greek referents. Neither do people talk and write English like this.

Such "formal correspondence translations" translate literally the word forms of the source language into the receptor language counterparts. When Paul employs a Greek word for "bowels" the KJV renders it "bowels" (e.g., Phil. 1:8, 2:1) because although the use is clearly figurative (signifying "affection" or "kindness") the basic meaning of the word when not used figuratively is "bowels." Likewise a formal correspondence translation renders each word in the source language mechanically by the same receptor language term. Thus RSV translates the Greek word *soma* as "body" in each of the following verses: Matthew 6:25; Mark 5:29; Luke 17:37; Romans 12:1 and Colossians 2:11, because "body" is the main meaning of the word, and the translators wanted to be consistent. However, the Greek and English words are far from exactly equivalent. The Greek word *soma* has many more meanings than simply "body," and a true translation should render whichever meaning the context indicates.

Literally thousands of such illustrations can be produced from the KJV, ASV and RSV of formal correspondence translations from Greek and Hebrew that obscure and sometimes obliterate the intended meanings. These translations were produced to adhere to older concepts of the nature of language, which regarded them simply as alternative codes for the same reality. Early in this century anthropologists and linguists recognized that understandings of reality are structured differently by different cultures and that these differences are strongly reflected in their languages. There is, therefore, no such thing as an exact correspondence between a given word in one language and the most nearly corresponding word in another language. By symbolizing cultures (including their languages) as geometrical figures divided by lines to indicate the way they segment reality, we may exemplify the differences between the older and modern concepts. (See figure below.)

Since cultures and their languages do not correspond exactly, formal correspondence translations frequently may create the misimpression that God requires us to learn a foreign (i.e., Hellenized or Hebraised) version of English before we can really understand him. They denote with English labels not English concepts but the segments into which the Greek or Hebrew languages are divided. Preachers using literal translations have to devote much time to explaining that in the Bible, the apparently English words don't have their English meanings, but, rather the Greek and Hebrew meanings, which only students of the biblical languages can properly understand and explain.

The Formal Correspondence Concept of Cultural and Linguistic Diversity:

Culture A   Culture B   Culture C

The Modern Formal Non-Correspondence Understanding of Cultural and Linguistic Diversity:

Culture A   Culture B   Culture C

The Phillips translation carried the task beyond mere formal correspondence, trying to be faithful both to the original message and to the intended impact of that message upon the original readers. For Phillips sought to elicit from modern readers a response equivalent to that elicited from the original audience of the slangy, communicative *koine* (= common people's) Greek. Recognizing the non-equitability of languages, he went beyond formal correspondence to function in today's English-speaking world in a way equivalent to that of the original in the New Testament Greek-speaking world. E. A. Nida calls this "dynamic equivalence translation." Such a translation is described as "the closest natural equivalent to the source-language message." It is "directed primarily toward equivalence of response rather than equivalence of form" (Nida 1964:166) and:

> is therefore to be defined in terms of the degree to which the receptors of the message in the receptor language respond to it in substantially the same manner as the receptors in the source language. This response can never be identical, for the cultural and historical settings are too different, but there should be a high degree of equivalence of response, or the translation will have failed to accomplish its purpose (Nida and Taber 1969:24).

Concomitant to this dynamic view of Bible translation is the fact that translation involves more than simply the conveying of information. According to Nida and Taber:

> It would be wrong to think . . . that the response of the receptors in the second language is merely in terms of comprehension of the information, for communication is not merely informative. It must also be expressive and imperative if it is to serve the principal purposes of communications such as those found in the Bible. That is to say, a translation of the Bible must not only provide information which people can understand but must present the message in such a

way that people can feel its relevance (the expressive element in communication) and can then respond to it in action (the imperative function) (1969:24).

This new concept of what is involved in translating the Bible allows for the complexity of each language and the process of moving concepts from one language to another. An oversimplified diagram of the formal correspondence understanding of the process of translation would look like this (C stands for concept):

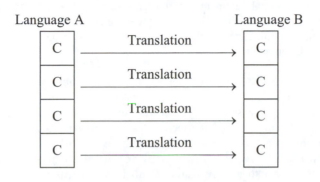

The translator seeks to understand the concept linguistically and to transfer it literally into the receptor language in roughly the same number of words as was required in the source language. If the cultural and/or linguistic situation contained implications that the reader of the receptor language could not understand (and they always did) it was considered invalid to add explanatory phrases since the process of translation was word-centered rather than idea-centered. Such additions were "paraphrases" and were not "translations."

The new understanding of what translation involves recognizes that the central aim is communication, not mere literalness even out of reverence for supposedly sacred words. The biblical writers intended to be understood. Faithful translation, involves doing whatever must be done (including paraphrase) to make sure the message originally phrased in the words and idioms of the source language is faithfully phrased in the functionally equivalent words and idioms of the receptor language. The real issue in translation lies not in the mere words but in the impact of the concepts embodied on the reader/hearer. If the impact results in wrong understanding, misunderstanding or lack of understanding on the part of the average (that is, unindoctrinated) reader/hearer, the translation has failed. A primary question asked by the new approach is, "What does the receptor language require that this concept be intelligible and convey an impact equivalent to that experienced by the original readers/hearers?" Whatever of paraphrase must be included then, is legitimately to be called "translation" since it is required by the receptor language, not optionally inserted at the whim of the translator.

All this is suggestive with respect to what churches should look like from culture to culture. Note the importance of each of the following basic understandings of the new approach both to Bible translation and to the concept of "dynamic equivalence churches" (Nida and Taber 1969:3–8):

1. "Each language has its own genius," its own distinctiveness, its own special character. Each has its own grammatical patterns, its own peculiar idioms, its own areas of vocabulary strength and its own weaknesses and limitations.

2. To communicate effectively in another language one must respect this uniqueness (both the strengths and the weaknesses) and work within its terms. Attempts to "remake" languages to conform to others have been unsuccessful. The effective translator is, prepared to make any and all formal changes necessary to reproduce the message in the distinctive structural forms of the receptor language."

3. "Anything that can be said in one language can be said in another, unless the form is an essential element of the message." Though translation and communication can never be absolute, they can be adequate if the focus is on the content being transmitted rather than on the mere preservation of the literal forms of the source language.

4. "To preserve the content of the message the form must be changed." Since different languages express similar concepts in very different ways and no concepts in exactly the same ways, the faithful translator must alter the form. Good (i.e., bad) examples of ineffective translation, due to the refusal of the translators to alter the Greek form, occur in the formal correspondence translations' (KJV, ASV, RSV) renderings of Mk 1:4 ("baptism of repentance" should be changed into a more natural English verbal expression such as "turn away from your sins and be baptized," TEV); Mt 3:8 ("bring forth . . . fruits meet for repentance" should be changed to something like "do the things that will show that you have turned from your sins," TEV); and Lk 20:47 ("which devour widows' houses" is more naturally rendered "who take advantage of widows and rob them of their homes," TEV).

If the source and the receptor languages participate in fairly similar cultures (as do English and the European languages) the changes of form will usually not be great. But the greater the linguistic and cultural distance between the source and receptor languages, the greater the number and extent of the formal changes required to preserve the meaning. And this need not always be distance along a "horizontal" axis as between, say, contemporary English and contemporary Zulu; it may be a "vertical" time distance between contemporary and seventeenth century (King James) English, or between a contemporary and first century Greek.

5. "The languages of the Bible are subject to the same limitations as any other natural languages" and are, therefore, not to be regarded as too sacred to analyze and translate in the modern sense. They are no more perfect or precise than other languages (e.g., over 700 grammatical and lexical ambiguities have been counted in the Greek Gospels alone!) but, in fact, just like all other languages, show both areas of strength and great liability. Furthermore, as will all languages, the biblical Greek and Hebrew vocabulary, idiom and grammar participate fully in and have meaning only in terms of the culture in which these languages were used. The authors did not invent unknown words or use them in unknown ways except as anyone is allowed by his culture to innovate on occasion to convey new insight or for cultural borrowing. "All the vocabulary was itself rooted in the finite experience of men and women, and all of the expressions must be understood in terms of this type of background." That is, it is the *message* of the Bible that is sacred, not the languages themselves, even though the sacred message was conveyed in terms of these finite, imperfect, culture-bound languages.

6. "The writers of the Biblical books expected to be understood." To many Americans, accustomed to hearing and reading God's Word from literal translations and hearing preachers trying to explain them, the idea that the authors

expected to be understood comes as a shock. Yet "the writers of the Bible were addressing themselves to concrete historical situations and were speaking to living people confronted with pressing issues." The translator is obligated to produce a translation that makes the same kind of sense in the receptor language if he is to keep faith with the original authors and the God for whom they spoke.

7. "The translator must attempt to reproduce the meaning of a passage as understood by the writer." We are to translate the writings of, say, Matthew and Luke, not the deduced Aramaic words of Jesus which these authors are reporting in Greek.

The dynamic equivalence model of translating, then, goes far beyond the formal correspondence model in its understanding of language, the cultural setting of language and the complexity of the translation process itself. This leads to a new and more demanding set of procedures which contrast markedly with the simplistic direct approach to translation diagrammed above. The new procedure may be briefly indicated by the following diagram.

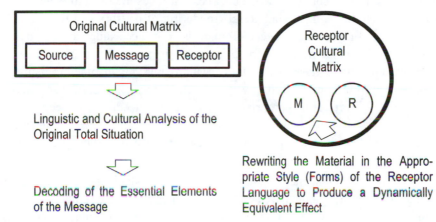

Dynamic Equivalence Churches

What is desired, then, is the kind of churchmen (indigenous or expatriate) who will regard the receptor culture and the biblical cultural expressions of "churchness" as the contemporary Bible translator regards the languages he works with. Such churchmen will work in accord with the basic propositions for translators outlined above. They will (1) recognize, (2) respect and work in terms of the unique genius of the receptor culture in recognition of the fact that (3) anything (such as the church) expressible in one culture is expressible in another. (4) They will not, however, hesitate to alter the (Hebrew and Greco-Roman) forms in terms of which the original churches were expressed because they recognize that it is the content expressed, not the forms in terms of which that content was originally expressed, that is sacred. (5) For the biblical cultures were fully human cultures, dignified by the fact that God worked within them but not sanctified thereby—demonstrating rather God's willingness to work in terms of any culture than his desire to perfect and impose any single culture. (6) The church is meant to be intelligible to the world around it—God expects to be understood by men by means of the church and the faithful churchman is to work toward this end in (7) consciously attempting to produce structures within the receptor culture that are dynamically equivalent to the churches portrayed (though but partially) for us in the pages of the New Testament.

Applying this model to church planting would mean the eschewing of attempts to produce mere formal correspondence between churches in one culture and those in another. A church that is merely a "literal" rendering of the forms of one church, be it American or first century Greco-Roman is not according to the dynamic equivalence model, since it is not structured in such a way that it can perform the functions and convey the meanings that a Christian church is intended to manifest in a culturally appropriate way. It will always smack of foreignness, of insensitivity to the surrounding culture, of inappropriateness to the real needs of the people and the real message of God to them, since its forms have not been translated or "transculturated" from those appropriate somewhere else into those appropriate in the new setting.

A "formal correspondence church" models itself slavishly after the foreign church that founded it. If that church has bishops or presbyters or elders, or operates according to a written constitution, or conducts business meetings according to Roberts' Rules of Order, the younger church will likewise. Similarly with regard to educational requirements for leadership, times of worship, style of worship, type of music, structures of church buildings, behavioral requirements for good standing, the types of educational, medical and benevolent activity entered into, even the expression of missionary concern (if any) will be modeled on the foreign prototype. And all of this in utter disregard for the culturally appropriate functional equivalents and the indigenously understood meanings of all of these things in the culture in which the young church is supposedly functioning and to which it is supposedly witnessing. The impression such churches give to the people of their cultural world is foreign and denominational even though the leadership may well be "their own people"—though again only in a formal sense, since these leaders have been carefully indoctrinated into the foreign system in order to attain the positions that they have within the system.

The true aim however, should be not formal correspondence, but the same kind of dynamic or functional equivalence discussed above for Bible translation. For, as Nida points out about what he terms "biblical relativism" Christianity is not like Islam which through the Koran "attempts to fix for all time the behavior of Muslims" by setting up an absolutely unbending set of forms which are simply to be adopted, never adapted. The Bible "clearly establishes the principle of relative relativism, which permits growth, adaptation, and freedom, under the Lordship of Jesus Christ . . . The Christian position is not one of static conformance to dead rules, but of dynamic obedience to a living God" (Nida 1954:48–52).

A "dynamic equivalence church" then, is the kind of church that produces the same kind of impact on its own society as the early church produced upon the original hearers. In that equivalence the younger church will have need of leadership, organization, education, worship, buildings, behavioral standards, means of expressing Christian love and concern to unconverted people. A dynamically equivalent church will employ familiar, meaningful, indigenous forms, adapting and infilling them with Christian content. At the beginning these may be only minimally adequate but the process of transformation will begin that is exemplified in the history of some of the word forms that the early church "possessed for Christ" (Kraft 1972b).

What is desired is a church that will possess indigenous forms for Christ, adapting them to Christian ends by fulfilling indigenous functions and conveying Christian meanings through them to the surrounding society. If this is what is intended by the term "indigenous Christian church" well and good. But such a designation must not be assigned on the basis of mere formal correspondence to the sending church.

Dynamic Equivalence to New Testament Models

According to the above conception, a dynamically equivalent church (1) conveys to its members truly Christian meanings, (2) functions within its own society in the name of Christ, meeting the felt needs of that society and producing within it the same Christian impact as the first century church in its day, and (3) is couched in cultural forms that are as nearly indigenous as possible.

What were the New Testament forms, functions and meanings the church in the receptor culture is expected to develop as dynamic equivalence? We look to the Book of Acts and the Pastoral Epistles for insights into matters of organization, leadership, fellowship, witness and worship. Insights into behavioral matters are in these books and also in the Corinthian epistles.

Developed techniques of exegesis enable us to discover these New Testament models for application in our own lives. All too easily we exegete well enough to discover culturally appropriate functional equivalents for our own culture and sub-culture only to impose these *forms* on the members of another culture. This is common when missionaries of some particular American religious heritage have organized the church in the receptor culture with their own denominational organizational, doctrinal, and behavioral emphases. This is certainly true with respect to modes of baptism and the apologetics that accompany them, the Lord's Supper and church organization, and the forms of worship, doctrine, witness and behavior which we recommend. Why, for example, should more time be given in Asian and

African Bible schools to discussions of the proofs of biblical inspiration (which is no problem to an African) and of historical theories of the atonement (problems in European church history) than to dealing with a Christian perspective on evil spirits and ancestor reverence (problems of vital importance within their cultures)?

In attempting to discover a dynamically equivalent form of preaching, I once asked a group of Nigerian church leaders how they would present the Christian message to the village council. They replied, "We would choose the oldest, most respected man in the group and ask him a question. He would discourse at length and then become silent, whereupon we would ask another question. As he talked others would comment as well. But eventually the discussion would lessen and the leader would talk more. In this way we would develop our message so it would become the topic for discussion of the whole village." I asked them why they didn't employ this approach in church. "Why, we've been taught that monologue is the Christian way," they replied. "Can this be why no old men come to church?" I asked. "Of course—we have alienated them by not showing them due respect in public meetings," was their reply. Thus it is that a preaching form that may (or may not) be appropriate (dynamic equivalent) in American culture—loses its equivalence when exported to another culture, and is counterproductive rather than facilitative with respect to the functions such a form is intended to fulfill.

The model is presented in the New Testament, as Anderson and Venn pointed out. It is equivalence to the churches displayed in the New Testament and to the ideal that lies behind them that we seek, but not, as has been stressed above, an equivalence of mere form. With regard to leadership, for example, simply because the New Testament churches appointed bishops, elders, and deacons does not mean that churches today must label their leaders by these terms. These were simply some of the types of leadership appropriate to the various New Testament cultures.

In the New Testament we see not a single leadership pattern set down for all time, but a series of experiments with cultural appropriateness ranging from a communal approach (Acts 2:42–47) to, apparently, a leadership council of "apostles and elders" (Acts 15:4, 6, 22), to the more highly structured patterns alluded to in the Pastoral Epistles. In each case the pattern alluded to was developed in response to the felt needs conditioned by the culturally inculcated expectations of the members of the culture and sub-culture in which the particular local church operated. Thus we observe certain organizational differences between the Jewish Jerusalem church and the Greek churches with which Timothy and Titus were concerned. Likewise we observe, in the Acts account of the appointment of deacons (Acts 6:1–6), the development in a culturally appropriate way of a new form to meet a need not anticipated at an earlier stage in the life of the Jerusalem church.

The Pastoral Epistles detail the attributes felt to be culturally appropriate to church leaders in the Greco-Roman part of the first century church picture. But the focus is constantly on appropriateness of function rather than on the standardization of form. The lists of characteristics simply catalogue for the original hearers (and for us) some of the things implicit in a person's qualifications for church leadership in that society at that time. Such a leader should, according to 1 Timothy 3:2 (NEB), be of unimpeachable character, which implies being "faithful to one wife, sober, temperate, courteous, hospitable," etc., to attain and maintain the proper reputation within and outside of the Christian community.

With both the specific forms of leadership and organization and those listed as characteristics of the leaders, it is not the specific forms that provide the model to which contemporary churches are to be equivalent, but the functions that lie behind these forms. Contemporary churches need leadership which functions in ways appropriate to the cultural context of our own day and generation and as varied as their cultures. And these leaders are to be of just as unimpeachable character, in terms of their societies' lists of qualifications.

Once again the forms in terms of which the content is presented are determined by the receptor culture and language. A dynamically equivalent church must fulfill its functions in and through the forms of its own culture and language. That is, Jesus Christ, in crossing the cultural barrier between the supracultural and the Hebrew cultural realms adopted the forms of the receptor culture (rather than maintaining allegiance to those of the supracultural realm from which he came—"stripped himself of all privilege," [Phil. 2:7—Phillips]) as the media for his life and work. And he so "indigenized" himself that at the formal level he was 100 percent Hebrew. He looked like a normal product of Hebrew parents at the formal level—not like a foreigner or a formal correspondence translation.

Thus, if the church in the receptor culture is dynamically equivalent to the New Testament models, its patterns of church government, leadership, etc., and even its definitions of what constitute proper qualifications (especially unimpeachability) for its leaders will correspond to the forms of the receptor culture rather than to the forms of the New Testament cultures or any other outside culture.

If the political structure of the receptor culture is one or another form of democracy, the dynamically equivalent church will manifest an appropriate kind of democratic government. Such a church, will be able to state its own culturally appropriate criteria of idealness on the part of its leaders—criteria which are functionally equivalent to those in 1 Timothy and Titus but not necessarily the same, since different cultures, while similar in some matters, focus in on slightly differing aspects according to their differing value systems.

In contemporary American culture this list would include such requirements as: sober, temperate, courteous, a good teacher (or preacher), not given to drink, not quarrelsome, self-controlled, upright, doctrinally sound. Such items as hospitable, dignified, no lover of money might or might not be specified in such a list but would probably also be expected. We would not, however, necessarily be so insistent that our leaders will have already demonstrated their ability to manage a home and family well, since we tend to choose younger leaders than seem to be in focus here—though such a factor would definitely be a consideration with an older man. Nor would we say, as it was necessary to say in Greco-Roman culture, that irreproachability demands that the person never have more than one marriage, since we allow and even encourage a man to remarry after the death of his first wife. Many churches, however, would disallow a pastor, at least, who had remarried after a divorce.

Our list would include most of the items on the Greek list, though some of those specifically mentioned by Paul would probably be left implicit rather than made explicit by us. We would probably want to add a few things such as administrative ability and perhaps even youth. Due, however, to similarities between Greco-Roman culture and our own the lists will be fairly similar.

If, however, we develop an equivalent list for a radically different culture such as many in Africa (e.g., Higi of northeastern Nigeria) we will find some additions and subtractions from the lists and at least one major reinterpretation of a criterion, though the criterion is basically the same. Greed, being the cardinal sin of Higiland, would be one of the major proscriptions and conformance to culturally expected patterns of politeness one of the more important prescriptions. Hospitality and its concomitant generosity would be highlighted to a much greater degree than would be true for either Greco-Roman or American culture. Soberness, temperance, patience and the like would appear on the Higi list and more highly valued than on the American list. Higis would, also focus on age and membership in the royal social class. They would, furthermore, strongly emphasize the family management aspect of the matter—certainly much more strongly than would Americans and probably even more strongly than Greco-Romans did.

And herein would lie the most significant formal difference between the Higi ideal and either of the others. For, in order for such a leader to effectively function in a way equivalent to that intended for the first century leaders, he would not only have to manage his household well but would have at least two wives in that household! "How," the Higi person would ask, "can one properly lead if he has not demonstrated his ability by managing well a household with more than one woman in it?" The Kru of Liberia with a similar ideal state that "You cannot trust a man with only one wife."

It must be made clear however, that we are here speaking only of God's starting point. Once God begins to work within the people of a culture his interaction with these people inevitably results in the *transformation* of at least certain of their customs. To maintain, therefore, as I have above that a dynamically equivalent Higi church would have polygamous leadership is not to say either that God's ultimate standard is polygamy or that this particular criterion for dynamically equivalent leadership will never be changed. It is, in fact, likely that it will be changed, just as, through God's interaction with the Hebrews, polygamy died out in Hebrew culture—over the course of a few thousand years. If, however, the missionary or other leader steps in and imposes foreign criteria on the Higi church he establishes formal correspondence to that foreign model rather than dynamic equivalence to the New Testament models and the dynamism apparent in the early churches is severely compromised.

This is so with each element in doctrine and worship. The New Testament needs to be interpreted in its cultural context if it is to meet the equivalent needs for the members of that culture. The priority, then, must be to convey an equivalent content in the receptor culture even if the cultural forms differ widely from those of the source culture. As with translation, so with the "transculturating" of the church—the extent of this divergence of forms will depend upon the distance between the cultures in question.

Formal Correspondence versus Dynamic Equivalence Transculturation of the Church

An approach to church planting and the evaluation of already established churches that goes beyond the current fuzzy notion of "indigenous church" is recommended. I have argued a case patterned after the theologically and anthropologically sound contemporary approach to Bible translation.

This approach would eschew the traditional formal correspondence model of church planting. In spite of high ideals many promoters of "indigenous church principles," continue to simplistically transplant their forms of worship, organization, behavior, witness, ceremonial, etc., for one culture to another with little or no understanding that Christianity is a matter of the content—functions, meanings—as perceived by the receptors rather than of the forms advocated by the source. In operating according to this formal correspondence model in church planting and nurture, its advocates betray the same kind of deficiency of cultural (and, ultimately, theological) understanding as do those who hold to the formal correspondence ideal for Bible translating.

Not infrequently those who demand formal correspondence churches are not thinking of correspondence to the New Testament models at all (of which they may know little due to serious lack of cultural understanding on the part of those who trained them in biblical interpretation) but, rather, of correspondence to their home-church models.

Euroamerican denominations, at least in their beginnings, often found their strength in the fact that they returned to dynamic equivalence to the New Testament models. Yet these churches that demand the right to a greater or lesser degree of dynamic equivalence themselves typically require of the churches they plant in other cultures formal correspondence, not to New Testament models but to Euroamerican cultural forms. That is, though to some extent we have moved in the direction of dynamic equivalence for ourselves, we now make the same mistake that the Judaizers made when they demanded that Gentiles first become Jews in order to truly follow Christ (see Acts 10 and 15; Kraft 1963); and that the Roman Catholic Church made in demanding that non-Latins convert to Roman culture in order to be Christian; and that the Lutheran Church made when, having broken from Roman culture and moved toward dynamic equivalence for themselves, they demanded that people of other cultures now convert to German culture in order to follow Christ. These all demanded formal cultural correspondence, thus eventually precipitating rebellion on the part of those who demanded greater dynamic equivalence. And such rebellion, for the same purpose, is even now a prominent feature in many lands.

The approach here outlined seeks to make explicit the relationship between the New Testament examples of churchness and contemporary expressions. We do this for two reasons: (1) to assist church planters in planting churches properly, and (2) to assist those involved in non-ideal church situations to better understanding wherein their non-idealness lies and where to look for correctives. For both purposes an analytic procedure is suggested, parallel to that described above as necessary to dynamic equivalence translation:

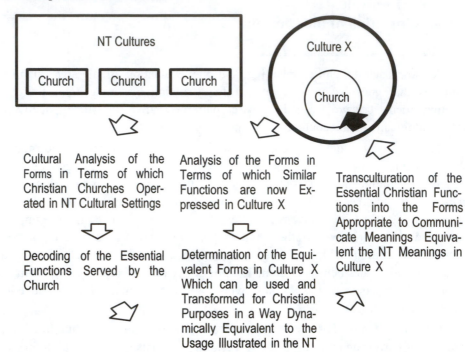

Through such analysis we arrive at more ideal bases for what both indigenous and expatriate church planters and builders are commissioned to be involved with God in. For integral to sound theology is sound anthropology. Dynamic equivalence is the model for churches that we should practice and teach. Formal correspondence models such as the "three-self" concept result in the same kind of foreign, stilted product as the Bible translations produced according to that model.

CHAPTER 34

MEASURING INDIGENEITY

Reprinted here with permission from
C. H Kraft and T. N. Wisley, eds. *Readings in Dynamic Indigeneity.*
Pasadena, CA: William Carey Library, 1979:118-152

Our ideal is to see churches planted and growing that are characterized by appropriately indigenous (or indigenized) forms fulfilling culturally relevant functions and conveying thoroughly Christian meanings. But to produce such an ideal church involves a particular use of the cultural patterns (forms, functions and meanings). And it is this aspect of the matter that is crucial in the production of the self and community-images (defined below) which are central to the dynamic equivalence that we seek. For it is the use that individuals and groups make of their culture that accounts for differences in life-style, belief systems and all other variations present within the culture.

In most aspects of life the members of a community respond rather habitually to the variety of personal and non-personal stimuli to which they are exposed. That is, we ordinarily do things in accordance with a previously arrived at set of patterns. The broad dimensions of these patterns we call cultural. This is the part of our environment that has been passed down to us while we were children by adult society. Over it we have no control at the point of its transmission to us.

We do not, however, accept our culture passively. We respond by interacting with this patterning. And, since into every cultural pattern is built a certain amount of leeway, we do not all choose to respond to the same cultural pattern in the same way, though more often than not once we have made a choice between the culturally allowed alternative responses, we install our chosen response. Thus at least two levels—the level of the overall cultural patterning which we have inherited and the level of the alternative response that we choose to each pattern—our cultural performance is habitual.

My culture says I may shave or not shave though it weights the choice for my peer group in favor of the former by assigning certain meanings such as nonconformity, insecurity, attempting to identify oneself with another age group, etc. to the growing of beard and/or mustache. In acquiescence, then, to the cultural pattern (including its meaning) I once chose to shave regularly, made shaving a habit and have continued to follow not only that habit but several other subsidiary habits (each reflecting a choice between alternatives made earlier in my life) such as the use of a safety razor rather than an electric razor, the order in which I treat the various parts of my face, the frequency with which I shave, the time when I shave, etc.

I do on occasion, however, review and revise my performance of these cultural patterns. And sometimes I choose to change the kind of razor I use or the time and place of shaving or the type of shaving cream I use. I even chose once (briefly) to grow a mustache. That is, I have chosen at various times to alter my use of this aspect of my culture. And certain of these usages have won my approval to the extent that I have installed them in my life in place of my previous habit—and they have become my habitual usage.

Thus, though the major part of our culture, including both broad and more specific patterns, is prescribed for us and the chosen alternatives within these patterns followed habitually by us, there is at every point a considerable amount of leeway for individual and group choice. And our activity in selecting between alternate (i.e., socially acceptable) courses of action, our use of culture or "performance" in relation to it is a highly significant aspect of our involvement in it. For in making the choices that we make from time to time we alter our use of one or another cultural pattern and effect changes of habit within our cultural performance. And such alterations of habitual behavior, especially those engaged in by influential persons, not infrequently "catch on" with others in the society, resulting in socially accepted habitual behavior which may ramify throughout the whole culture. Thus have rather trivial customs like lengthened sideburns for men and the wearing of slacks by women recently become widespread in American life. But thus too (over a longer period of time) have taken hold much more earthshaking changes such as the change from an understanding of the universe as God-centered and God-controlled to a very mechanistic understanding with man either actually or potentially in control at every point. In each case, however, the process of choice between allowed alternatives followed by the development of new habits has been the primary process accounting for the change.

A slightly less frequent but nonetheless very important type of choice has, however, often speeded up the process of change. This is the decision to go beyond the culturally allowed alternatives to either adopt a substitute pattern or to deliberately expand the scope of allowed alternatives within the existing pattern. Not very long ago, for example, the possibility of a woman choosing to wear slacks (now called "pants") on a dress-up occasion did not exist in American society. In recent years, however, the range of culturally allowed alternatives for female attire on such occasions has been widened to allow certain types of pant outfits as well as the previously allowed range of more traditionally acceptable possibilities. Likewise, with regard to the commercial use of evenings and Sunday. Not long ago the idea that business establishments such as grocery and department stores would be open in the evening or on Sunday was not only unacceptable to but unimagined by the majority of Americans. Now, however, through the widening of the range of allowed alternatives in this sector of our culture we not only have evening and Sunday shopping but, in certain cases, twenty-four hour shopping as well. Banks and certain other consumer establishments have not yet gone this route (though some now have

Saturday hours), but the widening of the range of allowed alternatives by other businesses makes it now at least imaginable that they someday might.

With respect to marriage customs we observe both the widening of the range of alternatives and the replacement of previous customs with innovative practices. The range of allowable (i.e., socially acceptable) places to be married and persons performing wedding ceremonies have recently undergone widening in America. With regard to who acceptably lives with whom, further, certain "respectable" segments of our society have begun to innovate by allowing couples to simply arrange to live together in place of formalized marriage of any kind. This kind of replacement or, often, partial replacement of one custom by another custom is a more drastic type of change which is presently forcing our society to reconsider a wide variety of definitions and practices with regard to marriage, adultery, legitimacy of children, the relationships of sex and marriage, etc.

The model of cultural patterning and process which I am here developing may be diagrammed as follows:

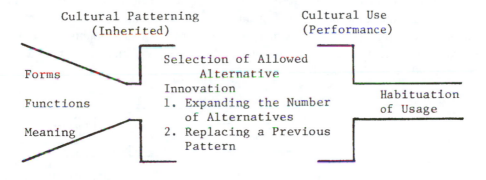

The stimulus for differential uses of cultural forms may either be generated from within the culture (as with women's use of pants) or be at least partially the result of exposure to another culture (as with "beat" music and, probably, at least certain aspects of the "trial marriage" forms). The selection of the socially allowed alternative or of a replacive practice is, however, always up to those within the society. And this is true even when the suggestion for change comes from outside of one's society (see Barnett 1953).[1] In Barnett's terminology, a change, only the members of a society may "innovate" though an outsider may "advocate," for that society. That is, how the cultural patterning is to be used—whether for the perpetuation, alteration or replacement of the present practice—is up to the members of the culture or group in question alone. An outsider, though he may appeal for change, is limited to his ability to win over some insider who will then effect the change(s) from within.

If, therefore, the kind of change that will result in dynamically equivalent churches is to come about it will be the result of choice on the part of the Christian members of a society to use existing, expanded, modified or replacive patterns in their society in a way equivalent to that of the first century churches. We may refer to this use of culture as "transformation" since it involves the conscious change (i.e.,

---

[1] Homer G. Barnett, *Innovation: The Basis of Cultural Change* (New York: McGraw-Hill, 1953).

"transforming") of cultural patterns in a particular direction for a particular end. "Transformational" culture change will in this usage contrast with "natural" culture change, though the difference is not in the kind of process involved but in the nature of the use made of these processes. In Christian transformational change the natural processes are used by the Christians in a society with 1) a different end in view, 2) a different "point of reference" for the change and 3) a different (i.e., supernatural) empowerment for change. By "point of reference" I mean the ideological considerations, with reference to which choice of cultural usage are made.

A factor that it is important to make explicit at this point, however, is that in our use of culture we not only act, we evaluate. That is, we monitor our activity (again in terms of our point of reference) with the aim of assessing the relationship of our performance to the goals and guidelines we have set for ourselves. And on the basis of this evaluation we develop a self-image which provides coordination and integration for the effort we expend in cultural performance. There is, however, in addition to our self-image what may be termed a "community-image" embodying a community evaluation of our efforts. The interplay between these two images and the self and group expectations and evaluations embodied in them set up for us a system which produces feedback which either confirms or raises doubts in use with regard to the way we are using our culture. Adding these factors to our model of culture yields a diagram like this:

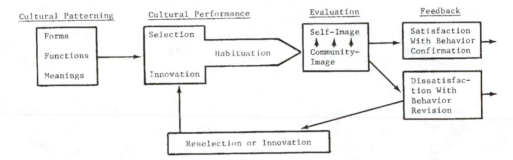

Returning to a consideration of how this process is used to bring about culture change, it is possible to diagram the natural process, used with a natural point of reference, natural empowerment and with a resultant natural end as follows:

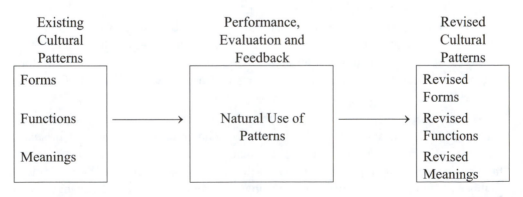

The Natural Culture Change Process

In the natural process change is effected by combining a felt need with the novel solution. The felt need always comes from within the culture—though the identification of the need as a need (rather than as an inevitable "fact of life") and the realization that it is possible to solve it may themselves be the result of suggestions originating outside of the culture (or subculture) in question, There are, however, three possible reference points in terms of which a solution to the felt need may be developed: 1) an in-culture reference point, 2) an other-culture reference point or 3) a supracultural (i.e., outside of any culture) reference point.

The vast majority of solutions to felt needs are generated in terms of reference points within the culture itself. The basic ideology and the values embodied in a culture provide primary in-culture reference points. Thus the development of mass production was the result of the application of a solution generated in terms of an in-culture reference point of the felt need for a cheaper, more efficient way to produce automobiles. Efficiency and inexpensiveness are important American values and easily become in-culture reference points for change.

Not infrequently, though, the reference point for change lies in another culture (or subculture) known to at least some of the members of the original group. Thus when the members of a non-western culture seek to solve one or another of their needs related to identity, power, prestige, freedom, etc. by aligning themselves with some aspect of western culture such as its schools, medicine, religion, politics, etc., they are employing an other-culture reference point for the generating of change within their culture. The culture change process in this case is essentially the same as that involving an in-culture reference point but the solution sought for the felt need is borrowed from a foreign source rather than internally generated. Not infrequently, then, this practice of looking to an outside culture for answers becomes habitual and incorporated into their ideology and value system. What comes from this foreign culture is evaluated as "better" than previous answers to problems or newly generated answers with in-culture points of reference. This attachment of change to other-culture points of reference is often done quite consciously at first but, as the practice becomes more habitual the consciousness of the foreigners of the solutions adopted typically recedes. In American culture, for example, the point of reference in terms of which medical scientists construct names for new medicines is the Latin language. Many Americans are more or less aware of this fact but are so used to it that they feel that this way of doing things is just "natural." Many, of course, are unaware of the process since it is so firmly entrenched even though they frequently have difficulty in pronouncing the names of the medicines they use.

The reference point for change may, however, be supracultural. In this case the reference point lies outside of any culture in God or Satan—and the solution to the felt need is generated with respect to the desire on the part of those seeking the solution to do what they feel will be pleasing to their supracultural reference point.

This concern, then, becomes a part of the people's ideology and partially or fully replaces the previous ideology in terms of which such decisions were formerly made.

Change of cultural usage in response to a supracultural point of reference is, however, liable to become a rather hit or miss thing unless there is some kind of in-culture guide in terms of which people can come to understand the desire of their supracultural point of reference. This purpose is served by a variety of written and experienced revelations purporting to cone partially or totally from the realm of the supracultural. In Christianity this purpose is served by the Bible and its Christian interpreters who, under the continuing leading of the holy Spirit are responsible under God for witnessing to others concerning the existence and implications of a supracultural reference point in God. The Bible, reporting as it does the experiences of previous witnesses—notably that of the God-become-man and of those who had direct experience with him provides contemporary witnesses with both a casebook of previous experience and a yardstick in terms of which to measure contemporary experience with the supracultural God.

In the cases of the in-culture and the other-culture point of reference the ends in view may be well or ill-defined and the empowerment for the change simply that of the human beings who operate the culture. In the third case, however, though the definition of the end in view may still be either well or poorly understood by the human participants, the empowerment for the change comes at least partially from a supernatural source (of which the human participants may or may not be aware). It is my understanding that this empowerment for change is ordinarily a cooperative matter between the human and the supracultural participants such as that referred to in Christianity as "following the leading of God."

When the third type of reference point for change is properly employed by Christians it uses the natural culture change processes with the supernatural empowerment of the Holy Spirit to effect ends defined by illustrated in or at least pointed to by the Scriptures. This is the process, here labeled "Christian transformational change." We may diagram this process to point up the differences between it and the natural process as follows:

Existing Cultural Patterns	Performance Evaluation and Feedback	Transformed Cultural Patterns
Forms ⎫ Functions ⎬ Employed to Natural Ends Meanings ⎭	→ Joint employment of these processes of Change by man + God in connection with a Supra-cultural point of Reference + Guided by the Scriptures	Revised Forms ⎫ Revised Functions ⎬ Employed to Christian Ends Revised Meanings ⎭

The Culture Change Process
Employed to Christian Ends

With respect to the dynamic equivalence of churches, the aim here advocated is to see existing cultural patterns and processes of change so employed jointly by man and God in relationship to the Christian Supracultural reference point that the churches produced are dynamically equivalent in the cultures in which they participate to the ideals portrayed for the people of God in the OT and NT. The key factor in the production of this dynamic equivalence is the use made of the cultural patterns and processes already existent in or potential to the culture. And one important result will be the transformation of these patterns and processes to more adequately serve the new ends. This transformation, though often impressive (e.g., elimination of slavery and polygamy), has never in history approached completeness and one despairs of the possibility of such cultural transformation ever proceeding far enough in any culture that one might accurately describe that culture as thoroughly Christian.

Self Image and Community
Image

As stated above the key to the evaluational aspect of the culture change process is the self-image of the person or group employing the process. This self-image provides coordination and integration of our efforts and also the monitoring mechanism producing feedback which leads to confirmation of or dissatisfaction with our performance. The self-image is, therefore, of extremely high importance in the whole process.

A dynamic equivalence church with the proper supracultural point of reference will develop the kind of self-image that enables it to see itself as the first-century church saw itself—as the body of Christ functioning in direct relationship to God (as its point of reference) and on his behalf in its use of the cultural patterns available to it. That is, the integrating, monitoring core—the self-image—of such a church will be functionally or dynamically equivalent to that of the New Testament churches. Such a church will "see itself as the Church of Jesus Christ in its own local situation, mediating the work, the mind, the word and the ministry of Christ in its own environment" (Tippett 1969:133).[2]

Such a church, functioning in dynamic equivalence to the New Testament churches, will not be content to establish (or retain) the fatherly mission or missionary as its point of reference—looking to and depending upon then for

---

[2] Alan R. Tippett, *Verdict Theology in Missionary Theory* (Lincoln, IL: Lincoln Christian College Press, 1969).

answers to pressing problems. It will, rather, in time of need, in accordance with its healthy self-image, muster its own forces in direct dependence upon its Lord, face both the crisis and its own responsibility in it and with him employ the situation as its opportunity to serve Christ in concerned witness to the surrounding society.

Word came to the missionary in charge of a series of village churches that the pastor of one of these churches was conducting services regularly in another village at some distance from that to which he was assigned. "How long has he been doing this?" the missionary asked his informant. "About three months" was the reply. "Has be left the work to which he was assigned, then?" the missionary asked. "Oh, no," came the reply, "he conducts the services first in the village to which he was assigned, then hops on his bicycle and goes to the other village." And the missionary was one of the last to know that the pastor conceived of his responsibility as more directly related to his relationship to God than to his relationship to the missionary. The pastor's self-image was dynamically equivalent to that of the early apostles and he did what lie did in response to God, not to man. Fortunately for all concerned, this missionary's concept of what should have been was such that the pastor was encouraged to continue and increase such direct dependence upon God for leading. There have been similar situations where such independent activity would have been discouraged or even forbidden.

A church with this kind of self-image will operate as a "self-functioning organic whole (characterized) by effective internal growth in grace within a developing organic structure, where members interact and cooperate and fulfill their natural functions" within the body (Tippett 1969:134). It will likewise be self-determining in governmental and all other matters. It will face up to its own affairs and make its own decisions freely according to culturally appropriate decision-making patterns. Such a church will support itself in a manner appropriate to its own resources and the economic patterns of the surrounding society. It will see the Great Commission as addressed directly to itself and propagate itself in its own society in culturally appropriate ways, giving itself to facing and alleviating both spiritual and social problems in direct response to the Master who called and commissioned it.

If, however, the church is working in terms merely of an in-culture or other-culture point of reference its self-image will not be dynamically equivalent to the New Testament models. It will, rather, see itself as merely a part of its own culture (if it employs an in-culture, indigenous point of reference for the use it makes of its culture) or as an outpost of some foreign culture (if it takes an other-cultural point of reference). And either of these pitfalls may be fallen into even if the church is operated according to "the three-self formula," since each of these "selfs" simply focuses on the formal outworking of the self-image of the church rather than on the kind and extent of approximation to the use of such forms manifested by the early churches.

The nature of the self-image of a church is, therefore, the primary feature to consider and evaluate when seeking to discover whether or not that church is the kind of dynamically equivalent church that God intends. But the community-image—what the society of which the church is a part thinks of it—is likewise important to consider for at least two reasons: 1) because what the community thinks of the church strongly affects the church's self-image and, therefore, the course that the church follows in its use of its culture and 2) because it is to the surrounding society that the church is responsible under God to communicate the gospel.

The community-image of the early Christians was such as to reinforce both their Christian self-image and their attachment to their supracultural point of reference in the Christian God. Of these early Christians it was said, the community "recognized that they (i.e., Peter and John in this case) had been with Jesus" (Acts 4:13). The members of the surrounding society marveled at the love that the Christians showed for one another. Tertullian, writing in the second century states, "It is our care for the helpers, our practice of loving-kindness that brands us in the eyes of many of our opponents "Only look!" they say, "look how they love one another!" (they themselves being given to mutual hatred). "Look how they are prepared to die for one another!" (they themselves being readier to kill each other)" (Apology 39; see also Eusebuis, ii.E. 9:8). The community learned to trust the Christians and "spoke highly of them" (Acts 5:13 NEB; see also Acts 2:47). The Jewish religious establishment whose community-image was apparently in pretty bad shape at this time felt threatened by the popularity the Christian cause was gaining to the extent that they even went against the advice of one of their distinguished leaders, Gamaliel (Acts 5:34-39), and attempted to stamp it out. The church leaders were dubbed "men who have turned the world upside down" (Acts 17:6). And history records the fact that that dedicated band of followers of Christ so used their culture that the impact of that use for Christ was to transform the first century world.

A church with a dynamically equivalent community-image will make an equivalent impact on its own society, communicating to that society an equivalent message and being perceived by that society in somewhat the same terms as those articulated by those of the first century. If the community-image is properly Christian, the surrounding community will see Christ in and through that church. The message heard will challenge the community to allegiance to Christ and his church, not merely to link up with some foreign or indigenous religious system. This message will have little to do with problems that are not live issues within the society in question but will be recognized by the society to be vitally related both to their own live issues and felt needs and to the God who through Christ has made provision for the meeting of these needs.

The surrounding society will see this kind of a church as the self-functioning organic whole that it seeks to be—growing, adapting, fulfilling its divinely appointed purposes within and according to culturally understandable and acceptable patterns. Such a church will not be seen by the surrounding society as dominated by, speaking for, supported by, governed by, and/or answering to the representatives (expatriate or national) of a foreign culture. It will be perceived to be directly related both to God and to the surrounding culture, faithfully representing and communicating the one in terms thoroughly appropriate to the other.

If, however, the community sees the church as an outpost of something foreign—propagating a foreign message, attached to a foreign point of reference, springing from a foreign ideology, organized and led according to foreign patterns and constantly addressing itself to foreign problems—the community-image of the church will be quite different. The foreign church may be regarded as attractive by many, especially those who seek or have been schooled to seek to escape from the reality of their own cultural experience because they have adopted the same other-cultural point(s) of reference to guide their use of the cultural processes in which they participate. But, attractive to some or not, this kind of a church is a long way from the dynamic equivalence to the New Testament models that is the ideal. And the future for such a church is not bright in the fact of increasing indications of the imminent demise of the (western) culture in which it finds its point(s) of reference—unless, of course, it is stimulated to evaluate and revise its present cultural performance in such a way that it adopts the proper supracultural point of reference, reworks its self and community images and sets its sights on the attainment of true dynamic equivalence to the biblical models.

Other churches, however, may be seen by the community to be so indigenous that there is little reason to get excited over or even interested in them unless one happens to particularly value the in-culture reference point(s) to which the church has attached itself. Such is the plight of many American churches whose point of reference has become mere social action and liberation or social and political conservatism. Such also is the plight of many "nativistic" movements in a number of different cultures which have set themselves to rally people to return to the "good old days" before their culture began to yield to the pressures to change in the direction of western culture. Such movements, whether in our culture or in someone else's, adopt an in-culture point of reference—even though they may verbally attach themselves to Christianity—and fail in this way to either attain or, often, even strive for dynamic equivalence to the biblical models.

Measuring Dynamic Equivalence

Though in any assessment of the degree to which a given contemporary church is dynamically equivalent to the biblical models primary attention should be given to the equivalence or lack of it between the self and community image of that church and those of the NT churches, it is important as well to evaluate representative numbers of the factors that go together to comprise and influence these images. For, though it is true that the self and community images both indicate the overall character of the church and vitally influence the direction in which it is moving, it is the composite of these other factors which both produces the images and, in turn, is acted upon if and when the church feels it necessary to attempt to change its self and community images. We do, however, want to distinguish between our evaluation of the component factors and that of the self and community images themselves.

In evaluating the component factors, further, we must be clear as to the point or points in the culture change process at which we seek to make our evaluations. It is not, for example, particularly instructive to evaluate the potential dynamic equivalence of the original cultural patterns before the entrance of Christianity into them. What we really want to know is how the church has used and is using these patterns, what modifications have been and are being made in them, what the commonly accepted Christian patterns and usages are and how all of this influences the self and community-images of the church in its society. If the culture pattern and performance diagram employed earlier is adapted as follows, it becomes clear that the phase of the process that most interests us here is that labeled "Stage 2."

Stage 1: The Original Culture Before the Coming of Christianity

Stage 2: The Use Made of the Cultural Patterns and Processes by the Christian Church and the Resultant Patterning

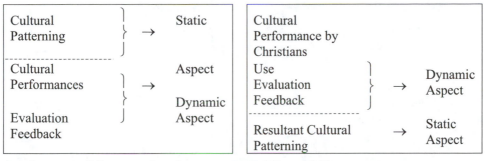

Another way of diagramming the process would be as follows:

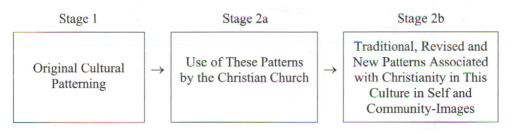

In any event it is our aim in what follows to attempt to evaluate first the patterns associated with Christianity (Stage 2b, above) and then the self and community-images of the sample churches treated as follows. In the final section of this paper, then, we will proceed to a consideration of remedies for deficient self-images.

In evaluating the patterns employed by a church it is possible to focus in at several levels. At this point the hierarchical arrangement of cultural elements into traits (the smallest units in focus), complexes of traits and patterns of complexes will be helpful. The listing that follows is intended to suggest areas of major importance to Christianity which need to be focused on in evaluating the potential dynamic equivalence of a given church within its culture to those portrayed in the NT within their cultures. This list is intended to be suggestive rather than exhaustive but is, I think, sufficiently detailed to indicate a bit of the complexity of the cultural patterning and performance that must be considered.

Items	Traits	Complexes	Patterns	Institutions

Singing
Prayer
Scripture   Corporate
Preaching   Worship
Ritual
Etc.
                                            Worship

Prayer   Private
Scripture   Worship
Etc.

Regulation
Procedures   Government
Decision Making
Etc.
                                            Organization

Qualification
Performance   Leadership
Interactions
Etc.

Salvation
God
Sin   Doctrine
Eschatology
Etc.
                                            Belief

World Views
Morals   Values
Various Value
Etc.

Verbal
Life   Individual
Personnel   Witness
Etc.
                                            Witness

Organizations
Personnel   Corporate
Own Society   Witness
Elsewhere
Etc.

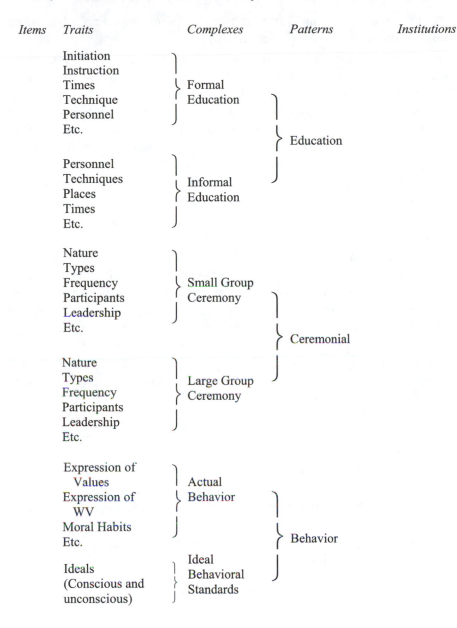

Items	Traits	Complexes	Patterns	Institutions
	Initiation Instruction Times Technique Personnel Etc.	Formal Education	Education	
	Personnel Techniques Places Times Etc.	Informal Education		
	Nature Types Frequency Participants Leadership Etc.	Small Group Ceremony	Ceremonial	
	Nature Types Frequency Participants Leadership Etc.	Large Group Ceremony		
	Expression of Values Expression of WV Moral Habits Etc.	Actual Behavior	Behavior	
	Ideals (Conscious and unconscious)	Ideal Behavioral Standards		

With this mass of potential elements to evaluate it will be necessary to choose in any given instance which level one wishes to focus in on. For purposes of illustration we will in what follows focus mainly at the highest (patterns) level but it would be possible to go into considerably more detail and indeed, it would not be possible to adequately treat the pattern level without a fair understanding of the complex and trait levels as well.

Evaluating the data once it is arranged in categories such as these can most easily be done by means of the development of a series of measurement scales which plot the findings in such a way that the nature of its approximation to the ideal can be easily grasped. These scales will be introduced and employed in the process of the development of the following illustrative case studies: Case Study I: "The

Evangelical Church of Vietnam" (data from Prof. S. Herendeen, Prof. of Missions, Regina Bible College, doctoral candidate, SWM).[3]

This church was established just after the turn of the century through the instrumentality of Christian and Missionary Alliance missionaries. It has operated since 1926 with formal autonomy and with the specific intent of embodying "three-self indigenous church principles." The church now numbers (in South Vietnam only) about 42,000 baptized members in an estimated Christian community of about 80,000-90,000 (of a total population of c. 15 million in South Vietnam). There are 348 workers c. 220 Bible School students. The church organizationally includes several large tribal groups which express themselves differently than the Vietnamese ethnic churches and would, no doubt, have to be evaluated differently from the Vietnamese (majority) churches. The following evaluation, however, is intended to apply mainly to the Vietnamese segments of this denomination.

The first measurement attempted will concern "The Extent of the Use By the Church of Cultural Patterns of the Surrounding Society." Since it is amply illustrated throughout the Bible that God works in terms of the culture of the people with whom he deals, we will assume that dynamic equivalence in this regard may be measured in terms of a high degree of use by the churches of Vietnamese culture in their expression of Christianity. This would involve Vietnamese Christians primarily in the selection of one or another of the behaviors allowed by Vietnamese culture at any given point as the preferred means of Christian expression. Though occasional borrowing from another culture would be appropriate, the greater the number of borrowed elements, the greater is the foreignness of the behavior, the less vital the functions of the behavior in the lives of the participants and the less relevant the answers to felt needs. Such behavior would, therefore, score low in dynamic equivalence to the first century models.

In the Vietnamese case the data shows a strong inclination toward using the change mechanisms of their culture mainly for the purpose of borrowing the forms of Christianity from western culture, rather than for the purpose of developing appropriate indigenous expression from within the culture. A charting of examples in this regard shows the following:

Scale I: Extent of Use of Surrounding Cultural Patterns

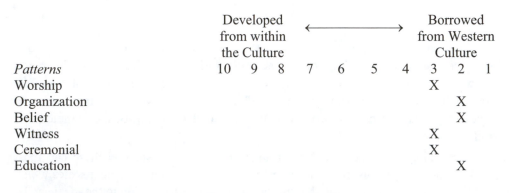

Patterns	Developed from within the Culture						Borrowed from Western Culture		
	10	9	8	7	6	5	4	3	2	1
Worship								X		
Organization									X	
Belief									X	
Witness								X		
Ceremonial								X		
Education									X	

---

[3] Dale S. Herendeen, "The Evangelical Church of Vietnam." Unpublished paper written as a doctoral student at School of World Mission, Fuller Seminary (1971).

With regard, then, to the source from which the various forms employed by the Vietnamese church come, the dynamic equivalence would seem to be generally very low. There are, however, a few bright spots such as the occasional elaboration of a ceremony or employment of a Vietnamese pattern of communication or interpretation. The vast number of cultural elements that could have been Vietnamese but which have been substituted for by western borrowings is such that the overall impression given is extremely western.

A second aspect to be measured is the Vitality of Function and Relevance of Meaning attached to the forms. But at this point a distinction has to be made between the understandings of the in-group—those who over the process of time have been indoctrinated into the meanings assigned by the church subculture—and the out-group—those who, though they may even belong to the church, have not been so indoctrinated. The reason why such a distinction must be made soon becomes apparent when dealing with the Vietnamese data since to many of the highly indoctrinated in-group even many of the western forms assume a high degree of relevance since they have been conditioned to be concerned with the questions answered by these forms and even to ask and to think about these questions in western ways.

For those not so thoroughly indoctrinated, however, what for the in-group appears to be relevant is found to "scratch" them elsewhere than where they itch—often not because the answers provided are in fact ultimately irrelevant to them but because they are packaged for western, not Vietnamese, consumption and are not, therefore, appropriateable except by those who are westernized enough to both understand the answer expressed in this way and to recognize the deep universally human question that it relates to. Examples of this include highly westernized forms for such things as funerals, marriages, child dedication, church music ("99 percent western tunes"), recruitment and training of leaders, evangelism, patterns of conversion, etc.: a pervasively western approach to "education" built on western classroom techniques, western Bible School curriculum and translated textbooks; and a thoroughly western approach to Christian doctrine which, though carefully teaching the founding denomination's perspectives on the "Truths of Scripture" regarded as important by the C&MA in America, merely condemns without, apparently, taking them seriously such genuinely Vietnamese live issues as ancestor reverence, polygamy, child and other types of arranged marriage, "idolatry and superstition," and the like.

What has happened, therefore, is that through the agency of the church a highly westernized "Christian" subculture has been created that has cultural contact only with other westernized subcultures within the country (who have likewise, largely through the western schools, been indoctrinated out of contact with the "rank and file" Vietnamese). Though the ministry of this kind of church to the westernized segments of society may well be challenging, the impression it gives to the non-westernized majority of Vietnamese society is that God is only concerned about those who exchange their own culture for western culture. This is the same message that the Judaizers proclaimed (i.e., that Gentile converts had to first become Jews to be accepted by God) and that God through Peter (Acts 10) and Paul (Acts 15) repudiated.

What develops, then, is the necessity of a kind of "split-image" of the vitality of function and relevance of meaning criteria. One part of the image will assess the functions and meanings to the in-group, the other for the out-group. In the following chart the symbols "I" (for in-group) and "O" (for out-group) will be employed to show this difference:

Scale II: Vitality of Function and Relevance of Meaning

	Vitality and Relevance ⟵⟶								Non-Vitality and Relevance	
Patterns	10	9	8	7	6	5	4	3	2	1
Worship						I			O	
Organization						I			O	
Belief					I			O		
Witness					I				O	
Ceremonial						I			O	
Education					I		O			

If this assessment is anywhere near accurate (and there are undoubtedly misinterpretations of the data—for which I apologize), the degree of dynamic equivalence between this church and the NT models is distressingly low precisely at the most crucial point—that of its contact with the non-Christian, non-westernized world around it. Though the relevance of the church is somewhat greater for the in-group it must be recognized that these persons and groups, too, are pervasively conditioned by Vietnamese culture. Though they are indeed strongly affected by western culture, there-fore they are not by any means completely westernized. Even for these, therefore, the church's relevance is not always high. A further factor that influences the total picture is the effect of the low degree of relevance to its own society manifested in certain areas of its life and doctrine by the denomination whose models have been employed in the Vietnamese church.

At this point it would be well to discuss the matter of the Vietnamese church's Point of Reference—the consideration(s) in terms of which the church determines its course of action with regard to any given set of circumstances, in our previous discussion (above) of points of reference it was indicated that there are basically three possibilities: in-cultural, other-cultural and supra-cultural. Though I did not make it explicit in that discussion, it is clear that for those groups who *choose a supracultural point of* reference it is all-important, since God works in terms of culture, whether they conceive of him as working in terms of their own culture or in terms of a foreign culture to which they must convert if they are to be in contact with him. The choice of point of reference for such groups is, therefore, a dual choice: they first choose the supracultural and then the cultural (theirs or another) in terms of which they understand him to work. Diagrammatically these alternatives may be expressed thus:

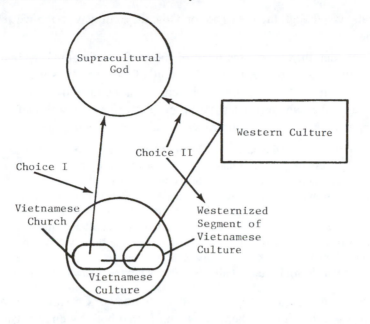

A dynamically equivalent church, in imitation of the Early Church would choose to relate to the supracultural point of reference (God) in terms of its own culture—expanding, adapting and replacing various elements of that culture as necessary but deriving the models for both its interaction with and service for God, in imitation of the Early Church, from its own society (choice I on the above diagram). Since, however, the Vietnamese church has (under strong external influence) sought its models for interaction with and service for God from a culture other than its own (i.e., choice II on the diagram) we may both indicate this "detoured" approach to its point of reference and, by employing a basic rectangle with rounded corners, indicate to some extent the lack of cultural correspondence between this church and its surrounding culture. If it had followed choice I it could appropriately be pictured as a small circle within the larger circle employed to depict Vietnamese culture as a whole.

On a scale similar to those above the fact that the church's point of reference is supra-cultural but largely via western culture may be indicated in the following way:

Scale III: Point of Reference

	10	9	8	7	6	5	4	3	2	1	
Supracultural via Vietnamese Culture								X			Supracultural via Western Culture

Vietnamese Culture	Western Culture

Note that with respect to point of reference there are four possibilities to be considered: the point(s) could be wholly within either culture or it/they could be supracultural as understood in terms of either culture. In the case of this church the ultimate reference point is supracultural—they look to God. But their understanding of him and of what he expects is so thoroughly "detoured" via western cultural models that, even though their eyes are on God, they fall way to the westernized end of the scale.

There remain, then, the assessment of the Self and Community Images plus a comment with regard to the future direction of change. In spite of the highly westernized nature of the Vietnamese church, when we turn to an attempt to assess its self-image, the whole matter takes on an encouraging hopefulness. Prof. Herendeen, who served for several years with this church, states that

> in spite of the fact that the basic organizational structure of the Evangelical Church is basically western, I believe that by now it has taken on a sense of "ours" that makes it indigenous. Since the years of the present war it has increasingly sensed its place in its own society and sought to feel the suffering and to identify with the people. Much foreign aid has slowed the church's own sense of responsibility, and many out of their poverty have looked to foreign aid and often to the mission. The present war came too soon for an adequate self-image [to develop] , hut the war has pressed upon the church this very same self-image... I have not the slightest doubt this church would stand if all missionaries left tomorrow (1971:11-12).

This church does, apparently, see itself as the body of Christ in Vietnam, at least in a formal way. They are, furthermore, being forced both by circumstances and by inclination to enter more and more into many of the implications of this responsibility that they had not been required to face previously. This is hopeful, though their extremely western approach to Christianity so insulates the church from effective communication of a dynamically equivalent message to Vietnamese society that in spite of am increasingly healthy self-image, their community-image appears to be decidedly unhealthy.

For the Vietnamese society at large, apparently (though predictably), sees the church as a thoroughly foreign enclave in their midst.

> Christianity continues to be regarded as foreign. That is simply to say, from a societal viewpoint, Christianity has yet to earn its way as a religion of the East.. as one intelligent young Vietnamese Christian told me, Christianity has not yet suffered with the people...long enough to find pro-found identity with the nation (Herendeen 1971:1).

Such a community-image profoundly affects the ability of the church to be understood by the surrounding society. Those whose attitude is positive toward western culture may show some inclination to listen—but because they are interested in the culture, not because they find Christ attractive. Or, if they have become westernized enough to discover that western culture no longer regards Christianity as relevant to its real interests, they may simply reject the church as "sophisticated" westerners have. In neither case are they basing their decision on issues integral to true Christianity. The unwesternized, of course, either hear nothing intelligible, because they and the church exist in widely divergent conceptual frames of reference, or they get the message that the first requirement for becoming a Christian is to renounce their own culture and to convert to that of the church. If, then, they are unwilling to take this step they simply disqualify themselves from membership in the church.

The reputation of the church, likewise, is dependent upon the attitude of the person or group toward western culture. Those who find western culture attractive may hold the church in high esteem or for one reason or another regard it as irrelevant. Those who are negatively disposed toward western culture are likely to be negative toward the church and to regard their brethren who belong to it as having "sold out" to foreigners. Either way they miss the point.

Scale IV: Self and Community Images

	Dynamically Equivalent to Early Church		$\longleftrightarrow$					Non-Dynamically Equivalent		
	10	9	8	7	6	5	4	3	2	1
Self-Image					X					
Community-Image										X

I would postulate a direct relationship between the lack of dynamic equivalence to NT models with respect to the community-image and the fact that the total Christian community claimed by this church amounts, even after sixty years of dedicated missionary effort (including a commitment to the "three-selfs" formula), to such an insignificant proportion of the South Vietnamese population. We see here a western religion (not essential Christianity) pitted competitively against Vietnamese culture and, predictably, losing rather than the type of dynamic that the Early Church manifested in employing Hebrew cultural forms to reach Hebrews, Greek and Roman cultural forms to reach Greeks and Romans.

But there is a ray of hope for the future—though it comes not so much from the Vietnamese situation as from history. For when the Early Church was exclusively Jewish, God led Peter (Acts 10) and Paul (Acts 15) to proclaim the gospel to Romans and Greeks without imposing Hebrew culture on them. When the gospel got too Roman, God raised up the Reformers and others to prove to the world that the gospel could be clothed in German, Swiss, English and other cultural forms. And sooner or later God is likely to demonstrate to the Evangelical Church of Vietnam that they don't have to become Americans to be Christian. Perhaps movement toward a dynamically equivalent Vietnamese church has already been started with the war as catalyst. Reports of church growth getting out of the control of the established church organization in certain areas are hopeful in this regard. Perhaps, then, even this westernized a church will, under the direction of the Holy Spirit learn to use the mechanisms of culture change which are a part of their westernized subculture just as they are a part of the indigenous culture which they have left, to move toward greater dynamic equivalence within whichever cultural frame of reference they choose to operate in terms of. Case Study II: "The African Israel Church Nineveh."[4]

In much briefer fashion I would like to apply these same scales to the independent African Israel Church Nineveh of Kenya. This denomination is the result of a 1942 split-off from a Canadian Pentecostal mission which by 1960 numbered more than 5000 members in over 100 churches. The specific intent of this

---

[4] Data from F. B. Welbourn and B. A. Ogot, *A Place to Feel at Home: A Study of Two Independent Churches in Western Kenya* (London: Oxford, 1966).

church is to enable its members to be "at home" as African (not western) Christians. In terms of our criteria it has made marvelous strides in that direction though it has not completely freed itself from the models of its parent mission, which, in the Kenyan context, fall short of dynamic equivalence. This church does, however, provide a neat contrast with the Evangelical Church of Vietnam and, thus, a useful second case to which to apply our evaluational scales.

For this church, then, we first ask, what is "The Extent of the Use by the Church of the Cultural Patterns of the Surrounding Society"? The answer to this question by nearly any set of criteria would be, "Considerable, though somewhat less than total." That is, the AICN has made magnificent strides toward the use of indigenous customs in such areas as ceremonial (e.g., harvest festivals, culturally appropriate funerals), many aspects of worship and organization (e.g., indigenous hymns, public confession, chief and tribe organizational model), and architecture (e.g., mud buildings with thatched roofs). The use of indigenous customs in their Christian expression is, however, not such as to leave them unmodified, for each custom employed is employed in accord with the supraculturally empowered Christian dynamic which transforms the function of each custom to serve something more than its "natural" purely cultural end. Thus, for example, such indigenous customs as that enjoining wrong-doers to confess their sin publicly and that of the reconciliation ceremony that follows are incorporated but reinterpreted. So also with circumcision, indigenous innovational and borrowing mechanisms ate also employed to produce, e.g., culturally appropriate (though not indigenous) customs such as the singing, drumming and dancing processionals on the way to church, the use and interpretation of long, white gowns to signify commonality of their cause and their purity (white-pure), the use of symbols such as A.I.N. and the star of David on clothes, doors, teapots, etc., the inclusion of cleanliness rules in their preaching, the use of Friday as a special day, and the like. There are, however, certain "undigested" customs, the forms of which have been borrowed legalistically and, probably, rather superstitiously such as the requirement that women keep their heads covered in church buildings, the forbidding of smoking and eating pork and certain aspects of their doctrinal statement.

Nevertheless, as the following scales attempt to show, the degree of dynamic equivalence to NT models appears very high.

Scale I: Extent of Use of Surrounding Cultural Patterns

	Developed from African Culture		← →				Borrowed from Western Culture		
Patterns	10	9	8	7	6	5	4	3	2	1
Worship			X							
Organization			X							
Belief				X						
Witness			X							
Ceremonial					?					
Education		X								

Scale II: Vitality of Function and Relevance of Meaning

	Vitality and Relevance			← →			Non-Vitality and Relevance		
Patterns	10	9	8	7	6	5	4	3	2	1
Worship		X								
Organization			X							
Belief				X						
Witness			X							
Ceremonial					?					
Education		X								

With regard to the AICN Point of Reference, a diagram similar to that produced for the Evangelical Church of Vietnam highlights some interesting differences:

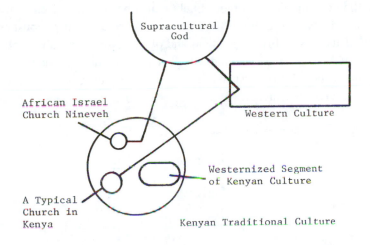

Note, in addition to the different routes to the supracultural point of reference, the greater cultural congruity (symbolized by the circle) between AICN and its surrounding culture than between the typical mission church and its surrounding culture. The latter situation is similar to the relationship between the Evangelical Church of Vietnam and the surrounding Vietnamese culture and results directly from the adoption of the "detoured" (i.e., via western culture) approach to its point of reference. The line between AICN and God is not, however, completely straight. They experience a "pull" toward western culture models which shows up frequently but not, in general, obtrusively.

A Point of Reference Scale for the African Israel Church Nineveh will, therefore, look like the following:

Scale III: Point of Reference

	10	9	8	7	6	5	4	3	2	1	
Supracultural via Kenyan Traditional Culture								X			Supracultural via Western Culture

Kenyan Traditional Culture											Western Culture

The AICN's Self and Community-Images likewise score high in dynamic equivalence. They see themselves as the Body of Christ in their own society—thoroughly African but thoroughly Christian. They find themselves "at home" as Christian Africans not, as with many African Christian churches, as foreigners (culturally as well as spiritually) in their own lands. And when they are faulted by the surrounding community it is more likely that it be for the "offense of the cross" than for the offense of cultural foreignness. A certain suspiciousness by the community of the possibility of political and/or other sub-Christian motivations on the part of AICN does, however, indicate that the community-image be lowered a bit—although the possibility exists that even in this suspicion is more rather than less equivalent to the Early Church.

Scale IV: Self and Community Images

AICN	Dynamically Equivalent to Early Church						← →			Non-Dynamically Equivalent	
	10	9	8	7	6	5	4	3	2	1	
Self-Image	X										
Community-Image		X									

Remedying Non-Dynamic Equivalence

We have seen two radically different types of churches and sought in much too brief and superficial fashion to evaluate their dynamic equivalence to the Early Church. The first of these we found to be seriously deficient in dynamic equivalence because it has, even in the name of an indigenous church approach to mission, been set up as a formal equivalent to the American home churches of the founding mission. The second church, however, shows a high degree of dynamic equivalence throughout its life and worship. But this dynamic equivalence was only attained by that church splitting off from the church established by its parent mission. Otherwise the evaluation of that church, as would be the case with a high percentage of mission-established churches in Africa, might have been as bad as that of the Vietnamese church.

Must we conclude, then, that the only road to dynamic equivalence is to break away from the parent mission or its daughter church? Perhaps—unless, of course, the church has been planted with the principle of dynamic equivalence in operation from the start.

There is, however, the possibility for non-dynamically equivalent churches to begin to use their present cultural patterning and processes to move in the right direction. They can learn how to transculturate themselves from the foreign culture in which they now find themselves into the culture of the community of which they are expected by God to be part and to which they are expected to communicate Christ.

And to make explicit the desirability of such use of culture, the cultural processes involved in such change and the possibility for non-dynamically equivalent churches to move in the right direction is the reason why I have written this article. For such change not only must come about—it *can* come about, and preferably with the help of missionaries rather than in spite of us. For, since it is we and our forebears who have led people into the present situation, if we now discover the situation to be less than ideal we have a responsibility to repent and assist them in working out of it. The steps are these:

1. First we must see it as the nature of the Scriptures to provide basically models of function not of form. The significance of the NT description of the interactions between the NT churches and the surrounding society lies in the functions they performed not in the forms in terms of which these functions were expressed. The forms came from the cultures in which the early churches participated and were not sacred then and certainly are not to be regarded as sacred now even though certain of them (e.g., baptism, Communion, the cross) have superstitiously been regarded as too sacred to tamper with. Worse yet, most of the forms regarded as sacred (or nearly so) by present-day cross-cultural carriers of Christianity have come not from biblical cultures but from Euroamerican culture (e.g., form B of church government, moral practices, times and methods of worship and preaching, doctrinal formulations, educational practices, etc.).

2. Secondly we must come to understand and endorse the principle of dynamic equivalence transculturation of the church—the bringing to birth and thence through growth to maturity churches that are as part and parcel a part of their contemporary culture as the NT churches were of theirs and that communicate the message of Christ to the cultures with an impact equivalent to that of the NT churches.

3. Thirdly, through coming to understand the workings of culture and the magnificent possibilities for using today's cultures for Christian ends (as the early churches did) we must give ourselves to influencing present situations toward greater approximation toward the ideal by:

   a. Working with Christians to understand the Scriptures functionally.

   b. Evaluating the various dimensions of the present situation in terms of its dynamic equivalence to NT models, and

   c. Actually beginning to move toward dynamic equivalence. God is still alive. And where there's God there's hope. But he seldom does his work alone.

REFERENCES CITED

Abraham, R. C. 1962. *Dictionary of the Hausa Language*. 2nd ed. London: University of London Press. Original edition, 1949.

Achebe, Chinua. 1958. *Things Fall Apart*. London: Heinemann.

Alford, Henry. 1871. *The Greek Testament*. 5th ed. Vol. 3. London: Rivingtons.

Archambault 1909. *Textes et documents sur l'etude du christianisne*, II, 0.280. Quoted by Gunnar Helander in *Must We Introduce Monogamy?* P. 26. Pietermaritzburg, South Africa: Shuter & Shooter, 1958.

Barbour, Ian C. 1974. *Myths, Models and Paradigms*. New York: Harper and Row.

Barnett, Homer G. 1953. *Innovation: The Basis of Cultural Change*. New York: McGraw-Hill.

Barney, G. Linwood. 1957. "The Meo—An Incipient Church." *Practical Anthropology* 4(2):31–50.

Barr, James. 1961. *The Semantics of Biblical Language*. London: Oxford.

Barrett, David. 1968. *Schism and Renewal*. London: Oxford.

Beals, R. L., and H. Hoijer. 1965. *An Introduction to Anthropology*. 3rd ed. New York: Macmillan.

Beekman, John, and John Callow. 1974. *Translating the Word of God*. Grand Rapids, MI: Zondervan.

Berlin, Brent, and Paul Kay. 1969. *Basic Color Terms: Their Universality and Evolution*. Berkeley, CA: University of California.

Berlo, David K. 1960. *The Process of Communication*. New York: Holt, Rinehart and Winston.

Bernard, J. H. 1906. *The Pastoral Epistles*. Vols. 15-17 of *Cambridge Greek Testament*. Cambridge, England: The University Press.

Bertsche, James E. 1966. "Kimbanguism: A Challenge to Missionary Statesmanship." *Practical Anthropology* 13(1):13-33. Reprinted in William A. Smalley, *Readings in Missionary Anthropology* pp. 373-393, Pasadena, CA: William Carey Library, 1978.

Bidney, David. 1967. *Theoretical Anthropology*. 2nd ed. New York: Schocken Books.

Blacking, John. 1961. "The Social Value of Venda Riddles." *African Studies* 20:5.

Bock, P. K. 1968. *Modern Cultural Anthropology*. New York: Alfred A. Knopf.

Bonino, José Miguez. 1975. "Whatever Happened to Theology?" *Christianity and Crisis* 35:112.

Boyd, R. H. S. 1969. *An Introduction to Indian Christian Theology*. Madras: Christian Literature Society.

Bratcher, R., and E. A. Nida. 1961. *Translator's Handbook on the Gospel of Mark*. Leiden: Brill (for United Bible Societies).

Brown, Ernest F. 1917. *The Pastoral Epistles. Westminster Commentaries*. New York: Methuen.

Bruce, A. B. 1898. *The Training of the Twelve*. 5th ed. Edinburgh, Scotland: T & T Clark.

Burling, Robbins. 1970. *Man's Many Voices*. New York: Holt, Rinehart and Winston.

Carroll, John B., ed. 1956. *Language, Thought and Reality: Selected Writings of Benjamin Lee Whorf*. New York: Wiley.

Christ, Carol. 1975. "Whatever Happened to Theology?" *Christianity and Crisis* 35:113.

Cobb, John. 1975. "Whatever Happened to Theology?" *Christianity and Crisis* 35:117-118.

Condon, John C. 1975. *Semantics and Communication*. 2nd ed. New York: Macmillan.

Conn, Harvie M. 1978. "Contextualization: A New Dimension For Cross-Cultural Hermeneutics." *Evangelical Missions Quarterly* 14:39–46.

Cox, Harvey. 1975. *Christianity and Crisis* 35:114-115.

Davies, W. D. 1962. *Christian Origins and Judaism*. London: Darton, Longman and Todd.

Davis, Linnell. 1968. "The Use of the Bible in the Kamba Tribal Setting." M.A. thesis, Fuller Theological Seminary.

Dickson, Kwesi, and Paul Ellingworth. 1969. *Biblical Revelation and African Beliefs*. London: Lutterworth.

Dictionary of the English Language. 1967. Random House Unabridged Edition. New York: Random House.

Easton, Burton Scott. 1948. *The Pastoral Epistles*. London: SCM Press.

Fletcher, Joseph. 1966. *Situation Ethics*. Philadelphia, PA: Westminster Press.

Foster, George H. 1973. *Traditional Societies and Technological Change*. New York: Harper and Row.

Fueter, Paul D. 1971. "Communicating the Bible." *International Review of Mission* 60:437–451.

Fuller, Daniel P. "Hermeneutics." Unpublished syllabus in use at Fuller Theological Seminary, Pasadena, California, in 1969.

Geertz, Clifford. 1966. "Religion as a Cultural System." In *Anthropological Approaches to the Study of Religion*. ASA Monographs 3. M. Banton, ed. Pp. 1-46. London: Tavistock.

Goldschmidt, Walter. 1966. *Comparative Functionalism*. Berkeley, CA: University of California Press.

Goody, Jack. 1968. *Literacy in Traditional Societies*. London: Cambridge.

Gottwald, Norman K. 1979. *The Tribes of Yahweh*. Maryknoll, NY: Orbis Books.

Guthrie, Donald. 1957. *The Pastoral Epistles*. Vol. 14 of *The Tyndale New Testament Commentaries*, R. V. G. Tasker, ed. Grand Rapids, MI: Eerdmans.

Hall, Edward T. 1974. *Handbook for Proxemic Analysis*. Washington D.C.: Society for the Anthropology of Visual Communication.

_____1976. *Beyond Culture*. New York: Doubleday.

Haring, Lee. 1972. "On Knowing the Answer." Paper presented at the African Studies Association meeting in Philadelphia.

Harries, Lyndon. 1971. "The Riddle in Africa." *Journal of American Folklore* 84:377–393.

Hatch, Elvin. 1983. *Culture and Morality*. New York: Columbia University Press.

Harjula, Raimo. n.d. "Towards a Theologia Africana." Unpublished paper. Lutheran Theological College, Tanzania.

Hawthorne, G. F., ed. 1975. *Current Issues in Biblical and Patristic Interpretation*. Grand Rapids, MI: Eerdmans.

Helander, Gunnar. 1958. *Must We Introduce Monogamy?* Pietermaritzburg, South Africa: Shuter & Shooter.

Henle, Paul, ed. 1958. *Language, Thought and Culture*. Ann Arbor, MI: University of Michigan Press. (Paperback edition 1965).

Herendeen, Dale S. 1971. "The Evangelical Church of Vietnam." Unpublished paper written as a doctoral student at School of World Mission, Fuller Seminary.

Herskovits, Melville J. 1948. *Man and His Works*. New York: Alfred Knopf.

Hesselgrave, David J. 1978. *Communicating Christ Cross-Culturally*. Grand Rapids, MI: Zondervan.

Hiebert, Paul G. 1976. *Cultural Anthropology*. Philadelphia, PA: Lippincott. Reprinted, Grand Rapids, MI: Baker, 1983.

_____1985. *Anthropological Insights for Missionaries*. Grand Rapids, MI: Baker.

Hillman, Eugene. 1975. *Polygamy Reconsidered*. Maryknoll, NY: Orbis.

Hoebel, E. Adamson. 1972. *Anthropology*. 4th ed. New York: McGraw-Hill.

Hughes, Charles C. 1960. *People of Cove and Woodlot*. New York: Basic Books.

Hulst, A. R. 1960. *Old Testament Translation Problems*. Leiden: Brill (for the United Bible Societies).

Hunter, David, and Mary Ann Foley. 1976. *Doing Anthropology*. New York: Harper and Row.

James, William. 1904. *The Will to Believe*. New York: Longmans, Green and Company.

_____1911. *Some Problems of Philosophy*. New York: Longmans.

_____1968. *Some Patterns of Philosophy*. New York: Greenwood Press.

Jeremias, Joachim. 1969. *Jerusalem in the Time of Jesus*. Philadelphia, PA: Fortress Press. Trans. of the 3rd edition of *Jerusalem zur Zeit Jesu*, by F. H. Cave and C. H. Cave, 1962–67.

Jorgensen, Knudsen. 1986. "The Role and Function of the Media in the Mission of the Church." Ph.D. diss., Fuller Theological Seminary. Ann Arbor, MI: University Microfilms.

Kaufman, Gordon D. 1975. "Whatever Happened to Theology?" *Christianity and Crisis* 35:111.

Kautzsch, E. 1904. "Religion of Israel." In *Dictionary of the Bible*. Vol. 5. James Hastings, ed. Pp. 612–634. New York: Charles Scribner's Sons.

Kearney, Michael. 1984. *World View*. Novato, CA: Chandler and Sharp.

Keesing, R. M., and F. M. Keesing. 1971. *New Perspectives in Cultural Anthropology*. New York: Holt, Rinehart and Winston.

King, Roberta. 1982. "Readings in Christian Music Communication." M.A. thesis, Fuller Theological Seminary.

_____1989. "Pathways in Christian Music Communication." Ph.D. diss., Fuller Theological Seminary. Ann Arbor, MI: University Microfilms.

Kittel, Gerhard. 1951. *Bible Key Words*. J. R. Coates, ed. and trans. New York: Harper.

_____1964 (ed.) *Theological Dictionary of the New Testament*. Vol. 1. G. W. Bromiley, trans. Grand Rapids, MI: Eerdmans.

_____1965 (ed.) *Theological Dictionary of the New Testament*. Vol. 3. G. W. Bromiley, trans. Grand Rapids, MI: Eerdmans.

Klem, Herbert V. 1982. *Oral Communication of the Scripture*. Pasadena, CA: William Carey Library.

Kluckhohn, Clyde. 1946. *The Navaho*. Garden City, NY: Doubleday.

_____1949. *Mirror for Man*. New York: McGraw-Hill.

Knudsen, Jorgen. 1986. "The Role and Function of the Media in the Mission of the Church." Dissertation. Ann Arbor, MI: University Microfilms.

Kraft, Charles H. 1963. "Christian Conversion or Cultural Conversion." *Practical Anthropology* 10(4):179–187. Reprinted in William A. Smalley, *Readings in Missionary Anthropology,* pp. 486-494, Pasadena, CA: William Carey Library, 1978.

_____1969. "What You Heard is Not What I Meant." *World Vision Magazine* 13(4):4, 10–12.

_____1971. "The New Wine of Independence." *World Vision Magazine* 15(2):7–9.

_____1973a. "Church Planters and Ethnolinguistics." In *God, Man and Church Growth*. Alan R. Tippett, ed. Pp. 226–249. Grand Rapids, MI: Eerdmans.

_____1973b. "Dynamic Equivalence Churches." *Missiology* 1:39–57.

_____1973c. "God's Model for Cross-Cultural Communication—The Incarnation." *Evangelical Missions Quarterly* 9:205–216.

_____1973d. "The Incarnation, Cross-Cultural Communication and Communication Theory." *Evangelical Missions Quarterly* 9:277–284.

____1973e. "Toward a Christian Ethnotheology." In *God, Man and Church Growth*. Alan R. Tippett, ed. Pp. 109–127. Grand Rapids, MI: Eerdmans.

____1975. "Toward an Ethnography of Hausa Riddling." *Ba Shiru* 6:17–24.

____1979a. *Christianity in Culture: A Study in Dynamic Biblical Theologizing in Cross-Cultural Perspective*. Maryknoll, NY: Orbis.

____1979b. *Communicating the Gospel God's Way*. Pasadena, CA: William Carey Library.

____1983. *Communication Theory for Christian Witness*. Nashville, TN: Abingdon. Revised ed., Maryknoll, NY: Orbis, 1991.

____1989. *Christianity with Power*. Ann Arbor, MI: Servant Publications.

____1996. *Anthropology for Christian Witness*. Maryknoll, NY: Orbis.

Kraft, Marguerite G. 1978. *Worldview and the Communication of the Gospel*. Pasadena, CA: William Carey Library.

Kraft, Robert A. 1975. "The Development of the Concept of 'Orthodox' in Early Christianity." In G. F. Hawthorne, ed. *Current Issues in Biblical and Patristic Interpretation*. Grand Rapids, MI: Eerdmans.

Kroeber, A. L. 1948. *Anthropology*. New York: Harcourt, Brace and World.

Kuhn, Thomas S. 1970. *The Structure of Scientific Revolutions*. 2nd ed. Chicago, IL: University of Chicago Press.

Leighton, A. A. 1959. *My Name is Legion*. New York: Basic Books.

Lessa, W. A., and E. Z. Vogt. 1958. *Reader in Comparative Religion*. New York: Harper and Row. Reprinted 1965, 1972.

Levy-Bruhl, Lucien. 1910. *Les functions mentales dans les sociétés inférieures*. Paris: F. Alcan.

____1922. *La mentalitéprimitive*. Paris: Librairie Félix Alcan.

Lewis, Oscar. 1959. *Five Families*. New York: Basic Books.

Lindsell, Harold. 1976. *The Battle for the Bible*. Grand Rapids, MI: Zondervan.

Linton, Ralph. 1936. *The Study Man*. New York: Appleton-Century-Crofts. Reprinted 1964.

Loewen, Jacob. 1960. "Identification in the Missionary Task." *Practical Anthropology* 7(1):1-15. Reprinted in William A. Smalley, *Readings in Missionary Anthropology,* pp. 746–760, Pasadena, CA: William Carey Library, 1978.

____1962. "Identification—Symptom or Sublimation?" *Practical Anthropology* 9(7):1–15. Reprinted in William A. Smalley, *Readings in Missionary Anthropology,* pp. 761–768, Pasadena, CA: William Carey Library, 1978.

____1975. *Culture and Human Values*. Pasadena, CA: William Carey Library.

Luzbetak, Louis. 1963. *The Church and Cultures*. Techny, IL: Divine Word Publications. Reprinted, Pasadena, CA: William Carey Library, 1975.

____1988. *The Church and Cultures*. Revised and enlarged. Maryknoll, NY: Orbis.

Maclean, A. J. 1916-18. "Marriage." In Vol. 2 of *Dictionary of the Apostolic Church*. James Hastings, ed. Pp. 11-17. New York: Charles Scribner's Sons.

Madsen, William. 1957. *Christo-Paganism: A Study of Mexican Religious Syncretism*. New Orleans, LA: Middle American Research Institute.

Malina, Bruce J. 1981. *The New Testament World*. Atlanta, GA: John Knox Press.

Maranda, Elli K. 1971. "The Logic of Riddles." In *Structural Analysis of Oral Tradition*. Pierre Maranda, and Elli Köngäs Maranda, eds. Pp. 189-232. Philadelphia, PA: University of Pennsylvania Press.

Maslow, Abraham. 1970. *Motivation and Personality*. 2nd. ed. New York: Harper and Row.

Maurier, Henri. 1968. *The Other Covenant: A Theology of Paganism*. New York: Newman Press.

Mayers, Marvin 1974. *Christianity Confronts Culture*. Grand Rapids, MI: Eerdmans.

Mbiti, John. 1969. "Eschatology." In *Biblical Revelation and African Beliefs*. K. A. Dickson and P. Ellingworth, eds. Pp. 159–184. London: Lutterworth,

____1971. *New Testament Eschatology in an African Background*. London: Oxford.

McGavran, Donald A. 1955. *Bridges of God*. New York: Friendship Press.

____1969. "What Says the Word of God?" *Church Growth Bulletin* 5(4):357-359.

____1970.*Understanding Church Growth*. Grand Rapids, MI: Eerdmans.

____1974. *The Clash Between Christianity and Culture*. Washington, D.C.: Canon Press.

McKim, Donald K., ed. 1986. *A Guide to Contemporary Hermeneutics*. Grand Rapids, MI: Eerdmans.

Mead, Margaret. 1943. "Our Educational Emphases in Primitive Perspective." *American Journal of Sociology* 48:633–639. Reprinted in Margaret Mead, *Anthropology: A Human Science*, pp. 162–174, New York: Van Nostrand, 1964.

____1964. *Anthropology: A Human Science*. New York: Van Nostrand.

Messenger, John. 1959. "The Christian Concept of Forgiveness and Anang Morality." *Practical Anthropology* 6(3):97–103.

____1960. "Anang Proverb-Riddlers." *Journal of American Folklore* 73:226.

Mickelsen, A. Berkeley. 1963. *Interpreting the Bible*. Grand Rapids, MI: Eerdmans.

Miller, Douglas J. 1975. "Seminary Education Tomorrow: A Forecast." *Christianity Today* 19(10):4–6.

Nash, Ronald H. 1977. "Truth By Any Other Name." *Christianity Today* 22(1):17-23.

Newman, B., and E. A. Nida. 1972. *A Translator's Handbook on The Acts of the Apostles*. London: United Bible Societies.

Nida, Eugene A. 1945. "Linguistics and Ethnology in Translation Problems." *Word* 1:194–208.

____1947. *Bible Translating*. New York: American Bible Society.

____1954. *Customs and Cultures*. New York: Harper and Row. Reprinted, Pasadena, CA: William Carey Library, 1975.

____1959. "Are We Really Monotheists?" *Practical Anthropology* 6(4):49-54.

____1960. *Message and Mission*. New York: Harper and Row. Revised ed., Pasadena, CA: William Carey Library, 1990.

_____1964. *Toward a Science of Translating.* Leiden: Brill.

_____1971. "Implications of Contemporary Linguistics for Biblical Scholarship." *Journal of Biblical Literature* 91:73–89. Reprinted in E. A. Nida, *Language Structure and Translation,* pp. 248–270, Stanford, CA: Stanford University Press, 1975.

_____1972. (ed.) The *Book of a Thousand Tongues.* London: United Bible Societies.

Nida, Eugene A., and Charles R. Taber. 1969. *The Theory and Practice of Translation.* Leiden: Brill.

Niebuhr, H. Richard. 1951. *Christ and Culture.* New York: Harper and Row.

Oden, Thomas C. 1966. *Kerygma and Counseling.* Philadelphia, PA: Westminster.

_____1974a. "The Diffusion of Therapeutic Agency." In *After Therapy, What? Lay Therapeutic Resources in Religious Perspective.* Thomas C. Oden and Neil Warren, eds. Pp. 3-26. Springfield, IL: Thomas.

_____1974b. "The Human Potential and Evangelical Hope." In *After Therapy, What? Lay Therapeutic Resources in Religious Perspective.* Thomas C. Oden and Neil Warren, eds. Pp. 59-79. Springfield, IL: Thomas.

_____1974c. "The Post-Therapeutic Situation." In *After Therapy, What? Lay Therapeutic Resources in Religious Perspective.* Thomas C. Oden and Neil Warren, eds. Pp. 27-58. Springfield, IL: Thomas.

Oden, Thomas C., and Neil Warren, eds. 1974. *After Therapy, What? Lay Therapeutic Resources in Religious Perspective.* Springfield, IL: Thomas.

Opler, Morris E. 1945. "Themes as Dynamic Forces in Culture." *American Journal of Sociology* 51:198–206.

Padilla, Rene. 1980. "Hermeneutics and Culture." In *Down to Earth.* John Stott and R. Coote, eds. Pp. 63–78. Grand Rapids, MI: Eerdmans.

Parrinder, Geoffrey. 1958. *The Bible and Polygamy.* London: SPCK.

Pelto, Perti. 1970. *Anthropological Research.* New York: Harper and Row.

Phillips, J. B. 1954. *Plain Christianity.* New York: Macmillan/London: Epworth.

_____1958. "Translator's Forward." *The New Testament in Modern English.* London: Bles.

Pike, Eunice, and Florence Cowan. 1959. "Mushroom Ritual Versus Christianity." *Practical Anthropology* 6(4):145–150. Reprinted in William A. Smalley, ed., *Readings in Missionary Anthropology,* pp. 52-57, Pasadena, CA: William Carey Library, 1974.

Ramm, Bernard. 1961. *Special Revelation and the Word of God.* Grand Rapids, MI: Eerdmans.

_____1970. *Protestant Biblical Interpretation.* 3rd rev. ed. Grand Rapids, MI: Baker.

Read, Margaret. 1955. *Education and Social Change in Tropical Areas.* Camden, NJ: Nelson.

Redfield, Robert. 1953. *The Primitive World and Its Transformations.* Ithaca, NY: Cornell University Press.

Reiling, J., and J. Swellengrebel. 1971. *A Translator's Handbook on the Gospel of Luke.* Leiden: Brill (for the United Bible Societies).

Reyburn, William D. 1957. "The Transformation of God and the Conversion of Man." *Practical Anthropology* 4(5):185–194. Reprinted in William A. Smalley, *Readings in Missionary Anthropology II*, pp. 481-485, Pasadena, CA: William Carey Library, 1978.

_____1970. "The Helping Relationship in Missionary Work." *Practical Anthropology* 17:49-59. Reprinted in William A. Smalley, *Readings in Missionary Anthropology II,* pp. 769–779, Pasadena, CA: William Carey Library, 1978.

Richardson, Don. 1974. *The Peace Child.* Ventura, CA: Regal Books.

Rogerson, J. W. 1978. *Anthropology and the Old Testament.* London: Basil Blackwell.

Ruether, Rosemary. 1975. "Whatever Happened to Theology?" *Christianity and Crisis* 35:109-110.

Sapir, Edward. 1929. "The Status of Linguistics as a Science." *Language* 5:207–214.

Schaeffer, Francis. 1968. *The God Who is There.* Chicago, IL: InterVarsity.

_____1976. *How Shall We Then Live?* Old Tappan, NJ: Revell.

Sire, James. 1976. *The Universe Next Door.* Downers Grove, IL: InterVarsity.

Smalley, William A. 1955. "Culture and Superculture." *Practical Anthropology* 2:58–71.

_____1958. "Cultural Implications of an Indigenous Church." *Practical Anthropology* 5:51–65.

_____1958. "The World Is Too Much with Us." *Practical Anthropology* 5:234–236.

_____1959. "What Are Indigenous Churches Like?" *Practical Anthropology* 6:135–139.

_____1974. (ed.) *Readings in Missionary Anthropology.* Pasadena, CA: William Carey Library. Original edition 1967.

_____1978. *Readings in Missionary Anthropology II.* Pasadena, CA: William Carey Library.

Smalley, William A., and Marie Fetzer. 1950. "A Christian View of Anthropology." In *Modern Science and Christian Faith: A Symposium on the Relationship of the Bible to Modern Science.* Pp. 98-195. F. A. Everest, ed. Wheaton, IL: Van Kampen Press.

Søgaard, Viggo. 1975. *Everything You Need to Know for a Cassette Ministry.* Minneapolis, MN: Bethany Fellowship.

_____1986. "Applying Christian Communication." Ph.D. diss., Fuller Theological Seminary. Ann Arbor, MI: University Microfilms.

Spradley, James P. 1979. *The Ethnographic Interview.* New York: Holt, Rinehart and Winston.

_____1980. *Participant Observation.* New York: Holt, Rinehart and Winston.

Spradley, James P., and David McCurdy. 1975. *Anthropology: The Cultural Perspective.* New York: Wiley.

Sproul, Robert C. 1976. "Controversy at Culture Gap." *Eternity* 27:13–15, 40.

Stock, Eugene. 1899. *History of the Church Missionary Society.* 3 vols. London: Church Missionary Society.

Strong, William E. 1910. *The Story of the American Board.* Boston, MA: Pilgrim Press.

Sundkler, Bengt. 1960. *The Christian Ministry in Africa.* London: SCM Press.

Taber, Charles R. 1980. "Hermeneutics and Culture." In *Down to Earth.* John Stott and R. Coote, eds. Pp. 79–94. Grand Rapids, MI: Eerdmans.

_____1978. "The Limits of Indigenization in Theology." *Missiology* 6(1):53-79.

Tanner, R. E. S. 1967. *Transition in African Beliefs.* Maryknoll, NY: Maryknoll Publications.

Taylor, John V. 1958. *The Growth of the Church in Buganda.* London: SCM.

_____1963. *The Primal Vision: Christian Presence Amid African Religion.* London: SCM.

Tennant, F. R. 1962. "Theology." *Encyclopedia Britannica.* Vol. 22. Harry S. Ashmore, editor in chief. P. 61B. Chicago, IL: Encyclopedia Britannica.

Thannickal, John. 1975. "Ashram: A Communicating Community." D.Miss. diss., Fuller Theological Seminary. Ann Arbor, MI: University Microfilms.

Thielicke, H. 1962. *A Little Exercise for Young Theologians.* Grand Rapids, MI: Eerdmans.

_____1965. *The Trouble With the Church.* New York: Harper Brothers.

Tillich, Paul. 1959. *Theology of Culture.* New York: Oxford.

Tippett, Alan R. 1958. "The Integrating Gospel." Unpublished manuscript in the library of Fuller Theological Seminary.

_____1971. "Patterns of Religious Change." In *Introduction to Missiology.* Pp. 157–182. Pasadena, CA: William Carey Library, 1987.

_____1973. *Verdict Theology in Missionary Theory.* Revised ed. Pasadena, CA: William Carey Library. Original edition, Lincoln, IL: Lincoln Christian College Press, 1969.

_____1973. (ed.) *God, Man and Church Growth.* Grand Rapids, MI: Eerdmans.

_____1975. *Christopaganism or Indigenous Christianity?* T. Yamamori and C. R. Taber, eds. Pasadena, CA: William Carey Library.

_____1987. *Introduction to Missiology.* Pasadena, CA: William Carey Library.

Trench, R. C. 1948. *Notes on the Parables of Our Lord.* Grand Rapids, MI: Baker. Original edition London: Macmillan, 1864. Revised 1874. Reprinted Philadelphia: Syckelmorre, 1878.

Von Allmen, Daniel. 1975. "The Birth of Theology." *International Review of Mission* 64:37–52.

Wagner, C. Peter. 1978a. "How Ethical Is the Homogeneous Unit Principle?" *Occasional Bulletin of Missionary Research* 2(1):12–19.

_____1978b. *Our Kind of People.* Atlanta, GA: John Knox Press.

_____1988. *How to Have a Healing Ministry Without Making Your Church Sick.* Ventura, CA: Regal.

Wallace, A. F. C. 1956. "Revitalization Movements." *American Anthropologist* 58:264–281.

____1966. *Religion: An Anthropological View*. New York: Random House.

Webber, Robert. 1980. *God Still Speaks*. Nashville, TN: Nelson.

Weber, Hans-Rudi. 1957. *The Communication of the Gospel to Illiterates*. London: SCM Press.

Welbourn, F. B., and B. A. Ogot. 1966. *A Place to Feel at Home: A Study of Two Independent Churches in Western Kenya*. London: Oxford.

Westermarck, Edward. 1922. *The History of Human Marriage*. 5th ed. 3 vols. New York: Allerton Book Company.

White, Newport J. D. 1909. *The First and Second Epistles to Timothy*. Vol. 4 of *The Expositor's Greek Testament*. W. Robertson Nicoll, ed. Grand Rapids, MI: Eerdmans. Reprinted 1951.

Whorf, Benjamin Lee. 1940. "Science and Linguistics." *Technological Review* 42:229–241, 247–248. Reprinted in John B. Carroll, ed., *Language, Thought and Reality: Selected Writings of Benjamin Lee Whorf*, pp. 207–219, New York: Wiley, 1956.

____1941, 1960. "The Relation of Habitual Thought and Behavior to Language." In *Language, Culture and Personality: Essays in Memory of Edward Sapir*. L. Spier, A. I. Hallowell and S. S. Newman. Pp. 75–93. Salt Lake City, UT: University of Utah Press. Reprinted in *Language, Thought and Reality: Selected Writings of Benjamin Lee Whorf*, John B. Carroll, ed., pp. 134–159, New York: Wiley, 1956.

Williams, Donald. 1989. *Signs, Wonders and the Kingdom of God*. Ann Arbor, MI: Servant.

Wimber, John. 1986. *Power Evangelism*. New York: Harper.

____1987. *Power Healing*. New York: Harper.

Wimsatt, William K. 1954. *The Verbal Icon*. Lexington, KY: University of Kentucky Press.

Winans, E. V. 1962. *Shambala*. Berkeley, CA: University of California Press.

Wold, Joseph C. 1968. *God's Impatience in Liberia*. Grand Rapids, MI: Eerdmans.

Wolff, Hans Walter. 1974. *Anthropology of the Old Testament*. London: SCM Press.

Wonderly, William L. 1958. "Pagan and Indian Concepts in a Mexican Indian Culture," *Practical Anthropology* 5(5-6):197-202. Reprinted in William A. Smalley, ed., *Readings in Missionary Anthropology*, pp. 229-234, Pasadena, CA: William Carey Library, 1974.

____1968. *Bible Translations for Popular Use*. London: United Bible Societies.

BIBLIOGRAPHY OF
CHARLES H. KRAFT

1958

Articles and Chapters in Books

1. "Missionary Interpersonal Relations: Younger Versus Older." *Practical Anthropology* 5:33-37.

1960

Book Reviews

1. Gunnar Helander, *Must We Introduce Monogamy?: A Study of Polygamy as a Mission Problem in South Africa* in *Practical Anthropology* 7:91-93.

1961

Articles and Chapters in Books

1. "Correspondence Courses in Anthropology." *Practical Anthropology* 8:168-175.

1963

Books

1. *A Study of Hausa Syntax* (3 volumes). Hartford Studies in Linguistics. Vols. 8, 9, 10. Hartford, CT: Hartford Seminary Foundation.

Articles and Chapters in Books

1. "Christian Conversion or Cultural Conversion." *Practical Anthropology* 10:179-187.

Book Reviews

1. Aidan Southall, *Social Change in Modern Africa*; Egbert DeVries, *Man in Rapid Social Change*; Paul Abrecht, *The Churches and Rapid Social Change*, in "Mission in a World of Rapid Social Change." *Practical Anthropology* 10:271-9.

1964

Articles and Chapters in Books

1. "A New Study of Hausa Syntax." *Journal of African Languages* 3:66-74.
2. "The Morpheme <u>na</u> in Relation to a Broader Classification of Hausa Verbals." *Journal of African Languages* 3:231-240.

Book Reviews
1. R. C. Abraham, *Dictionary of the Hausa Language,* in *Modern Language Journal* 68:252.
2. William A. Smalley, *Manual of Articulatory Phonetics*, in *Practical Anthropology* 11:191-192.
3. H. H. Wangler, *Zur Tonologie des Hausa,* in *Language* 40:504-507.

1965

Books
1. *An Introduction to Spoken Hausa* (textbook, workbook, tapes), African Language Monographs 5A, 5B. African Studies Center: Michigan State University.

1966

Books
1. *Cultural Materials in Hausa.* African Language Monograph 6A. African Studies Center: Michigan State University.
2. *Workbook in Intermediate and Advanced Hausa.* African Language Monograph 6B. African Studies Center: Michigan State University.
3. *Where Do I Go From Here?* (A Handbook for Continuing Language Study in the Field) with Marguerite G. Kraft. U.S. Peace Corps.

1969

Articles and Chapters in Books
1. "What You Heard is Not What I Meant." *World Vision Magazine* 13:10-12 (April). Reprinted in *Messenger* 16(118):20-22.

1970

Articles and Chapters in Books
1. "Tone in Hausa." Review article of H.H. Wangler, *Zur Tonologie des Hausa*, in *African Studies* 29:129-139.
2. "Hausa sai and da—A Couple of Overworked Particles." *Journal of African Languages* 9:92-109.

1971

Articles and Chapters in Books
1. "The New Wine of Independence." *World Vision* 15(2):6-9.
2. "Younger Churches—Missionaries and Indigeneity." *Church Growth Bulletin* 7:159-161.
3. "A Note on Lateral Fricatives in Chadic." *Studies in African Linguistics* 2:271-281.

1972

Articles and Chapters in Books

1. "Theology and Theologies I." *Theology, News and Notes* 18(2):4-6, 9.
2. "Spinoff From the Study of Cross-Cultural Mission." *Theology, News and Notes* 18(3):20-23.
3. "The Hutterites and Today's Church." *Theology, News and Notes* 18(3):15-16.
4. "Theology and Theologies II." *Theology, News and Notes* 18(3):17-20.

Book Reviews

1. Kwesi Dickson and Paul Ellingworth, eds., *Biblical Revelation and African Beliefs*, in *Evangelical Missions Quarterly* 8:244-247.

1973

Books

1. *Teach Yourself Hausa*, with A. H. M. Kirk-Greene. London: English Universities Press.
2. *Introductory Hausa*, with M. G. Kraft. Berkeley, CA: University of California Press.
3. *A Hausa Reader*. Berkeley, CA: University of California Press.

Articles and Chapters in Books

1. "Church Planters and Ethnolinguistics." In *God, Man and Church Growth*. A. R. Tippett, ed. Pp. 226-249. Grand Rapids, MI: Eerdmans.
2. "Dynamic Equivalence Churches: An Ethnological Approach to Indigeneity." *Missiology* 1:39-57. Reprinted in *Readings in Dynamic Indigeneity*. C. H. Kraft and T. N. Wisley, eds. Pp. 87-111. Pasadena, CA: William Carey Library, 1979.
3. "God's Model for Cross-Cultural Communication—The Incarnation." *Evangelical Missions Quarterly* 9:205-216.
4. "The Incarnation, Cross-Cultural Communication—The Incarnation." *Evangelical Missions Quarterly* 9:277-284.
5. "North America's Cultural Challenge: Pluralism's Challenge to Evangelism." *Christianity Today* 17:6-8.
6. "Toward a Christian Ethnotheology." In *God, Man and Church Growth*. A. R. Tippett, ed. Pp. 109-126. Grand Rapids, MI: Eerdmans.

Book Reviews

1. David J. Bosch, ed., *Church and Culture Change in Africa*, in *Evangelical Missions Quarterly* 9:249-252.
2. Modupe Oduyoye, *Yoruba Names: Their Structure and Their Meanings*, in *Missiology* 1:389-390.

1974

Articles and Chapters in Books

1. "Reconstructions of Chadic Pronouns I: Possessive, Object, and Independent Sets—An Interim Report." *Third Annual Conference on African Linguistics*, Erhard Voeltz, ed., Indiana University Publications: African Series 7:69-94.
2. "Ideological Factors in Intercultural Communication." *Missiology* 2:295-312.
3. "Christian Conversion as a Dynamic Process." *International Christian Broadcasters Bulletin* (Second Quarter): 8-9, 14.

4. "An Anthropologist's Response to Oden." In *After Therapy What?* Neil C. Warren, ed. Pp. 136-159. Springfield, IL: Charles C. Thomas.
5. "Why Have You Come," "Why Go to the Mission Field?," "What If I Hadn't Gone?" (3 lectures). *Missions Week Lectures 1974*. Eugene, OR: Northwest Christian College Missions Committee (mimeographed).
6. "Guidelines for Developing a Message Geared to the Horizon of Receptivity, Part I and 2." In *Media in Islamic Culture*. C. Richard Shumaker, ed. Pp. 17-33. Wheaton, IL: International Christian Broadcasters.
7. "Distinctive Religious Barriers to Outside Penetration." In *Media in Islamic Culture*. C. Richard Shumaker, ed. Pp. 65-76. Wheaton, IL: International Christian Broadcasters.
8. "Psychological Stress Factors Among Muslims." In *Media in Islamic Culture*. C. Richard Shumaker, ed. Pp. 137-144. Wheaton, IL: International Christian Broadcasters.
9. "Extent and Limitations of Media among Muslims." In *Media in Islamic Culture*. C. Richard Shumaker, ed. Pp 166-169. Wheaton, IL: International Christian Broadcasters.

Book Reviews
1. S. Neill, G. H. Anderson, and J. Goodwin, eds., *Concise Dictionary of the Christian World Mission*, in *Missiology* 2:142-144.

1975

Book Reviews
1. E. E. Evans-Pritchard, *Man and Woman Among the Azande*, in *Missiology* 3:390-393.
3. Roger S. Greenway, *A World to Win*; J. Herbert Kane, *The Making of a Missionary*; Richard R. DeRidder, *Discipling the Nations*; in *Christian Scholars Review* 7:225-227.

Sound Recordings
1. "Topics in Anthropology." 19 sound cassettes. Springfield, MO: Assemblies of God Audiovisual.

1976

Articles and Chapters in Books
1. "Toward an Ethnography of Hausa Riddling." *Ba Shiru* (1975) 6:171-24, and *Folia Orientalia* (Krakow, Poland) 17:231-43.
2. "Communicate or Compete?" *Spectrum* (Spring-Summer): 8-10.
3. "Cultural Concomitants of Higi Conversion: Early Periods." *Missiology* 4:431-442.
4. "An Ethnolinguistic Study of Hausa Epithets." *Studies in African Linguistics*, Supplement 6: *Papers in African Linguistics in Honor of Wm. E. Welmers*. Department of Linguistics, University of California, Los Angeles. Pp. 135-146.

1977

Articles and Chapters in Books

1. "Bible Translation and the Church" (editorial). *Theology, News and Notes* 23:2 (March).
2. "What is God Trying to Do?" *Theology, News and Notes* 23:9-11 (March). Reprinted in *Notes on Translation* 72:20-26 (December).
3. "Biblical Principles of Communication." *The Harvester* 56:262-264, 275. Edited and reprinted in *Buzz* New Malden, Surrey, December, pp. 17, 19.
4. "Can Anthropological Insight Assist Evangelical Theology?" *Christian Scholar's Review* 7:165-202.

Book Reviews

1. Sakae Kubo and Walter Specht, *So Many Versions?*, in *Theology News and Notes* 23:20-21.

1978

Articles and Chapters in Books

1. "The Contextualization of Theology." *Evangelical Missions Quarterly* 14:311-336.
2. "An Anthropological Apologetic for the Homogeneous Unit Principle in Missiology." *Occasional Bulletin of Missionary Research* 10:121-126.
3. "Worldview in Intercultural Communication." In *Intercultural and International Communication*, Fred L. Casmir, ed. Pp. 407-428. Lanham, MD: University Press of America.
4. "Christianity and Culture in Africa." *Facing the New Challenges—The Message of PACLA*. Pp. 286-291. Nairobi: Evangel Publishing House.
5. "What is an Indigenous Church?" *Facing the New Challenges—The Message of PACLA*. Pp. 304-307. Nairobi: Evangel Publishing House.
6. "Strategies for Reaching Africa's 300 Million Lost." *Facing the New Challenges—The Message of PACLA*. Pp. 490-500. Nairobi: Evangel Publishing House.
7. "The Church in Western Africa" (Response #2). *The Church in Africa 1977*, by Charles R. Taber. Pp. 166-175. Pasadena, CA: William Carey Library.
8. "Interpreting in Cultural Context." *Journal of the Evangelical Theological Society* 21:357-367.

1979

Books

1. *Christianity in Culture:A Study in Dynamic Biblical Theologizing in Cross-Cultural Perspective*. Maryknoll, NY: Orbis Books.
2. *Readings in Dynamic Indigeneity*, with T. Wisley. Pasadena, CA: William Carey Library.
4. *Communicating the Gospel God's Way*. Pasadena, CA: William Carey Library. Chinese (Mandarin) translation. D. Wang, trans. Hong Kong: Asian Outreach, 1983.

Articles and Chapters in Books
1. "Dynamic Equivalence Churches in Muslim Society." In *The Gospel and Islam: A 1978 Compendium*. Pp. 114-128. Donald M. McCurry, ed. Monrovia, CA: MARC.
2. "God's Model for Communication." *Ashland Theological Bulletin* 12(1):3-16. Reprinted in *Communicating the Gospel God's Way*, chapter 1.
3. "The Credibility of the Message and the Messenger." *Ashland Theological Bulletin* 12(1):17-32. Reprinted in *Communicating the Gospel God's Way*, chapter 2.
4. "What is the Receptor Up To?" *Ashland Theological Bulletin* 12(1):33-42. Reprinted in *Communicating the Gospel God's Way*, chapter 3.
5. "The Power of Life Involvement." *Ashland Theological Bulletin* 12(1):43-60. Reprinted in *Communicating the Gospel God's Way*, chapter 4.
6. "Dynamic Equivalence Theologizing." In *Readings in Dynamic Indigeneity*, by C. H. Kraft and T. N. Wisley. Pp. 258-285. Pasadena, CA: William Carey Library. Reprinted from *Christianity in Culture*. Pp. 231-311. Maryknoll, NY: Orbis, 1979.
7. "Measuring Indigeneity." In *Readings in Dynamic Indigeneity*, by C. H. Kraft and T. N. Wisley. Pp. 118-52. Pasadena, CA: William Carey Library.

Forward to a Book
1. Peter Falk, *The Growth of the Church in Africa*. Grand Rapids, MI: Zondervan.

1980

Articles and Chapters in Books
1. "Conservative Christians and Anthropologists: A Clash of Worldviews." *Journal of the American Scientific Affiliation* 32:140-145 (September).
2. "The Church in Culture: A Dynamic Equivalence Model." In *Down to Earth: Studies in Christianity and Culture*. John Stott and Robert Coote, eds. Pp. 211-230. Grand Rapids, MI: Eerdmans.

Book Reviews
1. E. Fashole-Luke, A. Hastings, and G. Tasie, *Christianity in Independent Africa* in *Theology Today* 36:618 (January).

1981

Books
1. *Chadic Wordlists* (3 vols.). Berlin: Verlag von Dietrich Reimer.

Articles and Chapters in Books
1. "The Place of the Receptor in Communication." *Theology, News and Notes* 28(3):13-15, 23.

1982

Articles and Chapters in Books
1. "My Distaste for the Combative Approach." *Evangelical Missions Quarterly* 18:139-142.

Forward to a Book
1. Herbert V. Klem, *Oral Communication of the Scripture*. Pasadena, CA: William Carey Library.

Book Reviews
1. J. S. Pobee, *Toward an African Theology*; K. Appiah-Kubi and S. Torres, *African Theology en Route*; K.O.K. Onyioha, *African Godianism*, in "Theology From African Perspectives," *Journal of Psychology and Theology* 11:74.

1983

Books
1. *Communication Theory for Christian Witness*. Nashville, TN: Abingdon Press.

Articles and Chapters in Books
1. "Can Anything Good Come Out of a Condensed Bible?" with R. Daniel Shaw. *Eternity* 34(2):28-9.

Forward to a Book
1. Osadolor Imasogie Achimota, *Guidelines for Christian Theology in Africa*. Ghana: Africa Christian Press.

Book Reviews
1. Choan-Seng Song, *Third-Eye Theology: Theology in Formation in Asian Settings* in *Journal of Psychology and Theology* 11:75.
2. Jung Young Lee, *The Theology of Change: A Christian Concept of God in an Eastern Perspective,* in *Journal of Psychology and Theology* 11:74.

Sound Recordings
1. "Communicating Christ to Americans." 4 sound cassettes. Carl G. Westerdahl lectures in evangelism, North Park Theological Seminary. Recorded January 18-19, 1998. Also available on videocassette.

1984

Book Reviews
1. Morris Inch, *Doing Theology Across Cultures*, in *TSF Bulletin* 7:24-25 (May/June).

1985

Articles and Chapters in Books
1. "Cultural Anthropology: Its Meaning for Theology." *Theology Today* 41:390-400.

2. "Gospel and Culture." *Christianity in Today's World*. Robin Keeley, organizing ed. Pp. 274-275. Grand Rapids, MI: Eerdmans. Also in British edition entitled *Christianity: A World Faith*. London: Lion Publishing.
3. "Why the Vineyard Should Move into Crosscultural Ministry." *First Fruits* 2(8):15-19 (November/December).
4. "'The Third Wave' in the Covenant Church." *Narthex* 5(1):5-15.

Book Reviews
1. G. H. Weber and L. M. Cohen, *Beliefs and Self-Help: Cross-Cultural Perspectives and Approaches* in *Journal of Psychology and Theology* 13:68-69.

1986
Articles and Chapters in Books
1. "The Question of Miracles." *The Pentecostal Minister* (Winter).
2. "Worldview and Bible Translation." *Notes on Anthropology* 6/7:46-57 (June-September).
3. "Missiology and SIL." *Current Concerns of Anthropologists and Missionaries*. Karl J. Franklin, ed. Pp. 133-142. Dallas, TX: Summer Institute of Linguistics.
4. "Five Years Later." *Signs and Wonders Today: The Remarkable Story of the MC510 Signs, Wonders and Church Growth at Fuller Theological Seminary*. C. Peter Wagner, ed. Pp. 115-124. Wheaton, IL: Christian Life Magazine.
5. "Let's Fight Staticosis." *Worship Times* Summer: 5.
6. "Sing *About* or Sing *To?*" *Worship Times* Fall: 4.
7. "Supracultural Meanings via Cultural Forms." *A Guide to Contemporary Hermeneutics*. Donald K. McKim, ed. Pp.309-343. Grand Rapids, MI: Eerdmans.
8. "Worldview and Bible Translation." *Anthropological and Missiological Issues*. Karl J. Franklin, ed. Dallas, TX: Summer Institute of Linguistics.
9. "Evangelicals Rediscover the Gifts." *Renewing Australia* December: 12-13.

1987
Articles and Chapters in Books
1. "A Shaky Stage?" *Worship Times* Winter: 1-2.
2. "The World Needs More Spiritual Power," *AD2000* May: 3.
3. "Organ or Guitar?" *Worship Times* Summer.
4. "Shifting Worldviews, Shifting Attitudes." *Equipping the Saints* (Sept-Oct).
5. "World View and Worship." *Worship Times* Spring.
6. "Shifting Worldviews, Shifting Attitudes." In *Riding the Third Wave*. John Wimber and Kevin Springer, eds. Pp. 122-134. England: Marshall Pickering.
7. "Worship is Up to the Worshippers," *Worship Times* Fall: 4.

Forward to a Book
1. A.R. Tippett, *Introduction to Missiology*. Pasadena, CA: William Carey Library. Foreword with Marguerite G. Kraft.

1988

Articles and Chapters in Books

1. "Follow the Leader?" *Worship Times* (Winter) 2(4):4.
2. "The Lord's Supper: A Live or Dead Ritual?" *Worship Times* (Spring): 3.

1989

Books

1. *Christianity with Power: Your Worldview and Your Experience of the Supernatural.* Ann Arbor, MI: Servant Publications.
   a. British edition: London: Marshall Pickering.
   b. German translation: Lorrach: Wolfgang Simson Verlag.
   c. Philippine edition: Manila: OMF Literature, 1990.
   d. Chinese (Mandarin) translation: Kaohsiung, Taiwan: Holy Light Theological Seminary, 1991.
   e. Korean translation: Seoul: Nathan Press, 1992.
   f. Japanese translation. Tokyo, 1994.

Articles and Chapters in Books

1. "The Hymnal Is Not Enough." *Christianity Today* 33(6):8.
2. "Who Was This Man: A Tribute to Alan Tippett." *Missiology* 17:269-281.
3. "Don't Worry About Ignorance: It's Our Knowledge That's the Problem." *Missions Tomorrow* (Spring/Summer): 27-34.
4. "Contextualizing Communication." *The Word Among Us*. Dean Gilliland, ed. Pp. 121-138. Dallas, TX: Word Books.

1990

Books

1. *Communicate With Power*. Manila: OMF Literature, Philippines. Korean translation, entitled, *Jesus, God's Model for Christian Communication*, 1992.

Articles and Chapters in Books

1. "A Third Wave Perspective on Pentecostal Missions." In *Called and Empowered: Pentecostal Perspective on Global Mission.* Pp. 299-312. Murray W. Dempster, Byron D. Klaus, Douglas Peterson, eds. Peabody, MA: Hendrickson Publications.
2. "Response to F. Douglas Pennoyer." In *Wrestling with Dark Angels*. C. Peter Wagner and F. Douglas Pennoyer, eds. Pp. 271-279. Ventura, CA: Regal Books.
3. "Shifting Worldviews, Sifting Attitudes." In *Conflict and Conquest*. Power Encounter Topics for Taiwan. Kenneth D. Shay, ed. P. 15-19. O C International, Taiwan.

Sound Recordings

1. "Anthropology." 18 sound cassettes. Pasadena, CA: Fuller Theological Seminary.

1991

Books

1. *Communication Theory for Christian Witness*. Revised edition. Maryknoll, NY: Orbis.

Articles and Chapters in Books

1. "Receptor-Oriented Ethics in Cross-Cultural Intervention." *Transformation* 8:1:20-25 (January-March).
2. "What Kind of Encounters Do We Need in our Christian Witness?" *Evangelical Missions Quarterly* 27:258-265.
3. "It's What We Think We Know—That's The Problem." *Renewing Australia* December: 14-15, 37.

Book Reviews

1. Louis J. Luzbetak, *The Church and Cultures: New Perspectives in Missiological Anthropology* in *International Bulletin of Missionary Research* 15:37-38.

1992

Books

1. *Defeating Dark Angels*. Ann Arbor, MI: Servant.
    a. British edition, Tonbridge, Kent: Sovereign World, 1993.
    b. German translation. Buchs (Zurich): Koinonia Verlag, 1995.
    c. Chinese (Mandarin) translation. Rosemead, CA: Evangelical Formosan Church, 1994.
    d. Korean translation. Seoul, 1995.
    e. Russian translation. Koinonia-Verlag, Switzerland, 2000.

Articles and Chapters in Books

1. "Changing What We Know." *Renewing Australia*, June: 19-21, 29.
2. "Worship: Tradition, or Just 'Follow the Leader?'" *Worship Leader* Feb/March: 7, 29.
3. "Hymns vs. Praise Songs: Which Shall We Sing?" *Worship Leader* April/May: 7, 44.
4. "How Our Worldview Affects the Way We Worship." *Worship Leader* June/July: 10, 53.
5. "Traditions Too Often Lose Meaning Over Time." *Worship Leader* Aug/Sept: 8, 53.
6. "Fear of Change Is Like Acting on a Shaky Stage." *Worship Leader* Oct/Nov: 9, 39.
7. "Do We Depend Too Much on Worship Leaders?" *Worship Leader* Dec1992/Jan 1993:7.
8. "Conversion in Group Settings." In *Handbook of Religious Conversion*. H. Newton Malony and Samuel Southard, eds. Pp. 259-275. Religious Education Press.
9. "Allegiance, Truth and Power Encounters in Christian Witness." In *Pentecost, Mission and Ecumenism, Essays on Intercultural Theology*. Pp. 215-230. Jan. A. B. Jongeneel, ed. New York: Peter Lang.

<u>1993</u>

Books

1. *Deep Wounds, Deep Healing: Discovering the Vital Link Between Spiritual Warfare and Inner Healing*. Ann Arbor, MI: Servant Books.
   a. British edition, Tonbridge, Kent: Sovereign World, 1994.
   b. Japanese translation, Vol. 1. Tokyo: Praise Publications, 1995. Vol. 2, 1997.
   c. Philippine edition. Manila: St Pauls, 1995.
   d. Korean translation. Seoul, 1995.
   e. German translation. Koinonia-Verlag, Oberweningen, Switzerland, 2000.

Articles and Chapters in Books

1. "Communication in Worship: To Whom Do We Sing?" *Worship Leader*, Feb/Mar: 7-8.
2. "Organ/Guitar Preference Reflects View of God." *Worship Leader* Apr/May: 7
3. "How Acts of Worship Help Defeat the Devil." *Worship Leader* June/July: 8, 44.
4. "Are We Really Communicating What We Intend?" *Worship Leader* Aug/Sept: 6, 8.
5. "Organs Vs. Guitar Question a Matter of Context." *Worship Leader* Oct/Nov: 9, 34.
6. "Shouldn't We Be Teaching People How to Worship?" *Worship Leader* Dec 1993/Jan
   1994: 4, 11, 30.
7. "Understanding and Valuing Multiethnic Diversity," with Marguerite G. Kraft. *Theology News and Notes* 40(4):6-8.
8. "Communicating and Ministering the Power of the Gospel Cross-Culturally: The Power of God for Christians Who Ride Two Horses," written with Marguerite G. Kraft. In *The Kingdom and the Power*. Gary S. Greig and Kevin N. Springer, eds. Pp. 346-356. Ventura, CA: Regal.

Book Reviews

1. Thomas H. McAlpine, *Facing the Powers: What Are the Options?* in *Missiology—An International Review* 21:226-227.

<u>1994</u>

Books

1. *Behind Enemy Lines: An Advanced Guide to Spiritual Warfare*, edited. Ann Arbor, MI: Servant Books.
   a. Korean translation. Seoul, 1996.
   b. Japanese translation. Tokyo, 1997.
   c. Reprint in English, Wipf and Stock, 2000.

Articles and Chapters in Books

1. "What Are We Communicating About Worship?" *Worship Leader* Apr: 8.
2. "Our Youth Need to Know that Worship Is Warfare." *Worship Leader* May/Jun: 8.
3. "Taking Out the Garbage and Exterminating the Rats." *Renewal News for Presbyterian and Reformed Churches* (Summer).
4. "The Concept of Power Encounter." *CMS Bulletin* III(2):1-2.

5. Condensation of "The Power of God for People Who Ride Two Horses," with M. G. Kraft. *CMS Bulletin* 3(2):9-13.
6. Article on Alan Tippett in *The Australian Dictionary of Evangelical Biography*. Brian Dickey, ed. Pp. 373-374. Sydney: Evangelical History Association.
7. "Two Kingdoms in Conflict." In *Behind Enemy Lines*, Charles Kraft, ed. Pp. 17-29. Ann Arbor, MI: Servant Books.
8. "Spiritual Power: Principles and Observations." In *Behind Enemy Lines*. Charles Kraft, ed. Pp. 31-62. Ann Arbor, MI: Servant Books.
9. "Dealing with Demonization." In *Behind Enemy Lines*. Charles Kraft, ed. Pp. 79-120. Ann Arbor, MI: Servant Books.
10. "Church Growth Needs to be for the Right Reasons?" *Worship Leader* Sept/Oct: 10.

Book Reviews
1. Stephen B. Bevans, *Models of Contextual Theology: The Struggle for Cultural Relevance,* in *International Bulletin of Missionary Research* 18(21):131.

Sound Recordings
1. "Contextualization, Encounter and Mission." 2 sound cassettes. Seminar in Missiology. Recorded at Asbury Theological Seminary, April 20, 1994.
2. "Deep Level Healing and Deliverance." 3 sound cassettes. Seminar in Missiology. Recorded at Asbury Theological Seminary, April 18, 1994.

1995

Articles and Chapters in Books
1. "Worship Isn't Very Important." *Worship Leader* Jan/Feb: 10.
2. "Media Are to Serve, Not to Be Served." *Worship Leader* May/June: 22, 42.
3. "'Christian Animism' or God-Given Authority." In *Spiritual Power and Missions.* Edward Rommen, ed. Pp 88-136. Pasadena, CA: William Carey Library.

Book Reviews
1. Charles H. Kraft, *Defeating Dark Angels* in *Reformation & Revival* 4:153-156.

1996

Books
1. *Anthropology for Christian Witness*. Maryknoll, NY: Orbis.

Articles and Chapters in Books
1. "Beneath Our Words." *Worship Leader* Sept/Oct: 17.

1997

Books
1. *I Give You Authority*. Grand Rapids, MI: Chosen (Baker).

Articles and Chapters in Books
1. "Information vs. Stimulus." *Worship Leader* Jan/Feb: 14.

2. "The Rule That Breaks All Rules." *Worship Leader* May/June: 14.
3. "Feel First, Think Later." *Worship Leader* Sept/Oct: 16.

1998

Articles and Chapters in Books
1. "Meaning by Association." *Worship Leader* Jan/Feb: 16.
2. "Communication Happens." *Worship Leader* May/June: 14.
3. "Source or Receptor?" *Worship Leader* Sept/Oct: 14.
4. "My Pilgrimage in Mission." *International Bulletin of Missionary Research* 22:162-164 (October).

1999

Books
1. *Communicating Jesus' Way*. Pasadena, CA: William Carey Library.

Articles and Chapters in Books
1. "Culture, Worldview and Contextualization." In *Perspectives on the World Christian Movement*. Pp. 384-391. Pasadena, CA: William Carey Library.
2. "Three Encounters in Christian Witness." In *Perspectives on the World Christian Movement*. Pp. 408-413. Pasadena, CA: William Carey Library.
3. "In With The Old, In With Two New." *Worship Leader* Jan/Feb: 16.

2000

Book
1. *The Rules of Engagement: Understanding the Principles that Govern the Spiritual Battles in Our Lives*. With David M. DeBord. Colorado Springs, CO: Wagner Publications.

Articles and Chapters in Books
1. "Anthropology." In *Evangelical Dictionary of World Missions*. A. Scott Moreau, ed. Pp. 66-68. Grand Rapids, MI: Baker.
2. "Cultural Conversion." *EDWM*. P. 251.
3. "Culture Shock." *EDWM*. Pp. 256-257.
4. "Curse, Curses." *EDWM*. Pp. 257-258.
5. "Divination, Diviners." *EDWM*. P. 282.
6. "Dynamic Equivalence." *EDWM*. P. 295.
7. "Interpersonal Communication." *EDWM*. Pp. 499-500.
8. "Polygamy and Church Membership." *EDWM*. P. 766.
9. "Power Encounter." *EDWM*. Pp. 774-775.
10. "Witchcraft and Sorcery," *EDWM*. Pp. 1019-1020.

Forward to a Book
1. Howard L. Foltz, *For Such a Time as This*. Pasadena, CA: William Carey Library.

<u>**2001**</u>

Books

1. *Culture, Communication and Christianity*. Pasadena, CA: William Carey Library.

BOOKS BY CHARLES H. KRAFT
September 2001

1. *A Study of Hausa Syntax*. 3 vols. Hartford Studies in Linguistics. Volumes 8, 9, 10. Hartford, CT: Hartford Seminary Foundation, 1963.
2. *An Introduction to Spoken Hausa.* African Language Monographs 5A. E. Lansing, MI: African Studies Center, Michigan State University, 1965.
3. *Workbook for An Introduction to Spoken Hausa.* African Language Monographs 5B. E. Lansing, MI: African Studies Center, Michigan State University, 1965.
4. *Cultural Materials in Hausa*. African Language Monograph 6A. African Studies Center: Michigan State University, 1966.
5. *Workbook in Intermediate and Advanced Hausa.* African Language Monograph 6B. African Studies Center: Michigan State University, 1966.
6. *Where Do I Go From Here?* (A Handbook for Continuing Language Study in the Field.) With Marguerite G. Kraft. U.S. Peace Corps, 1966.
7. *Introduction to Spoken Hausa*. With Marguerite G. Kraft. Berkeley, CA: University of California Press, 1973.
8. *Teach Yourself Hausa*. With A. Kirk-Greene. London: English Universities Press, 1973.
   a. American edition. Lincolnwood, IL: NTC Publishing Company, 1994.
9. *A Hausa Reader*. Berkeley, CA: University of California Press, 1973.
10. *Christianity in Culture: A Study in Dynamic Biblical Theologizing in Cross-Cultural Perspective*. Maryknoll, NY: Orbis, 1979.
11. *Communicating the Gospel God's Way*. Ashland Theological Journal. Ashland, OH: Ashland Seminary, 1979.
    a. (More formal publication) Pasadena, CA: William Carey Library, 1979
    b. Chinese (Mandarin) translation. D. Wang, trans. Hong Kong: Asian Outreach, 1983.
12. *Readings in Dynamic Indigeneity*. With Tom N. Wisley. Pasadena, CA: William Carey Library, 1979.
13. *Chadic Wordlists*. 3 vols. Berlin: Verlag von Dietrich Reimer, 1981.
14. *Communication Theory for Christian Witness*. Nashville, TN: Abingdon, 1983. Revised edition. Maryknoll, NY: Orbis, 1991.
15. *Christianity with Power: Your Worldview and Your Experience of the Supernatural*. Ann Arbor, MI: Servant Publications, 1989.
    a. British edition. London: Marshall Pickering, 1989.
    b. German translation. Lorrach: Wolfgang Simson Verlag, 1989.
    c. Philippine edition. Manila: OMF Literature, 1990.
    d. Chinese (Mandarin) translation. Kaohsiung, Taiwan: Holy Light Theological Seminary, 1991.
    e. Korean translation. Seoul: Nathan Press, 1992.
    f. Japanese translation. Tokyo, 1994.

16. *Communicate With Power*. Manila: OMF Literature, Philippines, 1990.
    a. Korean translation. Seoul: InterVarsity Press, 1991.

17. *Defeating Dark Angels: Breaking Demonic Oppression in the Believer's Life*. Ann Arbor, MI: Servant, 1992.
    a. British edition. Tonbridge, Kent: Sovereign World, 1993.
    b. German translation. Buchs (Zurich): Koinonia Verlag, 1995.
    c. Chinese (Mandarin) translation. Rosemead, CA: Evangelical Formosan Church, 1994.
    d. Korean translation. Seoul, 1995.
    e. Russian translation. Koinonia-Verlag, Switzerland, 2000.

18. *Deep Wounds, Deep Healing: Discovering the Vital Link Between Spiritual Warfare and Inner Healing*. Ann Arbor, MI: Servant, 1993.
    a. British edition. Tonbridge, Kent: Sovereign World, 1994.
    b. Japanese translation. Vol. 1. Tokyo: Praise Publications, 1995. Vol. 2, 1997.
    c. Philippine edition. Manila: St Pauls, 1995.
    d. Korean translation. Seoul, 1995.
    e. German translation. Koinonia-Verlag, Oberweningen, Switzerland, 2000.

19. *Behind Enemy Lines: An Advanced Guide to Spiritual Warfare*. (Edited). Ann Arbor, MI: Servant, 1994.
    a. Korean translation. Seoul, 1996.
    b. Japanese translation. Tokyo, 1997.

20. *Anthropology for Christian Witness*. Maryknoll, NY: Orbis, 1996.

21. *I Give You Authority*. Grand Rapids, MI: Chosen (Baker), 1997.
    a. British edition. East Sussex: Monarch Books, 1998, 2000.
    b. German translation. Ludenscheid: Asaph Verlag, 1998.
    c. Japanese translation. 2 Vols. Tokyo: Praise Publications, 1999.
    d. Korean translation. Seoul: Bethany Publishing House, 2000.

22. *Communicating Jesus' Way*. (A new edition of *Communicate with Power*, Manila, Philippines, 1990) Pasadena, CA: William Carey Library, 1999.

23. *The Rules of Engagement: Understanding the Principles that Govern the Spiritual Battles in Our Lives*. With David M. DeBord. Colorado Springs, CO: Wagner Publications, 2000.

24. *Culture, Communication and Christianity*. Pasadena, CA: William Carey Library, 2001.

INDEX

absolutes, 12, 15, 20, 25, 248, 250-251, 273, 315, 317, 320-321, 336, 348-350, 355, 365, 369-370, 373, 428, 434
  divine, 250
  theological, 12, 250, 313
absolutize, 11, 15, 29, 249, 274, 283, 320, 350, 362, 367, 373, 397
abstraction, level of, 307-308, 310, 333-335
acceptance, 28, 61, 67, 70, 94, 119-122, 126-127, 138, 154, 160, 218, 273, 289-290, 292, 296, 314, 351, 359, 372, 384-385, 398, 407, 416-417, 426
Achebe, Chinua, 122
adultery, 26, 73, 87, 257, 265, 273, 306, 321, 328, 372, 401, 403-404, 416, 443
Africa(n), 1-2, 4-5, 26-27, 34, 43, 52, 75, 77, 133, 141-145, 153-154, 158, 160, 162, 172-173, 175-180, 194-195, 228, 296, 309, 337, 345-346, 349, 352-353, 357-362, 367, 378, 399-401, 403-411, 413-416, 418-419, 424-425, 436, 438, 459, 460-462
African Israel Church Nineveh of Kenya (AICN), 459-462
African Studies Center, 4
agreements, multi-personal, 56
Akamba, 144-145, 154, 359
Alford, Henry, 418, 423-424
allegiances, 14, 36, 41, 62, 93, 97-100, 106-108, 114, 132, 142, 173, 191, 201, 215, 260, 289, 309, 336, 356, 388-389, 395, 397, 399-402, 406, 409-411, 414, 437, 449
American Bible Society, 2, 240, 279-280, 366, 379, 392
analysis
  contextual, 331
  cross-cultural, 307, 333
ancestors, 50, 56, 272, 321, 361, 436, 455
Anderson, Rufus, 427, 436
animism, 27
anthropological, 17, 61, 67, 85, 233, 244, 258, 263, 276, 279, 369
  generalizations, 263

insights, 2, 6, 14, 71, 73, 237-238, 257, 261, 263, 265, 267, 270, 272, 278-280, 288, 404
  linguistics, 257
  method, 276
  models, 259
  perspective, 14-18, 62, 71, 235, 237-238, 241, 246, 251, 259, 263-264, 266, 276, 313
  techniques, 261-262
  training, 2
anthropology/anthropologists, 1-2, 4-7, 9-18, 20, 22-25, 28, 39, 41, 44, 46-47, 50-52, 62, 64-65, 67, 71, 80, 85, 92, 97-98, 113, 115, 123, 129, 135, 138, 140, 160, 180, 234-238, 240-243, 246-248, 250-252, 257-258, 261, 263-265, 272-276, 278, 280-281, 283-284, 290, 294, 300-301, 306, 311-313, 319, 328, 349, 353, 364-366, 368-370, 372-375, 383, 403-404, 416, 429, 440
Aquinas, Thomas, 237, 362
Archambault, 420
Ashland Seminary, 2
Asia(n), 33, 43, 45, 346, 349
assumptions, 14, 44, 55-56, 58-59, 76, 79, 90, 97-103, 105-112, 114, 116-118, 129, 131-132, 134-135, 137, 246, 248-250, 260, 304, 326, 374, 387-388
  basic, 76, 103, 106, 111, 116, 129, 131, 240
  Christian, 101, 103, 114, 246
  core, 98-99
  culturally inculcated, 90, 159, 294, 436
  culturally structured, 56, 97, 114, 241, 388
  deep level, 55, 58, 79, 109, 131, 135, 241
  non-Christian, 246
  rationalistic, 134
  set of, 100, 258
  supernaturalistic, 14, 108
  western, 101
  worldview, 14, 44, 54-55, 79, 81, 98, 100-101, 104-105, 107-109, 111-114, 118, 131, 134-135, 197, 248, 383

489